CODE OF FEDERAL REGULATIONS

Title 45
Public Welfare

Parts 500 to 1199

Revised as of October 1, 2017

Containing a codification of documents
of general applicability and future effect

As of October 1, 2017

Published by the Office of the Federal Register
National Archives and Records Administration
as a Special Edition of the Federal Register

Table of Contents

	Page
Explanation	v

Title 45:

SUBTITLE B—REGULATIONS RELATING TO PUBLIC WELFARE (CONTINUED)

Chapter V—Foreign Claims Settlement Commission of the United States, Department of Justice	5
Chapter VI—National Science Foundation	39
Chapter VII—Commission on Civil Rights	249
Chapter VIII—Office of Personnel Management	291
Chapter IX—Denali Commission	311
Chapter X—Office of Community Services, Administration for Children and Families, Department of Health and Human Services	323
Chapter XI—National Foundation on the Arts and the Humanities	331

Finding Aids:

Table of CFR Titles and Chapters	511
Alphabetical List of Agencies Appearing in the CFR	531
List of CFR Sections Affected	541

Cite this Code: CFR

To cite the regulations in this volume use title, part and section number. Thus, 45 CFR 500.1 refers to title 45, part 500, section 1.

Explanation

The Code of Federal Regulations is a codification of the general and permanent rules published in the Federal Register by the Executive departments and agencies of the Federal Government. The Code is divided into 50 titles which represent broad areas subject to Federal regulation. Each title is divided into chapters which usually bear the name of the issuing agency. Each chapter is further subdivided into parts covering specific regulatory areas.

Each volume of the Code is revised at least once each calendar year and issued on a quarterly basis approximately as follows:

Title 1 through Title 16...as of January 1
Title 17 through Title 27 ....as of April 1
Title 28 through Title 41 ....as of July 1
Title 42 through Title 50...as of October 1

The appropriate revision date is printed on the cover of each volume.

LEGAL STATUS

The contents of the Federal Register are required to be judicially noticed (44 U.S.C. 1507). The Code of Federal Regulations is prima facie evidence of the text of the original documents (44 U.S.C. 1510).

HOW TO USE THE CODE OF FEDERAL REGULATIONS

The Code of Federal Regulations is kept up to date by the individual issues of the Federal Register. These two publications must be used together to determine the latest version of any given rule.

To determine whether a Code volume has been amended since its revision date (in this case, October 1, 2017), consult the "List of CFR Sections Affected (LSA)," which is issued monthly, and the "Cumulative List of Parts Affected," which appears in the Reader Aids section of the daily Federal Register. These two lists will identify the Federal Register page number of the latest amendment of any given rule.

EFFECTIVE AND EXPIRATION DATES

Each volume of the Code contains amendments published in the Federal Register since the last revision of that volume of the Code. Source citations for the regulations are referred to by volume number and page number of the Federal Register and date of publication. Publication dates and effective dates are usually not the same and care must be exercised by the user in determining the actual effective date. In instances where the effective date is beyond the cut-off date for the Code a note has been inserted to reflect the future effective date. In those instances where a regulation published in the Federal Register states a date certain for expiration, an appropriate note will be inserted following the text.

OMB CONTROL NUMBERS

The Paperwork Reduction Act of 1980 (Pub. L. 96–511) requires Federal agencies to display an OMB control number with their information collection request.

Many agencies have begun publishing numerous OMB control numbers as amendments to existing regulations in the CFR. These OMB numbers are placed as close as possible to the applicable recordkeeping or reporting requirements.

PAST PROVISIONS OF THE CODE

Provisions of the Code that are no longer in force and effect as of the revision date stated on the cover of each volume are not carried. Code users may find the text of provisions in effect on any given date in the past by using the appropriate List of CFR Sections Affected (LSA). For the convenience of the reader, a "List of CFR Sections Affected" is published at the end of each CFR volume. For changes to the Code prior to the LSA listings at the end of the volume, consult previous annual editions of the LSA. For changes to the Code prior to 2001, consult the List of CFR Sections Affected compilations, published for 1949-1963, 1964-1972, 1973-1985, and 1986-2000.

"[RESERVED]" TERMINOLOGY

The term "[Reserved]" is used as a place holder within the Code of Federal Regulations. An agency may add regulatory information at a "[Reserved]" location at any time. Occasionally "[Reserved]" is used editorially to indicate that a portion of the CFR was left vacant and not accidentally dropped due to a printing or computer error.

INCORPORATION BY REFERENCE

What is incorporation by reference? Incorporation by reference was established by statute and allows Federal agencies to meet the requirement to publish regulations in the Federal Register by referring to materials already published elsewhere. For an incorporation to be valid, the Director of the Federal Register must approve it. The legal effect of incorporation by reference is that the material is treated as if it were published in full in the Federal Register (5 U.S.C. 552(a)). This material, like any other properly issued regulation, has the force of law.

What is a proper incorporation by reference? The Director of the Federal Register will approve an incorporation by reference only when the requirements of 1 CFR part 51 are met. Some of the elements on which approval is based are:

(a) The incorporation will substantially reduce the volume of material published in the Federal Register.

(b) The matter incorporated is in fact available to the extent necessary to afford fairness and uniformity in the administrative process.

(c) The incorporating document is drafted and submitted for publication in accordance with 1 CFR part 51.

What if the material incorporated by reference cannot be found? If you have any problem locating or obtaining a copy of material listed as an approved incorporation by reference, please contact the agency that issued the regulation containing that incorporation. If, after contacting the agency, you find the material is not available, please notify the Director of the Federal Register, National Archives and Records Administration, 8601 Adelphi Road, College Park, MD 20740-6001, or call 202-741-6010.

CFR INDEXES AND TABULAR GUIDES

A subject index to the Code of Federal Regulations is contained in a separate volume, revised annually as of January 1, entitled CFR INDEX AND FINDING AIDS. This volume contains the Parallel Table of Authorities and Rules. A list of CFR titles, chapters, subchapters, and parts and an alphabetical list of agencies publishing in the CFR are also included in this volume.

An index to the text of "Title 3—The President" is carried within that volume.

The Federal Register Index is issued monthly in cumulative form. This index is based on a consolidation of the "Contents" entries in the daily Federal Register.

A List of CFR Sections Affected (LSA) is published monthly, keyed to the revision dates of the 50 CFR titles.

REPUBLICATION OF MATERIAL

There are no restrictions on the republication of material appearing in the Code of Federal Regulations.

INQUIRIES

For a legal interpretation or explanation of any regulation in this volume, contact the issuing agency. The issuing agency's name appears at the top of odd-numbered pages.

For inquiries concerning CFR reference assistance, call 202-741-6000 or write to the Director, Office of the Federal Register, National Archives and Records Administration, 8601 Adelphi Road, College Park, MD 20740-6001 or e-mail *fedreg.info@nara.gov*.

THIS TITLE

Title 45—PUBLIC WELFARE is composed of four volumes. The parts in these volumes are arranged in the following order: Parts 1–199, 200–499, 500–1199, and 1200 to end. Volume one (parts 1–199) contains all current regulations issued under subtitle A—Department of Health and Human Services. Volume two (parts 200–499) contains all current regulations issued under subtitle B—Regulations Relating to Public Welfare, chapter II—Office of Family Assistance (Assistance Programs), Administration for Children and Families, Department of Health and Human Services, chapter III—Office of Child Support Enforcement (Child Support Enforcement Program), Administration for Children and Families, Department of Health and Human Services, and chapter IV—Office of Refugee Resettlement, Administration for Children and Families, Department of Health and Human Services. Volume three (parts 500–1199) contains all current regulations issued under chapter V—Foreign Claims Settlement Commission of the United States, Department of Justice, chapter VI—National Science Foundation, chapter VII—Commission on Civil Rights, chapter VIII—Office of Personnel Management, chapter IX—Denali Commission, chapter X—Office of Community Services, Administration for Children and Families, Department of Health and Human Services, and chapter XI—National Foundation on the Arts and the Humanities. Volume four (part 1200 to end) contains all current regulations issued under chapter XII—Corporation for National and Community Service, chapter XIII—Administration for Children and Families, Department of Health and Human Services, chapter XVI—Legal Services Corporation, chapter XVII—National Commission on Libraries and Information Science, chapter XVIII—Harry S Truman Scholarship Foundation, chapter XXI—Commission of Fine Arts, chapter XXIII—Arctic Research Commission, chapter XXIV—James Madison Memorial Fellowship Foundation, and chapter XXV—Corporation for National and Community Service. The contents of these volumes represent all of the current regulations codified under this title of the CFR as of October 1, 2017.

For this volume, Ann Worley was Chief Editor. The Code of Federal Regulations publication program is under the direction of John Hyrum Martinez, assisted by Stephen J. Frattini.

Title 45—Public Welfare

(This book contains parts 500 to 1199)

SUBTITLE B—Regulations Relating to Public Welfare (Continued)

	Part
Chapter V—Foreign Claims Settlement Commission of the United States, Department of Justice	500
Chapter VI—National Science Foundation	601
Chapter VII—Commission on Civil Rights	701
Chapter VIII—Office of Personnel Management [Reserved]	
Chapter IX—Denali Commission	900
Chapter X—Office of Community Services, Administration for Children and Families, Department of Health and Human Services	1080
Chapter XI—National Foundation on the Arts and the Humanities	1100

Subtitle B—Regulations Relating to Public Welfare (Continued)

CHAPTER V—FOREIGN CLAIMS SETTLEMENT COMMISSION OF THE UNITED STATES, DEPARTMENT OF JUSTICE

SUBCHAPTER A—RULES OF PRACTICE

Part		Page
500	Appearance and practice	7
501	Subpoenas, depositions, and oaths	8
502	Public information-Freedom of Information Act	11
503	Privacy Act and Government in the Sunshine Regulations	17

SUBCHAPTER B—RECEIPT, ADMINISTRATION, AND PAYMENT OF CLAIMS UNDER TITLE I OF THE WAR CLAIMS ACT OF 1948, AS AMENDED

504	Filing of claims and procedures therefor	25
505	Provisions of general application	26
506	Eligibility requirements for compensation	27
507	Payment	30
508	Hearings	30

SUBCHAPTER C—RECEIPT, ADMINISTRATION, AND PAYMENT OF CLAIMS UNDER THE INTERNATIONAL CLAIMS SETTLEMENT ACT OF 1949, AS AMENDED, AND RELATED ACTS

509	Filing of claims and procedures therefor	33

SUBCHAPTER D—RECEIPT, ADMINISTRATION, AND PAYMENT OF CLAIMS UNDER THE GUAM WORLD WAR II LOYALTY RECOGNITION ACT

510	Filing of claims and procedures therefor	37
511–599	[Reserved]	

SUBCHAPTER A—RULES OF PRACTICE

PART 500—APPEARANCE AND PRACTICE

Sec.
500.1 Appearance and representation.
500.2 Notice of entry or withdrawal of counsel in claims.
500.3 Fees.
500.4 Suspension of attorneys.
500.5 Standards of Conduct.
500.6 Disqualification of former employees.

AUTHORITY: Sec. 2, Pub. L. 896, 80th Cong., 62 Stat. 1240, as amended (50 U.S.C. App. 2001); sec. 3, Pub. L. 455, 81st Cong., 64 Stat. 12, as amended (22 U.S.C. 1622); 18 U.S.C. 207; Sec.1705(a)(2), Pub. L. 114–328, 114th Cong., 130 Stat. 2644.

SOURCE: 66 FR 49844, Oct. 1, 2001, unless otherwise noted.

§ 500.1 Appearance and representation.

(a) An individual may appear in his or her own behalf, or may be represented by an attorney at law admitted to practice in any State or Territory of the United States, or the District of Columbia.

(b) A member of a partnership may represent the partnership.

(c) A bona fide officer of a corporation, trust or association may represent the corporation, trust or association.

(d) An officer or employee of the United States Department of Justice, when designated by the Attorney General of the United States, may represent the United States in a claim proceeding.

(e) In cases falling within the purview of subchapter B of this chapter, persons designated by veterans', service, and other organizations to appear before the Commission in a representative capacity on behalf of claimants will be deemed duly authorized to practice before the Commission if the designating organization has received a letter of accreditation from the Commission. Petitions for accreditation must be in writing, executed by duly authorized officer or officers, and addressed to the Foreign Claims Settlement Commission of the United States, Washington, DC 20579. Upon receipt of a petition setting forth pertinent facts as to the organization's history, purpose, number of posts or chapters and their locations, approximate number of paid-up memberships, statements that the organization will not charge any fee for services rendered by its designees in behalf of claimants and that it will not refuse on the grounds of non-membership to represent any claimant who applies for representation if the claimant has an apparently valid claim, accompanied by a copy of the organization's constitution, or charter, by-laws, and its latest financial statement, the Commission in its discretion will consider and in appropriate cases issue or deny letters of accreditation.

(f) A claimant may not be represented before the Commission except as authorized in paragraphs (a) through (e) of this section.

§ 500.2 Notice of entry or withdrawal of counsel in claims.

(a) Counsel entering an appearance in a claim originally filed by a claimant in the claimant's own behalf, or upon request for a substitution of attorneys, will be required to file an authorization signed by the claimant.

(b) When counsel seeks to withdraw from the prosecution of a claim, he or she will be required to demonstrate that the client (claimant) has been duly notified.

(c) When a claimant advises the Commission that counsel no longer represents that claimant, a copy of the Commission's acknowledgment will be forwarded to that counsel.

§ 500.3 Fees.

(a) The amount of attorney's fees that may be charged in connection with claims falling within the purview of title I of the International Claims Settlement Act of 1949, as amended (22 U.S.C. § 1621–1627), is governed by the provisions of 22 U.S.C.1623(f).

(b) The amount of attorney's fees that may be charged in connection with claims falling within the purview of subchapter B of this chapter is governed by the provisions of section 10 of the War Claims Act of 1948, as amended (50 U.S.C. App. 2009).

(c) The amount of attorney's fees that may be charged in connection with claims falling within the purview of subchapter D of this chapter is governed by the provisions of section 1705(b)(6) of the National Defense Authorization Act for Fiscal Year 2017, Title XVII, Guam World War II Loyalty Recognition Act, Public Law 114–328.

[66 FR 49844, Oct. 1, 2001, as amended at 82 FR 16126, Apr. 3, 2017]

§ 500.4 Suspension of attorneys.

(a) The Commission may disqualify, or deny, temporarily or permanently, the privilege of appearing or practicing before it in any way to any person who is found after a hearing in the matter—

(1) Not to possess the requisite qualifications to represent others before the Commission; or

(2) To be lacking in character or integrity or to have engaged in unethical or improper professional conduct; or

(3) To have violated sections 10 and 214 of the War Claims Act of 1948, as amended, section 4(f) of the International Claims Settlement Act of 1949, as amended, or section 1705(b)(6) of the National Defense Authorization Act for Fiscal Year 2017, Title XVII, Guam World War II Loyalty Recognition Act.

(b) Contemptuous or contumacious conduct at any hearing will be ground for exclusion from that hearing and for summary suspension without a hearing for the duration of the hearing.

[66 FR 49844, Oct. 1, 2001, as amended at 82 FR 16126, Apr. 3, 2017]

§ 500.5 Standards of Conduct.

The conduct of the members, officers and employees of the Commission, including its special Government employees, is governed by the *Standards of Ethical Conduct for Employees of the Executive Branch* set forth in 5 CFR part 2635 and the *Supplemental Standards of Conduct for Employees of the Department of Justice* set forth in 5 CFR part 3801.

§ 500.6 Disqualification of former employees.

The provisions of 18 U.S.C. 207 shall govern the post-employment appearance of former Commission members, officers, and employees, including special Government employees, in the capacity of agent, attorney or representative on behalf of claimants before the Commission.

PART 501—SUBPOENAS, DEPOSITIONS, AND OATHS

Sec.
501.1 Extent of authority.
501.2 Subpoenas.
501.3 Service of process.
501.4 Witnesses.
501.5 Depositions.
501.6 Documentary evidence.
501.7 Time.

AUTHORITY: Sec. 2, Pub. L. 896, 80th Cong., 62 Stat. 1240, as amended (50 U.S.C. App. 2001); sec. 3, Pub. L. 455, 81st Cong., 64 Stat. 12, as amended (22 U.S.C. 1622).

SOURCE: 66 FR 49844, Oct. 1, 2001, unless otherwise noted.

§ 501.1 Extent of authority.

(a) *Subpoenas, oaths and affirmations.* The issuance of subpoenas, the administration of oaths and affirmations, the taking of affidavits, the conduct of investigations, and the examination of witnesses by the Commission and its members, officers and employees is governed by the provisions of 22 U.S.C. 1623(c) and 50 U.S.C. App. 2001(c).

(b) *Certification.* The Commission or any member thereof may, for the purpose of a hearing, examination, or investigation, certify the correctness of any papers, documents, and other matters pertaining to the administration of any laws relating to the functions of the Commission.

§ 501.2 Subpoenas.

(a) *Issuance.* A member of the Commission or a designated employee may, on the member or employee's own volition or upon written application by any party and upon a showing of general relevance and reasonable scope of the evidence sought, issue subpoenas requiring persons to appear and testify or to appear and produce documents. Applications for issuance of subpoenas for production of documents shall specify the books, records, correspondence, or other documents sought. The subpoena will show on its face the

Foreign Claims Settlement Commission, Justice §501.3

name and address of the party at whose request the subpoena was issued.

(b) *Deposit for costs.* The Commission or designated employee, before issuing any subpoena in response to any application by an interested party, may require a deposit in an amount adequate to cover fees and mileage involved.

(c) *Motion to quash.* If any person subpoenaed does not intend to comply with the subpoena, that person must, within 15 days after the date of service of the subpoena, petition in writing to quash the subpoena. The basis for the motion must be stated in detail. Any party desiring to file an answer to a motion to quash must file the answer not later than 15 days after the filing of the motion. The Commission will rule on the motion to quash, duly recognizing any answer thereto filed. The motion, answer, and any ruling thereon will become part of the official record.

(d) *Appeal from interlocutory order.* An appeal may be taken to the Commission by the interested parties from the denial of a motion to quash or from the refusal to issue a subpoena for the production of documentary evidence.

(e) *Order of court upon failure to comply.* Upon the failure or refusal of any person to comply with a subpoena, the Commission may invoke the aid of the United States District Court within the jurisdiction of which the hearing, examination or investigation is being conducted, or wherein that person resides or transacts business, as provided in 22 U.S.C. 1623(c).

§ 501.3 Service of process.

(a) *By whom served.* The Commission will serve all orders, notices and other papers issued by it, together with any other papers which it is required by law to serve.

(b) *Kinds of service.* Subpoenas, orders, rulings, and other processes of the Commission may be served by delivering in person, by registered or certified mail, by overnight express delivery service, by first class mail, by telegraph, or by publication.

(c) *Personal service.* Service by delivering in person may be accomplished by:

(1) Delivering a copy of the document to the person to be served, to a member of the partnership to be served, to an executive officer or a director of the corporation to be served, or to a person competent to accept service; or

(2) By leaving a copy thereof at the residence, principal office or place of business of the person, partnership, or corporation.

(3) Proof of service. The return receipt for the order, other process or supporting papers, or the verification by the person serving, setting forth the manner of service, will be proof of the service of the document.

(4) Service upon attorney or agent. When any party has appeared by an authorized attorney or agent, service upon the party's attorney or agent will be deemed service upon the party.

(d) *Service by registered mail or certified mail.* Service by registered mail or certified mail will be regarded as complete on the date the return post office receipt for the orders, notices and other papers is received by the Commission.

(e) *Service by overnight express delivery service or by first class mail.* Service by overnight express delivery service or first class mail will be regarded as complete upon deposit, respectively, in the delivery service's package receptacle or in the United States mail properly stamped and addressed.

(f) *Service by telegraph.* Service by telegraph will be regarded as complete when deposited with a telegraph company properly addressed and with charges prepaid.

(g) *Service by publication.* Service by publication is completed when due notice has been given in the publication for the time and in the manner provided by law or rule.

(h) *Date of service.* The date of service is the day upon which the document is deposited in the United States mail or delivered in person, as the case may be.

(i) *Filing with Commission.* Papers required to be filed with the Commission will be deemed filed upon actual receipt by the Commission accompanied by proof of service upon parties required to be served. Upon the actual receipt, the filing will be deemed complete as of the date of deposit in the mail or with the telegraph company as provided in paragraphs (e) and (f) of this section.

§ 501.4 Witnesses.

(a) *Examination of witnesses.* Witnesses must appear in person and be examined orally under oath, except that for good cause shown, testimony may be taken by deposition.

(b) *Witness fees and mileage.* Witnesses summoned by the Commission on its own behalf or on behalf of a claimant or interested party will be paid the same fees and mileage that are allowed and paid witnesses in the District Courts of the United States. Witness fees and mileage will be paid by the Commission or by the party at whose request the witness appears.

(c) *Transcript of testimony.* Every person required to attend and testify will be entitled, upon payment of prescribed costs, to receive a copy of the recording of the testimony or a transcript of the recording. Every person required to submit documents or other evidence will be entitled to retain a copy thereof.

§ 501.5 Depositions.

(a) *Application to take.* (1) An application to take a deposition must be in writing setting forth the reason why the deposition should be taken, the name and address of the witness, the matters concerning which it is expected the witness will testify, and the time and place proposed for the taking of the deposition, together with the name and address of the person before whom it is desired that the deposition be taken. If the deposition is being offered in connection with a hearing or examination, the application for deposition must be made to the Commission at least 15 days prior to the proposed date of such hearing or examination.

(2) Application to take a deposition may be made during a hearing or examination, or subsequent to a hearing or examination, only where it is shown for good cause that the facts as set forth in the application to take the deposition were not within the knowledge of the person signing the application prior to the time of the hearing or examination.

(3) The Commission or its representative will, upon receipt of the application and a showing of good cause, make and cause to be served upon the parties an order which will specify the name of the witness whose deposition is to be taken, the time, the place, and where practicable the designation of the officer before whom the witness is to testify. The officer may or may not be the one specified in the application. The order will be served upon all parties at least 10 days prior to the date of the taking of the deposition.

(b) *Who may take.* The deposition may be taken before the designated officer or, if none is designated, before any officer authorized to administer oaths by the laws of the United States. If the examination is held in a foreign country, it may be taken before a secretary of an embassy or legation, consul-general, consul, vice consul, or consular agent of the United States.

(c) *Examination and certification of testimony.* At the time and place specified in the Commission's order, the officer taking the deposition will permit the witness to be examined and cross-examined under oath by all parties appearing, and the testimony will be reduced to writing by, or under the direction of, the presiding officer. All objections to questions or evidence will be deemed waived unless made in accordance with paragraph (d) of this section. The officer will not have power to rule upon any objections but will note them upon the deposition. The testimony must be subscribed by the witness in the presence of the officer who will attach a certificate stating that the witness was duly sworn, that the deposition is a true record of the testimony and exhibits given by the witness and that the officer is not counsel or attorney to any of the interested parties. The officer will immediately seal and deliver an original and two copies of the transcript, together with the officer's certificate, by registered mail to the Foreign Claims Settlement Commission, Washington, DC 20579 or, if applicable, to the designated Commission field office.

(d) *Admissibility in evidence.* The deposition will be admissible in evidence, subject to such objections to the questions and answers as were noted at the time of taking the deposition, or within ten (10) days after the return thereof, and would be valid were the witness personally present at the hearing.

(e) *Errors and irregularities.* All errors or irregularities occurring will be deemed waived unless a motion to suppress the deposition or some part thereof is made with reasonable promptness after the defect is, or with due diligence might have been, ascertained.

(f) *Scope of use.* The deposition of a witness, if relevant, may be used if the Commission finds:

(1) That the witness has died since the deposition was taken; or

(2) That the witness is at a distance greater than 100 miles radius of Washington, DC, the designated field office or the designated place of the hearing; or

(3) That the witness is unable to attend because of other good cause shown.

(g) *Interrogatories and cross-interrogatories.* Depositions may also be taken and submitted on written interrogatories in substantially the same manner as depositions taken by oral examination. When a deposition is taken upon interrogatories and cross-interrogatories, none of the parties may be present or represented, and no person, other than the witness, the person's representative or attorney, a stenographic reporter and the presiding officer, may be present at the examination of the witness, which fact will be certified by the officer, who will read the interrogatories and cross-interrogatories to the witness in their order and reduce the testimony to writing in the witness's own words.

(h) *Fees.* A witness whose deposition is taken pursuant to the regulations in this part, and the officer taking the deposition, will be entitled to the same fees and mileage allowed and paid for like service in the United States District Court for the district in which the deposition is taken. Such fees will be paid by the Commission or by the party at whose request the deposition is being taken.

§ 501.6 Documentary evidence.

Documentary evidence may consist of books, records, correspondence or other documents pertinent to any hearing, examination, or investigation within the jurisdiction of the Commission. The application for the issuance of subpoenas for production of documents must specify the books, records, correspondence or other documents sought. The production of documentary evidence will not be required at any place other than the witness's place of business. The production of such documents will not be required at any place if, prior to the return date specified in the subpoena, the person either has furnished the issuer of the subpoena with a properly certified copy of the documents or has entered into a stipulation as to the information contained in the documents.

§ 501.7 Time.

(a) *Computation.* In computing any period of time prescribed or allowed by the regulations, by order of the Commission, or by any applicable statute, the day of the act, event, or default after which the designated period of time begins to run is not to be included. The last day of the period so computed is to be included, unless it is a Saturday, Sunday or legal holiday, in which event the period runs until the end of the next day that is neither a Saturday, Sunday nor a holiday. When the period of time prescribed or allowed is less than 7 days, intermediate Saturdays, Sundays and holidays will be excluded in the computation.

(b) *Enlargement.* When by the regulations in this chapter, or by a notice given thereunder or by order of the Commission, an act is required or allowed to be done at or within a specific time, the Commission for good cause shown may, at any time in its discretion:

(1) With or without motion, notice, or previous order or

(2) Upon motion, permit the act to be done after the expiration of the specified period.

PART 502—PUBLIC INFORMATION-FREEDOM OF INFORMATION ACT

Sec.
502.1 Organization and authority—Foreign Claims Settlement Commission.
502.2 Material to be published in the Federal Register pursuant to the Freedom of Information Act.
502.3 Effect of nonpublication.
502.4 Incorporation by reference.
502.5 Records generally available.

502.6 Current index.
502.7 Additional documents and records generally available for inspection and copying.
502.8 Documents on-line.
502.9 Effect of noncompliance.
502.10 Availability of records.
502.11 Actions on requests.
502.12 Appeals.
502.13 Exemptions.
502.14 Fees for services.

AUTHORITY: 5 U.S.C. 552.

SOURCE: 66 FR 49844, Oct. 1, 2001, unless otherwise noted.

§ 502.1 Organization and authority—Foreign Claims Settlement Commission.

(a) The Foreign Claims Settlement Commission of the United States ("the Commission") is. an independent agency of the Federal Government created by Reorganization Plan No. 1 of 1954 (68 Stat. 1279) effective July 1, 1954. The Commission was transferred to the Department of Justice as an independent agency within that department as of October 1, 1980, under the terms of Public Law 96–209, approved March 14, 1980 (94 Stat. 96, 22 U.S.C. 1622a). Its duties and authority are defined in the International Claims Settlement Act of 1949, as amended (64 Stat. 12, 22 U.S.C. 1621–1645o) and the War Claims Act of 1948 (62 Stat. 1240, 50 U.S.C. App. 2001–2017p).

(b) The Commission has jurisdiction to determine the validity and amount of claims of United States nationals against foreign governments for compensation for losses and injuries sustained by those nationals, pursuant to programs authorized under either of the cited Acts. Funds for payment of claims are derived from international settlement agreements or through liquidation of foreign assets in the United States by the Department of Justice or Treasury, or from public funds when provided by the Congress.

(c) The Chair and the two part-time members of the Commission are appointed by the President with the advice and consent of the Senate to serve for 3-year terms of office as provided in 22 U.S.C. 1622c(c).

(d) All functions of the Commission are vested in the Chair with respect to the internal management of the affairs of the Commission, including but not limited to:

(1) The appointment of Commission employees;

(2) The direction of Commission employees and the supervision of their official duties;

(3) The distribution of business among employees and organizational units within the Commission;

(4) The preparation of budget estimates; and

(5) The use and expenditures of Commission funds appropriated for expenses of administration.

(e) Requests for records must be made in writing by mail or presented in person to the Administrative Officer, Foreign Claims Settlement Commission, Washington, DC 20579.

(f) The offices of the Commission are located at 600 E Street NW (Bicentennial Building), Room 6002, Washington, DC.

§ 502.2 Material to be published in the Federal Register pursuant to the Freedom of Information Act.

The Commission will separately state and concurrently publish the following materials in the FEDERAL REGISTER for the guidance of the public:

(a) Descriptions of its central and field organization and the established places at which, the officers from whom, and the methods whereby, the public may secure information, make submittals or requests, or obtain decisions.

(b) Statements of the general course and method by which its functions are channeled and determined, including the nature and requirements of all formal and informal procedures available.

(c) Rules of procedure, descriptions of forms available or the places at which forms may be obtained, and instructions as to the scope and contents of all papers, reports, or examinations.

(d) Substantive rules of general applicability adopted as authorized by law, and statements of general policy or interpretations of general applicability formulated and adopted by the agency.

(e) Every amendment, revision, or repeal of the foregoing.

§ 502.3 Effect of nonpublication.

Except to the extent that a person has actual and timely notice of the terms thereof, no person will in any manner be required to resort to, or be adversely affected by, any matter required to be published in the FEDERAL REGISTER and not so published.

§ 502.4 Incorporation by reference.

For purposes of this part, matter which is reasonably available to the class of persons affected thereby will be deemed published in the FEDERAL REGISTER when incorporated by reference therein with the approval of the Director of the Federal Register.

§ 502.5 Records generally available.

The Commission will make promptly available to any member of the public the following documents:

(a) Proposed and Final Decisions (including dissenting opinions) and all orders made with respect thereto, except when exempted from public disclosure by statute;

(b) Statements of policy and interpretations which have been adopted by the Commission which have not been published in the FEDERAL REGISTER; and

(c) A current index, which will be updated at least quarterly, covering the foregoing material adopted, issued or promulgated after July 4, 1967. Publication of an index is deemed both unnecessary and impractical. However, copies of the index are available upon request for a fee of the direct cost of duplication.

§ 502.6 Current index.

The Commission will maintain and make available for public inspection and copying, current indexes providing identifying information for the public as to any matter issued, adopted, or promulgated after July 4, 1967, as required by 5 U.S.C. 552(a)(2).

§ 502.7 Additional documents and records generally available for inspection and copying.

The following types of documents are also available for inspection and copying in the offices of the Commission:

(a) Rules of practice and procedure.

(b) Annual report of the Commission to the Congress of the United States.

(c) Bound volumes of Commission decisions.

(d) International Claims Settlement Act of 1949, with amendments; the War Claims Act of 1948, with amendments; and related Acts.

(e) Claims agreements with foreign governments effecting the settlement of claims under the jurisdiction of the Commission.

(f) Press releases and other miscellaneous material concerning Commission operations.

(g) Indexes of claims filed in the various claims programs administered by the Commission.

§ 502.8 Documents on-line.

Commission documents available in electronic format may be accessed via the Commission's World Wide Web site, the address of which is *http://www.usdoj.gov/fcsc.*

§ 502.9 Effect of non-compliance.

No decision, statement of policy, interpretation, or staff manual or instruction that affects any member of the public will be relied upon, used, or cited as precedent by the Commission against any private party unless it has been indexed and either made available or published as provided by this part, or unless that private party has actual and timely notice of the terms thereof.

§ 502.10 Availability of records.

(a) Each person desiring access to a record covered by this part must comply with the following provisions:

(1) A written request must be made for the record.

(2) Such request must indicate that it is being made under the Freedom of Information Act.

(3) The envelope in which the request is sent must be prominently marked with the letters "FOIA."

(4) The request must be addressed to the appropriate official or employee of the Commission as set forth in paragraph (c) of this section.

(5) The foregoing requirements must be complied with whether the request is mailed or hand-delivered to the Commission.

(b) If the requirements of paragraph (a) of this section are not met, the twenty-day time limit described in § 502.10(a) will not begin to run until the request has been identified by an official or employee of the Commission as a request under the Freedom of Information Act and has been received by the appropriate official or employee of the Commission.

(c) Each person desiring access to a record covered in this part that is located in the Commission, or to obtain a copy of such a record, must make a written request to the Administrative Officer, Foreign Claims Settlement Commission, 600 E Street NW, Room 6002, Washington, DC 20579.

(d) Each request should reasonably describe the particular record requested. The request should specify the subject matter, the date when it was made and the person or office that made it. If the description is insufficient, the official or employee handling the request may notify the person making the request and, to the extent possible, indicate the additional data required.

(e) Each record made available under this section is available for inspection and copying during regular working hours. Original documents may be copied but may not be released from custody.

(f) Authority to administer this part in connection with Commission records is delegated to the Administrative Officer or the Commission employee acting in that official's capacity.

§ 502.11 Actions on requests.

(a) The Administrative Officer or any employee acting in that official's capacity will determine within twenty days (excepting Saturdays, Sundays, and legal public holidays) after the receipt of any a request whether to comply with the request. Upon receipt of a request for a Commission record which is available, the Administrative Officer or other employee will notify the requester as to the time the record is available, and will promptly make the record available after advising the requester of the applicable fees under § 502.13. The person making the request will be notified immediately after any adverse determination, the reasons for making the adverse determination and the right of the person to appeal.

(b) Any denial of a request for a record will be written and signed by the Administrative Officer or other employee, including a statement of the reason for denial. That statement will contain, as applicable:

(1) A reference to the specific exemption under the Freedom of Information Act authorizing the withholding of a record, and to the extent consistent with the purpose of the exemption, an explanation of how the exemption applies to the record withheld.

(2) If a record requested does not exist, or has been legally disposed of, the requester will be so notified.

(c) In unusual circumstances, the time limit prescribed in paragraph (a) of this section may be extended by written notice to the person making the request setting forth the reasons for the extension and the date on which a determination is expected to be dispatched. No extension notice will specify a date that would result in an extension for more than twenty working days. As used in this paragraph, "unusual circumstances" means, but only to the extent reasonably necessary to the proper processing of the particular request—

(1) The need to search for and collect the requested records from other establishments that are separate from the office processing the request;

(2) The need to search for, collect, and appropriately examine a voluminous amount of separate and distinct records which are demanded in a single request; or

(3) The need for consultation, which will be conducted with all practicable speed, with another agency having a substantial interest in the determination of the request or among two or more components of the agency having substantial subject-matter interest therein.

§ 502.12 Appeals.

(a) Any person to whom a record has not been made available within the time limits established by paragraph (b) of § 502.11, and any person who has been given an adverse determination pursuant to paragraph (b) of § 503.10 of this chapter, that a requested record will not be disclosed, may apply to the Office of Information and Privacy, U.S. Department of Justice, Washington,

Foreign Claims Settlement Commission, Justice § 502.13

DC 20530, for reconsideration of the request. The person making such a request will also be notified of the provisions for judicial review provided in 5 U.S.C. 552(a)(4).

(b) Each application for reconsideration must be made in writing within sixty days from the date of receipt of the original denial and must include all information and arguments relied upon by the person making the request. The application must indicate that it is an appeal from a denial of a request made under the Freedom of Information Act. The envelope in which the application is sent must be prominently marked with the letters "FOIA." If these requirements are not met, the twenty day limit described in § 502.10 will not begin to run until the application has been identified as an application under the Freedom of Information Act and has been received by the Office of Information and Privacy of the Department of Justice.

(c) Whenever it is to be determined necessary, the person making the request may be required to furnish additional information, or proof of factual allegations and other proceedings appropriate in the circumstances may be ordered.

(d) The decision not to disclose a record under this part is considered to be a withholding for the purposes of 5 U.S.C. 552(a)(3).

§ 502.13 Exemptions.

In the event any document or record requested hereunder should contain material which is exempt from disclosure under this section, any reasonably segregable portion of the record will, notwithstanding that fact, and to the extent feasible, be provided to any person requesting it, after deletion of the portions which are exempt under this section. Documents or records determined to be exempt from disclosure hereunder may nonetheless be provided upon request in the event it is determined that the provision of the document would not violate the public interest or the right of any person to whom the information may pertain, and the disclosure is not prohibited by law or Executive Order. The following categories of records are exempt from disclosure under the provisions of 5 U.S.C. 552(b):

(a) Records which are specifically required by Executive Order to be kept secret in the interest of national defense or foreign policy and are in fact properly classified pursuant to such Executive Order. This exception may apply to records in the custody of the Commission which have been transmitted to the Commission by another agency which has designated the record as nonpublic under Executive Order.

(b) Records related solely to the internal personnel rules and practices of the Commission.

(c) Records specifically exempted from disclosure by statute.

(d) Information given in confidence. This includes information obtained by or given to the Commission which constitutes confidential commercial or financial information, privileged information, or other information which was given to the Commission in confidence or would not customarily be released by the person from whom it was obtained.

(e) Inter-agency or intra-agency memoranda or letters which would not be available by law to a private party in litigation with the Commission. Such communications include inter-agency memoranda, drafts, staff memoranda transmitted to the Commission, written communications between the Commission and its staff regarding the preparation of Commission decisions, other documents received or generated in the process of issuing a decision or regulation, and reports and other work papers of staff attorneys, accountants, and investigators.

(f) Personnel and medical files and similar files, the disclosure of which would constitute a clearly unwarranted invasion of personal privacy.

(g) Records or information compiled for law enforcement purposes, but only to the extent that the production of such law enforcement records or information:

(1) Could reasonably be expected to interfere with enforcement proceedings;

(2) Would deprive a person of a right to a fair trial or an impartial adjudication;

(3) Could reasonably be expected to constitute an unwarranted invasion of personal privacy;

(4) Could reasonably be expected to disclose the identity of a confidential source, including a state, local or foreign agency or authority or any private institution which furnished information on a confidential basis and, in the case of a record or information compiled by a criminal law enforcement authority in the course of a criminal investigation, or by an agency conducting a lawful security intelligence investigation, information furnished by a confidential source;

(5) Would disclose techniques and procedures for law enforcement investigations or prosecutions if such disclosure could reasonably be expected to risk circumvention of the law; or

(6) Could reasonably be expected to endanger the life or physical safety of any individual.

§ 502.14 Fees for services.

The following provisions shall apply in the assessment and collection of fees for services rendered in processing requests for disclosure of Commission records under this part.

(a) *Fee for duplication of records:* $0.15 per page.

(b) *Search and review fees:*

(1) Searches for records by clerical personnel—$3.00 per quarter hour, including time spent searching for and copying any record.

(2) Search for and review of records by professional and supervisory personnel—$6.00 per quarter hour spent searching for any record or reviewing a record to determine whether it may be disclosed, including time spent in copying any record.

(c) *Certification and validation fee:* $1.00 for each certification, validation or authentication of a copy of any record.

(d) *Imposition of fees:*

(1) Commercial use requests—Where a request appears to seek disclosure of records for a commercial use, the requester shall be charged for the time spent by Commission personnel in searching for the requested record and in reviewing the record to determine whether it should be disclosed, and for the cost of each page of duplication. *Commercial use* is defined as a use or purpose that furthers the commercial, trade or profit interests of the requester or the person on whose behalf the request is made. The request also must reasonably identify the records sought.

(2) Requests from representatives of news media—Where a request seeks disclosure of records to a representative of the news media, the requester shall be charged only for the actual duplication cost of the records and only to the extent that the number of duplications exceeds 100 pages; provided, however, that the request must reasonably describe the records sought, and it must appear that the records are for use by the requester in such person's capacity as a news media representative. "Representative of the news media" refers to any person actively gathering news for an entity that is organized and operated to publish or broadcast news to the public. The term *news* means information that is about current events or that would be of current interest to the public. A "freelance" journalist not actually employed by a news organization shall be eligible for inclusion under this category if the person can demonstrate a solid basis for expecting publication by a news organization.

(3) Requests from educational and non-commercial scientific institutions—Where a request seeks disclosure of records to an educational or non-commercial scientific institution, the requester shall be charged only for the actual duplication cost of the records and only to the extent that the number of duplications exceeds 100 pages; provided, however, that the request must reasonably describe the records sought and it must appear that the records are to be used by the requester in furtherance of its educational or non-commercial scientific research programs. "Educational institution" refers to a preschool, a public or private elementary or secondary school, or an institution of undergraduate, graduate, professional or vocational education, which operates a program or programs of scholarly research. "Non-commercial scientific institution" refers to an institution that is not operated on a "commercial" basis, within the meaning of paragraph (d)(1) of this section

Foreign Claims Settlement Commission, Justice

and which is operated solely for the purpose of conducting scientific research, the results of which are not intended to promote any particular product or industry.

(4) *All other requests*—Where a request seeks disclosure of records to a person or entity other than one coming within paragraphs (d) (1), (2) and (3) of this section, the requester shall be charged the full cost of search and duplication. However, the first two hours of search time and the first 100 pages of duplication shall be furnished without charge.

(e) *Aggregating of requests.* If there exists a solid basis for concluding that a requester or group of requesters has submitted a series of partial requests for disclosure of records in an attempt to evade assessment of fees, the requests may be aggregated so as to constitute a single request, with fees charged accordingly.

(f) *Unsuccessful searches.* Except as provided in paragraph (d) of this section, the cost of searching for a requested record shall be charged even if the search fails to locate the record or it is determined that the record is exempt from disclosure.

(g) *Interest.* In the event a requester fails to remit payment of fees charged for processing a request under this part within 30 days from the date those fees were billed, interest on the fees may be assessed beginning on the 31st day after the billing date, to be calculated at the rate prescribed in 31 U.S.C. 3717.

(h) *Advance payments.* (1) If, but only if, it is estimated or determined that processing of a request for disclosure of records will result in a charge of fees of more than $250.00, the requester may be required to pay the fees in advance in order to obtain completion of the processing.

(2) If a requester has previously failed to make timely payment (i.e., within 30 days of billing date) of fees charged under this part, the requester may be required to pay those fees and interest accrued thereon, and to make an advance payment of the full amount of estimated fees chargeable in connection with any pending or new request, in order to obtain processing of the pending or new request.

(3) With regard to any request coming within paragraphs (h) (1) and (2) of this section, the administrative time limits set forth in §§ 502.11 and 502.12 of this part will begin to run only after the requisite fee payments have been received.

(i) *Non-payment.* In the event of non-payment of billed charges for disclosure of records, the provisions of the Debt Collection Act of 1982 (Pub. L. 97–365), including disclosure to consumer credit reporting agencies and referral to collection agencies, may be utilized to obtain payment.

(j) *Waiver or reduction of charges.* Fees otherwise chargeable in connection with a request for disclosure of a record shall be waived or reduced where—

(1) It is determined that disclosure is in the public interest because it is likely to contribute significantly to public understanding of the operations or activities of the government and is not primarily in the commercial interest of the requester; or

(2) It is determined that the cost of collection would be equal to or exceed the amount of those fees. No charges shall be assessed if the fees amount to $8.00 or less.

PART 503—PRIVACY ACT AND GOVERNMENT IN THE SUNSHINE REGULATIONS

Subpart A—Privacy Act Regulations

Sec.
503.1 Definitions—Privacy Act.
503.2 General policies—Privacy Act.
503.3 Conditions of disclosure.
503.4 Accounting of certain disclosures.
503.5 Access to records or information.
503.6 Determination of requests for access to records.
503.7 Amendment of a record.
503.8 Appeals from denial of requests for amendment to records.
503.9 Fees.
503.10 Exemptions.
503.11 Reports.
503.12 Notices.

Subpart B—Government in the Sunshine Regulations

503.20 Definitions.
503.21 Notice of public observation.
503.22 Scope of application.
503.23 Open meetings.

§ 503.1

503.24 Grounds for closing a meeting.
503.25 Announcement of meetings.
503.26 Procedures for closing of meetings.
503.27 Reconsideration of opening or closing, or rescheduling a meeting.
503.28 Record of closed meetings, or closed portion of a meeting.
503.29 Requests for information.

AUTHORITY: 5 U.S.C. 552a(f).

SOURCE: 66 FR 49844, Oct. 1, 2001, unless otherwise noted.

Subpart A—Privacy Act Regulations

§ 503.1 Definitions—Privacy Act.

For the purpose of this part:

Agency includes any executive department, military department, government corporation, government controlled corporation, or other establishment in the executive branch of the government (including the Executive Office of the President) or any independent regulatory agency. The Foreign Claims Settlement Commission ("Commission") is an *agency* within the meaning of the term.

Individual means a citizen of the United States or an alien lawfully admitted for permanent residence.

Maintain includes maintain, collect, use or disseminate.

Record means any item, collection, or grouping of information about an individual that is maintained by an agency, including, but not limited to, an individual's education, financial transactions, medical history, and criminal or employment history, and that contains an individual's name, or the identifying number, symbol, or other identifying particular assigned to the individual, such as a finger or voice print or a photograph.

Routine use means, with respect to the disclosure of a record, the use of that record for a purpose which is compatible with the purpose for which it was collected.

Statistical record means a record in a system of records maintained for statistical research or reporting purposes only and not used in whole or in part in making any determination about an identifiable individual except as provided by section 13 U.S.C. 8.

System of records means a group of any records under the control of any agency from which information is retrieved by the name of the individual or by some identifying number, symbol, or other identifying particular assigned to the individual.

§ 503.2 General policies—Privacy Act.

The Commission will protect the privacy of an individual identified in any information or record systems which it maintains. Accordingly, its officials and employees, except as otherwise provided by law or regulation, will:

(a) Permit an individual to determine what records pertaining to that individual are collected, maintained, used or disseminated by the Commission.

(b) Permit an individual to prevent a record pertaining to that individual obtained by the Commission for a particular purpose from being used or made available for another purpose without the individual's consent.

(c) Permit an individual to gain access to information pertaining to that individual in Commission records, to have a copy made of all or any portion thereof, and to correct or amend those records.

(d) Collect, maintain, use, or disseminate any record of identifiable personal information in a manner that assures that the Commission's action is for a necessary and lawful purpose, that the information is current and accurate for its intended use, and that adequate safeguards are provided to prevent misuse of the information.

(e) Permit exemptions from record requirements provided under the Privacy Act only where an important public policy use for the exemption has been determined in accordance with specific statutory authority.

§ 503.3 Conditions of disclosure.

The Commission will not disclose any record contained in a system of records by any means of communication to any person or any other agency except by written request of or prior written consent of the individual to whom the record pertains unless the disclosure is:

(a) To those officers and employees of the Commission who have a need for the record in the performance of their duties;

(b) Required under the Freedom of Information Act, 5 U.S.C. 552;

(c) For a routine use;

(d) To the Bureau of Census for purposes of planning or carrying out a census or survey or related activity under the provisions of Title 13, United States Code;

(e) To a recipient who has provided the Commission with adequate advance assurance that the record will be used solely as a statistical research or reporting record, and the record is to be transferred in a form that is not individually identifiable;

(f) To the National Archives of the United States as a record which has sufficient historical or other value to warrant its continued preservation by the United States Government or for evaluation to determine whether the record has that value;

(g) To another agency or to an instrumentality of any government jurisdiction within or under control of the United States for a civil or criminal law enforcement activity authorized by law, provided the head of the agency or instrumentality has made a prior written request to the Commission, specifying the particular record and the law enforcement activity for which it is sought;

(h) To a person pursuant to a showing of compelling circumstances affecting the health or safety of an individual if, upon disclosure, notification is transmitted to the last known address of the individual;

(i) To either House of Congress, or, to the extent of matter within its jurisdiction, any committee or subcommittee thereof, any joint committee of Congress or subcommittee of the joint committee;

(j) To the Comptroller General, or any of that official's authorized representatives, in the course of the performance of the duties of the General Accounting Office; or

(k) Pursuant to the order of a court of competent jurisdiction.

§ 503.4 Accounting of certain disclosures.

(a) Except for disclosures under § 503.3(a) and (b) of this part, the Administrative Officer will keep an accurate accounting of each disclosure of a record to any person or to another agency made under § 503.3(c), (d), (e), (f), (g), (h), (i), (j), and (k) of this part.

(b) Except for a disclosure made to another agency or to an instrumentality of any governmental jurisdiction under § 503.3(g) of this part, the Administrative Officer will make the accounting as required under paragraph (a) of this section available to any individual upon written request made in accordance with § 503.5.

(c) The Administrative Officer will inform any person or other agency about any correction or notation of dispute made in accordance with § 503.7 of this part of any record that has been disclosed to the person or agency if an accounting of the disclosure was made.

(d) An accounting of disclosures of records within this section will consist of the date, nature, the purpose of each disclosure of a record to any person or to another agency, and the name and address of the person or agency to whom the disclosure is made.

(e) This accounting shall be retained for 5 years or the life of the record, whichever is longer, after the disclosure for which the accounting is made.

§ 503.5 Access to records or information.

(a) Upon request in person or by mail, any individual will be informed whether or not a system of records maintained by the Commission contains a record or information pertaining to that individual.

(b) Any individual requesting access to a record or information in person must appear in person at the offices of the Foreign Claims Settlement Commission, 600 E Street, NW., Room 6002, Washington, DC, between the hours of 9 a.m. and 5:30 p.m., Monday through Friday, and

(1) Provide information sufficient to identify the record, *e.g.*, the individual's own name, claim and decision number, date and place of birth, etc.;

(2) Provide identification sufficient to verify the individual's identity, *e.g.*, driver's license, identification or Medicare card; and

(3) Any individual requesting access to records or information pertaining to himself or herself may be accompanied by a person of the individual's own choosing while reviewing the records or

§ 503.6

information. If an individual elects to be so accompanied, advance notification of the election will be required along with a written statement authorizing disclosure and discussion of the record in the presence of the accompanying person at any time, including the time access is granted.

(c) Any individual making a request for access to records or information pertaining to himself or herself by mail must address the request to the Administrative Officer (Privacy Officer), Foreign Claims Settlement Commission, 600 E Street, NW., Room 6002, Washington, DC 20579, and must provide information acceptable to the Administrative Officer to verify the individual's identity.

(d) Responses to requests under this section normally will be made within ten (10) days of receipt (excluding Saturdays, Sundays, and legal holidays). If it is not possible to respond to requests within that period, an acknowledgment will be sent to the individual within ten (10) days of receipt of the request (excluding Saturdays, Sundays, and legal holidays).

§ 503.6 Determination of requests for access to records.

(a) Upon request made in accordance with § 503.5, the Administrative Officer will:

(1) Determine whether or not the request will be granted;

(2) Make that determination and provide notification within a reasonable period of time after receipt of the request.

(b) If access to a record is denied because information has been compiled by the Commission in reasonable anticipation of a civil or criminal action or proceeding, the Administrative Officer will notify the individual of that determination and the reason therefor.

(c) If access to the record is granted, the individual making the request must notify the Administrative Officer whether the record requested is to be copied and mailed to the individual.

(d) If a record is to be made available for personal inspection, the individual must arrange with the Administrative Officer a mutually agreeable time and place for inspection of the record.

§ 503.7 Amendment of a record.

(a) Any individual may request amendment of a record pertaining to himself or herself according to the procedure in paragraph (b) of this section, except in the case of records described under paragraph (d) of this section.

(b) After inspection by an individual of a record pertaining to himself or herself, the individual may file a written request, presented in person or by mail, with the Administrative Officer, for an amendment to a record. The request must specify the particular portions of the record to be amended, the desired amendments and the reasons therefor.

(c) Not later than ten (10) days (excluding Saturdays, Sundays, and legal holidays) after the receipt of a request made in accordance with this section to amend a record in whole or in part, the Administrative Officer will:

(1) Make any correction of any portion of the record which the individual believes is not accurate, relevant, timely or complete and thereafter inform the individual of such correction; or

(2) Inform the individual, by certified mail return receipt requested, of the refusal to amend the record, setting forth the reasons therefor, and notify the individual of the right to appeal that determination as provided under Sec. 503.8 of this part.

(d) The provisions for amending records do not apply to evidence presented in the course of Commission proceedings in the adjudication of claims, nor do they permit collateral attack upon what has already been subject to final agency action in the adjudication of claims in programs previously completed by the Commission pursuant to statutory time limitations.

§ 503.8 Appeals from denial of requests for amendment to records.

(a) An individual whose request for amendment of a record pertaining to the individual is denied may request a review of that determination. The request must be addressed to the Chair of the Commission, and must specify the reasons for which the refusal to amend is challenged.

Foreign Claims Settlement Commission, Justice § 503.20

(b) If on appeal the refusal to amend the record is upheld, the Commission will permit the individual to file a statement setting forth the reasons for disagreement with the determination. The statement must also be submitted within 30 days of receipt of the denial. The statement will be included in the system of records in which the disputed record is maintained and will be marked so as to indicate:

(1) That a statement of disagreement has been filed, and

(2) Where in the system of records the statement may be found.

§ 503.9 Fees.

Fees to be charged, if any, to any individual for making copies of that individual's record excluding the cost of any search for and review of the record will be as follows:

(a) Photocopy reproductions: each copy $0.15.

(b) Where the Commission undertakes to perform for a requester, or any other person, services which are clearly not required to be performed under the Privacy Act, either voluntarily or because those services are required by some other law, the question of charging fees for those services will be determined by the official or designee authorized to release the information, under the Federal user charge statute, 31 U.S.C. 583a, any other applicable law, and the provisions of § 502.13 of part 502 of this chapter.

§ 503.10 Exemptions.

No system of records maintained by the Foreign Claims Settlement Commission is exempt from the provisions of 5 U.S.C. 552a as permitted under certain conditions by 5 U.S.C. 552a(j) and (k). However, the Chair of the Commission reserves the right to promulgate rules in accordance with the requirements of 5 U.S.C. 553(b)(1), (2) and (3), and 5 U.S.C. 553(c) and (e) to exempt any system of records maintained by the Commission in accordance with the provisions of 5 U.S.C. 552a(k).

§ 503.11 Reports.

(a) The Administrative Officer or designee will provide adequate advance notice to Congress and the Office of Management and Budget of any proposal to establish or alter any Commission system of records, as required by 5 U.S.C. 552a(o).

(b) If at any time a system of records maintained by the Commission is determined to be exempt from the application of 5 U.S.C. 552a in accordance with the provisions of 5 U.S.C. 552a(j) and (k), the number of records contained in such system will be separately listed and reported to the Office of Management and Budget.

§ 503.12 Notices.

The Commission will publish in the FEDERAL REGISTER at least annually a notice of the existence and character of the systems of records which it maintains. Such notice will include:

(a) The name and location of each system;

(b) The categories of individuals on whom the records are maintained in each system;

(c) The categories of records maintained in each system;

(d) Each routine use of the records contained in each system including the categories of users and the purpose of each use;

(e) The policies and practices of the Commission regarding storage, retrievability, access controls, retention, and disposal of the records;

(f) The title and business address of the agency official who is responsible for each system of records;

(g) Commission procedures whereby an individual can be notified if a system of records contains a record pertaining to that individual;

(h) Commission procedures whereby an individual can be notified how to gain access to any record pertaining to that individual contained in a system of records, and how to contest its content, and

(i) The categories of sources of records in each system.

Subpart B—Government in the Sunshine Regulations

AUTHORITY: 5 U.S.C. 552b.

§ 503.20 Definitions.

For purposes of this part: *Closed meeting* and *closed portion of a meeting* mean, respectively, a meeting or that part of a meeting designated as provided in § 503.27 as closed to the public by reason of one or more of the closure provisions listed in § 503.24.

Commission means the Foreign Claims Settlement Commission, which is a collegial body that functions as a unit composed of three individual members, appointed by the President with the advice and consent of the Senate.

Meeting means the deliberations of at least two (quorum) members of the Commission where such deliberations determine or result in joint conduct or disposition of official Commission business.

Member means any one of the three members of the Commission.

Open meeting means a meeting or portion of a meeting which is not a closed meeting or a closed portion of a meeting.

Public observation means the right of any member of the public to attend and observe, but not participate or interfere in any way, in an open meeting of the Commission within the limits of reasonable and comfortable accommodations made available for such purpose by the Commission.

§ 503.21 Notice of public observation.

(a) A member of the public is not required to give advance notice of an intention to exercise the right of public observation of an open meeting of the Commission. However, in order to permit the Commission to determine the amount of space and number of seats which must be made available to accommodate individuals who desire to exercise the right of public observation, those individuals are requested to give notice to the Commission at least two business days before the start of the open meeting of the intention to exercise that right.

(b) Notice of intention to exercise the right of public observation may be given in writing, in person, or by telephone to the official designated in § 503.29.

(c) Individuals who have not given advance notice of intention to exercise the right of public observation will not be permitted to attend and observe the open meeting of the Commission if the available space and seating are necessary to accommodate individuals who gave advance notice of such intention.

§ 503.22 Scope of application.

The provisions of this part 503, §§ 503.20 through 503.29, apply to meetings of the Commission, and do not apply to conferences or other gatherings of employees of the Commission who meet or join with others, except at meetings of the Commission to deliberate on or conduct official agency business.

§ 503.23 Open meetings.

Every meeting of the Commission will be open to public observation except as provided in § 503.24.

§ 503.24 Grounds for closing a meeting.

(a) Except in a case where the Commission determines otherwise, a meeting or portion of a meeting may be closed to public observation where the Commission determines that the meeting or portion of the meeting is likely to:

(1) Disclose matters that are:

(i) Specifically authorized under criteria established by an Executive Order to be kept secret in the interests of national defense or foreign policy and

(ii) In fact properly classified pursuant to such Executive order;

(2) Relate solely to the internal personnel rules and practices of the Commission;

(3) Disclose matters specifically exempted from disclosure by statute (other than 5 U.S.C. 552) provided that such statute:

(i) Requires that the matters be withheld from the public in such a manner as to leave no discretion on the issue, or

(ii) Establishes particular criteria for withholding or refers to particular types of matters to be withheld;

(4) Disclose trade secrets and commercial or financial information obtained from a person and privileged or confidential;

(5) Involve accusing any person of a crime, or formally censuring any person;

(6) Disclose information of a personal nature where disclosure would constitute a clearly unwarranted invasion of personal privacy;

Foreign Claims Settlement Commission, Justice § 503.26

(7) Disclose investigatory records compiled for law enforcement purposes, or information which if written would be contained in such records, but only to the extent that the production of the records or information would:

(i) Interfere with enforcement proceedings,

(ii) Deprive a person of a right to a fair trial or an impartial adjudication,

(iii) Constitute an unwarranted invasion of personal privacy,

(iv) Disclose the identity of a confidential source and, in the case of a record compiled by a criminal law enforcement authority in the course of a criminal investigation, or by an agency conducting a lawful national security intelligence investigation, confidential information furnished only by the confidential source,

(v) Disclose investigative techniques and procedures, or

(vi) Endanger the life or physical safety of law enforcement personnel;

(8) Disclose information contained in or related to examination, operating, or condition reports prepared by, on behalf of, or for the use of the Commission;

(9) Disclose information the premature disclosure of which would be likely to significantly frustrate implementation of a proposed action of the Commission, provided the Commission has not already disclosed to the public the content or nature of its proposed action, or is not required by law to make the disclosure on its own initiative prior to taking final action on the proposal; or

(10) Specifically concern the Commission's issuance of a subpoena or the Commission's participation in a civil action or proceeding, an action in a foreign court or international tribunal, or an arbitration, or the initiation, conduct, or disposition by the Commission of a particular case of formal agency adjudication pursuant to the procedures in 5 U.S.C. 554, or otherwise involve a determination on the record after opportunity for a hearing.

(b) If the Commission determines that the public interest would require that a meeting to be open, it may nevertheless so hold.

§ 503.25 Announcement of meetings.

(a) The Commission meets in its offices at 600 E Street, NW, Washington, DC, from time to time as announced by timely notice published in the FEDERAL REGISTER.

(b) At the earliest practicable time, which is estimated to be not later than eight days before the beginning of a meeting of the Commission, the Commission will make available for public inspection in its offices, and, if requested, will furnish by telephone or in writing, a notice of the subject matter of the meeting, except to the extent that the information is exempt from disclosure under the provisions of § 503.24.

§ 503.26 Procedures for closing of meetings.

(a) The closing of a meeting will occur when:

(1) A majority of the membership of the Commission votes to take that action. A separate vote of the Commission members will be taken with respect to each Commission meeting, a portion or portions of which are proposed to be closed to the public pursuant to § 503.24, or with respect to any information which is proposed withheld under § 503.24. A single vote may be taken with respect to a series of meetings, a portion or portions of which are proposed to be closed to the public, or with respect to any information concerning that series of meetings, so long as each meeting in the series involves the same particular matters and is scheduled to be held no more than thirty days after the initial meeting in the series. The vote of each Commission member participating in the voting will be recorded and no proxies will be allowed.

(2) Whenever any person whose interests may be directly affected by a portion of a meeting requests that the Commission close that portion to the public for any of the reasons referred to in § 503.24(e), (f), or (g), the Commission, upon request of any one of its Commission members, will take a recorded vote, whether to close that portion of the meeting.

(b) Within one day of any vote taken, the Commission will make publicly available a written copy of the voting reflecting the vote of each member on the question and a full written explanation of its action closing the entire or portion of the meeting together with a list of all persons expected to attend the meeting and their affiliation.

(c) The Commission will announce the time, place and subject matter of the meeting at least eight days before the meeting.

(d) For every closed meeting, before the meeting is closed, the Commission's Chair will publicly certify that the meeting may be closed to the public, and will state each relevant closure provision. A copy of the certification, together with a statement setting forth the time and place of the meeting, and the persons present, will be retained by the Commission.

§ 503.27 Reconsideration of opening or closing, or rescheduling a meeting.

The time or place of a Commission meeting may be changed following the public announcement only if the Commission publicly announces such changes at the earliest practicable time. The subject matter of a meeting, or the determination of the Commission to open or close a meeting, or portion of a meeting, to the public, may be changed following the public announcement only if a majority of the Commission members determines by a recorded vote that Commission business so requires and that no earlier announcement of the changes was possible, and the Commission publicly announces the changes and the vote of each member upon the changes at the earliest practicable time.

§ 503.28 Record of closed meetings, or closed portion of a meeting.

(a) The Commission will maintain a complete transcript or electronic recording adequate to record fully the proceedings of each closed meeting or closed portion of a meeting, except that in the case of a meeting or portion of a meeting closed to the public pursuant to § 503.24(d), (h), or (j), the Commission will maintain either a transcript or recording, or a detailed set of minutes.

(b) Any minutes so maintained will fully and clearly describe all matters discussed and shall provide a full and accurate summary of any actions taken, and the reasons therefor, including a description of each of the views expressed on any item and the record of any rollcall vote. All documents considered in connection with any action will be identified in the minutes.

(c) The Commission will promptly make available to the public, in its offices, the transcript, electronic recording, or minutes, of the discussion of any item on the agenda of a closed meeting, or closed portion of a meeting, except for the item or items of discussion which the Commission determines to contain information which may be withheld under § 503.24. Copies of the transcript or minutes, or a transcription of the recording, disclosing the identity of each speaker, will be furnished to any person at the actual cost of duplication or transcription.

(d) The Commission will maintain a complete verbatim copy of the transcript, a complete copy of the minutes, or a complete electronic recording of each closed meeting or closed portion of a meeting for a period of two years after the date of the closed meeting or closed portion of a meeting.

(e) All actions required or permitted by this section to be undertaken by the Commission will be by or under the authority of the Chair of the Commission.

§ 503.29 Requests for information.

Requests to the Commission for information about the time, place, and subject matter of a meeting, whether it or any portions thereof are closed to the public, and any requests for copies of the transcript or minutes or of a transcript of an electronic recording of a closed meeting, or closed portion of a meeting, to the extent not exempt from disclosure by the provisions of § 503.24, must be addressed to the Administrative Officer, Foreign Claims Settlement Commission, 600 E Street, NW, Room 6002, Washington, DC 20579, telephone (202) 616–6975.

SUBCHAPTER B—RECEIPT, ADMINISTRATION, AND PAYMENT OF CLAIMS UNDER TITLE I OF THE WAR CLAIMS ACT OF 1948, AS AMENDED

PART 504—FILING OF CLAIMS AND PROCEDURES THEREFOR

Sec.
504.1 Claim defined.
504.2 Time within which claims may be filed.
504.3 Official claim forms.
504.4 Place of filing claims.
504.5 Documents to accompany forms.
504.6 Receipt of claims.

AUTHORITY: Sec. 2, Pub. L. 896, 80th Cong., as amended (50 U.S.C. App. 2001).

SOURCE: 66 FR 49844, Oct. 1, 2001, unless otherwise noted.

§ 504.1 Claim defined.

(a) This subchapter is included solely in order to provide for the adjudication of any additional claims that may arise on behalf of survivors of deceased civilians and military veterans who had been listed as missing during the Vietnam conflict but were subsequently determined to have been interned, in hiding, or captured by a hostile force in Southeast Asia (see § 504.2(a)(3) and (b)(3)). The Commission no longer has authority to receive or consider any other types of claims based on the internment of civilians or the maltreatment of military servicemen held as prisoners of war by forces hostile to the United States.

(b) A properly completed and executed application made on an official form provided by the Foreign Claims Settlement Commission for such purpose constitutes a claim and will be processed under the laws administered by the Commission.

(c) Any communication, letter, note, or memorandum from a claimant, or the claimant's duly authorized representative, or a person acting as next friend of a claimant who is not legally competent, setting forth sufficient facts to apprise the Commission of an interest to apply under the provisions of sections 5(i) and 6(f) of the Act, will be deemed to be an informal claim. Where an informal claim is received and an official form is forwarded for completion and execution by the applicant, that official form will be considered as evidence necessary to complete the initial claim, and unless that official form is received within thirty (30) days from the date it was transmitted for execution, if the claimant resides in the continental United States, or forty-five (45) days if outside the continental United States, the claim may be disallowed.

§ 504.2 Time within which claims may be filed.

(a) Claims of individuals entitled to benefits under section 5(i) of the War Claims Act of 1948, as added by Public Law 91–289, will be accepted by the Commission during the period beginning June 24, 1970, and ending:

(1) June 24, 1973, inclusive;

(2) 3 years from the date the civilian American citizen by whom the claim is filed returned to the jurisdiction of the United States; or

(3) 3 years from the date upon which the Commission, at the request of a potentially eligible survivor, makes a determination that the civilian American citizen has actually died or may be presumed to be dead, in the case of any civilian American citizen who has not returned to the jurisdiction of the United States, whichever of the preceding dates last occurs.

(b) Claims of individuals entitled to benefits under section 6(f) of the War Claims Act of 1948, as added by Public Law 91–289, will be accepted by the Commission during the period beginning June 24, 1970, and ending:

(1) June 24, 1973, inclusive;

(2) 3 years from the date the prisoner of war by whom the claim is filed returned to the jurisdiction of the Armed Forces of the United States; or

(3) 3 years from the date the Department of Defense makes a determination that the prisoner of war has actually died or is presumed to be dead, in the case of any prisoner of war who has not returned to the jurisdiction of the Armed Forces of the United States,

§ 504.3

whichever of the preceding dates last occurs.

§ 504.3 Official claim forms.

Official forms are provided for use in the preparation of claims for submission to the Commission for processing. Claim forms are available at the Washington offices of the Commission and through other offices as the Commission may designate. The official claim form for all claims under section 5(i) and 6(f) has been designated FCSC Form 289, "Application for Compensation for Members of the Armed Forces of the United States Held as Prisoner of War in Vietnam; for Persons Assigned to Duty on board the 'U.S.S. Pueblo' Captured by Military Forces of North Korea; for Civilian American Citizens Captured or Who Went into Hiding to Avoid Capture or Internment in Southeast Asia During the Vietnam Conflict and, in Case of Death of any Such Person, for Their Survivors."

§ 504.4 Place of filing claims.

Claims must be mailed or delivered in person to the Foreign Claims Settlement Commission, 600 E Street, NW, Room 6002, Washington, DC 20579.

§ 504.5 Documents to accompany forms.

All claims filed pursuant to sections 5(a) and 6(f) of the Act must be accompanied by evidentiary documents, instruments, and records as outlined in the instruction sheet attached to the claim form.

§ 504.6 Receipt of claims.

(a) *Claims deemed received.* A claim will be deemed to have been received by the Commission on the date postmarked, if mailed, or if delivery is made in person, on the date of delivery at the offices of the Commission in Washington, DC.

(b) *Claims developed.* In the event that a claim has been insufficiently prepared so as to preclude processing thereof, the Commission may request the claimant to furnish whatever supplemental evidence, including the completion and execution of an official claim form, as may be essential to the processing of the claim. In case the evidence or official claim form requested is not returned within the time which may be designated by the Commission, the claim may be deemed to have been abandoned and may be disallowed.

PART 505—PROVISIONS OF GENERAL APPLICATION

Sec.
505.1 Persons eligible to file claims.
505.2 Persons under legal disability.
505.3 Definitions applicable under the Act.

AUTHORITY: Sec. 2, Pub. L. 896, 80th Cong., as amended (50 U.S.C. App. 2001).

SOURCE: 66 FR 49844, Oct. 1, 2001, unless otherwise noted.

§ 505.1 Persons eligible to file claims.

Persons eligible to file claims with the Commission under the provisions of sections 5(i) and 6(f) of the War Claims Act of 1948, as amended, are:

(a) Civilian American citizens captured and held in Southeast Asia or their eligible survivors, under the provisions of section 5(i) of the Act; and

(b) Members of the Armed Forces of the United States held as prisoners of war during the Vietnam conflict or their eligible survivors, under section 6(f) of the Act.

§ 505.2 Persons under legal disability.

(a) Claims may be submitted on behalf of persons who, being otherwise eligible to make claims under the provisions of sections 5(i) and 6(f), are incompetent or otherwise under any legal disability, by the natural or legal guardian, committee, conservator, curator, or any other person, including the spouse of the claimant, whom the Commission determines is charged with the care of the claimant.

(b) Upon the death of any individual for whom an award has been made, the Commission may consider the initial application filed by or in behalf of the decedent as a formal claim for the purpose of reissuing the award to the next eligible survivor in the order of preference as set forth under sections 5(i) and 6(d)(4) of the Act.

§ 505.3 Definitions applicable under the Act.

Child means:

(1) A natural or adopted son or daughter of a deceased prisoner of war

or a deceased civilian prisoner of war or a deceased American citizen including any posthumous son or daughter of such deceased person.

(2) Any son or daughter of a deceased person born out of wedlock will be deemed to be a child of the deceased for the purpose of this Act, if:

(i) Legitimated by a subsequent marriage of the parents,

(ii) Recognized as a child of the deceased by his or her admission, or

(iii) So declared by an order or decree of any court of competent jurisdiction.

Husband means the surviving male spouse of a deceased prisoner of war or of a deceased civilian American citizen who was married to the deceased at the time of her death by a marriage valid under the applicable law of the place entered into.

Natural guardian means father and mother who shall be deemed to be the natural guardians of the person of their minor children. If either dies or is incapable of action, the natural guardianship of the person shall devolve upon the other. In the event of death or incapacity of both parents, then the blood relative, paternal or maternal, standing in loco parentis to the minor shall be deemed the natural guardian.

Parent means:

(1)(i) The natural or adoptive father or mother of a deceased prisoner of war, or any other individual standing in loco parentis to the deceased person for a period of not less than 1 year immediately preceding the date of that person's entry into active service and during at least 1 year of the person's minority. Not more than one mother or one father as defined shall be recognized in any case. An individual will not be recognized as standing in loco parentis if the natural parents or adoptive parents are living, unless there is affirmative evidence of abandonment and renunciation of parental duties and obligations by the natural or adoptive parent or parents prior to entry into active service by the deceased prisoner or war;

(ii) An award in the full amount allowable had the deceased prisoner of war survived may be made to only one parent when it is shown that the other parent has died or if there is affirmative evidence of abandonment and renunciation of parental duties and obligations by the other parent.

(2) The father of an illegitimate child will not be recognized as such for purposes of the Act unless evidence establishes that:

(i) He has legitimated the child by subsequent marriage with the mother;

(ii) Recognized the child as his by written admission prior to enlistment of the deceased in the armed forces or entry into an overseas duty status; or

(iii) Prior to death of the child he has been declared by decree of a court of competent jurisdiction to be the father.

Widow means the surviving female spouse of a deceased prisoner of war or a deceased civilian American citizen who was married to the deceased at the time of his death by marriage valid under the applicable law of the place where entered into.

PART 506—ELIGIBILITY REQUIREMENTS FOR COMPENSATION

Subpart A—Civilian American Citizens

Sec.
506.1 "Civilian American citizen" defined.
506.2 Other definitions.
506.3 Rate of benefits payable.
506.4 Survivors entitled to award of detention benefits.
506.5 Persons not eligible to award of civilian detention benefits.

Subpart B—Prisoners of War

506.10 "Vietnam conflict" defined.
506.11 "Prisoner of war" defined.
506.12 Membership in the Armed Forces of the United States; establishment of.
506.13 "Armed Forces of the United States" defined.
506.14 "Force hostile to the United States" defined.
506.15 Geneva Convention of August 12, 1949.
506.16 Failure to meet the conditions and requirements prescribed under the Geneva Convention of August 12, 1949.
506.17 Rate of and basis for award of compensation.
506.18 Entitlement of survivors to award in case of death of prisoner of war.
506.19 Members of the Armed Forces of the United States precluded from receiving award of compensation.

AUTHORITY: Sec. 2, Pub. L. 896, 80th Cong., as amended (50 U.S.C. App. 2001).

SOURCE: 66 FR 49844, Oct. 1, 2001, unless otherwise noted.

Subpart A—Civilian American Citizens

§ 506.1 "Civilian American citizen" defined.

Civilian American citizen means any person who, being then a citizen of the United States, was captured in Southeast Asia during the Vietnam conflict by any force hostile to the United States, or who went into hiding in Southeast Asia in order to avoid capture or internment by any such hostile force.

§ 506.2 Other definitions.

Calendar month means the period of time between a designated day of any given month and the date preceding a similarly designated day of the following month.

Citizen of the United States means a person who under applicable law acquired citizenship of the United States by birth, by naturalization, or by derivation.

Dependent husband means the surviving male spouse of a deceased civilian American citizen who was married to the deceased at the time of her death by a marriage valid under the applicable law of the place where entered into.

Force hostile to the United States means any organization or force in Southeast Asia, or any agent or employee thereof, engaged in any military or civil activities designed to further the prosecution of its armed conflict against the Armed Forces of the United States during the Vietnam conflict.

Southeast Asia means, but is not necessarily restricted to, the areas of Vietnam, Laos, and Cambodia.

Went into hiding means the action taken by a civilian American citizen when that person initiated a course of conduct consistent with an intention to evade capture or detention by a hostile force in Southeast Asia.

§ 506.3 Rate of benefits payable.

Detention benefits awarded to a civilian American citizen will be paid at the rate of $150 for each calendar month of internment or during the period in which that civilian American citizen went into hiding to avoid capture and internment by a hostile force. Awards shall take account of fractional parts of a calendar month.

§ 506.4 Survivors entitled to award of detention benefits.

In case of death of a civilian American citizen who would have been entitled to detention benefits under the War Claims Act of 1948, as amended, benefits will be awarded, if claim is made, only to the following persons:

(a) Widow or husband if there is no child or children of the deceased;

(b) Widow or dependent husband and child or children of the deceased, one-half to the widow or dependent husband and the other half to the child or children in equal shares;

(c) The child or children of the deceased in equal shares if there is no widow or dependent husband, if otherwise qualified.

§ 506.5 Persons not eligible to award of civilian detention benefits.

An individual is disqualified as a "civilian American citizen" under the Act, and thus is precluded from receiving an award of detention benefits, if that person:

(a) Voluntarily, knowingly, and without duress, gave aid to or collaborated with or in any manner served the detaining hostile force; or

(b) While detained, was a regularly appointed, enrolled, enlisted, or inducted member of the Armed Forces of the United States.

Subpart B—Prisoners of War

§ 506.10 "Vietnam conflict" defined.

Vietnam conflict refers to the period beginning February 28, 1961, and ending on a date to be determined by Presidential proclamation or concurrent resolution of the Congress. (For purposes of determining eligibility for certain veterans' benefits, the President has proclaimed the date of May 7, 1975, to be the ending date of the "Vietnam era" (Presidential Proclamation No. 4373, 38 U.S.C. 101 note). In addition, Congress has set May 7, 1975, as the ending date of the "Vietnam conflict" for purposes of payment of interest on missing military service members' deposits in the United States Treasury under 10 U.S.C. 1035. However, neither the President nor the Congress has set an ending date for the Vietnam conflict for purposes of determining eligibility for compensation under 50 U.S.C. App. 2004 and 2005.)

§ 506.11 "Prisoner of war" defined.

Prisoner of war means any regularly appointed, enrolled, enlisted or inducted member of the Armed Forces of the United States who was held by any force hostile to the United States for any period of time during the Vietnam conflict.

§ 506.12 Membership in the Armed Forces of the United States; establishment of.

Regular appointment, enrollment, enlistment or induction in the Armed Forces of the United States must be established by certification obtained from the Department of Defense.

§ 506.13 "Armed Forces of the United States" defined.

Armed Forces of the United States means the United States Air Force, Army, Navy, Marine Corps and Coast Guard, and commissioned officers of the U.S. Public Health Service who were detailed for active duty with the Armed Forces of the United States.

§ 506.14 "Force hostile to the United States" defined.

Force hostile to the United States means any organization or force in Southeast Asia, or any agent or employee thereof, engaged in any military or civil activities designed to further the prosecution of its armed conflict against the Armed Forces of the United States during the Vietnam conflict.

§ 506.15 Geneva Convention of August 12, 1949.

The Geneva Convention of August 12, 1949, as identified in section 6(f) of the War Claims Act of 1948, as amended, is the "Geneva Convention Relative to the Treatment of Prisoners of War of August 12, 1949" which is included under the "Geneva Convention of August 12, 1949, for the Protection of War Victims," entered into by the United States and other governments, including the former government in North Vietnam which acceded to it on June 28, 1957.

§ 506.16 Failure to meet the conditions and requirements prescribed under the Geneva Convention of August 12, 1949.

For the purpose of this part, obligations under the Geneva Convention of August 12, 1949, consist of the responsibility assumed by the contracting parties thereto with respect to prisoners of war within the meaning of the Convention, to comply with and to fully observe the provisions of the Convention, and particularly those articles relating to food rations of prisoners of war, humane treatment, protection, and labor of prisoners of war, and the failure to abide by the conditions and requirements established in such Convention by any hostile force with which the Armed Forces of the United States were engaged in armed conflict.

§ 506.17 Rate of and basis for award of compensation.

(a) Compensation allowed a prisoner of war during the Vietnam conflict under section 6(f)(2) of the War Claims Act of 1948, as amended, will be paid at the rate of $2 per day for each day on which that person was held as prisoner of war and on which the hostile force, or its agents, failed to furnish the quantity and quality of food prescribed for prisoners of war under the Geneva Convention of August 12, 1949.

(b) Compensation allowed a prisoner of war during the Vietnam conflict under section 6(f)(3) of the Act, will be paid at the rate of $3 per day for each day on which that person was held as a prisoner of war and on which the hostile force failed to meet the conditions and requirements under the provisions of the Geneva Convention of August 12, 1949 relating to labor of prisoners of war or for inhumane treatment by the hostile force by which such person was held.

(c) Compensation under paragraphs (a) and (b) of this section will be paid to the prisoner of war or qualified applicant on a lump-sum basis at a total rate of $5 per day for each day the prisoner of war was entitled to compensation.

§ 506.18 **Entitlement of survivors to award in case of death of prisoner of war.**

In case of death of a prisoner of war who would have been entitled to an award of compensation under section 6(f) (2) and (3) of the War Claims Act of 1948, as amended, the compensation will be awarded, if claim is made, only to the following persons:

(a) Widow or husband if there is no child or children of the deceased;

(b) Widow or husband and child or children of the deceased, one-half to the widow or husband and the other half to the child or children of the deceased in equal shares;

(c) Child or children of the deceased (in equal shares) if there is no widow or husband; and

(d) Parents (in equal shares) if there is no widow, husband or child.

§ 506.19 **Members of the Armed Forces of the United States precluded from receiving award of compensation.**

Any member of the Armed Forces of the United States, who at any time, voluntarily, knowingly, and without duress gave aid to or collaborated with, or in any manner served any force hostile to the United States, is precluded from receiving an award of compensation based on that member's capture and internment.

PART 507—PAYMENT

Sec.
507.1 Payments under the War Claims Act of 1948, as amended by Pub. L. 91-289.
507.2 Payments to persons under legal disability.
507.3 Reissuance of awards.

AUTHORITY: Sec. 2, Pub. L. 80-896, as amended (50 U.S.C. App. 2001).

SOURCE: 66 FR 49844, Oct. 1, 2001, unless otherwise noted.

§ 507.1 **Payments under the War Claims Act of 1948, as amended by Public Law 91-289.**

(a) Upon a determination by the Commission as to the amount and validity of each claim filed pursuant to section 5(i) and 6(f) of the War Claims Act of 1948, as amended, any award made thereunder will be certified by the Commission to the Secretary of the Treasury for payment out of funds appropriated for this purpose, in favor of the civilian internee or prisoner of war found entitled thereto.

(b) Awards made to survivors of deceased civilian internees or prisoners of war will be certified to the Secretary of the Treasury for payment to the individual member or members of the class or classes of survivors entitled to receive compensation in the full amount of the share to which each survivor is entitled, and if applicable, under the procedure set forth in § 507.3, except that as to persons under legal disability, payment will be made as specified in § 507.2.

§ 507.2 **Payments to persons under legal disability.**

Any awards or any part of an award payable under sections 5(i) and 6(f) of the Act to any person under legal disability may, in the discretion of the Commission, be certified for payment for the use of the claimant, to the natural or legal guardian, committee, conservator or curator, or if there is no natural or legal guardian, committee, conservator or curator, then, in the discretion of the Commission, to any person, including the spouse of such person, or the Chief Officer of the hospital in which the claimant may be a patient, whom the Commission may determine is charged with the care of the claimant. In the case of a minor, any part of the amount payable may, in the discretion of the Commission, be certified for payment to that minor.

§ 507.3 **Reissuance of awards.**

Upon the death of any claimant entitled to payment of an award, the Commission will cause the award to be canceled and the amount of the award will be redistributed to the survivors of the same class or to members of the next class of eligible survivors, if appropriate, in the order of preference as set forth under the Act.

PART 508—HEARINGS

Sec.
508.1 Basis for hearing.
508.2 Request for hearing.
508.3 Notification to claimant.
508.4 Failure to file request for hearing.

Foreign Claims Settlement Commission, Justice § 508.8

508.5 Purpose of hearing.
508.6 Resume of hearing, preparation of.
508.7 Action by the Commission.
508.8 Application of other regulations.

AUTHORITY: Sec. 2, Pub. L. 896, 80th Cong., as amended (50 U.S.C. App. 2001).

SOURCE: 66 FR 49844, Oct. 1, 2001, unless otherwise noted.

§ 508.1 Basis for hearing.

Any claimant whose application is denied or is approved for less than the full allowable amount of his or her claim will be entitled to a hearing before the Commission or its representative with respect to that claim. Hearings may also be held on the Commission's own motion.

§ 508.2 Request for hearing.

Within 30 days after the Commission's notice of denial of a claim, or approval for a lesser amount than claimed, has been posted by the Commission, the claimant, if a hearing is desired, must notify the Commission in writing, and must set forth in full the reasons for requesting the hearing, including any statement of law or facts upon which the claimant relies.

§ 508.3 Notification to claimant.

Upon receipt of such a request, the Commission will schedule a hearing and notify the claimant as to the date and place the hearing is to be held. No later than 10 days prior to the scheduled hearing date, the claimant must submit all documents, briefs, or other additional evidence relevant to his or her appeal.

§ 508.4 Failure to file request for hearing.

The failure to file a request for a hearing within the period specified in § 509.2 of this chapter will be deemed to constitute a waiver of right to a hearing and the decision of the Commission will constitute a full and final disposition of the case.

§ 508.5 Purpose of hearing.

(a) Hearings will be conducted by the Commission, its designee or designees. Oral testimony and documentary evidence, including depositions that may have been taken as provided by statute and the rules of practice, may be offered in evidence on claimant's behalf or by counsel for the Commission designated by it to represent the public interest opposed to the allowance of an unjust or unfounded claim or portion thereof, and either may cross-examine as to evidence offered through witnesses on behalf of the other. Objections to the admission of any such evidence will be ruled upon by the presiding officer.

(b) Hearings may be stenographically recorded either at the request of the claimant or at the discretion of the Commission. A claimant making such a request must notify the Commission at least 10 days prior to the hearing date. When a stenographic record of a hearing is ordered at the claimant's request, the cost of such reporting and transcription may be charged to the claimant.

(c) Such hearings will be open to the public.

§ 508.6 Résumé of hearing, preparation of.

Following each hearing, the hearing officer will prepare a résumé of the hearing, specifying the issues on which the hearing was based, and including a list of documents and contents and other items relative to the issues that were introduced as evidence. A brief analysis of oral testimony will also be prepared and included in the résumé of each hearing not stenographically reported.

§ 508.7 Action by the Commission.

After the conclusion of the hearing and a review of the résumé, the Commission may affirm, modify, or reverse its former action with respect to the claim, including a denial or reduction in the amount of the award theretofore approved. All findings of the Commission concerning the persons to whom compensation is payable, and the amounts thereof, are conclusive and not reviewable by any court.

§ 508.8 Application of other regulations.

To the extent they are not inconsistent with the regulations set forth under provisions of this subchapter, the other regulations of the Commission will also be applicable to the claims filed hereunder.

SUBCHAPTER C—RECEIPT, ADMINISTRATION, AND PAYMENT OF CLAIMS UNDER THE INTERNATIONAL CLAIMS SETTLEMENT ACT OF 1949, AS AMENDED, AND RELATED ACTS

PART 509—FILING OF CLAIMS AND PROCEDURES THEREFOR

Sec.
509.1 Time for filing.
509.2 Form, content and filing of claims.
509.3 Exhibits and documents in support of claim.
509.4 Acknowledgment and numbering.
509.5 Procedure for determination of claims.
509.6 Hearings.
509.7 Presettlement conference.

AUTHORITY: Sec. 3, Pub. L. 455, 81st Cong., as amended (22 U.S.C. 1622).

SOURCE: 66 FR 49844, Oct. 1, 2001, unless otherwise noted.

§ 509.1 Time for filing.

Claims must be filed as specified by the Commission by duly promulgated notice published in the FEDERAL REGISTER, or as specified in legislation passed by Congress, as applicable.

§ 509.2 Form, content and filing of claims.

(a) Unless otherwise specified by law, or by regulations published in the FEDERAL REGISTER, claims must be filed on official forms, which will be provided by the Commission upon request in writing addressed to the Commission at its office at 600 E Street, NW, Suite 6002, Washington, DC 20579. Each form must include all of the information called for in it and must be completed and signed in accordance with the instructions accompanying the form.

(b) Notice to the Foreign Claims Settlement Commission, the Department of State, or any other governmental office or agency of an intention to file a claim against a foreign government, prior to the enactment of the statute authorizing a claims program, prior to a referral of claims to the Commission by the Secretary for pre-adjudication, or prior to the effective date of a lump-sum claims settlement agreement, will *not* be considered as a timely filing of a claim under the statute, referral, or agreement.

(c) Any initial written indication of an intention to file a claim received within 30 days prior to the expiration of the filing period thereof will be considered as a timely filing of a claim if formalized within 30 days after the expiration of the filing period.

§ 509.3 Exhibits and documents in support of claim.

(a) *Original documents.* If available, all exhibits and documents must be filed with and at the same time as the claim, and must, wherever possible, be in the form of original documents, or copies or originals certified as such by their public or other official custodian.

(b) *Documents in a foreign language.* Each copy of a document, exhibit or paper filed, which is written or printed in a language other than English, must be accompanied by an English translation thereof duly verified under oath by its translator to be a true and accurate translation thereof, together with the name and address of the translator.

(c) *Preparation of papers.* All claims, briefs, and memoranda filed shall be typewritten or printed and, if typewritten, must be on business letter (8½″ × 11″) size paper.

§ 509.4 Acknowledgment and numbering.

The Commission will acknowledge the receipt of a claim in writing and will notify the claimant of the claim number assigned to it, which number must be used on all further correspondence and papers filed with regard to the claim.

§ 509.5 Procedure for determination of claims.

(a) The Commission may on its own motion order a hearing upon any claim, specifying the questions to which the hearing shall be limited.

(b) Without previous hearing, the Commission or a designated member of the staff may issue a Proposed Decision in determination of a claim. This Proposed Decision will set forth findings of

§ 509.5

fact and conclusions of law on the relevant elements of the claim, to the extent that evidence and information relevant to such elements is before the Commission. The claimant will have the burden of proof in submitting evidence and information sufficient to establish the elements necessary for a determination of the validity and amount of his or her claim.

(c) The Proposed Decision will be delivered to the claimant or the claimant's attorney of record in person or by mail. Delivery by mail will be deemed completed 5 days after the mailing of the Proposed Decision addressed to the last known address of the claimant or the claimant's attorney of record. A copy of the Proposed Decision will be available for public inspection at the offices of the Commission, except in cases where public disclosure of the names of claimants is barred by statute.

(d) It will be the policy of the Commission to post on a bulletin board and on its World Wide Web site (*http://www.usdoj.gov/fcsc*), any information of general interest to claimants before the Commission.

(e) When the Proposed Decision denies a claim in whole or in part, the claimant may file notice of objection to the denial within 15 days of delivery of the decision. If the claimant wishes to appear at an oral hearing before the Commission to present his or her objection, the claimant must request the oral hearing at the time of submission of his or her objection, stating the reasons for objection, and may request a hearing on the claim, specifying whether for the taking of evidence or for oral argument on the legal issues which are the subject of the objection.

(f) Copies of objections to or requests for hearings on Proposed Decisions will be available for public inspection at the Commission's offices.

(g) Upon the expiration of 30 days after delivery to the claimant or claimant's attorney, if no objection under this section has in the meantime been filed, a staff Proposed Decision, upon approval by the Commission, will become the Commission's final determination and decision on the claim. A Proposed Decision issued by the Commission will become final 30 days after delivery to the claimant or the claimant's attorney without further order or decision by the Commission.

(h) If an objection has in the meantime been filed, but no hearing requested, the Commission may, after due consideration thereof:

(1) Issue a Final Decision affirming or modifying its Proposed Decision,

(2) Issue an Amended Proposed Decision, or

(3) On its own motion order hearing thereon, indicating whether for the taking of evidence on specified questions or for the hearing of oral arguments.

(i) After the conclusion of a hearing, upon the expiration of any time allowed by the Commission for further submissions, the Commission may proceed to issue a Final Decision in determination of the claim.

(j)(1) In case an individual claimant dies prior to the issuance of the Final Decision, that person's legal representative will be substituted as party claimant. However, upon failure of a representative to qualify for substitution, the Commission may issue its decision in the name of the estate of the deceased and, in case of an award, certify the award in the same manner to the Secretary of the Treasury for payment, if the payment of the award is provided for by statute.

(2) Notice of the Commission's action under this paragraph will be forwarded to the claimant's attorney of record, or if the claimant is not represented by an attorney, the notice will be addressed to the estate of the claimant at the last known place of residence.

(3) The term *legal representative* as applied in this paragraph means, in general, the administrator or executor, heir(s), next of kin, or descendant(s).

(k) After the date of filing with the Commission no claim may be amended to reflect the assignment thereof by the claimant to any other person or entity except as otherwise provided by statute.

(l) At any time after a final Decision has been issued on a claim, or a Proposed Decision has been entered as the Final Decision on a claim, but not later than 60 days before the completion date of the Commission's affairs in connection with the program under which such claim is filed, a petition to reopen on the ground of newly discovered evidence may be filed. No such petition will be entertained unless it appears therein that the newly discovered evidence came to the knowledge of the party filing the petition subsequent to the date of issuance of the Final Decision or the date on which the Proposed Decision was entered as the Final Decision; that it was not for want of due diligence that the evidence did not come sooner to the claimant's knowledge; and that the evidence is material, and not merely cumulative, and that reconsideration of the matter on the basis of that evidence would produce a different decision. The petition must include a statement of the facts which the petitioner expects to prove, the name and address of each witness, the identity of documents, and the reasons for failure to make earlier submission of the evidence.

§ 509.6 Hearings.

(a) Hearings, whether upon the Commission's own motion or upon request of claimant, will be held upon not less than fifteen days' notice of the time and place thereof.

(b) The hearings will be open to the public unless otherwise requested by claimant and ordered by the Commission, or when required by law.

(c) The hearings will be conducted by the Commission, its designee or designees. Oral testimony and documentary evidence, including depositions that may have been taken as provided by statute and the rules of practices, may be offered in evidence on the claimant's behalf or by counsel for the Commission designated by it to represent the public interest opposed to the allowance of any unjust or unfounded claim or portion thereof; and either may cross-examine as to evidence offered through witnesses on behalf of the other. Objections to the admission of any such evidence will be ruled upon by the presiding officer.

(d) The hearings will be conducted as non-adversarial proceedings. However, the claimant will be the moving party, and will have the burden of proof on all issues involved in the determination of his or her claim.

(e) Hearings may be stenographically reported or electronically recorded, either at the request of the claimant or upon the discretion of the Commission. A claimant making such a request must notify the Commission at least ten (10) days prior to the hearing date. When a stenographic record or transcript of a hearing is ordered at the claimant's request, the cost of the reporting and transcription will be charged to the claimant.

(f) The following rules of procedure will apply in the conduct of hearings held by the Commission for presentation of objections to Proposed Decisions:

(1) *Presentation of objections to Proposed Decisions.* (i) Objections should focus either on the presentation of new evidence, or on the presentation of arguments demonstrating that, in the claimant's view, the Commission erred in considering the evidence previously submitted. Restatements of facts, evidence or materials already established in the record should be avoided.

(ii) The Chief Counsel of the Commission or designated staff attorney will first introduce the objecting claimant and any witnesses to the Commission, and will then present a brief summary of the case, together with reasons supporting the decision as issued.

(iii) The objecting claimant and all witnesses will be sworn.

(iv) The objecting claimant, or the claimant's attorney, will then present the claimant's objections to the Commission, specifically setting forth the basis for the claimant's disagreement with the Proposed Decision, and the reasons supporting the claimant's contention that a more favorable decision should be rendered. Claimants will normally be limited to fifteen (15) minutes for their presentation of objections, but may request additional time if needed.

(v) Following presentation of the claimant's objection, the Chief Counsel or designated staff attorney will be allotted an equivalent amount of time to question the claimant and the claimant's witnesses with respect to the testimony and other evidence presented in support of the objection.

(vi) The objecting claimant or the claimant's attorney, and the Chief

Counsel or designated staff attorney, will then be allotted up to five (5) minutes each for follow-up or rebuttal.

(vii) The Chair and Commissioners may direct questions to the objecting claimant and the claimant's attorney, and to the Chief Counsel or designated staff attorney, at any time during the proceedings described in the foregoing.

(viii) The foregoing provisions may be modified at the discretion of the Chair as circumstances may require.

(ix) At the conclusion, the Chair will inform the participants that the Commission will take the matter under advisement, and that a written Final Decision disposing of the objection will issue in due course.

(2) *Submission to Questioning/Conduct of Proceedings* (i) Presentation of the claimant's objection by the objecting claimant or the claimant's attorney, and of follow-up and rebuttal by the claimant or the claimant's attorney and by the Chief Counsel or designated staff attorney, must be directed to the Commission. Verbal exchanges between the objecting claimant or the claimant's attorney, and the Chief Counsel or designated staff attorney, will be limited to questions and answers during the questioning phase of the proceeding described in paragraph (f)(1)(v) of this section, unless otherwise necessary for clarification or exchange of documents.

(ii) Professional conduct and courtesies of the kind normally accorded in appellate judicial proceedings must be observed in all appearances and proceedings before the Commission.

§ 509.7 **Presettlement conference.**

The Commission on its own motion or initiative, or upon the application of a claimant for good cause shown, may direct that a presettlement conference be held with respect to any issue involved in a claim.

SUBCHAPTER D—RECEIPT, ADMINISTRATION, AND PAYMENT OF CLAIMS UNDER THE GUAM WORLD WAR II LOYALTY RECOGNITION ACT

PART 510—FILING OF CLAIMS AND PROCEDURES THEREFOR

Sec.
510.1 Definitions.
510.2 Time for filing.
510.3 Applicability of administrative provisions concerning claims under the International Claims Settlement Act of 1949.

AUTHORITY: Sec.1705(a)(2), Pub. L. 114–328, 114th Cong., 130 Stat. 2644.

SOURCE: 82 FR 16126, Apr. 3, 2017, unless otherwise noted.

§ 510.1 Definitions.

For purposes of this subchapter:

Personal injury means a discernible injury (such as disfigurement, scarring, or burns) that is more serious than a superficial injury.

Severe personal injury means loss of a limb, dismemberment, paralysis, or any injury of a similar type or that is comparable in severity.

§ 510.2 Time for filing.

Claims for payments under the Guam World War II Loyalty Recognition Act, Title XVII, Public Law 114–328 (the "Act"), must be filed not later than one year after the date on which the Commission publishes the notice described in section 1705(b)(2)(B) of the Act.

§ 510.3 Applicability of administrative provisions concerning claims under the International Claims Settlement Act of 1949.

To the extent they are not inconsistent with the provisions of the Act, the following provisions of subchapter C of this chapter shall be applicable to claims under this subchapter: §§ 509.2, 509.3, 509.4, 509.5, and 509.6.

PARTS 511–599 [RESERVED]

CHAPTER VI—NATIONAL SCIENCE FOUNDATION

Part		Page
600	[Reserved]	
601	Classification and declassification of national security information	41
604	New restrictions on lobbying	43
605	Nondiscrimination on the basis of handicap in programs or activities receiving Federal financial assistance	55
606	Enforcement of nondiscrimination on the basis of handicap in programs or activities conducted by the National Science Foundation	71
607	Salary offset	77
608	Claims collection and administrative offset	81
611	Nondiscrimination in federally-assisted programs of the National Science Foundation—effectuation of title VI of the Civil Rights Act of 1964	85
612	Availability of records and information	95
613	Privacy Act regulations	108
614	Government in the Sunshine Act regulations of the National Science Board	112
615	Testimony and production of records	115
617	Nondiscrimination on the basis of age in programs or activities receiving Federal financial assistance from NSF	117
618	Nondiscrimination on the basis of sex in education programs or activities receiving Federal financial assistance	121
630	Governmentwide requirements for drug-free workplace (financial assistance)	138
640	Compliance with the National Environmental Policy Act	143
641	Environmental assessment procedures for proposed National Science Foundation actions in Antarctica	147
650	Patents	152

Part		Page
660	Intergovernmental review of the National Science Foundation programs and activities	161
670	Conservation of Antarctic animals and plants	164
671	Waste regulation	177
672	Enforcement and hearing procedures	185
673	Antarctic non-governmental expeditions	198
674	Antarctic meteorites	199
675	Medical clearance process for deployment to Antarctica	201
680	National Science Foundation Rules of Practice	202
681	Program Fraud Civil Remedies Act regulations	205
689	Research misconduct	218
690	Protection of human subjects	223
691–699	[Reserved]	

PART 600 [RESERVED]

PART 601—CLASSIFICATION AND DECLASSIFICATION OF NATIONAL SECURITY INFORMATION

Sec.
601.1 Purpose.
601.2 Classification authority.
601.3 Security program.
601.4 Classification Review Committee.
601.5 Derivative classification.
601.6 Downgrading and declassification.
601.7 Mandatory declassification review.
601.8 Access to classified materials.
601.9 Access by historical researchers and former Presidential appointees.

AUTHORITY: E.O. 12958, 3 CFR, 1995 Comp. p. 333.

SOURCE: 47 FR 57284, Dec. 23, 1983, unless otherwise noted.

§ 601.1 Purpose.

Pursuant to Executive Order 12958 and Information Security Oversight Office Directive No. 1, the National Science Foundation [Foundation] issues the following regulations. The regulations identify the information to be protected, prescribe classification, declassification, downgrading, and safeguarding procedures to be followed, and establish a monitoring system to ensure the regulations' effectiveness.

[47 FR 57284, Dec. 23, 1983, as amended at 61 FR 51021, Sept. 30, 1996]

§ 601.2 Classification authority.

The Foundation does not have original classification authority under Executive Order 12958. In any instance where a Foundation employee develops information that appears to warrant classification because of its national security character, the material will be afforded protection and sent to the Division of Administrative Services (DAS). Upon determination that classification is warranted, DAS will submit such material to the agency that has appropriate subject matter interest and classification authority.

[47 FR 57284, Dec. 23, 1983, as amended at 61 FR 51021, Sept. 30, 1996]

§ 601.3 Security program.

The Director, Division of Administrative Services, is responsible for conducting a security program that ensures effective implementation of Executive Order 12958, to include:

(a) Maintaining active training and orientation programs for employees concerned with classified information or material.

(b) Encouraging Foundation personnel to challenge those classification decisions they believe to be improper.

(c) Issuing directives that ensure classified information is used, processed, stored, reproduced and transmitted only under conditions that will provide adequate protection and prevent access by unauthorized persons.

(d) Recommending to the Director appropriate administrative action to correct abuse or violation of any provision of these regulations, including notification by warning letters, formal reprimand, and to the extent permitted by law, suspension without pay and removal.

[47 FR 57284, Dec. 23, 1983, as amended at 61 FR 51021, Sept. 30, 1996]

§ 601.4 Classification Review Committee.

The Security Officer (Information) chairs the Foundation's Classification Review Committee which has authority to act on all suggestions and complaints with respect to the Foundation's administration of the regulations. The Assistant Directors and the Heads of other offices reporting to the Director serve as members of the Committee. All suggestions and complaints including those regarding overclassification, failure to classify, or delay in declassifying not otherwise resolved, shall be referred to the Committee for resolution. The Committee shall establish procedures to review and act within 30 days upon all appeals regarding requests for declassification. The Committee is authorized to overrule previous determinations in whole or in part when in its judgment, continued protection is no longer required. If the Committee determines that continued classification is required under the criteria of the Executive Order, it shall promptly so notify the requester and advise him that he may file an application for review with the Foundation. In addition, the Committee shall review all appeals of requests for records under section 552 of title 5 U.S.C. (Freedom of Information Act) when the proposed denial is based on their continued classification under Executive Order 12958.

[47 FR 57284, Dec. 23, 1983, as amended at 61 FR 51021, Sept. 30, 1996]

§ 601.5 Derivative classification.

Distinct from "original" classification is the determination that information is in substance the same as information currently classified, because of incorporating, paraphrasing, restating or generating in new form information that is already classified, and marking the newly developed material consistent with the marking of the source information. Persons who only reproduce, extract, or summarize classified information, or who only apply classification markings derived from source material or as directed by a classification guide, need not possess original classification authority.

(a) If a person who applies derivative classification markings believes that the paraphrasing, restating, or summarizing of classified information has changed the level of or removed the basis for classification, that person must consult for a determination an appropriate official of the originating agency or office of origin who has the authority to upgrade, downgrade, or declassify the information.

(b) The person who applies derivative classification markings shall observe and respect original classification decisions; and carry forward to any newly created documents any assigned authorized markings. The declassification date or event that provides the longest period of classification shall be used for documents classified on the basis of multiple sources.

§ 601.6 Downgrading and declassification.

Executive Order 12958 prescribes a uniform system for classifying, declassifying, and safeguarding national security information.

(a) Information shall be declassified or downgraded as soon as national security considerations permit. The National Science Foundation shall coordinate their review of classified information with other agencies that have a direct interests in the subject matter. Information that continues to meet the classification requirements prescribed by Section 1.3 despite the passage of time will continue to be protected in accordance with Executive Order 12958.

(b) Foundation documents may be declassified or downgraded by the official who authorized the original classification, if that official is still serving in the same position; the originator's successor; a supervisory official of either; or officials delegated such authority in writing by the Director.

(c) The Director shall conduct internal systematic review programs for classified information originated by the Foundation contained in records determined by the Archivist to be permanently valuable but that have not been accessioned into the National Archives of the United States.

(d) The Archivist of the United States shall, in accordance with procedures and timeframes prescribed in the Information Security Oversight Office's directives implementing Executive Order 12958, systematically review for declassification or downgrading, classified records accessioned into the National Archives of the United States. Such information shall be reviewed by the Archivist for declassification or downgrading in accordance with systematic review guidelines that shall be provided by the head of the agency that originated the information, or in the case of foreign government information, by the Director of Information Security Oversight Office in consultation with interested agency heads.

[47 FR 57284, Dec. 23, 1983, as amended at 61 FR 51021, Sept. 30, 1996]

§ 601.7 Mandatory declassification review.

(a) The Division of Administrative Services is hereby designated as the office to which members of the public or Departments may direct requests for mandatory review for declassification under this provision. In the case of documents originally classified by the Foundation, this office shall, in turn, assign the request to the appropriate office for action within 60 days. In each instance, receipt of the request will be acknowledged in writing immediately by the office that has been assigned action. A request for classification review must reasonably describe the document.

(b) Whenever a request is deficient in its description of the record sought, the requester should be asked to provide additional identifying information to the extent possible. Whenever a request does not reasonably describe the information sought, the requester shall be notified that unless additional information is provided or the scope of the request is narrowed, no further action will be undertaken. Upon a determination that the requested material no longer warrants classification, it shall be declassified and made promptly available to the requester, if not otherwise exempt from disclosure under 5 U.S.C. 552(b) (Freedom of Information Act) or other provision of law. If the information may not be released in whole or in part the requester shall be given a brief statement as to the reasons for denial, a notice of the right to appeal the determination of the Classification Review Committee, and a notice that such an appeal must be filed with the Foundation within 60 days in order to be considered.

(c) When the request relates to a document given derivative classification by the Foundation or originated by another agency, the request and the document will be forwarded to the originator of the source document, and the requestor notified of such referral.

(d) Employees presently cleared for access to classified information are encouraged to challenge classification in cases where there is reasonable cause to believe that information is classified unnecessarily, improperly, or for an inappropriate period of time. Such challenges should be brought to the attention of the Security Officer (Information) who will act thereon within 30 days, informing the challenger of actions taken. Requests for confidentiality will be honored.

§ 601.8 Access to classified materials.

No person may be given access to classified information unless that person has been determined to be trustworthy and unless access is essential to the accomplishment of lawful and authorized Government purposes.

§ 601.9 Access by historical researchers and former Presidential appointees.

The requirement in § 601.8 that access to classified information may be granted only as is essential to the accomplishment of lawful and authorized Government purposes may be waived for persons who are engaged in historical research projects, or previously have occupied policymaking positions to which they were appointed by the President, provided they execute written agreements to safeguard the information and written consent to the Foundation's review of their notes and manuscripts solely for the purpose of determining that no classified information is disclosed. A precondition to any such access is the favorable completion of an appropriate investigative inquiry.

PART 604—NEW RESTRICTIONS ON LOBBYING

Subpart A—General

Sec.
604.100 Conditions on use of funds.
604.105 Definitions.
604.110 Certification and disclosure.

Subpart B—Activities by Own Employees

604.200 Agency and legislative liaison.
604.205 Professional and technical services.
604.210 Reporting.

Subpart C—Activities by Other Than Own Employees

604.300 Professional and technical services.

Subpart D—Penalties and Enforcement

604.400 Penalties.
604.405 Penalty procedures.
604.410 Enforcement.

Subpart E—Exemptions

604.500 Secretary of Defense.

Subpart F—Agency Reports

604.600 Semi-annual compilation.
604.605 Inspector General report.
APPENDIX A TO PART 604—CERTIFICATION REGARDING LOBBYING
APPENDIX B TO PART 604—DISCLOSURE FORM TO REPORT LOBBYING

AUTHORITY: Sec. 319, Pub. L. 101–121 (31 U.S.C. 1352); 42 U.S.C. 1870.

§ 604.100

SOURCE: 55 FR 6737, 6754, Feb. 26, 1990, unless otherwise noted.

CROSS REFERENCE: See also Office of Management and Budget notice published at 54 FR 52306, December 20, 1989.

Subpart A—General

§ 604.100 Conditions on use of funds.

(a) No appropriated funds may be expended by the recipient of a Federal contract, grant, loan, or cooperative ageement to pay any person for influencing or attempting to influence an officer or employee of any agency, a Member of Congress, an officer or employee of Congress, or an employee of a Member of Congress in connection with any of the following covered Federal actions: the awarding of any Federal contract, the making of any Federal grant, the making of any Federal loan, the entering into of any cooperative agreement, and the extension, continuation, renewal, amendment, or modification of any Federal contract, grant, loan, or cooperative agreement.

(b) Each person who requests or receives from an agency a Federal contract, grant, loan, or cooperative agreement shall file with that agency a certification, set forth in appendix A, that the person has not made, and will not make, any payment prohibited by paragraph (a) of this section.

(c) Each person who requests or receives from an agency a Federal contract, grant, loan, or a cooperative agreement shall file with that agency a disclosure form, set forth in appendix B, if such person has made or has agreed to make any payment using nonappropriated funds (to include profits from any covered Federal action), which would be prohibited under paragraph (a) of this section if paid for with appropriated funds.

(d) Each person who requests or receives from an agency a commitment providing for the United States to insure or guarantee a loan shall file with that agency a statement, set forth in appendix A, whether that person has made or has agreed to make any payment to influence or attempt to influence an officer or employee of any agency, a Member of Congress, an officer or employee of Congress, or an employee of a Member of Congress in connection with that loan insurance or guarantee.

(e) Each person who requests or receives from an agency a commitment providing for the United States to insure or guarantee a loan shall file with that agency a disclosure form, set forth in appendix B, if that person has made or has agreed to make any payment to influence or attempt to influence an officer or employee of any agency, a Member of Congress, an officer or employee of Congress, or an employee of a Member of Congress in connection with that loan insurance or guarantee.

§ 604.105 Definitions.

For purposes of this part:

(a) *Agency*, as defined in 5 U.S.C. 552(f), includes Federal executive departments and agencies as well as independent regulatory commissions and Government corporations, as defined in 31 U.S.C. 9101(1).

(b) *Covered Federal action* means any of the following Federal actions:

(1) The awarding of any Federal contract;

(2) The making of any Federal grant;

(3) The making of any Federal loan;

(4) The entering into of any cooperative agreement; and,

(5) The extension, continuation, renewal, amendment, or modification of any Federal contract, grant, loan, or cooperative agreement.

Covered Federal action does not include receiving from an agency a commitment providing for the United States to insure or guarantee a loan. Loan guarantees and loan insurance are addressed independently within this part.

(c) *Federal contract* means an acquisition contract awarded by an agency, including those subject to the Federal Acquisition Regulation (FAR), and any other acquisition contract for real or personal property or services not subject to the FAR.

(d) *Federal cooperative agreement* means a cooperative agreement entered into by an agency.

(e) *Federal grant* means an award of financial assistance in the form of money, or property in lieu of money, by the Federal Government or a direct

National Science Foundation § 604.105

appropriation made by law to any person. The term does not include technical assistance which provides services instead of money, or other assistance in the form of revenue sharing, loans, loan guarantees, loan insurance, interest subsidies, insurance, or direct United States cash assistance to an individual.

(f) *Federal loan* means a loan made by an agency. The term does not include loan guarantee or loan insurance.

(g) *Indian tribe* and *tribal organization* have the meaning provided in section 4 of the Indian Self-Determination and Education Assistance Act (25 U.S.C. 450B). Alaskan Natives are included under the definitions of Indian tribes in that Act.

(h) *Influencing or attempting to influence* means making, with the intent to influence, any communication to or appearance before an officer or employee or any agency, a Member of Congress, an officer or employee of Congress, or an employee of a Member of Congress in connection with any covered Federal action.

(i) *Loan guarantee* and *loan insurance* means an agency's guarantee or insurance of a loan made by a person.

(j) *Local government* means a unit of government in a State and, if chartered, established, or otherwise recognized by a State for the performance of a governmental duty, including a local public authority, a special district, an intrastate district, a council of governments, a sponsor group representative organization, and any other instrumentality of a local government.

(k) *Officer or employee of an agency* includes the following individuals who are employed by an agency:

(1) An individual who is appointed to a position in the Government under title 5, U.S. Code, including a position under a temporary appointment;

(2) A member of the uniformed services as defined in section 101(3), title 37, U.S. Code;

(3) A special Government employee as defined in section 202, title 18, U.S. Code; and,

(4) An individual who is a member of a Federal advisory committee, as defined by the Federal Advisory Committee Act, title 5, U.S. Code appendix 2.

(l) *Person* means an individual, corporation, company, association, authority, firm, partnership, society, State, and local government, regardless of whether such entity is operated for profit or not for profit. This term excludes an Indian tribe, tribal organization, or any other Indian organization with respect to expenditures specifically permitted by other Federal law.

(m) *Reasonable compensation* means, with respect to a regularly employed officer or employee of any person, compensation that is consistent with the normal compensation for such officer or employee for work that is not furnished to, not funded by, or not furnished in cooperation with the Federal Government.

(n) *Reasonable payment* means, with respect to perfessional and other technical services, a payment in an amount that is consistent with the amount normally paid for such services in the private sector.

(o) *Recipient* includes all contractors, subcontractors at any tier, and subgrantees at any tier of the recipient of funds received in connection with a Federal contract, grant, loan, or cooperative agreement. The term excludes an Indian tribe, tribal organization, or any other Indian organization with respect to expenditures specifically permitted by other Federal law.

(p) *Regularly employed* means, with respect to an officer or employee of a person requesting or receiving a Federal contract, grant, loan, or cooperative agreement or a commitment providing for the United States to insure or guarantee a loan, an officer or employee who is employed by such person for at least 130 working days within one year immediately preceding the date of the submission that initiates agency consideration of such person for receipt of such contract, grant, loan, cooperative agreement, loan insurance commitment, or loan guarantee commitment. An officer or employee who is employed by such person for less than 130 working days within one year immediately preceding the date of the submission that initiates agency consideration of such person shall be considered to be regularly employed as

45

soon as he or she is employed by such person for 130 working days.

(q) *State* means a State of the United States, the District of Columbia, the Commonwealth of Puerto Rico, a territory or possession of the United States, an agency or instrumentality of a State, and a multi-State, regional, or interstate entity having governmental duties and powers.

§ 604.110 **Certification and disclosure.**

(a) Each person shall file a certification, and a disclosure form, if required, with each submission that initiates agency consideration of such person for:

(1) Award of a Federal contract, grant, or cooperative agreement exceeding $100,000; or

(2) An award of a Federal loan or a commitment providing for the United States to insure or guarantee a loan exceeding $150,000.

(b) Each person shall file a certification, and a disclosure form, if required, upon receipt by such person of:

(1) A Federal contract, grant, or cooperative agreement exceeding $100,000; or

(2) A Federal loan or a commitment providing for the United States to insure or guarantee a loan exceeding $150,000,

unless such person previously filed a certification, and a disclosure form, if required, under paragraph (a) of this section.

(c) Each person shall file a disclosure form at the end of each calendar quarter in which there occurs any event that requires disclosure or that materially affects the accuracy of the information contained in any disclosure form previously filed by such person under paragraph (a) or (b) of this section. An event that materially affects the accuracy of the information reported includes:

(1) A cumulative increase of $25,000 or more in the amount paid or expected to be paid for influencing or attempting to influence a covered Federal action; or

(2) A change in the person(s) or individual(s) influencing or attempting to influence a covered Federal action; or,

(3) A change in the officer(s), employee(s), or Member(s) contacted to influence or attempt to influence a covered Federal action.

(d) Any person who requests or receives from a person referred to in paragraph (a) or (b) of this section:

(1) A subcontract exceeding $100,000 at any tier under a Federal contract;

(2) A subgrant, contract, or subcontract exceeding $100,000 at any tier under a Federal grant;

(3) A contract or subcontract exceeding $100,000 at any tier under a Federal loan exceeding $150,000; or,

(4) A contract or subcontract exceeding $100,000 at any tier under a Federal cooperative agreement,

shall file a certification, and a disclosure form, if required, to the next tier above.

(e) All disclosure forms, but not certifications, shall be forwarded from tier to tier until received by the person referred to in paragraph (a) or (b) of this section. That person shall forward all disclosure forms to the agency.

(f) Any certification or disclosure form filed under paragraph (e) of this section shall be treated as a material representation of fact upon which all receiving tiers shall rely. All liability arising from an erroneous representation shall be borne solely by the tier filing that representation and shall not be shared by any tier to which the erroneous representation is forwarded. Submitting an erroneous certification or disclosure constitutes a failure to file the required certification or disclosure, respectively. If a person fails to file a required certification or disclosure, the United States may pursue all available remedies, including those authorized by section 1352, title 31, U.S. Code.

(g) For awards and commitments in process prior to December 23, 1989, but not made before that date, certifications shall be required at award or commitment, covering activities occurring between December 23, 1989, and the date of award or commitment. However, for awards and commitments in process prior to the December 23, 1989 effective date of these provisions, but not made before December 23, 1989, disclosure forms shall not be required at time of award or commitment but shall be filed within 30 days.

(h) No reporting is required for an activity paid for with appropriated funds if that activity is allowable under either subpart B or C.

Subpart B—Activities by Own Employees

§ 604.200 Agency and legislative liaison.

(a) The prohibition on the use of appropriated funds, in § 604.100 (a), does not apply in the case of a payment of reasonable compensation made to an officer or employee of a person requesting or receiving a Federal contract, grant, loan, or cooperative agreement if the payment is for agency and legislative liaison activities not directly related to a covered Federal action.

(b) For purposes of paragraph (a) of this section, providing any information specifically requested by an agency or Congress is allowable at any time.

(c) For purposes of paragraph (a) of this section, the following agency and legislative liaison activities are allowable at any time only where they are not related to a specific solicitation for any covered Federal action:

(1) Discussing with an agency (including individual demonstrations) the qualities and characteristics of the person's products or services, conditions or terms of sale, and service capabilities; and,

(2) Technical discussions and other activities regarding the application or adaptation of the person's products or services for an agency's use.

(d) For purposes of paragraph (a) of this section, the following agencies and legislative liaison activities are allowable only where they are prior to formal solicitation of any covered Federal action:

(1) Providing any information not specifically requested but necessary for an agency to make an informed decision about initiation of a covered Federal action;

(2) Technical discussions regarding the preparation of an unsolicited proposal prior to its official submission; and,

(3) Capability presentations by persons seeking awards from an agency pursuant to the provisions of the Small Business Act, as amended by Public Law 95–507 and other subsequent amendments.

(e) Only those activities expressly authorized by this section are allowable under this section.

§ 604.205 Professional and technical services.

(a) The prohibition on the use of appropriated funds, in § 604.100 (a), does not apply in the case of a payment of reasonable compensation made to an officer or employee of a person requesting or receiving a Federal contract, grant, loan, or cooperative agreement or an extension, continuation, renewal, amendment, or modification of a Federal contract, grant, loan, or cooperative agreement if payment is for professional or technical services rendered directly in the preparation, submission, or negotiation of any bid, proposal, or application for that Federal contract, grant, loan, or cooperative agreement or for meeting requirements imposed by or pursuant to law as a condition for receiving that Federal contract, grant, loan, or cooperative agreement.

(b) For purposes of paragraph (a) of this section, "professional and technical services" shall be limited to advice and analysis directly applying any professional or technical discipline. For example, drafting of a legal document accompanying a bid or proposal by a lawyer is allowable. Similarly, technical advice provided by an engineer on the performance or operational capability of a piece of equipment rendered directly in the negotiation of a contract is allowable. However, communications with the intent to influence made by a professional (such as a licensed lawyer) or a technical person (such as a licensed accountant) are not allowable under this section unless they provide advice and analysis directly applying their professional or technical expertise and unless the advice or analysis is rendered directly and solely in the preparation, submission or negotiation of a covered Federal action. Thus, for example, communications with the intent to influence made by a lawyer that do not provide legal advice or analysis directly and solely related to the legal aspects of

§ 604.210

his or her client's proposal, but generally advocate one proposal over another are not allowable under this section because the lawyer is not providing professional legal services. Similarly, communications with the intent to influence made by an engineer providing an engineering analysis prior to the preparation or submission of a bid or proposal are not allowable under this section since the engineer is providing technical services but not directly in the preparation, submission or negotiation of a covered Federal action.

(c) Requirements imposed by or pursuant to law as a condition for receiving a covered Federal award include those required by law or regulation, or reasonably expected to be required by law or regulation, and any other requirements in the actual award documents.

(d) Only those services expressly authorized by this section are allowable under this section.

§ 604.210   Reporting.

No reporting is required with respect to payments of reasonable compensation made to regularly employed officers or employees of a person.

Subpart C—Activities by Other Than Own Employees

§ 604.300   Professional and technical services.

(a) The prohibition on the use of appropriated funds, in § 604.100 (a), does not apply in the case of any reasonable payment to a person, other than an officer or employee of a person requesting or receiving a covered Federal action, if the payment is for professional or technical services rendered directly in the preparation, submission, or negotiation of any bid, proposal, or application for that Federal contract, grant, loan, or cooperative agreement or for meeting requirements imposed by or pursuant to law as a condition for receiving that Federal contract, grant, loan, or cooperative agreement.

(b) The reporting requirements in § 604.110 (a) and (b) regarding filing a disclosure form by each person, if required, shall not apply with respect to professional or technical services rendered directly in the preparation, submission, or negotiation of any commitment providing for the United States to insure or guarantee a loan.

(c) For purposes of paragraph (a) of this section, "professional and technical services" shall be limited to advice and analysis directly applying any professional or technical discipline. For example, drafting or a legal document accompanying a bid or proposal by a lawyer is allowable. Similarly, technical advice provided by an engineer on the performance or operational capability of a piece of equipment rendered directly in the negotiation of a contract is allowable. However, communications with the intent to influence made by a professional (such as a licensed lawyer) or a technical person (such as a licensed accountant) are not allowable under this section unless they provide advice and analysis directly applying their professional or technical expertise and unless the advice or analysis is rendered directly and solely in the preparation, submission or negotiation of a covered Federal action. Thus, for example, communications with the intent to influence made by a lawyer that do not provide legal advice or analysis directly and solely related to the legal aspects of his or her client's proposal, but generally advocate one proposal over another are not allowable under this section because the lawyer is not providing professional legal services. Similarly, communications with the intent to influence made by an engineer providing an engineering analysis prior to the preparation or submission of a bid or proposal are not allowable under this section since the engineer is providing technical services but not directly in the preparation, submission or negotiation of a covered Federal action.

(d) Requirements imposed by or pursuant to law as a condition for receiving a covered Federal award include those required by law or regulation, or reasonably expected to be required by law or regulation, and any other requirements in the actual award documents.

(e) Persons other than officers or employees of a person requesting or receiving a covered Federal action include consultants and trade associations.

(f) Only those services expressly authorized by this section are allowable under this section.

Subpart D—Penalties and Enforcement

§ 604.400 Penalties.

(a) Any person who makes an expenditure prohibited herein shall be subject to a civil penalty of not less than $10,000 and not more than $100,000 for each such expenditure.

(b) Any person who fails to file or amend the disclosure form (see appendix B) to be filed or amended if required herein, shall be subject to a civil penalty of not less than $10,000 and not more than $100,000 for each such failure.

(c) A filing or amended filing on or after the date on which an administrative action for the imposition of a civil penalty is commenced does not prevent the imposition of such civil penalty for a failure occurring before that date. An administrative action is commenced with respect to a failure when an investigating official determines in writing to commence an investigation of an allegation of such failure.

(d) In determining whether to impose a civil penalty, and the amount of any such penalty, by reason of a violation by any person, the agency shall consider the nature, circumstances, extent, and gravity of the violation, the effect on the ability of such person to continue in business, any prior violations by such person, the degree of culpability of such person, the ability of the person to pay the penalty, and such other matters as may be appropriate.

(e) First offenders under paragraphs (a) or (b) of this section shall be subject to a civil penalty of $10,000, absent aggravating circumstances. Second and subsequent offenses by persons shall be subject to an appropriate civil penalty between $10,000 and $100,000, as determined by the agency head or his or her designee.

(f) An imposition of a civil penalty under this section does not prevent the United States from seeking any other remedy that may apply to the same conduct that is the basis for the imposition of such civil penalty.

§ 604.405 Penalty procedures.

Agencies shall impose and collect civil penalties pursuant to the provisions of the Program Fraud and Civil Remedies Act, 31 U.S.C. sections 3803 (except subsection (c)), 3804, 3805, 3806, 3807, 3808, and 3812, insofar as these provisions are not inconsistent with the requirements herein.

§ 604.410 Enforcement.

The head of each agency shall take such actions as are necessary to ensure that the provisions herein are vigorously implemented and enforced in that agency.

Subpart E—Exemptions

§ 604.500 Secretary of Defense.

(a) The Secretary of Defense may exempt, on a case-by-case basis, a covered Federal action from the prohibition whenever the Secretary determines, in writing, that such an exemption is in the national interest. The Secretary shall transmit a copy of each such written exemption to Congress immediately after making such a determination.

(b) The Department of Defense may issue supplemental regulations to implement paragraph (a) of this section.

Subpart F—Agency Reports

§ 604.600 Semi-annual compilation.

(a) The head of each agency shall collect and compile the disclosure reports (see appendix B) and, on May 31 and November 30 of each year, submit to the Secretary of the Senate and the Clerk of the House of Representatives a report containing a compilation of the information contained in the disclosure reports received during the six-month period ending on March 31 or September 30, respectively, of that year.

(b) The report, including the compilation, shall be available for public inspection 30 days after receipt of the report by the Secretary and the Clerk.

§ 604.605

(c) Information that involves intelligence matters shall be reported only to the Select Committee on Intelligence of the Senate, the Permanent Select Committee on Intelligence of the House of Representatives, and the Committees on Appropriations of the Senate and the House of Representatives in accordance with procedures agreed to by such committees. Such information shall not be available for public inspection.

(d) Information that is classified under Executive Order 12356 or any successor order shall be reported only to the Committee on Foreign Relations of the Senate and the Committee on Foreign Affairs of the House of Representatives or the Committees on Armed Services of the Senate and the House of Representatives (whichever such committees have jurisdiction of matters involving such information) and to the Committees on Appropriations of the Senate and the House of Representatives in accordance with procedures agreed to by such committees. Such information shall not be available for public inspection.

(e) The first semi-annual compilation shall be submitted on May 31, 1990, and shall contain a compilation of the disclosure reports received from December 23, 1989 to March 31, 1990.

(f) Major agencies, designated by the Office of Management and Budget (OMB), are required to provide machine-readable compilations to the Secretary of the Senate and the Clerk of the House of Representatives no later than with the compilations due on May 31, 1991. OMB shall provide detailed specifications in a memorandum to these agencies.

(g) Non-major agencies are requested to provide machine-readable compilations to the Secretary of the Senate and the Clerk of the House of Representatives.

(h) Agencies shall keep the originals of all disclosure reports in the official files of the agency.

§ 604.605 Inspector General report.

(a) The Inspector General, or other official as specified in paragraph (b) of this section, of each agency shall prepare and submit to Congress each year, commencing with submission of the President's Budget in 1991, an evaluation of the compliance of that agency with, and the effectiveness of, the requirements herein. The evaluation may include any recommended changes that may be necessary to strengthen or improve the requirements.

(b) In the case of an agency that does not have an Inspector General, the agency official comparable to an Inspector General shall prepare and submit the annual report, or, if there is no such comparable official, the head of the agency shall prepare and submit the annual report.

(c) The annual report shall be submitted at the same time the agency submits its annual budget justifications to Congress.

(d) The annual report shall include the following: All alleged violations relating to the agency's covered Federal actions during the year covered by the report, the actions taken by the head of the agency in the year covered by the report with respect to those alleged violations and alleged violations in previous years, and the amounts of civil penalties imposed by the agency in the year covered by the report.

APPENDIX A TO PART 604—
CERTIFICATION REGARDING LOBBYING

Certification for Contracts, Grants, Loans, and Cooperative Agreements

The undersigned certifies, to the best of his or her knowledge and belief, that:

(1) No Federal appropriated funds have been paid or will be paid, by or on behalf of the undersigned, to any person for influencing or attempting to influence an officer or employee of an agency, a Member of Congress, an officer or employee of Congress, or an employee of a Member of Congress in connection with the awarding of any Federal contract, the making of any Federal grant, the making of any Federal loan, the entering into of any cooperative agreement, and the extension, continuation, renewal, amendment, or modification of any Federal contract, grant, loan, or cooperative agreement.

(2) If any funds other than Federal appropriated funds have been paid or will be paid to any person for influencing or attempting to influence an officer or employee of any agency, a Member of Congress, an officer or employee of Congress, or an employee of a Member of Congress in connection with this Federal contract, grant, loan, or cooperative agreement, the undersigned shall complete and submit Standard Form-LLL, "Disclosure

Form to Report Lobbying," in accordance with its instructions.

(3) The undersigned shall require that the language of this certification be included in the award documents for all subawards at all tiers (including subcontracts, subgrants, and contracts under grants, loans, and cooperative agreements) and that all subrecipients shall certify and disclose accordingly.

This certification is a material representation of fact upon which reliance was placed when this transaction was made or entered into. Submission of this certification is a prerequisite for making or entering into this transaction imposed by section 1352, title 31, U.S. Code. Any person who fails to file the required certification shall be subject to a civil penalty of not less than $10,000 and not more than $100,000 for each such failure.

Statement for Loan Guarantees and Loan Insurance

The undersigned states, to the best of his or her knowledge and belief, that:

If any funds have been paid or will be paid to any person for influencing or attempting to influence an officer or employee of any agency, a Member of Congress, an officer or employee of Congress, or an employee of a Member of Congress in connection with this commitment providing for the United States to insure or guarantee a loan, the undersigned shall complete and submit Standard Form-LLL, "Disclosure Form to Report Lobbying," in accordance with its instructions.

Submission of this statement is a prerequisite for making or entering into this transaction imposed by section 1352, title 31, U.S. Code. Any person who fails to file the required statement shall be subject to a civil penalty of not less than $10,000 and not more than $100,000 for each such failure.

DISCLOSURE OF LOBBYING ACTIVITIES

Complete this form to disclose lobbying activities pursuant to 31 U.S.C. 1352
(See reverse for public burden disclosure.)

Approved by OMB
0348-0046

1. **Type of Federal Action:**
   - ☐ a. contract
   - ☐ b. grant
   - ☐ c. cooperative agreement
   - ☐ d. loan
   - ☐ e. loan guarantee
   - ☐ f. loan insurance

2. **Status of Federal Action:**
   - ☐ a. bid/offer/application
   - ☐ b. initial award
   - ☐ c. post-award

3. **Report Type:**
   - ☐ a. initial filing
   - ☐ b. material change

   For Material Change Only:
   year _____ quarter _____
   date of last report _____

4. **Name and Address of Reporting Entity:**
   ☐ Prime   ☐ Subawardee
   Tier _____ , if known:

   Congressional District, if known:

5. **If Reporting Entity in No. 4 is Subawardee, Enter Name and Address of Prime:**

   Congressional District, if known:

6. **Federal Department/Agency:**

7. **Federal Program Name/Description:**

   CFDA Number, if applicable: _____

8. **Federal Action Number,** if known:

9. **Award Amount,** if known:
   $

10. a. **Name and Address of Lobbying Entity**
    (if individual, last name, first name, MI):

    b. **Individuals Performing Services** (including address if different from No. 10a)
    (last name, first name, MI):

(attach Continuation Sheet(s) SF-LLL-A, if necessary)

11. **Amount of Payment** (check all that apply):
    $ _____ ☐ actual ☐ planned

13. **Type of Payment** (check all that apply):
    - ☐ a. retainer
    - ☐ b. one-time fee
    - ☐ c. commission
    - ☐ d. contingent fee
    - ☐ e. deferred
    - ☐ f. other; specify: _____

12. **Form of Payment** (check all that apply):
    - ☐ a. cash
    - ☐ b. in-kind; specify: nature _____
      value _____

14. **Brief Description of Services Performed or to be Performed and Date(s) of Service, including officer(s), employee(s), or Member(s) contacted, for Payment Indicated in Item 11:**

(attach Continuation Sheet(s) SF-LLL-A, if necessary)

15. **Continuation Sheet(s) SF-LLL-A attached:** ☐ Yes ☐ No

16. Information requested through this form is authorized by title 31 U.S.C. section 1352. This disclosure of lobbying activities is a material representation of fact upon which reliance was placed by the tier above when this transaction was made or entered into. This disclosure is required pursuant to 31 U.S.C. 1352. This information will be reported to the Congress semi-annually and will be available for public inspection. Any person who fails to file the required disclosure shall be subject to a civil penalty of not less than $10,000 and not more than $100,000 for each such failure.

Signature: _____
Print Name: _____
Title: _____
Telephone No.: _____ Date: _____

Federal Use Only:

Authorized for Local Reproduction
Standard Form - LLL

National Science Foundation   Pt. 604, App. B

INSTRUCTIONS FOR COMPLETION OF SF-LLL, DISCLOSURE OF LOBBYING ACTIVITIES

This disclosure form shall be completed by the reporting entity, whether subawardee or prime Federal recipient, at the initiation or receipt of a covered Federal action, or a material change to a previous filing, pursuant to title 31 U.S.C. section 1352. The filing of a form is required for each payment or agreement to make payment to any lobbying entity for influencing or attempting to influence an officer or employee of any agency, a Member of Congress, an officer or employee of Congress, or an employee of a Member of Congress in connection with a covered Federal action. Use the SF-LLL-A Continuation Sheet for additional information if the space on the form is inadequate. Complete all items that apply for both the initial filing and material change report. Refer to the implementing guidance published by the Office of Management and Budget for additional information.

1. Identify the type of covered Federal action for which lobbying activity is and/or has been secured to influence the outcome of a covered Federal action.

2. Identify the status of the covered Federal action.

3. Identify the appropriate classification of this report. If this is a followup report caused by a material change to the information previously reported, enter the year and quarter in which the change occurred. Enter the date of the last previously submitted report by this reporting entity for this covered Federal action.

4. Enter the full name, address, city, state and zip code of the reporting entity. Include Congressional District, if known. Check the appropriate classification of the reporting entity that designates if it is, or expects to be, a prime or subaward recipient. Identify the tier of the subawardee, e.g., the first subawardee of the prime is the 1st tier. Subawards include but are not limited to subcontracts, subgrants and contract awards under grants.

5. If the organization filing the report in item 4 checks "Subawardee", then enter the full name, address, city, state and zip code of the prime Federal recipient. Include Congressional District, if known.

6. Enter the name of the Federal agency making the award or loan commitment. Include at least one organizational level below agency name, if known. For example, Department of Transportation, United States Coast Guard.

7. Enter the Federal program name or description for the covered Federal action (item 1). If known, enter the full Catalog of Federal Domestic Assistance (CFDA) number for grants, cooperative agreements, loans, and loan commitments.

8. Enter the most appropriate Federal identifying number available for the Federal action identified in item 1 (e.g., Request for Proposal (RFP) number; Invitation for Bid (IFB) number; grant announcement number; the contract, grant, or loan award number; the application/proposal control number assigned by the Federal agency). Include prefixes, e.g., "RFP-DE-90-001."

9. For a covered Federal action where there has been an award or loan commitment by the Federal agency, enter the Federal amount of the award/loan commitment for the prime entity identified in item 4 or 5.

10. (a) Enter the full name, address, city, state and zip code of the lobbying entity engaged by the reporting entity identified in item 4 to influence the covered Federal action.

    (b) Enter the full names of the individual(s) performing services, and include full address if different from 10 (a). Enter Last Name, First Name, and Middle Initial (MI).

11. Enter the amount of compensation paid or reasonably expected to be paid by the reporting entity (item 4) to the lobbying entity (item 10). Indicate whether the payment has been made (actual) or will be made (planned). Check all boxes that apply. If this is a material change report, enter the cumulative amount of payment made or planned to be made.

12. Check the appropriate box(es). Check all boxes that apply. If payment is made through an in-kind contribution, specify the nature and value of the in-kind payment.

13. Check the appropriate box(es). Check all boxes that apply. If other, specify nature.

14. Provide a specific and detailed description of the services that the lobbyist has performed, or will be expected to perform, and the date(s) of any services rendered. Include all preparatory and related activity, not just time spent in actual contact with Federal officials. Identify the Federal official(s) or employee(s) contacted or the officer(s), employee(s), or Member(s) of Congress that were contacted.

15. Check whether or not a SF-LLL-A Continuation Sheet(s) is attached.

16. The certifying official shall sign and date the form, print his/her name, title, and telephone number.

Public reporting burden for this collection of information is estimated to average 30 mintues per response, including time for reviewing instructions, searching existing data sources, gathering and maintaining the data needed, and completing and reviewing the collection of information. Send comments regarding the burden estimate or any other aspect of this collection of information, including suggestions for reducing this burden, to the Office of Management and Budget, Paperwork Reduction Project (0348-0046), Washington, D.C. 20503.

**DISCLOSURE OF LOBBYING ACTIVITIES
CONTINUATION SHEET**

Approved by OMB
0348-0046

Reporting Entity: _____   Page _____ of _____

Authorized for Local Reproduction
Standard Form - LLL-A

National Science Foundation

PART 605—NONDISCRIMINATION ON THE BASIS OF HANDICAP IN PROGRAMS OR ACTIVITIES RECEIVING FEDERAL FINANCIAL ASSISTANCE

Subpart A—General Provisions

Sec.
605.0 Adoption of HHS regulations.
605.1 Purpose.
605.2 Application.
605.3 Definitions.
605.4 Discrimination prohibited.
605.5 Assurances required.
605.6 Remedial action, voluntary action, and self-evaluation.
605.7 Designation of responsible employee and adoption of grievance procedures.
605.8 Notice.
605.9 Administrative requirements for small recipients.
605.10 Effect of state or local law or other requirements and effect of employment opportunities.

Subpart B—Employment Practices

605.11 Discrimination prohibited.
605.12 Reasonable accommodation.
605.13 Employment criteria.
605.14 Preemployment inquiries.
605.15–605.20 [Reserved]

Subpart C—Accessibility

605.21 Discrimination prohibited.
605.22 Existing facilities.
605.23 New construction.
605.24–605.30 [Reserved]

Subpart D—Preschool, Elementary, and Secondary Education

605.31 Application of this subpart.
605.32 Location and notification.
605.33 Free appropriate public education.
605.34 Educational setting.
605.35 Evaluation and placement.
605.36 Procedural safeguards.
605.37 Nonacademic services.
605.38 Preschool and adult education.
605.39 Private education.
605.40 [Reserved]

Subpart E—Postsecondary Education

605.41 Application of this subpart.
605.42 Admissions and recruitment.
605.43 Treatment of students; general.
605.44 Academic adjustments.
605.45 Housing.
605.46 Financial and employment assistance to students.
605.47 Nonacademic services.
605.48–605.50 [Reserved]

Subpart F—Health, Welfare, and Social Services

605.51 Application of this subpart.
605.52 Health, welfare, and other social services.
605.53 Drug and alcohol addicts.
605.54 Education of institutionalized persons.
605.55–605.60 [Reserved]

Subpart G—Procedures

605.61 Procedures.
605.62–605.90 [Reserved]

AUTHORITY: 29 U.S.C. 794.

SOURCE: 47 FR 8573, Mar. 1, 1982, unless otherwise noted.

Subpart A—General Provisions

§ 605.0 Adoption of HHS regulations.

The regulations of the Department of Health and Human Services on Nondiscrimination on the Basis of Handicap, 45 CFR part 84, including any amendments thereto, have been adopted almost in their entirety to programs or activities receiving Federal financial assistance from the National Science Foundation. The few changes in the Foundation's rules include a newly added sub-paragraph (5) to paragraph (k) of § 605.3; and modifications in paragraph (j), § 605.3; paragraph (a) of § 605.5; paragraph (b) of § 605.46; and § 605.61. Paragraph (c) of § 605.5 has been removed, and "qualified handicapped persons" has been substituted for "handicapped persons" wherever that phrase appears in § 605.4(b)(5) and in subpart C (§§ 605.21 through 605.23). The date for compliance with § 605.33(d) has been changed.

[47 FR 8573, Mar. 1, 1982, as amended at 61 FR 51021, Sept. 30, 1996; 68 FR 51381, Aug. 26, 2003]

§ 605.1 Purpose.

The purpose of this part is to effectuate section 504 of the Rehabilitation Act of 1973, which is designed to eliminate discrimination on the basis of handicap in any program or activity receiving Federal financial assistance.

§ 605.2 Application.

This part applies to each recipient of Federal financial assistance from the National Science Foundation and to each program or activity that receives such assistance.

[47 FR 8573, Mar. 1, 1982, as amended at 68 FR 51381, Aug. 26, 2003]

§ 605.3 Definitions.

As used in this part, the term:

(a) *The Act* means the Rehabilitation Act of 1973, Public Law 93–112, as amended by the Rehabilitation Act Amendments of 1974, Public Law 93–516, 29 U.S.C. 794.

(b) *Section 504* means section 504 of the Act.

(c) *Education of the Handicapped Act* means that statute as amended by the Education for all Handicapped Children Act of 1975, Public Law 94–142, 20 U.S.C. 1401 et seq.

(d) *Foundation* means the National Science Foundation.

(e) *Director* means the Director of the National Science Foundation.

(f) *Recipient* means any state or its political subdivision, any instrumentality of a state or its political subdivision, any public or private agency, institution, organization, or other entity, or any person to which Federal financial assistance is extended directly or through another recipient, including any successor, assignee, or transferee of a recipient, but excluding the ultimate beneficiary of the assistance.

(g) *Applicant for assistance* means one who submits an application, request, or plan required to be approved by a Foundation official or by a recipient as a condition to becoming a recipient.

(h) *Federal financial assistance* means any grant, loan, contract (other than a procurement contract or a contract of insurance or guaranty), or any other arrangement by which the Foundation provides or otherwise makes available assistance in the form of:

(1) Funds;

(2) Services of Federal personnel; or

(3) Real and personal property or any interest in or use of such property, including:

(i) Transfers or leases of such property for less than fair market value or for reduced consideration; and

(ii) Proceeds from a subsequent transfer or lease of such property if the Federal share of its fair market value is not returned to the Federal Government.

(i) *Facility* means all or any portion of buildings, structures, equipment, roads, walks, parking lots, or other real or personal property or interest in such property.

(j) *Handicapped person*—(1) *Handicapped persons* means any person in the United States who (i) has a physical or mental impairment which substantially limits one or more major life activities, (ii) has a record of such an impairment, or (iii) is regarded as having such an impairment.

(2) As used in paragraph (j)(1) of this section, the phrase:

(i) *Physical or mental impairment* means (A) any physiological disorder or condition, cosmetic disfigurement, or anatomical loss affecting one or more of the following body systems: neurological; musculoskeletal; special sense organs; respiratory, including speech organs; cardiovascular; reproductive, digestive, genito-urinary; hemic and lymphatic; skin; and endocrine; or (B) any mental or psychological disorder, such as mental retardation, organic brain syndrome, emotional or mental illness, and specific learning disabilities.

(ii) *Major life activities* means functions such as caring for one's self, performing manual tasks, walking, seeing, hearing, speaking, breathing, learning, and working.

(iii) *Has a record of such an impairment* means has a history of, or has been misclassified as having, a mental or physical impairment that substantially limits one or more major life activities.

(iv) *Is regarded as having an impairment* means (A) has a physical or mental impairment that does not subtantially limit major life activities but that is treated by a recipient as constituting such a limitation; (B) has a physical or mental impairment that substantially limits major life activities only as a result of the attitudes of others toward such impairment; or (C) has none of the impairments defined in paragraph (j)(2)(i) of this section but is treated by a recipient as having such an impairment.

(k) *Qualified handicapped person* means:

National Science Foundation § 605.4

(1) With respect to employment, a handicapped person who, with reasonable accommodation, can perform the essential functions of the job in question;

(2) With respect to public preschool elementary, secondary, or adult educational services, a handicapped person (i) of an age during which nonhandicapped persons are provided such services, (ii) of any age during which it is mandatory under state law to provide such services to handicapped persons, or (iii) to whom a state is required to provide a free appropriate public education under section 612 of the Education of the Handicapped Act; and

(3) With respect to postsecondary and vocational education services, a handicapped person who meets the academic and technical standards requisite to admission or participation in the recipient's education program or activity;

(4) With respect to other services, a handicapped person who meets the essential eligibility requirements for the receipt of such services.

(5) With respect to scientific and technical experimentation, observation, or field work a person who meets the academic, scientific and technical standards for participation and any reasonable physical qualifications for participation. Physical qualifications are not "reasonable," however, if they can be obviated without unreasonable burden by modifying facilities or aid, benefits, or services or by providing auxiliary aids. In determining whether the burdens are unreasonable, factors such as cost, risks, or sacrifice of legitimate objectives may be considered. In exceptional cases psychological qualifications may be considered 'reasonable physical qualifications' under this paragraph. Nothing in this provision or these regulations requires reversal of scientific judgments on research, including choice of experiments, protocols for experiments, location of observing sites, or the like that are considered necessary to any line of scientific inquiry by the research scientists involved.

(1) *Handicap* means any condition or characteristic that renders a person a handicapped person as defined in paragraph (j) of this section.

(m) *Program or activity* means all of the operations of any entity described in paragraphs (m)(1) through (4) of this section, any part of which is extended Federal financial assistance:

(1)(i) A department, agency, special purpose district, or other instrumentality of a State or of a local government; or

(ii) The entity of such State or local government that distributes such assistance and each such department or agency (and each other State or local government entity) to which the assistance is extended, in the case of assistance to a State or local government;

(2)(i) A college, university, or other postsecondary institution, or a public system of higher education; or

(ii) A local educational agency (as defined in 20 U.S.C. 7801), system of vocational education, or other school system;

(3)(i) An entire corporation, partnership, or other private organization, or an entire sole proprietorship—

(A) If assistance is extended to such corporation, partnership, private organization, or sole proprietorship as a whole; or

(B) Which is principally engaged in the business of providing education, health care, housing, social services, or parks and recreation; or

(ii) The entire plant or other comparable, geographically separate facility to which Federal financial assistance is extended, in the case of any other corporation, partnership, private organization, or sole proprietorship; or

(4) Any other entity which is established by two or more of the entities described in paragraph (m)(1), (2), or (3) of this section.

[47 FR 8573, Mar. 1, 1982, as amended at 68 FR 51380, Aug. 26, 2003]

§ 605.4 Discrimination prohibited.

(a) *General.* No qualified handicapped person shall, on the basis of handicap, be excluded from participation in, be denied the benefits of, or otherwise be subjected to discrimination under any program or activity which receives Federal financial assistance.

(b) *Discriminatory actions prohibited.* (1) A recipient, in providing any aid, benefit, or service, may not, directly or

§ 605.4

through contractual, licensing, or other arrangements, on the basis of handicap:

(i) Deny a qualified handicapped person the opportunity to participate in or benefit from the aid, benefit, or service;

(ii) Afford a qualified handicapped person an opportunity to participate in or benefit from the aid, benefit, or service that is not equal to that afforded others;

(iii) Provide a qualified handicapped person with an aid, benefit, or service that is not as effective as that provided to others;

(iv) Provide different or separate aid, benefits, or services to handicapped persons or to any class of handicapped persons unless such action is necessary to provide qualified handicapped persons with aid, benefits, or services that are as effective as those provided to others;

(v) Aid or perpetuate discrimination against a qualified handicapped person by providing significant assistance to an agency, organization, or person that discriminates on the basis of handicap in providing any aid, benefit, or service to beneficiaries of the recipient's program or activity;

(vi) Deny a qualified handicapped person the opportunity to participate as a member of planning or advisory boards; or

(vii) Otherwise limit a qualified handicapped person in the enjoyment of any right, privilege, advantage, or opportunity enjoyed by others receiving an aid, benefit, or service.

(2) For purposes of this part, aids, benefits, and services, to be equally effective, are not required to produce the identical result or level of achievement for handicapped and nonhandicapped persons, but must afford handicapped persons equal opportunity to obtain the same result, to gain the same benefit, or to reach the same level of achievement, in the most integrated setting appropriate to the person's needs.

(3) Despite the existence of separate or different aid, benefits, or services provided in accordance with this part, a recipient may not deny a qualified handicapped person the opportunity to participate in such programs or activities that are not separate or different.

(4) A recipient may not, directly or through contractual or other arrangements, utilize criteria or methods of administration (i) that have the effect of subjecting qualified handicapped persons to discrimination on the basis of handicap, (ii) that have the purpose or effect of defeating or substantially impairing accomplishment of the objectives of the recipient's program or activity with respect to handicapped persons, or (iii) that perpetuate the discrimination of another recipient if both recipients are subject to common administrative control or are agencies of the same State.

(5) In determining the site or location of a facility, an applicant for assistance or a recipient may not make selections (i) that have the effect of excluding qualified handicapped persons from, denying them the benefits of, or otherwise subjecting them to discrimination under any program or activity that receives Federal financial assistance or (ii) that have the purpose or effect of defeating or substantially impairing the accomplishment of the objectives of the program or activity with respect to qualified handicapped persons.

(6) As used in this section, the aid, benefit, or service provided under a program or activity receiving Federal financial assistance includes any aid, benefit, or service provided in or through a facility that has been constructed, expanded, altered, leased or rented, or otherwise acquired, in whole or in part, with Federal financial assistance.

(c) *Aid, benefits, or services limited by Federal law.* The exclusion of nonhandicapped persons from aid, benefits, or services limited by Federal statute or executive order to handicapped persons or the exclusion of a specific class of handicapped persons from aid, benefits, or services limited by Federal statute or executive order to a different class of handicapped persons is not prohibited by this part.

[47 FR 8573, Mar. 1, 1982, as amended at 68 FR 51381, Aug. 26, 2003]

§ 605.5 Assurances required.

(a) *Assurances.* Recipients of Federal financial assistance to which this part applies will assure NSF, in a manner specified by the Director, that the programs or activities will be operated in compliance with this part.

(b) *Duration of obligation.* (1) In the case of Federal financial assistance extended in the form of real property or to provide real property or structures on the property, the assurance will obligate the recipient or, in the case of a subsequent transfer, the transferee, for the period during which the real property or structures are used for the purpose for which Federal financial assistance is extended or for another purpose involving the provision of similar services or benefits.

(2) In the case of Federal financial assistance extended to provide personal property, the assurance will obligate the recipient for the period during which it retains ownership or possession of the property.

(3) In all other cases the assurance will obligate the recipient for the period during which Federal financial assistance is extended.

[47 FR 8573, Mar. 1, 1982, as amended at 68 FR 51381, Aug. 26, 2003]

§ 605.6 Remedial action, voluntary action, and self-evaluation.

(a) *Remedial action.* (1) If the Director finds that a recipient has discriminated against persons on the basis of handicap in violation of section 504 or this part, the recipient shall take such remedial action as the Director deems necessary to overcome the effects of the discrimination.

(2) Where a recipient is found to have discriminated against persons on the basis of handicap in violation of section 504 or this part and where another recipient exercises control over the recipient that has discriminated, the Director, where appropriate, may require either or both recipients to take remedial action.

(3) The Director may, where necessary to overcome the effects of discrimination in violation of section 504 or this part, require a recipient to take remedial action (i) with respect to handicapped persons who are no longer participants in the recipient's program or activity but who were participants in the program when such discrimination occurred or (ii) with respect to handicapped persons who would have been participants in the program or activity had the discrimination not occurred.

(b) *Voluntary action.* A recipient may take steps, in addition to any action that is required by this part, to overcome the effects of conditions that resulted in limited participation in the recipient's program or activity by qualified handicapped persons.

(c) *Self-evaluation.* (1) A recipient shall, within one year of the effective date of this part:

(i) Evaluate, with the assistance of interested persons, including handicapped persons or organizations representing handicapped persons, its current policies and practices and the effects thereof that do not or may not meet the requirements of this part;

(ii) Modify, after consultation with interested persons, including handicapped persons or organizations representing handicapped persons, any policies and practices that do not meet the requirements of this part; and

(iii) Take, after consultation with interested persons, including handicapped persons or organizations representing handicapped persons, appropriate remedial steps to eliminate the effects of any discrimination that resulted from adherence to these policies and practices.

(2) A recipient that employs fifteen or more persons shall, for at least three years following completion of the evaluation required under paragraph (c)(1) of this section, maintain on file, make available for public inspection, and provide to the Director upon request: (i) A list of the interested person consulted (ii) a description of areas examined and any problems identified, and (iii) a description of any modifications made and any remedial steps taken.

[47 FR 8573, Mar. 1, 1982, as amended at 68 FR 51381, Aug. 26, 2003]

§ 605.7 Designation of responsible employee and adoption of grievance procedures.

(a) *Designation of responsible employee.* A recipient that employs fifteen or

§ 605.8

more persons shall designate at least one person to coordinate its efforts to comply with this part.

(b) *Adoption of grievance procedures.* A recipient that employs fifteen or more persons shall adopt grievance procedures that incorporate appropriate due process standards and that provide for the prompt and equitable resolution of complaints alleging any action prohibited by this part. Such procedures need not be established with respect to complaints from applicants for employment or from applicants for admission to postsecondary educational institutions.

§ 605.8 Notice.

(a) A recipient that employs fifteen or more persons shall take appropriate initial and continuing steps to notify participants, beneficiaries, applications, and employees, including those with impaired vision or hearing, and unions or professional organizations holding collective bargaining or professional agreements with the recipient that it does not discriminate on the basis of handicap in violation of section 504 and this part. The notification shall state, where appropriate, that the recipient does not discriminate in admission or access to, or treatment or employment in, its programs or activities. The notification shall also include an identification of the responsible employee designated pursuant to § 605.7(a). A recipient shall make the initial notification required by this paragraph within 90 days of the effective date of this part. Methods of initial and continuing notification may include the posting of notices, publication in newspapers and magazines, placement of notices in recipient's publication, and distribution of memoranda or other written communications.

(b) If a recipient publishes or uses recruitment materials or publications containing general information that it makes available to participants, beneficiaries, applicants, or employees, it shall include in those materials or publications a statement of the policy described in paragraph (a) of this section. A recipient may meet the requirement of this paragraph either by including appropriate inserts in existing materials and publications or by revising and reprinting the materials and publications.

[47 FR 8573, Mar. 1, 1982, as amended at 68 FR 51381, Aug. 26, 2003]

§ 605.9 Administrative requirements for small recipients.

The Director may require any recipient with fewer than fifteen employees, or any class of such recipients, to comply with §§ 605.7 and 605.8, in whole or in part, when the Director finds a violation of this part or finds that such compliance will not significantly impair the ability of the recipient or class or recipients to provide benefits or services.

§ 605.10 Effect of state or local law or other requirements and effect of employment opportunities.

(a) The obligation to comply with this part is not obviated or alleviated by the existence of any state or local law or other requirement that, on the basis of handicap, imposes prohibitions or limits upon the eligibility of qualified handicapped persons to receive services or to practice any occupation or profession.

(b) The obligation to comply with this part is not obviated or alleviated because employment opportunities in any occupation or profession are or may be more limited for handicapped persons than for nonhandicapped persons.

Subpart B—Employment Practices

§ 605.11 Discrimination prohibited.

(a) *General.* (1) No qualified handicapped person shall, on the basis of handicap, be subjected to discrimination in employment under any program or activity to which this part applies.

(2) A recipient that receives assistance under the Education of the Handicapped Act shall take positive steps to employ and advance in employment qualified handicapped persons in programs or activities assisted under that Act.

(3) A recipient shall make all decisions concerning employment under any program or activity to which this part applies in a manner which ensures that discrimination on the basis of handicap does not occur and may not

limit, segregate, or classify applicants or employees in any way that adversely affects their opportunities or status because of handicap.

(4) A recipient may not participate in a contractual or other relationship that has the effect of subjecting qualified handicapped applicants or employees to discrimination prohibited by this subpart. The relationships referred to in this subparagraph include relationships with employment and referral agencies, with labor unions, with organizations providing or administering fringe benefits to employees of the recipient, and with organizations providing training and apprenticeships.

(b) *Specific activities.* The provisions of this subpart apply to:

(1) Recruitment, advertising, and the processing of applications for employment;

(2) Hiring, upgrading, promotion, award of tenure, demotion, transfer, layoff, termination, right of return from layoff and rehiring;

(3) Rates of pay or any other form of compensation and changes in compensation;

(4) Job assignments, job classifications, organizational structures, position descriptions, lines of progression, and seniority lists;

(5) Leaves of absence, sick leave, or any other leave;

(6) Fringe benefits available by virtue of employment, whether or not administered by the recipient;

(7) Selection and financial support for training, including apprenticeship, professional meetings, conferences, and other related activities, and selection for leaves of absence to pursue training;

(8) Employer sponsored activities, including those that are social or recreational; and

(9) Any other term, condition, or privilege of employment.

(c) A recipient's obligation to comply with this subpart is not affected by any inconsistent term of any collective bargaining agreement to which it is a party.

[47 FR 8573, Mar. 1, 1982, as amended at 68 FR 51381, Aug. 26, 2003]

§ 605.12 Reasonable accommodation.

(a) A recipient shall make reasonable accommodation to the known physical or mental limitations of an otherwise qualified handicapped applicant or employee unless the recipient can demonstrate that the accommodation would impose an undue hardship on the operation of its program or activity.

(b) Reasonable accommodation may include: (1) Making facilities used by employees readily accessible to and usable by handicapped persons, and (2) job restructuring, part-time or modified work schedules, acquisition or modification or equipment or devices, the provision of readers or interpreters, and other similar actions.

(c) In determining pursuant to paragraph (a) of this section whether an accommodation would impose an undue hardship on the operation of a recipient's program or activity, factors to be considered include:

(1) The overall size of the recipient's program or activity with respect to number of employees, number and type of facilities, and size of budget;

(2) The type of the recipient's operation, including the composition and structure of the recipient's workforce; and

(3) The nature and cost of the accommodation needed.

(d) A recipient may not deny any employment opportunity to a qualified handicapped employee or applicant if the basis for the denial is the need to make reasonable accommodation to the physical or mental limitations of the employee or applicant.

[47 FR 8573, Mar. 1, 1982, as amended at 68 FR 51381, Aug. 26, 2003]

§ 605.13 Employment criteria.

(a) A recipient may not make use of any employment test or other selection criterion that screens out or tends to screen out handicapped persons or any class of handicapped persons unless: (1) The test score or other selection criterion, as used by the recipient, is shown to be job-related for the position in question, and (2) alternative job-related tests or criteria that do not screen out or tend to screen out as many handicapped persons are not shown by the Director to be available.

(b) A recipient shall select and administer tests concerning employment so as best to ensure that, when administered to an applicant or employee who has a handicap that impairs sensory, manual, or speaking skills, the test results accurately reflect the applicant's or employee's job skills, aptitude, or whatever other factor the test purports to measure, rather than reflecting the applicant's or employee's impaired sensory, manual, or speaking skills (except where those skills are the factors that the test purports to measure).

§ 605.14 Preemployment inquiries.

(a) Except as provided in paragraphs (b) and (c) of this section, a recipient may not conduct a preemployment medical examination or may not make preemployment inquiry of an applicant as to whether the applicant is a handicapped person or as to the nature or severity of a handicap. A recipient may, however, make preemployment inquiry into an applicant's ability to perform job-related functions.

(b) When a recipient is taking remedial action to correct the effects of past discrimination pursuant to § 605.6(a), when a recipient is taking voluntary action to overcome the effects of conditions that resulted in limited participation in its federally assisted program or activity pursuant to § 605.6(b), or when a recipient is taking affirmative action pursuant to section 503 of the Act, the recipient may invite applicants for employment to indicate whether and to what extent they are handicapped, *Provided*, That:

(1) The recipient states clearly on any written questionnaire used for this purpose or makes clear orally if no written questionnaire is used that the information requested is intended for use solely in connection with its remedial action obligations or its voluntary or affirmative action efforts; and

(2) The recipient states clearly that the information is being requested on a voluntary basis, that it will be kept confidential as provided in paragraph (d) of this section, that refusal to provide it will not subject the applicant or employee to any adverse treatment, and that it will be used only in accordance with this part.

(c) Nothing in this section shall prohibit a recipient from conditioning an offer of employment on the results of a medical examination conducted prior to the employee's entrance on duty, *Provided*, That: (1) All entering employees are subjected to such an examination regardless of handicap, and (2) the results of such an examination are used only in accordance with the requirements of this part.

(d) Information obtained in accordance with this section as to the medical condition or history of the applicant shall be collected and maintained on separate forms that shall be accorded confidentiality as medical records, except that:

(1) Supervisors and managers may be informed regarding restrictions on the work or duties of handicapped persons and regarding necessary accommodations;

(2) First aid and safety personnel may be informed, where appropriate, if the condition might require emergency treatment; and

(3) Government officials investigating compliance with the Act shall be provided relevant information upon request.

§§ 605.15–605.20 [Reserved]

Subpart C—Accessibility

§ 605.21 Discrimination prohibited.

No qualified handicapped person shall, because a recipient's facilities are inaccessible to or unusable by handicapped persons, be denied the benefits of, be excluded from participation in, or otherwise be subjected to discrimination under any program or activity to which this part applies.

§ 605.22 Existing facilities.

(a) *Accessibility*. A recipient shall operate each program or activity to which this part applies so that when each part is viewed in its entirety it is readily accessible to qualified handicapped persons. This paragraph does not require a recipient to make each of its existing facilities or every part of a facility accessible to and usable by qualified handicapped persons.

(b) *Methods*. A recipient may comply with the requirements of paragraph (a) of this section through such means as redesign of equipment, reassignment of classes or other services to accessible buildings, assignment of aides to beneficiaries, home visits, delivery of health, welfare, or other social services at alternate accessible sites, alteration of existing facilities and construction of new facilities in conformance with the requirements of § 605.23, or any other methods that result in making its program or activity accessible to qualified handicapped persons. A recipient is not required to make structural changes in existing facilities where other methods are effective in achieving compliance with paragraph (a) of this section. In choosing among available methods for meeting the requirement of paragraph (a) of this section, a recipient shall give priority to those methods that serve qualified handicapped persons in the most integrated setting appropriate.

(c) *Small health, welfare, or other social service providers.* If a recipient with fewer than fifteen employees that provides health, welfare, or other social services finds, after consultation with a qualified handicapped person seeking its services, that there is no method of complying with paragraph (a) of this section other than making a significant alteration in its existing facilities, the recipient may, as an alternative, refer the qualified handicapped person to other providers of those services that are accessible.

(d) *Time period.* A recipient shall comply with the requirement of paragraph (a) of this section within sixty days of the effective date of this part except that where structural changes in facilities are necessary, such changes shall be made within three years of the effective date of this part, but in any event as expeditiously as possible.

(e) *Transition plan.* In the event that structural changes to facilities are necessary to meet the requirement of paragraph (a) of this section, a recipient shall develop, within six months of the effective date of this part, a transition plan setting forth the steps necessary to complete such changes. The plan shall be developed with the assistance of interested persons, including qualified handicapped persons or organizations representing qualified handicapped persons. A copy of the transition plan shall be made available for public inspection. The plan shall, at a minimum:

(1) Identify physical obstacles in the recipient's facilities that limit the accessibility of its program or activity to qualified handicapped persons;

(2) Describe in detail the methods that will be used to make the facilities accessible;

(3) Specify the schedule for taking the steps necessary to achieve full accessibility under paragraph (a) of this section and, if the time period of the transition plan is longer than one year, identify the steps of that will be taken during each year of the transition period; and

(4) Indicate the person responsible for implementation of the plan.

(f) *Notice.* The recipient shall adopt and implement procedures to ensure that interested persons, including persons with impaired vision or hearing, can obtain information as to the existence and location of services, activities, and facilities that are accessible to and usuable by qualified handicapped persons.

[47 FR 8573, Mar. 1, 1982, as amended at 68 FR 51381, Aug. 26, 2003]

§ 605.23 New construction.

(a) *Design and construction.* Each facility or part of a facility constructed by, on behalf of, or for the use of a recipient shall be designed and constructed in such manner that the facility or part of the facility is readily accessible to and usable by qualified handicapped persons, if the construction was commenced after the effective date of this part.

(b) *Alteration.* Each facility or part of a facility which is altered by, on behalf of, or for the use of a recipient after the effective date of this part in a manner that affects or could affect the usability of the facility or part of the facility shall, to the maximum extent feasible, be altered in such manner that the altered portion of the facility is readily accessible to and usable by qualified handicapped persons.

(c) *Conformance with Uniform Federal Accessibility Standards.* (1) Effective as of January 18, 1991, design, construction, or alteration of buildings in conformance with sections 3-8 of the Uniform Federal Accessibility Standards (USAF) (appendix A to 41 CFR subpart 101–19.6) shall be deemed to comply with the requirements of this section with respect to those buildings. Departures from particular technical and scoping requirements of UFAS by the use of other methods are permitted where substantially equivalent or greater access to and usability of the building is provided.

(2) For purposes of this section, section 4.1.6(1)(g) of UFAS shall be interpreted to exempt from the requirements of UFAS only mechanical rooms and other spaces that, because of their intended use, will not require accessibility to the public or beneficiaries or result in the employment or residence therein of persons with physical handicaps.

(3) This section does not require recipients to make building alterations that have little likelihood of being accomplished without removing or altering a load-bearing structural member.

[47 FR 8573, Mar. 1, 1982, as amended at 55 FR 52138, 52142, Dec. 19, 1990]

§§ 605.24–605.30 [Reserved]

Subpart D—Preschool, Elementary, and Secondary Education

§ 605.31 Application of this subpart.

Subpart D applies to preschool, elementary, secondary, and adult education programs or activities that receive or benefit from Federal financial assistance and to recipients that operate, or that receive Federal financial assistance for the operation of, such programs or activities.

[47 FR 8573, Mar. 1, 1982, as amended at 68 FR 51381, Aug. 26, 2003]

§ 605.32 Location and notification.

A recipient that operates a public elementary or secondary education program shall annually:

(a) Undertake to identify and locate every qualified handicapped person residing in the recipient's jurisdiction who is not receiving a public education; and

(b) Take appropriate steps to notify handicapped persons and their parents or guardians or the recipient's duty under this subpart.

§ 605.33 Free appropriate public education.

(a) *General.* A recipient that operates a public elementary or secondary education program shall provide a free appropriate public education to each qualified handicapped person who is in the recipient's jurisdiction, regardless of the nature or severity of the person's handicap.

(b) *Appropriate education.* (1) For the purpose of this subpart, the provision of an appropriate education is the provision of regular or special education and related aids and services that (i) are designed to meet individual educational needs of handicapped persons as adequately as the needs of nonhandicapped persons are met and (ii) are based upon adherence to procedures that satisfy the requirements of §§ 605.34, 605.35 and 605.36.

(2) Implementation of an Individualized Education Program developed in accordance with the Education of the Handicapped Act is one means of meeting the standard established in paragraph (b)(1)(i) of this section.

(3) A recipient may place a handicapped person or refer such person for aid, benefits, or services other than those that it operates or provides as its means of carrying out the requirements of this subpart. If so, the recipient remains responsible for ensuring that the requirements of this subpart are met with respect to any handicapped person so placed or referred.

(c) *Free education*—(1) *General.* For the purpose of this section, the provision of a free education is the provision of educational and related services without cost to the handicapped person or to his or her parents or guardian, except for those fees that are imposed on non-handicapped persons or their parents or guardian. It may consist either of the provision of free services or, if a recipient places a handicapped person or refers such person for aid, benefits, or services not operated or provided by the recipient as its means of carrying out the requirements of this subpart, of payment for the costs of the aid, benefits, or services. Funds available from any public or private agency may be used to meet the requirements of this subpart. Nothing in this section shall be construed to relieve an insurer or similar third party from an otherwise valid obligation to provide or pay for services provided to a handicapped person.

(2) *Transportation.* If a recipient places a handicapped person or refers such person for aid, benefits, or services not operated or provided by the recipient as its means of carrying out the requirements of this subpart, the recipient shall ensure that adequate transportation to and from the aid, benefits, or services is provided at no greater cost than would be incurred by the person or his or her parents or guardian if the person were placed in the program operated by the recipient.

(3) *Residential placement.* If a public or private residential placement is necessary to provide a free appropriate public education to a handicapped person because of his or her handicap, the placement, including non-medical care and room and board, shall be provided at no cost to the person or his or her parents or guardian.

(4) *Placement of handicapped persons by parents.* If a recipient has made available, in conformance with the requirements of this section and § 605.34, a free appropriate public education to a handicapped person and the person's parents or guardian chooses to place the person in a private school, the recipient is not required to pay for the person's education in the private school. Disagreements between a parent or guardian and a recipient regarding whether the recipient has made a free appropriate public education available or otherwise regarding the question of financial responsibility are subject to the due process procedures of § 605.36.

(d) *Compliance.* A recipient may not exclude any qualified handicapped person from a public elementary or secondary education after the effective date of this part. A recipient that is not, on the effective date of this regulation, in full compliance with the other requirements of the preceding paragraphs of this section shall meet such requirements at the earliest practicable time and in no event later than July 1, 1983.

[47 FR 8573, Mar. 1, 1982, as amended at 68 FR 51381, Aug. 26, 2003]

§ 605.34 Educational setting.

(a) *Academic setting.* A recipient to which this subpart applies shall educate, or shall provide for the education of, each qualified handicapped person in its jurisdiction with persons who are not handicapped to the maximum extent appropriate to the needs of the handicapped person. A recipient shall place a handicapped person in the regular educational environment operated by the recipient unless it is demonstrated by the recipient that the education of the person in the regular environment with the use of supplementary aids and services cannot be achieved satisfactorily. Whenever a recipient places a person in a setting other than the regular educational environment pursuant to this paragraph, it shall take into account the proximity of the alternate setting to the person's home.

(b) *Nonacademic settings.* In providing or arranging for the provision of nonacademic and extracurricular services and activities, including meals, recess periods, and the services and activities set forth in § 605.37(a)(2), a recipient shall ensure that handicapped persons participate with nonhandicapped persons in such activities and services to the maximum extent appropriate to the needs of the handicapped person in question.

(c) *Comparable facilities.* If a recipient, in compliance with paragraph (a) of this section, operates a facility that is identifiable as being for handicapped persons, the recipient shall ensure that the facility and the services and activities provided therein are comparable to the other facilities, services, and activities of the recipient.

§ 605.35 Evaluation and placement.

(a) *Preplacement evaluation.* A recipient that operates a public elementary or secondary education program or activity shall conduct an evaluation in accordance with the requirements of paragraph (b) of this section of any person who, because of handicap, needs or is believed to need special education or related services before taking any action with respect to the initial placement of the person in regular or special education and any subsequent significant change in placement.

(b) *Evaluation procedures.* A recipient to which this subpart applies shall establish standards and procedures for the evaluation and placement of persons who, because of handicap, need or are believed to need special education or related services which ensure that:

(1) Tests and other evaluation materials have been validated for the specific purpose for which they are used and are administered by trained personnel in conformance with the instructions provided by their producer;

(2) Tests and other evaluation materials include those tailored to assess specific areas of educational need and not merely those which are designed to provide a single general intelligence quotient; and

(3) Tests are selected and administered so as best to ensure that, when a test is administered to a student with impaired sensory, manual, or speaking skills, the test results accurately reflect the student's aptitude or achievement level or whatever other factor the test purports to measure, rather than reflecting the student's impaired sensory, manual, or speaking skills (except where those skills are the factors that the test purports to measure).

(c) *Placement procedures.* In interpreting evaluation data and in making placement decisions, a recipient shall (1) draw upon information from a variety of sources, including aptitude and achievement tests, teacher recommendations, physical condition, social or cultural background, and adaptive behavior, (2) establish procedures to ensure that information obtained from all such sources is documented and carefully considered, (3) ensure that the placement decision is made by a group of persons, including persons knowledgeable about the child, the meaning of the evaluation data, and the placement options, and (4) ensure that the placement decision is made in conformity with §605.34.

(d) *Reevaluation.* A recipient to which this section applies shall establish procedures, in accordance with paragraph (b) of this section, for periodic reevaluation of students who have been provided special education and related services. A reevaluation procedure consistent with the Education for the Handicapped Act is one means of meeting this requirement.

[47 FR 8573, Mar. 1, 1982, as amended at 68 FR 51381, Aug. 26, 2003]

§605.36 Procedural safeguards.

A recipient that operates a public elementary or secondary education program shall establish and implement, with respect to actions regarding the identification, evaluation, or educational placement of persons who, because of handicap, need or are believed to need special instruction or related services, a system of procedural safeguards that includes notice, an opportunity for the parents or guardian of the person to examine relevant records, an impartial hearing with opportunity for participation by the person's parents or guardian and representation by counsel, and a review procedure. Compliance with the procedural safeguards of section 615 of the Education of the Handicapped Act is one means of meeting this requirement.

§605.37 Nonacademic services.

(a) *General.* (1) A recipient to which this subpart applies shall provide nonacademic and extracurricular services and activities in such manner as is necessary to afford handicapped students an equal opportunity for participation in such services and activities.

(2) Nonacademic and extracurricular services and activities may include counseling services, physical recreational athletics, transportation, health services, recreational activities, special interest groups or clubs sponsored by the recipients, referrals to agencies which provide assistance to handicapped persons, and employment of students, including both employment by the recipient and assistance in making available outside employment.

(b) *Counseling services.* A recipient to which this subpart applies that provides personal, academic, or vocational counseling, guidance, or placement services to its students shall provide these services without discrimination on the basis of handicap. The recipient shall ensure that qualified handicapped students are not counseled toward more restrictive career objectives than are nonhandicapped students with similar interests and abilities.

(c) *Physical education and athletics.* (1) In providing physical education courses and athletics and similar aid, benefits, or services to any of its students, a recipient to which this subpart applies may not discriminate on the basis of handicap. A recipient that offers physical education courses or that operates or sponsors interscholastic, club, or intramural athletics shall provide to qualified handicapped students an equal opportunity for participation.

(2) A recipient may offer to handicapped students physical education and athletic activities that are separate or different from those offered to nonhandicapped students only if separation or differentiation is consistent with the requirements of §605.34 and only if no qualified handicapped student is denied the opportunity to compete for teams or to participate in courses that are not separate or different.

[47 FR 8573, Mar. 1, 1982, as amended at 68 FR 51381, Aug. 26, 2003]

§ 605.38 Preschool and adult education.

A recipient to which this subpart applies that provides preschool education or day care or adult education may not, on the basis of handicap, exclude qualified handicapped persons and shall take into account the needs of such persons in determining the aid, benefits, or services to be provided.

[47 FR 8573, Mar. 1, 1982, as amended at 68 FR 51381, Aug. 26, 2003]

§ 605.39 Private education.

(a) A recipient that provides private elementary or secondary education may not, on the basis of handicap, exclude a qualified handicapped person if the person can, with minor adjustments, be provided an appropriate education, as defined in §605.33(b)(1), within that recipient's program or activity.

(b) A recipient to which this section applies may not charge more for the provision of an appropriate education to handicapped persons than to nonhandicapped persons except to the extent that any additional charge is justified by a substantial increase in cost to the recipient.

(c) A recipient to which this section applies that provides special education shall do so in accordance with the provisions of §§ 605.35 and 605.36. Each recipient to which this section applies is subject to the provisions of §§ 605.34, 605.37 and 605.38.

[47 FR 8573, Mar. 1, 1982, as amended at 68 FR 51381, Aug. 26, 2003]

§ 605.40 [Reserved]

Subpart E—Postsecondary Education

§ 605.41 Application of this subpart.

Subpart E applies to postsecondary education programs or activities, including postsecondary vocational education programs or activities, that receive Federal financial assistance and to recipients that operate, or that receive Federal financial assistance for the operation of, such programs or activities.

[47 FR 8573, Mar. 1, 1982, as amended at 68 FR 51381, Aug. 26, 2003]

§ 605.42 Admissions and recruitment.

(a) *General.* Qualified handicapped persons may not, on the basis of handicap, be denied admission or be subjected to discrimination in admission or recruitment by a recipient to which this subpart applies.

(b) *Admissions.* In administering its admission policies, a recipient to which this subpart applies:

(1) May not apply limitations upon the number or proportion of handicapped persons who may be admitted;

(2) May not make use of any test or criterion for admission that has a disproportionate, adverse effect on handicapped persons or any class of handicapped persons unless (i) the test or criterion, as used by the recipient, has been validated as a predictor of success in the education program or activity in question and (ii) alternate tests or criteria that have a less disproportionate, adverse effect are not shown by the Director to be available.

§ 605.43

(3) Shall assure itself that (i) admissions tests are selected and administered so as best to ensure that, when a test is administered to an applicant who has a handicap that impairs sensory, manual, or speaking skills, the test results accurately reflect the applicant's aptitude or achievement level or whatever other factor the test purports to measure, rather than reflecting the applicant's impaired sensory, manual, or speaking skills (except where those skills are the factors that the test purports to measure); (ii) admissions tests that are designed for persons with impaired sensory, manual, or speaking skills are offered as often and in as timely a manner as are other admissions tests; and (iii) admissions tests are administered in facilities that, on the whole, are accessible to handicapped persons; and

(4) Except as provided in paragraph (c) of this section, may not make preadmission inquiry as to whether an applicant for admission is a handicapped person but, after admission, may make inquiries on a confidential basis as to handicaps that may require accommodation.

(c) *Preadmission inquiry exception.* When a recipient is taking remedial action to correct the effects of past discrimination pursuant to § 605.6(a) or when a recipient is taking voluntary action to overcome the effects of conditions that resulted in limited participation in its federally assisted program or activity pursuant to § 605.6(6), the recipient may invite applicants for admission to indicate whether and to what extent they are handicapped, *Provided,* That:

(1) The recipient states clearly on any written questionnaire used for this purpose or makes clear orally if no written questionnaire is used that the information requested is intended for use solely in connection with its remedial action obligations or its voluntary action efforts; and

(2) The recipient states clearly that the information is being requested on a voluntary basis, that it will be kept confidential, that refusal to provide it will not subject the applicant to any adverse treatment, and that it will be used only in accordance with this part.

(d) *Validity studies.* For the purpose of paragraph (b)(2) of this section, a recipient may base prediction equations on first year grades, but shall conduct periodic validity studies against the criterion of overall success in the education program or activity in question in order to monitor the general validity of the test scores.

§ 605.43 Treatment of students; general.

(a) No qualified handicapped student shall, on the basis of handicap, be excluded from participation in, be denied the benefits of, or otherwise be subjected to discrimination under any academic, research, occupational training, housing, health insurance, counseling, financial aid, physical education, athletics, recreation, transportation, other extracurricular, or other postsecondary education aid, benefits, or services to which this subpart applies.

(b) A recipient to which this subpart applies that considers participation by students in education programs or activities not operated wholly by the recipient as part of, or equivalent to, an education program or activity operated by the recipient shall assure itself that the other education program or activity, as a whole, provides an equal opportunity for the participation of qualified handicapped persons.

(c) A recipient to which this subpart applies may not, on the basis of handicap, exclude any qualified handicapped student from any course, course of study, or other part of its education program or activity.

(d) A recipient to which this subpart applies shall operate its program or activity in the most integrated setting appropriate.

[47 FR 8573, Mar. 1, 1982, as amended at 68 FR 51381, Aug. 26, 2003]

§ 605.44 Academic adjustments.

(a) *Academic requirements.* A recipient to which this subpart applies shall make such modifications to its academic requirements as are necessary to ensure that such requirements do not discriminate or have the effect of discriminating, on the basis of handicap, against a qualified handicapped applicant or student. Academic requirements that the recipient can demonstrate are essential to the instruction being pursued by such student or to any directly related licensing requirement will not be regarded as discriminatory within the meaning of this section. Modifications may include changes in the length of time permitted for the completion of degree requirements, substitution of specific courses required for the completion of degree requirements, and adaptation of the manner in which specific courses are conducted.

(b) *Other rules.* A recipient to which this subpart applies may not impose upon handicapped students other rules, such as the prohibition of tape recorders in classrooms or of dog guides in campus buildings, that have the effect of limiting the participation of handicapped students in the recipient's education program or activity.

(c) *Course examinations.* In its course examinations or other procedures for evaluating students' academic achievement, a recipient to which this subpart applies shall provide such methods for evaluating the achievement of students who have a handicap that impairs sensory, manual, or speaking skills as will best ensure that the results of the evaluation represents the student's achievement in the course, rather than reflecting the student's impaired sensory, manual, or speaking skills (except where such skills are the factors that the test purports to measure).

(d) *Auxiliary aids.* (1) A recipient to which this subpart applies shall take such steps as are necessary to ensure that no handicapped student is denied the benefits of, excluded from participation in, or otherwise subjected to discrimination under the education program or activity operated by the recipient because of the absence of educational auxiliary aids for students with impaired sensory, manual, or speaking skills.

(2) Auxiliary aids may include taped texts, interpreters or other effective methods of making orally delivered materials available to students with hearing impairments, readers in libraries for students with visual impairments, classroom equipment adapted for use by students with manual impairments, and other similar services and actions. Recipients need not provide attendents, individually prescribed devices, readers for personal use or study, or other devices or services of a personal nature.

[47 FR 8573, Mar. 1, 1982, as amended at 68 FR 51381, Aug. 26, 2003]

§ 605.45 Housing.

(a) *Housing provided by the recipient.* A recipient that provides housing to its nonhandicapped students shall provide comparable, convenient, and accessible housing to handicapped students at the same cost as to others. At the end of the transition period provided for in subpart C, such housing shall be available in sufficient quantity and variety so that the scope of handicapped students' choice of living accommodations is, as a whole, comparable to that of nonhandicapped students.

(b) *Other housing.* A recipient that assists any agency, organization, or person in making housing available to any of its students shall take such action as may be necessary to assure itself that such housing is, as a whole, made available in a manner that does not result in discrimination on the basis of handicap.

§ 605.46 Financial and employment assistance to students.

(a) *Provision of financial assistance.* (1) In providing financial assistance to qualified handicapped persons, a recipient to which this subpart applies may not (i), on the basis of handicap, provide less assistance than is provided to nonhandicapped persons, limit eligibility for assistance, or otherwise discriminate or (ii) assist any entity or person that provides assistance to any of the recipient's students in a manner that discriminates against qualified handicapped persons on the basis of handicap.

(2) A recipient may administer or assist in the administration of scholarships, fellowships, or other forms of financial assistance established under wills, trusts, bequests, or similar legal instruments that require awards to be made on the basis of factors that discriminate or have the effect of discriminating on the basis of handicap

only if the overall effect of the award of scholarships, fellowships, and other forms of financial assistance is not discriminatory on the basis of handicap.

(b) *Assistance in making available outside employment.* A recipient that helps its students to obtain employment shall assure itself that the employment opportunities it helps to make available to students are, as a whole, made available in a manner that would not violate subpart B if they were provided by the recipient.

(c) *Employment of students by recipients.* A recipient that employs any of its students may not do so in a manner that violates subpart B.

§ 605.47 Nonacademic services.

(a) *Physical education and athletics.* (1) In providing physical education courses and athletics and similar aid, benefits, or services to any of its students, a recipient to which this subpart applies may not discriminate on the basis of handicap. A recipient that offers physical education courses or that operates or sponsors intercollegiate, club, or intramural athletics shall provide to qualified handicapped students an equal opportunity for participation in these activities.

(2) A recipient may offer to handicapped students physical education and athletic activities that are separate or different only if separation or differentiation is consistent with the requirements of § 605.43(d) and only if no qualified handicapped student is denied the opportunity to compete for teams or to participate in courses that are not separate or different.

(b) *Counseling and placement services.* A recipient to which this subpart applies that provides personal, academic, or vocational counseling, guidance, or placement services to its students shall provide these services without discrimination on the basis of handicap. The recipient shall ensure that qualified handicapped students are not counseled toward more restrictive career objectives than are nonhandicapped students with similar interests and abilities. This requirement does not preclude a recipient from providing factual information about licensing and certification requirements that may present obstacles to handicapped persons in their pursuit of particular careers.

(c) *Social organizations.* A recipient that provides significant assistance to fraternities, sororities, or similar organizations shall assure itself that the membership practices of such organizations do not permit discrimination otherwise prohibited by this subpart.

[47 FR 8573, Mar. 1, 1982, as amended at 68 FR 51381, Aug. 26, 2003]

§§ 605.48–605.50 [Reserved]

Subpart F—Health, Welfare, and Social Services

§ 605.51 Application of this subpart.

Subpart F applies to health, welfare, and other social service programs or activities that receive Federal financial assistance and to recipients that operate, or that receive Federal financial assistance for the operation of, such programs or activities.

[47 FR 8573, Mar. 1, 1982, as amended at 68 FR 51381, Aug. 26, 2003]

§ 605.52 Health, welfare, and other social services.

(a) *General.* In providing health, welfare, or other social services or benefits, a recipient may not, on the basis of handicap:

(1) Deny a qualified handicapped person these benefits or services;

(2) Afford a qualified handicapped person an opportunity to receive benefits or services that is not equal to that offered nonhandicapped persons;

(3) Provide a qualified handicapped person which benefits or services that are not as effective (as defined in § 605.4(b)) as the benefits or services provided to others;

(4) Provide benefits or services in a manner that limits or has the effect of limiting the participation of qualified handicapped persons; or

(5) Provide different or separate benefits or services to handicapped persons except where necessary provide qualified handicapped persons with benefits and services that are as effective as those provided to others.

(b) *Notice.* A recipient that provides notice concerning benefits or services or written material concerning waivers of rights or consent to treatment shall take such steps as are necessary to ensure that qualified handicapped persons, including those with impaired sensory or speaking skills, are not denied effective notice because of their handicap.

(c) *Emergency treatment for the hearing impaired.* A recipient hospital that provides health services or benefits shall establish a procedure for effective communication with persons with impaired hearing for the purpose of providing emergency health care.

(d) *Auxiliary aids.* (1) A recipient to which this subpart applies that employs fifteen or more persons shall provide appropriate auxiliary aids to persons with impaired sensory, manual, or speaking skills, where necessary to afford such persons an equal opportunity to benefit from the service in question.

(2) The Director may require recipients with fewer than fifteen employees to provide auxiliary aids where the provision of aids would not significantly impair the ability of the recipient to provide its benefits or services.

(3) For the purpose of this paragraph, auxiliary aids may include brailled and taped material, interpreters, and other aids for persons with impaired hearing or vision.

§ 605.53 Drug and alcohol addicts.

A recipient to which this subpart applies that operates a general hospital or outpatient facility may not discriminate in admission or treatment against a drug or alcohol abuser or alcoholic who is suffering from a medical condition, because of the person's drug or alcohol abuse or alcoholism.

§ 605.54 Education of institutionalized persons.

A recipient to which this subpart applies and that operates or supervises a program or activity that provides aid, benefits, or services for persons who are institutionalized because of handicap shall ensure that each qualified handicapped person, as defined in § 605.3(k)(2), in its program or activity is provided an appropriate education, as defined in § 605.33(b). Nothing in this section shall be interpreted as altering in any way the obligations of recipients under subpart D.

[47 FR 8573, Mar. 1, 1982, as amended at 68 FR 51381, Aug. 26, 2003]

§§ 605.55–605.60 [Reserved]

Subpart G—Procedures

§ 605.61 Procedures.

The procedural provisions applicable to title VI of the Civil Rights Act of 1964 apply to this part. These procedures are found in §§ 611.6 through 611.10 of this title (45 CFR). In the event that the Department of Education or the Department of Health and Human Services conducts a hearing under this part on behalf of NSF, the provisions of 45 CFR 84.61 shall also apply except that the Director of NSF or his designee shall also be "the responsible Department official" for purposes of 45 CFR 81.102 and 81.121 and "the reviewing authority" for purposes of 45 CFR 81.103, 81.104, and 81.105. Also, in such cases, the Director of NSF rather than the Secretary of HHS or Education shall conduct the review provided for in 45 CFR 81.106.

§§ 605.62–605.90 [Reserved]

PART 606—ENFORCEMENT OF NONDISCRIMINATION ON THE BASIS OF HANDICAP IN PROGRAMS OR ACTIVITIES CONDUCTED BY THE NATIONAL SCIENCE FOUNDATION

Sec.
606.1 Purpose.
606.2 Application.
606.3 Definitions.
606.4–606.9 [Reserved]
606.10 Self-evaluation.
606.11 Notice.
606.12–606.29 [Reserved]
606.30 General prohibitions against discrimination.
606.31–606.39 [Reserved]
606.40 Employment.
606.41–606.49 [Reserved]
606.50 Program accessibility: Discrimination prohibited.
606.51 Program accessibility: Existing facilities.
606.52 Program accessibility: New construction and alterations.
606.53–606.59 [Reserved]
606.60 Communications.

§ 606.1

606.61–606.69 [Reserved]
606.70 Complaint procedures.
606.71–606.99 [Reserved]

AUTHORITY: 29 U.S.C. 794.

SOURCE: 54 FR 4791, Jan. 31, 1989, unless otherwise noted.

§ 606.1 Purpose.

The purpose of this part is to effectuate section 119 of the Rehabilitation, Comprehensive Services, and Developmental Disabilities Amendments of 1978, which amended section 504 of the Rehabilitation Act of 1973 to prohibit discrimination on the basis of handicap in programs or activities conducted by Executive agencies or the United States Postal Service.

§ 606.2 Application.

This part applies to all programs or activities conducted by the Foundation, except for programs or activities conducted outside the United States that do not involve individuals with handicaps in the United States. Programs and activities receiving Federal financial assistance from the Foundation are covered by 45 CFR part 605.

§ 606.3 Definitions.

For purposes of this part, the term—

Assistant Attorney General means the Assistant Attorney General, Civil Rights Division, Department of Justice.

Auxiliary aids means services or devices that enable persons with impaired sensory, manual, or speaking skills to have an equal opportunity to participate in, and enjoy the benefits of, programs or activities conducted by the Foundation. For example, auxiliary aids useful for persons with impaired vision include readers, Brailled materials, audio recordings, and other similar services and devices. Auxiliary aids useful for persons with impaired hearing include telephone handset amplifiers, telephones compatible with hearing aids, telecommunication devices for deaf persons (TDD's), interpreters, note takers, written materials, and other similar services and devices.

Complete complaint means a written statement that contains the complainant's name and address and describes the Foundation's alleged discriminatory action in sufficient detail to inform the Foundation of the nature and date of the alleged violation of section 504. It shall be signed by the complainant or by someone authorized to do so on his or her behalf. Complaints filed on behalf of classes or third parties shall describe or identify (by name, if possible) the alleged victims of discrimination.

Facility means all or any portion of buildings, structures, equipment, roads, walks, parking lots, rolling stock or other conveyances, or other real or personal property.

Foundation means the National Science Foundation.

Individual with handicaps means any person in the United States who has a physical or mental impairment that substantially limits one or more major life activities, has a record of such an impairment, or is regarded as having such an impairment. As used in this definition, the phrase:

(1) *Physical or mental impairment* includes—

(i) Any physiological disorder or condition, cosmetic disfigurement, or anatomical loss affecting one or more of the following body systems: neurological; musculoskeletal; special sense organs; respiratory, including speech organs; cardiovascular; reproductive; digestive; genitourinary; hemic and lymphatic; skin; and endocrine; or

(ii) Any mental or psychological disorder, such as mental retardation, organic brain syndrome, emotional or mental illness, and specific learning disabilities. The term *physical or mental impairment* includes, but is not limited to, such diseases and conditions as orthopedic, visual, speech, and hearing impairments, cerebral palsy, epilepsy, muscular dystrophy, multiple sclerosis, cancer, heart disease, diabetes, mental retardation, emotional illness, and drug addiction and alcoholism.

(2) *Major life activities* includes functions such as caring for one's self, performing manual tasks, walking, seeing, hearing, speaking, breathing, learning, and working.

(3) *Has a record of such an impairment* means has a history of, or has been misclassified as having, a mental or physical impairment that substantially limits one or more major life activities.

National Science Foundation § 606.30

(4) *Is regarded as having an impairment* means—

(i) Has a physical or mental impairment that does not substantially limit major life activities but is treated by the Foundation as constituting such a limitation;

(ii) Has a physical or mental impairment that substantially limits major life activities only as a result of the attitudes of others toward such impairment; or

(iii) Has none of the impairments defined in paragraph (1) of this definition but is treated by the Foundation as having such an impairment.

Qualified individual with handicaps means—

(1) With respect to any Foundation program or activity under which a person is required to perform services or to achieve a level of accomplishment, an individual with handicaps who meets the essential eligibility requirements and who can achieve the purpose of the program or activity without modifications in the program or activity that the Foundation can demonstrate would result in a fundamental alteration in its nature;

(2) With respect to any other program or activity, an individual with handicaps who meets the essential eligibility requirements for participation in, or receipt of benefits from, that program or activity; and

(3) *Qualified handicapped person* as that term is defined for purposes of employment in 29 CFR 1613.702(f), which is made applicable to this part by § 606.40.

Section 504 means section 504 of the Rehabilitation Act of 1973 (Pub. L. 93–112, 87 Stat. 394 (29 U.S.C. 794)), as amended by the Rehabilitation Act Amendments of 1974 (Pub. L. 93–516, 88 Stat. 1617); and the Rehabilitation, Comprehensive Services, and Developmental Disabilities Amendments of 1978 (Pub. L. 95–602, 92 Stat. 2955); the Rehabilitation Act Amendments of 1986 (Pub. L. 99–506, 100 Stat. 1810; and the Civil Rights Restoration Act of 1987 (Pub. L. 100–259, 102 Stat. 28). As used in this part, section 504 applies only to programs or activities conducted by Executive agencies and not to federally assisted programs.

§§ 606.4–606.9 [Reserved]

§ 606.10 Self-evaluation.

(a) The Foundation shall, within one year of the effective date of this part, evaluate its current policies and practices, and the effects thereof, that do not or may not meet the requirements of this part, and, to the extent modification of any such policies and practices is required, the Foundation shall proceed to make the necessary modifications.

(b) The Foundation shall provide an opportunity to interested persons, including individuals with handicaps or organizations representing individuals with handicaps, to participate in the self-evaluation process by submitting comments (both oral and written).

(c) The Foundation shall, for at least three years following completion of the evaluation required under paragraph (a) of this section, maintain on file and make available for public inspection:

(1) A list of the interested persons who made comments;

(2) A description of areas examined and any problems identified; and

(3) A description of any modifications made.

§ 606.11 Notice.

The Foundation shall make available to employees, applicants, participants, beneficiaries, and other interested persons such information regarding the provisions of this part and its applicability to the programs or activities conducted by the Foundation and make such information available to them in such manner as the Director of the Foundation finds necessary to apprise such persons of the protections against discrimination assured them by section 504 and this regulation.

§§ 606.12–606.29 [Reserved]

§ 606.30 General prohibitions against discrimination.

(a) No qualified individual with handicaps shall, on the basis of handicap, be excluded from participation in, be denied the benefits of, or otherwise be subjected to discrimination under any program or activity conducted by the Foundation.

(b)(1) The Foundation, in providing any aid, benefit, or service, may not, directly or through contractual, licensing, or other arrangements, on the basis of handicap—

(i) Deny a qualified individual with handicaps the opportunity to participate in or benefit from the aid, benefit, or service;

(ii) Afford a qualified individual with handicaps an opportunity to participate in or benefit from the aid, benefit, or service that is not equal to that afforded others;

(iii) Provide a qualified individual with handicaps with an aid, benefit, or service that is not as effective in affording equal opportunity to obtain the same result, to gain the same benefit, or to reach the same level of achievement as that provided to others;

(iv) Provide different or separate aid, benefits, or services to individuals with handicaps or to any class of individuals with handicaps than is provided to others unless such action is necessary to provide qualified individuals with handicaps with aid, benefits, or services that are as effective as those provided to others;

(v) Deny a qualified individual with handicaps the opportunity to participate as a member of planning or advisory boards; or

(vi) Otherwise limit a qualified individual with handicaps in the enjoyment of any right, privilege, advantage, or opportunity enjoyed by others receiving the aid, benefit, or service.

(2) The Foundation may not deny a qualified individual with handicaps the opportunity to participate in programs or activities that are not separate or different, despite the existence of permissibly separate or different programs or activities.

(3) The Foundation may not, directly or through contractual or other arrangements, utilize criteria or methods of administration the purpose or effect of which would—

(i) Subject qualified individuals with handicaps to discrimination on the basis of handicap; or

(ii) Defeat or substantially impair accomplishment of the objectives of a program or activity with respect to individuals with handicaps.

(4) The Foundation may not, in determining the site or location of a facility, make selections the purpose or effect of which would—

(i) Exclude qualified individuals with handicaps from, deny them the benefits of, or otherwise subject them to discrimination under any program or activity conducted by the Foundation; or

(ii) Defeat or substantially impair the accomplishment of the objectives of a program or activity with respect to individuals with handicaps.

(5) The Foundation, in the selection of procurement contractors, may not use criteria that subject qualified individuals with handicaps to discrimination on the basis of handicap.

(c) The exclusion of nonhandicapped persons from the benefits of a program limited by Federal statute or Executive order to individuals with handicaps or the exclusion of a specific class of individuals with handicaps from a program limited by Federal statute or Executive order to a different class of individuals with handicaps is not prohibited by this part.

(d) The Foundation shall administer programs and activities in the most integrated setting appropriate to the needs of qualified individuals with handicaps.

§§ 606.31–606.39 [Reserved]

§ 606.40 Employment.

No qualified individual with handicaps shall, on the basis of handicap, be subjected to discrimination in employment under any program or activity conducted by the Foundation. The definitions, requirements, and procedures of section 501 of the Rehabilitation Act of 1973 (29 U.S.C. 791), as established by the Equal Employment Opportunity Commission in 29 CFR part 1613, shall apply to employment in federally conducted programs or activities.

§§ 606.41–606.49 [Reserved]

§ 606.50 Program accessibility: Discrimination prohibited.

Except as otherwise provided in § 606.51, no qualified individual with handicaps shall, because the Foundation's facilities are inaccessible to or

National Science Foundation § 606.51

unusable by individuals with handicaps, be denied the benefits of, be excluded from participation in, or otherwise be subjected to discrimination under any program or activity conducted by the Foundation.

§ 606.51 Program accessibility: Existing facilities.

(a) *General.* The Foundation shall operate each program or activity so that the program or activity, when viewed in its entirety, is readily accessible to and usable by individuals with handicaps. This paragraph does not—

(1) Necessarily require the Foundation to make each of its existing facilities accessible to and usable by individuals with handicaps; or

(2) Require the Foundation to take any action that it can demonstrate would result in a fundamental alteration in the nature of a program or activity or in undue financial and administrative burdens. In those circumstances where Foundation personnel believe that the proposed action would fundamentally alter the program or activity or would result in undue financial and administrative burdens, the Foundation has the initial burden of establishing that compliance with § 606.51(a) would result in such alteration or burdens. The decision that compliance would result in such alteration or burdens must be made by the Foundation Director or his or her designee after considering all Foundation resources available for use in the funding and operation of the conducted program or activity, and must be accompanied by a written statement of the reasons for reaching that conclusion. If an action would result in such an alteration or burdens, the Foundation shall take any other action that would not result in such an alteration or such burdens but would nevertheless ensure that individuals with handicaps receive the benefits and services of the program or activity.

(b) *Methods.* The Foundation may comply with the requirements of this section through such means as redesign of equipment, reassignment of services to accessible buildings, assignment of aides to beneficiaries, home visits, delivery of services at alternate accessible sites, alteration of existing facilities and construction of new facilities, use of accessible rolling stock, or any other methods that result in making its programs or activities readily accessible to and usable by individuals with handicaps. The Foundation is not required to make structural changes in existing facilities where other methods are effective in achieving compliance with this section. The Foundation, in making alterations to existing buildings, shall meet accessibility requirements to the extent compelled by the Architectural Barriers Act of 1968, as amended (42 U.S.C. 4151–4157), and any regulations implementing it. In choosing among available methods for meeting the requirements of this section, the Foundation shall give priority to those methods that offer programs and activities to qualified individuals with handicaps in the most integrated setting appropriate.

(c) *Time period for compliance.* The Foundation shall comply with the obligations established under this section within 60 days of the effective date of this part except that where structural changes in facilities are undertaken, such changes shall be made within three years of the effective date of this part, but in any event as expeditiously as possible.

(d) *Transition plan.* In the event that structural changes to facilities will be undertaken to achieve program accessibility, the Foundation shall develop, within six months of the effective date of this part, a transition plan setting forth the steps necessary to complete such changes. The Foundation shall provide an opportunity to interested persons, including individuals with handicaps or organizations representing individuals with handicaps, to participate in the development of the transition plan by submitting comments (both oral and written). A copy of the transition plan shall be made available for public inspection. The plan shall, at a minimum—

(1) Identify physical obstacles in the Foundation's facilities that limit the accessibility of its programs or activities to individuals with handicaps;

(2) Describe in detail the methods that will be used to make the facilities accessible;

(3) Specify the schedule for taking the steps necessary to achieve compliance with this section and, if the time period of transition plan is longer than one year, identify steps that will be taken during each year of the transition period; and

(4) Indicate the official responsible for implementation of the plan.

§ 606.52 Program accessibility: New construction and alterations.

Each building or part of a building that is constructed or altered by, on behalf of, or for the use of the Foundation shall be designed, constructed, or altered so as to be readily accessible to and usable by individuals with handicaps. The definitions, requirements, and standards of the Architectural Barriers Act (42 U.S.C. 4151–4157), as established in 41 CFR 101–19.600 to 101–19.607, apply to buildings covered by this section.

§§ 606.53–606.59 [Reserved]

§ 606.60 Communications.

(a) The Foundation shall take appropriate steps to ensure effective communication with applicants, participants, personnel of other Federal entities, and members of the public.

(1) The Foundation shall furnish appropriate auxiliary aids where necessary to afford an individual with handicaps an equal opportunity to participate in, and enjoy the benefits of, a program or activity conducted by the Foundation.

(i) In determining what type of auxiliary aid is necessary, the Foundation shall give primary consideration to the requests of the individual with handicaps.

(ii) The Foundation need not provide individually prescribed devices, readers for personal use or study, or other devices of a personal nature.

(2) Where the Foundation communicates with applicants and beneficiaries by telephone, telecommunications devices for deaf persons (TDD's) or equally effective telecommunication systems shall be used to communicate with persons with impaired hearing.

(b) The Foundation shall ensure that interested persons, including persons with impaired vision or hearing, can obtain information as to the existence and location of accessible services, activities, and facilities.

(c) The Foundation shall provide signage at a primary entrance to each of its inaccessible facilities, directing users to a location at which they can obtain information about accessible facilities. The international symbol for accessibility shall be used at each primary entrance of an accessible facility.

(d) This section does not require the Foundation to take any action that it can demonstrate would result in a fundamental alteration in the nature of a program or activity or in undue financial and administrative burdens. In those circumstances where Foundation personnel believe that the proposed action would fundamentally alter the program or activity or would result in undue financial and administrative burdens, the Foundation has the initial burden of establishing that compliance with § 606.60 would result in such alteration or burdens. The decision that compliance would result in such alteration or burdens must be made by the Foundation Director or his or her designee after considering all Foundation resources available for use in the funding and operation of the conducted program or activity and must be accompanied by a written statement of the reasons for reaching that conclusion. If an action required to comply with this section would result in such an alteration or such burdens, the Foundation shall take any other action that would not result in such an alteration or such burdens but would nevertheless ensure that, to the maximum extent possible, individuals with handicaps receive the benefits and services of the program or activity.

§§ 606.61–606.69 [Reserved]

§ 606.70 Complaint procedures.

(a) Except as provided in paragraph (b) of this section, this section applies to all allegations of discrimination on the basis of handicap in programs or activities conducted by the Foundation.

(b) The Foundation shall process complaints alleging violations of section 504 with respect to employment

National Science Foundation

according to the procedures established by the Equal Employment Opportunity Commission in 29 CFR part 1613 pursuant to section 501 of the Rehabilitation Act of 1973 (29 U.S.C. 791).

(c) The Director, Office of Equal Opportunity Programs (OEOP), shall coordinate implementation of this section.

(d) Persons wishing to submit complaints should submit complete complaints (see §606.03) to the Office of Equal Opportunity Programs, National Science Foundation, 4201 Wilson Boulevard, Arlington, VA 22230. In accordance with the procedures outlined below, the Foundation will accept all complete complaints and will either undertake to investigate them if they are within the jurisdiction of the Foundation and submitted within 180 days of the alleged acts of discrimination or in the case of complaints not within the jurisdiction of the Foundation, it shall promptly notify the complainant and shall make reasonable efforts to refer the complaint to the appropriate government entity. Complete complaints submitted after the 180 day time limit may also be acted upon at the discretion of the Foundation if good cause for the delay in submission is found.

(e) The Foundation shall notify the Architectural and Transportation Barriers Compliance Board upon receipt of any complaint alleging that a building or a facility that is subject to the Architectural Barriers Act of 1968, as amended (42 U.S.C. 4151–4157), is not readily accessible to and usable by individuals with handicaps.

(f) Within 180 days of the receipt of a complete complaint, the Director, Office of Equal Opportunity Programs (OEOP), or his or her designee or delegate, will investigate the complaint and shall notify the complainant of the results of the investigation in a letter containing—

(1) Findings of fact and conclusions of law;

(2) A description of a remedy for each violation found; and

(3) A notice of a right to appeal to the Director of the Foundation.

(g)(1) A complainant may appeal findings of fact, conclusions of law, or remedies to the Director of the Foundation. Such appeals must be in writing and must state fully the basis for the appeal, proposed alternative findings of fact, conclusions of law, or remedies. They must be sent (as evidenced by an appropriate postmark or other satisfactory evidence) within 90 days after the date of receipt from the Foundation of the letter described in paragraph (f) of this section. The Foundation may extend this time for good cause.

(2) The Director shall notify the complainant of the results of the appeal within 30 days of the receipt of the appeal. If the Director determines that additional information is needed from the complainant, the Director shall have 30 days from the date such additional information is received from the complainant to make a determination on the appeal.

(h) The time limits for sending a letter to the complainant in paragraph (f) and for deciding an appeal in paragraph (g)(2) of this section may be extended with the permission of the Assistant Attorney General.

[54 FR 4791, Jan. 31, 1989, as amended at 59 FR 37437, July 22, 1994]

§§ 606.71–606.99 [Reserved]

PART 607—SALARY OFFSET

Sec.
607.1 Purpose and scope.
607.2 Definitions.
607.3 Applicability.
607.4 Notice requirements before offset.
607.5 Hearing.
607.6 Written decision.
607.7 Coordinating offset with another Federal agency.
607.8 Procedures for salary offset.
607.9 Refunds.
607.10 Statute of limitations.
607.11 Non-waiver of rights.
607.12 Interest, penalties, and administrative costs.

AUTHORITY: 5 U.S.C. 5514; E.O. 12107, 3 CFR, 1978 Comp., p. 264; 5 CFR part 550, subpart K.

SOURCE: 58 FR 68769, Dec. 29, 1993, unless otherwise noted.

§ 607.1 Purpose and scope.

(a) This part provides procedures for the collection by administrative offset of a federal employee's salary without his or her consent to satisfy certain

§ 607.2

debts owed to the Federal government. This part applies to all Federal employees who owe debts to the National Science Foundation (NSF) and to current employees of NSF who owe debts to other Federal agencies. This part does not apply when the employee consents to recovery from his or her current pay account.

(b) This part does not apply to debts or claims arising under:

(1) The Internal Revenue Code of 1954, as amended, 26 U.S.C. 1 *et seq.*;

(2) The Social Security Act, 42 U.S.C. 301 *et seq.*;

(3) The tariff laws of the United States; or

(4) Any case where a collection of a debt by salary offset is explicitly provided for or prohibited by another statute.

(c) This part does not apply to any adjustment to pay arising out of an employee's selection of coverage or a change in coverage under a Federal benefits program requiring periodic deductions from pay if the amount to be recovered was accumulated over four pay periods or less.

(d) This part does not preclude the compromise, suspension, or termination of collection action where appropriate under the standards implementing the Federal Claims Collection Act, 31 U.S.C. 3711 *et seq.*, and 4 CFR parts 101 through 105.

(e) This part does not preclude an employee from requesting waiver of an overpayment under 5 U.S.C. 5584, 10 U.S.C. 2774, or 32 U.S.C. 716, or in any way questioning the amount or validity of the debt by submitting a subsequent claim to the General Accounting Office. This part does not preclude an employee from requesting a waiver pursuant to other statutory provisions applicable to the particular debt being collected.

(f) Matters not addressed in this part should be reviewed in accordance with the Federal Claims Collection Standards at 4 CFR 101.1 *et seq.*

§ 607.2 Definitions.

For the purposes of this part the following definitions will apply:

Agency means an executive agency as defined at 5 U.S.C. 105, including the U.S. Postal Service and the U.S. Postal Rate Commission; a military department as defined at 5 U.S.C. 102; an agency or court in the judicial branch; an agency of the legislative branch, including the U.S. Senate and House of Representatives; and other independent establishments that are entities of the Federal government.

Certification means a written debt claim received from a creditor agency which requests the paying agency to offset the salary of an employee.

Chief Financial Officer means the Chief Financial Officer of NSF or such other official of NSF who is designated by the Chief Financial Officer to determine whether an employee is indebted to the United States and to take action to collect such debts.

Creditor agency means an agency of the Federal Government to which the debt is owed.

Debt means an amount owed by a Federal employee to the United States from sources which include loans insured or guaranteed by the United States and all other amounts due the United States from fees, leases, rents, royalties, services, sales of real or personal property, overpayments, penalties, damages, interests, fines, forfeitures (except those arising under the Uniform Code of Military Justice), and all other similar sources.

Disposable pay means the amount that remains from an employee's Federal pay after required deductions for social security, Federal, State or local income tax, health insurance premiums, retirement contributions, life insurance premiums, Federal employment taxes, and any other deductions that are required to be withheld by law.

Hearing official means an individual responsible for conducting a hearing with respect to the existence or amount of a debt claimed, or the repayment schedule of a debt, and who renders a decision on the basis of such hearing. A hearing official may not be under the supervision or control of the Chief Financial Officer or of persons having supervision or control over the Chief Financial Officer.

NSF means the National Science Foundation.

Paying agency means the agency that employs the individual who owes the debt and authorizes the payment of his or her current pay.

Salary offset means an administrative offset to collect a debt pursuant to 5 U.S.C. 5514 by deduction(s) at one or more officially established pay intervals from the current pay account of an employee without his or her consent.

§ 607.3 Applicability.

The regulations in this part are to be followed when:

(a) NSF is owed a debt by an individual who is a current employee of the NSF; or

(b) NSF is owed a debt by an individual currently employed by another Federal agency; or

(c) NSF employs an individual who owes a debt to another Federal agency.

§ 607.4 Notice requirements before offset.

(a) Salary offset shall not be made against an employee's pay unless the employee is provided with written notice signed by the Chief Financial Officer of the debt at least 30 days before salary offset commences.

(b) The written notice shall contain:

(1) A statement that the debt is owed and an explanation of its nature and amount;

(2) The agency's intention to collect the debt by deducting from the employee's current disposable pay account;

(3) The amount, frequency, proposed beginning date, and duration of the intended deduction(s);

(4) An explanation of interest, penalties, and administrative charges, including a statement that such charges will be assessed unless excused in accordance with the Federal Claims Collections Standards at 4 CFR 101.1;

(5) The employee's right to inspect, request, and receive a copy of government records relating to the debt;

(6) The employee's opportunity to establish a written schedule for the voluntary repayment of the debt in lieu of offset;

(7) The employee's right to an oral hearing or a determination based on a review of the written record ("paper hearing") conducted by an impartial hearing official concerning the existence or the amount of the debt, or the terms of the repayment schedule;

(8) The procedures and time period for petitioning for a hearing;

(9) A statement that a timely filing of a petition for a hearing will stay the commencement of collection proceedings;

(10) A statement that a final decision on the hearing (if requested) will be issued by the hearing official not later than 60 days after the filing of the petition requesting the hearing unless employee requests and the hearing official grants a delay in the proceedings;

(11) A statement that knowingly false or frivolous statements, representations, or evidence may subject the employee to appropriate disciplinary procedures and/or statutory penalties;

(12) A statement of other rights and remedies available to the employee under statutes or regulations governing the program for which the collection is being made;

(13) Unless there are contractual or statutory provisions to the contrary, a statement that amounts paid on or deducted for the debt which are later waived or found not owed to the United States will be promptly refunded to the employee; and

(14) A statement that the proceedings regarding such debt are governed by section 5 of the Debt Collection Act of 1982 (5 U.S.C. 5514).

§ 607.5 Hearing.

(a) *Request for hearing.* (1) An employee may file a petition for an oral or paper hearing in accordance with the instructions outlined in the agency's notice to offset.

(2) A hearing may be requested by filing a written petition addressed to the Chief Financial Officer stating why the employee disputes the existence or amount of the debt or, in the case of an individual whose repayment schedule has been established other than by a written agreement, concerning the terms of the repayment schedule. The petition for a hearing must be received by the Chief Financial Officer not later than fifteen (15) calendar days after the employee's receipt of the offset notice, or notice of the terms of the payment schedule, unless the employee can show

§ 607.6

good cause for failing to meet the filing deadline.

(b) *Hearing procedures.* (1) The hearing will be presided over by an impartial hearing official.

(2) The hearing shall conform to procedures contained in the Federal Claims Collection Standards, 4 CFR 102.3(c). The burden shall be on the employee to demonstrate that the existence or the amount of the debt is in error.

§ 607.6 Written decision.

(a) The hearing official shall issue a final written opinion no later than 60 days after the filing of the petition.

(b) The written opinion will include a statement of the facts presented to demonstrate the nature and origin of the alleged debt; the hearing official's analysis, findings, and conclusions; the amount and validity of the debt, if any; and the repayment schedule, if any.

§ 607.7 Coordinating offset with another Federal agency.

(a) When the NSF is the creditor agency and the Chief Financial Officer determines that an employee of another agency (i.e., the paying agency) owes a debt to the NSF, the Chief Financial Officer shall, as appropriate:

(1) Certify in writing to the paying agency that the employee owes the debt, the amount and basis of the debt, the date on which payment was due, and the date the Government's right to collect the debt accrued, and that this part 607 has been approved by the Office of Personnel Management.

(2) Unless the employee has consented to salary offset in writing or signed a statement acknowledging receipt of the required procedures, and the written consent is sent to the paying agency, the Chief Financial Officer must advise the paying agency of the action(s) taken under this part 607, and the date(s) they were taken.

(3) Request the paying agency to collect the debt by salary offset. If deductions must be made in installments, the Chief Financial Officer may recommend to the paying agency the amount or percentage of disposable pay to be collected in each installment;

(4) Arrange for a hearing upon the proper petitioning by the employee.

(b) When the NSF is the creditor agency and the employee is in the process of separating from the Federal service, the NSF must submit its debt claim to the paying agency as provided in this part. The paying agency must certify the total amount collected, give a copy of the certification to the employee, and send a copy of the certification and notice of the employee's separation to the NSF. If the paying agency is aware that the employee is entitled to Civil Service Retirement and Disability Fund or other similar payments, it must certify to the agency responsible for making such payments that the debtor owes a debt, including the amount of the debt, and that the provisions of 5 CFR 550.1108 have been followed.

(c) When the NSF is the creditor agency and the employee has already separated from Federal service and all payments due from the paying agency have been paid, the Chief Financial Officer may request, unless otherwise prohibited, that money payable to the employee from the Civil Service Retirement and Disability Fund or other similar funds be collected by administrative offset.

(d) When the NSF is the paying agency, upon receipt of a properly certified debt claim from another agency, deductions will be scheduled to begin at the next established pay interval. The employee must receive written notice that NSF has received a certified debt claim from the creditor agency, the amount of the debt, the date salary offset will begin, and the amount of the deduction(s). NSF shall not review the merits of the creditor agency's determination of the validity or the amount of the certified claim. If the employee transfers to another agency after the creditor agency has submitted its debt claim to NSF and before the debt is collected completely, NSF must certify the amount collected. One copy of the certification must be furnished to the employee. A copy must be furnished to the creditor agency with notice of the employee's transfer.

§ 607.8 Procedures for salary offset.

(a) Deductions to liquidate an employee's debt will be by the method and

National Science Foundation § 608.1

in the amount stated in the Chief Financial Officer's notice of intention to offset as provided in § 607.4. Debts will be collected in one lump sum where possible. If the employee is financially unable to pay in one lump sum, collection must be made in installments.

(b) Debts will be collected by deduction at officially established pay intervals from an employee's current pay account unless alternative arrangements for repayment are made.

(c) Installment deductions will be made over a period not greater than the anticipated period of employment. The size of installment deductions must bear a reasonable relationship to the size of the debt and the employee's ability to pay. The deduction for the pay intervals for any period must not exceed 15% of disposable pay unless the employee has agreed in writing to a deduction of a greater amount.

(d) Unliquidated debts may be offset against any financial payment due to a separated employee including but not limited to final salary or leave payment in accordance with 31 U.S.C. 3716.

§ 607.9 Refunds.

(a) NSF will promptly refund to an employee any amounts deducted to satisfy debts owed to NSF when the debt is waived, found not owed to NSF, or when directed by an administrative or judicial order.

(b) Another creditor agency will promptly return to NSF any amounts deducted by NSF to satisfy debts owed to the creditor agency when the debt is waived, found not owed, or when directed by an administrative or judicial order.

(c) Unless required by law, refunds under this section shall not bear interest.

§ 607.10 Statute of limitations.

If a debt has been outstanding for more than 10 years after NSF's right to collect the debt first accrued, the agency may not collect by salary offset unless facts material to the Government's right to collect were not known and could not reasonably have been known by the official or officials who were charged with the responsibility for discovery and collection of such debts.

§ 607.11 Non-waiver of rights.

An employee's involuntary payment of all or any part of a debt collected under the regulations in this part will not be construed as a waiver of any rights that the employee may have under 5 U.S.C. 5514 or any other provision of law.

§ 607.12 Interest, penalties, and administrative costs.

Charges may be assessed on a debt for interest, penalties, and administrative costs in accordance with 31 U.S.C. 3717 and the Federal Claims Collection Standards, 4 CFR 101.1.

PART 608—CLAIMS COLLECTION AND ADMINISTRATIVE OFFSET

Sec.
608.1 Purpose and scope.
608.2 Collection, compromise, and use of consumer reporting agencies.
608.3 Administrative offset.
608.4 Reductions of tax refunds.

AUTHORITY: 31 U.S.C. 3711, 3716, 3718 and 3720A.

SOURCE: 58 FR 68772, Dec. 29, 1993, unless otherwise noted.

§ 608.1 Purpose and scope.

(a) This part sets forth policies and procedures for the collection and compromise claims and the administrative offset of claims by the National Science Foundation (NSF) pursuant to 31 U.S.C. 3711, 3716, 3718 and 3720A. It is not intended to limit or govern the rights of the NSF or the United States to collect, compromise, or administratively offset debts or claims under other authority and procedures that may be legally available to it.

(b) Matters not addressed in this part should be reviewed and handled in accordance with applicable statutory provisions and the Federal Claims Collection Standards issued jointly by the Attorney General and the Comptroller General (4 CFR parts 101 through 105).

(c) Any action other than the issuance of regulations specifically required to be done by the head of the agency by any of the statutes or regulations referred to in paragraphs (a) and (b) of this section shall be done on behalf of NSF by its Chief Financial

§ 608.2

Officer or by those to whom the Chief Financial Officer delegates authority. This is not intended to prevent the Chief Financial Officer from issuing additional internal procedures and guidance consistent with this part.

§ 608.2 Collection, compromise, and use of consumer reporting agencies.

(a) Subject to the specific limitations and procedures of 31 U.S.C. 3711 and in accordance with the applicable provisions of the Federal Claims Collection Standards, NSF, acting through its Chief Financial Officer or those to whom he or she delegates authority or assigns responsibilities, shall try to collect claims of the United States Government for money or property arising out of the activities of NSF or that are referred to NSF and may compromise or suspend or end collection action of certain claims. In making demands for payment, NSF will follow the guidance set forth at 4 CFR 102.2. In appropriate cases, as authorized by and subject to 31 U.S.C. 3718 and 4 CFR 102.6, NSF may contract for collection services. Before compromising or suspending or ending the collection of a claim in excess of $5,000, the matter shall be referred to the NSF Office of General Counsel for legal review.

(b) When trying to collect a claim of the Government (except for claims under the Internal Revenue Code of 1986, 26 U.S.C. 1 et seq.), NSF may disclose to a consumer reporting agency information from a system of records that an individual is responsible for a claim if (1) a notice published pursuant to 5 U.S.C. 552a(3)(4) indicates that information in the system of records may be disclosed to a consumer reporting agency that an individual is responsible for a claim and (2) if the Chief Financial Officer of NSF decides that the claim is valid and overdue. Such disclosures to a consumer reporting agency will be done only under the conditions and procedures specified in 31 U.S.C. 3711(f) and in the Federal Claims Collections Standards. Specifically, before NSF provides the information to the consumer reporting agency, the individual will be given the notice required by 31 U.S.C. 3711(f)(1)(C); and in accordance with 4 CFR 102.5(c), the right of administrative review to be provided to the individual shall be consistent with the provisions of 4 CFR 102.3(c). If NSF does not have a current address for the individual in its files, it will take reasonable action to locate the individual, but if unsuccessful will mail the notice to the individual's last known address. NSF will disclose information only to a consumer reporting agency that gives satisfactory assurances that it is complying with all laws of the United States relating to providing consumer credit information. The information provided by NSF shall be limited to the type of information described in 31 U.S.C. 3711(f)(1)(F). Moreover, NSF will not provide such information until it has established internal procedures to disclose promptly to a consumer reporting agency to which disclosure is made of any substantial changes in the condition or amount of the claim and to verify or correct promptly information about the claim on request of a consumer reporting agency for verification of information disclosed.

(c) If in response to the notice referred to in paragraph (b) of this section, the individual repays or agrees in writing with NSF to a repayment plan, the information will not be disclosed to a consumer reporting agency. If in response to the notice referred to in paragraph (b) the individual requests a review or reconsideration of the claim, information shall not be disclosed to the consumer reporting agency until such a review is provided.

(d) The review referred to in paragraph (c) of this section shall be based only on the written documentation in the file, including any additional written information provided by the individual in response to the notice referred to in paragraph (b). A written summary briefly describing the nature of the review performed and the conclusion reached shall be made. The written summary and conclusion shall be referred to the NSF Office of General Counsel for legal review. After legal review, a copy of the written summary shall be sent to the individual.

§ 608.3 Administrative offset.

(a) If NSF is unable to collect a claim from a person after trying to do so in accordance with § 608.2, NSF may collect the claim by administrative offset subject to the procedures and limitations of 31 U.S.C. 3716 and the applicable provisions of the Federal Claims Collection Standards. Determinations to pursue administrative offset shall be made on a case-by-case basis taking into account the considerations specified at 31 U.S.C. 3716(b) and 4 CFR 102.3(a). Before employing administrative offset, NSF will comply with the notice, hearing, review, or other procedural requirements of 31 U.S.C. 3716(a) and 4 CFR 102.3(b) and (c). Furthermore, before an administrative offset is taken by NSF pursuant to the authority of this part 608, the matter shall be referred to the Office of General Counsel for legal review to ensure that the required procedures have been followed.

(b) When another agency requests NSF to administratively offset a claim owing to that agency, NSF will normally comply with such request if the requesting agency has provided the certification required by 4 CFR 102.3(f) and offset would not be contrary to law. Before imposing administrative offsets at the request of another agency under this part 608, the matter shall be referred to the NSF Office of General Counsel for legal review.

(c)(1) In appropriate cases, NSF may request another agency to administratively setoff a claim owed to NSF. Before making the certification to the other agency required by 4 CFR 102.3(f), the matter shall be referred to the NSF Office of General Counsel for legal review.

(2) Unless otherwise prohibited by law, NSF may request that moneys that are due and payable to a debtor from the Civil Service Retirement and Disability Fund, the Foreign Service Retirement Fund or any other Federal retirement fund be administratively offset in reasonable amounts in order to collect in one full payment or a minimal number of payments debts owed the United States by the debtor. Such requests shall be made to the appropriate officials of the respective fund servicing agency in accordance with such regulations as may be prescribed by that agency. The requests for administrative offset will certify in writing that (i) the debtor owes the United States a debt and the amount of the debt; (ii) NSF has complied with applicable regulations and procedures; and (iii) NSF has followed the requirements of the Federal Claims Collection Standards as made applicable by this section. Once NSF decides to request offset from a Federal retirement fund, it will make the request as soon as practical after completion of the applicable procedures in order that the fund servicing agency may identify and flag the debtor's account in anticipation of the time when the debtor requests or becomes eligible to receive payments from the fund and to ensure that offset will be initiated prior to the expiration of the statute of limitations.

(3) If NSF collects part or all of the debt by other means before deductions are made or completed pursuant to this paragraph (c), NSF shall act promptly to modify or terminate its request for offset.

(4) This paragraph (c) does not require or authorize the fund servicing agency to review the merits of (i) NSF's determination with respect to the amount and validity of the debt, (ii) NSF's determination as to waiver under an applicable statute, or (iii) NSF's determination to provide or not provide an oral hearing.

(d) No collection by administrative offset shall be made on any debt that has been outstanding for more than ten years unless facts material to the Government's right to collect the debt were not known, and reasonably could not have been known, by the official or officials responsible for discovering the debt.

(e) Administrative offset under this section will not be initiated against:

(1) A debt in which administrative offset of the type of debt involved is explicitly provided for or prohibited by a statutes other than 31 U.S.C. 3716, including debts subject to the Salary offset procedures at 45 CFR part 607;

(2) Debts owed by other agencies of the United States or by any State or local Government; or

(3) Debts arising under the Internal Revenue Code of 1954; the Social Security Act; or the tariff laws of the United States.

§ 608.4 Reductions of tax refunds.

(a) In accordance with regulations and guidance issued by the Secretary of the Treasury at 26 CFR 301.6402–6 and the requirements of 31 U.S.C. 3720A, NSF will participate in the Federal Tax Refund Offset Program for offset against income tax refunds of persons owing past due legally enforceable debts to NSF.

(b) For purposes of this section, a past-due legally enforceable debt referable to the IRS is a debt which is owed to the United States and:

(1) Except in the case of a judgment debt, has been delinquent for at least three months but has not been delinquent for more than ten years at the time the offset is made;

(2) Cannot be currently collected pursuant to the salary offset provisions of 5 U.S.C. 5514(a)(1);

(3) Is ineligible for administrative offset under 31 U.S.C. 3716(a) by reason of 31 U.S.C. 3716(c)(2) or cannot be collected by administrative offset under 31 U.S.C. 3716(a) by NSF against amounts payable to or on behalf of the debtor by or on behalf of NSF;

(4) With respect to which NSF has notified or has made a reasonable attempt to notify the taxpayer that the debt is past-due and, unless repaid within 60 days thereafter, the debt will be referred to the IRS for offset against any overpayment of tax;

(5) With respect to which NSF has given the taxpayer at least 60 days from the date of notification to present evidence that all or part of the debt is not past-due or legally enforceable, has considered the evidence presented by such taxpayer, and has determined that an amount of such debt is past-due and legally enforceable;

(6) Has been disclosed by NSF to a consumer reporting agency as authorized by 31 U.S.C. 3711(f), unless a consumer reporting agency would be prohibited from using such information by 15 U.S.C. 1681c, or unless the amount of the debt does not exceed $100.00;

(7) Is at least $25.00;

(8) All other requirements of 31 U.S.C. 3720A and the Internal Revenue Service regulations at 26 CFR 301.6402–6 relating to the eligibility of a debt for tax return offset have been satisfied.

(c) NSF will make a request for reduction of an IRS tax refund only after the NSF determines that an amount is owed and past-due and provides the debtor with 60 days written notice. NSF's notice of intention to collect by IRS tax refund offset (Notice of Intent) will state:

(1) The amount of the debt;

(2) That unless the debt is repaid within 60 days from the date of the NSF's Notice of Intent, NSF intends to collect the debt by requesting the IRS to reduce any amounts payable to the debtor as refunds of Federal taxes paid by an amount equal to the amount of the debt and all accumulated interest and other charges;

(3) That the debtor has a right to present evidence that all or part of the debt is not past-due or legally enforceable; and

(4) A mailing address for forwarding any written correspondence and a contact name and phone number for any questions.

(d) A debtor who receives a Notice of Intent has the right to present evidence that all or part of the debt is not past-due or not legally enforceable. To exercise this right, the debtor must:

(1) Send a written request for a review of the evidence to the address provided in the notice.

(2) State in the request the amount disputed and the reasons why the debtor believes that the debt is not past-due or is not legally enforceable.

(3) Include with the request any documents which the debtor wishes to be considered or state that additional information will be submitted within the remainder of the 60-day period.

(e) The failure of a debtor to respond as provided in paragraph (d) of this section will result in an automatic referral of the debt to the IRS without further action by NSF. If the debtor responds, NSF will consider all available evidence related to the debt and issue a written determination, including supporting rationale, whether its prior determination that the debt is past-due and legally enforceable is sustained, amended, or canceled. Before this determination is made the matter shall be referred to the NSF Office of General Counsel for legal review. NSF will give prompt notification of this determination to the debtor.

PART 611—NONDISCRIMINATION IN FEDERALLY-ASSISTED PROGRAMS OF THE NATIONAL SCIENCE FOUNDATION—EFFECTUATION OF TITLE VI OF THE CIVIL RIGHTS ACT OF 1964

Sec.
611.1 Purpose.
611.2 Application of part.
611.3 Discrimination prohibited.
611.4 Assurances required.
611.5 Illustrative applications.
611.6 Compliance information.
611.7 Conduct of investigations.
611.8 Procedure for effecting compliance.
611.9 Hearings.
611.10 Decisions and notices.
611.11 Judicial review.
611.12 Effect on other regulations; forms and instructions.
611.13 Definitions.
APPENDIX A TO PART 611

AUTHORITY: Sec. 11(a), National Science Foundation Act of 1950, as amended, 42 U.S.C. 1870(a); 42 U.S.C. 2000d-1.

SOURCE: 29 FR 16305, Dec. 4, 1964, unless otherwise noted.

§ 611.1 Purpose.

The purpose of this part is to effectuate the provisions of title VI of the Civil Rights Act of 1964 (hereafter referred to as the "Act") to the end that no person in the United States shall, on the grounds of race, color, or national origin, be excluded from participation in, be denied the benefits of, or be otherwise subjected to discrimination under any program or activity receiving Federal financial assistance from the National Science Foundation.

§ 611.2 Application of part.

This part applies to any program for which Federal financial assistance is authorized under a law administered by the Foundation, including the types of Federal financial assistance listed in appendix A of this part. It applies to money paid, property transferred, or other Federal financial assistance extended after the effective date of the regulation pursuant to an application approved prior to such effective date. This part does not apply to (a) any Federal financial assistance by way of insurance or guaranty contract, (b) money paid, property transferred, or other assistance extended before the effective date of this part, (c) any assistance to any individual who is the ultimate beneficiary, or (d) any employment practice, under any such program, of any employer, employment agency, or labor organization, except to the extent described in § 611.3. The fact that a type of Federal financial assistance is not listed in the appendix shall not mean, if title VI of the Act is otherwise applicable, that a program is not covered. Other types of Federal financial assistance under statutes now in force or hereafter enacted may be added to this list by notice published in the FEDERAL REGISTER.

[29 FR 16305, Dec. 4, 1964, as amended at 68 FR 51382, Aug. 26, 2003]

§ 611.3 Discrimination prohibited.

(a) *General.* No person in the United States, shall, on grounds of race, color, or national origin be excluded from participation in, be denied the benefits of, or be otherwise subjected to discrimination under any program to which this part applies.

(b) *Specific discriminatory actions prohibited.* (1) A recipient to which this part applies may not directly or through contractual or other arrangements, on the ground of race, color, or national origin:

(i) Deny an individual any service, financial aid, or other benefit provided under the program;

(ii) Provide any service, financial aid, or other benefit to an individual which is different, or is provided in a different manner, from that provided to others under the program;

(iii) Subject an individual to segregation or separate treatment in any matter related to his receipt of any service, financial aid, or other benefit under the program;

(iv) Restrict an individual in any way in the enjoyment of any advantage or privilege enjoyed by others receiving any service, financial aid, or other benefit under the program;

(v) Treat an individual differently from others in determining whether he satisfies any admission, enrollment, quota, eligibility, membership or other

§ 611.3

requirement or condition which individuals must meet in order to be provided any service, financial aid, or other benefit provided under the program;

(vi) Deny an individual an opportunity to participate in the program through the provision of services or otherwise or afford him an opportunity to do so which is different from that afforded others under the program (including the opportunity to participate in the program of an employee but only to the extent set forth in paragraph (c) of this section).

(2) A recipient, in determining the types of services, financial aid, or other benefits, or facilities which will be provided under any such program, or the class of individuals to whom, or the situations in which, such services, financial aid, other benefits, or facilities will be provided under any such program, or the class of individuals to be afforded an opportunity to participate in any such program, may not directly or through contractual or other arrangements, utilize criteria or methods of administration which have the effect of subjecting individuals to discrimination because of their race, color, or national origin, or have the effect of defeating or substantially impairing accomplishment of the objectives of the program as respects individuals of a particular race, color, or national origin.

(3) In determining the site or location of facilities, a recipient or applicant may not make selections with the purpose or effect of excluding individuals from, denying them the benefits of, or subjecting them to discrimination under any program to which this regulation applies, on the grounds of race, color, or national origin; or with the purpose or effect of defeating or substantially impairing the accomplishment of the objectives of the Act or this regulation.

(4) As used in this section the services, financial aid, or other benefits provided under a program receiving Federal financial assistance shall be deemed to include any service, financial aid, or other benefit provided in or through a facility provided with the aid of Federal financial assistance.

(5) The enumeration of specific forms of prohibited discrimination in this paragraph and paragraph (c) of this section does not limit the generality of the prohibition in paragraph (a) of this section.

(6) This regulation does not prohibit the consideration of race, color, or national origin if the purpose and effect are to remove or overcome the consequences of practices or impediments which have restricted the availability of, or participation in, the program or activity receiving Federal financial assistance, on the grounds of race, color, or national origin. Where previous discriminatory practice or usage tends, on the grounds of race, color, or national origin, to exclude individuals from participation in, to deny them the benefits of, or to subject them to discrimination under any program or activity to which this regulation applies the applicant or recipient has an obligation to take reasonable action to remove or overcome the consequences of the prior discriminatory practice or usage, and to accomplish the purposes of the Act.

(c) *Employment practices.* (1) Where a primary objective of the Federal financial assistance to a program to which this part applies is to provide employment, a recipient may not directly or through contractual or other arrangements subject an individual to discrimination on the ground of race, color, or national origin in its employment practices under such program (including recruitment or recruitment advertising, employment, layoff or termination, upgrading, demotion, or transfer, rates of pay or other forms of compensation and use of facilities), including programs where a primary objective of the Federal financial assistance is (i) to assist such individuals through employment to meet expenses incident to the commencement or continuation of their education or training or (ii) to provide work experience which contributes to the education or training of such individuals.

(2) Types of Federal financial assistance listed in appendix A as respects employment opportunities provided thereunder, or in facilities provided thereunder, which are limited, or for which preference is given, to students,

National Science Foundation

fellows, or other persons, including research associates, where in training for the same or related employments, have one of the above purposes as a primary purpose.

(3) The requirements applicable to construction employment under any such program shall be those specified in or pursuant to part III of Executive Order 11246 or any Executive order which supersedes it.

(4) Where a primary objective of the Federal financial assistance is not to provide employment, but discrimination on the grounds of race, color, or national origin in the employment practices of the recipient or other persons subject to the regulation tends, on the grounds of race, color, or national origin, to exclude individuals from participation in, to deny them the benefits of, or to subject them to discrimination under any program to which this regulation applies, the provisions of paragraph (c)(3) of this section shall apply to the employment practices of the recipient or other persons subject to the regulation, to the extent necessary to assure equality of opportunity to, and nondiscriminatory treatment of, beneficiaries.

(d) *Medical emergencies.* Notwithstanding the foregoing provisions of this section, a recipient of Federal financial assistance shall not be deemed to have failed to comply with paragraph (a) of this section if immediate provision of a service or other benefit to an individual is necessary to prevent his death or serious impairment of his health, and such service or other benefit cannot be provided except by or through a medical institution which refuses or fails to comply with paragraph (a) of this section.

[29 FR 16305, Dec. 4, 1964, as amended at 38 FR 17985, July 5, 1973; 68 FR 51382, Aug. 26, 2003]

§ 611.4 Assurances required.

(a) *General.* (1) Every application for Federal financial assistance to which this part applies, and every application for Federal financial assistance to provide a facility shall, as a condition to its approval and the extension of any Federal financial assistance pursuant to the application, contain or be accompanied by an assurance that the program will be conducted or the facility operated in compliance with all requirements imposed by or pursuant to this part. In the case where the Federal financial assistance is to provide or is in the form of personal property, or real property or interest therein or structures thereon, the assurance shall obligate the recipient, or, in the case of a subsequent transfer, the transferee, for the period during which the property is used for a purpose for which the Federal financial assistance is extended or for another purpose involving the provision of similar services and benefits, or for as long as the recipient retains ownership or possession of the property, whichever is longer. In all other cases the assurance shall obligate the recipient for the period during which Federal Financial assistance is extended pursuant to the application. The responsible Foundation official shall specify the form of the foregoing assurances and the extent to which like assurances will be required of subgrantees, contractors and subcontractors, successors in interest, and other participants. Any such assurance shall include provisions which give the United States a right to seek its judicial enforcement.

(2) In the case where Federal financial assistance is provided in the form of a transfer of real property, structures, or improvements thereon, or interest therein, from the Federal Government, the instrument effecting or recording the transfer shall contain a covenant running with the land assuring nondiscrimination for the period during which the real property is used for a purpose for which the Federal financial assistance is extended or for another purpose involving the provision of similar services or benefits. Where no transfer of property or interest therein from the Federal Government is involved, but property is acquired or improved with Federal financial assistance, the recipient shall agree to include such covenant in any subsequent transfer of such property. When the property is obtained from the Federal Government, such covenant may also include a condition coupled with a right to be reserved by the

Foundation to revert title to the property in the event of a breach of the covenant where, in the discretion of the responsible Foundation official, such a condition and right of reverter is appropriate to the statute under which the real property is obtained and to the nature of the grant and the grantee. In such event if a transferee of real property proposes to mortgage or otherwise encumber the real property as security for financing construction of new, or improvement of existing, facilities on such property for the purposes for which the property was transferred, the responsible Foundation official may agree, upon request of the transferee and if necessary to accomplish such financing, and upon such conditions as he deems appropriate, to subordinate such right of reversion to the lien of such mortgage or other encumbrance.

(3) Transfers of surplus property are subject to regulations issued by the Administrator of the General Services Administration. (41 CFR 101–6.2.)

(b) *Elementary and secondary schools.* The requirements of paragraph (a) of this section with respect to any elementary or secondary school or school system shall be deemed to be satisfied if such school or school system (1) is subject to a final order of a court of the United States for the desegregation of such school or school system, and provides an assurance that it will comply with such order, including any future modification of such order, or (2) submits a plan for the desegregation of such school or school system which the responsible Official of the Department of Health, Education, and Welfare determines is adequate to accomplish the purposes of the Act and this part, and provides reasonable assurance that it will carry out such plan. In any case of continuing Federal financial assistance the responsible Official of the Department of Health, Education, and Welfare may reserve the right to redetermine, after such period as may be specified by him, the adequacy of the plan to accomplish the purposes of the Act and this part. In any case in which a final order of a court of the United States for the desegregation of such school or school system is entered after submission of such a plan, such plan shall be revised to conform to such final order, including any future modification of such order.

(c) *Assurances from institutions.* (1) In the case of any application for Federal financial assistance to an institution of higher education (including assistance for construction, for research for a special training project, or for any other purpose), the assurance required by this section shall extend to admission practices and to all other practices relating to the treatment of students.

(2) The assurance required with respect to an institution of higher education, hospital, or any other institution, insofar as the assurance relates to the institution's practices with respect to admission or other treatment of individuals as students, patients, or clients of the institution or to the opportunity to participate in the provision of services or other benefits to such individuals, shall be applicable to the entire institution.

[29 FR 16305, Dec. 4, 1964, as amended at 38 FR 17985, July 5, 1973; 68 FR 51382, Aug. 26, 2003]

§ 611.5 Illustrative applications.

The following examples will illustrate the application of the foregoing provisions to some of the programs aided by the Foundation. (In all cases the discrimination prohibited is discrimination on the ground of race, color, or national origin prohibited by title VI of the Act and this part, as a condition of the receipt of Federal financial assistance.)

1. For support to elementary or secondary schools such as for the acquisition of equipment discrimination by the recipient school district in any of its elementary or secondary schools, or by the recipient private institution, in the admission of students, or in the treatment of its students in any aspect of the educational process, is prohibited. In this and the following illustration the prohibition of discrimination in the treatment of students or other trainees includes the prohibition of discrimination among the students or trainees in the availability or use of any academic, dormitory, eating, recreational, or other facilities of the grantee or other recipient.

2. In a research, training, or other grant to a university for activities to be conducted in a graduate school, discrimination in the admission and treatment of students in the

National Science Foundation §611.6

graduate school is prohibited, and the prohibition extends to the entire university.

3. In a training grant to a hospital or other nonacademic institution, discrimination is prohibited in the selection of individuals to be trained and in their treatment by the grantee during their training. In a research or demonstration grant to such an institution, discrimination is prohibited with respect to any educational activity, any provision of medical or other services and any financial aid to individuals incident to the program.

4. In grants to assist in the construction of facilities for research or for the provision of educational services, assurances will be required that services will be provided without discrimination, to the same extent that discrimination would be prohibited as a condition of Federal operating grants for the support of such services. Thus, as a condition of grants for the construction of academic, research, or other facilities at institutions of higher education, assurances will be required that there will be no discrimination in the admission or treatment of students. In other construction grants the assurances required will similarly be adapted to the nature of the activities to be conducted in the facilities for construction of which the grants have been authorized by Congress.

5. Upon transfers of real or personal property for research or educational uses, discrimination is prohibited to the same extent as in the case of grants for the construction of facilities or the provision of equipment for like purposes.

6. In some situations even though past discriminatory practices have been abandoned, the consequences of such practices continue to impede the full availability of a benefit. If the efforts required of the applicant or recipient under §611.6(d) to provide information as to the availability of the program or activity, and the rights of beneficiaries under this regulation, have failed to overcome these consequences, it will become necessary for such applicant or recipient to take additional steps to make the benefits fully available to racial and nationality groups previously subjected to discrimination. This action might take the form, for example, of special arrangements for obtaining referrals which will insure that groups previously subjected to discrimination are adequately served but not the establishment of discriminatory qualifications for participation in any program.

7. Even though an applicant or recipient has never used discriminatory policies, the services and benefits of the program or activity it administers may not in fact be equally available to some racial or nationality groups. In such circumstances an applicant or recipient may properly give special consideration to race, color, or national origin to make the benefits of its program more widely available to such groups, not then being adequately served. For example, where a university is not adequately serving members of a particular racial or nationality group, it may establish special recruitment policies to make its program better known and more readily available to such group, and take other steps to provide that group with more adequate service.

[29 FR 16305, Dec. 4, 1964, as amended at 38 FR 17985, July 5, 1973; 68 FR 51382, Aug. 26, 2003]

§611.6 Compliance information.

(a) *Cooperation and assistance.* The responsible Foundation official shall, to the fullest extent practicable, seek the cooperation of recipients in obtaining compliance with this part and shall provide assistance and guidance to recipients to help them comply voluntarily with this part.

(b) *Compliance reports.* Each recipient shall keep such records and submit to the responsible Foundation official timely, complete and accurate compliance reports at such times, and in such form and containing such information, as the responsible Foundation official may determine to be necessary to enable him to ascertain whether the recipient has complied or is complying with this part. In the case in which a primary recipient extends Federal financial assistance to any other recipient, such other recipient shall also submit such compliance reports to the primary recipient as may be necessary to enable the primary recipient to carry out its obligations under this part.

(c) *Access to sources of information.* Each recipient shall permit access by the responsible Foundation official or his designee during normal business hours to such of its books, records, accounts, and other sources of information, and its facilities as may be pertinent to ascertain compliance with this part. Where any information required of a recipient is in the exclusive possession of any other agency, institution or person and this agency, institution or person shall fail or refuse to furnish this information, the recipient shall so certify in its report and shall set forth what efforts it has made to obtain the information.

(d) *Information to beneficiaries and participants.* Each recipient shall make available to participants, beneficiaries,

§ 611.7

and other interested persons such information regarding the provisions of this part and its applicability to the program for which the recipient receives Federal financial assistance, and make such information available to them in such manner, as the responsible Foundation official finds necessary to apprise such persons of the protections against discrimination assured them by the Act and this part.

(Approved by the Office of Management and Budget under control number 3145–0087)

[29 FR 16305, Dec. 4, 1964, as amended at 49 FR 37595, Sept. 25, 1984; 68 FR 51382, Aug. 26, 2003]

§ 611.7 Conduct of investigations.

(a) *Periodic compliance reviews.* The responsible Foundation official shall from time to time review the practices of recipients to determine whether they are complying with this part.

(b) *Complaints.* Any person who believes himself or any specific class of individuals to be subjected to discrimination prohibited by this part may by himself or by a representative file with the responsible Foundation official a written complaint. A complaint must be filed not later than 90 days from the date of the alleged discrimination, unless the time for filing is extended by the responsible Foundation official.

(c) *Investigations.* The responsible Foundation official will make a prompt investigation whenever a compliance review, report, complaint, or any other information indicates a possible failure to comply with this part. The investigation should include, where appropriate, a review of the pertinent practices and policies of the recipient, the circumstances under which the possible noncompliance with this part occurred, and other factors relevant to a determination as to whether the recipient has failed to comply with this part.

(d) *Resolution of matters.* (1) If an investigation pursuant to paragraph (c) of this section indicates a failure to comply with this regulation, the responsible Foundation official will so inform the recipient and the matter will be resolved by informal means whenever possible. If it has been determined that the matter cannot be resolved by informal means, action will be taken as provided for in § 611.8.

(2) If an investigation does not warrant action pursuant to paragraph (d)(1) of this section the responsible Foundation official will so inform the recipient and the complainant, if any, in writing.

(e) *Intimidatory or retaliatory acts prohibited.* No recipient or other person shall intimidate, threaten, coerce, or discriminate against any individual for the purpose of interfering with any right or privilege secured by section 601 of the Act or this part, or because he has made a complaint, testified, assisted, or participated in any manner in an investigation, proceeding, or hearing under this part. The identity of complainants shall be kept confidential except to the extent necessary to carry out the purposes of this part, including the conduct of any investigation, hearing, or judicial proceeding arising thereunder.

§ 611.8 Procedure for effecting compliance.

(a) *General.* If there appears to be a failure or threatened failure to comply with this part, and if the noncompliance or threatened noncompliance cannot be corrected by informal means, compliance with this part may be effected by the suspension or termination of or refusal to grant or to continue Federal financial assistance or by any other means authorized by law. Such other means may include, but are not limited to (1) a reference to the Department of Justice with a recommendation that appropriate proceedings be brought to enforce any rights of the United States under any law of the United States (including other titles of the Act), or any assurance or other contractual undertaking, and (2) any applicable proceeding under State or local law.

(b) *Noncompliance with § 611.4.* If an applicant fails or refuses to furnish an assurance required under § 611.4 or otherwise fails to comply with that section, Federal financial assistance may be refused in accordance with the procedures of paragraph (c) of this section. The Foundation shall not be required to provide assistance in such a case during the pendency of the administrative proceedings under such subsection, except that the Foundation shall continue assistance during the pendency of such proceedings where such assistance is due and payable pursuant to an application therefor approved prior to the effective date of this part.

(c) *Termination of or refusal to grant or to continue Federal financial assistance.* No order suspending, terminating, or refusing to grant or continue Federal financial assistance shall become effective until:

(1) The responsible Foundation official has advised the applicant or recipient of his failure to comply and has determined that compliance cannot be secured by voluntary means,

(2) There has been an express finding on the record, after opportunity for hearings, of a failure by the applicant or recipient to comply with a requirement imposed by or pursuant to this part,

(3) The action has been approved by the Director pursuant to §611.10(e) and

(4) The expiration of thirty days after the Director has filed with the Committee of the House and the Committee of the Senate having legislative jurisdiction over the program involved, a full written report of the circumstances and the grounds for such action.

Any action to suspend or terminate or to refuse to grant or to continue Federal financial assistance shall be limited to the particular political entity, or part thereof, or other applicant or recipient as to whom such a finding has been made and shall be limited in its effect to the particular program, or part thereof, in which such noncompliance has been so found.

(d) *Other means authorized by law.* No action to effect compliance by any other means authorized by law shall be taken until (1) the responsible Foundation official has determined that compliance cannot be secured by voluntary means, (2) the recipient or other person has been notified of its failure to comply and of the action to be taken to effect compliance, and (3) the expiration of at least ten days from the mailing of such notice to the recipient or other person. During this period of at least ten days additional efforts shall be made to persuade the recipient or other person to comply with this part and to take such corrective action as may be appropriate.

[29 FR 16305, Dec. 4, 1964, as amended at 38 FR 17985, July 5, 1973; 51 FR 22938, June 24, 1986]

§ 611.9 Hearings.

(a) *Opportunity for hearing.* Whenever an opportunity for a hearing is required by §611.8(b), reasonable notice shall be given by registered or certified mail, return receipt requested, to the affected applicant or recipient. This notice shall advise the applicant or recipient of the action proposed to be taken, the specific provision under which the proposed action against it is to be taken, and the matters of fact or law asserted as the basis for this action, and either (1) fix a date not less than twenty days after the date of such notice within which the applicant or recipient may request of the responsible Foundation official that the matter be scheduled for hearing or (2) advise the applicant or recipient that the matter in question has been set down for hearing at a stated place and time. The time and place so fixed shall be reasonable and shall be subject to change for cause. The complainant, if any, shall be advised of the time and place of the hearing. An applicant or recipient may waive a hearing and submit written information and argument for the record. The failure of an applicant or recipient to request a hearing under this paragraph or to appear at a hearing for which a date has been set shall be deemed to be a waiver of the right to a hearing under section 602 of the Act and §611.8(c) and consent to the making of a decision on the basis of such information as is available.

(b) *Time and place of hearing.* Hearings shall be held at the offices of the Foundation in Arlington, VA, at a time fixed by the responsible Foundation official unless he determines that the convenience of the applicant or recipient or of the Foundation requires that another place be selected. Hearings shall be held before the responsible Foundation official or, at the discretion of the Director, a hearing examiner designated in accordance with 5 U.S.C. 3105 and 3344.

(c) *Right to counsel.* In all proceedings under this section, the applicant or recipient and the Foundation shall have the right to be represented by counsel.

(d) *Procedures, evidence, and record.* (1) The hearing, decision, and any administrative review thereof shall be conducted in conformity with 5 U.S.C. 554 through 557, and in accordance with such rules of procedure as are proper (and not inconsistent with this section) relating to the conduct of the hearing, giving of notices subsequent to those provided for in paragraph (a) of this section, taking of testimony, exhibits, arguments and briefs, requests for findings, and other related matters. Both the Foundation and the applicant or recipient shall be entitled to introduce all relevant evidence on the issues as stated in the notice for hearing or as determined by the officer conducting the hearing at the outset of or during the hearing.

(2) Technical rules of evidence shall not apply to hearings conducted pursuant to this part, but rules or principles designed to assure production of the most credible evidence available and to subject testimony to test by cross-examination shall be applied where reasonably necessary by the officer conducting the hearing. The hearing officer may exclude irrelevant, immaterial, or unduly repetitious evidence. All documents and other evidence offered or taken for the record shall be open to examination by the parties and opportunity shall be given to refute facts and arguments advanced on either side of the issues. A transcript shall be made of the oral evidence except to the extent the substance thereof is stipulated for the record. All decisions shall be based upon the hearing record and written findings shall be made.

(e) *Consolidated or joint hearings.* In cases in which the same or related facts are asserted to constitute noncompliance with this part with respect to two or more Federal statutes, authorities, or other means by which Federal financial assistance is extended and to which this part applies or noncompliance with this part and the regulations of one or more other Federal departments or agencies issued under title VI of the Act, the Director may, by agreement with such other departments or agencies, where applicable, provide for the conduct of consolidated or joint hearings, and for the application to such hearings of rules of procedure not inconsistent with this part. Final decisions in such cases, insofar as this part is concerned, shall be made in accordance with §611.10.

[29 FR 16305, Dec. 4, 1964, as amended at 38 FR 17985, July 5, 1973; 59 FR 37437, July 22, 1994; 68 FR 51382, Aug. 26, 2003]

§ 611.10 Decisions and notices.

(a) *Decision by a person or persons other than the responsible Foundation official.* If the hearing is held by a hearing examiner, such hearing examiner shall either make an initial decision, if so authorized, or certify the entire record including recommended findings and proposed decision to the responsible Foundation official for a final decision, and a copy of such initial decision or certification shall be mailed to the applicant or recipient. Where the initial decision is made by the hearing examiner, the applicant or recipient may within 30 days of the mailing of such notice of initial decision file with the responsible Foundation official his exceptions to the initial decision, with his reasons therefor. In the absence of exceptions, the responsible Foundation official may on his own motion within 45 days after the initial decision serve on the applicant or recipient a notice that he will review the decision. Upon the filing of such exceptions or of such notice of review the responsible Foundation official shall review the initial decision and issue his own decision thereon including the reasons therefor. In the absence of either exceptions or a notice of review the initial decision shall constitute the final decision of the responsible Foundation official.

(b) *Decisions on record or review by the responsible Foundation official.* Whenever, after hearing, a record is certified to the responsible Foundation official for decision or he reviews the decision of a hearing examiner pursuant to paragraph (a) of this section, or whenever the responsible Foundation official conducts the hearing, the applicant or recipient shall be given reasonable opportunity to file with him briefs

National Science Foundation § 611.12

or other written statements of its contentions, and a copy of the final decision of the responsible Foundation official shall be given in writing to the applicant or recipient, and to the complainant, if any.

(c) *Decisions on record where a hearing is waived.* Whenever a hearing is waived pursuant to § 611.9(a), a decision shall be made by the responsible Foundation official on the record and a copy of such decision shall be given in writing to the applicant or recipient, and to the complainant, if any.

(d) *Rulings required.* Each decision of a hearing officer, panel, or responsible Foundation official shall set forth the ruling on each finding, conclusion, or exception presented, and shall identify the requirement or requirements imposed by or pursuant to this part with which it is found that the applicant or recipient has failed to comply.

(e) *Approval by Director.* Any final decision of a responsible Foundation official (other than the Director) which provides for the suspension or termination of, or the refusal to grant or continue Federal financial assistance, or the imposition of any other sanction available under this part or the Act, shall promptly be transmitted to the Director who may approve such decision, may vacate it, or remit or mitigate any sanction imposed.

(f) *Content of orders.* The final decision may provide for suspension or termination of, or refusal to grant or continue Federal financial assistance, in whole or in part, to which this regulation applies, and may contain such terms, conditions, and other provisions as are consistent with and will effectuate the purposes of the Act and this part, including provisions designed to assure that no Federal financial assistance to which this regulation applies will thereafter be extended to the applicant or recipient determined by such decision to be in default in its performance of an assurance given by it pursuant to this part, or to have otherwise failed to comply with this part, unless and until it corrects its noncompliance and satisfies the responsible Foundation official that it will fully comply with this part.

(g) *Posttermination proceedings.* (1) An applicant or recipient adversely affected by an order issued under paragraph (f) of this section shall be restored to full eligibility to receive Federal financial assistance if it satisfies the terms and conditions of that order for such eligibility or if it brings itself into compliance with this regulation and provides reasonable assurance that it will fully comply with this regulation.

(2) Any applicant or recipient adversely affected by an order entered pursuant to paragraph (f) of this section may at any time request the responsible Foundation official to restore fully its eligibility to receive Federal financial assistance. Any such request shall be supported by information showing that the applicant or recipient has met the requirements of paragraph (g)(1) of this section. If the responsible Foundation official determines that those requirements have been satisfied, he shall restore such eligibility.

(3) If the responsible Foundation official denies any such request, the applicant or recipient may submit a request for a hearing in writing, specifying why it believes such official to have been in error. It shall thereupon be given an expeditious hearing, with a decision on the record, in accordance with rules of procedure issued by the responsible Foundation official. The applicant or recipient will be restored to such eligibility if it proves at such a hearing that it satisfied the requirements of paragraph (g)(1) of this section. While proceedings under this paragraph are pending, the sanctions imposed by the order issued under paragraph (f) of this section shall remain in effect.

[29 FR 16305, Dec. 4, 1964, as amended at 38 FR 17985, July 5, 1973; 51 FR 22939, June 24, 1986; 68 FR 51382, Aug. 26, 2003]

§ 611.11 Judicial review.

Action taken pursuant to section 602 of the Act is subject to judicial review as provided in section 603 of the Act.

§ 611.12 Effect on other regulations; forms and instructions.

(a) *Effect on other regulations.* All regulations, orders, or like directions heretofore issued by any officer of the Foundation which impose requirements designed to prohibit any discrimination against individuals on the ground of race, color, or national origin under any program to which this part applies, and which authorize the suspension or termination of or refusal to grant or to continue Federal financial assistance to any applicant for or recipient of such assistance for failure to comply with such requirements, are hereby superseded to the extent that such discrimination is prohibited by this part, except that nothing in this part shall be deemed to relieve any person of any obligation assumed or imposed under any such superseded regulation, order, instruction, or like direction prior to the effective date of this part. Nothing in this part, however, supersedes any of the following (including future amendments thereof): (1) Executive Order 11246 and regulation issued thereunder, or (2) any other orders, regulations, or instructions, insofar as such orders, regulations, or instructions prohibit discrimination on the ground of race, color, or national origin in any program or situation to which this part is inapplicable, or prohibit discrimination on any other ground.

(b) *Forms and instructions.* Each responsible Foundation official shall issue and promptly make available to interested persons forms and detailed instructions and procedures for effectuating this part as applied to programs to which this part applies and for which he is responsible.

(c) *Supervision and coordination.* The Director may from time to time assign to officials of other departments or agencies of the Government, with the consent of such departments or agencies, responsibilities in connection with the effectuation of the purposes of title VI of the Act and this part (other than responsibility for final decision as provided in §611.10), including the achievement of effective coordination and maximum uniformity within the Foundation and within the Executive Branch of the Government in the application of title VI and this regulation to similar programs and in similar situations. Any action taken, determination made, or requirement imposed by an official of another Department or agency acting pursuant to an assignment of responsibility under this subsection shall have the same effect as though such action had been taken by the responsible official of this agency.

[29 FR 16305, Dec. 4, 1964, as amended at 38 FR 17985, July 5, 1973; 68 FR 51382, Aug. 26, 2003]

§ 611.13 Definitions.

As used in this part:

(a) The term *Foundation* means the National Science Foundation, and includes each of its organizational units.

(b) The term *Director* means the Director of the National Science Foundation.

(c) The term *responsible Foundation official* with respect to any program receiving Federal financial assistance means the Director or other official of the Foundation designated by the Director.

(d) The term *United States* means the States of the United States, the District of Columbia, Puerto Rico, the Virgin Islands, American Samoa, Guam, Wake Island, the Canal Zone, and the territories and possessions of the United States, and the term *State* means any one of the foregoing.

(e) The term *Federal financial assistance* includes (1) grants and loans of Federal funds, (2) the grant or the donation of Federal property and interests in property, (3) the detail of Federal personnel, (4) the sale and lease of, and the permission to use (on other than a casual or transient basis), Federal property or any interest in such property without consideration or at a nominal consideration, or at a consideration which is reduced for the purpose of assisting the recipient, or in recognition of the public interest to be served by such sale or lease to the recipient, and (5) any Federal agreement, arrangement, or other contract which has as one of its purposes the provision of assistance.

(f) The terms *program or activity* and *program* mean all of the operations of any entity described in paragraphs (f)(1) through (4) of this section, any part of which is extended Federal financial assistance:

(1)(i) A department, agency, special purpose district, or other instrumentality of a State or of a local government; or

(ii) The entity of such State or local government that distributes such assistance and each such department or agency (and each other State or local government entity) to which the assistance is extended, in the case of assistance to a State or local government;

(2)(i) A college, university, or other postsecondary institution, or a public system of higher education; or

(ii) A local educational agency (as defined in 20 U.S.C. 7801), system of vocational education, or other school system;

(3)(i) An entire corporation, partnership, or other private organization, or an entire sole proprietorship—

(A) If assistance is extended to such corporation, partnership, private organization, or sole proprietorship as a whole; or

(B) Which is principally engaged in the business of providing education, health care, housing, social services, or parks and recreation; or

(ii) The entire plant or other comparable, geographically separate facility to which Federal financial assistance is extended, in the case of any other corporation, partnership, private organization, or sole proprietorship; or

(4) Any other entity which is established by two or more of the entities described in paragraph (f)(1), (2), or (3) of this section.

(g) The term *facility* includes all or any portion of structures, equipment, or other real or personal property or interests therein, and the provision of facilities includes the construction, expansion, renovation, remodeling, alteration or acquisition of facilities.

(h) The term *recipient* means any State, political subdivision of any State, or instrumentality of any State or political subdivision, any public or private agency, institution, or organization, or other entity or any individual, in any State, to whom Federal financial assistance is extended, directly or through another recipient, including any successor, assign, or transferee thereof, but such term does not include any ultimate beneficiary.

(i) The term *primary recipient* means any recipient which is authorized or required to extend Federal financial assistance to another recipient.

(j) The term *applicant* means one who submits an application, request, or plan required to be approved by a responsible Foundation official, or by a primary recipient, as a condition to eligibility for Federal financial assistance, and the term *application* means such an application, request, or plan.

[29 FR 16305, Dec. 4, 1964, as amended at 68 FR 51382, Aug. 26, 2003]

Appendix A to Part 611

Statutory Provisions under which the National Science Foundation provides Federal financial assistance:
The National Science Foundation Act of 1950, as amended (42 U.S.C. 1861–1875).

[38 FR 17986, July 5, 1973, as amended at 59 FR 37437, July 22, 1994]

PART 612—AVAILABILITY OF RECORDS AND INFORMATION

Sec.
612.1 General provisions.
612.2 Public reading room.
612.3 Requirements for making requests.
612.4 Responding to requests.
612.5 Timing of responses to requests.
612.6 Responses to requests.
612.7 Exemptions.
612.8 Business information.
612.9 Appeals.
612.10 Fees.
612.11 Other rights and services.

AUTHORITY: 5 U.S.C. 552, as amended.

SOURCE: 78 FR 53278, Aug. 29, 2013, unless otherwise noted.

§ 612.1 General provisions.

(a) This part contains the rules that the National Science Foundation (NSF) follows in processing requests for records under the Freedom of Information Act (FOIA), 5 U.S.C. 552. Information routinely made available to the public as part of a regular Foundation activity (for example, program announcements and solicitations, summary of awarded proposals, statistical reports on U.S. science, press releases issued by the Office of Legislative and Public Affairs) may be provided to the public without reliance on this part. As a matter of policy, the Foundation also makes discretionary disclosures of

§ 612.2

records or information otherwise exempt under the FOIA whenever disclosure would not foreseeably harm an interest protected by a FOIA exemption. This policy, however, does not create any right enforceable in court. When individuals seek records about themselves under the Privacy Act of 1974, 5 U.S.C. 552a, NSF processes those requests under both NSF's Privacy regulations at part 613 of this chapter, and this part.

(b) As used in this part, NSF includes one component, the Office of the Inspector General (OIG) of the National Science Foundation.

§ 612.2 Public reading room.

(a) The Foundation maintains a public reading room located in the NSF Library at 4201 Wilson Boulevard, Suite 225, Arlington, Virginia, open during regular working hours Monday through Friday. It contains the records that the FOIA requires to be made regularly available for public inspection and copying and has computers and printers available for public use in accessing records. Also available for public inspection and copying are current subject matter indexes of reading room records.

(b) Information about FOIA and Privacy at NSF and copies of frequently requested FOIA releases are available online at *www.nsf.gov/policies/foia/jsp*. Most NSF policy documents, staff instructions, manuals, and other publications that affect a member of the public, are available in electronic form through the "Publications" option on the tool bar on NSF's Home Page on the World Wide Web at *www.nsf.gov*.

§ 612.3 Requirements for making requests.

(a) *Where to send a request.* You may make a FOIA request for records of the National Science Foundation by writing directly to the NSF FOIA Officer, Office of the General Counsel, National Science Foundation, 4201 Wilson Boulevard, Suite 1265, Arlington, VA 22230. Requests may also be sent by facsimile to (703) 292–9041 or by email to *foia@nsf.gov*. The National Science Foundation includes one agency component, the NSF Office of the Inspector General (OIG). For records maintained by the NSF OIG, you may write directly to the Office of Inspector General, National Science Foundation, 4201 Wilson Boulevard, Suite 1135, Arlington, VA 22230. Requests may also be sent to the OIG by facsimile to (703) 292–9158. The NSF FOIA Officer and the OIG component will also forward requests as appropriate.

(b) *Form of request.* A FOIA request need not be in any particular format, but it must be in writing, include the requester's name and mailing address, and be clearly identified both on the envelope and in the letter, or in a facsimile or electronic mail message as a Freedom of Information Act or "FOIA" request. It must describe the records sought with sufficient specificity to permit identification, and include agreement to pay applicable fees as described in § 612.10. NSF and its OIG component are not obligated to act upon a request until it meets these procedural requirements.

(c) *Personal records.* (1) If you are making a request for records about yourself and the records are not contained in a Privacy Act system of records, your request will be processed only under the FOIA, since the Privacy Act does not apply. If the records about you are contained in a Privacy Act system of records, NSF will respond with information on how to make a Privacy Act request (see NSF Privacy Act regulations at 45 CFR 613.2).

(2) If you are making a request for personal information about another individual, either a written authorization signed by that individual in accordance with § 613.2(f) of this chapter permitting disclosure of those records to you, or proof that that individual is deceased (for example, a copy of a death certificate or a published obituary) will help the agency process your request.

(d) *Description of records sought.* Your request must describe the records that you seek in enough detail to enable NSF personnel to locate them with a reasonable amount of effort. A record must have been created or obtained by NSF and be under the control of NSF at the time of the request to be subject to the FOIA. NSF has no obligation under the FOIA to create, compile, or obtain a record to satisfy a FOIA request. Whenever possible, your request should include specific descriptive information about each record sought, such as the date, title or name, author, recipient, and subject matter of the record. As a general rule, the more specific you are about the records or type of records that you want, the more likely the Foundation will be able to locate those records in response to your request, and the more likely fees will be reduced or eliminated. If NSF determines that your request does not reasonably describe records, you will be advised what additional information is needed to perfect your request or why your request is otherwise insufficient.

(e) *Agreement to pay fees.* Your request must state that you will promptly pay the total fees chargeable under this regulation or set a maximum amount you are willing to pay. NSF does not charge if fees total less than $25.00. If you seek a waiver of fees, please see § 612.10(k) for a discussion of the factors you must address. If you place an inadequate limit on the amount you will pay, or have failed to make payments for previous requests, NSF may require advance payment (see § 612.10(i)).

(f) *Receipt date.* A request that meets the requirements of this section will be considered received on the date it is properly received by the Office of the General Counsel or the Office of the Inspector General. In determining which records are responsive to a FOIA request, the NSF will include only records in its possession as of the date the NSF or OIG begins its search. If any other date is used, the NSF or OIG shall inform the requester of that date.

(g) *Publications excluded.* For the purpose of public requests for records the term "record" does not include publications which are available to the public in the FEDERAL REGISTER, or by sale or free distribution. Such publications may be obtained from the Government Printing Office, the National Technical Information Service, or through NSF's Home Page on the World Wide Web at *http://www.nsf.gov/publications/*. Requests for such publications will be referred to or the requester informed of the appropriate source.

§ 612.4 Processing requests.

(a) *Monitoring of requests.* The NSF Office of the General Counsel (OGC), or such other office as may be designated by the Director, will serve as the central office for administering these regulations. For records maintained by the Office of Inspector General, that Office will control incoming requests made directly or referred to it, dispatch response letters, and maintain administrative records. For all other records maintained by NSF, OGC (or such other office as may be designated by the Director) will control incoming requests, assign them to appropriate action offices, monitor compliance, consult with action offices on disclosure, approve necessary extensions, dispatch denial and other letters, and maintain administrative records.

(b) *Consultations and referrals.* When the NSF receives a request for a record in its possession that originated with another agency or in which another agency has a substantial interest, it may decide that the other agency of the Federal Government is better able to determine whether the record should or should not be released under the FOIA.

(1) If the NSF determines that it is the agency best able to process the record in response to the request, then it will do so, after consultation with the other interested agencies where appropriate.

(2) If it determines that it is not the agency best able to process the record, then it will refer the request regarding that record (or portion of the record) to the agency that originated or has a substantial interest in the record in question (but only if that agency is subject to the FOIA). Ordinarily, the agency that originated a record will be presumed to be best able to determine whether to disclose it.

(3) Whenever NSF refers all or any part of the responsibility for responding to a request to another agency, it ordinarily will notify the requester of the referral and inform the requester of the name of each agency to which the request has been referred and of the part of the request that has been referred, unless such notification would disclose information otherwise exempt.

§ 612.5 Timing of responses to requests.

(a) *In general.* The NSF and its component, OIG, ordinarily will initiate processing of requests according to their order of receipt.

(b) *Multitrack processing.* (1) NSF and OIG may use two or more processing tracks by distinguishing between simple and more complex requests based on the amount of work and/or time needed to process the request, including through limits based on the number of pages involved. If NSF or OIG does so, it shall advise requesters in its slower track(s) of the limits of its faster track(s).

(2) NSF or OIG using multitrack processing may provide requesters in its slower track(s) with an opportunity to limit the scope of their requests in order to qualify for faster processing within the specified limits of the NSF's or OIG's faster track(s). The requester may be contacted by telephone, email, or letter, whichever is more efficient in each case.

(c) *Time for response.* The NSF will seek to take appropriate action within 20 days of when a request is properly received or is perfected (excluding the date of receipt, weekends, and legal holidays), whichever is later. A request which otherwise meets the requirements of § 612.3 is perfected when you have reasonably described the records sought under § 612.3(d), and agreed to pay fees under § 612.3(e), or otherwise met the fee requirements under § 612.10.

(d) *Unusual circumstances.* (1) Where the time limits for processing a request cannot be met because of unusual circumstances, as defined in the FOIA, the NSF FOIA Officer or the OIG component will notify the requester as soon as practicable in writing of the unusual circumstances and may extend the response period for up to ten working days.

(2) Where the extension is for more than ten working days, the FOIA Officer or the OIG component will provide the requester with an opportunity either to modify the request so that it may be processed within the ten day extension period or to arrange an agreed upon alternative time period with the FOIA Officer or the OIG component for processing the request or a modified request.

(3) Where the NSF reasonably believes that multiple requests submitted by a requester, or by a group of requesters acting in concert, constitute a single request that would otherwise involve unusual circumstances, and the requests involve clearly related matters, they may be aggregated. Multiple requests involving unrelated matters will not be aggregated.

(e) *Expedited processing.* (1) If you want to receive expedited processing, you must submit a statement, certified to be true and correct to the best of your knowledge and belief, explaining in detail the basis for requesting expedited processing.

(2)(i) Requests and appeals will be given expedited treatment whenever it is determined that a requester has demonstrated compelling need by presenting:

(A) Circumstances in which the lack of expedited treatment could reasonably be expected to pose an imminent threat to the life or physical safety of an individual; or

(B) An urgency to inform the public about an actual or alleged Federal government activity, if made by a person primarily engaged in disseminating information.

(ii) For example, a requester who is not a full-time member of the news media must establish that he or she is a person whose main professional activity or occupation is information dissemination, though it need not be his or her sole occupation. Such requester also must establish a particular urgency to inform the public about the government activity involved in the request, beyond the public's right to know about government activity generally, and that the information sought has particular value that would be lost if not disseminated quickly.

(3) Within ten calendar days of receipt of a request for expedited processing, the NSF FOIA Officer or OIG component will decide whether to grant it, and will notify the requester of the decision orally or in writing. If a request for expedited treatment is granted, the request will be processed as soon as practicable. If a request for

National Science Foundation § 612.7

expedited processing is denied, any appeal of that decision will be acted on expeditiously.

§ 612.6 Responses to requests.

(a) *Acknowledgment of requests.* The NSF or OIG will ordinarily send an email acknowledgment of all FOIA requests with an assigned request number for further reference and an estimated response date.

(b) *Grants of requests.* Once the NSF makes a determination to grant a request in whole or in part, it will notify the requester in writing. The NSF will inform the requester in the notice of any applicable fee and will disclose records to the requester promptly on payment of applicable fees. Records disclosed in part will be marked or annotated to show both the amount and the location of the information deleted where practicable.

(c) *Denials of requests.* (1) Denials of FOIA requests will be made by the Office of the General Counsel, the Office of the Inspector General, or such other office as may be designated by the Director. The response letter will briefly set forth the reasons for the denial, including any FOIA exemption(s) applied in denying the request. It will also provide the name and title or position of the person responsible for the denial, will inform the requester of the right to appeal, and will, where appropriate, include an estimate of the volume of any requested materials withheld. An estimate need not be provided when the volume is otherwise indicated through deletions on records disclosed in part, or if providing an estimate would harm an interest protected by an applicable exemption.

(2) Requesters can appeal an agency determination to withhold all or part of any requested record; a determination that a requested record does not exist or cannot be located; a determination that what has been requested is not a record subject to the Act; a disapproval of a fee category claim by a requester; denial of a fee waiver or reduction; or a denial of a request for expedited treatment (see § 612.9).

§ 612.7 Exemptions.

(a) *Exemptions from disclosure.* The following types of records or information may be withholdable as exempt in full or in part from mandatory public disclosure:

(1) *Exemption 1–5 U.S.C. 552(b)(1).* Records specifically authorized and properly classified pursuant to Executive Order to be kept secret in the interest of national defense or foreign policy. NSF does not have classifying authority and normally does not deal with classified materials.

(2) *Exemption 2–5 U.S.C. 552(b)(2).* Records related solely to the internal personnel rules and practices of NSF. Examples of records normally exempt from disclosure include, but are not limited to: Information relating to position management and manpower utilization, such as internal staffing plans, authorizations or controls, or involved in determination of the qualifications of candidates for employment, advancement, or promotion including examination questions and answers.

(3) *Exemption 3–5 U.S.C. 552(b)(3).* Records specifically exempted from disclosure by another statute that either requires that the information be withheld in a such way that the agency has no discretion in the matter; or establishes particular criteria for withholding or refers to particular types of information to be withheld; and, if enacted after the date of enactment of the OPEN FOIA Act of 2009, October 28, 2009, specifically cites to 5 U.S.C. 552(b)(3). Examples of records exempt from disclosure include, but are not limited to:

(i) Records that disclose any invention in which the Federal Government owns or may own a right, title, or interest (including a nonexclusive license), 35 U.S.C. 205;

(ii) Contractor proposals not specifically set forth or incorporated by reference into a contract, 41 U.S.C. 253b(m);

(iii) Information protected by the Procurement Integrity Act, 41 U.S.C. 423;

(iv) Statistical information protected by section 14(i) of the NSF Act of 1950, as amended, 42 U.S.C. 1873(i) and/or the Confidential Information Protection and Statistical Efficiency Act of 2002, 44 U.S.C. 3501 note.

§ 612.7

(4) *Exemption 4–5 U.S.C. 552(b)(4).* Trade secrets and commercial or financial information obtained from a person, and privileged or confidential. Information subject to this exemption is that customarily held in confidence by the originator(s), including nonprofit organizations and their employees. Release of such information is likely to cause substantial harm to the competitive position of the originator or submitter, or impair the Foundation's ability to obtain such information in the future. NSF will process information potentially exempted from disclosure by Exemption 4 under § 612.8.

Examples of records or information normally exempt from disclosure include, but are not limited to:

(i) Information received in confidence, such as grant applications, fellowship applications, and research proposals prior to award;

(ii) Confidential scientific and manufacturing processes or developments, and technical, scientific, statistical data or other information developed by a grantee;

(iii) Technical, scientific, or statistical data, and commercial or financial information privileged or received in confidence from an existing or potential contractor or subcontractor, in connection with bids, proposals, or contracts, concerning contract performance, income, profits, losses, and expenditures, as well as trade secrets, inventions, discoveries, or other proprietary data. When the provisions of 41 U.S.C. 253b(m) or 41 U.S.C. 423 are met, certain proprietary and source selection information may also be withheld under Exemption 3;

(iv) Confidential proprietary information submitted on a voluntary basis;

(v) Statements or information collected in the course of inspections, investigations, or audits, when such statements are received in confidence from the individual and retained in confidence because they reveal trade secrets or commercial or financial information normally considered confidential or privileged.

(5) *Exemption 5–5 U.S.C. 552(b)(5).* Inter-agency or intra-agency memoranda or letters which would not be available by law to a private party in litigation with NSF. Factual material contained in such records will be considered for release if it can be reasonably segregated and is not otherwise exempt. Examples of records exempt from disclosure include, but are not limited to:

(i) Those portions of reports, memoranda, correspondence, workpapers, minutes of meetings, and staff papers, containing evaluations, advice, opinions, suggestions, or other deliberative material that are prepared for use within NSF or within the Executive Branch of the Government by agency personnel and others acting in a consultant or advisory capacity;

(ii) Advance information on proposed NSF plans to procure, lease, or otherwise acquire, or dispose of materials, real estate, facilities, services or functions, when such information would provide undue or unfair competitive advantage to private interests or impede legitimate government functions;

(iii) Negotiating positions or limits at least until the execution of a contract (including a grant or cooperative agreement) or the completion of the action to which the negotiating positions were applicable. They may also be exempt pursuant to other provisions of this section;

(iv) Trade secret or other confidential research development, or commercial information owned by the Government, where premature release is likely to affect the Government's negotiating position or other commercial interest;

(iv) Records prepared for use in proceedings before any Federal or State court or administrative body;

(vi) Evaluations of and comments on specific grant applications, research projects or proposals, fellowship applications or nominations or other individual awards, or potential contractors and their products, whether made by NSF personnel or by external reviewers acting either individually or in panels, committees or similar groups;

(vii) Preliminary, draft or unapproved documents, such as opinions, recommendations, evaluations, decisions, or studies conducted or supported by NSF;

(viii) Proposed budget requests, and supporting projections used or arising in the preparation and/or execution of

National Science Foundation § 612.7

a budget; proposed annual and multi-year policy, priorities, program and financial plan and supporting papers;

(ix) Those portions of official reports of inspection, reports of the Inspector General, audits, investigations, or surveys pertaining to safety, security, or the internal management, administration, or operation of NSF, when these records have traditionally been treated by the courts as privileged against disclosure in litigation.

(6) *Exemption 6–5 U.S.C. 552(b)(6).* Personnel and medical files and similar files, the disclosure of which would constitute a clearly unwarranted invasion of personal privacy. The exemption may apply to protect the privacy of living persons and of living close survivors of a deceased person identified in a record. Information in such files which is not otherwise exempt from disclosure pursuant to other provisions of this section will be released to the subject or to his designated legal representative, and may be disclosed to others with the subject's written consent. Examples of records exempt from disclosure include, but are not limited to:

(i) Reports, records, and other materials pertaining to individual cases in which disciplinary or other administrative action has been or may be taken. Opinions and orders resulting from those administrative or disciplinary proceedings shall be disclosed without identifying details if used, cited, or relied upon as precedent;

(ii) Records compiled to evaluate or adjudicate the suitability of candidates for employment, and the eligibility of individuals (civilian or contractor employees) for security clearances, or for access to classified information;

(iii) Reports and evaluations which reflect upon the qualifications or competence of individuals;

(iv) Personal information such as home addresses and telephone and facsimile numbers, private email addresses, social security numbers, dates of birth, marital status and the like;

(v) The exemption also applies when the fact of the existence or nonexistence of a responsive record would itself reveal personal, private information, and the public interest in disclosure is not sufficient to outweigh the privacy interest.

(7) *Exemption 7–5 U.S.C. 552(b)(7).* Records or information compiled for civil or criminal law enforcement purposes, including the implementation of Executive Orders or regulations issued pursuant to law. This exemption may exempt from mandatory disclosure records not originally created, but later gathered, for law enforcement purposes.

(i) This exemption applies only to the extent that the production of such law enforcement records or information:

(A) Could reasonably be expected to interfere with enforcement proceedings;

(B) Would deprive a person of the right to a fair trial or an impartial adjudication;

(C) Could reasonably be expected to constitute an unwarranted invasion of personal privacy of a living person, or living close survivors of a deceased person identified in a record;

(D) Could reasonably be expected to disclose the identity of a confidential source, including a source within the Federal Government, or a State, local, or foreign agency or authority, or any private institution, that furnished information on a confidential basis; and information furnished by a confidential source and obtained by a criminal law enforcement authority in a criminal investigation;

(E) Would disclose techniques and procedures for law enforcement investigations or prosecutions, or would disclose guidelines for law enforcement investigations or prosecutions if such disclosure could reasonably be expected to risk circumvention of the law, or

(F) Could reasonably be expected to endanger the life or physical safety of any individual.

(ii) Examples of records normally exempt from disclosure include, but are not limited to:

(A) The identity and statements of complainants or witnesses, or other material developed during the course of an investigation and all materials prepared in connection with related government litigation or adjudicative proceedings;

§ 612.8

(B) The identity of firms or individuals investigated for alleged irregularities involving NSF grants, contracts or other matters when no indictment has been obtained, no civil action has been filed against them by the United States, or no government-wide public suspension or debarment has occurred;

(C) Information obtained in confidence, expressed or implied, in the course of a criminal investigation by the NSF Office of the Inspector General.

(iii) The exclusions contained in 5 U.S.C. 552(c)(1) and (2) may also apply to these records.

(8) *Exemption 8–5 U.S.C. 552(b)(8).* Records contained in or related to examination, operating, or condition reports prepared by, on behalf of, or for the use of any agency responsible for the regulation or supervision of financial institutions.

(9) *Exemption 9–5 U.S.C. 552(b)(9).* Records containing geological and geophysical information and data, including maps, concerning wells.

(b) *Deletion of exempt portions and identifying details.* Any reasonably segregable portion of a record will be provided to requesters after deletion of the portions which are exempt. Whenever any final opinion, order, or other materials required to be made available relates to a private party or parties and the release of the name(s) or other identifying details will constitute a clearly unwarranted invasion of personal privacy, the record shall be published or made available with such identifying details left blank, or shall be published or made available with obviously fictitious substitutes and with a notification such as the following: Names of parties and certain other identifying details have been removed (and fictitious names substituted) in order to prevent a clearly unwarranted invasion of the personal privacy of the individuals involved.

§ 612.8 Business information.

(a) *In general.* Business information obtained by the Foundation from a submitter of that information will be disclosed under the FOIA only under this section's procedures.

(b) *Definitions.* For purposes of this section:

(1) *Business Information* means commercial or financial information obtained by the Foundation from a submitter that may be protected from disclosure under Exemption 4 of the FOIA and § 612.7(a)(4).

(2) *Submitter* means any person or entity from whom the Foundation obtains business information, directly or indirectly. The term includes corporations; state, local, and tribal governments; and foreign governments.

(c) *Designation of business information.* A submitter of business information must use good faith efforts to designate, by appropriate markings, either at the time of submission or at a reasonable time thereafter, any portions of its submission that it considers to be protected from disclosure under Exemption 4. These designations will expire ten years after the date of the submission unless the submitter requests, and provides justification for, a longer designation period.

(d) *Notice to submitters.* The Foundation will provide a submitter with prompt written notice of a FOIA request or administrative appeal that seeks its business information wherever required under this section, in order to give the submitter an opportunity to object to disclosure of any specified portion of that information under paragraph (f) of this section. The notice shall either describe the business information requested or include copies of the requested records or record portions containing the information.

(e) *Where notice is required.* Notice will be given to a submitter wherever:

(1) The information has been designated in good faith by the submitter as information considered protected from disclosure under Exemption 4; or

(2) The Foundation has reason to believe that the information may be protected from disclosure under Exemption 4.

(f) *Opportunity to object to disclosure.* NSF will allow a submitter a reasonable time, consistent with statutory requirements, to respond to the notice described in paragraph (d) of this section. If a submitter has any objection to disclosure, it must submit a detailed written statement. The statement must specify all grounds for withholding any portion of the information under any exemption of the FOIA and, in the case of Exemption 4, must show why the information is a trade secret, or commercial or financial information that is privileged or confidential. In the event that a submitter fails to respond within the time specified in the notice, the submitter will be considered to have no objection to disclosure of the information. Information provided by a submitter under this paragraph may itself be a record subject to disclosure under the FOIA.

(g) *Notice of intent to disclose.* The Foundation will consider a submitter's objections and specific grounds for nondisclosure in deciding whether to disclose business information. Whenever it decides to disclose business information over the objection of a submitter, the Foundation will give the submitter written notice, which will include:

(1) A statement of the reason(s) why the submitter's disclosure objections were not sustained;

(2) A description of the business information to be disclosed; and

(3) A specified disclosure date, which will be a reasonable time subsequent to the notice.

(h) *Exceptions to notice requirements.* The notice requirements of paragraphs (d) and (g) of this section will not apply if:

(1) The Foundation determines that the information should not be disclosed (the Foundation protects from disclosure to third parties information about specific unfunded applications, including pending, withdrawn, or declined proposals);

(2) The information lawfully has been published or has been officially made available to the public;

(3) Disclosure of the information is required by statute (other than the FOIA) or by a regulation issued in accordance with the requirements of Executive Order 12600 (3 CFR, 1988 Comp., p. 235); or

(4) The designation made by the submitter under paragraph (c) of this section appears obviously frivolous, in which case the Foundation will, within a reasonable time prior to a specified disclosure date, give the submitter written notice of any final decision to disclose the information.

(i) *Notice of FOIA lawsuit.* Whenever a requester files a lawsuit seeking to compel the disclosure of business information, the Foundation will promptly notify the submitter(s). Whenever a submitter files a lawsuit seeking to prevent the disclosure of business information, the Foundation will notify the requester(s).

§ 612.9 Appeals.

(a) *Appeals of denials.* You may appeal a denial of your request to the General Counsel, National Science Foundation, 4201 Wilson Boulevard, Suite 1265, Arlington, VA 22230. You must make your appeal in writing and it must be received by the Office of the General Counsel within ten days of the receipt of the denial (weekends, legal holidays, and the date of receipt excluded). You must clearly mark your appeal letter and the envelope or your electronic submission as a "Freedom of Information Act Appeal." Your appeal letter must include a copy of your written request and the denial together with any written argument you wish to submit.

(b) *Responses to appeals.* A written decision on your appeal will be made by the General Counsel. A decision affirming an adverse determination in whole or in part will contain a statement of the reason(s) for the affirmance, including any FOIA exemption(s) applied, and will inform you of the FOIA provisions for court review of the decision. If the adverse determination is reversed or modified on appeal, in whole or in part, you will be notified in a written decision and your request will be reprocessed in accordance with that appeal decision.

(c) *When appeal is required.* If you wish to seek review by a court of any denial, you must first appeal it under this section.

§ 612.10 Fees

(a) *In general.* NSF will charge for processing requests under the FOIA in accordance with paragraph (c) of this section, except where fees are limited under paragraph (d) of this section or where a waiver or reduction of fees is granted under paragraph (k) of this section. If fees are applicable, NSF will itemize the amounts charged. NSF may collect all applicable fees before sending copies of requested records to a requester. Requesters must pay fees by check or money order made payable to the Treasury of the United States.

(b) *Definitions.* For purposes of this section:

(1) *Commercial use request* means a request from or on behalf of a person who seeks information for a use or purpose that furthers his or her commercial, trade, or profit interests, which can include furthering those interests through litigation. When it appears that the requester will put the records to a commercial use, either because of the nature of the request itself or because NSF has reasonable cause to doubt a requester's stated use, NSF will provide the requester a reasonable opportunity to submit further clarification.

(2) *Direct costs* means those expenses that an agency actually incurs in searching for and duplicating (and, in the case of commercial use requests, reviewing) records to respond to a FOIA request. Direct costs include, for example, the salary of the employee performing the work (the basic rate of pay for the employee, plus 16 percent of that rate to cover benefits) and the cost of operating duplication machinery. Not included in direct costs are overhead expenses such as the costs of space and heating or lighting of the facility in which the records are kept.

(3) *Duplication* means the making of a copy of a record, or of the information contained in it, necessary to respond to a FOIA request. Copies can take the form of paper, microform, audiovisual materials, or electronic records (for example, magnetic tape or compact disk) among others. NSF will honor a requester's specified preference of form or format of disclosure if the record is readily reproducible by NSF, with reasonable effort, in the requested form or format.

(4) *Educational institution* means a preschool, a public or private elementary or secondary school, an institution of undergraduate higher education, an institution of graduate higher education, an institution of professional education, or an institution of vocational education that operates a program of scholarly research. To be in this category, a requester must show that the request is authorized by and made under the auspices of a qualifying institution and that the records are not sought for a commercial use, but are sought to further scholarly research.

(5) *Noncommercial scientific institution* means an institution that is not operated on a "commercial" basis, as that term is defined in paragraph (b)(1) of this section, and that is operated solely for the purpose of conducting scientific research, the results of which are not intended to promote any particular product or industry. To be in this category, a requester must show that the request is authorized by and made under the auspices of a qualifying institution and that the records are not sought for a commercial use or to promote any particular product or industry, but are sought to further scientific research.

(6) *Representative of the news media or news media requester* means any person actively gathering news for an entity that is organized and operated to publish or broadcast news to the public. The term *news* means information that is about current events or that would be of current interest to the public. Examples of news media entities include television or radio stations broadcasting to the public at large and publishers of periodicals (but only in those instances where they can qualify as disseminators of "news") who make their products available for purchase or subscription by the general public. For "freelance" journalists to be regarded as working for a news organization, they must demonstrate a solid basis for expecting publication through that organization. A publication contract would be the clearest proof, but NSF shall also look to the past publication record of a requester in making this determination. To be in this category, a requester must not be seeking the requested records for a commercial use. However, a request for records supporting the news dissemination function of the requester will not be considered to be for a commercial use.

(7) *Review* means the examination of a record located in response to a request in order to determine whether

National Science Foundation § 612.10

any portion of it is exempt from disclosure. It also includes processing any record for disclosure, for example, doing all that is necessary to redact it and prepare it for disclosure. Review costs are recoverable even if a record ultimately is not disclosed. Review time includes time spent considering any formal objection to disclosure made by a business submitter under § 612.8, but does not include time spent resolving general legal or policy issues regarding the application of exemptions.

(8) *Search* means the process of looking for and retrieving records or information responsive to a request. It includes page by page or line by line identification of information within records and also includes reasonable efforts to locate and retrieve information from records maintained in paper or electronic form or format, or stored in Federal Records Centers. NSF will ensure that searches are done in the most efficient and least expensive manner reasonably possible. For example, NSF will not search line by line where duplicating an entire document would be quicker and less expensive.

(c) *Fees*. In responding to FOIA requests, NSF will charge the following fees unless a waiver or reduction of fees has been granted under paragraph (k) of this section:

(1) *Search*. (i) Search fees will be charged for all requests, other than requests made by educational institutions, noncommercial scientific institutions, or representatives of the news media, subject to the limitations of paragraph (d) of this section. NSF may charge for time spent searching even if responsive records are not located or are withheld entirely as exempt from disclosure.

(ii) *Manual searches for records*. Whenever feasible, NSF will charge at the salary rate(s) (*i.e.*, basic pay plus 16 percent) of the employee(s) conducting the search. Where a homogeneous class of personnel is used exclusively (e.g., all administrative/clerical or all professional/executive), NSF has established an average rate for the range of grades typically involved. Routine search for records by administrative personnel are charged at $5.50 for each quarter hour. When a non-routine, non-clerical search by professional personnel is conducted (for example, where the task of determining which records fall within a request requires professional time) the charge is $11.50 for each quarter hour.

(iii) *Computer searches of records*. NSF will charge at the actual direct cost of conducting the search. This will include the cost of operating the computer system(s) for that portion of operating time that is directly attributable to searching for records responsive to a FOIA request and operator/programmer salary (*i.e.*, basic pay plus 16 percent) apportionable to the search. When NSF can establish a reasonable agency-wide average rate for computer operating costs and operator/programmer salaries involved in FOIA searches, the Foundation will do so and charge accordingly.

(iv) *Archived records*. For requests that require the retrieval of records stored by NSF at a Federal records center operated by the National Archives and Records Administration (NARA), additional costs will be charged in accordance with the Transactional Billing Rate Schedule established by NARA.

(2) *Duplication*. Duplication fees will be charged to all requesters, subject to the limitations of paragraph (d) of this section. For a paper photocopy of a record (no more than one copy of which need be supplied), the fee will be ten cents per page. For copies produced by computer, such as print outs, tapes, compact disks, or other electronic media, NSF will charge the direct costs, including operator time, of producing the copy. Where paper documents must be scanned in order to comply with a requester's preference to receive the records in an electronic format, the requester shall pay the direct costs associated with scanning those materials. For other forms of duplication, NSF will charge the direct costs of that duplication.

(3) *Review*. Review fees will be charged to requesters who make a commercial use request. Review fees will be charged only for the initial record review, in other words, the review done when NSF determines whether an exemption applies to a particular record or record portion at the initial request level. NSF may charge for review even

if a record ultimately is not disclosed. No charge will be made for review at the administrative appeal level for an exemption already applied. However, records or record portions withheld under an exemption that is subsequently determined not to apply may be reviewed again to determine whether any other exemption not previously considered applies; the costs of that review are chargeable where it is made necessary by a change of circumstances. Review fees will be charged at the salary rate (basic pay plus 16%) of the employee(s) performing the review.

(d) *Limitations on charging fees.* (1) No search fee will be charged for requests by educational institutions, noncommercial scientific institutions, or representatives of the news media. (2) Except for requesters seeking records for a commercial use, NSF will provide without charge:

(i) The first 100 pages of duplication (or the cost equivalent); and

(ii) The first two hours of search (or the cost equivalent).

(3) Whenever a total fee calculated under paragraph (c) of this section is $25.00 or less for any request, no fee will be charged.

(4) The provisions of paragraphs (d)(2) and (3) of this section work together. This means that noncommercial requesters will be charged no fees unless the cost of search in excess of two hours plus the cost of duplication in excess of 100 pages totals more than $25.00. Commercial requesters will not be charged unless the costs of search, review, and duplication total more than $25.00.

(e) *Notice of anticipated fees in excess of $25.00.* When NSF determines or estimates that the fees to be charged under this section will exceed $25.00, it will notify the requester of the actual or estimated amount of the fees, unless the requester has indicated a willingness to pay fees as high as those anticipated. If only a portion of the fee can be estimated readily, NSF will advise the requester that the estimated fee may be only a portion of the total fee. In cases in which a requester has been notified that actual or estimated fees exceed $25.00, the request will not be considered perfected and further work will not be done until the requester agrees to pay the anticipated total fee. Any such agreement should be memorialized in writing. A notice under this paragraph will offer the requester an opportunity to discuss the matter with Foundation personnel in order to reformulate the request to meet the requester's needs at a lower cost, if possible. If a requester fails to respond within 60 days of notice of actual or estimated fees with an agreement to pay those fees, NSF may administratively close the request.

(f) *Charges for other services.* Apart from the other provisions of this section, when NSF chooses as a matter of administrative discretion to provide a requested special service such as certifying that records are true copies or sending them by other than ordinary mail, the direct costs of providing the service will be charged to the requester.

(g) *Charging interest.* NSF may charge interest on any unpaid bill starting on the 31st day following the date of billing the requester. Interest charges will be assessed at the rate provided in 31 U.S.C. 3717 and will accrue from the date of the billing until payment is received by NSF. NSF may follow the provisions of the Debt Collection Act of 1982 (Pub. L. 97–365, 96 Stat. 1749), as amended, and its administrative procedures, including the use of consumer reporting agencies, collection agencies, and offset.

(h) *Aggregating requests.* Where NSF reasonably believes that a requester or a group of requesters acting together is attempting to divide a request into a series of requests for the purpose of avoiding fees, the agency may aggregate those requests and charge accordingly. NSF may presume that multiple requests of this type made within a 30-day period have been made in order to avoid fees. Where requests are separated by a longer period, NSF will aggregate them only where there exists a solid basis for determining that aggregation is warranted under all the circumstances involved. Multiple requests involving unrelated matters will not be aggregated.

(i) *Advance payments.* (1) For requests other than those described in paragraphs (i) (2) and (3) of this section,

National Science Foundation §612.10

NSF will not require the requester to make an advance payment, -in other words, a payment made before work is begun or continued on a request. Payment owed for work already completed (i.e., a prepayment before copies are sent to a requester) is not an advance payment.

(2) Where NSF determines or estimates that a total fee to be charged under this section will be more than $250.00, it may require the requester to make an advance payment of an amount up to the amount of the entire anticipated fee before beginning to process the request, except where it receives a satisfactory assurance of full payment from a requester that has a history of prompt payment.

(3) Where a requester has previously failed to pay a properly charged fee to any agency within 30 days of the date of billing, NSF may require the requester to pay the full amount due, plus any applicable interest, and to make an advance payment of the full amount of any anticipated fee, before NSF begins to process a new request or continues to process a pending request from that requester.

(4) In cases in which NSF requires advance payment or payment due under paragraph (i)(2) or (3) of this section, the request will not be considered perfected and further work will not be done on it until the required payment is received.

(j) *Other statutes specifically providing for fees.* The fee schedule of this section does not apply to fees charged under any statute that specifically requires an agency to set and collect fees for particular types of records. Where records responsive to requests are maintained for distribution by agencies operating such statutorily based fee schedule programs, NSF will inform requesters of the steps for obtaining records from those sources so that they may do so most economically.

(k) *Waiver or reduction of fees.* (1) Records responsive to a request will be furnished without charge or at a charge reduced below that established under paragraph (c) of this section where NSF determines, based on all available information, that disclosure of the requested information is in the public interest because it is likely to contribute significantly to public understanding of the operations or activities of the government and is not primarily in the commercial interest of the requester.

(2) To determine whether the first fee waiver requirement is met, NSF will consider the following factors:

(i) The subject of the request: Whether the subject of the requested records concerns "the operations or activities of the government." The subject of the requested records must concern identifiable operations or activities of the federal government, with a connection that is direct and clear, not remote or attenuated.

(ii) The informative value of the information to be disclosed: Whether disclosure is "likely to contribute" to an understanding of government operations or activities. The disclosable portions of the requested records must be meaningfully informative about government operations or activities in order to be "likely to contribute" to an increased public understanding of those operations or activities. Disclosure of information already in the public domain, in either duplicative or substantially identical form, is unlikely to contribute to such understanding where nothing new would be added to the public's understanding.

(iii) The contribution to an understanding of the subject by the public likely to result from disclosure: Whether disclosure of the requested information will contribute to "public understanding." The disclosure must contribute to the understanding of a reasonably broad audience of persons interested in the subject as opposed to the individual understanding of the requester. A requester's expertise in the subject area and ability and intention to effectively convey information to the public will be considered. A representative of the news media as defined in paragraph (b)(6) of this section will normally be presumed to satisfy this consideration.

(iv) The significance of the contribution to public understanding: Whether disclosure is likely to contribute "significantly" to public understanding of government operations or activities. The public's understanding of the subject in question must be enhanced by the disclosure to a significant extent as compared to the level of public understanding existing prior to the disclosure. NSF will make no value judgments about whether information that would contribute significantly to public understanding of the operations or activities of the government is "important" enough to be made public.

(3) To determine whether the second fee waiver requirement is met, NSF will consider the following factors:

(i) The existence and magnitude of a commercial interest: Whether the requester has a commercial interest that would be furthered by the requested disclosure. NSF will consider any commercial interest of the requester (with reference to the definition of "commercial use" in paragraph (b)(1) of this section), or of any person on whose behalf the requester may be acting, that would be furthered by the requested disclosure. Requesters will be given an opportunity in the administrative process to provide explanatory information regarding this consideration.

(ii) The primary interest in disclosure: Whether any identified commercial interest of the requester is sufficiently large, in comparison with the public interest in disclosure, that disclosure is "primarily in the commercial interest of the requester." A fee waiver or reduction is justified where the public interest standard is satisfied and that public interest is greater in magnitude than that of any identified commercial interest in disclosure. NSF ordinarily will presume that where a news media requester has satisfied the public interest standard, the public interest will be the interest primarily served by disclosure to that requester. Disclosure to data brokers or others who merely compile and market government information for direct economic return will not be presumed to primarily serve the public interest.

(4) Where only some of the requested records satisfy the requirements for a waiver of fees, a waiver will be granted for those records.

(5) Requests for the waiver or reduction of fees should address the factors listed in paragraphs (k)(2) and (3) of this section, insofar as they apply to each request.

§ 612.11 Other rights and services.

Nothing in this part will be construed to entitle any person, as of right, to any service or to the disclosure of any record to which such person is not entitled under the FOIA.

PART 613—PRIVACY ACT REGULATIONS

Sec.
613.1 General provisions.
613.2 Requesting access to records.
613.3 Responding to requests for access to records.
613.4 Amendment of records.
613.5 Exemptions.
613.6 Other rights and services.

AUTHORITY: 5 U.S.C. 552a.

SOURCE: 70 FR 43068, July 26, 2005, unless otherwise noted.

§ 613.1 General Provisions.

This part sets forth the National Science Foundation procedures under the Privacy Act of 1974. The rules in this part apply to all records in systems of records maintained by NSF that are retrieved by an individual's name or personal identifier. They describe the procedures by which individuals, as defined in the Privacy Act, may request access to records about themselves and request amendment or correction of those records. All Privacy Act requests for access to records are also processed under the Freedom of Information Act, 5 U.S.C. 552 (as provided in part 612 of this chapter), which gives requesters the benefit of both statutes. Notice of systems of records maintained by the National Science Foundation are published in the FEDERAL REGISTER.

§ 613.2 Requesting access to records.

(a) *Where to make a request.* You may make a request for access to NSF records about yourself by appearing in person at the National Science Foundation or by making a written request. If you choose to visit the Foundation, you must contact the NSF Security Desk and ask to speak with the Foundation's Privacy Act Officer of the General Counsel. Written requests should be sent to the NSF Privacy Act Officer, National Science Foundation,

National Science Foundation §613.3

4201 Wilson Boulevard, Suite 1265, Arlington, VA 22230. Written requests are recommended, since in many cases it may take several days to determine whether a record exists, and additional time may be required for record(s) retrieval and processing.

(b) *Description of requested records.* You must describe the records that you seek in enough detail to enable NSF personnel to locate the system of records containing them with a reasonable amount of effort. Providing information about the purpose for which the information was collected, applicable time periods, and name or identifying number of each system of records in which you think records about you may be kept, will help speed the processing of your request. NSF publishes notices in the FEDERAL REGISTER that describe the systems of records maintained by the Foundation. The Office of the Federal Register publishes a biennial "Privacy Act compilation" that includes NSF system notices. This compilation is available in many large reference and university libraries, and can be accessed electronically at the Government Printing Office's Web site at *www.access.gpo/su_docs/aces/PrivacyAct.shtml.*

(c) *Verification of identity.* When requesting access to records about yourself, NSF requires that you verify your identity in an appropriate fashion. Individuals appearing in person should be prepared to show reasonable picture identification such as driver's license, government or other employment identification card, or passport. Written requests must state your full name and current address. you must sign your request and your signature must either be notarized, or submitted by you under 28 U.S.C. 1746, a law that permits statements to be made under penalty of perjury as a substitute for notarization. While no specific form is required, you may obtain information about these required elements for requests from the NSF Privacy Act Officer, Suite 1265, 4201 Wilson Blvd, Arlington, VA 22230, or from the NSF Home Page under "Public & media Information—FOIA and Privacy Act" at *http://www.nsf.gov/home/pubinfo/foia.htm.* In order to help agency personnel in locating and identifying requested records, you may also, at your option, include your social security number, and/or date and place of birth. An individual reviewing his or her record(s) in person may be accompanied by an individual of his or her choice after signing a written statement authorizing that individual's presence. Individuals requesting or authorizing the disclosure of records to a third party must verify their identity and specifically name the third party and identify the information to be disclosed.

(d) *Verification of guardianship.* When making a request as the parent or guardian of a minor or as the guardian of someone determined by a court of competent jurisdiction to be incompetent, for access to records about that individual, you must establish:

(1) The identity of the record subject, by stating individuals' name and current address and, at your option, the social security number and/or date and place of birth of the individual;

(2) Your own identity, as required in paragraph (c) of this section;

(3) That you are the parent or guardian of that individual, which you may prove by providing a copy of the individual's birth certificate showing your parentage or by providing a court order establishing your guardianship; and

(4) That you are acting on behalf of that individual in making the request.

(e) The procedures of paragraphs (a) through (d) of this section shall also apply to requests made pursuant to 5 U.S.C. 552a(c)(3).

§613.3 Responding to requests for access to records.

(a) *Timing of responses to requests.* The Foundation will make reasonable effort to act on a request for access to records within 20 days of its receipt by the Privacy Act Officer (excluding date of receipt, weekends, and legal holidays) or from the time any required identification is received by the Privacy Act Officer, whichever is later. In determining which records are responsive to a request, the Foundation will include only records in its possession as of the date of receipt. When the agency cannot complete processing of a request within 20 working days, the foundation will send a letter explaining the delay and notifying the requester

§613.4

of the date by which processing is expected to be completed.

(b) *Authority to grant or deny requests.* The Privacy Act Officer, or his or her designee in the office with responsibility for the requested records, is authorized to grant or deny access to a Foundation record.

(c) *Granting access to records.* When a determination is made to grant a request for access in whole or part, the requester will be notified as soon as possible of the Foundation's decision. Where a requester has previously failed to pay a properly charged fee to any agency within 30 days of the date of billing, NSF may require the requester to pay the full amount due, plus any applicable interest, and to make an advance payment of the full amount of any anticipated fee, before NSF begins to process a new request or continues to process a pending request from that requester.

(1) *Requests made in person.* When a request is made in person, if the records can be found, and reviewed for access without unreasonable disruption of agency operations, the Foundation may disclose the records to the requester directly upon payment of any applicable fee. A written record should be made documenting the granting of the request. If a requester is accompanied by another person, the requester shall be required to authorize in writing any discussion of the records in the presence of the other person.

(2) *Requests made in writing.* The Foundation will send the records to the requester promptly upon payment of any applicable fee.

(d) *Denying access to records.* The requester will be notified in writing of any determination to deny a request for access to records. The notification letter will be signed by the Privacy Act Officer, or his or designee, as the individual responsible for the denial and will include a brief statement of the reason(s) for the denial, including any Privacy Act exemption(s) applied in denying the request.

(e) *Fees.* The Foundation will charge for duplication of records requested under the Privacy Act in the same way it charges for duplication under the Freedom of Information Act (see CFR 612.10). No search or review fee may be charged for the record unless the record has been exempted from access under Exemptions (j)(2) or (k)(2) of the Privacy Act.

§613.4 Amendment of records.

(a) *Where to make a request.* An individual may request amendment of records pertaining to him or her that are maintained in an NSF Privacy Act system of records, except that certain records described in paragraph (h) of this section are exempt from amendment. Request for amendment of records must be made in writing to the NSF Privacy Act Officer, National Science Foundation, Suite 1265, 4201 Wilson Boulevard, Arlington, VA 22230.

(b) *How to make a request.* Your request should identify each particular record in question, state the amendment you want to take place and specify why you believe that the record is not accurate, relevant, timely, or complete. You may submit any documentation that you think would be helpful. Providing an edited copy of the record(s) showing the desired change will assist the agency in making a determination about your request. If you believe that the same information is maintained in more than one NSF system of records you should include that information in your request. You must sign your request and provide verification of your identity as specified in 613.2(c).

(c) *Timing of responses to requests.* The Privacy Act Officer, or his or her designee, will acknowledge receipt of request for amendment within 10 working days of receipt. Upon receipt of a proper request the Privacy Act Officer will promptly confer with the NSF Directorate or Office with responsibility for the record to determine if the request should be granted in whole or part.

(d) *Granting request for amendment.* When a determination is made to grant a request for amendment in whole or part, notification to the requester will be made as soon as possible, normally within 30 wording days of the Privacy Act Officer receiving the request, describing the amendment made and including a copy of the amended record, in disclosable form.

(e) *Denying request for amendment.* When a determination is made that amendment, in whole or part, is unwarranted, the matter shall be brought to the attention of the Inspector General, if it pertains to records maintained by the Office of the Inspector General, or to the attention of the General Counsel, if it pertains to other NSF records. If the General Counsel or Inspector General or their designee agrees with the determination that amendment is not warranted, the Privacy Act Officer will notify the requester in writing, normally within 30 working days of the Privacy Act Officer receiving the request. The notification letter will be signed by the Privacy Act Officer or his or her designee, and will include a statement of the reason(s) for the denial and how to appeal the decision.

(f) *Appealing a denial.* You may appeal a denial of a request to amend records to the General Counsel, National Science Foundation, 4201 Wilson Blvd., Suite 1265, Arlington, VA 22230. You must make your appeal in writing and it must be received by the Office of the General Counsel within ten days of the receipt of the denial (weekends, legal holidays, and the date of receipt excluded). Clearly mark your appeal letter and envelope "Privacy Act Appeal." Your appeal letter must include a copy of your original request for amendment and the denial letter, along with any additional documentation or argument you wish to submit in favor of amending the records. It must be signed by you or your officially designated representative.

(g) *Responses to appeals.* The General Counsel, or his or her designee, will normally render a decision on the appeal within thirty working days after proper receipt of the written appeal by the General Counsel. If additional time to make a determination is necessary you will be advised in writing of the need for an extension.

(1) *Amendment appeal granted.* If on appeal the General Counsel, or his or her designee, determines that amendment of the record should take place, you will be notified as soon as possible of the Foundation's decision. The notification will describe the amendment made and include a copy of the amended record, in disclosable form.

(2) *Amendment appeal denied—Statement of disagreement.* If on appeal the General Counsel, or his or her designee, upholds a denial of a request for amendment of records, you will be notified in writing of the reasons why the appeal was denied and advised of your right to seek judicial review of the decision. The letter will also notify you of your right to file with the Foundation a concise statement setting forth the reasons for your disagreement with the refusal of the Foundation to amend the record. The statement should be sent to the Privacy Act Officer, who will ensure that a copy of the statement is placed with the disputed record. A copy of the statement will be included with any subsequent disclosure of the record.

(h) *Records not subject to amendment.* The following records are not subject to amendment:

(1) Transcripts of testimony given under oath or written statements made under oath;

(2) Transcripts of grand jury proceedings, judicial proceedings, or quasi-judicial proceedings, which are the official record of those proceedings;

(3) Pre-sentence records that originated with the courts; and

(4) Records in systems of records that have been exempted from amendment under Privacy Act, 5 U.S.C. 552a(j) or (k) by notice published in the FEDERAL REGISTER.

§ 613.5 **Exemptions.**

(a) *Fellowships and other support.* Pursuant to 5 U.S.C. 552a(k)(6), the Foundation hereby exempts from the application of 5 U.S.C. 552a(c)(3) and (d) any materials which would reveal the identity of references of fellowship or other award applicants or nominees, or reviewers of applicants for Federal contracts (including grants and cooperative agreements) contained in any of the following systems of records:

(1) "Fellowships and Other Awards,"

(2) "Principal Investigator/Proposal File and Associated Records,"

(3) "Reviewer/Proposal File and Associated Records," and

(4) "Reviewer/Fellowship and Other Awards File and Associated Records."

(b) *OIG Files Compiled for the Purpose of a Criminal Investigation and for Related Purposes.* Pursuant to 5 U.S.C. 552a(j)(2), the Foundation hereby exempts the system of records entitled "Office of Inspector General Investigative Files," insofar as it consists of information compiled for the purpose of a criminal investigation or for other purposes within the scope of 5 U.S.C. 552a(j)(2), from the application of 5 U.S.C. 552a, except for subsections (b), (c)(1) and (2), (e)(4)(A) through (F), (e)(6), (7), (9), (10) and (11), and (i).

(c) *OIG and ACA Files Compiled for Other Law Enforcement Purposes.* Pursuant to 5 U.S.C. 552a(k)(2), the Foundation hereby exempts the systems of records entitled "Office of Inspector General Investigative Files" and "Antarctic Conservation Act Files" insofar as they consist of information compiled for law enforcement purposes other than material within the scope of 5 U.S.C. 552a(j)(2), from the application of 5 U.S.C. 552a(c)(3), (d), (e)(1), (e)(4)(G), (H), and (I), and (f).

(d) *Investigations of Scientific Misconduct.* Pursuant to 5 U.S.C. 552a(k)(2) and (k)(5), the Foundation hereby exempts from the application of 5 U.S.C. 552a(c)(3) and (d) any materials which would reveal the identity of confidential sources of information contained in the following system of records: "Debarment/Scientific Misconduct Files."

(e) *Personnel Security Clearances.* Pursuant to 5 U.S.C. 552a(k)(5), the Foundation hereby exempts from the application of 5 U.S.C. 552a(c)(3) and (d) any materials which would reveal the identity of confidential sources of information contained in the following system of records: "Personnel Security."

(f) *Applicants for Employment.* Records on applicants for employment at NSF are covered by the Office of Personnel Management (OPM) government-wide system notice "Recruiting, Examining and Placement Records." These records are exempted as claimed in 5 CFR 297.501(b)(7).

(g) *Statistical records.* Pursuant to 5 U.S.C. 552a(k)(4), the Foundation hereby exempts the systems of records entitled "Doctorate Records Files," "Doctorate Work History Files," and "National Survey of Recent College Graduates & Follow-up Files" from the application of 5 U.S.C. 552a(c)(3), (d), (e)(1), (e)(4)(G), (H), and (I), and (f).

(h) *Other records.* The Foundation may also assert exemptions for records received from another agency that could properly be claimed by that agency in responding to a request.

§ 613.6 Other rights and services.

Nothing in this subpart shall be construed to entitle any person, as of right, to any service or to the disclosure of any record to which such person is not entitled under the Privacy Act.

PART 614—GOVERNMENT IN THE SUNSHINE ACT REGULATIONS OF THE NATIONAL SCIENCE BOARD

Sec.
614.1 General rule.
614.2 Grounds for closing meetings.
614.3 Materials relating to closed portions of meetings.
614.4 Opening of transcript or recording.
614.5 Public announcement.
614.6 Meeting changes.
614.7 Record vote.
614.8 Application to Board Executive Committee.

AUTHORITY: Government in the Sunshine Act, sec. 552b of title 5, U.S.C.; 90 Stat. 1241.

SOURCE: 42 FR 14719, Mar. 16, 1977, unless otherwise noted.

§ 614.1 General rule.

Except as otherwise provided in these regulations, every portion of every meeting of the National Science Board will be open to public observation.

§ 614.2 Grounds for closing meetings.

(a) The National Science Board may by record vote close any portion of any meeting if it properly determines that an open meeting:

(1) Is likely to disclose matters that (i) are specifically authorized under criteria established by Executive Order to be kept secret in the interests of national defense or foreign policy and (ii) are in fact properly classified pursuant to the Executive Order;

(2) Is likely to relate solely to the internal personnel rules and practices of the National Science Foundation;

(3) Is likely to disclose matters specifically exempted from disclosure by

statute (other than 5 U.S.C. 552): *Provided,* That the statute (i) requires in such a manner as to leave no discretion on the issue that the matters be withheld from the public, or (ii) establishes particular criteria for withholding or refers to particular types of matters to be withheld;

(4) Is likely to disclose trade secrets and commercial or financial information obtained from a person and privileged or confidential;

(5) Is likely to involve accusing any person of a crime, or formally censuring any person;

(6) Is likely to disclose personal information where the disclosure would constitute a clearly unwarranted invasion of personal privacy;

(7) Is likely to disclose investigatory law-enforcement records, or information which, if written, would be contained in such records, but only to the extent provided in 5 U.S.C. 552b(c)(7);

(8) Is likely to disclose information contained in or related to examination, operating, or condition reports prepared by, on behalf of, or for the use of an agency responsible for the regulation or supervision of financial institutions;

(9) Is likely to disclose information, the premature disclosure of which would:

(i) In the case of information received from an agency which regulates currencies, securities, commodities, or financial institutions, be likely to (A) lead to significant financial speculation in currencies, securities, or commodities, or (B) significantly endanger the stability of any financial institution; or

(ii) Be likely to significantly frustrate implementation of a proposed Foundation action, unless the Foundation has already disclosed to the public the content or nature of its proposed action or is required by law to make such disclosure on its own initiative before taking final action; or

(10) Is likely to specifically concern the Foundation's participation in a civil action or proceeding, an action in a foreign court or international tribunal, or an arbitration.

(b) Anyone who believes his interests may be directly affected by a portion of a meeting may request that the Board close it to the public for any reason referred to in paragraph (a) (5), (6), or (7) of this section. The request should be addressed to the Executive Officer, National Science Board, National Science Foundation, 4201 Wilson Boulevard, Arlington, VA 22230. It will be circulated to Members of the Board if received at least three full days before the meeting, and on motion of any Member the Board will determine by record vote whether to close the affected portion of the meeting.

[42 FR 14719, Mar. 16, 1977, as amended at 59 FR 37438, July 22, 1994]

§ 614.3 Materials relating to closed portions of meetings.

If a portion or portions of any meeting of the National Science Board are closed to the public under § 614.2:

(a) The General Counsel of the National Science Foundation shall publicly certify that, in his opinion, that portion or portions may properly be closed to the public. The certificate shall state the exemptions under 5 U.S.C. 552b(c) that make the closings proper.

(b) The presiding officer of the meeting (usually the Chairman of the Board) shall furnish a statement setting forth the time and place of the meeting and the persons present.

(c) The Board shall make a complete transcript or electronic recording adequate to record fully the proceedings of each portion of the meeting that is closed to the public.

(d) The National Science Board Office shall maintain the General Counsel's certificate, the presiding officer's statement, and the transcript or recording of the meeting for at least three years after the meeting and at least one year after the Board completes consideration of any proposal, report, resolution, or similar matter discussed in any closed portion of the meeting.

[42 FR 14719, Mar. 16, 1977, as amended at 75 FR 40755, July 14, 2010]

§ 614.4 Opening of transcript or recording.

(a) Except as otherwise provided in this section, the transcript or electronic recording of every portion of every meeting closed to the public will

§ 614.5

promptly be made available on request to any member of the public in an easily accessible place.

(b) Informal requests to inspect or copy the transcript or electronic recording of a closed session may be made to the staff of the National Science Board and will be handled informally and expeditiously. Written requests to inspect or copy such a transcript or recording that cite the Freedom of Information Act or the Sunshine Act will be treated as formal requests made under the Freedom of Information Act. They will be handled under the Foundation's Freedom of Information procedures described in 45 CFR part 612. The exemptions of these Sunshine Act regulations, 45 CFR 614.2, will govern, however, in determining what portions of the transcript or recording may be withheld.

(c) A request to inspect or copy a transcript or electronic recording should specify the date of the meeting and the agenda item or items to which the request pertains. It should contain a promise to pay the costs of any duplication requested.

(d) No search or transcription fees will be charged. Duplication fees may be charged as provided in 45 CFR 612.6.

[42 FR 55619, Oct. 18, 1977]

§ 614.5 Public announcement.

(a) Except as provided in paragraphs (c) and (d) of this section, the National Science Board will make a public announcement of each Board meeting at least one week before the meeting takes place. The announcement will cover:

(1) The time, place, and subject matter of the meeting;

(2) What portions of the meeting, if any, are to be closed to the public; and

(3) The name and telephone number of the official designated to respond to requests for information on the meeting.

(b) Each such announcement will be promptly posted on the National Science Foundation's Web site at *http://www.nsf.gov/nsb/notices/*. Immediately following the issuance of such an announcement, it will be submitted for publication in the FEDERAL REGISTER.

(c) The announcement may be made less than a week before the meeting it announces or after the meeting only if (1) the Board by record vote determines that agency business requires the meeting to be called on such short or after-the-fact notice and (2) an announcement is made at the earliest practicable time.

(d) All or any portion of the announcement of any meeting may be omitted if the Board by record vote determines that the announcement would disclose information which should be withheld under the same standards as apply for closing meetings under § 614.2.

[42 FR 14719, Mar. 16, 1977, as amended at 75 FR 40755, July 14, 2010]

§ 614.6 Meeting changes.

(a) The time or place of a meeting of the National Science Board that has been publicly announced as provided in § 614.5 may subsequently be changed, but any such change will be publicly announced at the earliest practicable time.

(b) The subject matter of any portion of any meeting of the Board that has been publicly announced as provided in § 614.5 or the determination whether any portion of any meeting so publicly announced will be open or closed may subsequently be changed, but only when:

(1) The Board determines by record vote that agency business so requires and that no earlier announcement of the change was possible; and

(2) The Board publicly announces the change and the vote of each Member on the change at the earliest practicable time.

§ 614.7 Record vote.

(a) For purposes of this part a vote of the National Science Board is a "record vote" if:

(1) It carries by a majority of all those holding office as Board Members at the time of the vote;

(2) No proxies are counted toward the necessary majority; and

(3) The individual vote of each Member present and voting is recorded.

(b) Within one day of any such record vote or any attempted record vote that fails to achieve the necessary majority under paragraph (a)(1) of this section, the Board Office will make publicly available a written record showing the vote of each Member on the question.

(c) Within one day of any record vote under which any portion or portions of a Board meeting are to be closed to the public, the Board Office will make available a full written explanation of the Board's action and a list of all persons expected to attend the meeting, showing their affiliations.

§ 614.8 Application to Board Executive Committee.

All the provisions of this part applicable to the National Science Board shall apply equally to the Executive Committee of the Board whenever the Executive Committee is meeting pursuant to its authority to act on behalf of the Board.

PART 615—TESTIMONY AND PRODUCTION OF RECORDS

Sec.
615.1 Purpose.
615.2 Applicability.
615.3 Definitions.
615.4 Legal proceedings before NSF or in which the United States is a party.
615.5 Legal proceedings between private litigants: Testimony and production of documents.
615.6 Legal proceedings between private litigants: Procedure when demand is made.
615.7 Legal proceedings between private litigants: Office of Inspector General employees.

AUTHORITY: 42 U.S.C. 1870(a).

SOURCE: 59 FR 44056, Aug. 26, 1994, unless otherwise noted.

§ 615.1 Purpose.

(a) This part sets forth policies and procedures to be followed when, in connection with a legal proceeding, an NSF employee is issued a demand to provide testimony or produce official records and information.

(b) The provisions of this part are intended to promote economy and efficiency in NSF's programs and operations; minimize the possibility of involving NSF in controversial issues not related to its functions; maintain the impartiality of NSF among private litigants; and protect sensitive, confidential information and the deliberative process.

(c) This part is not intended to and does not waive the sovereign immunity of the United States.

(d) This part is intended only to provide guidance for the internal operations of NSF, and is not intended to, and does not, and may not be relied upon to create any right or benefit, substantive or procedural, enforceable at law by a party against the United States.

§ 615.2 Applicability.

This part applies to demands and requests for factual or expert testimony or for official records or information in legal proceedings, whether or not the United States is a party, except that it does not apply to:

(a) Demands upon or requests for an NSF employee to testify as to facts or events that are in no way related to his or her official duties or to the functions of NSF;

(b) Demands upon or requests for a former NSF employee to testify as to matters in which the former employee was not directly or materially involved while at NSF;

(c) Demands upon or requests for an NSF reviewer to testify as to matters not directly related to that individual's employment by or service to NSF; and

(d) Congressional demands and requests for testimony or records.

§ 615.3 Definitions.

(a) *Demand*—A subpoena, order, or other demand of a court or other competent authority for the production of records or for the appearance and testimony of an NSF employee, issued in a legal proceeding between private litigants.

(b) *Foundation* or *NSF* means the National Science Foundation.

(c) *General Counsel* means the General Counsel of the Foundation, or any person to whom the General Counsel has delegated authority under this part.

(d) *Legal proceeding* means any proceeding before a court of law, administrative board or commission, hearing officer, or other body conducting a legal or administrative proceeding.

(e) *Official records and information* means all documents and material which are records of the Foundation under the Freedom of Information Act,

5 U.S.C. 552; all other records contained in NSF's files; and all other information or material acquired by an NSF employee in the performance of his or her official duties or because of his or her official status.

(f) *NSF employee or employee* means any present or former officer or employee of NSF; any other individual hired through contractual agreement by or on behalf of NSF, or who has performed or is performing services under such an agreement for NSF; and any individual who served or is serving on any advisory committee or in any advisory capacity, whether formal or informal.

(g) *Request* means any informal request, by whatever method, for the production of official records and information or for testimony which has not been ordered by a court or other competent authority.

(h) *Testimony* means any written or oral statement by a witness, including depositions, answers to interrogatories, affidavits, declarations, and statements at a hearing or trial.

§ 615.4 **Legal proceedings before NSF or in which the United States is a party.**

In any legal proceeding before NSF or to which the United States is a party, the General Counsel shall arrange for a current employee to testify as a witness for the United States whenever the attorney representing the United States requests it. The employee may testify for the United States both as to facts within the employee's personal knowledge and as an expert or opinion witness. For any party other than the United States, the employee may testify only as to facts within his or her personal knowledge.

§ 615.5 **Legal proceedings between private litigants: Testimony and production of documents.**

(a) No employee may produce official records and information or provide any testimony in response to a demand or request unless authorized to do so by the General Counsel in accordance with this part.

(b) The General Counsel, in his or her discretion, may grant an employee permission to testify or produce official records and information in response to a demand or request. In making this decision, the General Counsel shall consider whether:

(1) The purposes of this part are met;

(2) Allowing such testimony or production of records would be necessary to prevent a miscarriage of justice;

(3) NSF has an interest in the decision that may be rendered in the legal proceeding; and

(4) Allowing such testimony or production of records would be in the best interest of NSF or the United States.

(c) If authorized to testify pursuant to this part, an employee may testify as to facts within his or her personal knowledge, but, unless specifically authorized to do so by the General Counsel, shall not:

(1) Disclose confidential or privileged information;

(2) Testify as to facts when the General Counsel determines such testimony would not be in the best interest of the Foundation or the United States; or

(3) Testify as an expert or opinion witness with regard to any matter arising out of the employee's official duties or the functions of the Foundation.

§ 615.6 **Legal proceedings between private litigants: Procedure when demand is made.**

(a) Whenever an employee is served with a demand to testify in his or her official capacity, or to produce official records and information, the employee shall immediately notify the General Counsel.

(b) The General Counsel shall review the demand and, in accordance with the provisions of § 615.5, determine whether, or on what conditions, to authorize the employee to testify and/or produce official records and information.

(c) If a response to a demand is required before the General Counsel has made the determination referred to in § 615.6(b), the General Counsel shall provide the court or other competent authority with a copy of this part, inform the court or other competent authority that the demand is being reviewed, and seek a stay of the demand pending a final determination. If the court fails to stay the demand, the employee must appear at the stated time and place, produce a copy of this part, and respectfully decline to comply with the demand. *"United States ex rel Touhy* v. *Ragen,"* 340 US 462 (1951).

(d) If a court or other competent authority orders that a demand be complied with notwithstanding a final decision by the General Counsel to the contrary, or at any other stage in the process, the General Counsel may take steps to arrange for legal representation for the employee, and shall advise the employee on how to respond to the demand.

§ 615.7 Legal proceedings between private litigants: Office of Inspector General employees.

Notwithstanding the requirements set forth in §§ 615.1 through 615.6, when an employee of the Office of Inspector General is issued a demand or receives a request to provide testimony or produce official records and information, the Inspector General or his or her designee shall be responsible for performing the functions assigned to the General Counsel with respect to such demand or request pursuant to the provisions of this part.

[73 FR 21549, Apr. 22, 2008]

PART 617—NONDISCRIMINATION ON THE BASIS OF AGE IN PROGRAMS OR ACTIVITIES RECEIVING FEDERAL FINANCIAL ASSISTANCE FROM NSF

Sec.
617.1 Purpose.
617.2 Definitions.
617.3 Standards.
617.4 General duties of recipients.
617.5 Self-evaluation.
617.6 Information requirements.
617.7 Compliance reviews.
617.8 Pre-award reviews.
617.9 Complaints.
617.10 Mediation.
617.11 Investigation.
617.12 Compliance procedure.
617.13 Hearings, decisions, post-termination proceedings.
617.14 Remedial action by recipients.
617.15 Exhaustion of administrative remedies.
617.16 Prohibition against intimidation or retaliation.

APPENDIX I TO PART 617—LIST OF AGE DISTINCTIONS PROVIDED IN FEDERAL STATUTES OR REGULATIONS AFFECTING FEDERAL FINANCIAL ASSISTANCE ADMINISTERED BY NSF

AUTHORITY: Age Discrimination Act of 1975, as amended, 42 U.S.C. 6101, *et seq.;* 45 CFR part 90.

SOURCE: 49 FR 49628, Dec. 21, 1984, unless otherwise noted.

§ 617.1 Purpose.

This part prescribes NSF's policies and procedures under the Age Discrimination Act of 1975 and the Department of Health and Human Services government-wide age discrimination regulations at 45 CFR part 90. The Act and part 90 prohibit discrimination on the basis of age in programs or activities receiving Federal financial assistance. The Act and part 90 permit federally assisted programs or activities and recipients of Federal funds to continue to use age distinctions and factors other than age which meet the requirements of the Act and part 90.

[49 FR 49628, Dec. 21, 1984, as amended at 68 FR 51383, Aug. 26, 2003]

§ 617.2 Definitions.

The following terms used in this part are defined in part 90:

Act
Action
Age
Age distinction
Age-related term
Agency
Federal financial assistance
Program or activity
Recipient (including subrecipients)
United States

[49 FR 49628, Dec. 21, 1984, as amended at 68 FR 51383, Aug. 26, 2003]

§ 617.3 Standards.

Standards for determining whether an age distinction or age-related term is prohibited are set out in part 90 of this title 45. See also appendix I to this part.

§ 617.4 General duties of recipients.

Each recipient of Federal financial assistance from NSF shall comply with the Act, part 90, and this part. Each

§ 617.5

NSF award of Federal financial assistance shall contain the following provision:

COMPLIANCE WITH AGE DISCRIMINATION ACT

The recipient agrees to comply with the Age Discrimination Act of 1975 as implemented by the Department of Health and Human Services regulations at 45 CFR part 90 and the regulations of the Foundation at 45 CFR part 617. In the event the recipient passes on NSF financial assistance to sub-recipients, this provision shall apply to the subrecipients, and the instrument under which the Federal financial assistance is passed to the subrecipient shall contain a provision identical to this provision.

§ 617.5 Self-evaluation.

(a) Each recipient (including sub-recipients) employing the equivalent of fifteen or more full-time employees shall complete a written self-evaluation of its compliance under this part within 18 months of the effective date of these regulations, unless a similar evaluation has been completed for another agency.

(b) In its self-evaluation, each recipient shall identify all age distinctions it uses and justify each age distinction it imposes on the program or activity receiving Federal financial assistance from NSF.

(c) Each recipient shall take corrective action whenever a self-evaluation indicates a violation of the Act.

(d) Each recipient shall make the self-evaluation available on request to NSF and the public for three years after its completion.

§ 617.6 Information requirements.

Each recipient shall:

(a) Make available upon request to NSF information necessary to determine whether the recipient is complying with the Act.

(b) Permit reasonable access by NSF or its designee to the books, records, accounts, and other recipient facilities and sources of information to the extent necessary to determine whether a recipient is complying with the Act.

§ 617.7 Compliance reviews.

(a) NSF may conduct compliance reviews of recipients that will permit it to investigate and correct violations of the Act. NSF may conduct these reviews even in the absence of a complaint against a recipient. The review may be as comprehensive as necessary to determine whether a violation of the Act has occurred.

(b) If a compliance review indicates a violation of the Act, NSF will attempt to achieve voluntary compliance with the Act. If voluntary compliance cannot be achieved, NSF may arrange for enforcement as described in § 617.12.

§ 617.8 Pre-award reviews.

NSF reserves the right to conduct pre-award reviews of applicants for Federal financial assistance from NSF in cases where the NSF has substantial reason to believe that a potential recipient who is not then a recipient of other NSF financial assistance under the same program or activity may engage in practices under that program or activity that would violate the Act. However, the results of any such review shall not constitute a basis for NSF refusal to grant financial assistance to the applicant under that program or activity unless the procedural requirements of the Act (42 U.S.C. 6104) and §§ 617.12 and 617.13 of this part have been followed.

[49 FR 49628, Dec. 21, 1984, as amended at 68 FR 51383, Aug. 26, 2003]

§ 617.9 Complaints.

(a) Any person, individually or as a member of a class or on behalf of others, may file a complaint with NSF, alleging discrimination prohibited by the Act. A complainant shall file a complaint within 180 days from the date the complainant first had knowledge of the alleged act of discrimination. However, for good cause shown, NSF may extend this time limit.

(b) NSF will accept as a sufficient complaint, any written statement which identifies the parties involved and the date the complainant first had knowledge of the alleged violation, describes generally the action or practice complained of, and is signed by the complainant. If an insufficient complaint is amended within 10 working days after notice by NSF to the complainant of the deficiency, NSF will consider the amended complaint as filed on the date the original insufficient complaint was filed for purposes

National Science Foundation § 617.11

of determining if it was timely filed. However, all other time requirements established by the Act and this part shall run from the date the amended complaint was filed.

(c) On receipt of any complaint NSF shall promptly send written acknowledgement to the complainant, and a copy of the complaint to the recipient. In addition, NSF shall send either copies of this part or other pertinent information describing the rights and obligations of the parties.

(d) NSF will return to the complainant any complaint outside the coverage of this part, and will state why it is outside the coverage of this part.

§ 617.10 Mediation.

(a) NSF will refer to the Federal Mediation and Conciliation Service all complaints that fall within the jurisdiction of this part and contain all information necessary for further processing.

(b) Both the complainant and the recipient shall participate in the mediation process to the extent necessary to reach an agreement or for a mediator to make an informed judgement that an agreement is not possible. NSF will take no further administrative action on any complaint if the complainant refuses to participate in the mediation process.

(c) If the complainant and the recipient reach an agreement, the mediator shall prepare a written statement of the agreement and have the complainant and recipient sign it. The mediator shall send a copy of the agreement to NSF. NSF shall take no further action on the complaint unless the complainant or the recipient fails to comply with the agreement, in which case the other party may request that the complaint be reopened.

(d) The mediator shall protect the confidentiality of all information obtained in the course of the mediation process. No mediator shall testify in any adjudicative proceeding, produce any document, or otherwise disclose any information obtained in the course of the mediation process without prior approval of the head of the Federal Mediation and Conciliation Service.

(e) NSF will use the mediation process for a maximum of 60 days after receiving a complaint. Mediation ends if:

(1) 60 days elapse from the time NSF receives a sufficient complaint; *or*

(2) Before the end of the 60 day period, an agreement is reached; *or*

(3) Before the end of the 60 day period, the mediator determines that an agreement cannot be reached.

(f) The mediator shall return unresolved complaints to NSF.

§ 617.11 Investigation.

(a) *Informal investigation.* (1) NSF will investigate complaints that are unresolved after mediation or are reopened because of violation of a mediation agreement.

(2) As part of the initial investigation, NSF will use informal fact finding methods, including joint or separate discussions with the complainant and recipient, to establish the facts, and, if possible, will settle the complaint on terms that are agreeable to the parties. NSF may seek the assistance of any involved State agency.

(3) NSF will put any agreement in writing and have it signed by the parties and an authorized official of NSF.

(4) A settlement shall not affect other enforcement efforts of NSF, including compliance reviews, or individual complaints that involve the recipient.

(5) A settlement is not a finding of discrimination against the recipient.

(b) *Formal investigation.* If NSF cannot resolve the complaint through informal investigation, it will begin to develop formal findings through further investigation of the complaint. If the investigation indicates a violation of the Act, NSF will try to obtain voluntary compliance. If NSF cannot obtain voluntary compliance, it will begin enforcement as described in § 617.12. If the investigation does not indicate a violation of the Act, NSF will issue a written determination in favor of the recipient.

[49 FR 49628, Dec. 21, 1984, as amended at 68 FR 51383, Aug. 26, 2003]

§ 617.12 Compliance procedure.

(a) NSF may enforce this part by either termination of a recipient's financial asistance from NSF for the program or activity involved where the recipient has violated the Act or this part or refusal to grant further financial assistance under the program or activity involved where the recipient has violated the Act or this part. The determination of the recipient's violation may be made only after a recipient has had an opportunity for a hearing on the record before an administrative law judge. Therefore, cases settled in the mediation process or before a hearing will not involve termination of a recipient's Federal financial assistance from NSF.

(b) NSF may also enforce this part by any other means authorized by law, including but not limited to:

(1) Referral to the Department of Justice for proceedings to enforce any rights of the United States or obligations by this part.

(2) Use of any requirement of or referral to any Federal, State, or local government agency that will have the effect of correcting a violation of the Act or this part.

(c) NSF will limit any termination or refusal to grant further financial assistance to the particular recipient and the particular program or activity found to be in violation of the Act. NSF will not base any part of a termination or refusal on a finding with respect to any program or activity of the recipient which does not receive Federal financial assistance for NSF.

(d) NSF will not begin any hearing under paragraph (a) until the Director has advised the recipient of its failure to comply with this part and has determined that voluntary compliance cannot be obtained.

(e) NSF will not terminate or refuse to grant financial assistance until thirty days have elapsed after the Director has sent a written report of the circumstances and grounds of the action to the committees of the Congress having legislative jurisdiction over the program or activity involved. The Director will file a report whenever any action is taken under paragraph (f) of this section.

(f) *Alternate Funds Disbursal Procedures.* (1) When NSF withholds funds from a recipient under these regulations, the Secretary may disburse the withheld funds directly to an alternate recipient: Any public or non-profit private organization or agency, or State or political subdivision of the State.

(2) The Director will require any alternate recipient to demonstrate:

(i) The ability to comply with these regulations; and

(ii) The ability to achieve the goals of the Federal statute authorizing the Federal financial assistance.

[49 FR 49628, Dec. 21, 1984, as amended at 68 FR 51383, Aug. 26, 2003]

§ 617.13 Hearings, decisions, post-termination proceedings.

Procedures prescribed in 45 CFR 611.9 and 611.10 for NSF enforcement of Title VI of the Civil Rights Act of 1964 shall apply also for NSF enforcement of this part. At the conclusion of any action taken under § 617.12, NSF, shall remind both parties of the right to judicial review established by 42 U.S.C. 6105.

§ 617.14 Remedial action by recipients.

Where the Director finds that a recipient has discriminated on the basis of age, the recipient shall take any remedial action the Director may require to overcome the effects of the discrimination. If another recipient exercises control over the recipient that has discriminated, the Director may require both recipients to take remedial action.

§ 617.15 Exhaustion of administrative remedies.

(a) A complainant may file a civil action after exhausting administrative remedies under the Act. Administrative remedies are exhausted if:

(1) 180 days have elapsed since the complainant filed a sufficient complaint and NSF has made no finding with regard to the complaint; or

(2) NSF issues any finding in favor of the recipient.

(b) If NSF fails to make a finding within 180 days or issues a finding in favor of the recipient, NSF will:

(1) Promptly advise the complainant of this fact; and

(2) Advise the complainant of his or her right to bring a civil action for injunctive relief under 42 U.S.C. 6104; and

(3) Inform the complainant that under 42 U.S.C. 6104:

(i) The complainant may bring a civil action only in a United States District court for the district in which the recipient is located or transacts business;

(ii) A complainant prevailing in a civil action has the right to be awarded the costs of the action, including reasonable attorney's fees, but that the complainant must demand these costs in the complaint;

(iii) Before commencing the action the complainant shall give 30 days notice by registered mail to the Director, the Attorney General of the United States, and the recipient;

(iv) The notice must state the alleged violation of the Act; the relief requested; the court in which the complainant is bringing the action; and whether or not attorney's fees are demanded in the event the complainant prevails; and

(v) The complainant may not bring an action if the same alleged violation of the Act by the same recipient is the subject of a pending action in any court of the United States.

§ 617.16 Prohibition against intimidation or retaliation.

A recipient may not engage in acts of intimidation or retaliation against a person who:

(a) Attempts to assert a right protected by the Act, or

(b) Cooperates in any mediation, investigation, hearing or other part of NSF's investigation, conciliation, and enforcement process.

APPENDIX I TO PART 617—LIST OF AGE DISTINCTIONS PROVIDED IN FEDERAL STATUTES OR REGULATIONS AFFECTING FEDERAL FINANCIAL ASSISTANCE ADMINISTERED BY NSF

I. Section 6 of Pub. L. 94–86, 42 U.S.C. 1881a: This statute authorizes the Foundation to establish the Alan T. Waterman Award to recognize and encourage the work of "younger" scientists. Under NSF procedures awards have been limited to persons 35 years of age or under.

PART 618—NONDISCRIMINATION ON THE BASIS OF SEX IN EDUCATION PROGRAMS OR ACTIVITIES RECEIVING FEDERAL FINANCIAL ASSISTANCE

Subpart A—Introduction

Sec.
618.100 Purpose and effective date.
618.105 Definitions.
618.110 Remedial and affirmative action and self-evaluation.
618.115 Assurance required.
618.120 Transfers of property.
618.125 Effect of other requirements.
618.130 Effect of employment opportunities.
618.135 Designation of responsible employee and adoption of grievance procedures.
618.140 Dissemination of policy.

Subpart B—Coverage

618.200 Application.
618.205 Educational institutions and other entities controlled by religious organizations.
618.210 Military and merchant marine educational institutions.
618.215 Membership practices of certain organizations.
618.220 Admissions.
618.225 Educational institutions eligible to submit transition plans.
618.230 Transition plans.
618.235 Statutory amendments.

Subpart C—Discrimination on the Basis of Sex in Admission and Recruitment Prohibited

618.300 Admission.
618.305 Preference in admission.
618.310 Recruitment.

Subpart D—Discrimination on the Basis of Sex in Education Programs or Activities Prohibited

618.400 Education programs or activities.
618.405 Housing.
618.410 Comparable facilities.
618.415 Access to course offerings.
618.420 Access to schools operated by LEAs.
618.425 Counseling and use of appraisal and counseling materials.
618.430 Financial assistance.
618.435 Employment assistance to students.
618.440 Health and insurance benefits and services.
618.445 Marital or parental status.
618.450 Athletics.

618.455 Textbooks and curricular material.

Subpart E—Discrimination on the Basis of Sex in Employment in Education Programs or Activities Prohibited

618.500 Employment.
618.505 Employment criteria.
618.510 Recruitment.
618.515 Compensation.
618.520 Job classification and structure.
618.525 Fringe benefits.
618.530 Marital or parental status.
618.535 Effect of state or local law or other requirements.
618.540 Advertising.
618.545 Pre-employment inquiries.
618.550 Sex as a bona fide occupational qualification.

Subpart F—Procedures

618.600 Notice of covered programs.
618.605 Enforcement procedures.

AUTHORITY: 20 U.S.C. 1681, 1682, 1683, 1685, 1686, 1687, 1688.

SOURCE: 65 FR 52865, 52893, Aug. 30, 2000, unless otherwise noted.

Subpart A—Introduction

§ 618.100 Purpose and effective date.

The purpose of these Title IX regulations is to effectuate Title IX of the Education Amendments of 1972, as amended (except sections 904 and 906 of those Amendments) (20 U.S.C. 1681, 1682, 1683, 1685, 1686, 1687, 1688), which is designed to eliminate (with certain exceptions) discrimination on the basis of sex in any education program or activity receiving Federal financial assistance, whether or not such program or activity is offered or sponsored by an educational institution as defined in these Title IX regulations. The effective date of these Title IX regulations shall be September 29, 2000.

§ 618.105 Definitions.

As used in these Title IX regulations, the term:

Administratively separate unit means a school, department, or college of an educational institution (other than a local educational agency) admission to which is independent of admission to any other component of such institution.

Admission means selection for part-time, full-time, special, associate, transfer, exchange, or any other enrollment, membership, or matriculation in or at an education program or activity operated by a recipient.

Applicant means one who submits an application, request, or plan required to be approved by an official of the Federal agency that awards Federal financial assistance, or by a recipient, as a condition to becoming a recipient.

Designated agency official means General Counsel and head of the policy office, Division of Contracts, Policy, and Oversight.

Educational institution means a local educational agency (LEA) as defined by 20 U.S.C. 8801(18), a preschool, a private elementary or secondary school, or an applicant or recipient that is an institution of graduate higher education, an institution of undergraduate higher education, an institution of professional education, or an institution of vocational education, as defined in this section.

Federal financial assistance means any of the following, when authorized or extended under a law administered by the Federal agency that awards such assistance:

(1) A grant or loan of Federal financial assistance, including funds made available for:

(i) The acquisition, construction, renovation, restoration, or repair of a building or facility or any portion thereof; and

(ii) Scholarships, loans, grants, wages, or other funds extended to any entity for payment to or on behalf of students admitted to that entity, or extended directly to such students for payment to that entity.

(2) A grant of Federal real or personal property or any interest therein, including surplus property, and the proceeds of the sale or transfer of such property, if the Federal share of the fair market value of the property is not, upon such sale or transfer, properly accounted for to the Federal Government.

(3) Provision of the services of Federal personnel.

(4) Sale or lease of Federal property or any interest therein at nominal consideration, or at consideration reduced for the purpose of assisting the recipient or in recognition of public interest

to be served thereby, or permission to use Federal property or any interest therein without consideration.

(5) Any other contract, agreement, or arrangement that has as one of its purposes the provision of assistance to any education program or activity, except a contract of insurance or guaranty.

Institution of graduate higher education means an institution that:

(1) Offers academic study beyond the bachelor of arts or bachelor of science degree, whether or not leading to a certificate of any higher degree in the liberal arts and sciences;

(2) Awards any degree in a professional field beyond the first professional degree (regardless of whether the first professional degree in such field is awarded by an institution of undergraduate higher education or professional education); or

(3) Awards no degree and offers no further academic study, but operates ordinarily for the purpose of facilitating research by persons who have received the highest graduate degree in any field of study.

Institution of professional education means an institution (except any institution of undergraduate higher education) that offers a program of academic study that leads to a first professional degree in a field for which there is a national specialized accrediting agency recognized by the Secretary of Education.

Institution of undergraduate higher education means:

(1) An institution offering at least two but less than four years of college-level study beyond the high school level, leading to a diploma or an associate degree, or wholly or principally creditable toward a baccalaureate degree; or

(2) An institution offering academic study leading to a baccalaureate degree; or

(3) An agency or body that certifies credentials or offers degrees, but that may or may not offer academic study.

Institution of vocational education means a school or institution (except an institution of professional or graduate or undergraduate higher education) that has as its primary purpose preparation of students to pursue a technical, skilled, or semiskilled occupation or trade, or to pursue study in a technical field, whether or not the school or institution offers certificates, diplomas, or degrees and whether or not it offers full-time study.

Recipient means any State or political subdivision thereof, or any instrumentality of a State or political subdivision thereof, any public or private agency, institution, or organization, or other entity, or any person, to whom Federal financial assistance is extended directly or through another recipient and that operates an education program or activity that receives such assistance, including any subunit, successor, assignee, or transferee thereof.

Student means a person who has gained admission.

Title IX means Title IX of the Education Amendments of 1972, Public Law 92–318, 86 Stat. 235, 373 (codified as amended at 20 U.S.C. 1681–1688) (except sections 904 and 906 thereof), as amended by section 3 of Public Law 93–568, 88 Stat. 1855, by section 412 of the Education Amendments of 1976, Public Law 94–482, 90 Stat. 2234, and by Section 3 of Public Law 100–259, 102 Stat. 28, 28–29 (20 U.S.C. 1681, 1682, 1683, 1685, 1686, 1687, 1688).

Title IX regulations means the provisions set forth at §§ 618.100 through 618.605.

Transition plan means a plan subject to the approval of the Secretary of Education pursuant to section 901(a)(2) of the Education Amendments of 1972, 20 U.S.C. 1681(a)(2), under which an educational institution operates in making the transition from being an educational institution that admits only students of one sex to being one that admits students of both sexes without discrimination.

§ 618.110 **Remedial and affirmative action and self-evaluation.**

(a) *Remedial action.* If the designated agency official finds that a recipient has discriminated against persons on the basis of sex in an education program or activity, such recipient shall take such remedial action as the designated agency official deems necessary to overcome the effects of such discrimination.

(b) *Affirmative action.* In the absence of a finding of discrimination on the basis of sex in an education program or activity, a recipient may take affirmative action consistent with law to overcome the effects of conditions that resulted in limited participation therein by persons of a particular sex. Nothing in these Title IX regulations shall be interpreted to alter any affirmative action obligations that a recipient may have under Executive Order 11246, 3 CFR, 1964–1965 Comp., p. 339; as amended by Executive Order 11375, 3 CFR, 1966–1970 Comp., p. 684; as amended by Executive Order 11478, 3 CFR, 1966–1970 Comp., p. 803; as amended by Executive Order 12086, 3 CFR, 1978 Comp., p. 230; as amended by Executive Order 12107, 3 CFR, 1978 Comp., p. 264.

(c) *Self-evaluation.* Each recipient education institution shall, within one year of September 29, 2000:

(1) Evaluate, in terms of the requirements of these Title IX regulations, its current policies and practices and the effects thereof concerning admission of students, treatment of students, and employment of both academic and nonacademic personnel working in connection with the recipient's education program or activity;

(2) Modify any of these policies and practices that do not or may not meet the requirements of these Title IX regulations; and

(3) Take appropriate remedial steps to eliminate the effects of any discrimination that resulted or may have resulted from adherence to these policies and practices.

(d) *Availability of self-evaluation and related materials.* Recipients shall maintain on file for at least three years following completion of the evaluation required under paragraph (c) of this section, and shall provide to the designated agency official upon request, a description of any modifications made pursuant to paragraph (c)(2) of this section and of any remedial steps taken pursuant to paragraph (c)(3) of this section.

§ 618.115 Assurance required.

(a) *General.* Either at the application stage or the award stage, Federal agencies must ensure that applications for Federal financial assistance or awards of Federal financial assistance contain, be accompanied by, or be covered by a specifically identified assurance from the applicant or recipient, satisfactory to the designated agency official, that each education program or activity operated by the applicant or recipient and to which these Title IX regulations apply will be operated in compliance with these Title IX regulations. An assurance of compliance with these Title IX regulations shall not be satisfactory to the designated agency official if the applicant or recipient to whom such assurance applies fails to commit itself to take whatever remedial action is necessary in accordance with §618.110(a) to eliminate existing discrimination on the basis of sex or to eliminate the effects of past discrimination whether occurring prior to or subsequent to the submission to the designated agency official of such assurance.

(b) *Duration of obligation.* (1) In the case of Federal financial assistance extended to provide real property or structures thereon, such assurance shall obligate the recipient or, in the case of a subsequent transfer, the transferee, for the period during which the real property or structures are used to provide an education program or activity.

(2) In the case of Federal financial assistance extended to provide personal property, such assurance shall obligate the recipient for the period during which it retains ownership or possession of the property.

(3) In all other cases such assurance shall obligate the recipient for the period during which Federal financial assistance is extended.

(c) *Form.* (1) The assurances required by paragraph (a) of this section, which may be included as part of a document that addresses other assurances or obligations, shall include that the applicant or recipient will comply with all applicable Federal statutes relating to nondiscrimination. These include but are not limited to: Title IX of the Education Amendments of 1972, as amended (20 U.S.C. 1681–1683, 1685–1688).

(2) The designated agency official will specify the extent to which such assurances will be required of the applicant's or recipient's subgrantees, contractors, subcontractors, transferees, or successors in interest.

National Science Foundation

§ 618.120 Transfers of property.

If a recipient sells or otherwise transfers property financed in whole or in part with Federal financial assistance to a transferee that operates any education program or activity, and the Federal share of the fair market value of the property is not upon such sale or transfer properly accounted for to the Federal Government, both the transferor and the transferee shall be deemed to be recipients, subject to the provisions of §§ 618.205 through 618.235(a).

§ 618.125 Effect of other requirements.

(a) *Effect of other Federal provisions.* The obligations imposed by these Title IX regulations are independent of, and do not alter, obligations not to discriminate on the basis of sex imposed by Executive Order 11246, 3 CFR, 1964–1965 Comp., p. 339; as amended by Executive Order 11375, 3 CFR, 1966–1970 Comp., p. 684; as amended by Executive Order 11478, 3 CFR, 1966–1970 Comp., p. 803; as amended by Executive Order 12087, 3 CFR, 1978 Comp., p. 230; as amended by Executive Order 12107, 3 CFR, 1978 Comp., p. 264; sections 704 and 855 of the Public Health Service Act (42 U.S.C. 295m, 298b-2); Title VII of the Civil Rights Act of 1964 (42 U.S.C. 2000e *et seq.*); the Equal Pay Act of 1963 (29 U.S.C. 206); and any other Act of Congress or Federal regulation.

(b) *Effect of State or local law or other requirements.* The obligation to comply with these Title IX regulations is not obviated or alleviated by any State or local law or other requirement that would render any applicant or student ineligible, or limit the eligibility of any applicant or student, on the basis of sex, to practice any occupation or profession.

(c) *Effect of rules or regulations of private organizations.* The obligation to comply with these Title IX regulations is not obviated or alleviated by any rule or regulation of any organization, club, athletic or other league, or association that would render any applicant or student ineligible to participate or limit the eligibility or participation of any applicant or student, on the basis of sex, in any education program or activity operated by a recipient and that receives Federal financial assistance.

§ 618.130 Effect of employment opportunities.

The obligation to comply with these Title IX regulations is not obviated or alleviated because employment opportunities in any occupation or profession are or may be more limited for members of one sex than for members of the other sex.

§ 618.135 Designation of responsible employee and adoption of grievance procedures.

(a) *Designation of responsible employee.* Each recipient shall designate at least one employee to coordinate its efforts to comply with and carry out its responsibilities under these Title IX regulations, including any investigation of any complaint communicated to such recipient alleging its noncompliance with these Title IX regulations or alleging any actions that would be prohibited by these Title IX regulations. The recipient shall notify all its students and employees of the name, office address, and telephone number of the employee or employees appointed pursuant to this paragraph.

(b) *Complaint procedure of recipient.* A recipient shall adopt and publish grievance procedures providing for prompt and equitable resolution of student and employee complaints alleging any action that would be prohibited by these Title IX regulations.

§ 618.140 Dissemination of policy.

(a) *Notification of policy.* (1) Each recipient shall implement specific and continuing steps to notify applicants for admission and employment, students and parents of elementary and secondary school students, employees, sources of referral of applicants for admission and employment, and all unions or professional organizations holding collective bargaining or professional agreements with the recipient, that it does not discriminate on the basis of sex in the educational programs or activities that it operates, and that it is required by Title IX and

§ 618.200

these Title IX regulations not to discriminate in such a manner. Such notification shall contain such information, and be made in such manner, as the designated agency official finds necessary to apprise such persons of the protections against discrimination assured them by Title IX and these Title IX regulations, but shall state at least that the requirement not to discriminate in education programs or activities extends to employment therein, and to admission thereto unless §§ 618.300 through 618.310 do not apply to the recipient, and that inquiries concerning the application of Title IX and these Title IX regulations to such recipient may be referred to the employee designated pursuant to § 618.135, or to the designated agency official.

(2) Each recipient shall make the initial notification required by paragraph (a)(1) of this section within 90 days of September 29, 2000 or of the date these Title IX regulations first apply to such recipient, whichever comes later, which notification shall include publication in:

(i) Newspapers and magazines operated by such recipient or by student, alumnae, or alumni groups for or in connection with such recipient; and

(ii) Memoranda or other written communications distributed to every student and employee of such recipient.

(b) *Publications.* (1) Each recipient shall prominently include a statement of the policy described in paragraph (a) of this section in each announcement, bulletin, catalog, or application form that it makes available to any person of a type, described in paragraph (a) of this section, or which is otherwise used in connection with the recruitment of students or employees.

(2) A recipient shall not use or distribute a publication of the type described in paragraph (b)(1) of this section that suggests, by text or illustration, that such recipient treats applicants, students, or employees differently on the basis of sex except as such treatment is permitted by these Title IX regulations.

(c) *Distribution.* Each recipient shall distribute without discrimination on the basis of sex each publication described in paragraph (b)(1) of this section, and shall apprise each of its admission and employment recruitment representatives of the policy of nondiscrimination described in paragraph (a) of this section, and shall require such representatives to adhere to such policy.

Subpart B—Coverage

§ 618.200 Application.

Except as provided in §§ 618.205 through 618.235(a), these Title IX regulations apply to every recipient and to each education program or activity operated by such recipient that receives Federal financial assistance.

§ 618.205 Educational institutions and other entities controlled by religious organizations.

(a) *Exemption.* These Title IX regulations do not apply to any operation of an educational institution or other entity that is controlled by a religious organization to the extent that application of these Title IX regulations would not be consistent with the religious tenets of such organization.

(b) *Exemption claims.* An educational institution or other entity that wishes to claim the exemption set forth in paragraph (a) of this section shall do so by submitting in writing to the designated agency official a statement by the highest-ranking official of the institution, identifying the provisions of these Title IX regulations that conflict with a specific tenet of the religious organization.

§ 618.210 Military and merchant marine educational institutions.

These Title IX regulations do not apply to an educational institution whose primary purpose is the training of individuals for a military service of the United States or for the merchant marine.

§ 618.215 Membership practices of certain organizations.

(a) *Social fraternities and sororities.* These Title IX regulations do not apply to the membership practices of social fraternities and sororities that are exempt from taxation under section 501(a) of the Internal Revenue Code of 1954, 26 U.S.C. 501(a), the active membership of which consists primarily of students in attendance at institutions of higher education.

(b) *YMCA, YWCA, Girl Scouts, Boy Scouts, and Camp Fire Girls.* These Title IX regulations do not apply to the membership practices of the Young Men's Christian Association (YMCA), the Young Women's Christian Association (YWCA), the Girl Scouts, the Boy Scouts, and Camp Fire Girls.

(c) *Voluntary youth service organizations.* These Title IX regulations do not apply to the membership practices of a voluntary youth service organization that is exempt from taxation under section 501(a) of the Internal Revenue Code of 1954, 26 U.S.C. 501(a), and the membership of which has been traditionally limited to members of one sex and principally to persons of less than nineteen years of age.

§ 618.220 Admissions.

(a) Admissions to educational institutions prior to June 24, 1973, are not covered by these Title IX regulations.

(b) *Administratively separate units.* For the purposes only of this section, §§ 618.225 and 618.230, and §§ 618.300 through 618.310, each administratively separate unit shall be deemed to be an educational institution.

(c) *Application of §§ 618.300 through .310.* Except as provided in paragraphs (d) and (e) of this section, §§ 618.300 through 618.310 apply to each recipient. A recipient to which §§ 618.300 through 618.310 apply shall not discriminate on the basis of sex in admission or recruitment in violation of §§ 618.300 through 618.310.

(d) *Educational institutions.* Except as provided in paragraph (e) of this section as to recipients that are educational institutions, §§ 618.300 through 618.310 apply only to institutions of vocational education, professional education, graduate higher education, and public institutions of undergraduate higher education.

(e) *Public institutions of undergraduate higher education.* §§ 618.300 through 618.310 do not apply to any public institution of undergraduate higher education that traditionally and continually from its establishment has had a policy of admitting students of only one sex.

§ 618.225 Educational institutions eligible to submit transition plans.

(a) *Application.* This section applies to each educational institution to which §§ 618.300 through 618.310 apply that:

(1) Admitted students of only one sex as regular students as of June 23, 1972; or

(2) Admitted students of only one sex as regular students as of June 23, 1965, but thereafter admitted, as regular students, students of the sex not admitted prior to June 23, 1965.

(b) *Provision for transition plans.* An educational institution to which this section applies shall not discriminate on the basis of sex in admission or recruitment in violation of §§ 618.300 through 618.310.

§ 618.230 Transition plans.

(a) *Submission of plans.* An institution to which § 618.225 applies and that is composed of more than one administratively separate unit may submit either a single transition plan applicable to all such units, or a separate transition plan applicable to each such unit.

(b) *Content of plans.* In order to be approved by the Secretary of Education, a transition plan shall:

(1) State the name, address, and Federal Interagency Committee on Education Code of the educational institution submitting such plan, the administratively separate units to which the plan is applicable, and the name, address, and telephone number of the person to whom questions concerning the plan may be addressed. The person who submits the plan shall be the chief administrator or president of the institution, or another individual legally authorized to bind the institution to all actions set forth in the plan.

(2) State whether the educational institution or administratively separate unit admits students of both sexes as regular students and, if so, when it began to do so.

(3) Identify and describe with respect to the educational institution or administratively separate unit any obstacles to admitting students without discrimination on the basis of sex.

(4) Describe in detail the steps necessary to eliminate as soon as practicable each obstacle so identified and

indicate the schedule for taking these steps and the individual directly responsible for their implementation.

(5) Include estimates of the number of students, by sex, expected to apply for, be admitted to, and enter each class during the period covered by the plan.

(c) *Nondiscrimination.* No policy or practice of a recipient to which § 618.225 applies shall result in treatment of applicants to or students of such recipient in violation of §§ 618.300 through 618.310 unless such treatment is necessitated by an obstacle identified in paragraph (b)(3) of this section and a schedule for eliminating that obstacle has been provided as required by paragraph (b)(4) of this section.

(d) *Effects of past exclusion.* To overcome the effects of past exclusion of students on the basis of sex, each educational institution to which § 618.225 applies shall include in its transition plan, and shall implement, specific steps designed to encourage individuals of the previously excluded sex to apply for admission to such institution. Such steps shall include instituting recruitment programs that emphasize the institution's commitment to enrolling students of the sex previously excluded.

§ 618.235 **Statutory amendments.**

(a) This section, which applies to all provisions of these Title IX regulations, addresses statutory amendments to Title IX.

(b) These Title IX regulations shall not apply to or preclude:

(1) Any program or activity of the American Legion undertaken in connection with the organization or operation of any Boys State conference, Boys Nation conference, Girls State conference, or Girls Nation conference;

(2) Any program or activity of a secondary school or educational institution specifically for:

(i) The promotion of any Boys State conference, Boys Nation conference, Girls State conference, or Girls Nation conference; or

(ii) The selection of students to attend any such conference;

(3) Father-son or mother-daughter activities at an educational institution or in an education program or activity, but if such activities are provided for students of one sex, opportunities for reasonably comparable activities shall be provided to students of the other sex;

(4) Any scholarship or other financial assistance awarded by an institution of higher education to an individual because such individual has received such award in a single-sex pageant based upon a combination of factors related to the individual's personal appearance, poise, and talent. The pageant, however, must comply with other nondiscrimination provisions of Federal law.

(c) *Program or activity* or *program* means:

(1) All of the operations of any entity described in paragraphs (c)(1)(i) through (iv) of this section, any part of which is extended Federal financial assistance:

(i)(A) A department, agency, special purpose district, or other instrumentality of a State or of a local government; or

(B) The entity of such State or local government that distributes such assistance and each such department or agency (and each other State or local government entity) to which the assistance is extended, in the case of assistance to a State or local government;

(ii)(A) A college, university, or other postsecondary institution, or a public system of higher education; or

(B) A local educational agency (as defined in section 8801 of title 20), system of vocational education, or other school system;

(iii)(A) An entire corporation, partnership, or other private organization, or an entire sole proprietorship—

(*1*) If assistance is extended to such corporation, partnership, private organization, or sole proprietorship as a whole; or

(*2*) Which is principally engaged in the business of providing education, health care, housing, social services, or parks and recreation; or

(B) The entire plant or other comparable, geographically separate facility to which Federal financial assistance is extended, in the case of any other corporation, partnership, private organization, or sole proprietorship; or

(iv) Any other entity that is established by two or more of the entities described in paragraphs (c)(1)(i), (ii), or (iii) of this section.

(2)(i) *Program or activity* does not include any operation of an entity that is controlled by a religious organization if the application of 20 U.S.C. 1681 to such operation would not be consistent with the religious tenets of such organization.

(ii) For example, all of the operations of a college, university, or other postsecondary institution, including but not limited to traditional educational operations, faculty and student housing, campus shuttle bus service, campus restaurants, the bookstore, and other commercial activities are part of a "program or activity" subject to these Title IX regulations if the college, university, or other institution receives Federal financial assistance.

(d)(1) Nothing in these Title IX regulations shall be construed to require or prohibit any person, or public or private entity, to provide or pay for any benefit or service, including the use of facilities, related to an abortion. Medical procedures, benefits, services, and the use of facilities, necessary to save the life of a pregnant woman or to address complications related to an abortion are not subject to this section.

(2) Nothing in this section shall be construed to permit a penalty to be imposed on any person or individual because such person or individual is seeking or has received any benefit or service related to a legal abortion. Accordingly, subject to paragraph (d)(1) of this section, no person shall be excluded from participation in, be denied the benefits of, or be subjected to discrimination under any academic, extracurricular, research, occupational training, employment, or other educational program or activity operated by a recipient that receives Federal financial assistance because such individual has sought or received, or is seeking, a legal abortion, or any benefit or service related to a legal abortion.

Subpart C—Discrimination on the Basis of Sex in Admission and Recruitment Prohibited

§ 618.300 Admission.

(a) *General.* No person shall, on the basis of sex, be denied admission, or be subjected to discrimination in admission, by any recipient to which §§ 618.300 through 618.310 apply, except as provided in §§ 618.225 and 618.230.

(b) *Specific prohibitions.* (1) In determining whether a person satisfies any policy or criterion for admission, or in making any offer of admission, a recipient to which §§ 618.300 through 618.310 apply shall not:

(i) Give preference to one person over another on the basis of sex, by ranking applicants separately on such basis, or otherwise;

(ii) Apply numerical limitations upon the number or proportion of persons of either sex who may be admitted; or

(iii) Otherwise treat one individual differently from another on the basis of sex.

(2) A recipient shall not administer or operate any test or other criterion for admission that has a disproportionately adverse effect on persons on the basis of sex unless the use of such test or criterion is shown to predict validly success in the education program or activity in question and alternative tests or criteria that do not have such a disproportionately adverse effect are shown to be unavailable.

(c) *Prohibitions relating to marital or parental status.* In determining whether a person satisfies any policy or criterion for admission, or in making any offer of admission, a recipient to which §§ 618.300 through 618.310 apply:

(1) Shall not apply any rule concerning the actual or potential parental, family, or marital status of a student or applicant that treats persons differently on the basis of sex;

(2) Shall not discriminate against or exclude any person on the basis of pregnancy, childbirth, termination of pregnancy, or recovery therefrom, or establish or follow any rule or practice that so discriminates or excludes;

(3) Subject to § 618.235(d), shall treat disabilities related to pregnancy, childbirth, termination of pregnancy, or recovery therefrom in the same manner

§ 618.305

and under the same policies as any other temporary disability or physical condition; and

(4) Shall not make pre-admission inquiry as to the marital status of an applicant for admission, including whether such applicant is "Miss" or "Mrs." A recipient may make pre-admission inquiry as to the sex of an applicant for admission, but only if such inquiry is made equally of such applicants of both sexes and if the results of such inquiry are not used in connection with discrimination prohibited by these Title IX regulations.

§ 618.305 Preference in admission.

A recipient to which §§ 618.300 through 618.310 apply shall not give preference to applicants for admission, on the basis of attendance at any educational institution or other school or entity that admits as students only or predominantly members of one sex, if the giving of such preference has the effect of discriminating on the basis of sex in violation of §§ 618.300 through 618.310.

§ 618.310 Recruitment.

(a) *Nondiscriminatory recruitment.* A recipient to which §§ 618.300 through 618.310 apply shall not discriminate on the basis of sex in the recruitment and admission of students. A recipient may be required to undertake additional recruitment efforts for one sex as remedial action pursuant to § 618.110(a), and may choose to undertake such efforts as affirmative action pursuant to § 618.110(b).

(b) *Recruitment at certain institutions.* A recipient to which §§ 618.300 through 618.310 apply shall not recruit primarily or exclusively at educational institutions, schools, or entities that admit as students only or predominantly members of one sex, if such actions have the effect of discriminating on the basis of sex in violation of §§ 618.300 through 618.310.

Subpart D—Discrimination on the Basis of Sex in Education Programs or Activities Prohibited

§ 618.400 Education programs or activities.

(a) *General.* Except as provided elsewhere in these Title IX regulations, no person shall, on the basis of sex, be excluded from participation in, be denied the benefits of, or be subjected to discrimination under any academic, extracurricular, research, occupational training, or other education program or activity operated by a recipient that receives Federal financial assistance. Sections 618.400 through 618.455 do not apply to actions of a recipient in connection with admission of its students to an education program or activity of a recipient to which §§ 618.300 through 618.310 do not apply, or an entity, not a recipient, to which §§ 618.300 through 618.310 would not apply if the entity were a recipient.

(b) *Specific prohibitions.* Except as provided in §§ 618.400 through 618.455, in providing any aid, benefit, or service to a student, a recipient shall not, on the basis of sex:

(1) Treat one person differently from another in determining whether such person satisfies any requirement or condition for the provision of such aid, benefit, or service;

(2) Provide different aid, benefits, or services or provide aid, benefits, or services in a different manner;

(3) Deny any person any such aid, benefit, or service;

(4) Subject any person to separate or different rules of behavior, sanctions, or other treatment;

(5) Apply any rule concerning the domicile or residence of a student or applicant, including eligibility for instate fees and tuition;

(6) Aid or perpetuate discrimination against any person by providing significant assistance to any agency, organization, or person that discriminates on the basis of sex in providing any aid, benefit, or service to students or employees;

(7) Otherwise limit any person in the enjoyment of any right, privilege, advantage, or opportunity.

(c) *Assistance administered by a recipient educational institution to study at a foreign institution.* A recipient educational institution may administer or assist in the administration of scholarships, fellowships, or other awards established by foreign or domestic wills, trusts, or similar legal instruments, or by acts of foreign governments and restricted to members of one sex, that are designed to provide opportunities to study abroad, and that are awarded to students who are already matriculating at or who are graduates of the recipient institution; *Provided,* that a recipient educational institution that administers or assists in the administration of such scholarships, fellowships, or other awards that are restricted to members of one sex provides, or otherwise makes available, reasonable opportunities for similar studies for members of the other sex. Such opportunities may be derived from either domestic or foreign sources.

(d) *Aids, benefits or services not provided by recipient.* (1) This paragraph (d) applies to any recipient that requires participation by any applicant, student, or employee in any education program or activity not operated wholly by such recipient, or that facilitates, permits, or considers such participation as part of or equivalent to an education program or activity operated by such recipient, including participation in educational consortia and cooperative employment and student-teaching assignments.

(2) Such recipient:

(i) Shall develop and implement a procedure designed to assure itself that the operator or sponsor of such other education program or activity takes no action affecting any applicant, student, or employee of such recipient that these Title IX regulations would prohibit such recipient from taking; and

(ii) Shall not facilitate, require, permit, or consider such participation if such action occurs.

§ 618.405 Housing.

(a) *Generally.* A recipient shall not, on the basis of sex, apply different rules or regulations, impose different fees or requirements, or offer different services or benefits related to housing, except as provided in this section (including housing provided only to married students).

(b) *Housing provided by recipient.* (1) A recipient may provide separate housing on the basis of sex.

(2) Housing provided by a recipient to students of one sex, when compared to that provided to students of the other sex, shall be as a whole:

(i) Proportionate in quantity to the number of students of that sex applying for such housing; and

(ii) Comparable in quality and cost to the student.

(c) *Other housing.* (1) A recipient shall not, on the basis of sex, administer different policies or practices concerning occupancy by its students of housing other than that provided by such recipient.

(2)(i) A recipient which, through solicitation, listing, approval of housing, or otherwise, assists any agency, organization, or person in making housing available to any of its students, shall take such reasonable action as may be necessary to assure itself that such housing as is provided to students of one sex, when compared to that provided to students of the other sex, is as a whole:

(A) Proportionate in quantity; and

(B) Comparable in quality and cost to the student.

(ii) A recipient may render such assistance to any agency, organization, or person that provides all or part of such housing to students of only one sex.

§ 618.410 Comparable facilities.

A recipient may provide separate toilet, locker room, and shower facilities on the basis of sex, but such facilities provided for students of one sex shall be comparable to such facilities provided for students of the other sex.

§ 618.415 Access to course offerings.

(a) A recipient shall not provide any course or otherwise carry out any of its education program or activity separately on the basis of sex, or require or refuse participation therein by any of its students on such basis, including health, physical education, industrial, business, vocational, technical, home economics, music, and adult education courses.

§ 618.420

(b)(1) With respect to classes and activities in physical education at the elementary school level, the recipient shall comply fully with this section as expeditiously as possible but in no event later than one year from September 29, 2000. With respect to physical education classes and activities at the secondary and post-secondary levels, the recipient shall comply fully with this section as expeditiously as possible but in no event later than three years from September 29, 2000.

(2) This section does not prohibit grouping of students in physical education classes and activities by ability as assessed by objective standards of individual performance developed and applied without regard to sex.

(3) This section does not prohibit separation of students by sex within physical education classes or activities during participation in wrestling, boxing, rugby, ice hockey, football, basketball, and other sports the purpose or major activity of which involves bodily contact.

(4) Where use of a single standard of measuring skill or progress in a physical education class has an adverse effect on members of one sex, the recipient shall use appropriate standards that do not have such effect.

(5) Portions of classes in elementary and secondary schools, or portions of education programs or activities, that deal exclusively with human sexuality may be conducted in separate sessions for boys and girls.

(6) Recipients may make requirements based on vocal range or quality that may result in a chorus or choruses of one or predominantly one sex.

§ 618.420 Access to schools operated by LEAs.

A recipient that is a local educational agency shall not, on the basis of sex, exclude any person from admission to:

(a) Any institution of vocational education operated by such recipient; or

(b) Any other school or educational unit operated by such recipient, unless such recipient otherwise makes available to such person, pursuant to the same policies and criteria of admission, courses, services, and facilities comparable to each course, service, and facility offered in or through such schools.

§ 618.425 Counseling and use of appraisal and counseling materials.

(a) *Counseling.* A recipient shall not discriminate against any person on the basis of sex in the counseling or guidance of students or applicants for admission.

(b) *Use of appraisal and counseling materials.* A recipient that uses testing or other materials for appraising or counseling students shall not use different materials for students on the basis of their sex or use materials that permit or require different treatment of students on such basis unless such different materials cover the same occupations and interest areas and the use of such different materials is shown to be essential to eliminate sex bias. Recipients shall develop and use internal procedures for ensuring that such materials do not discriminate on the basis of sex. Where the use of a counseling test or other instrument results in a substantially disproportionate number of members of one sex in any particular course of study or classification, the recipient shall take such action as is necessary to assure itself that such disproportion is not the result of discrimination in the instrument or its application.

(c) *Disproportion in classes.* Where a recipient finds that a particular class contains a substantially disproportionate number of individuals of one sex, the recipient shall take such action as is necessary to assure itself that such disproportion is not the result of discrimination on the basis of sex in counseling or appraisal materials or by counselors.

§ 618.430 Financial assistance.

(a) *General.* Except as provided in paragraphs (b) and (c) of this section, in providing financial assistance to any of its students, a recipient shall not:

(1) On the basis of sex, provide different amounts or types of such assistance, limit eligibility for such assistance that is of any particular type or source, apply different criteria, or otherwise discriminate;

(2) Through solicitation, listing, approval, provision of facilities, or other

services, assist any foundation, trust, agency, organization, or person that provides assistance to any of such recipient's students in a manner that discriminates on the basis of sex; or

(3) Apply any rule or assist in application of any rule concerning eligibility for such assistance that treats persons of one sex differently from persons of the other sex with regard to marital or parental status.

(b) *Financial aid established by certain legal instruments.* (1) A recipient may administer or assist in the administration of scholarships, fellowships, or other forms of financial assistance established pursuant to domestic or foreign wills, trusts, bequests, or similar legal instruments or by acts of a foreign government that require that awards be made to members of a particular sex specified therein; *Provided,* that the overall effect of the award of such sex-restricted scholarships, fellowships, and other forms of financial assistance does not discriminate on the basis of sex.

(2) To ensure nondiscriminatory awards of assistance as required in paragraph (b)(1) of this section, recipients shall develop and use procedures under which:

(i) Students are selected for award of financial assistance on the basis of nondiscriminatory criteria and not on the basis of availability of funds restricted to members of a particular sex;

(ii) An appropriate sex-restricted scholarship, fellowship, or other form of financial assistance is allocated to each student selected under paragraph (b)(2)(i) of this section; and

(iii) No student is denied the award for which he or she was selected under paragraph (b)(2)(i) of this section because of the absence of a scholarship, fellowship, or other form of financial assistance designated for a member of that student's sex.

(c) *Athletic scholarships.* (1) To the extent that a recipient awards athletic scholarships or grants-in-aid, it must provide reasonable opportunities for such awards for members of each sex in proportion to the number of students of each sex participating in interscholastic or intercollegiate athletics.

(2) A recipient may provide separate athletic scholarships or grants-in-aid for members of each sex as part of separate athletic teams for members of each sex to the extent consistent with this paragraph (c) and § 618.450.

§ 618.435 **Employment assistance to students.**

(a) *Assistance by recipient in making available outside employment.* A recipient that assists any agency, organization, or person in making employment available to any of its students:

(1) Shall assure itself that such employment is made available without discrimination on the basis of sex; and

(2) Shall not render such services to any agency, organization, or person that discriminates on the basis of sex in its employment practices.

(b) *Employment of students by recipients.* A recipient that employs any of its students shall not do so in a manner that violates §§ 618.500 through 618.550.

§ 618.440 **Health and insurance benefits and services.**

Subject to § 618.235(d), in providing a medical, hospital, accident, or life insurance benefit, service, policy, or plan to any of its students, a recipient shall not discriminate on the basis of sex, or provide such benefit, service, policy, or plan in a manner that would violate §§ 618.500 through 618.550 if it were provided to employees of the recipient. This section shall not prohibit a recipient from providing any benefit or service that may be used by a different proportion of students of one sex than of the other, including family planning services. However, any recipient that provides full coverage health service shall provide gynecological care.

§ 618.445 **Marital or parental status.**

(a) *Status generally.* A recipient shall not apply any rule concerning a student's actual or potential parental, family, or marital status that treats students differently on the basis of sex.

(b) *Pregnancy and related conditions.* (1) A recipient shall not discriminate against any student, or exclude any student from its education program or activity, including any class or extracurricular activity, on the basis of such student's pregnancy, childbirth, false pregnancy, termination of pregnancy, or recovery therefrom, unless the student requests voluntarily to participate in a separate portion of the program or activity of the recipient.

(2) A recipient may require such a student to obtain the certification of a physician that the student is physically and emotionally able to continue participation as long as such a certification is required of all students for other physical or emotional conditions requiring the attention of a physician.

(3) A recipient that operates a portion of its education program or activity separately for pregnant students, admittance to which is completely voluntary on the part of the student as provided in paragraph (b)(1) of this section, shall ensure that the separate portion is comparable to that offered to non-pregnant students.

(4) Subject to § 618.235(d), a recipient shall treat pregnancy, childbirth, false pregnancy, termination of pregnancy and recovery therefrom in the same manner and under the same policies as any other temporary disability with respect to any medical or hospital benefit, service, plan, or policy that such recipient administers, operates, offers, or participates in with respect to students admitted to the recipient's educational program or activity.

(5) In the case of a recipient that does not maintain a leave policy for its students, or in the case of a student who does not otherwise qualify for leave under such a policy, a recipient shall treat pregnancy, childbirth, false pregnancy, termination of pregnancy, and recovery therefrom as a justification for a leave of absence for as long a period of time as is deemed medically necessary by the student's physician, at the conclusion of which the student shall be reinstated to the status that she held when the leave began.

§ 618.450 Athletics.

(a) *General.* No person shall, on the basis of sex, be excluded from participation in, be denied the benefits of, be treated differently from another person, or otherwise be discriminated against in any interscholastic, intercollegiate, club, or intramural athletics offered by a recipient, and no recipient shall provide any such athletics separately on such basis.

(b) *Separate teams.* Notwithstanding the requirements of paragraph (a) of this section, a recipient may operate or sponsor separate teams for members of each sex where selection for such teams is based upon competitive skill or the activity involved is a contact sport. However, where a recipient operates or sponsors a team in a particular sport for members of one sex but operates or sponsors no such team for members of the other sex, and athletic opportunities for members of that sex have previously been limited, members of the excluded sex must be allowed to try out for the team offered unless the sport involved is a contact sport. For the purposes of these Title IX regulations, contact sports include boxing, wrestling, rugby, ice hockey, football, basketball, and other sports the purpose or major activity of which involves bodily contact.

(c) *Equal opportunity.* (1) A recipient that operates or sponsors interscholastic, intercollegiate, club, or intramural athletics shall provide equal athletic opportunity for members of both sexes. In determining whether equal opportunities are available, the designated agency official will consider, among other factors:

(i) Whether the selection of sports and levels of competition effectively accommodate the interests and abilities of members of both sexes;

(ii) The provision of equipment and supplies;

(iii) Scheduling of games and practice time;

(iv) Travel and per diem allowance;

(v) Opportunity to receive coaching and academic tutoring;

(vi) Assignment and compensation of coaches and tutors;

(vii) Provision of locker rooms, practice, and competitive facilities;

(viii) Provision of medical and training facilities and services;

(ix) Provision of housing and dining facilities and services;

(x) Publicity.

(2) For purposes of paragraph (c)(1) of this section, unequal aggregate expenditures for members of each sex or unequal expenditures for male and female teams if a recipient operates or sponsors separate teams will not constitute noncompliance with this section, but

the designated agency official may consider the failure to provide necessary funds for teams for one sex in assessing equality of opportunity for members of each sex.

(d) *Adjustment period.* A recipient that operates or sponsors interscholastic, intercollegiate, club, or intramural athletics at the elementary school level shall comply fully with this section as expeditiously as possible but in no event later than one year from September 29, 2000. A recipient that operates or sponsors interscholastic, intercollegiate, club, or intramural athletics at the secondary or postsecondary school level shall comply fully with this section as expeditiously as possible but in no event later than three years from September 29, 2000.

§ 618.455 Textbooks and curricular material.

Nothing in these Title IX regulations shall be interpreted as requiring or prohibiting or abridging in any way the use of particular textbooks or curricular materials.

Subpart E—Discrimination on the Basis of Sex in Employment in Education Programs or Activities Prohibited

§ 618.500 Employment.

(a) *General.* (1) No person shall, on the basis of sex, be excluded from participation in, be denied the benefits of, or be subjected to discrimination in employment, or recruitment, consideration, or selection therefor, whether full-time or part-time, under any education program or activity operated by a recipient that receives Federal financial assistance.

(2) A recipient shall make all employment decisions in any education program or activity operated by such recipient in a nondiscriminatory manner and shall not limit, segregate, or classify applicants or employees in any way that could adversely affect any applicant's or employee's employment opportunities or status because of sex.

(3) A recipient shall not enter into any contractual or other relationship which directly or indirectly has the effect of subjecting employees or students to discrimination prohibited by §§ 618.500 through 618.550, including relationships with employment and referral agencies, with labor unions, and with organizations providing or administering fringe benefits to employees of the recipient.

(4) A recipient shall not grant preferences to applicants for employment on the basis of attendance at any educational institution or entity that admits as students only or predominantly members of one sex, if the giving of such preferences has the effect of discriminating on the basis of sex in violation of these Title IX regulations.

(b) *Application.* The provisions of §§ 618.500 through 618.550 apply to:

(1) Recruitment, advertising, and the process of application for employment;

(2) Hiring, upgrading, promotion, consideration for and award of tenure, demotion, transfer, layoff, termination, application of nepotism policies, right of return from layoff, and rehiring;

(3) Rates of pay or any other form of compensation, and changes in compensation;

(4) Job assignments, classifications, and structure, including position descriptions, lines of progression, and seniority lists;

(5) The terms of any collective bargaining agreement;

(6) Granting and return from leaves of absence, leave for pregnancy, childbirth, false pregnancy, termination of pregnancy, leave for persons of either sex to care for children or dependents, or any other leave;

(7) Fringe benefits available by virtue of employment, whether or not administered by the recipient;

(8) Selection and financial support for training, including apprenticeship, professional meetings, conferences, and other related activities, selection for tuition assistance, selection for sabbaticals and leaves of absence to pursue training;

(9) Employer-sponsored activities, including social or recreational programs; and

(10) Any other term, condition, or privilege of employment.

§ 618.505 Employment criteria.

A recipient shall not administer or operate any test or other criterion for any employment opportunity that has a disproportionately adverse effect on persons on the basis of sex unless:

(a) Use of such test or other criterion is shown to predict validly successful performance in the position in question; and

(b) Alternative tests or criteria for such purpose, which do not have such disproportionately adverse effect, are shown to be unavailable.

§ 618.510 Recruitment.

(a) *Nondiscriminatory recruitment and hiring.* A recipient shall not discriminate on the basis of sex in the recruitment and hiring of employees. Where a recipient has been found to be presently discriminating on the basis of sex in the recruitment or hiring of employees, or has been found to have so discriminated in the past, the recipient shall recruit members of the sex so discriminated against so as to overcome the effects of such past or present discrimination.

(b) *Recruitment patterns.* A recipient shall not recruit primarily or exclusively at entities that furnish as applicants only or predominantly members of one sex if such actions have the effect of discriminating on the basis of sex in violation of §§ 618.500 through 618.550.

§ 618.515 Compensation.

A recipient shall not make or enforce any policy or practice that, on the basis of sex:

(a) Makes distinctions in rates of pay or other compensation;

(b) Results in the payment of wages to employees of one sex at a rate less than that paid to employees of the opposite sex for equal work on jobs the performance of which requires equal skill, effort, and responsibility, and that are performed under similar working conditions.

§ 618.520 Job classification and structure.

A recipient shall not:

(a) Classify a job as being for males or for females;

(b) Maintain or establish separate lines of progression, seniority lists, career ladders, or tenure systems based on sex; or

(c) Maintain or establish separate lines of progression, seniority systems, career ladders, or tenure systems for similar jobs, position descriptions, or job requirements that classify persons on the basis of sex, unless sex is a bona fide occupational qualification for the positions in question as set forth in § 618.550.

§ 618.525 Fringe benefits.

(a) *"Fringe benefits" defined.* For purposes of these Title IX regulations, *fringe benefits* means: Any medical, hospital, accident, life insurance, or retirement benefit, service, policy or plan, any profit-sharing or bonus plan, leave, and any other benefit or service of employment not subject to the provision of § 618.515.

(b) *Prohibitions.* A recipient shall not:

(1) Discriminate on the basis of sex with regard to making fringe benefits available to employees or make fringe benefits available to spouses, families, or dependents of employees differently upon the basis of the employee's sex;

(2) Administer, operate, offer, or participate in a fringe benefit plan that does not provide for equal periodic benefits for members of each sex and for equal contributions to the plan by such recipient for members of each sex; or

(3) Administer, operate, offer, or participate in a pension or retirement plan that establishes different optional or compulsory retirement ages based on sex or that otherwise discriminates in benefits on the basis of sex.

§ 618.530 Marital or parental status.

(a) *General.* A recipient shall not apply any policy or take any employment action:

(1) Concerning the potential marital, parental, or family status of an employee or applicant for employment that treats persons differently on the basis of sex; or

(2) Which is based upon whether an employee or applicant for employment is the head of household or principal wage earner in such employee's or applicant's family unit.

(b) *Pregnancy.* A recipient shall not discriminate against or exclude from employment any employee or applicant for employment on the basis of pregnancy, childbirth, false pregnancy, termination of pregnancy, or recovery therefrom.

(c) *Pregnancy as a temporary disability.* Subject to § 618.235(d), a recipient shall treat pregnancy, childbirth, false pregnancy, termination of pregnancy, recovery therefrom, and any temporary disability resulting therefrom as any other temporary disability for all job-related purposes, including commencement, duration, and extensions of leave, payment of disability income, accrual of seniority and any other benefit or service, and reinstatement, and under any fringe benefit offered to employees by virtue of employment.

(d) *Pregnancy leave.* In the case of a recipient that does not maintain a leave policy for its employees, or in the case of an employee with insufficient leave or accrued employment time to qualify for leave under such a policy, a recipient shall treat pregnancy, childbirth, false pregnancy, termination of pregnancy, and recovery therefrom as a justification for a leave of absence without pay for a reasonable period of time, at the conclusion of which the employee shall be reinstated to the status that she held when the leave began or to a comparable position, without decrease in rate of compensation or loss of promotional opportunities, or any other right or privilege of employment.

§ 618.535 Effect of state or local law or other requirements.

(a) *Prohibitory requirements.* The obligation to comply with §§ 618.500 through 618.550 is not obviated or alleviated by the existence of any State or local law or other requirement that imposes prohibitions or limits upon employment of members of one sex that are not imposed upon members of the other sex.

(b) *Benefits.* A recipient that provides any compensation, service, or benefit to members of one sex pursuant to a State or local law or other requirement shall provide the same compensation, service, or benefit to members of the other sex.

§ 618.540 Advertising.

A recipient shall not in any advertising related to employment indicate preference, limitation, specification, or discrimination based on sex unless sex is a bona fide occupational qualification for the particular job in question.

§ 618.545 Pre-employment inquiries.

(a) *Marital status.* A recipient shall not make pre-employment inquiry as to the marital status of an applicant for employment, including whether such applicant is "Miss" or "Mrs."

(b) *Sex.* A recipient may make pre-employment inquiry as to the sex of an applicant for employment, but only if such inquiry is made equally of such applicants of both sexes and if the results of such inquiry are not used in connection with discrimination prohibited by these Title IX regulations.

§ 618.550 Sex as a bona fide occupational qualification.

A recipient may take action otherwise prohibited by §§ 618.500 through 618.550 provided it is shown that sex is a bona fide occupational qualification for that action, such that consideration of sex with regard to such action is essential to successful operation of the employment function concerned. A recipient shall not take action pursuant to this section that is based upon alleged comparative employment characteristics or stereotyped characterizations of one or the other sex, or upon preference based on sex of the recipient, employees, students, or other persons, but nothing contained in this section shall prevent a recipient from considering an employee's sex in relation to employment in a locker room or toilet facility used only by members of one sex.

Subpart F—Procedures

§ 618.600 Notice of covered programs.

Within 60 days of September 29, 2000, each Federal agency that awards Federal financial assistance shall publish in the FEDERAL REGISTER a notice of the programs covered by these Title IX regulations. Each such Federal agency shall periodically republish the notice of covered programs to reflect changes

§ 618.605

in covered programs. Copies of this notice also shall be made available upon request to the Federal agency's office that enforces Title IX.

§ 618.605 Enforcement procedures.

The investigative, compliance, and enforcement procedural provisions of Title VI of the Civil Rights Act of 1964 (42 U.S.C. 2000d) ("Title VI") are hereby adopted and applied to these Title IX regulations. These procedures may be found at 45 CFR part 611.

PART 630—GOVERNMENTWIDE REQUIREMENTS FOR DRUG-FREE WORKPLACE (FINANCIAL ASSISTANCE)

Subpart A—Purpose and Coverage

Sec.
630.100 What does this part do?
630.105 Does this part apply to me?
630.110 Are any of my Federal assistance awards exempt from this part?
630.115 Does this part affect the Federal contracts that I receive?

Subpart B—Requirements for Recipients Other Than Individuals

630.200 What must I do to comply with this part?
630.205 What must I include in my drug-free workplace statement?
630.210 To whom must I distribute my drug-free workplace statement?
630.215 What must I include in my drug-free awareness program?
630.220 By when must I publish my drug-free workplace statement and establish my drug-free awareness program?
630.225 What actions must I take concerning employees who are convicted of drug violations in the workplace?
630.230 How and when must I identify workplaces?

Subpart C—Requirements for Recipients Who Are Individuals

630.300 What must I do to comply with this part if I am an individual recipient?
630.301 [Reserved]

Subpart D—Responsibilities of National Science Foundation Awarding Officials

630.400 What are my responsibilities as a National Science Foundation awarding official?

Subpart E—Violations of This Part and Consequences

630.500 How are violations of this part determined for recipients other than individuals?
630.505 How are violations of this part determined for recipients who are individuals?
630.510 What actions will the Federal Government take against a recipient determined to have violated this part?
630.515 Are there any exceptions to those actions?

Subpart F—Definitions

630.605 Award.
630.610 Controlled substance.
630.615 Conviction.
630.620 Cooperative agreement.
630.625 Criminal drug statute.
630.630 Debarment.
630.635 Drug-free workplace.
630.640 Employee.
630.645 Federal agency or agency.
630.650 Grant.
630.655 Individual.
630.660 Recipient.
630.665 State.
630.670 Suspension.

AUTHORITY: 41 U.S.C. 701 et seq.

SOURCE: 68 FR 66557, 66634, Nov. 26, 2003, unless otherwise noted.

Subpart A—Purpose and Coverage

§ 630.100 What does this part do?

This part carries out the portion of the Drug-Free Workplace Act of 1988 (41 U.S.C. 701 et seq., as amended) that applies to grants. It also applies the provisions of the Act to cooperative agreements and other financial assistance awards, as a matter of Federal Government policy.

§ 630.105 Does this part apply to me?

(a) Portions of this part apply to you if you are either—

(1) A recipient of an assistance award from the National Science Foundation; or

(2) A(n) National Science Foundation awarding official. (See definitions of award and recipient in §§ 630.605 and 630.660, respectively.)

(b) The following table shows the subparts that apply to you:

National Science Foundation

§ 630.220

If you are . . .	see subparts . . .
(1) A recipient who is not an individual	A, B and E.
(2) A recipient who is an individual	A, C and E.
(3) A(n) National Science Foundation awarding official.	A, D and E.

§ 630.110 Are any of my Federal assistance awards exempt from this part?

This part does not apply to any award that the Director or designee determines that the application of this part would be inconsistent with the international obligations of the United States or the laws or regulations of a foreign government.

§ 630.115 Does this part affect the Federal contracts that I receive?

It will affect future contract awards indirectly if you are debarred or suspended for a violation of the requirements of this part, as described in § 630.510(c). However, this part does not apply directly to procurement contracts. The portion of the Drug-Free Workplace Act of 1988 that applies to Federal procurement contracts is carried out through the Federal Acquisition Regulation in chapter 1 of Title 48 of the Code of Federal Regulations (the drug-free workplace coverage currently is in 48 CFR part 23, subpart 23.5).

Subpart B—Requirements for Recipients Other Than Individuals

§ 630.200 What must I do to comply with this part?

There are two general requirements if you are a recipient other than an individual.

(a) First, you must make a good faith effort, on a continuing basis, to maintain a drug-free workplace. You must agree to do so as a condition for receiving any award covered by this part. The specific measures that you must take in this regard are described in more detail in subsequent sections of this subpart. Briefly, those measures are to—

(1) Publish a drug-free workplace statement and establish a drug-free awareness program for your employees (see §§ 630.205 through 630.220); and

(2) Take actions concerning employees who are convicted of violating drug statutes in the workplace (see § 630.225).

(b) Second, you must identify all known workplaces under your Federal awards (see § 630.230).

§ 630.205 What must I include in my drug-free workplace statement?

You must publish a statement that—
(a) Tells your employees that the unlawful manufacture, distribution, dispensing, possession, or use of a controlled substance is prohibited in your workplace;
(b) Specifies the actions that you will take against employees for violating that prohibition; and
(c) Lets each employee know that, as a condition of employment under any award, he or she:
(1) Will abide by the terms of the statement; and
(2) Must notify you in writing if he or she is convicted for a violation of a criminal drug statute occurring in the workplace and must do so no more than five calendar days after the conviction.

§ 630.210 To whom must I distribute my drug-free workplace statement?

You must require that a copy of the statement described in § 630.205 be given to each employee who will be engaged in the performance of any Federal award.

§ 630.215 What must I include in my drug-free awareness program?

You must establish an ongoing drug-free awareness program to inform employees about—
(a) The dangers of drug abuse in the workplace;
(b) Your policy of maintaining a drug-free workplace;
(c) Any available drug counseling, rehabilitation, and employee assistance programs; and
(d) The penalties that you may impose upon them for drug abuse violations occurring in the workplace.

§ 630.220 By when must I publish my drug-free workplace statement and establish my drug-free awareness program?

If you are a new recipient that does not already have a policy statement as described in § 630.205 and an ongoing awareness program as described in

§ 630.225, you must publish the statement and establish the program by the time given in the following table:

If...	then you...
(a) The performance period of the award is less than 30 days.	must have the policy statement and program in place as soon as possible, but before the date on which performance is expected to be completed.
(b) The performance period of the award is 30 days or more.	must have the policy statement and program in place within 30 days after award.
(c) You believe there are extraordinary circumstances that will require more than 30 days for you to publish the policy statement and establish the awareness program.	may ask the National Science Foundation awarding official to give you more time to do so. The amount of additional time, if any, to be given is at the discretion of the awarding official.

§ 630.225 What actions must I take concerning employees who are convicted of drug violations in the workplace?

There are two actions you must take if an employee is convicted of a drug violation in the workplace:

(a) First, you must notify Federal agencies if an employee who is engaged in the performance of an award informs you about a conviction, as required by § 630.205(c)(2), or you otherwise learn of the conviction. Your notification to the Federal agencies must—

(1) Be in writing;

(2) Include the employee's position title;

(3) Include the identification number(s) of each affected award;

(4) Be sent within ten calendar days after you learn of the conviction; and

(5) Be sent to every Federal agency on whose award the convicted employee was working. It must be sent to every awarding official or his or her official designee, unless the Federal agency has specified a central point for the receipt of the notices.

(b) Second, within 30 calendar days of learning about an employee's conviction, you must either—

(1) Take appropriate personnel action against the employee, up to and including termination, consistent with the requirements of the Rehabilitation Act of 1973 (29 U.S.C. 794), as amended; or

(2) Require the employee to participate satisfactorily in a drug abuse assistance or rehabilitation program approved for these purposes by a Federal, State or local health, law enforcement, or other appropriate agency.

§ 630.230 How and when must I identify workplaces?

(a) You must identify all known workplaces under each National Science Foundation award. A failure to do so is a violation of your drug-free workplace requirements. You may identify the workplaces—

(1) To the National Science Foundation official that is making the award, either at the time of application or upon award; or

(2) In documents that you keep on file in your offices during the performance of the award, in which case you must make the information available for inspection upon request by National Science Foundation officials or their designated representatives.

(b) Your workplace identification for an award must include the actual address of buildings (or parts of buildings) or other sites where work under the award takes place. Categorical descriptions may be used (e.g., all vehicles of a mass transit authority or State highway department while in operation, State employees in each local unemployment office, performers in concert halls or radio studios).

(c) If you identified workplaces to the National Science Foundation awarding official at the time of application or award, as described in paragraph (a)(1) of this section, and any workplace that you identified changes during the performance of the award, you must inform the National Science Foundation awarding official.

Subpart C—Requirements for Recipients Who Are Individuals

§ 630.300 What must I do to comply with this part if I am an individual recipient?

As a condition of receiving a(n) National Science Foundation award, if you are an individual recipient, you must agree that—

(a) You will not engage in the unlawful manufacture, distribution, dispensing, possession, or use of a controlled substance in conducting any activity related to the award; and

(b) If you are convicted of a criminal drug offense resulting from a violation occurring during the conduct of any award activity, you will report the conviction:

(1) In writing.
(2) Within 10 calendar days of the conviction.
(3) To the National Science Foundation awarding official or other designee for each award that you currently have, unless § 630.301 or the award document designates a central point for the receipt of the notices. When notice is made to a central point, it must include the identification number(s) of each affected award.

§ 630.301 [Reserved]

Subpart D—Responsibilities of National Science Foundation Awarding Officials

§ 630.400 What are my responsibilities as a(n) National Science Foundation awarding official?

As a(n) National Science Foundation awarding official, you must obtain each recipient's agreement, as a condition of the award, to comply with the requirements in—

(a) Subpart B of this part, if the recipient is not an individual; or
(b) Subpart C of this part, if the recipient is an individual.

Subpart E—Violations of This Part and Consequences

§ 630.500 How are violations of this part determined for recipients other than individuals?

A recipient other than an individual is in violation of the requirements of this part if the Director or designee determines, in writing, that—

(a) The recipient has violated the requirements of subpart B of this part; or
(b) The number of convictions of the recipient's employees for violating criminal drug statutes in the workplace is large enough to indicate that the recipient has failed to make a good faith effort to provide a drug-free workplace.

§ 630.505 How are violations of this part determined for recipients who are individuals?

An individual recipient is in violation of the requirements of this part if the Director or designee determines, in writing, that—

(a) The recipient has violated the requirements of subpart C of this part; or
(b) The recipient is convicted of a criminal drug offense resulting from a violation occurring during the conduct of any award activity.

§ 630.510 What actions will the Federal Government take against a recipient determined to have violated this part?

If a recipient is determined to have violated this part, as described in § 630.500 or § 630.505, the National Science Foundation may take one or more of the following actions—

(a) Suspension of payments under the award;
(b) Suspension or termination of the award; and
(c) Suspension or debarment of the recipient under 45 CFR part 620, for a period not to exceed five years.

§ 630.515 Are there any exceptions to those actions?

The Director, National Science Foundation may waive with respect to a particular award, in writing, a suspension of payments under an award, suspension or termination of an award, or suspension or debarment of a recipient if the Director, National Science Foundation determines that such a waiver would be in the public interest. This exception authority cannot be delegated to any other official.

Subpart F—Definitions

§ 630.605 Award.

Award means an award of financial assistance by the National Science Foundation or other Federal agency directly to a recipient.

(a) The term award includes:
(1) A Federal grant or cooperative agreement, in the form of money or property in lieu of money.
(2) A block grant or a grant in an entitlement program, whether or not the grant is exempted from coverage under

§ 630.610

the Governmentwide rule 45 CFR part 602 that implements OMB Circular A-102 (for availability, see 5 CFR 1310.3) and specifies uniform administrative requirements.

(b) The term award does not include:

(1) Technical assistance that provides services instead of money.

(2) Loans.

(3) Loan guarantees.

(4) Interest subsidies.

(5) Insurance.

(6) Direct appropriations.

(7) Veterans' benefits to individuals (*i.e.*, any benefit to veterans, their families, or survivors by virtue of the service of a veteran in the Armed Forces of the United States).

§ 630.610 Controlled substance.

Controlled substance means a controlled substance in schedules I through V of the Controlled Substances Act (21 U.S.C. 812), and as further defined by regulation at 21 CFR 1308.11 through 1308.15.

§ 630.615 Conviction.

Conviction means a finding of guilt (including a plea of nolo contendere) or imposition of sentence, or both, by any judicial body charged with the responsibility to determine violations of the Federal or State criminal drug statutes.

§ 630.620 Cooperative agreement.

Cooperative agreement means an award of financial assistance that, consistent with 31 U.S.C. 6305, is used to enter into the same kind of relationship as a grant (see definition of grant in § 630.650), except that substantial involvement is expected between the Federal agency and the recipient when carrying out the activity contemplated by the award. The term does not include cooperative research and development agreements as defined in 15 U.S.C. 3710a.

§ 630.625 Criminal drug statute.

Criminal drug statute means a Federal or non-Federal criminal statute involving the manufacture, distribution, dispensing, use, or possession of any controlled substance.

§ 630.630 Debarment.

Debarment means an action taken by a Federal agency to prohibit a recipient from participating in Federal Government procurement contracts and covered nonprocurement transactions. A recipient so prohibited is debarred, in accordance with the Federal Acquisition Regulation for procurement contracts (48 CFR part 9, subpart 9.4) and the common rule, Government-wide Debarment and Suspension (Nonprocurement), that implements Executive Order 12549 and Executive Order 12689.

§ 630.635 Drug-free workplace.

Drug-free workplace means a site for the performance of work done in connection with a specific award at which employees of the recipient are prohibited from engaging in the unlawful manufacture, distribution, dispensing, possession, or use of a controlled substance.

§ 630.640 Employee.

(a) *Employee* means the employee of a recipient directly engaged in the performance of work under the award, including—

(1) All direct charge employees;

(2) All indirect charge employees, unless their impact or involvement in the performance of work under the award is insignificant to the performance of the award; and

(3) Temporary personnel and consultants who are directly engaged in the performance of work under the award and who are on the recipient's payroll.

(b) This definition does not include workers not on the payroll of the recipient (*e.g.*, volunteers, even if used to meet a matching requirement; consultants or independent contractors not on the payroll; or employees of subrecipients or subcontractors in covered workplaces).

§ 630.645 Federal agency or agency.

Federal agency or agency means any United States executive department, military department, government corporation, government controlled corporation, any other establishment in

§ 630.650 Grant.

Grant means an award of financial assistance that, consistent with 31 U.S.C. 6304, is used to enter into a relationship—

(a) The principal purpose of which is to transfer a thing of value to the recipient to carry out a public purpose of support or stimulation authorized by a law of the United States, rather than to acquire property or services for the Federal Government's direct benefit or use; and

(b) In which substantial involvement is not expected between the Federal agency and the recipient when carrying out the activity contemplated by the award.

§ 630.655 Individual.

Individual means a natural person.

§ 630.660 Recipient.

Recipient means any individual, corporation, partnership, association, unit of government (except a Federal agency) or legal entity, however organized, that receives an award directly from a Federal agency.

§ 630.665 State.

State means any of the States of the United States, the District of Columbia, the Commonwealth of Puerto Rico, or any territory or possession of the United States.

§ 630.670 Suspension.

Suspension means an action taken by a Federal agency that immediately prohibits a recipient from participating in Federal Government procurement contracts and covered nonprocurement transactions for a temporary period, pending completion of an investigation and any judicial or administrative proceedings that may ensue. A recipient so prohibited is suspended, in accordance with the Federal Acquisition Regulation for procurement contracts (48 CFR part 9, subpart 9.4) and the common rule, Government-wide Debarment and Suspension (Nonprocurement), that implements Executive Order 12549 and Executive Order 12689. Suspension of a recipient is a distinct and separate action from suspension of an award or suspension of payments under an award.

PART 640—COMPLIANCE WITH THE NATIONAL ENVIRONMENTAL POLICY ACT

Sec.
640.1 Purpose.
640.2 Committee on Environmental Matters.
640.3 Actions requiring an environmental assessment and categorical exclusions.
640.4 Responsibilities and procedures for preparation of an environmental assessment.
640.5 Responsibilities and procedures for preparation of an environmental impact statement.

AUTHORITY: NEPA; the Environmental Quality Improvement Act of 1970, as amended (42 U.S.C. 4371 *et seq.*); sec. 309 of the Clean Air Act, as amended (42 U.S.C. 7609); E.O. 11514, "Protection and Enhancement of Environmental Quality" (March 5, 1970, as amended by E.O. 11991, May 24, 1977); and CEQ regulations at 40 CFR Parts 1500 through 1508.

SOURCE: 45 FR 40, Jan. 2, 1980, unless otherwise noted.

§ 640.1 Purpose.

The purpose of this regulation is to adopt NSF procedures to supplement regulations at 40 CFR parts 1500 through 1508 (hereafter referred to as "CEQ regulations").

§ 640.2 Committee on Environmental Matters.

(a) There is established an NSF Committee on Environmental Matters (hereafter referred to as the Committee) to consist of one representative from each directorate. The General Counsel, or his or her designee, shall serve as Chairman. At the discretion of the Chairman and with the concurrence of the Committee, additional members may be appointed.

(b) All incoming correspondence from CEQ and other agencies concerning matters related to NEPA, including draft and final environmental impact statements, shall be brought to the attention of the Chairman. The Chairman will prepare or, at his or her discretion, coordinate replies to such correspondence.

(c) The Committee shall meet regularly to discuss NSF policies and practices regarding NEPA, and make recommendations on the need for or adequacy of environmental impact assessments or statements.

(d) With respect to actions of NSF, the Committee will:

(1) Maintain a list of actions for which environmental impact statements are being prepared.

(2) Revise this list at regular intervals, based on input from the directorates, and send revisions to CEQ.

(3) Make the list available for public inspection on request.

(4) Maintain a list of environmental impact assessments.

(5) Maintain a file of draft and final environmental impact statements.

(e) The Committee and/or the Chairman will perform such additional functions as are set forth elsewhere in this part and in other NSF issuances.

[45 FR 40, Jan. 2, 1980, as amended at 49 FR 37596, Sept. 25, 1984; 59 FR 37438, July 22, 1994]

§ 640.3 Actions requiring an environmental assessment and categorical exclusions.

(a) The types of actions to be classified as "major Federal actions" subject to NEPA procedures are discussed generally in the CEQ regulations. Paragraph (b) of this section describes various classes of NSF actions that normally require the preparation of an environmental assessment or an EIS, and those classes that are categorically excluded. (Categorical exclusion is defined at 40 CFR 1508.4.) The word "normally" is stressed; there may be individual cases in which specific factors require contrary action. NSF directorates and offices are responsible for identifying situations in which an environmental assessment or an EIS should be prepared even if not normally required by paragraph (b) of this paragraph.

(b) Most NSF awards support individual scientific research projects and are not "major Federal actions significantly affecting the quality of the human environment" except in the sense that the long term effect of the accumulation of human knowledge is likely to affect the quality of the human environment. However, such long term effects are basically speculative and unknowable in advance; thus they normally do not provide a sufficient basis for classifying research as subject to NEPA (See 40 CFR 1508.8) and are categorically excluded from an environmental assessment. Nevertheless, in some cases the actual procedures used in carrying out the research may have potential environmental effects, particularly where the project requires construction of facilities or major disturbance of the local environment brought about by blasting, drilling, excavating, or other means. Accordingly, except as provided in paragraph (c) of this section, the following types of activities require at least an environmental assessment:

(1) Cases where developmental efforts are supported, if the project supports the transition of a particular technology from the development stage to large-scale commercial utilization.

(2) Any project supporting construction, other than interior remodelling.

(3) Cases where field work affecting the natural environment will be conducted.

(4) Any project that will involve drilling of the earth, excavation, explosives, weather modification, or other techniques that may alter a local environment.

(5) Any project that provides for the testing and release of biological-control agents for purposes of ecosystem manipulation and assessment of short- and long-term effects of major ecosystem perturbation.

(c) Directorates having divisions or programs with a substantial number of projects that fall within categories (3), (4), and (5) in (b) of this section, are authorized to issue supplemental guidelines to Division Directors and Program Officers establishing subcategories of research methodologies or techniques for which environmental assessments need not be prepared. For example, if a program regularly supports research that involves noninvasive techniques or nonharmful invasive techniques (such as taking water or soil samples, or collecting non-protected species of flora and fauna) the directorate may determine that field projects otherwise coming under paragraph (b)(3) of this section

National Science Foundation § 640.5

which involve only the use of such techniques do not require an environmental assessment. However, any such guidelines must be submitted to the Chairman for approval.

(d) In some cases within the categories listed in paragraph (b) of this section, it will be evident at the outset or after the assessment process is begun that an EIS should be prepared. In such cases an assessment need not be completed, but the process of preparing an EIS (See § 640.5, of this part) should be started.

§ 640.4 Responsibilities and procedures for preparation of an environmental assessment.

(a) Program Officers, as the first point of decision in the review process, shall determine into which category incoming proposals fall, according to the criteria set forth in § 640.3 of this part. Notwithstanding this responsibility of the Program Officer, the appropriate Division Director, Assistant Director, and other reviewing policy officials must assure that adequate analysis is being made.

(b) Where appropriate, programs, divisions, or directorates will advise prospective applicants in program announcements, requests for proposals, and other NSF-prepared brochures of the requirement to furnish information regarding any environmental impact that the applicant's proposed study may have.

(c) Should an environmental assessment be required, the directorate supporting the activity shall be responsible for its preparation. The grant or contract applicant may be asked to submit additional information in order that a reasonable and accurate assessment may be made. Though no specific format for an environmental assessment is prescribed, it shall be a separate document suitable for public review and shall serve the purpose described in 40 CFR 1508.9, which is quoted in full as follows:

Section 1508.9 Environmental Assessment

"Environmental Assessment":
(a) Means a concise public document for which a Federal agency is responsible that serves to:
(1) Briefly provide sufficient evidence and analysis for determining whether to prepare an environmental impact statement or a finding of no significant impact.
(2) Aid an agency's compliance with the Act when no environmental impact statement is necessary.
(3) Facilitate preparation of a statement when one is necessary.
(b) Shall include brief discussions of the need for the proposal, of alternatives as required by section 102(2)(E), of the environmental impacts of the proposed action and alternatives, and a listing of agencies and persons consulted.

(d) A copy of the assessment or drafts shall accompany the appropriate proposal throughout the NSF internal review and approval process. At the option of the directorate preparing the assessment, a draft may be submitted to the Committee for its review and comments. Prior to an award decision, one copy of all completed assessments shall be sent to the Chairman for review and updating of the Committee listing of assessments.

(e) If, on the basis of an environmental assessment, it is determined that an EIS is not required, a Finding of No Significant Impact (FNSI) as described in 40 CFR 1508.13 will be prepared. The FNSI shall include the environmental assessment or a summary of it and be available to the public from the Committee. If the proposed action is one that normally requires an EIS, is closely similar to an action normally requiring an EIS, or is without precedent, the FNSI shall be made available for a 30 day public review period before any action is taken.

§ 640.5 Responsibilities and procedures for preparation of an environmental impact statement.

(a) If initially or after an environmental assessment has been completed, it is determined that an environmental impact statement should be prepared, it and other related documentation will be prepared by the directorate responsible for the action in accordance with section 102(2)(c) of the Act, this part, and the CEQ regulations. The responsible directorate will be in close communication with the grant or contract applicant and may have to rely extensively on his or her input in preparing the EIS. However, once a document is prepared it shall be submitted to the Chairman who, after such review by the Committee as is deemed necessary by the Chairman, shall transmit the document as required by CEQ regulations and this part. If the Chairman considers a document unsatisfactory, he or she shall return it to the responsible directorate for revision prior to an award decision.

Specifically, the following steps, as discussed in the CEQ regulations, will be followed in preparing an EIS:

(1) A notice of intent to prepare a draft EIS will be published as described in 40 CFR 1501.7.

(2) Scoping, as described in 40 CFR 1501.7, will be conducted.

(3) The format and contents of the draft and final EIS shall be as discussed in 40 CFR part 1502.

(4) Comments on the draft EIS shall be invited as set forth in 40 CFR 1503.1. The minimum period to be afforded for comments on a draft EIS shall be 45 days, unless a lesser period is necessary to comply with other specific statutory requirements or in case of emergency circumstances, as described in 40 CFR 1506.11.

(5) The requirements of 40 CFR 1506.9 for filing of documents with the Environmental Protection Agency shall be followed.

(6) The responsible directorate shall examine carefully the basis on which supportive studies have been conducted to assure that such studies are objective and comprehensive in scope and in depth.

(7) The Act requires that the decisionmaking involved "utilize a systematic, interdisciplinary approach that will insure the integrated use of the natural and social sciences and the environmental design arts." If such disciplines are not present on the NSF staff, appropriate use should be made of personnel of Federal, State, and local agencies, universities, non-profit organizations, or private industry.

(8) A copy of the draft EIS or the final EIS (or a summary, if the size of the EIS does not make this practical) shall be included in and accompany the appropriate proposal throughout the NSF internal review and approval process.

(b)(1) 40 CFR 1506.1 describes the types of actions that should not be taken during the NEPA process. Such actions shall be avoided by NSF personnel during the process of preparation of an EIS and for a period of thirty days after the final EIS is filed with EPA, unless such actions are necessary to comply with other specific statutory requirements.

(2) 40 CFR 1506.10 also places certain limitations on the timing of agency decisions on taking "major Federal actions". In some cases the actual "decision point" may be more clear-cut than others. If the "action" that necessitated the preparation of an EIS is one that would be carried out under grant, contract, or cooperative agreement, then the award shall not be made before the times set forth in 40 CFR 1506.10, unless such action is necessary to comply with other specific statutory requirements, or as exceptions are needed as provided in 40 CFR 1506.10, 1506.11, or 1507.3. However, an award for preliminary planning proposals may be made before such times if it is so structured as to require further NSF approvals for funding the actual actions that might adversely affect the quality of the human environment. In such cases, the subsequent approvals for funding these actions will be considered the "decision". This is consistent with the requirement that environmental considerations undergo concurrent review with all other project planning considerations.

(c) In appropriate cases, if the action involves other agencies, the Chairman may agree to designate another agency as "lead agency" and to cooperate as discussed in 40 CFR 1501.5 and 1501.6. In such cases, the Chairman has authority to alter the procedures described in (a) to the extent they are inconsistent with functions assigned to NSF under the "cooperating agency" arrangements.

(d) A public record of decision stating what the decision was; identifying alternatives that were considered, including the environmentally preferable one(s); discussing any national policy considerations that entered into the decision; and summarizing a monitoring and enforcement program if applicable for mitigation, will be prepared. This record of decision will be prepared at the time the decision is

National Science Foundation

§ 641.14

made, or if appropriate, when the agency makes its recommendation for action to Congress. (See 40 CFR 1505.2.)

PART 641—ENVIRONMENTAL ASSESSMENT PROCEDURES FOR PROPOSED NATIONAL SCIENCE FOUNDATION ACTIONS IN ANTARCTICA

Sec.
641.10 Purpose.
641.11 Policy.
641.12 Applicability.
641.13 Right of action.
641.14 Definitions.
641.15 Preliminary environmental review.
641.16 Preparation of environmental documents, generally.
641.17 Initial environmental evaluation.
641.18 Comprehensive environmental evaluation.
641.19 Modification of environmental documents.
641.20 Notification of the availability of environmental documents and other information.
641.21 Monitoring.
641.22 Cases of emergency.

AUTHORITY: E.O. 12114, 44 FR 1957, 3 CFR 1979 Comp., p. 356.

SOURCE: 57 FR 40339, Sept. 3, 1992, unless otherwise noted.

§ 641.10 Purpose.

These procedures are designed to elicit and evaluate information that will inform the National Science Foundation (NSF) of the potential environmental consequences of proposed U.S. Antarctic Program (USAP) actions, so that relevant environmental considerations are taken into account by decisionmakers before reaching final decisions on whether or how to proceed with proposed actions. These procedures are consistent with and implement the requirements of:

(a) Executive Order 12114 as it relates to NSF's Antarctic activities, and

(b) the environmental assessment provisions of the Protocol on Environmental Protection to the Antarctic Treaty.

§ 641.11 Policy.

It is the policy of NSF to use all practicable means, consistent with its authority, to ensure that potential environmental effects of actions undertaken by NSF in Antarctica, either independently or in cooperation with another country, are appropriately identified and considered during the decisionmaking process, and that appropriate environmental safeguards which would limit, mitigate or prevent adverse impacts on the Antarctic environment are identified.

§ 641.12 Applicability.

The requirements set forth in this part apply to all proposed projects, programs and actions authorized or approved by, or subject to the control and responsibility of NSF that may have an impact on the Antarctic environment.

§ 641.13 Right of action

The procedures set forth in this part establish internal procedures to be followed by NSF in considering the potential environmental effects of actions taken in Antarctica. Nothing in this part shall be construed to create a cause of action.

§ 641.14 Definitions.

As used in these procedures, the term:

(a) *Action* means a project, program or other activity, including the adoption of an official policy or formal plan, that is undertaken, authorized, adopted or approved by, or subject to the control or responsibility of NSF, the decommissioning of a physical plant or facility, and any change in the scope or intensity of a project, program or action.

(b) *Antarctica* means the area south of 60 degrees south latitude.

(c) *Antarctic environment* means the natural and physical environment of Antarctica and its dependent and associated ecosystems, but excludes social, economic and other environments.

(d) *Antarctic Treaty Consultative Meeting* means a meeting of the Parties to the Antarctic Treaty, held pursuant to Article IX(1) of the Treaty.

(e) *Comprehensive Environmental Evaluation* or *CEE* means a study of the reasonably foreseeable potential effects of a proposed action on the antarctic environment, prepared in accordance with the provisions of § 641.18, and includes all comments thereon received during the comment period described

147

§ 641.15

in § 641.18(c). A Comprehensive Environmental Evaluation shall constitute an environmental impact statement for purposes of the Executive Order.

(f) *Environmental Action Memorandum* means a document briefly describing a proposed action and its potential impacts, if any, on the antarctic environment prepared by the responsible official when he or she determines that a proposed action will have less than a minor or transitory impact on the Antarctic environment.

(g) *Environmental document* means an initial environmental evaluation or a comprehensive environmental evaluation.

(h) *Environmental review* means the environmental review required by the provisions of this part, and includes preliminary environmental review and preparation of an environmental document, and review by the parties to the Protocol, and committees established under the Protocol for that purpose, and the public, as applicable.

(i) *Executive Order* means Executive Order 12114, Environmental Effects Abroad of Major Federal Actions, 44 FR 1957.

(j) *Initial Environmental Evaluation* or *IEE* means a study of the reasonably foreseeable potential effects of a proposed action on the antarctic environment, prepared in accordance with the provisions of § 641.17.

(k) *Preliminary environmental review* means the environmental review described in § 641.15(a).

(l) *Protocol* means the Protocol on Environmental Protection to the Antarctic Treaty, adopted on October 4, 1991, in Madrid, at the fourth session of the Eleventh Special Antarctic Treaty Consultative Meeting and signed by the United States on that date, and all annexes thereto.

(m) *Responsible official* means the Director of the Office of Polar Programs, or any NSF employee(s) designated by the Director to be principally responsible for the preparation of environmental action memoranda or environmental documents under this part.

(n) *Treaty* means the Antarctic Treaty signed in Washington, D.C., on December 1, 1959, T.I.A.S No. 4780.

[57 FR 40339, Sept. 3, 1992, as amended at 59 FR 37438, July 22, 1994]

§ 641.15 Preliminary environmental review.

(a) The responsible official shall be notified early in the general planning process of actions proposed by USAP components that may have impacts on the Antarctic environment, so that environmental review may be integrated into the planning and decisionmaking processes. The responsible official shall conduct a preliminary environmental review of each action, including consideration of the potential direct and reasonably foreseeable indirect effects of a proposed action on the Antarctic environment.

(b) If, on the basis of the preliminary environmental review, the responsible official determines that an action will have less than a minor or transitory impact on the Antarctic environment, he will prepare an Environmental Action Memorandum briefly summarizing the environmental issues considered and conclusions drawn from the review. No further environmental review shall be necessary.

§ 641.16 Preparation of environmental documents, generally.

(a) *Preparation of an environmental document.* If the responsible official determines, either initially or on the basis of a preliminary environmental review, that a proposed action may have at least a minor or transitory impact on the Antarctic environment, he will prepare an environmental document in accordance with the provisions of this part. In making this determination, the responsible official should consider whether and to what degree the proposed action:

(1) Has the potential to adversely affect the Antarctic environment;

(2) May adversely affect climate and weather patterns;

(3) May adversely affect air or water quality;

(4) May affect atmospheric, terrestrial (including aquatic), glacial or marine environments;

(5) May detrimentally affect the distribution, abundance or productivity or species, or populations of species of fauna and flora;

(6) May further jeopardize endangered or threatened species or populations of such species;

(7) May degrade, or pose substantial risk to, areas of biological, scientific, historic, aesthetic or wilderness significance;

(8) Has highly uncertain environmental effects, or involves unique or unknown environmental risks; or

(9) Together with other actions, the effects of any one of which is individually insignificant, may have at least minor or transitory cumulative environmental effects.

(b) *Prior assessments.* Notwithstanding the provisions of § 641.16(a), if (1) An environmental document (including a generic or programmatic CEE) or its equivalent has been prepared for a particular type of action; (2) That document includes an analysis of potential environmental effects that are directly relevant to the potential effects of the proposed action, taking in account factors such as the similarity of the actions and of the locations within which they take place; and (3) There are no potential site specific or other impacts that would require further evaluation, then a new environmental document need not be prepared. Instead, the responsible official shall prepare an Environmental Action Memorandum for the proposed action, cross-referencing the previously prepared environmental document.

(c) *Exclusions.* NSF has determined that the following actions will have less than a minor or transitory impact on the Antarctic environment, and are not subject to the procedures set forth in this part, except to the extent provided herein:

(1) Scientific research activities involving:

(i) Low volume collection of biological or geologic specimens, provided no more mammals or birds are taken than can normally be replaced by natural reproduction in the following season;

(ii) Small-scale detonation of explosives in connection with seismic research conducted in the continental interior or Antarctica where there will be no potential for impact on native flora and fauna;

(iii) Use of weather/research balloons, research rockets, and automatic weather stations that are to be retrieved; and

(iv) Use of radioisotopes, provided such use complies with applicable laws and regulations, and with NSF procedures for handling and disposing of radioisotopes.

(2) Interior remodelling and renovation of existing facilities.

Notwithstanding the foregoing, if information developed during the planning of any of the actions described in this paragraph (c) indicates the possibility that the action may have at least a minor or transitory impact on the Antarctic environment, the environmental effects of the action shall be reviewed to determine the need for the preparation of an environmental document.

(d) *Coordination with other committees, offices and federal agencies.* The responsible official shall notify NSF's Committee of Environmental Matters when he intends to prepare an environmental document, and will coordinate preparation of the document with those entities. Responsibility for preparation of the environmental document rests primarily with the responsible official, but, as soon as is feasible, he should consult with and encourage the participation of other knowledgeable individuals within NSF, and, where appropriate, with other individuals, government agencies and entities with relevant knowledge and expertise.

(e) *Type of environmental document.* The type of environmental document required under this part depends on the nature of the proposed action under consideration. An IEE must be prepared for proposed actions which the responsible official concludes may have at least a minor or transitory impact on the Antarctic environment and for which a CEE is not prepared. A CEE must be prepared if an IEE indicates, or if it is otherwise determined, that a proposed action is likely to have more than a minor or transitory impact on the Antarctic environment.

(f) *Obligation of funds.* Because of logistic constraints (*i.e.,* constraints due to transportation difficulties, inaccessibility of Antarctic bases for much of the year, and the need to obtain items or materials requiring long lead times), it may not be possible to complete the environmental review of a proposed action before funds must be committed and/or disbursed. In such cases, funds for the proposed action may be committed and/or disbursed, provided:

(1) The appropriate environmental review is completed before implementation of the proposed action in Antarctica, and

(2) Implementation plans for the proposed action will be modified or canceled, if appropriate, in light of the completed environmental review (including public comments, if applicable).

[57 FR 40339, Sept. 3, 1992, as amended at 59 FR 37438, July 22, 1994]

§ 641.17 Initial environmental evaluation.

(a) *Contents.* An IEE shall contain sufficient detail to assess whether a proposed action may have more than a minor or transitory impact on the Antarctic environment, and shall include the following information:

(1) A description of the proposed action, including its purpose, location, duration and intensity; and

(2) Consideration of alternatives to the proposed action and any impacts that the proposed action may have on the Antarctic environment, including cumulative impacts in light of existing and known planned actions and existing information on such actions.

(b) *Further environmental review.* If an IEE indicates that a proposed action is likely to have no more than a minor or transitory impact on the Antarctic environment, no further environmental review of the action is necessary provided that appropriate procedures, which may include monitoring, are put in place to assess and verify the impact of the action.

(c) *Availability to public.* An annual list of IEEs and a description of any decisions taken in consequence thereof shall be provided to the Department of State for circulation to all Parties to the Protocol and to organizations or committees established pursuant to the Protocol or the Treaty, as required. The Environmental Officer, Division of Polar Programs, shall also make the list and copies of final IEEs available to the public upon request.

§ 641.18 Comprehensive environmental evaluation.

(a) *Scoping.* If it is determined that a CEE will be prepared, the responsible official shall publish a notice of intent to prepare a CEE in the FEDERAL REGISTER, inviting interested persons and government agencies to participate in the process of identifying significant issues relating to the proposed action and determining the scope of the issues to be addressed in the CEE.

(b) *Contents of CEE.* A CEE shall be a concise and analytical document, prepared in accordance with the range of relevant issues identified in the scoping process. It shall contain sufficient information to permit informed consideration of the reasonably foreseeable potential environmental effects of a proposed action and possible alternatives to that proposed action. Such information shall include the following:

(1) A description of the proposed action including its purpose, location, duration and intensity;

(2) A description of the initial baseline environmental state with which predicted changes are to be compared, and a prediction of the future environmental state in the absence of the proposed action;

(3) A description of the methods and data used to forecast the potential impacts of the proposed action;

(4) An estimate of the nature, extent, duration and intensity of the likely direct potential impacts of the proposed action;

(5) A consideration of the potential indirect or second order impacts from the proposed action;

(6) A consideration of potential cumulative impacts of the proposed action in light of existing activities and other known planned actions and available information on those actions;

(7) A description of possible alternatives to the proposed action, including the alternative of not proceeding, and the potential consequences of those alternatives, in sufficient detail to allow a clear basis for choice among the alternatives and the proposed action;

(8) Identification of measures, including monitoring, that could be employed

to minimize, mitigate or prevent potential impacts of the proposed action, detect unforeseen impacts, provide early warning of any adverse effects, and carry out prompt and effective response to accidents;

(9) Identification of unavoidable potential impacts of the proposed action;

(10) Consideration of the potential effects of the proposed action on the conduct of scientific research and on other existing uses and values;

(11) Identification of gaps in knowledge and uncertainties encountered in compiling the information required by this paragraph (b);

(12) A non-technical summary of the information included in the CEE; and

(13) The name and address of the person and/or organization which prepared the CEE, and the address to which comments thereon should be directed.

(c) *Circulation of draft CEE.* A draft of each CEE shall be provided to the Department of State for circulation to all Parties to the Protocol and to organizations or committees established pursuant to the Protocol or Treaty, as required by the Protocol, and shall be made publicly available. Notice of such public availability shall be published in the FEDERAL REGISTER. All such parties shall have a period of not less than ninety (90) days within which to review and comment upon the draft CEE.

(d) *Final CEE.* A final CEE shall address, and shall include or summarize, comments received on the draft CEE. The final CEE, notice of any decisions related thereto, and any evaluation of the significance of the predicted impacts in relation to the advantages of the proposed action shall be provided to the Department of State for circulation to all Parties to the Protocol, and shall be available to the public upon request, at least sixty (60) days prior to the commencement of the proposed activity in Antarctica. Notice of such public availability shall be published in the FEDERAL REGISTER.

(e) *Implementation of proposed action.* No final decision shall be taken to proceed in Antarctica with an action for which a final CEE is required until after the earlier of:

(1) The first Antarctic Treaty Consultative Meeting taking place at least one hundred and twenty days after circulation of the draft CEE, or

(2) Fifteen months following the circulation of the draft CEE.

§ 641.19 Modification of environmental documents.

The responsible official should revise or supplement an environmental document if there is a change in a proposed action that may have more than a minor or transitory effect on the antarctic environment, or if there are new circumstances or information that indicate the action may have impacts not anticipated in the original environmental document.

§ 641.20 Notification of the availability of environmental documents and other information.

The Environmental Officer, Office of Polar Programs, shall make Environmental Action Memoranda, environmental documents and final data obtained under § 641.21, available to the public upon request. However, notice of such availability need not be given, except as specifically provided in this part.

[57 FR 40339, Sept. 3, 1992, as amended at 59 FR 37438, July 22, 1994]

§ 641.21 Monitoring.

Scientific, analytic and/or reporting procedures shall be put in place, including appropriate monitoring of key environmental indicators, to assess and verify the potential environmental impacts of actions which are the subject of a CEE. All proposed actions for which an environmental document has been prepared shall include procedures designed to provide a regular and verifiable record of the actual impacts of those actions, in order, *inter alia,* to

(a) Enable assessments to be made of the extent to which such impacts are consistent with the Protocol; and

(b) Provide information useful for minimizing or mitigating those impacts, and, where appropriate, information on the need for suspension, cancellation or modification of the action.

§ 641.22 Cases of emergency.

This part shall not apply to actions taken in cases of emergency relating to the safety of human life or of ships, aircraft or equipment and facilities of high value, or the protection of the environment which require an action to be taken without completion of the environmental review required by this part. Notice of any such actions which would otherwise have required the preparation of a CEE shall be provided immediately to the Department of State for circulation to all Parties to the Protocol and to committees and organizations established pursuant to the Treaty or Protocol, as required. A description of the emergency action undertaken shall also be provided to the Department of State for appropriate circulation within ninety days of the action.

PART 650—PATENTS

Sec.
650.1 Scope of part.
650.2 National Science Foundation patent policy.
650.3 Source of authority.
650.4 Standard patent rights clause.
650.5 Special patent provisions.
650.6 Awards not primarily for research.
650.7 Awards affected by international agreements.
650.8 Retention of rights by inventor.
650.9 Unwanted inventions.
650.10 Inventions also supported by another Federal agency.
650.11 Utilization reports.
650.12 Waivers and approvals.
650.13 Exercise of march-in rights.
650.14 Request for conveyance of title to NSF.
650.15 Appeals.
650.16 Background rights.
650.17 Subcontracts.
650.18 Delegation of authority.
650.19 Electronic invention handling.
APPENDIX A TO PART 650—OPTIONAL FORMAT FOR CONFIRMATORY LICENSE

AUTHORITY: 35 U.S.C. 200–212, 42 U.S.C. 1870(e) and 1871; and the Presidential Memorandum entitled "Government Patent Policy", issued February 18, 1983.

SOURCE: 57 FR 18053, Apr. 28, 1992, unless otherwise noted.

§ 650.1 Scope of part.

This part contains the policies, procedures, and clauses that govern allocation of rights to inventions made in performance of NSF-assisted research. It applies to all current and future funding agreements entered into by the Foundation that relate to performance of scientific or engineering research. As stated in the NSF Acquisition Regulation (chapter 25 of title 48 of the Code of Federal Regulations), this part applies to contracts as well as to grants and cooperative agreements.

§ 650.2 National Science Foundation patent policy.

As authorized by the National Science Board at its 230th meeting, October 15–16, 1981, the Director of the National Science Foundation has adopted the following statement of NSF patent policy.

(a) In accordance with the Bayh-Dole Act and the Presidential Memorandum entitled "Government Patent Policy" issued February 18, 1983, the Foundation will use the Patent Rights clause prescribed by the Department of Commerce in all its funding agreements for the performance of experimental, developmental, or research work, including awards made to foreign entities, unless the Foundation determines that some other provision would better serve the purposes of that Act or the interests of the United States and the general public.

(b) In funding agreements covered by a treaty or agreement that provides that an international organization or foreign government, research institute, or inventor will own or share patent rights, the Foundation will acquire such patent rights as are necessary to comply with the applicable treaty or agreement.

(c) If an awardee elects not to retain rights to an invention, the Foundation will allow the inventor to retain the principal patent rights unless the awardee, or the inventor's employer if other than the awardee, shows that it would be harmed by that action.

(d) The Foundation will normally allow any patent rights not wanted by the awardee or inventor to be dedicated to the public through publication in scientific journals or as a statutory invention registration. However, if another Federal agency is known to be interested in the relevant technology, the Foundation may give it an opportunity to review and patent the invention so long as that does not inhibit

National Science Foundation § 650.4

the dissemination of the research results to the scientific community.

§ 650.3 Source of authority.

(a) 35 U.S.C. 200–212, commonly called the Bayh-Dole Act, as amended by title V of Public Law 98–620 (98 stat. 3335, 3364). That law controls the allocation of rights to inventions made by employees of small business firms and domestic nonprofit organizations, including universities, during federally-supported experimentation, research, or development. Government-wide implementing regulations are contained in part 401 of title 37 of the Code of Federal Regulations.

(b) Section 11(e) of the National Science Foundation Act of 1950, as amended, (42 U.S.C. 1870(e)) provides that the Foundation shall have the authority to do all things necessary to carry out the provisions of this Act, including, but without being limited thereto, the authority—to acquire by purchase, lease, loan, gift, or condemnation, and to hold and dispose of by grant, sale, lease, or loan, real and personal property of all kinds necessary for, or resulting from, the exercise of authority granted by this Act.

(c) Section 12 of the NSF Act (42 U.S.C. 1871) provides that each contract or other arrangement executed pursuant to this Act which relates to scientific research shall contain provisions governing the disposition of inventions produced thereunder in a manner calculated to protect the public interest and the equities of the individual or organization with which the contract or other arrangement is executed.

(d) The Presidential Memorandum entitled "Government Patent Policy" issued February 18, 1983, directs Federal agencies, to the extent permitted by law, to apply to all research performers the policies of the Bayh-Dole Act. Under the provisions of the National Science Foundation Act quoted above, the Foundation is permitted to apply the Bayh-Dole policies without restriction.

§ 650.4 Standard patent rights clause.

(a) The following Patent Rights clause will be used in every funding agreement awarded by the Foundation that relates to scientific or engineering research unless a special patent clause has been negotiated (see § 650.5).

PATENT RIGHTS (AUGUST, 2005)

(a) *Definitions*—(1) *Invention* means any invention or discovery which is or may be patentable or otherwise protectable under title 35 of the United States Code, to any novel variety of plant which is or may be protected under the Plant Variety Protection Act (7 U.S.C. 2321 et seq.).

(2) *Subject invention* means any invention of the grantee conceived or first actually reduced to practice in the performance of work under this grant, provided that in the case of a variety of plant, the date of determination (as defined in section 41(d) of the Plant Variety Protection Act (7 U.S.C. 2401(d)) must also occur during the period of grant performance.

(3) *Practical application* means to manufacture in the case of a composition or product, to practice in the case of a process or method, or to operate in the case of a machine or system; and, in each case, under such conditions as to establish that the invention is being utilized and that its benefits are to the extent permitted by law or Government regulations available to the public on reasonable terms.

(4) *Made* when used in relation to any invention means the conception or first actual reduction to practice of such invention.

(5) *Small business firm* means a domestic small business concern as defined at section 2 of Public Law 85–536 (15 U.S.C. 632) and implementing regulations of the Administrator of the Small Business Administration. For the purpose of this Patents Rights clause, the size standard for small business concerns involved in Government procurement and subcontracting at 13 CFR 121.3–8 and 13 CFR 121.3–12, respectively, will be used.

(6) *Nonprofit organization* means a domestic university or other institution of higher education or an organization of the type described in section 501(c)(3) of the Internal Revenue Code of 1954 (26 U.S.C. 501(c)) and exempt from taxation under section 501(a) of the Internal Revenue Code (26 U.S.C. 501(a)) or any domestic nonprofit scientific or educational organization qualified under a State nonprofit organization statute.

(b) *Allocation of Principal Rights.* The grantee may retain the entire right, title, and interest throughout the world to each subject invention subject to the provisions of this Patents Rights clause and 35 U.S.C. 203. With respect to any subject invention in which the grantee retains title, the Federal Government shall have a nonexclusive, nontransferable, irrevocable, paid-up license to practice or have practiced for or on behalf of the United States the subject invention throughout the world. If the award indicates it is

§ 650.4

subject to an identified international agreement or treaty, the National Science Foundation (NSF) also has the right to direct the grantee to convey to any foreign participant such patent rights to subject inventions as are required to comply with that agreement or treaty.

(c) *Invention Disclosure, Election of Title and Filing of Patent Applications by Grantee.* (1) The grantee will disclose each subject invention to NSF within two months after the inventor discloses it in writing to grantee personnel responsible for the administration of patent matters. The disclosure to NSF will be submitted via the iEdison Invention Information Management System maintained by the National Institutes of Health and shall identify the grant under which the invention was made and the inventor(s). It shall be sufficiently complete in technical detail to convey a clear understanding of the nature, purpose, operation, and, to the extent known, the physical, chemical, biological or electrical characteristics of the invention. The disclosure shall also identify any publication, on sale or public use of the invention and whether a manuscript describing the invention has been submitted for publication and, if so, whether it has been accepted for publication at the time of disclosure. In addition, after disclosure to NSF, the grantee will promptly notify NSF of the acceptance of any manuscript describing the invention for publication or of any on sale or public use planned by the grantee.

(2) The grantee will elect in writing whether or not to retain title to any such invention by notifying NSF within two years of disclosure to NSF. However, in any case where publication, on sale, or public use has initiated the one year statutory period wherein valid patent protection can still be obtained in the United States, the period for election of title may be shortened by NSF to a date that is no more than 60 days prior to the end of the statutory period.

(3) The grantee will file its initial patent application on an invention to which it elects to retain title within one year after election of title or, if earlier, prior to the end of any statutory period wherein valid patent protection can be obtained in the United States after a publication, on sale, or public use. The grantee will file patent applications in additional countries or international patent offices within either ten months of the corresponding initial patent application, or six months from the date when permission is granted by the Commissioner of Patents and Trademarks to file foreign patent applications when such filing has been prohibited by a Secrecy Order.

(4) Requests for extension of the time for disclosure to NSF, election, and filing under subparagraphs (c) (1), (2), and (3) of this clause may, at the discretion of NSF, be granted.

(d) *Conditions When the Government May Obtain Title.* The grantee will convey to NSF, upon written request, title to any subject invention:

(1) If the grantee fails to disclose or elect the subject invention within the times specified in paragraph (c) above, or elects not to retain title; provided that NSF may only request title within 60 days after learning of the failure of the grantee to disclose or elect within the specified times.

(2) In those countries in which the grantee fails to file patent applications within the times specified in paragraph (c) above; provided, however, that if the grantee has filed a patent application in a country after the times specified in paragraph (c) above, but prior to its receipt of the written request of NSF, the grantee shall continue to retain title in that country.

(3) In any country in which the grantee decides not to continue the prosecution of any application for, to pay the maintenance fees on, or defend in a reexamination or opposition proceeding on, a patent on a subject invention.

(e) *Minimum Rights to Grantee.* (1) The grantee will retain a nonexclusive royalty-free license throughout the world in each subject invention to which the Government obtains title, except if the grantee fails to disclose the subject invention within the times specified in paragraph (c) above. The grantee's license extends to its domestic subsidiaries and affiliates, if any, within the corporate structure of which the grantee is a party and includes the right to grant sublicenses of the same scope to the extent the grantee was legally obligated to do so at the time the grant was awarded. The license is transferable only with the approval of NSF except when transferred to the successor of that part of the grantee's business to which the invention pertains.

(2) The grantee's domestic license may be revoked or modified by NSF to the extent necessary to achieve expeditious practical application of the subject invention pursuant to an application for an exclusive license submitted in accordance with applicable provisions at 37 CFR part 404. This license will not be revoked in that field of use or the geographical areas in which the grantee has achieved practical application and continues to make the benefits of the invention reasonably accessible to the public. The license in any foreign country may be revoked or modified at the discretion of NSF to the extent the grantee, its licensees, or its domestic subsidiaries or affiliates have failed to achieve practical application in that foreign country.

(3) Before revocation or modification of the license, NSF will furnish the grantee a written notice of its intention to revoke or modify the license, and the grantee will be allowed thirty days (or such other time as may

National Science Foundation § 650.4

be authorized by NSF for good cause shown by the grantee) after the notice to show cause why the license should not be revoked or modified. The grantee has the right to appeal, in accordance with applicable regulations in 37 CFR part 404 concerning the licensing of Government-owned inventions, any decision concerning the revocation or modification of its license.

(f) *Grantee Action to Protect Government's Interest.* (1) The grantee agrees to execute or to have executed and promptly deliver to NSF all instruments necessary to:

(i) Establish or confirm the rights the Government has throughout the world in those subject inventions for which the grantee retains title, and

(ii) Convey title to NSF when requested under paragraph (d) above, and to enable the Government to obtain patent protection throughout the world in that subject invention.

(2) The grantee agrees to require, by written agreement, its employees, other than clerical and non-technical employees, to disclose promptly in writing to personnel identified as responsible for the administration of patent matters and in a format suggested by the grantee each subject invention made under this grant in order that the grantee can comply with the disclosure provisions of paragraph (c) above, and to execute all papers necessary to file patent applications on subject inventions and to establish the Government's rights in the subject inventions. The disclosure format should require, at a minimum, the information requested by paragraph (c)(1) above. The grantee shall instruct such employees through the employee agreements or other suitable educational programs on the importance of reporting inventions in sufficient time to permit the filing of patent applications prior to U.S. or foreign statutory bars.

(3) The grantee will notify NSF of any decision not to continue prosecution of a patent application, pay maintenance fees, or defend in a reexamination or opposition proceeding on a patent, in any country, not less than thirty days before the expiration of the response period required by the relevant patent office.

(4) The grantee agrees to include, within the specification of any United States patent application and any patent issuing thereon covering a subject invention, the following statement: "This invention was made with Government support under (identify the grant) awarded by the National Science Foundation. The Government has certain rights in this invention."

(5) The grantee or its representative will complete, execute, and submit electronically to NSF via the iEdison Invention Information Management System maintained by the National Institutes of Health a confirmation of a License to the United States Government and the page of a United States patent application that contains the Federal support clause within two months of filing any domestic or foreign patent application.

(g) *Subcontracts.* (1) The grantee will include this Patents Rights clause, suitably modified to identify the parties, in all subcontracts, regardless of tier, for experimental, developmental, or research work. The subcontractor will retain all rights provided for the grantee in this Patents Rights clause, and the grantee will not, as part of the consideration for awarding the subcontract, obtain rights in the subcontractor's subject inventions.

(2) In the case of subcontracts, at any tier, when the prime award by the Foundation was a contract (but not a grant or cooperative agreement), NSF, subcontractor, and contractor agree that the mutual obligations of the parties created by this Patents Rights clause constitute a contract between the subcontractor and the Foundation with respect to those matters covered by this Patents Rights clause.

(h) *Reporting on Utilization of Subject Inventions.* The grantee agrees to submit on request periodic reports no more frequently than annually on the utilization of a subject invention or on efforts at obtaining such utilization that are being made by the grantee or its licensees or assignees. Such reports shall include information regarding the status of development, date of first commercial sale or use, gross royalties received by the grantee, and such other data and information as NSF may reasonably specify. The grantee also agrees to provide additional reports in connection with any march-in proceeding undertaken by NSF in accordance with paragraph (j) of this Patents Rights clause. As required by 35 U.S.C. 202(c)(5), NSF agrees it will not disclose such information to persons outside the Government without the permission of the grantee.

(i) *Preference for United States Industry.* Notwithstanding any other provision of this Patents Rights clause, the grantee agrees that neither it nor any assignee will grant to any person the exclusive right to use or sell any subject invention in the United States unless such person agrees that any products embodying the subject invention or produced through the use of the subject invention will be manufactured substantially in the United States. However, in individual cases, the requirement for such an agreement may be waived by NSF upon a showing by the grantee or its assignee that reasonable but unsuccessful efforts have been made to grant licenses on similar terms to potential licensees that would be likely to manufacture substantially in the United States or that under the circumstances domestic manufacture is not commercially feasible.

(j) *March-in Rights.* The grantee agrees that with respect to any subject invention in which it has acquired title, NSF has the right in accordance with procedures at 37 CFR 401.6 and NSF regulations at 45 CFR 650.13 to require the grantee, an assignee or exclusive licensee of a subject invention to grant a nonexclusive, partially exclusive, or exclusive license in any field of use to a responsible applicant or applicants, upon terms that are reasonable under the circumstances, and if the grantee, assignee, or exclusive licensee refuses such a request, NSF has the right to grant such a license itself if NSF determines that:

(1) Such action is necessary because the grantee or assignee has not taken, or is not expected to take within a reasonable time, effective steps to achieve practical application of the subject invention in such field of use;

(2) Such action is necessary to alleviate health or safety needs which are not reasonably satisfied by the grantee, assignee, or their licensees;

(3) Such action is necessary to meet requirements for public use specified by Federal regulations and such requirements are not reasonably satisfied by the grantee, assignee, or licensee; or

(4) Such action is necessary because the agreement required by paragraph (i) of this Patents Rights clause has not been obtained or waived or because a licensee of the exclusive right to use or sell any subject invention in the United States is in breach of such agreement.

(k) *Special Provisions for Grants with Nonprofit Organizations.* If the grantee is a nonprofit organization, it agrees that:

(1) Rights to a subject invention in the United States may not be assigned without the approval of NSF, except where such assignment is made to an organization which has as one of its primary functions the management of inventions, provided that such assignee will be subject to the same provisions as the grantee;

(2) The grantee will share royalties collected on a subject invention with the inventor, including Federal employee co-inventors (when NSF deems it appropriate) when the subject invention is assigned in accordance with 35 U.S.C. 202(e) and 37 CFR 401.10;

(3) The balance of any royalties or income earned by the grantee with respect to subject inventions, after payment of expenses (including payments to inventors) incidental to the administration of subject inventions, will be utilized for the support of scientific research or education; and

(4) It will make efforts that are reasonable under the circumstances to attract licensees of subject inventions that are small business firms and that it will give preference to a small business firm if the grantee determines that the small business firm has a plan or proposal for marketing the invention which, if executed, is equally likely to bring the invention to practical application as any plans or proposals from applicants that are not small business firms; provided that the grantee is also satisfied that the small business firm has the capability and resources to carry out it plan or proposal. The decision whether to give a preference in any specific case will be at the discretion of the grantee. However, the grantee agrees that the Secretary of Commerce may review the grantee's licensing program and decisions regarding small business applicants, and the grantee will negotiate changes to its licensing policies, procedures, or practices with the Secretary when the Secretary's review discloses that the grantee could take reasonable steps to implement more effectively the requirements of this paragraph (k)(4).

(1) *Communications.* All communications required by this Patents Rights clause must be submitted through the iEdison Invention Information Management System maintained by the National Institutes of Health unless prior permission for another form of submission is obtained from the Patent Assistant at *patents@nsf.gov* or at Office of the General Counsel, National Science Foundation, 4201 Wilson Boulevard, Arlington, VA 22230.

(b) When the above Patent Rights clause is used in a funding agreement other than a grant, "grant" and "grantee" may be replaced by "contract" and "contractor" or other appropriate terms.

(Approved by the Office of Management and Budget under control number 3145–0084)

[57 FR 18053, Apr. 28, 1992, as amended at 59 FR 37438, July 22, 1994; 62 FR 49938, Sept. 24, 1997; 70 FR 43071, July 26, 2005]

§ 650.5 Special patent provisions.

At the request of the prospective awardee or on recommendation from NSF staff, a Grants or Contracts Officer, with the concurrence of the cognizant Program Manager, may negotiate special patent provisions when he or she determines that exceptional circumstances require restriction or elimination of the right of a prospective awardee to retain title to any subject invention in order to better promote the policy and objectives of chapter 18 of title 35 of the United States Code or the National Science Foundation Act. The Grants or Contracts Officer will prepare the written determination required by § 401.3(e) of title 37 of the Code of Federal Regulations and assure that appropriate reports are made to the Secretary of Commerce and Chief Counsel for Advocacy of the Small Business Administration as required in § 401.3(f). Unless doing so would be inconsistent with an obligation imposed on the Foundation by statute, international agreement, or pact with other participants in or supporters of the research, every special patent provision will allow the awardee, after an invention has been made, to request that it be allowed to retain principal rights to that invention under § 650.12(e) of this regulation.

§ 650.6 Awards not primarily for research.

(a) Awards not primarily intended to support scientific or engineering research need contain no patent provision. Examples of such awards are travel and conference grants.

(b) NSF fellowships and traineeships are primarily intended to support education or training, not particular research. Therefore, in accordance with section 212 of title 35 of the United States Code, the Foundation claims no rights to inventions made by fellows or trainees. The following provision will be included in each fellowship or traineeship program announcement and made part of the award:

INTELLECTUAL PROPERTY RIGHTS

The National Science Foundation claims no rights to any inventions or writings that might result from its fellowship or traineeship awards. However, fellows and trainees should be aware that the NSF, another Federal agency, or some private party may acquire such rights through other support for particular research. Also, fellows and trainees should note their obligation to include an Acknowledgment and Disclaimer in any publication.

§ 650.7 Awards affected by international agreements.

(a) Some NSF awards are made as part of international cooperative research programs. The agreements or treaties underlying many of these programs require an allocation of patent rights different from that provided by the Patent Rights clause in § 650.4(a). Therefore, as permitted by § 401.5(d) of the implementing regulations for the Bayh-Dole Act (37 CFR 401.5(d)), paragraph (b) of the standard Patent Rights clause in § 650.4(a) has been modified to provide that the Foundation may require the grantee to transfer to a foreign government or research performer such rights in any subject invention as are contemplated in the international agreement. The award instrument will identify the applicable agreement or treaty.

(b) After an invention is disclosed to the Patent Assistant, the recipient of an award subject to an international agreement will be informed as to what rights, if any, it must transfer to foreign participants. Recipients may also ask the Program Manager to provide them with copies of the identified international agreements before or after accepting an award.

§ 650.8 Retention of rights by inventor.

If an awardee elects not to retain rights to an invention, the inventor may request the NSF Patent Assistant for permission to retain principal patent rights. Such requests should be made as soon as possible after the awardee notifies the Patent Assistant that it does not want to patent the invention. Such requests will normally be granted unless either the awardee or the employer of the inventor shows that it would be harmed by that action. As required by § 401.9 of the implementing regulations for the Bayh-Dole Act (37 CFR 401.9), the inventor will be subject to the same conditions that the awardee would have been, except that the special restrictions imposed on nonprofit organizations will not apply to the inventor.

§ 650.9 Unwanted inventions.

(a) The Foundation will normally allow any patent rights not wanted by the awardee or inventor to be dedicated to the public through publication in scientific and engineering journals or as a statutory invention registration under section 157 of title 35 of the United States Code. Except as provided in paragraph (b) of this section, the NSF Patent Assistant will acknowledge a negative election by encouraging the awardee and inventor to promptly make all research results available to the scientific and engineering community.

(b) If the NSF Patent Assistant believes that another Federal agency is

§ 650.10

interested in the relevant technology, he or she may, after receiving the awardee's election not to patent and ascertaining that the inventor also does not want to patent, send a copy of the invention disclosure to that agency to give it an opportunity to review and patent the invention. Unless the agency expresses an interest in the invention within thirty days, the Patent Assistant will acknowledge the awardee's negative election by encouraging prompt publication of all research results. If the agency does express an interest in patenting the invention, the Patent Assistant will transfer to it all rights to the invention.

§ 650.10 Inventions also supported by another Federal Agency.

Section 401.13(a) of the implementing regulation for the Bayh-Dole Act (37 CFR 401.13(a)) provides that in the event that an invention is made under funding agreements of more than one federal agency, the agencies involved will, at the request of the grantee or contractor or on their own initiative, designate one agency to be responsible for the administration of the invention. Whenever the NSF Patent Assistant finds that another agency also supported an NSF subject invention, he or she will consult with the grantee or contractor and appropriate personnel in the other agency to determine if a single agency should be designated to administer the Government's rights in the invention. The Patent Assistant may transfer to, or accept from, any other Federal agency, responsibility for administering a jointly-supported invention.

§ 650.11 Utilization reports.

Paragraph (h) of the standard Patent Rights clause set forth in § 650.4 obliges grantees "to submit on request periodic reports no more frequently than annually on the utilization of a subject invention or on efforts at obtaining such utilization". At this time, the Foundation does not plan to request such reports except in connection with march-in investigations conducted under § 650.13. This section will be amended to describe periodic reporting requirements if such are ever established.

[57 FR 18053, Apr. 28, 1992, as amended at 59 FR 37438, July 22, 1994]

§ 650.12 Waivers and approvals.

(a) Requests for extension of time to disclose to the NSF Patent Assistant, make an election to retain title to, or file a patent on a subject invention will be granted by the NSF Patent Assistant unless he or she determines that such an extension would either imperil the securing of valid patent protection or unacceptably restrict the publication of the results of the NSF-supported research.

(b) Approval of assignments by nonprofit organizations (required by subparagraph (k)(1) of the Patent Rights clause in § 650.4(a)) will be given by the Patent Assistant unless he or she determines that the interests of the United States Government will be adversely affected by such assignment.

(c) Approval of long-term exclusive licensing of NSF-assisted inventions by nonprofit organizations (restricted by earlier versions of the NSF Patents Rights clause and by pre-Bayh-Dole Institutional Patent Agreements and waiver conditions) will be given by the Patent Assistant unless he or she determines that the interests of the United States Government will be adversely affected by such waiver.

(d) The preference for United States industry imposed by paragraph (i) of the Patent Rights clause in § 650.4(a) may be waived by the NSF Patent Assistant as provided in that paragraph.

(e) Special restrictions on or limitation of the right of an awardee to retain title to subject inventions imposed under § 650.5 of this regulation may be waived by the Grants or Contracting Officer whenever he or she determines, after consultation with the cognizant Program Manager, that the reasons for imposing the restrictions or limitations do not require their application to a particular invention.

(f) Requests for approvals and waiver under this section should be addressed to the NSF Patent Assistant as provided in paragraph (1) of the Patent Rights clause in § 650.4(a). Requests under paragraph (a) of this section for extensions of time to disclose, elect, or file may be made by telephone or electronic mail as well as in writing. A written request for extension of time to disclose, elect, or file can be assumed to have been approved unless the Patent Assistant replies negatively within ten business days of the date such request was mailed, telecopied, or otherwise dispatched. Requests for approvals or waivers under paragraphs (b), (c), (d), and (e) of this section must be in writing and should explain why an approval or waiver is justified under the stated criteria. The requester will be given a written explanation of the reasons for denial of a request covered by this section.

§ 650.13 Exercise of march-in rights.

(a) The procedures established by this section supplement those prescribed by § 401.6 of the implementing regulation for the Bayh-Dole Act (37 CFR § 401.6) and apply to all march-in rights held by NSF including those resulting from funding agreements not covered by the Bayh-Dole Act.

(b) Petitions requesting that the NSF exercise a march-in right should be addressed to the NSF Patent Assistant. Such petitions should:

(1) Identify the patent or patent application involved and the relevant fields of use of the invention;

(2) State the grounds for the proposed march-in;

(3) Supply evidence that one or more of the four conditions creating a march-in right (lack of practical application, unsatisfied health or safety needs, unmet requirements for public use, or failure to prefer United States industry) is present; and

(4) Explain what action by the Foundation is necessary to correct that condition.

(c) If evidence received from a petitioner or from the Foundation's administration of the Patent Rights clause indicates that one or more of the four conditions creating a march-in right might exist, the NSF Patent Assistant will informally review the matter as provided in § 401.6(b) of the implementing regulation. If that informal review indicates that one or more of the four conditions creating a march-in right probably exists, the Patent Assistant will initiate a formal march-in proceeding by issuing a written notice to the patent holder. That notice will provide all the information required by § 401.6(c) of the implementing regulation. The patent holder may submit information and argument in opposition to the proposed march-in in person, in writing, or through a representative.

(d) If the NSF Patent Assistant determines that a genuine dispute over material facts exists, he or she will identify the disputed facts and notify the NSF General Counsel. The General Counsel will create a cross-directorate fact-finding panel, which will establish its own fact-finding procedures within the requirements of § 401.6(e) of the implementing regulation based on the dimensions of the particular dispute. The Patent Assistant will serve as secretary to the panel, but will not take part in its deliberations. Written findings of facts will be submitted to the General Counsel, sent by certified mail to the patent holder, and made available to all other interested parties.

(e) The NSF General Counsel will determine whether and how the Foundation should exercise a march-in right as provided in § 401.6(g) of the implementing regulation.

§ 650.14 Request for conveyance of title to NSF.

(a) The procedures established by this section apply to the exercise of the Foundation's right under paragraph (d) of the Patent Rights clause in § 650.4(a) to request conveyance of title to a subject invention if certain conditions exist.

(b) The NSF Patent Assistant may request the recipient of an NSF award to convey to the Foundation or a designee title in one or more countries to any invention to which the awardee has elected not to retain title. The NSF Patent Assistant may request immediate conveyance of title to a subject invention if the awardee fails (1) to submit a timely invention disclosure, (2) to make a timely election to retain patent rights, or (3) to file a timely patent application; but only if he or she determines that such action is required to preserve patent rights.

(c) The NSF Patent Assistant will informally review any apparent failure by an awardee to comply with the requirements of paragraph (c) of the Patent Rights clause in § 650.4(a). The interested institution, the inventor, the patent holder, and any other interested party will be given an opportunity to explain why a particular invention was not disclosed, why an election was not made, or why a patent application was not filed. If the Patent Assistant determines that a genuine dispute over material facts exists, a cross-directorate fact-finding panel will be appointed by the General Counsel. The panel will establish its own fact-finding procedures based on the dimensions of the particular dispute. Written findings of facts will be submitted to the General Counsel, sent by certified mail to the patent holder, and made available to all other interested parties.

(d) The NSF General Counsel will determine whether the Foundation should request conveyance of title or if it should retain title obtained under § 650.14(b).

§ 650.15 Appeals.

(a) All actions by the NSF Patent Assistant under § 650.8 denying an inventor's request to retain rights to a subject invention, under § 650.12 denying a request for waiver, or under § 650.14(d) denying the existence of a material dispute may be appealed to the Director of the NSF Division of Grants and Contracts by an affected party within thirty days. A request under § 650.14(b) to immediately convey title to the Foundation may be appealed to the DGC Director by the title holder within five days.

(b) All actions by a Grants and Agreements Officer or Contracting Officer refusing to eliminate restrictions on or limitation of the right of an awardee to retain title to subject inventions imposed under § 650.5 of this regulation may be appealed to the Director of the NSF Division of Contracts, Policy, and Oversight (CPO) by an affected party within thirty days.

(c) A decision by the General Counsel to exercise a march-in right or to request conveyance of title may be appealed by the patent holder or any affected licensee to the NSF Deputy Director within thirty days. When a march-in was initiated in response to a petition, the General Counsel's decision not to exercise a march-in right or to exercise it in a manner different from that requested in the petition may be appealed by the petitioner to the NSF Deputy Director within thirty days.

(d) In reviewing the actions of the NSF Patent Assistant, a Grants and Agreements Officer, a Contracting Officer, or the General Counsel, the CPO Director or NSF Deputy Director will consider both the factual and legal basis for the action or determination and its consistency with the policies and objectives of the Foundation and, if applicable, the Bayh-Dole Act (35 U.S.C. 200–212) and implementing regulations at part 401 of title 37 of the Code of Federal Regulations.

[57 FR 18053, Apr. 28, 1992, as amended at 61 FR 51022, Sept. 30, 1996]

§ 650.16 Background rights.

The Foundation will acquire rights to a research performer's pre-existing technology only in exceptional circumstances where, due to the nature of the research being supported, the Foundation requires greater control over resulting inventions. The NSF Grants or Contracts Officer, with concurrence of the cognizant Program Manager, will negotiate a background rights provision. If the affected awardee is a small business firm or nonprofit organization, the provision will conform to the requirements of the Bayh-Dole Act (35 U.S.C. 202(f)) as implemented by 37 CFR 401.12).

§ 650.17 Subcontracts.

As provided in paragraph (g) of the Patent Rights clause in § 650.4(a), awardees should normally use that clause in all subcontracts. At the request of the awardee or subcontractor or on recommendation from NSF staff, the cognizant Grants or Contracts Officer may direct the awardee to insert into subcontracts relating to scientific research a special patent provision negotiated under § 650.5.

§ 650.18 Delegation of authority.

The General Counsel is responsible for implementing this regulation and is authorized to make any exceptions to or extensions of the NSF Patent Policy as may be required by particular circumstances. The General Counsel will designate the NSF Patent Assistant and that individual is authorized to carry out the functions assigned by this regulation.

§ 650.19 Electronic invention handling.

(a) Grantees must use the iEdison Invention Information Management System maintained by the National Institutes of Health to disclose NSF subject inventions. Detailed instructions for use of that system are provided at *http://s-edison.info.nih.gov/iEdison/* and should be followed for NSF subject inventions except that:

(1) All communications required must be provided electronically as a PDF or TIFF file through iEdison unless prior permission for another form of submission is obtained from the Patent Assistant.

(2) NSF does not require either an Annual Utilization Report or a Final Invention Statement and Certification.

(b) Questions on use of iEdison and requests for permission to submit material in other forms may be sent to the NSF Patent Assistant at *patents@nsf.gov* or at Office of the General Counsel, National Science Foundation, 4201 Wilson Boulevard, Arlington, VA 22230.

[70 FR 43071, July 26, 2005]

APPENDIX A TO PART 650—OPTIONAL FORMAT FOR CONFIRMATORY LICENSE

The following format may be used for the confirmatory license to the Government required by subparagraph (f)(5) of the Patent Rights clause in § 650.4(a). Any equivalent instrument may also be used.

LICENSE TO THE UNITED STATES GOVERNMENT

This instrument confirms to the United States Government, as represented by the National Science Foundation, an irrevocable, nonexclusive, nontransferable, royalty-free license to practice or have practiced on its behalf throughout the world the following subject invention:

(invention title)

(inventor[s] name[s])

(patent application number and filing date)

(country, if other than United States)

(NSF Disclosure No.).

This subject invention was made with NSF support through:

(grant or contract number)

(grantee or contractor).

Principal rights to this subject invention have been left with the licensor.

Signed: _____
Name: _____
Title: _____
Date: _____

Accepted on behalf of the Government:

NSF Patent Assistant

Date: _____

PART 660—INTERGOVERNMENTAL REVIEW OF THE NATIONAL SCIENCE FOUNDATION PROGRAMS AND ACTIVITIES

Sec.
660.1 What is the purpose of these regulations?
660.2 What definitions apply to these regulations?
660.3 What programs and activities of the Foundation are subject to these regulations?
660.4 [Reserved]
660.5 What is the Director's obligation with respect to Federal interagency coordination?
660.6 What procedures apply to the selection of programs and activities under these regulations?
660.7 How does the Director communicate with state and local officials concerning the Foundation's programs and activities?
660.8 How does the Director provide states an opportunity to comment on proposed Federal financial assistance and direct Federal development?
660.9 How does the Director receive and respond to comments?
660.10 How does the Director make efforts to accommodate intergovernmental concerns?
660.11 What are the Director's obligations in interstate situations?
660.12 [Reserved]
660.13 May the Director waive any provision of these regulations?

AUTHORITY: E.O. 12372, July 14, 1982 (47 FR 30959), as amended Apr. 8, 1983 (48 FR 15887); and sec. 401 of the Intergovernmental Cooperation Act of 1968 and as amended (31 U.S.C. 6506).

SOURCE: 48 FR 29365, June 24, 1983, unless otherwise noted.

§ 660.1 What is the purpose of these regulations?

(a) The regulations in this part implement Executive Order 12372, "Intergovernmental Review of Federal Programs," issued July 14, 1982 and amended on April 8, 1983. These regulations also implement applicable provisions of section 401 of the Intergovernmental Cooperation Act of 1968.

(b) These regulations are intended to foster an intergovernmental partnership and a strengthened Federalism by relying on state processes and on state, areawide, regional and local coordination for review of proposed Federal financial assistance and direct Federal development.

(c) These regulations are intended to aid the internal management of the Foundation, and are not intended to create any right or benefit enforceable at law by a party against the Foundation or its officers.

§ 660.2 What definitions apply to these regulations?

Foundation means the National Science Foundation.

Order means Executive Order 12372, issued July 14, 1982, and amended April 8, 1983 and titled "Intergovernmental Review of Federal Programs."

Director means the Director of the National Science Foundation or an official or employee of the Foundation acting for the Director under a delegation of authority.

State means any of the 50 states, the District of Columbia, the Commonwealth of Puerto Rico, the Commonwealth of the Northern Mariana Islands, Guam, American Samoa, the U.S. Virgin Islands, or the Trust Territory of the Pacific Islands.

§ 660.3 What programs and activities of the Foundation are subject to these regulations?

The Director publishes in the FEDERAL REGISTER a list of the Foundation's programs and activities that are subject to these regulations.

§ 660.4 [Reserved]

§ 660.5 What is the Director's obligation with respect to Federal interagency coordination?

The Director, to the extent practicable, consults with and seeks advice from all other substantially affected Federal departments and agencies in an effort to assure full coordination between such agencies and the Foundation regarding programs and activities covered under these regulations.

§ 660.6 What procedures apply to the selection of programs and activities under these regulations?

(a) A state may select any program or activity published in the FEDERAL REGISTER in accordance with § 660.3 of this part for intergovernmental review under these regulations. Each state, before selecting programs and activities, shall consult with local elected officials.

(b) Each state that adopts a process shall notify the Director of the Foundation's programs and activities selected for that process.

(c) A state may notify the Director of changes in its selections at any time. For each change, the state shall submit to the Director an assurance that the state has consulted with elected local elected officials regarding the change. The Foundation may establish deadlines by which states are required to inform the Director of changes in their program selections.

(d) The Director uses a state's process as soon as feasible, depending on individual programs and activities, after the Director is notified of its selections.

§ 660.7 How does the Director communicate with state and local officials concerning the Foundation's programs and activities?

(a) For those programs and activities covered by a state process under § 660.6, the Director, to the extent permitted by law:

(1) Uses the state process to determine views of state and local elected officials; and

(2) Communicates with state and local elected officials, through the state process, as early in a program

National Science Foundation

planning cycle as is reasonably feasible to explain specific plans and actions.

(b) The Director provides notice to directly affected state, areawide, regional, and local entities in a state of proposed Federal financial assistance or direct Federal development if:

(1) The state has not adopted a process under the Order; or

(2) The assistance or development involves a program or activity not selected for the state process.

This notice may be made by publication in the FEDERAL REGISTER or other appropriate means, which the Foundation in its discretion deems appropriate.

§ 660.8 How does the Director provide states an opportunity to comment on proposed Federal financial assistance and direct Federal development?

(a) Except in unusual circumstances, the Director gives state processes or directly affected state, areawide, regional and local officials and entities:

(1) At least 30 days from the date established by the Director to comment on proposed Federal financial assistance in covered programs (i.e., those referenced in § 660.3) in the form of continuation awards that are not peer reviewed; and

(2) At least 60 days from the date established by the Director to comment on proposed direct Federal development or Federal financial assistance in covered programs (i.e., those referenced § 660.3) other than continuation awards that are not peer reviewed.

(b) This section also applies to comments in cases in which the review, coordination, and communication with the Foundation have been delegated.

§ 660.9 How does the Director receive and respond to comments?

(a) The Director follows the procedures in § 660.10 if:

(1) A state office or official is designated to act as a single point of contact between a state process and all Federal agencies, and

(2) That office or official transmits a state process recommendation for a program selected under § 660.6.

(b)(1) The single point of contact is not obligated to transmit comments from state, areawide, regional or local officials and entities where there is no state process recommendation.

(2) If a state process recommendation is transmitted by a single point of contact, all comments from state, areawide, regional, and local officials and entities that differ from it must also be transmitted.

(c) If a state has not established a process, or is unable to submit a state process recommendation, state, areawide, regional and local officials and entities may submit comments either to the applicant or to the Foundation.

(d) If a program or activity is not selected for a state process, state, areawide, regional and local officials and entities may submit comments either to the applicant or to the Foundation. In addition, if a state process recommendation for a nonselected program or activity is transmitted to the Foundation by the single point of contact, the Director follows the procedures of § 660.10 of this part.

(e) The Director considers comments which do not constitute a state process recommendation submitted under these regulations and for which the Director is not required to apply the procedures of § 660.10 of this part, when such comments are provided by a single point of contact, by the applicant, or directly to the Foundation by a commenting party.

§ 660.10 How does the Director make efforts to accommodate intergovernmental concerns?

(a) If a state process provides a state process recommendation to the Foundation through its single point of contact, the Director either:

(1) Accepts the recommendation;

(2) Reaches a mutually agreeable solution with the state process; or

(3) Provides the single point of contact with a written explanation of the decision in such form as the Director in his or her discretion deems appropriate. The Director may also supplement the written explanation by providing the explanation to the single point of contact by telephone, other telecommunication, or other means.

(b) In any explanation under paragraph (a)(3) of this section, the Director informs the single point of contact that:

(1) The Foundation will not implement its decision for at least ten days after the single point of contact receives the explanation; or

(2) The Director has reviewed the decision and determined that, because of unusual circumstances, the waiting period of at least ten days is not feasible.

(c) For purposes of computing the waiting period under paragraph (b)(1) of this section, a single point of contact is presumed to have received written notification 5 days after the date of mailing of such notification.

§ 660.11 What are the Director's obligations in interstate situations?

(a) The Director is responsible for:

(1) Identifying proposed Federal financial assistance and direct Federal development that have an impact on interstate areas;

(2) Notifying appropriate officials and entities in states which have adopted a process and which select the Foundation's program or activity.

(3) Making efforts to identify and notify the affected state, areawide, regional, and local officials and entities in those states that have not adopted a process under the Order or do not select the Foundation's program or activity;

(4) Responding pursuant to § 660.10 of this part if the Director receives a recommendation from a designated areawide agency transmitted by a single point of contact, in cases in which the review, coordination, and communication with the Foundation have been delegated.

(b) The Director uses the procedures in § 660.10 if a state process provides a state process recommendation to the Foundation through a single point of contact.

§ 660.12 [Reserved]

§ 660.13 May the Director waive any provision of these regulations?

In an emergency, the Director may waive any provision of these regulations.

PART 670—CONSERVATION OF ANTARCTIC ANIMALS AND PLANTS

Subpart A—Introduction

Sec.
670.1 Purpose of regulations.
670.2 Scope.
670.3 Definitions.

Subpart B—Prohibited Acts, Exceptions

670.4 Prohibited acts.
670.5 Exception in extraordinary circumstances.
670.6 Prior possession exception.
670.7 Food exception.
670.8 Foreign permit exception.
670.9 Antarctic Conservation Act enforcement exception.
670.10 [Reserved]

Subpart C—Permits

670.11 Applications for permits.
670.12 General issuance criteria.
670.13 Permit administration.
670.14 Conditions of permits.
670.15 Modification, suspension, and revocation.
670.16 [Reserved]

Subpart D—Native Mammals, Birds, Plants, and Invertebrates

670.17 Specific issuance criteria.
670.18 Content of permit applications.
670.19 Designation of native mammals.
670.20 Designation of native birds.
670.21 Designation of native plants.
670.22 [Reserved]

Subpart E—Specially Protected Species of Mammals, Birds, and Plants

670.23 Specific issuance criteria.
670.24 Content of permit applications.
670.25 Designation of specially protected species of native mammals, birds, and plants.
670.26 [Reserved]

Subpart F—Antarctic Specially Protected Areas

670.27 Specific issuance criteria.
670.28 Content of permit applications.
670.29 Designation of Antarctic specially protected areas, specially managed areas and historic sites and monuments.
670.30 [Reserved]

Subpart G—Import Into and Export From the United States

670.31 Specific issuance criteria for imports.
670.32 Specific issuance criteria for exports.

National Science Foundation

670.33 Content of permit applications.
670.34 Entry and exit ports.
670.35 [Reserved]

Subpart H—Introduction of Non-Indigenous Plants and Animals

670.36 Specific issuance criteria.
670.37 Content of permit applications.
670.38 Conditions of permits.
670.39 [Reserved]

AUTHORITY: 16 U.S.C. 2405, as amended.

SOURCE: 63 FR 50164, Sept. 21, 1998, unless otherwise noted.

Subpart A—Introduction

§ 670.1 Purpose of regulations.

The purpose of the regulations in this part is to conserve and protect the native mammals, birds, plants, and invertebrates of Antarctica and the ecosystem upon which they depend and to implement the Antarctic Conservation Act of 1978, Public Law 95–541, as amended by the Antarctic Science, Tourism, and Conservation Act of 1996, Public Law 104–227.

§ 670.2 Scope.

The regulations in this part apply to:
(a) Taking mammals, birds, or plants native to Antarctica.
(b) Engaging in harmful interference of mammals, birds, invertebrates, or plants native to Antarctica.
(c) Entering or engaging in activities within Antarctic Specially Protected Areas.
(d) Receiving, acquiring, transporting, offering for sale, selling, purchasing, importing, exporting or having custody, control, or possession of any mammal, bird, or plant native to Antarctica that was taken in violation of the Act.
(e) Introducing into Antarctica any member of a non-native species.

§ 670.3 Definitions.

In this part:

Act means the Antarctic Conservation Act of 1978, Public Law 95–541 (16 U.S.C. 2401 et seq.) as amended by the Antarctic Science, Tourism, and Conservation Act of 1996, Public Law 104–227.

Antarctic Specially Protected Area means an area designated by the Antarctic Treaty Parties to protect outstanding environmental, scientific, historic, aesthetic, or wilderness values or to protect ongoing or planned scientific research, designated in subpart F of this part.

Antarctica means the area south of 60 degrees south latitude.

Director means the Director of the National Science Foundation, or an officer or employee of the Foundation designated by the Director.

Harmful interference means—

(a) Flying or landing helicopters or other aircraft in a manner that disturbs concentrations of birds or seals;
(b) Using vehicles or vessels, including hovercraft and small boats, in a manner that disturbs concentrations of birds or seals;
(c) Using explosives or firearms in a manner that disturbs concentrations of birds or seals;
(d) Willfully disturbing breeding or molting birds or concentrations of birds or seals by persons on foot;
(e) Significantly damaging concentrations of native terrestrial plants by landing aircraft, driving vehicles, or walking on them, or by other means; and
(f) Any activity that results in the significant adverse modification of habitats of any species or population of native mammal, native bird, native plant, or native invertebrate.

Import means to land on, bring into, or introduce into, or attempt to land on, bring into or introduce into, any place subject to the jurisdiction of the United States, including the 12-mile territorial sea of the United States, whether or not such act constitutes an importation within the meaning of the customs laws of the United States.

Management plan means a plan to manage the activities and protect the special value or values in an Antarctic Specially Protected Area designated by the United States as such a site consistent with plans adopted by the Antarctic Treaty Consultative Parties.

Native bird means any member, at any stage of its life cycle, of any species of the class Aves which is indigenous to Antarctica or occurs there seasonally through natural migrations, that is designated in subpart D of this part. It includes any part, product, egg, or offspring of or the dead body or parts thereof excluding fossils.

Native invertebrate means any terrestrial or freshwater invertebrate, at any stage of its life cycle, which is indigenous to Antarctica. It includes any part thereof, but excludes fossils.

Native mammal means any member, at any stage of its life cycle, of any species of the class Mammalia, which is indigenous to Antarctica or occurs there seasonally through natural migrations, that is designated in subpart D of this part. It includes any part, product, offspring of or the dead body or parts thereof but excludes fossils.

Native plant means any terrestrial or freshwater vegetation, including bryophytes, lichens, fungi, and algae, at any stage of its life cycle which is indigenous to Antarctica that is designated in subpart D of this part. It includes seeds and other propagules, or parts of such vegetation, but excludes fossils.

Person has the meaning given that term in section 1 of title 1, United States Code, and includes any person subject to the jurisdiction of the United States and any department, agency, or other instrumentality of the Federal Government or of any State or local government.

Protocol means the Protocol on Environmental Protection to the Antarctic Treaty, signed October 4, 1991, in Madrid, and all annexes thereto, including any future amendments to which the United States is a Party.

Specially Protected Species means any native species designated as a Specially Protected Species that is designated in subpart E of this part.

Take or taking means to kill, injure, capture, handle, or molest a native mammal or bird, or to remove or damage such quantities of native plants that their local distribution or abundance would be significantly affected or to attempt to engage in such conduct.

Treaty means the Antarctic Treaty signed in Washington, DC on December 1, 1959.

United States means the several states of the Union, the District of Columbia, the Commonwealth of Puerto Rico, American Samoa, the Virgin Islands, Guam, the Commonwealth of the Northern Mariana Islands, and other commonwealth, territory, or possession of the United States.

Subpart B—Prohibited Acts, Exceptions

§ 670.4 Prohibited acts.

Unless a permit has been issued pursuant to subpart C of this part or unless one of the exceptions stated in §§ 670.5 through 670.9 is applicable, it is unlawful to commit, attempt to commit, or cause to be committed any of the acts described in paragraphs (a) through (g) of this section.

(a) *Taking of native mammal, bird or plants.* It is unlawful for any person to take within Antarctica a native mammal, a native bird, or native plants.

(b) *Engaging in harmful interference.* It is unlawful for any person to engage in harmful interference in Antarctica of native mammals, native birds, native plants or native invertebrates.

(c) *Entry into Antarctic specially designated areas.* It is unlawful for any person to enter or engage in activities within any Antarctic Specially Protected Area.

(d) *Possession, sale, export, and import of native mammals, birds, and plants.* It is unlawful for any person to receive, acquire, transport, offer for sale, sell, purchase, export, import, or have custody, control, or possession of, any native bird, native mammal, or native plant which the person knows, or in the exercise of due care should have known, was taken in violation of the Act.

(e) *Introduction of non-indigenous animals and plants into Antarctica.* It is unlawful for any person to introduce into Antarctica any animal or plant which is not indigenous to Antarctica or which does not occur there seasonally through natural migrations, as specified in subpart H of this part, except as provided in §§ 670.7 and 670.8.

(f) *Violations of regulations.* It is unlawful for any person to violate the regulations set forth in this part.

(g) *Violation of permit conditions.* It is unlawful for any person to violate any term or condition of any permit issued under subpart C of this part.

§ 670.5 Exception in extraordinary circumstances.

(a) *Emergency exception.* No act described in § 670.4 shall be unlawful if the person committing the act reasonably believed that the act was committed under emergency circumstances involving the safety of human life or of ships, aircraft, or equipment or facilities of high value, or the protection of the environment.

(b) *Aiding or salvaging native mammals or native birds.* The prohibition on taking shall not apply to any taking of native mammals or native birds if such action is necessary to:

(1) Aid a sick, injured or orphaned specimen;

(2) Dispose of a dead specimen; or

(3) Salvage a dead specimen which may be useful for scientific study.

(c) *Reporting.* Any actions taken under the exceptions in this section shall be reported promptly to the Director.

§ 670.6 Prior possession exception.

(a) *Exception.* Section 670.4 shall not apply to:

(1) any native mammal, bird, or plant which is held in captivity on or before October 28, 1978; or

(2) Any offspring of such mammal, bird, or plant.

(b) *Presumption.* With respect to any prohibited act set forth in § 670.4 which occurs after April 29, 1979, the Act creates a rebuttable presumption that the native mammal, native bird, or native plant involved in such act was not held in captivity on or before October 28, 1978, or was not an offspring referred to in paragraph (a) of this section.

§ 670.7 Food exception.

Paragraph (e) of § 670.4 shall not apply to the introduction of animals and plants into Antarctica for use as food as long as animals and plants used for this purpose are kept under carefully controlled conditions. This exception shall not apply to living species of animals. Unconsumed poultry or its parts shall be removed from Antarctica unless incinerated, autoclaved or otherwise sterilized.

§ 670.8 Foreign permit exception.

Paragraphs (d) and (e) of § 670.4 shall not apply to transporting, carrying, receiving, or possessing native mammals, native plants, or native birds or to the introduction of non-indigenous animals and plants when conducted by an agency of the United States Government on behalf of a foreign national operating under a permit issued by a foreign government to give effect to the Protocol.

§ 670.9 Antarctic Conservation Act enforcement exception.

Paragraphs (a) through (d) of § 670.4 shall not apply to acts carried out by an Antarctic Conservation Act Enforcement Officer (designated pursuant to 45 CFR 672.3) if undertaken as part of the Antarctic Conservation Act Enforcement Officer's official duties.

§ 670.10 [Reserved]

Subpart C—Permits

§ 670.11 Applications for permits.

(a) *General content of permit applications.* All applications for a permit shall be dated and signed by the applicant and shall contain the following information:

(1) The name and address of the applicant;

(i) Where the applicant is an individual, the business or institutional affiliation of the applicant must be included; or

(ii) Where the applicant is a corporation, firm, partnership, or institution, or agency, either private or public, the name and address of its president or principal officer must be included.

(2) Where the applicant seeks to engage in a taking,

(i) The scientific names, numbers, and description of native mammals, native birds or native plants to be taken; and

(ii) Whether the native mammals, birds, or plants, or part of them are to be imported into the United States, and if so, their ultimate disposition.

(3) Where the applicant seeks to engage in a harmful interference, the scientific names, numbers, and description of native birds or native seals to be disturbed; the scientific names, numbers, and description of native

plants to be damaged; or the scientific names, numbers, and description of native invertebrates, native mammals, native plants, or native birds whose habitat will be adversely modified;

(4) A complete description of the location, time period, and manner in which the taking or harmful interference would be conducted, including the proposed access to the location;

(5) Where the application is for the introduction of non-indigenous plants or animals, the scientific name and the number to be introduced;

(6) Whether agents as referred to in § 670.13 will be used; and

(7) The desired effective dates of the permit.

(b) *Content of specific permit applications.* In addition to the general information required for permit applications set forth in this subpart, the applicant must submit additional information relating to the specific action for which the permit is being sought. These additional requirements are set forth in the sections of this part dealing with the subject matter of the permit applications as follows:

Native Mammals, Birds, Plants, and Invertebrates—Section 670.17
Specially Protected Species—Section 670.23
Specially Protected Areas—Section 670.27
Import and Export—Section 670.31
Introduction of Non-Indigenous Plants and Animals—Section 670.36

(c) *Certification.* Applications for permits shall include the following certification:

I certify that the information submitted in this application for a permit is complete and accurate to the best of my knowledge and belief. Any false statement will subject me to the criminal penalties of 18 U.S.C. 1001.

(d) *Address to which applications should be sent.* Each application shall be in writing, addressed to:

Permit Officer, Office of Polar Programs, National Science Foundation, Room 755, 4201 Wilson Boulevard, Arlington, Virginia 22230.

(e) *Sufficiency of application.* The sufficiency of the application shall be determined by the Director. The Director may waive any requirement for information, or request additional information as determined to be relevant to the processing of the application.

(f) *Withdrawal.* An applicant may withdraw an application at any time.

(g) *Publication of permit applications.* The Director shall publish notice in the FEDERAL REGISTER of each application for a permit. The notice shall invite the submission by interested parties, within 30 days after the date of publication of the notice, of written data, comments, or views with respect to the application. Information received by the Director as a part of any application shall be available to the public as a matter of public record.

§ 670.12 General issuance criteria.

Upon receipt of a complete and properly executed application for a permit and the expiration of the applicable public comment period, the Director will decide whether to issue the permit. In making the decision, the Director will consider, in addition to the specific criteria set forth in the appropriate subparts of this part:

(a) Whether the authorization requested meets the objectives of the Act and the requirements of the regulations in this part;

(b) The judgment of persons having expertise in matters germane to the application; and

(c) Whether the applicant has failed to disclose material information required or has made false statements about any material fact in connection with the application.

§ 670.13 Permit administration.

(a) *Issuance of the permits.* The Director may approve any application in whole or part. Permits shall be issued in writing and signed by the Director. Each permit may contain such terms and conditions as are consistent with the Act and this part.

(b) *Denial.* The applicant shall be notified in writing of the denial of any permit request or part of a request and of the reason for such denial. If authorized in the notice of denial, the applicant may submit further information or reasons why the permit should not be denied. Such further submissions shall not be considered a new application.

(c) *Amendment of applications or permits.* An applicant or permit holder desiring to have any term or condition of his application or permit modified must submit full justification and supporting information in conformance with the provisions of this subpart and the subpart governing the activities sought to be carried out under the modified permit. Any application for modification of a permit that involves a material change beyond the terms originally requested will normally be subject to the same procedures as a new application.

(d) *Notice of issuance or denial.* Within 10 days after the date of the issuance or denial of a permit, the Director shall publish notice of the issuance or denial in the FEDERAL REGISTER.

(e) *Agents of the permit holder.* The Director may authorize the permit holder to designate agents to act on behalf of the permit holder.

(f) *Marine mammals, endangered species, and migratory birds.* If the Director receives a permit application involving any native mammal which is a marine mammal as defined by the Marine Mammal Protection Act of 1972 (16 U.S.C. 1362(5)), any species which is an endangered or threatened species under the Endangered Species Act of 1973 (16 U.S.C. 1531 *et seq.*) or any native bird which is protected under the Migratory Bird Treaty Act (16 U.S.C. 701 *et seq.*), the Director shall submit a copy of the application to the Secretary of Commerce or to the Secretary of the Interior, as appropriate. If the appropriate Secretary determines that a permit should not be issued pursuant to any of the cited acts, the Director shall not issue a permit. The Director shall inform the applicant of any denial by the appropriate Secretary and no further action shall be taken on the application. If, however, the appropriate Secretary issues a permit pursuant to the requirements of the cited acts, the Director still must determine whether the proposed action is consistent with the Act and the regulations in this part.

§ 670.14 Conditions of permits.

(a) *Possession of permits.* Permits issued under the regulations in this part, or copies of them, must be in the possession of persons to whom they are issued and their agents when conducting the authorized action.

(b) *Display of permits.* Any permit issued shall be displayed for inspection upon request to the Director, designated agents of the Director, or any person with enforcement responsibilities.

(c) *Filing of reports.* Permit holders are required to file reports of the activities conducted under a permit. Reports shall be submitted to the Director not later than June 30 for the preceding 12 months.

§ 670.15 Modification, suspension, and revocation.

(a) The Director may modify, suspend, or revoke, in whole or in part, any permit issued under this subpart:

(1) In order to make the permit consistent with any change to any regulation in this part made after the date of issuance of this permit;

(2) If there is any change in conditions which make the permit inconsistent with the purpose of the Act and the regulations in this part; or

(3) In any case in which there has been any violation of any term or condition of the permit, any regulation in this part, or any provision of the Act.

(b) Whenever the Director proposes any modifications, suspension, or revocation of a permit under this section, the permittee shall be afforded opportunity, after due notice, for a hearing by the Director with respect to such proposed modification, suspension or revocation. If a hearing is requested, the action proposed by the Director shall not take effect before a decision is issued by him after the hearing, unless the proposed action is taken by the Director to meet an emergency situation.

(c) Notice of the modification, suspension, or revocation of any permit by the Director shall be published in the FEDERAL REGISTER, within 10 days from the date of the Director's decision.

§ 670.16 [Reserved]

Subpart D—Native Mammals, Birds, Plants, and Invertebrates

§ 670.17 Specific issuance criteria.

With the exception of specially protected species of mammals, birds, and plants designated in subpart E of this part, permits to engage in a taking or harmful interference:

(a) May be issued only for the purpose of providing—

(1) Specimens for scientific study or scientific information; or

(2) Specimens for museums, zoological gardens, or other educational or cultural institutions or uses; or

(3) For unavoidable consequences of scientific activities or the construction and operation of scientific support facilities; and

(b) Shall ensure, as far as possible, that—

(1) No more native mammals, birds, or plants are taken than are necessary to meet the purposes set forth in paragraph (a) of this section;

(2) No more native mammals or native birds are taken in any year than can normally be replaced by net natural reproduction in the following breeding season;

(3) The variety of species and the balance of the natural ecological systems within Antarctica are maintained; and

(4) The authorized taking, transporting, carrying, or shipping of any native mammal or bird is carried out in a humane manner.

§ 670.18 Content of permit applications.

In addition to the information required in subpart C of this part, an applicant seeking a permit to take a native mammal or native bird shall include a complete description of the project including the purpose of the proposed taking, the use to be made of the native mammals or native birds, and the ultimate disposition of the native mammals and birds. An applicant seeking a permit to engage in a harmful interference shall include a complete description of the project including the purpose of the activity which will result in the harmful interference. Sufficient information must be provided to establish that the taking, harmful interference, transporting, carrying, or shipping of a native mammal or bird shall be humane.

§ 670.19 Designation of native mammals.

The following are designated native mammals:

Pinnipeds:
  Crabeater seal—*Lobodon carcinophagus.*
  Leopard seal—*Hydrurga leptonyx.*
  Ross seal—*Ommatophoca rossi.*[1]
  Southern elephant seal—*Mirounga leonina.*
  Southern fur seals—*Arctocephalus spp.*[1]
  Weddell seal—Leptonychotes weddelli.
Large Cetaceans (Whales):
  Blue whale—*Balaenoptera musculus.*
  Fin whale—*Balaenoptera physalus.*
  Humpback whale—*Megaptera novaeangliae.*
  Minke whale—*Balaenoptera acutrostrata.*
  Pygmy blue whale—*Balaenoptera musculus brevicauda*
  Sei whale—*Balaenoptera borealis*
  Southern right whale—*Balaena glacialis australis*
  Sperm whale—*Physeter macrocephalus*
Small Cetaceans (Dolphins and porpoises):
  Arnoux's beaked whale—*Berardius arnuxii.*
  Commerson's dolphin—*Cephalorhynchus commersonii*
  Dusky dolphin—*Lagenorhynchus obscurus*
  Hourglass dolphin—*Lagenorhynchus cruciger*
  Killer whale—*Orcinus orca*
  Long-finned pilot whale—*Globicephala melaena*
  Southern bottlenose whale—*Hyperoodon planifrons.*
  Southern right whale dolphin—*Lissodelphis peronii*
  Spectacled porpoise—*Phocoena dioptrica*

§ 670.20 Designation of native birds.

The following are designated native birds:

Albatross

Black-browed—*Diomedea melanophris.*
Gray-headed—*Diomedea chrysostoma.*
Light-mantled sooty—*Phoebetria palpebrata.*
Wandering—*Diomedea exulans.*

Fulmar

Northern Giant—*Macronectes halli.*
Southern—*Fulmarus glacialoides.*
Southern Giant—*Macronectes giganteus.*

Gull

Southern Black-backed—*Larus dominicanus.*

Jaeger

Parasitic—*Stercorarius parasiticus.*
Pomarine—*Stercorarius pomarinsus*

Penguin

Adelie—*Pygoscelis adeliae.*
Chinstrap—*Pygoscelis antarctica.*

---

[1] These species of mammals have been designated as specially protected species and are subject to subpart E of this part.

Emperor—*Aptenodytes forsteri.*
Gentoo—*Pygoscelis papua.*
King—*Aptenodytes patagonicus.*
Macaroni—*Eudyptes chrysolophus.*
Rockhopper—*Eudyptes crestatus.*

Petrel

Antarctic—*Thalassoica antarctica.*
Black-bellied Storm—*Fregetta tropica.*
Blue—*Halobaena caerulea.*
Gray—*Procellaria cinerea.*
Great-winged—*Pterodroma macroptera.*
Kerguelen—*Pterodroma brevirostris.*
Mottled—*Pterodroma inexpectata.*
Snow—*Pagodroma nivea.*
Soft-plumaged—*Pterodroma mollis.*
South-Georgia Diving—*Pelecanoides georgicus.*
White-bellied Storm—*Fregetta grallaria.*
White-chinned—*Procellaria aequinoctialis.*
White-headed—*Pterodroma lessoni.*
Wilson's Storm—*Oceanites oceanicus.*

Pigeon

Cape—*Daption capense.*

Pintail

South American Yellow-billed—*Anas georgica spinicauda.*

Prion

Antarctic—*Pachyptila desolata.*
Narrow-billed—*Pachyptila belcheri.*

Shag

Blue-eyed—*Phalacrocorax atriceps.*

Shearwater

Sooty—*Puffinus griseus.*

Skua

Brown—*Catharacta lonnbergi*
South Polar—*Catharacta maccormicki.*

Swallow

Barn—*Hirundo rustica.*

Sheathbill

American—*Chionis alba.*

Tern

Antarctic—*Sterna vittata.*
Arctic—*Sterna paradisaea.*

[66 FR 46739, Sept. 7, 2001]

§ 670.21 Designation of native plants.

All plants whose normal range is limited to, or includes Antarctica are designated native plants, including:

Bryophytes
Freshwater algae
Fungi
Lichens
Marine algae
Vascular Plants

§ 670.22 [Reserved]

Subpart E—Specially Protected Species of Mammals, Birds, and Plants

§ 670.23 Specific issuance criteria.

Permits authorizing the taking of mammals, birds, or plants designated as a Specially Protected Species of mammals, birds, and plants in § 670.25 may only be issued if:

(a) There is a compelling scientific purpose for such taking;

(b) The actions allowed under any such permit will not jeopardize the existing natural ecological system, or the survival of the affected species or population;

(c) The taking involves non-lethal techniques, where appropriate; and

(d) The authorized taking, transporting, carrying or shipping will be carried out in a humane manner.

§ 670.24 Content of permit applications.

In addition to the information required in subpart C of this part, an applicant seeking a permit to take a Specially Protected Species shall include the following in the application:

(a) A detailed scientific justification of the need for taking the Specially Protected Species, including a discussion of possible alternative species;

(b) Information demonstrating that the proposed action will not jeopardize the existing natural ecological system or the survival of the affected species or population; and

(c) Information establishing that the taking, transporting, carrying, or shipping of any native bird or native mammal will be carried out in a humane manner.

§ 670.25 Designation of specially protected species of native mammals, birds, and plants.

The following species has been designated as Specially Protected Species by the Antarctic Treaty Parties and is hereby designated Specially Protected Species:

Common Name and Scientific Name
Ross Seal—Ommatophoca rossii

[73 FR 14939, Mar. 20, 2008]

§ 670.26 [Reserved]

Subpart F—Antarctic Specially Protected Areas

§ 670.27 Specific issuance criteria.

Permits authorizing entry into any Antarctic Specially Protected Area designated in § 670.29 may only be issued if:

(a) The entry and activities to be engaged in are consistent with an approved management plan, or

(b) A management plan relating to the area has not been approved by the Antarctic Treaty Parties, but

(1) There is a compelling scientific purpose for such entry which cannot be served elsewhere, and

(2) The actions allowed under the permit will not jeopardize the natural ecological system existing in such area.

§ 670.28 Content of permit application.

In addition to the information required in subpart C of this part, an applicant seeking a permit to enter an Antarctic Specially Protected Area shall include the following in the application:

(a) A detailed justification of the need for such entry, including a discussion of alternatives;

(b) Information demonstrating that the proposed action will not jeopardize the unique natural ecological system in that area; and

(c) Where a management plan exists, information demonstrating the consistency of the proposed actions with the management plan.

§ 670.29 Designation of Antarctic Specially Protected Areas, Specially Managed Areas and Historic Sites and Monuments.

(a) The following areas have been designated by the Antarctic Treaty Parties for special protection and are hereby designated as Antarctic Specially Protected Areas (ASPA). The Antarctic Conservation Act of 1978, as amended, prohibits, unless authorized by a permit, any person from entering or engaging in activities within an ASPA. Detailed maps and descriptions of the sites and complete management plans can be obtained from the National Science Foundation, Office of Polar Programs, National Science Foundation, Room 755, 4201 Wilson Boulevard, Arlington, Virginia 22230.

ASPA 101 Taylor Rookery, Mac. Robertson Land
ASPA 102 Rookery Islands, Holme Bay, Mac. Robertson Land
ASPA 103 Ardery Island and Odbert Island, Budd Coast, Wilkes Land
ASPA 104 Sabrina Island, Northern Ross Sea, Antarctica
ASPA 105 Beaufort Island, McMurdo Sound, Ross Sea
ASPA 106 Cape Hallett, Northern Victoria Land, Ross Sea
ASPA 107 Emperor Island, Dion Islands, Marguerite Bay, Antarctic Peninsula
ASPA 108 Green Island, Berthelot Islands, Antarctic Peninsula
ASPA 109 Moe Island, South Orkney Islands
ASPA 110 Lynch Island, South Orkney Islands
ASPA 111 Southern Powell Island and adjacent islands, South Orkney Islands
ASPA 112 Coppermine Peninsula, Robert Island, South Shetland Islands
ASPA 113 Litchfield Island, Arthur Harbour, Anvers Island, Palmer Archipelago
ASPA 114 Northern Coronation Island, South Orkney Islands
ASPA 115 Lagotellerie Island, Marguerite Bay, Graham Land
ASPA 116 New College Valley, Caughley Beach, Cape Bird, Ross Island
ASPA 117 Avian Island, Marguerite Bay, Antarctic Peninsula
ASPA 118 Summit of Mount Melbourne, Victoria Land
ASPA 119 Davis Valley and Forlidas Pond, Dufek Massif, Pensacola Mountains
ASPA 120 Pointe-Geologie Archipelago, Terre Adelie
ASPA 121 Cape Royds, Ross Island
ASPA 122 Arrival Heights, Hut Point Peninsula, Ross Island
ASPA 123 Barwick and Balham Valleys, Southern Victoria Land
ASPA 124 Cape Crozier, Ross Island

National Science Foundation § 670.29

ASPA 125 Fildes Peninsula, King George Island (25 de Mayo)
ASPA 126 Byers Peninsula, Livingston Island, South Shetland Islands
ASPA 127 Haswell Island
ASPA 128 Western shore of Admiralty Bay, King George Island, South Shetland Islands
ASPA 129 Rothera Point, Adelaide Island
ASPA 130 Tramway Ridge, Mount Erebus, Ross Island
ASPA 131 Canada Glacier, Lake Fryxell, Taylor Valley, Victoria Land
ASPA 132 Potter Peninsula, King George Island (Isla 25 de Mayo) (South Shetland Islands)
ASPA 133 Harmony Point, Nelson Island, South Shetland Islands
ASPA 134 Cierva Point and offshore islands, Danco Coast, Antarctic Peninsula
ASPA 135 North-eastern Bailey Peninsula, Budd Coast, Wilkes Land
ASPA 136 Clark Peninsula, Budd Coast, Wilkes Land
ASPA 137 North-west White Island, McMurdo Sound
ASPA 138 Linnaeus Terrace, Asgard Range, Victoria Land
ASPA 139 Biscoe Point, Anvers Island, Palmer Archipelago
ASPA 140 Parts of Deception Island, South Shetland Islands
ASPA 141 Yukidori Valley, Langhovde, Lutzow-Holm Bay
ASPA 142 Svarthamaren
ASPA 143 Marine Plain, Mule Peninsula, Vestfold Hills, Princess Elizabeth Land
ASPA 144 Chile Bay (Discovery Bay), Greenwich Island, South Shetland Islands
ASPA 145 Port Foster, Deception Island, South Shetland Islands
ASPA 146 South Bay, Doumer Island, Palmer Archipelago
ASPA 147 Ablation Valley and Ganymede Heights, Alexander Island
ASPA 148 Mount Flora, Hope Bay, Antarctic Peninsula
ASPA 149 Cape Shirreff and San Talmo Island, Livingston Island, South Shetland Islands
ASPA 150 Ardley Island, Maxwell Bay, King George Island (25 de Mayo)
ASPA 151 Lions Rump, King George Island, South Shetland Islands
ASPA 152 Western Bransfield Strait
ASPA 153 Eastern Dallmann Bay
ASPA 154 Botany Bay, Cape Geology, Victoria Land
ASPA 155 Cape Evans, Ross Island
ASPA 156 Lewis Bay, Mount Erebus, Ross Island
ASPA 157 Backdoor Bay, Cape Royds, Ross Island
ASPA 158 Hut Point, Ross Island
ASPA 159 Cape Adare, Borchgrevink Coast
ASPA 160 Frazier Islands, Windmill Islands, Wilkes Land, East Antarctica
ASPA 161 Terra Nova Bay, Ross Sea
ASPA 162 Mawson's Huts, Cape Denison, Commonwealth Bay, George V Land, East Antarctica
ASPA 163 Dakshin Gangotri Glacier, Dronning Maud Land
ASPA 164 Scullin and Murray Monoliths, Mac. Robertson Land
ASPA 165 Edmonson Point, Wood Bay, Ross Sea
ASPA 166 Port-Martin, Terre Adelie
ASPA 167 Hawker Island, Vestfold Hills, Ingrid Christensen Coast, Princess Elizabeth Land, East Antarctica
ASPA 168 Mount Harding, Grove Mountains, East Antarctica
ASPA 169 Amanda Bay, Ingrid Christensen Coast, Princess Elizabeth Land, East Antarctica
ASPA 170 Marion Nunataks, Charcot Island, Antarctic Peninsula ASPA 171 Narebski Point, Barton Peninsula, King George Island

(b) The following areas have been designated by the Antarctic Treaty Parties for special management and have been designated as Antarctic Specially Managed Areas (ASMA). Detailed maps and descriptions of the sites and complete management plans can be obtained from the National Science Foundation, Office of Polar Programs, Room 755, 4201 Wilson Boulevard, Arlington, Virginia 22230.

ASMA 1 Admiralty Bay, King George Island
ASMA 2 McMurdo Dry Valleys, Southern Victoria Land
ASMA 3 Cape Denison, Commonwealth Bay, George V Land, East Antarctica
ASMA 4 Deception Island
ASMA 5 Amundsen-Scott South Pole Station, South Pole

§ 670.29

ASMA 6 Larsemann Hills, East Antarctica

ASMA 7 Southwest Anvers Island and Palmer Basin

(c) The following areas have been designated by the Antarctic Treaty Parties as historic sites or monuments (HSM). The Antarctic Conservation Act of 1978, as amended, prohibits any damage, removal or destruction of a historic site or monument listed pursuant to Annex V to the Protocol.

Descriptions of the sites or monuments can be obtained from the National Science Foundation, Office of Polar Programs, Room 755, 4201 Wilson Boulevard, Arlington, Virginia 22230.

HSM 1 Flag mast erected in December 1965 at South Geographical Pole by the First Argentine Overland Polar Expedition.

HSM 2 Rock cairn and plaques erected in January 1961 at Syowa Station in memory of Shun Fukushima.

HSM 3 Rock cairn and plaque erected in January 1930 by Sir Douglas Mawson on Proclamation Island, Enderby Land.

HSM 4 Station building to which a bust of V.I. Lenin is fixed together with a plaque in memory of the conquest of the Pole of Inaccessibility, by Soviet Antarctic Explorers in 1958.

HSM 5 Rock cairn and plaque at Cape Bruce, Mac. Robertson Land, erected in February 1931 by Sir Douglas Mawson.

HSM 6 Rock cairn and canister at Walkabout Rocks, Vestfold Hills, Princess Elizabeth Land, erected in 1939 by Sir Hubert Wilkins.

HSM 7 Stone with inscribed plaque, erected at Mirny Observatory, Mabus Point, in memory of driver-mechanic Ivan Kharma.

HSM 8 Metal Monument sledge and plaque at Mirny Observatory, Mabus Point, in memory of driver-mechanic Anatoly Shcheglov.

HSM 9 Cemetery on Buromskiy Island, near Mirny Observatory.

HSM 10 Building (Magnetic Observatory) at Dobrowolsky Station, Bunger Hills, with plaque in memory of the opening of Oasis Station in 1956.

HSM 11 Heavy Tractor at Vostock Station with plaque in memory of the opening of the Station in 1957.

HSM 14 Site of ice cave at Inexpressible Island, Terra Nova Bay, constructed in March 1912 by Victor Campbell's Northern Party.

HSM 15 Hut at Cape Royds, Ross Island, built in February 1908 by the British Antarctic Expedition.

HSM 16 Hut at Cape Evans, Ross Island, built in January 1911 by the British Antarctic Expedition.

HSM 17 Cross on Wind Vane Hill, Cape Evans, Ross Island, erected by the Ross Sea Party in memory of three members of the party who died in the vicinity in 1916.

HSM 18 Hut at Hut Point, Ross Island, built in February 1902 by the British Antarctic Expedition.

HSM 19 Cross at Hut Point, Ross Island, erected in February 1904 by the British Antarctic Expedition in memory of George Vince.

HSM 20 Cross on Observation Hill, Ross Island, erected in January 1913 by the British Antarctic Expedition in memory of Captain Robert F Scott's party which perished on the return journey from the South Pole.

HSM 21 Remains of stone hut at Cape Crozier, Ross Island, constructed in July 1911 by the British Antarctic Expedition.

HSM 22 Three huts and associated relics at Cape Adare Two built in February 1899 the third was built in February 2011 all by the British Antarctic Expedition.

HSM 23 Grave at Cape Adare of Norwegian biologist Nicolai Hanson.

HSM 24 Rock cairn, known as "Amundsen's cairn," at Mount Betty, Queen Maud Range erected by Roald Amundsen in January 1912.

HSM 26 Abandoned installations of Argentine Station "General San Martin" on Barry Island, Debenham Islands, Marguerite Bay, Antarctic Peninsula.

HSM 27 Cairn with a replica of a lead plaque erected at Megalestris Hill, Petermann Island in 1909 by the second French expedition.

HSM 28 Rock Cairn at Port Charcot, Booth Island, with wooden pillar and plaque.

HSM 29 Lighthouse named "Primero de Mayo" erected on Lambda Island, Melchior Islands, by Argentina in 1942.

HSM 30 Shelter at Paradise Harbour erected in 1950.

HSM 32 Concrete Monolith erected in 1947 near Capitan Arturo Prat Base on Greenwich Island, South Shetland Islands.

HSM 33 Shelter and cross with plaque near Capitan Arturo Prat Base Greenwich Island, South Shetland Islands.

HSM 34 Bust at Capitan Arturo Prat base Greenwich Island, South Shetland Islands, of Chilean naval hero Arturo Prat.

HSM 35 Wooden cross and statue of the Virgin of Carmen erected in 1947 near Capitan Arturo Prat base Greenwich Island, South Shetland Islands.

HSM 36 Replica of a metal plaque erected by Eduard Dallman at Potter Cove, King George Island, South Shetland Islands.

HSM 37 Statue erected in 1948 at General Bernando O'Higgins Base (Chile) Trinity Peninsula.

HSM 38 Wooden hut on Snow Hill Island built in February 1902 by the Swedish South Polar Expedition.

HSM 39 Stone hut at Hope Bay, Trinity Peninsula built in January 1903 by the Swedish South Polar Expedition.

HSM 40 Bust of General San Martin, grotto with statue of the Virgin Lujan, a flag mast and graveyard at Base Esperanza, Hope Bay Trinity Peninsula, erected by Argentina in 1955.

HSM 41 Stone hut and grave at Paulet Island built in 1903 by members of the Swedish South Polar Expedition.

HSM 42 Area of Scotia bay, Laurie Island, South Orkney containing stone huts built in 1903 by the Scottish Antarctic Expedition, Argentine meteorological hut and magnetic observatory (Moneta house) and graveyard.

HSM 43 Cross erected in 1955 and subsequently moved to Belgrano II Station, Nunatak Bertrab, Confin Coast, Coats Land in 1979.

HSM 44 Plaque erected at temporary Indian Station "Dakshin Gangotri," Princess Astrid Kyst, Droning Maud Land, listing the names of the first Indian Antarctic Expedition.

HSM 45 Plaque on Brabant Island, on Metchnikoff Point, at a height of 70m on the crest of the moraine separating this point from the glacier and bearing an inscription.

HSM 46 All of the buildings and installations of Port-Martin Base, Terre Ad6lie, constructed in 1950 by the 3rd French expedition in Terre Ad6lie.

HSM 47 Wooden building called "Base Marret" on the Ile des Petrels, Terre Ad6lie.

HSM 48 Iron Cross on the North-East headland of the Ile des Petrels, Terre Ad6lie.

HSM 49 Concrete pillar erected by the First Polish Antarctic Expedition at Dobrowski Station on Bunger Hill in January 1959, to measure acceleration due to gravity.

HSM 50 Brass Plaque bearing the Polish Eagle at Fildes Peninsula, King George Island, South Shetland Islands.

HSM 51 Grave of Wlodzimierz Puchalski, surmounted by an iron cross south of Arctowski station on King George Island, South Shetland Islands.

HSM 52 Monolith commemorating the establishment on 20 February 1985 of the "Great Wall Station" on Fildes Peninsula, King George Island, South Shetland Islands.

HSM 53 Bust of Captain Luis Alberto Pardo, monolith and plaques on Point Wild, Elephant Island, South Shetland Islands.

HSM 54 Richard E. Byrd Historic Monument, a bronze bust at McMurdo Station.

HSM 55 East Base, Antarctica, Stonington Island (Buildings and artifacts) erected by the Antarctic Service Expedition (1939–1941) and the Ronne Antarctic Research Expedition (1947–1948).

HSM 56 Waterboat Point, Danco Coast, (remains of hut and environs).

HSM 57 Plaque at "Yankee Bay" (Yankee Harbour), MacFarlane Strait, Greenwich Island, South Shetland Islands.

HSM 59 Cairn on Half Moon Beach, Cape Shirreff, Livingston Island, South Shetland Islands and a Plaque on 'Cerro Gaviota' opposite San Telmo Islets.

HSM 60 Wooden plaque and cairn placed in November 1903 at "Penguins Bay," Seymour Island (Marambio), James Ross Archipelago.

§ 670.30

HSM 61 "Base A" at Port Lockroy, Goudier Island, off Wiencke Island.
HSM 62 "Base F" (Wordie House), on Winter Island, Argentine Islands.
HSM 63 "Base Y" on Horseshoe Island, Marguerite Bay, western Graham Land.
HSM 64 "Base E" on Stonington Island, Marguerite Bay, western Graham Land.
HSM 65 Message post erected in January 1895 on Svend Foyn Island, Possession Islands.
HSM 66 Prestrud's cairn, Scott Nunataks, Alexandra Mountains, Edward VII Peninsula erected in December 1911.
HSM 67 Rock shelter known as "Granite House," erected in 1911 at Cape Geology, Granite Harbour.
HSM 68 Site of depot at Hells Gate Moraine, Inexpressible Island, Terra Nova Bay.
HSM 69 Message post at Cape Crozier, Ross Island, erected January 1902 by Capt. Robert F. Scott's Discovery Expedition.
HSM 70 Message post at Cape Wadworth, Coulman Island, erected January 1902 by Capt. Robert F. Scott.
HSM 71 Whalers Bay, Deception Island, South Shetland Islands (includes whaling artifacts).
HSM 72 Mikkelsen Cairn, Tryne Islands, Vestfold Hills.
HSM 73 Memorial Cross for the 1979 Mount Erebus crash victims, erected in January 1987 at Lewis Bay, Ross Island.
HSM 74 Unnamed cove on the southwest coast of Elephant Island, South Shetland Islands, including the foreshore and intertidal area, in which the wreckage of a large wooden sailing vessel is located.
HSM 75 "A Hut" of Scott base, Pram Point, Ross Island.
HSM 76 Ruins of base Pedro Aguirre Cerda, Pendulum Cove, Deception Island, South Shetland Islands.
HSM 77 Cape Denison, Commonwealth Bay, George V Land, including Boat Harbour and the historic artifacts contained within its waters.
HSM 78 Memorial Plaque at India Point, Humboldt Mountains, Wohlthat Massif, central Dronning Maud Land.
HSM 79 Lillie Marleen Hut, Mt. Dockery, Everett Range, Northern Victoria Land.
HSM 80 Amundsen's Tent erected in December 1911 at the South Pole.
HSM 81 Rocher du Debarquement (Landing Rock).
HSM 82 Monument to the Antarctic Treaty and Plaques, Fildes Peninsula, King George Island, South Shetland Islands.
HSM 83 Base "W" established in 1956 at Detaille Island, Lallemande Fjord, Loubert Coast.
HSM 84 Hut erected in 1973 at Damoy Point, Dorian Bay, Wiencke Island, Palmer Archipelago.
HSM 85 Plaque Commemorating the PM-3A Nuclear Power Plant at McMurdo Station.
HSM 86 No.1 Building Commemorating China's Antarctic Expedition at Great Wall/Station.

[77 FR 5404, Feb. 3, 2012]

§ 670.30 [Reserved]

Subpart G—Import Into and Export From the United States

§ 670.31 Specific issuance criteria for imports.

Subject to compliance with other applicable law, any person who takes a native mammal, bird, or plant under a permit issued under the regulations in this part may import it into the United States unless the Director finds that the importation would not further the purpose for which it was taken. If the importation is for a purpose other than that for which the native mammal, bird, or plant was taken, the Director may permit importation upon a finding that importation would be consistent with the purposes of the Act, the regulations in this part, or the permit under which they were taken.

§ 670.32 Specific issuance criteria for exports.

The Director may permit export from the United States of any native mammal, bird, or native plants taken within Antarctica upon a finding that exportation would be consistent with the purposes of the Act, the regulations in this part, or the permit under which they were taken.

§ 670.33 Content of permit applications.

In addition to the information required in subpart C of this part, an applicant seeking a permit to import into or export from the United States a native mammal, a native bird, or native plants taken within Antarctica shall include the following in the application:

(a) Information demonstrating that the import or export would further the purposes for which the species was taken;

(b) Information demonstrating that the import or export is consistent with the purposes of the Act or the regulations in this part;

(c) A statement as to which U.S. port will be used for the import or export, and

(d) Information describing the intended ultimate disposition of the imported or exported item.

§ 670.34 Entry and exit ports.

(a) Any native mammal, native bird, or native plants taken within Antarctica that are imported into or exported from the United States must enter or leave the United States at ports designated by the Secretary of Interior in 50 CFR part 14. The ports currently designated are:

(1) Los Angeles, California.
(2) San Francisco, California.
(3) Miami, Florida.
(4) Honolulu, Hawaii.
(5) Chicago, Illinois.
(6) New Orleans, Louisiana.
(7) New York, New York.
(8) Seattle, Washington.
(9) Dallas/Fort Worth, Texas.
(10) Portland, Oregon.
(11) Baltimore, Maryland.
(12) Boston, Massachusetts.
(13) Atlanta, Georgia.

(b) Permits to import or export at non-designated ports may be sought from the Secretary of Interior pursuant to subpart C, 50 CFR part 14.

§ 670.35 [Reserved]

Subpart H—Introduction of Non-Indigenous Plants and Animals

§ 670.36 Specific issuance criteria.

For purposes consistent with the Act, only the following plants and animals may be considered for a permit allowing their introduction into Antarctica:

(a) Domestic plants; and

(b) Laboratory animals and plants including viruses, bacteria, yeasts, and fungi.

Living non-indigenous species of birds shall not be introduced into Antarctica.

§ 670.37 Content of permit applications.

Applications for the introduction of plants and animals into Antarctica must describe:

(a) The species, numbers, and if appropriate, the age and sex, of the animals or plants to be introduced into Antarctica;

(b) The need for the plants or animals;

(c) What precautions the applicant will take to prevent escape or contact with native fauna and flora; and

(d) How the plants or animals will be removed from Antarctica or destroyed after they have served their purpose.

§ 670.38 Conditions of permits.

All permits allowing the introduction of non-indigenous plants and animals will require that the animal or plant be kept under controlled conditions to prevent its escape or contact with native fauna and flora and that after serving its purpose the plant or animal shall be removed from Antarctica or be destroyed in manner that protects the natural system of Antarctica.

§ 670.39 [Reserved]

PART 671—WASTE REGULATION

Subpart A—Introduction

Sec.
671.1 Purpose of regulations.
671.2 Scope.
671.3 Definitions.

Subpart B—Prohibited Acts, Exceptions

671.4 Prohibited acts.
671.5 Exceptions.

Subpart C—Permits

671.6 Applications for permits.
671.7 General issuance criteria.
671.8 Permit administration.
671.9 Conditions of permit.
671.10 Review, modification, suspension, and revocation.

Subpart D—Waste Management

671.11 Waste storage.
671.12 Waste disposal.
671.13 Waste management for the USAP.

Subpart E—Designation of Banned Substances; Reclassification of Pollutants

671.14 Annual review.
671.15 Publication of preliminary determination.
671.16 Designation and redesignation of pollutants.

Subpart F—Cases of Emergency

671.17 Cases of emergency.

AUTHORITY: 16 U.S.C. 2405.

SOURCE: 58 FR 34719, June 29, 1993, unless otherwise noted.

Subpart A—Introduction

§671.1 Purpose of regulations.

The purposes of these regulations in part 671 are to protect the Antarctic environment and dependent and associated ecosystems, to preserve Antarctica's value as an area for the conduct of scientific research, and to implement the Antarctic Conservation Act of 1978, Public Law 95–541, consistent with the provisions of the Protocol on Environmental Protection to the Antarctic Treaty, signed in Madrid, Spain, on October 4, 1991.

§671.2 Scope.

These regulations in part 671 apply to any U.S. citizen's use or release of a banned substance, designated pollutant or waste in Antarctica.

[58 FR 34719, June 29, 1993, as amended at 59 FR 37438, July 22, 1994]

§671.3 Definitions.

(a) *Definitions.* In this part:

Act means the Antarctic Conservation Act of 1978, Public Law 95–541, 92 Stat. 2048 (16 U.S.C. 2401 *et seq.*).

Antarctic hazardous waste means any waste consisting of or containing one or more designated pollutants.

Antarctica means the area south of 60 degrees south latitude.

Banned substance means any polychlorinated biphenyls (PCBs), non-sterile soil, polystyrene beads, plastic chips or similar loose polystyrene packing material, pesticides (other than those required for scientific, medical or hygiene purposes) or other substance designated as such under subpart E of this part.

Designated pollutant means any substance designated as such by the Director pursuant to subpart E of this part; any pesticide, radioactive substance, or substance consisting of or containing any chemical listed by source, generic or chemical name at 40 CFR 61.01, Table 116.4A of 40 CFR 116.4; subpart D of 40 CFR part 261, 40 CFR 302.4, part 355, and part 372; and any substance which exhibits a hazardous waste characteristic as defined in subparts B and C of 40 CFR part 261; but shall not include any banned substance.

Director means the Director of the National Science Foundation, or an officer or employee of the Foundation designated by the Director.

Incinerate or *Incineration* means the processing of material by mechanisms that (1) involve the control of combustion air and/or fuel so as to maintain adequate temperature for efficient combustion; (2) contain the combustion reaction in an enclosed device with sufficient residence time and mixing for complete processing; and (3) control emission of gaseous or particulate combustion products.

Master permit means a permit issued to a federal agency, or its agents or contractors, or any other entity, covering activities conducted in connection with USAP or other group activities in Antarctica.

NSF or *Foundation* means the National Science Foundation.

Open burning means combustion of any material by means other than incineration.

Permit means a permit issued pursuant to subpart C of this part.

Private permit means any permit other than a master permit.

Protocol means the Protocol on Environmental Protection to the Antarctic Treaty, signed by the United States in Madrid on October 4, 1991, and any and all Annexes thereto, as amended or supplemented from time to time.

Release means any spilling, leaking, pumping, pouring, emitting, emptying, discharging, injecting, leaching, dumping, burying or disposing of a substance, whether intentionally or accidentally.

Station means McMurdo Station, Palmer Station, Amundsen-Scott South Pole Station and any other permanent USAP facility in Antarctica designed to accommodate at least 50 persons at any one time.

Substance means any gas, liquid, or solid, or mixture thereof, including biological material.

Treaty means the Antarctic Treaty signed in Washington, D.C., on December 1, 1959.

United States means the several States of the Union, the District of Columbia, the Commonwealth of Puerto Rico, American Samoa, the Virgin Islands, Guam and the Trust Territory of the Pacific Islands, including the Federated States of Micronesia and the Commonwealth of the Northern Mariana Islands.

United States Antarctic Program or *USAP* means the United States national program in Antarctica.

U.S. citizen means any individual who is a citizen or national of the United States; any corporation, partnership, trust, association, or other legal entity existing or organized under the laws of any of the United States; and any department agency or other instrumentality of the Federal government or of any State, and any officer, employee, or agent of such instrumentality.

Use means to use, generate or create a substance, or to import a substance into Antarctica, but does not include the shipboard use of a substance, provided that substance is not released or removed from the vessel.

Waste means any substance that will no longer be used for any useful purpose, but does not include substances to be recycled in Antarctica, or substances to be reused in a manner different than their initial use, provided such substances are stored in a manner that will prevent their dispersal into the environment, and further provided that they are recycled, reused or disposed of in accordance with the provisions of this part within three years. Recycling includes, but is not limited to, the reuse, further use, reclamation or extraction of a waste through a process or activity that is separate from the process or activity that produced the waste.

(b) *Pollutants, generally.* All banned substances, designated pollutants and waste shall be considered pollutants for purposes of the Antarctic Conservation Act.

Subpart B—Prohibited Acts, Exceptions

§ 671.4 Prohibited acts.

Unless one of the exceptions stated in § 671.5 is applicable, it is unlawful for any U.S. citizen to:

(a) Use or release any banned substance in Antarctica;

(b) Use or release any designated pollutant in Antarctica, except pursuant to a permit issued by NSF under subpart C of this part;

(c) Release any waste in Antarctica, except pursuant to a permit issued by NSF under subpart C of this part; or

(d) Violate any term or condition of a permit issued by NSF under subpart C of this part, or any term or condition of any of the regulations issued under this part.

§ 671.5 Exceptions

A permit shall not be required for any use or release of designated pollutants or waste allowed under the Act to Prevent Marine Pollution from Ships (33 U.S.C. 1901 *et seq.*), as amended, or for any shipboard use of banned substances or designated pollutants, provided such substances are not removed from the vessel in Antarctica.

Subpart C—Permits

§ 671.6 Applications for permits.

(a) *General content of permit applications.* Each application for a permit shall be dated and signed by the applicant, and shall include the following information:

(1) The applicant's name, address and telephone number, the business or institutional affiliation of the applicant, or the name, address and telephone number of the president, principal officer or managing partner of the applicant, as applicable;

(2) A description of the types, expected concentrations and volumes of wastes and designated pollutants to be released in Antarctica; the nature and timing of such releases; arrangements for waste management, including, without limitation, plans for waste reduction, minimization, treatment and processing, recycling, storage, transportation and disposal; arrangements for training and educating personnel to comply with these waste management requirements and procedures, and arrangements for monitoring compliance; and other arrangements for minimizing and monitoring the environmental impacts of proposed operations and activities;

(3) A description of the types, expected concentrations and volumes of designated pollutants to be used in Antarctica; the nature and timing of such uses; the method of storage of designated pollutants; and a contingency plan for controlling releases in a manner designed to minimize any resulting hazards to health and the environment;

(4) The desired effective date and duration of the permit; and

(5) The following certification:

"I certify that, to the best of my knowledge and belief, and based upon due inquiry, the information submitted in this application for a permit is complete and accurate. Any knowing or intentional false statement will subject me to the criminal penalties of 18 U.S.C. 1001."

(b) *Address to which application should be sent.* Each application shall be in writing, and sent to:

Permits Office, Office of Polar Programs, National Science Foundation, 4201 Wilson Boulevard, Arlington, VA 22230.

(c) *Sufficiency of application.* The sufficiency of the application shall be determined by the Director. The Director may waive any requirement for information, or require such additional information as he determines is relevant to the processing and evaluation of the application.

(d) *Publication of permit applications.* The Director shall publish notice in the FEDERAL REGISTER of each application for a permit and the proposed conditions of its issuance (including duration). The notice shall invite the submission by interested parties, the Environmental Protection Agency and other federal agencies, within 30 days after the date of publication of notice, of written data, comments, or views with respect to the application. Information received by the Director as a part of any application shall be available to the public as a matter of public record.

[58 FR 34719, June 29, 1993, as amended at 59 FR 37438, July 22, 1994]

§ 671.7 General issuance criteria.

(a) Upon receipt of a complete and properly executed application for a permit, the Director will decide whether and on what conditions he will issue a permit. In making this decision, the Director will carefully consider any comments or suggestions received from interested parties, the Environmental Protection Agency and other federal agencies pursuant to § 671.6(d), and will determine whether the permit requested meets the objectives of the Act, the Protocol, and the requirements of these regulations.

(b) Permits authorizing the use or release of designated pollutants or wastes may be issued only if, based on relevant available information, the Director determines that such use or release will not pose a substantial hazard to health or the environment, taking into account available information on the possible cumulative impact of multiple releases.

§ 671.8 Permit administration.

(a) *Issuance of permits.* The Director may approve an application for a permit in whole or in part, and may condition such approval upon compliance with additional terms and conditions. Permits shall be issued in writing, shall be signed by the Director, shall specify duration, and shall contain such terms and conditions as may be established by the Director and as are consistent with the Act and this part.

(b) *Denial.* An applicant shall be notified in writing of the denial of any permit request or part of a request, and the reason for such denial. If authorized in the notice of denial, the applicant may submit further information, or reasons why the permit should not be denied. Such further submissions shall constitute amendments of the application.

(c) *Amendment of applications or permits.* An applicant or permit holder desiring to have any term or condition of his application or permit modified must submit full justification and supporting information in conformance with the provisions of this part. Any application for modification of a permit that involves a material change beyond the terms originally requested will be subject to the same procedures as a new application.

(d) *Public notice of issuance or denial.* Within 10 days after the date of the issuance or denial of a permit, the Director shall publish notice of the issuance or denial in the FEDERAL REGISTER, including the conditions of issuance or basis for denial, as appropriate.

§ 671.9 Conditions of permit.

(a) *Conditions.* All permits issued pursuant to subpart C of this part shall be conditioned upon compliance with the relevant provisions of the ACA, the Treaty, the Protocol, such specific conditions or restrictions as may be imposed by the Director under § 671.7, and the provisions of subpart D of this part.

(b) *Possession of permits.* Permits issued under this part, or copies of them, must be in the possession of persons to whom they are issued or their agents when conducting the authorized action. Any permit issued shall be shown to the Director or to any other person with enforcement authority upon request.

(c)(1) *Reports.* Permit holders must provide the Director with written reports of:

(i) Any non-permitted release of designated pollutants or waste within fourteen days after the occurrence of such release, including the date, quantity and cause of the release, and plans for remediation;

(ii) The identity and quantity of all designated pollutants removed from Antarctica or otherwise disposed of, and the method of disposal; and

(iii) Any other violations of the terms and conditions of their permits.

(2) The Director may also require permit holders to file reports of activities conducted under their permits. Such reports shall be submitted to the Director not later than June 30 for the preceding 12 month period ending May 31.

§ 671.10 Review, modification, suspension, and revocation.

(a) The Director may modify, suspend or revoke, in whole or in part, any permit issued under this part:

(1) In order to make the permit consistent with any change to any regulation in this part made after the date of issuance of the permit;

(2) If there is any change in conditions which makes the permit inconsistent with the Act and any regulation in this part; or

(3) In any case in which there has been any violation of any term or condition of the permit, any regulation in this part, or any provision of the Act.

(b) The Director shall review all unexpired permits issued under this part at least biennially to determine whether those permits should be modified, suspended or revoked as set forth in paragraph (a) of this section.

(c) Whenever the Director proposes any modifications, suspensions or revocations of a permit under this § 671.10, the permittee shall be afforded the opportunity, after due notice, for a hearing by the Director with respect to such proposed modification, suspension, or revocation. If a hearing is requested, the action proposed by the Director shall not take effect before a decision is issued by him after the hearing, unless the proposed action is taken by the Director to meet an emergency situation.

(d) Notice of the modification, suspension, or revocation of any permit shall be published in the FEDERAL REGISTER within 10 days from the date of the Director's decision.

Subpart D—Waste Management

§ 671.11 Waste storage.

(a) Pending the treatment, disposal or removal of any wastes pursuant to § 671.12, all wastes shall be contained, confined or stored in a manner that will prevent dispersal into the environment;

(b) All Antarctic hazardous wastes generated at or transported to any USAP station may be temporarily stored at such station prior to the treatment, disposal or removal of any wastes pursuant to § 671.12, provided all such Antarctic hazardous waste is stored in either closed containers or tanks labeled to indicate their contents and the beginning date of accumulation of such waste, and further provided the following conditions are satisfied:

(1) If Antarctic hazardous wastes, radioactive wastes, or medical wastes, are generated at or transported to McMurdo Station, they may be temporarily stored at that station for a period not to exceed 15 months;

(2) If Antarctic hazardous wastes, radioactive wastes, or medical wastes, are generated at or transported to South Pole Station, they may be temporarily stored at that station while awaiting transport to McMurdo Station, for a period not to exceed 15 months;

(3) If Antarctic hazardous wastes, radioactive wastes, or medical wastes, are generated at or transported to Palmer Station, they may be temporarily stored at that station while awaiting transport to McMurdo Station or other disposition, for a period not to exceed 28 months;

(4) Containers holding Antarctic hazardous wastes must be:

(i) In good, non-leaking condition with sufficient structural integrity for the storage of Antarctic hazardous waste;

(ii) Made of or lined with materials which will not react with, and are otherwise compatible with, the Antarctic hazardous waste to be stored, so that the ability of the containers to contain such waste is not impaired;

(iii) Stored in a manner that allows access for inspection and response to emergencies; and

(iv) Inspected at least weekly for leakage and deterioration. All inspections must be appropriately documented.

(5) Tank systems used for storing Antarctic hazardous wastes must be in good, non-leaking condition with sufficient structural integrity for the storing of hazardous wastes; and systems must be inspected weekly to detect corrosion or releases of waste and to collect data from monitoring and leak detection equipment, to the extent available, to ensure that they are functioning properly. All inspections must be appropriately documented. Prior to the expiration of the 15 month period referred to in § 671.11(b)(1), all Antarctic hazardous wastes shall be treated or removed from Antarctica in accordance with § 671.12.

(6) Ignitable, reactive or incompatible wastes shall be properly segregated and protected from sources of ignition or reaction, as appropriate.

(c) All Antarctic hazardous wastes generated at a location other than a permanent station may be temporarily stored at such location for a period not to exceed 12 months, in closed, non-leaking containers marked to indicate their contents. Such containers must be in good condition and made of or lined with material which will not react with and is otherwise compatible with the Antarctic hazardous waste stored therein so as not to impair the ability of the container to contain the waste. Prior to the expiration of the 12 month period referred to above, all such hazardous wastes shall be either:

(1) Treated or processed, disposed of or removed from Antarctica pursuant to § 671.12, or

(2) Removed to a permanent station and temporarily stored at that station in accordance with paragraph (b) of this section.

§ 671.12 Waste disposal.

(a)(1) The following wastes shall be removed from Antarctica:

(i) Radioactive materials;

(ii) Electrical batteries;

(iii) Fuel (both liquid and solid);

(iv) Waste containing harmful levels of heavy metals or acutely toxic or harmful persistent compounds;

(v) Poly-vinyl chloride (PVC), polyurethane foam, polystyrene foam, rubber and lubricating oils, treated timbers and other products containing additives which can produce harmful emissions or releases;

(vi) All other plastic wastes except low density polyethylene containers (such as bags for storing wastes) provided such containers are incinerated in accordance with paragraph (e) of this section;

(vii) Solid, non-combustible wastes; and

(viii) Fuel, oil and chemical drums that constitute waste.

(2) Notwithstanding paragraph (a)(1) of this section, the obligations set forth in paragraphs (a)(1) (vii) and (viii) of this section shall not apply if the Director determines that the removal of such wastes by any practicable option would cause greater adverse environmental impacts than would be caused by leaving them in their existing locations.

(b) All liquid wastes other than sewage and domestic liquid wastes and wastes referred in paragraph (a) of this section shall be removed from Antarctica to the maximum extent practicable.

(c) Sewage and domestic liquid wastes may be discharged directly into the sea, taking into account the assimilative capacity of the receiving marine environment, and provided that such discharge occurs, wherever practicable, where conditions exist for initial dilution and rapid dispersal, and further provided that large quantities of such wastes (generated in a station where the average weekly occupancy over the austral summer is approximately 30 individuals or more) shall be treated at least by maceration. If biological treatment processes are used, the by-product of such treatment may be disposed of into the sea provided disposal does not adversely affect the local environment.

(d) Residues of introduced animal carcasses, laboratory culture of microorganisms and plant pathogens, and introduced avian products must be removed from Antarctica unless incinerated, autoclaved or otherwise sterilized.

(e) Combustible wastes not removed from Antarctica other than wastes referred to in paragraph (a) of this section, shall be burnt in incinerators which reduce harmful emissions or discharges to the maximum extent practicable and the solid residue of such incineration shall be removed from Antarctica; provided, however, that USAP may continue to bury such combustible wastes in snow pits at South Pole Station, but must phase out such practices before March 1, 1995. Any emission or discharge standards and equipment guidelines which may be recommended by the Committee for Environmental Protection constituted or to be constituted pursuant to the Protocol or by the Scientific Committee on Antarctic Research shall be taken into account.

(f) Sewage and domestic liquid wastes and other liquid wastes not removed from Antarctica in accordance with other provisions of this section, shall, to the maximum extent practicable, not be disposed of onto sea ice, ice shelves or grounded ice-sheet unless such wastes were generated by stations located inland on ice shelves or on the grounded ice-sheet. In such event, the wastes may be disposed of in deep ice pits if that is the only practicable option, provided the ice pits are not located on known ice-flow lines which terminate at ice-free land areas or in blue ice areas of high ablation. .

(g) No wastes may be disposed of onto ice-free areas or into any fresh water system.

(h) Open burning of wastes is prohibited at all permanent stations, and shall be phased out at all other locations by March 1, 1994. If it is necessary to dispose of waste by open burning prior to March 1, 1994, allowance shall be made for the wind direction and speed and the type of waste to be burnt to limit particulate deposition and to avoid such deposition over areas of special biological, scientific, historic, aesthetic or wilderness significance.

(i) Each unauthorized release of waste in Antarctic shall be, to the maximum extent practicable, promptly cleaned up by the person responsible for such release.

§ 671.13 Waste management for the USAP.

(a) In order to provide a basis for tracking USAP wastes, and to facilitate studies aimed at evaluating the environmental impacts of scientific activity and logistic support, the USAP shall classify its wastes in one of the following categories:

(1) Sewage and domestic liquid wastes;

(2) Other liquid wastes and chemicals, including fuels and lubricants;

(3) Solid wastes to be combusted;

(4) Other solid wastes; and

(5) Radioactive material.

(b) USAP shall prepare and annually review and update a waste management plan (including plans for waste reduction, storage and disposal) specifying for each of its permanent stations, field camps and ships (other than small boats that are part of the operations of permanent stations or are otherwise taken into account in existing management plans for ships):

(1) Current and planned waste management arrangements, including final disposal;

(2) Current and planned arrangement for assessing the environmental effects of waste and waste management;

(3) Other efforts to minimize environmental effects of wastes and waste management; and

(4) Programs for cleaning up existing waste disposal sites and abandoned work sites.

(c) USAP shall designate one or more waste management officials to develop and monitor waste management plans and ensure that members of expeditions receive training so as to limit the impact of their activities on the Antarctic environment, and to inform them of the requirements of the Protocol and of this part.

(d) USAP shall, to the extent practicable, prepare an inventory of locations of past activities (i.e., traverses, fuel depots, field bases, crashed aircraft) so that such locations can be taken into account in planning future scientific, logistic and waste management programs.

(e) USAP shall clean up its past and present waste disposal sites on land and abandoned work sites, except that it shall not be required to:

(1) Remove any structure designated as a historic site or monument; or

(2) Remove any structure or waste in circumstances where the removal would result in greater adverse environmental impact than leaving the structure or waste in its existing location.

(f) USAP shall circulate waste management plans and inventories described in this section in accordance with the requirements of the Treaty and the Protocol.

Subpart E—Designation of Banned Substances; Reclassification of Pollutants

§ 671.14 Annual review.

The Director shall review the list of banned substances and designated pollutants at least annually, and may propose the designation or redesignation of any substance as a banned substance, designated pollutant or other waste, based on the following criteria:

(a) If the Director determines that a substance, including a designated pollutant, poses a substantial immediate hazard to health or the environment and such hazard cannot be eliminated through waste management practices or other methods, or if the Parties to the Protocol or Treaty agree that a substance should be banned from use in Antarctica, the Director may designate such substance a banned substance.

(b) If the Director determines that a substance is liable to create a hazard to health or the environment if improperly treated or processed, stored, transported, or disposed of, the Director may designate such substance a designated pollutant.

(c) If the Director determines that a substance previously designated a banned substance no longer displays the characteristics described in paragraph (a) of this section, the Director may remove such substance from the list of banned substances (to the extent consistent with the provisions of the Protocol), but if the Director determines that such substance has the characteristics described in paragraph (b) of this section, it shall be redesignated a designated pollutant.

(d) If the Director determines that a substance previously designated a designated pollutant no longer displays the characteristics described in paragraph (b) of this section, the Director may remove such substance from the list of designated pollutants.

(e) In making the determinations referred to in paragraphs (a) through (d) of this section, the Director shall take into account all relevant new information obtained through monitoring activities or otherwise.

§ 671.15 Publication of preliminary determination

Prior to any designation or redesignation of substances pursuant to § 671.14 (including removal of such substances from lists of banned substances or designated pollutants), the Director shall publish notice in the FEDERAL REGISTER of any proposed designation or redesignation, including the basis therefor. The notice shall invite the submission by interested parties, the Environmental Protection Agency and other federal agencies, within 30 days after the date of publication of notice, of written data, comments, or views with respect to such action.

§ 671.16 Designation and redesignation of pollutants

After review of any comments or suggestions received from interested parties, the Environmental Protection Agency and other Federal agencies pursuant to § 671.15, the Director will make a final determination to designate and redesignate various substances as set forth above. Within 10 days after the date of such final determination, the Director shall publish notice of any action taken in the FEDERAL REGISTER. Such action shall become effective no earlier than thirty days following publication of notice.

Subpart F—Cases of Emergency

§ 671.17 Cases of emergency.

The provisions of this part shall not apply in cases of emergency relating to the safety of human life or of ships, aircraft or other equipment and facilities of high value, or the protection of the environment. Notice of any acts or omissions resulting from such emergency situations shall be reported promptly to the Director, who shall notify the Treaty parties in accordance with the requirements of the Treaty and the Protocol, and publish notice of such acts or omissions in the FEDERAL REGISTER.

PART 672—ENFORCEMENT AND HEARING PROCEDURES

Sec.
672.1 Hearing procedures—Scope of these rules.
672.2 Definitions.
672.3 Powers and duties of the Director; Presiding Official; Office of Polar Programs.
672.4 Filing, service, and form of pleadings and documents.
672.5 Filing and service of rulings, orders, and decisions.
672.6 Appearances.
672.7 Issuance of complaint.
672.8 Answer to the complaint.
672.9 Motions.
672.10 Default order.
672.11 Informal settlement; consent agreement and order.
672.12 Prehearing conference.
672.13 Accelerated decision; decision to dismiss.
672.14 Scheduling the hearing.
672.15 Evidence.
672.16 Objections and offers of proof.
672.17 Burden of presentation; burden of persuasion.
672.18 Filing the transcript.
672.19 Proposed findings, conclusions, and order.
672.20 Initial decision.
672.21 Appeal from or review of interlocutory orders or rulings.
672.22 Appeal from or review of initial decision.
672.23 Final order on appeal.
672.24 Maximum civil monetary penalties for violations.

AUTHORITY: 16 U.S.C. 2401 et seq., 28 U.S.C. 2461 note.

SOURCE: 54 FR 7132, Feb. 16, 1989, unless otherwise noted. Redesignated at 58 FR 34718, June 29, 1993.

§ 672.1 Hearing procedures—Scope of these rules.

(a) These hearing rules govern all adjudicatory proceedings for the assessment of civil penalties or imposition of other sanctions pursuant to the Antarctic Conservation Act of 1978, 16 U.S.C. 2407; 2404(f); 2401–2412; and

(b) Other adjudicatory proceedings that the Foundation, in its discretion, determines are appropriate for handling under these rules, including proceedings governed by the Administrative Procedure Act requirements for "hearings on the record." 5 U.S.C. 554 (1982).

(c) Questions arising at any stage of the proceeding which are not addressed in these rules shall be resolved at the discretion of the Director or Presiding Officer.

§ 672.2 Definitions.

(a) Throughout these rules, words in the singular also include the plural, and words in the masculine gender also include the feminine, and vice versa.

(b) *Act* means the particular statute authorizing the initiation of the proceeding.

(c) *Administrative Law Judge* means an Administrative Law Judge appointed under 5 U.S.C. 3105 (see also Pub. L. 95–251, 92 Stat. 183).

(d) *Complainant* means any person authorized to issue a complaint on behalf of the Agency to persons alleged to be in violation of the Act. The complainant shall not be the Presiding Officer or any other person who will participate or advise in the decision.

(e) *Complaint* means a written communication, alleging one or more violations of specific provisions of the Act, Treaties, NSF regulations or a permit promulgated thereunder, issued by the complainant to a person under this subpart.

(f) *Consent Agreement* means any written document, signed by the parties, containing stipulations or conclusions of fact or law, and a proposed penalty, revocation or suspension of a permit, or other sanction.

(g) *Director* means the Director of the National Science Foundation (NSF) or his delegatee.

(h) *Final Order* means (1) an order issued by the Director after an appeal of an initial decision, accelerated decision, a decision to dismiss, or default order, or (2) an initial decision which becomes a final order.

(i) *Foundation, Agency,* or *NSF* means the National Science Foundation.

(j) *Hearing* means a hearing on the record open to the public and conducted under these rules.

(k) *Hearing Clerk* is the person with whom all pleadings, motions, and other documents required under this subpart are filed.

(l) *Initial Decision* means the decision issued by the Presiding Officer based upon the official record of the proceedings.

(m) *Party* means any person that participates in a hearing as complainant, respondent, or intervenor.

(n) *Permit* means a permit issued under section 5 of the Antarctic Conservation Act of 1978, 16 U.S.C. section 2404.

(o) *Person* includes any individual, partnership, association, corporation, and any trustee, assignee, receiver or legal successor thereof; any organized group of persons whether incorporated or not; and any officer, employee, agent, department, agency or instrumentality of the Federal Government. of any State or local unit of government, or of any foreign government.

(p) *Presiding Officer* means the attorney designated by the Director to conduct hearings or other proceedings under this subpart.

(q) *Respondent* means any person proceeded against in the complaint.

(r) Terms defined in the Act and not defined in these rules of practice are used consistent with the meanings given in the Act.

§ 672.3 Powers and duties of the Director; Presiding Official; Office of Polar Programs.

(a) *Director.* The Director of NSF shall exercise all powers and duties as prescribed or delegated under the Act and these rules.

(b) The Director may delegate all or part of his authority. Partial delegation does not prevent the Presiding Officer from referring any motion or case to the Director.

(c) *Presiding Officer.* The Director may designate one or more Presiding Officers to perform the functions described below. The Presiding Officers shall be attorneys who are permanent or temporary employees of the Foundation or some other Federal Agency and may perform other duties compatible with their authority as hearing officers. Administrative Law Judges may perform the functions of Presiding Officers. The Presiding Officer shall have performed no prosecutorial or investigatory functions in connection with any matter related to the hearing.

(d) The Presiding Officer shall conduct a fair and impartial proceeding, assure that the facts are fully elicited, adjudicate all issues, and avoid delay. The Presiding Officer shall have authority to:

(1) Conduct administrative hearings under these rules of practice;

(2) Rule upon motions, requests, and offers of proof, dispose of procedural requests, and issue all necessary orders;

(3) Administer oaths and affirmations and take affidavits;

(4) Examine witnesses and receive documentary or other evidence;

(5) For good cause, upon motion or sua sponte, order a party, or an officer or agent thereof, to produce testimony, documents, or other nonprivileged evidence, and failing the production thereof without good cause being shown, draw adverse inferences against that party;

(6) Admit or exclude evidence;

(7) Hear and decide questions of facts, law or discretion;

(8) Require parties to attend conferences for the settlement or simplification of the issues, or the expedition of facts, law or discretion;

(9) Issue subpoenas authorized by the Act; and

(10) Take all actions necessary for the maintenance of order and for the efficient, fair and impartial adjudication of issues arising in proceedings governed by these rules.

(e) *Disqualification; Withdrawal.* (1) The Presiding Officer may not participate in any matter in which he (i) has a financial interest or (ii) has any relationship with a party or with the subject matter which would make it inappropriate for him to act. Any party may at any time by motion made to the Director, or his delegatee, request that the Presiding Officer be disqualified from the proceeding.

(2) If the Presiding Officer is disqualified or withdraws from the proceeding, the Director shall assign a qualified replacement who has none of the infirmities listed in paragraph (e)(1) of this section. The Director, should he withdraw or disqualify himself, shall assign the Deputy Director to be his replacement.

(f) *Office of Polar Programs.* The Office of Polar Programs (OPP) manages and operates the national program in Antarctica, including administration of the Antarctic Conservation Act (ACA) permit system. OPP is responsible for investigating alleged violations of the "prohibited acts" section of the ACA and alleged noncompliance with ACA permits. OPP will act as the official complainant in all proceedings under the ACA governed by these rules. OPP may delegate all or part of its investigatory duties to other appropriate NSF employees, other qualified federal employees, or consultants. OPP will prepare complaints with the assistance of designated prosecuting attorneys within NSF's Office of the General Counsel, other qualified federal attorneys, or other appropriate legal representative selected jointly by OPP and OGC. The designated prosecuting attorney will represent OPP in all proceedings governed by these rules.

(g) The Office of Polar Programs, acting on behalf of the Director, may designate qualified individuals as enforcement officers empowered to execute all of the law enforcement functions set forth in section 10 of the ACA, 16 U.S.C. 2409, as well as any other appropriate actions ancillary to those statutory duties. OPP will provide each enforcement officer with official enforcement credentials for identification purposes and use during execution of official duties.

OPP may also designate knowledgeable individuals to provide educational and other information regarding the Antarctic to tour operators, their clients and employees, and other visitors to the Antarctic.

(h) The Office of the General Counsel, with the concurrence of the Office of Polar Programs, may refer appropriate cases to the Department of Justice for

§672.4

possible prosecution of criminal violations of the Antarctic Conservation Act.

[54 FR 7132, Feb. 16, 1989. Redesignated at 58 FR 34718, June 29, 1993, and amended at 59 FR 37438, July 22, 1994; 61 FR 51022, Sept. 30, 1996; 66 FR 42451, Aug. 13, 2001]

§672.4 Filing, service, and form of pleadings and documents.

(a) *Filing of pleadings and documents.* (1) Except as otherwise provided, the original and one copy of the complaint, and the original of the answer and of all other documents served in the proceeding, shall be filed with the Hearing Clerk.

(2) A certificate of service shall accompany each document filed or served. Except as otherwise provided, a party filing documents with the Hearing Clerk, after the filing of the answer, shall serve copies thereof upon all other parties and the Presiding Officer. The Presiding Officer shall maintain a duplicate file during the course of the proceeding.

(3) When the Presiding Officer corresponds directly with the parties, he shall file the original of the correspondence with the Hearing Clerk, maintain a copy in the duplicate file, and send a copy to all parties. Parties who correspond directly with the Presiding Officer shall in addition to serving all other parties send a copy of all such correspondence to the Hearing Clerk. A certificate of service shall accompany each document served under this subsection.

(b) *Service of pleadings and documents*—(1) *Service of complaint.* (i) Service of a copy of the signed original of the complaint, together with a copy of these rules, may be made personally or by certified mail, return receipt requested, on the respondent or his representative.

(ii) Service upon a domestic or foreign corporation or upon a partnership or other unincorporated association which is subject to suit under a common name shall be made by personal service or certified mail, as prescribed by paragraph (b)(1)(i) of this section, directed to an officer, partner, a managing or general agent, or to any other person authorized by appointment or by Federal or State law to receive service of process.

(iii) Service upon an officer or agency of the United States shall be made by delivering a copy of the complaint to the officer or agency, or in any manner prescribed for service by applicable regulations. If the agency is a corporation, the complaint shall be served as prescribed in paragraph (b)(1)(ii) of this section.

(iv) Service upon a State or local unit of government, or a State or local officer, agency, department, corporation or other instrumentality shall be made by serving a copy of the complaint in the manner prescribed by the law of the State for the service of process on any such persons, or

(A) If upon a State or local unit of government, or a State or local department, agency, corporation or other instrumentality, by delivering a copy of the complaint to the chief executive officer thereof; or

(B) If upon a State or local officer by delivering a copy to such officer.

(v) Proof of service of the complaint shall be made by affidavit of the person making personal service, or by properly executed return receipt. Such proof of service shall be filed with the complaint immediately upon completion of service.

(2) The first page of every pleading, letter, or other document shall contain a caption identifying the respondent and the docket number which is exhibited on the complaint.

(3) The original of any pleading, letter, or other document (other than exhibits) shall be signed by the party filing it or by his representative. The signature constitutes a representation by the signer that he has read the pleading, letter or other document, that to the best of his knowledge, information and belief, the statements made therein are true, and that it is not interposed for delay.

(4) The initial document filed by any person shall contain his name, address and telephone number. Any changes in this information shall be communicated promptly to the Hearing Clerk, Presiding Officer, and all parties to the proceeding. A party who fails to furnish such information and any changes thereto shall be deemed to have waived

§ 672.5 Filing and service of rulings, orders, and decisions.

(a) All rulings, orders, decisions, and other documents issued by the Presiding Officer shall be filed with the Hearing Clerk. Copies of all such documents shall be served personally, or by certified mail, return receipt requested, upon all parties.

(b) *Computation.* In computing any period of time prescribed or allowed in these rules, except as otherwise provided, computation is by calendar days and does not include the day of the event from which the designated period begins to run. When a stated time expires on a Saturday, Sunday or legal holiday, the stated time period shall be extended to include the next business day.

(c) *Extensions of time.* The Presiding Officer may grant an extension of time for the filing of any pleading, document, or motion (1) upon timely motion of a party to the proceeding, for good cause shown, and after consideration of prejudice to other parties, or (2) upon his own motion. Such a motion by a party may only be made after notice to all other parties, unless the movant can show good cause why serving notice is impracticable. The motion shall be filed in advance of the date on which the pleading, document or motion is due to be filed, unless the failure of a party to make timely motion for extension of time was the result of excusable neglect.

(d) *Service by mail.* Service of the complaint is complete when the return receipt is signed. Service of all other pleadings and documents is complete upon mailing. Where a pleading or document is served by mail, five (5) days shall be added to the time allowed by these rules for the filing of a responsive pleading or document.

(e) *Ex parte discussion of proceeding.* At no time after the issuance of the complaint shall the Presiding Officer, or any other person who is likely to advise these officials in the decision on the case, discuss ex parte the merits of the proceeding with any interested person outside the Agency, with any Agency staff member who performs a prosecutorial or investigative function in the proceeding or other factually related proceeding, or with any representative of such person. Any ex parte memorandum or other communication addressed to the Presiding Officer during the pendency of the proceeding and relating to the merits thereof, by or on behalf of any party, shall be regarded as argument made in the proceeding and shall be served upon all other parties. The Presiding Officer shall give the other parties an opportunity to reply.

(f) Subject to the provisions of law restricting the public disclosure of confidential information, any person may, during Agency business hours, inspect and copy any document filed in any proceeding. Such documents shall be made available by the Hearing Clerk.

(g) The person seeking copies of any documents filed in a proceeding shall bear the cost of duplication. Upon a formal request the Agency may waive this cost in appropriate cases.

§ 672.6 Appearances.

(a) *Appearances.* Any party may appear in person or by counsel or other representative. A partner may appear on behalf of a partnership and an officer may appear on behalf of a corporation. Persons who appear as counsel or other representative must conform to the standards of conduct and ethics required of practitioners before the courts of the United States.

(b) *Intervention.* A motion for leave to intervene in any proceeding conducted under these rules must set forth the grounds for the proposed intervention, the position and interest of the movant, and whether the intervention will cause delay. Any person already a party to the proceeding may file an answer to a motion to intervene, making specific reference to the factors set forth in the foregoing sentence and paragraph (c) of this section, within ten (10) days after service of the motion for leave to intervene.

(c) A motion for leave to intervene in a proceeding must ordinarily be filed before the first prehearing conference, or if there is no such conference, prior to the setting of a time and place for a hearing. Any motion filed after that time must include, in addition to the information set forth in paragraph (b) of this section, a statement of good cause for the failure to file in a timely manner. Agreements, arrangements, and other matters previously resolved during the proceeding are binding on the intervenor.

(d) *Disposition.* The Presiding Officer may grant leave to intervene only if the movant demonstrates that (1) his presence in the proceeding would not unduly prolong or otherwise prejudice the adjudication of the rights of the original parties; (2) the movant will be adversely affected by a final order; and (3) the interests of the movant are not being adequately represented by the original parties. The intervenor becomes a full party to the proceeding upon the granting of leave to intervene.

(e) *Amicus curiae.* Persons not parties to the proceeding who wish to file briefs may so move. The motion shall identify the interest of the applicant and shall state the reasons why the proposed amicus brief is desirable. If the motion is granted, the Presiding Officer or Director shall issue an order setting the time for filing such brief. An amicus curiae is eligible to participate in any briefing after his motion is granted, and shall be served with all briefs, motions, and orders relating to issues to be briefed.

(f) *Consolidation.* The Presiding Officer may, by motion or sua sponte, consolidate any or all matters at issue in two or more proceedings docketed under these rules where (1) there exists common parties or common questions of fact or law; (2) consolidation would expedite and simplify consideration of the issues; and (3) consolidation would not adversely affect the rights of parties engaged in otherwise separate proceedings.

(g) *Severance.* The Presiding Officer may, by motion or sua sponte, for good cause shown order any proceedings severed with respect to any or all parties or issues.

§ 672.7 Issuance of complaint.

(a) *General.* If the complainant has reason to believe that a person has violated any provision of the Antarctic Conservation Act, other Act or attendant regulations, or a permit issued under the ACA, he may institute a proceeding for the assessment of a civil penalty or other sanctions by issuing a complaint under the Act and these rules.

(b) If the complainant has reason to believe that (1) a permittee violated any term or condition of the permit, or (2) a permittee misrepresented or inaccurately described any material fact in the permit application or failed to disclose all relevant facts in the permit application, or (3) other good cause exists for such action, he may institute a proceeding for the revocation or suspension of a permit by issuing a complaint under the Act and these rules. A complaint may seek suspension or revocation of a permit in addition to the assessment of a civil penalty.

(c) *Content and amendment of the complaint.* All complaints shall include:

(1) A statement reciting the section(s) of the Act, regulations, and/or permit authorizing the issuance of the complaint;

(2) A concise statement of the factual basis for all alleged violations; and

(3) Notice of the respondent's right to request a hearing on any material fact contained in the complaint, or on the appropriateness of the proposed sanction.

(d) Each complaint for the assessment of a civil penalty shall also include:

(1) Specific reference to each provision of the Act and implementing regulations which respondent is alleged to have violated;

(2) The amount of the civil penalty which is proposed to be assessed; and

(3) A statement explaining the reasoning behind the proposed penalty;

(e) Each complaint for the revocation or suspension of a permit shall also include:

(1) Specific reference to each term or condition of the permit which the respondent is alleged to have violated, to each alleged inaccuracy or misrepresentation in respondent's permit application, to each fact which the respondent allegedly failed to disclose in his permit application, or to other reasons which form the basis for the complaint;

(2) A request for an order to either revoke or suspend the permit and a statement of the terms and conditions

National Science Foundation § 672.9

of any proposed partial suspension or revocation; and

(3) A statement indicating the basis for recommending the revocation, rather than the suspension, of the permit, or vice versa.

A copy of these rules shall accompany each complaint served.

(f) *Derivation of proposed civil penalty.* The complainant shall determine the dollar amount of the proposed civil penalty in accordance with any criteria set forth in the Act and with any civil penalty guidance issued by NSF.

(g) *Amendment of the complaint.* The complainant may amend the complaint once as a matter of right at any time before the answer is filed. Otherwise the complainant may amend the complaint only upon motion granted by the Presiding Officer. Respondent shall have twenty (20) additional days from the date of service of the amended complaint to file his answer.

(h) *Withdrawal of the complaint.* The complainant may withdraw the complaint, or any part thereof, without prejudice one time before the answer has been filed. After one withdrawal before the filing of an answer, or after the filing of an answer, the complainant may withdraw the complaint, or any part thereof, without prejudice, only upon motion granted by the Presiding Officer.

(i) Complainant, in cooperation with the Office of General Counsel, may refer cases to the Department of Justice for possible criminal prosecution if there is reason to believe that respondent willfully violated the Antarctic Conservation Act or its attendant regulations. Such referral does not automatically preclude NSF from proceeding administratively under the Act and these rules against the same respondent.

§ 672.8 Answer to the complaint.

(a) *General.* Where respondent (1) contests any material fact upon which the complaint is based; (2) contends that the amount of the penalty proposed in the complaint or the proposed revocation or suspension, as the case may be, is inappropriate; or (3) contends that he is entitled to judgment as a matter of law, he shall file a written answer to the complaint with the Hearing Clerk. Any such answer to the complaint must be filed with the Hearing Clerk within twenty (20) days after service of the complaint.

(b) *Contents of the answer.* The answer shall clearly and directly admit, deny or explain each of the factual allegations contained in the complaint. If respondent asserts he has no knowledge of a particular factual allegation, the allegation is deemed denied. The answer shall also state (1) the circumstances or arguments which are alleged to constitute the grounds of defense; (2) the facts which respondent intends to place at issue; and (3) whether a hearing is requested.

(c) *Request for hearing.* A hearing upon the issues raised by the complaint and answer shall be held upon request of respondent in the answer. The Presiding Officer may deem the right to a hearing waived if it is not requested by respondent. In addition, a hearing may be held at the discretion of the Presiding Officer, sua sponte, to examine issues raised in the answer.

(d) *Failure to admit, deny, or explain.* Failure of respondent to admit, deny, or explain any material factual allegation contained in the complaint constitutes an admission of the allegation.

(e) *Amendment of the answer.* The respondent may amend the answer to the complaint upon motion granted by the Presiding Officer.

§ 672.9 Motions.

(a) *General.* All motions, except those made orally on the record during a hearing, shall (1) be in writing; (2) state the basis or grounds with particularity; (3) set forth the relief or order sought; and (4) be accompanied by any affidavit, certificate, or other evidence or legal memorandum relied upon.

(b) *Response to motions.* A party must file a response to any written motion within ten (10) days after service of such motion, unless the Presiding Officer allows additional time. The response shall be accompanied by any affidavit, certificate, other evidence, or legal memorandum relied upon. If no response is filed within the designated period, the Presiding Officer may deem the parties to have waived any objection to the granting of the motion. The

Presiding Officer may also set a shorter time for response, or make such other appropriate orders concerning the disposition of motions.

(c) *Ruling on Motions.* The Presiding Officer shall rule on all motions, unless otherwise provided in these rules. The Presiding Officer may permit oral argument if he considers it necessary or desirable.

§ 672.10 Default order.

(a) *Default.* The Presiding Officer may find a party in default (1) after motion, upon failure to file a timely answer to the complaint; (2) after motion or sua sponte, upon failure to comply with a prehearing or hearing order of the Presiding Officer; or (3) after motion or sua sponte, upon failure to appear at a conference or hearing without good cause being shown. No finding of default on the basis of a failure to appear at a hearing shall be made against the respondent unless the complainant presents sufficient evidence to the Presiding Officer to establish a prima facie case against the respondent. Any motion for a default order shall include a proposed default order and shall be served upon all parties. The alleged defaulting party shall have twenty (20) days from service to reply to the motion. Default by respondent constitutes, for purposes of the pending action only, an admission of all facts alleged in the complaint and a waiver of respondent's right to a hearing on such factual allegations. If the complaint is for the assessment of a civil penalty, the penalty proposed in the complaint shall become due and payable by respondent without further proceedings sixty (60) days after a final order issued upon default. If the complaint is for the revocation or suspension of a permit, the conditions of revocation or suspension proposed in the complaint shall become effective without further proceedings on the date designated by the Presiding Officer in his final order issued upon default. Default by the complainant shall result in the dismissal of the complaint with prejudice.

(b) *Procedures upon default.* When the Presiding Officer finds a default has occurred, he shall issue a default order against the defaulting party. This order shall constitute the initial decision, and shall be filed with the Hearing Clerk.

(c) *Contents of a default order.* A default order shall include findings of fact showing the grounds for the order, conclusions regarding all material issues of law or discretion, and the penalty which is recommended, or the terms and conditions of permit revocation or suspension, or other sanctions.

(d) The Presiding Officer may set aside a default order for good cause shown.

§ 672.11 Informal settlement; consent agreement and order.

(a) *Settlement policy.* The Agency encourages settlement of a proceeding at any time if the settlement is consistent with the provisions and objectives of the Act and applicable regulations. The respondent may confer with complainant concerning settlement whether or not the respondent requests a hearing. Settlement conferences shall not affect the respondent's obligation to file a timely answer.

(b) *Consent agreement.* The parties shall forward a written consent agreement and a proposed consent order to the Presiding Officer whenever settlement or compromise is proposed. The consent agreement shall state that, for the purpose of this proceeding, respondent (1) admits the jurisdictional allegations of the complaint; (2) admits the facts stipulated in the consent agreement or neither admits nor denies specific factual allegations contained in the complaint; and (3) consents to the assessment of a stated civil penalty or to the stated permit revocation or suspension, or to other sanctions or actions in mitigation. The consent agreement shall include any and all terms of the agreement, and shall be signed by all parties or their counsel or representatives.

(c) *Consent order.* No settlement or consent agreement shall dispose of any proceeding under the rules without a consent order from the Director or his delegatee. Before signing such an order, the Director or his delegatee may require that the parties to the settlement appear before him to answer inquiries relating to the consent agreement or order.

National Science Foundation § 672.12

(d) *Actions by respondent to clean, protect, enhance, or benefit the environment.* NSF may accept from respondent environmentally beneficial actions, in lieu of penalties, in whole or in part, assessed under the Antarctic Conservation Act. An assessment of the monetary value of any action in mitigation shall be made before that action is incorporated as a part of any consent agreement and order.

§ 672.12 Prehearing conference.

(a) *Purpose of prehearing conference.* Unless a conference appears unnecessary, the Presiding Officer, at any time before the hearing begins, shall direct the parties and their counsel or other representatives to appear at a conference before him to consider:

(1) The settlement of the case;

(2) The simplification of issues and stipulation of facts not in dispute;

(3) The necessity or desirability of amendments to pleadings;

(4) The exchange of exhibits, documents, prepared testimony, and admissions or stipulations of fact which will avoid unnecessary proof;

(5) The limitation of the number of expert or other witnesses;

(6) Setting a time and place for the hearing; and

(7) Any other matters which may expedite the proceeding.

(b) *Exchange of witness lists and documents.* Unless otherwise ordered by the Presiding Officer, each party at the prehearing conference shall make available to all other parties (1) the names of the expert and other witnesses he intends to call, together with a brief narrative summary of their expected testimony, and (2) copies of all documents and exhibits which each party intends to introduce into evidence. Documents and exhibits shall be marked for identification as ordered by the Presiding Officer. The Presiding Officer may exclude from evidence any document or testimony not disclosed at the prehearing conference. If the Presiding Officer permits the submittal of new evidence, he will grant parties a reasonable opportunity to respond.

(c) *Record of the prehearing conference.* No transcript of a prehearing conference relating to settlement shall be made. With respect to other prehearing conferences, no transcript of any prehearing conferences shall be made unless ordered by the Presiding Officer upon motion of a party or sua sponte. The Presiding Officer shall prepare and file for the record a written summary of the action taken at the conference. The summary shall incorporate any written stipulations or agreements of the parties and all rulings and appropriate orders containing directions to the parties.

(d) *Unavailability of a prehearing conference.* If a prehearing conference is unnecessary or impracticable, the Presiding Officer, on motion or sua sponte, may conduct a telephonic conference or direct the parties to correspond with him to accomplish any of the objectives set forth in this section.

(e) *Other discovery.* (1) Except as provided by paragraph (b) of this section, further discovery shall be permitted only upon determination by the Presiding Officer that (i) such discovery will not in any way unreasonably delay the proceeding; (ii) the information to be obtained is not otherwise obtainable; and (iii) such information has significant probative value.

(2) The Presiding Officer shall order depositions upon oral questions only upon a showing of good cause and upon a finding that (i) the information sought cannot be obtained by alternative methods; or (ii) there is substantial reason to believe that relevant and probative evidence may otherwise not be preserved for presentation by a witness at the hearing.

(3) Any party may request further discovery by motion. Such a motion shall set forth (i) the circumstances warranting the taking of the discovery; (ii) the nature of the information expected to be discovered; and (iii) the proposed time and place where it will be taken. If the Presiding Officer determines that the motion should be granted, he shall issue an order granting discovery, with any qualifying conditions and terms.

(4) When the information sought to be obtained is within the control of one of the parties, failure to comply with an order issued pursuant to this paragraph may lead to (i) the inference that the information to be discovered would be adverse to the party from whom the

§ 672.13

information was sought; or (ii) the issuance of a default.

§ 672.13 Accelerated decision; decision to dismiss.

(a) *General.* The Presiding Officer, upon motion of any party or sua sponte, may at any time render an accelerated decision in favor of the complainant or the respondent as to all or any part of the proceeding, without further hearing or upon such limited additional evidence, such as affidavits, as he may require, if no genuine issue of material fact exists and a party is entitled to judgment as a matter of law regarding all or any part of the proceeding. In addition, the Presiding Officer, upon motion of the respondent, may at any time dismiss an action without further hearing or upon such limited additional evidence as he requires, if complainant fails to establish a prima facie case, or if other grounds show complainant has no right to relief.

(b) *Effect.* (1) If an accelerated decision or a decision to dismiss is issued as to all the issues and claims in the proceeding, the decision constitutes an initial decision of the Presiding Officer, and shall be filed with the Hearing Clerk.

(2) If an accelerated decision or a decision to dismiss is rendered on less than all issues or claims in the proceeding, the Presiding Officer shall determine what material facts exist without substantial controversy and what material facts remain controverted in good faith. He shall then issue an interlocutory order specifying the facts which appear substantially uncontroverted, and the issues and claims upon which the hearing will proceed.

§ 672.14 Scheduling the hearing.

(a) When an answer is filed, the Hearing Clerk shall forward the complaint, the answer, and any other documents filed thus far in the proceeding to the Presiding Officer, who will notify the parties of his assignment.

(b) *Notice of hearing.* If the respondent requests a hearing in his answer, or one is ordered by the Presiding Officer, the Presiding Officer shall serve upon the parties a notice setting forth a time and place for the hearing. The Presiding Officer may issue the notice of hearing at any appropriate time, but not later than twenty (20) days prior to the date set for the hearing.

(c) *Postponement of hearing.* The Presiding Officer will not grant a request for postponement of a hearing except upon motion and for good cause shown.

§ 672.15 Evidence.

(a) *General.* The Presiding Officer shall admit all evidence which is not irrelevant, immaterial, unduly repetitious, or otherwise unreliable or of little probative value. Notwithstanding the preceding sentence, evidence relating to settlement which would be excluded in the federal courts under Rule 408 of the Federal Rules of Evidence is inadmissible. In the presentation, admission, disposition, and use of evidence, the Presiding Officer shall preserve the confidentiality of trade secrets and other commercial and financial information. The confidential or trade secret status of any information shall not, however, preclude its introduction into evidence. The Presiding Officer may review such evidence in camera, and issue appropriate protective orders.

(b) *Examination of witnesses.* Parties shall examine witnesses orally, under oath or affirmation, except as otherwise provided in these rules or by the Presiding Officer. Parties shall have the right to cross-examine a witness who appears at the hearing.

(c) *Verified statements.* The Presiding Officer may admit into the record as evidence, in lieu of oral testimony, statements of fact or opinion prepared by a witness. The admissibility of the evidence contained in the statement shall be subject to the same rules as if the testimony were produced under oral examination. Before any such statement is read or admitted into evidence, the witness shall deliver a copy of the statement to the Presiding Officer, the reporter, and opposing counsel. The witness presenting the statement shall swear to or affirm the statement and shall be subject to appropriate oral cross-examination.

(d) *Admission of affidavits where the witness is unavailable.* The Presiding Officer may admit into evidence affidavits of witnesses who are "unavailable," within the meaning of that term under Rule 804(a) of the Federal Rules of Evidence.

(e) *Exhibits.* Where practicable, an original and one copy of each exhibit shall be filed with the Presiding Officer for the record and a copy shall be furnished to each party. A true copy of any exhibit may be substituted for the original.

(f) *Official notice.* Official notice may be taken of any matter judicially noticeable in the Federal courts and of other facts within the specialized knowledge and experience of the Agency. Opposing parties shall be given adequate opportunity to show that such facts are erroneously noticed.

§ 672.16 Objections and offers of proof.

(a) *Objection.* Any objection concerning the conduct of the hearing may be made orally or in writing during the hearing. The party raising the objection must supply a short statement of its grounds. The ruling by the Presiding Officer on any objection and the reasons given for it shall be part of the record. An exception to each objection overruled shall be automatic and is not waived by further participation in the hearing.

(b) *Offer of proof.* Whenever evidence is excluded from the record, the party offering the evidence may make an offer of proof, which shall be included in the record. The offer of proof for excluded oral testimony shall consist of a brief statement describing the nature of the evidence excluded. The offer of proof for excluded documents or exhibits shall consist of the insertion in the record of the documents or exhibits excluded.

§ 672.17 Burden of presentation; burden of persuasion.

The complainant has the burden of going forward with and of proving that the violation occurred as set forth in the complaint and that the proposed civil penalty, revocation, suspension, or other sanction, is appropriate. Following the establishment of a prima facie case, respondent has the burden of presenting and of going forward with any defense to the allegations set forth in the complaint. The Presiding Officer shall decide all controverted matters upon a preponderance of the evidence.

§ 672.18 Filing the transcript.

The hearing shall be transcribed verbatim. After the Presiding Officer closes the record, the reporter shall promptly transmit the original and certified copies to the Hearing Clerk, and one certified copy directly to the Presiding Officer. A certificate of service shall accompany each copy of the transcript. The Hearing Clerk shall notify all parties of the availability of the transcript and shall furnish the parties with a copy of the transcript upon payment of the cost of reproduction, unless a party can show that the cost is unduly burdensome. Any person not a party to the proceeding may obtain a copy of the transcript upon payment of the reproduction fee, except for those parts of the transcript ordered to be kept confidential by the Presiding Officer.

§ 672.19 Proposed findings, conclusions, and order.

Unless otherwise ordered by the Presiding Officer, any party may submit proposed findings of fact, conclusions of law, and a proposed order, together with supporting briefs, within twenty (20) days after the parties are notified of the availability of the transcript. The Presiding Officer shall set a time by which reply briefs must be submitted. All submissions shall be in writing, shall be served upon all parties, and shall contain adequate references to the record and relied-upon authorities.

§ 672.20 Initial decision.

(a) *Filing and contents.* The Presiding Officer shall issue and file with the Hearing Clerk an initial decision as soon as practicable after the period for filing reply briefs, if any, has expired. The initial decision shall contain findings of fact, conclusions regarding all material issues of law or discretion, the reasons for the findings and conclusions, a recommended civil penalty assessment or other sanction, if appropriate, and a proposed final order. Upon receipt of an initial decision, the Hearing Clerk shall forward a copy to all parties, and shall send the original, along with the record of the proceeding, to the Director.

(b) *Amount of civil penalty.* If the Presiding Officer determines that a violation has occurred, he shall set the dollar amount of the recommended civil penalty in the initial decision in accordance with any criteria set forth in the Act, and must consider any civil penalty guidelines issued by NSF. If the Presiding Officer decides to assess a penalty different in amount from the penalty recommended in the complaint, he shall set forth in the initial decision the specific reasons for the increase or decrease. The Presiding Officer shall not raise a penalty from that recommended in the complaint if the respondent has defaulted.

(c) *Effect of initial decision.* The initial decision of the Presiding Officer shall become the final order of the Agency within forty-five (45) days after its service upon the parties and without further proceedings unless (1) an appeal to the Director is filed by a party to the proceedings; or (2) the Director elects, sua sponte, to review the initial decision.

(d) *Motion to reopen a hearing.* A motion to reopen a hearing to take further evidence must be made no later than twenty (20) days after service of the initial decision on the parties and shall (1) state the specific grounds upon which relief is sought; (2) state briefly the nature and purpose of the evidence to be adduced; (3) show that such evidence is not cumulative; and (4) show good cause why such evidence was not adduced at the hearing. The motion shall be made to the Presiding Officer and filed with the Hearing Clerk. Parties shall have ten (10) days following service to respond. The Presiding Officer shall grant or deny such motion as soon as practicable. The conduct of any proceeding which may be required as a result of the granting of any motion to reopen shall be governed by the provisions of the applicable sections of these rules. The filing of a motion to reopen a hearing shall automatically stay the running of all time periods specified under these Rules until such time as the motion is denied or the reopened hearing is concluded.

§ 672.21 Appeal from or review of interlocutory orders or rulings.

(a) *Request for interlocutory orders or rulings.* Except as provided in this section, appeals to the Director or, upon delegation, to the General Counsel, shall obtain as a matter of right only from a default order, an accelerated decision or decision to dismiss, or an initial decision rendered after an evidentiary hearing. Appeals from other orders or rulings shall lie only if the Presiding Officer, upon motion of a party, certifies such orders or rulings to the Director on appeal. Requests for such certification shall be filed in writing within six (6) days of notice of the ruling or service of the order, and shall state briefly the grounds to be relied upon on appeal.

(b) *Availability of interlocutory appeal.* The Presiding Officer may certify any ruling for appeal to the Director when (1) the order or ruling involves an important question of law or policy and there is substantial grounds for difference of opinion; and (2) either (i) an immediate appeal from the order or ruling will materially advance the ultimate resolution of the proceeding, or (ii) review after the final order is issued will be inadequate or ineffective.

(c) *Decision.* If the Director or the General Counsel takes no action within thirty (30) days of the certification, the appeal is dismissed. If the Director or the General Counsel decides to hear the interlocutory appeal, he shall make and transmit his findings and conclusions to the Presiding Officer. When the Presiding Officer declines to certify an order or ruling to the Director on interlocutory appeal, it may be reviewed by the Director only upon appeal from the initial decision.

(d) *Stay of proceedings.* The Presiding Officer may stay the proceedings for an interlocutory appeal. Proceedings will not be stayed except in extraordinary circumstances. Where the Presiding Officer grants a stay of more than thirty (30) days, such stay must be separately approved by the Director.

§ 672.22 Appeal from or review of initial decision.

(a) *Notice of appeal.* Any party may appeal any adverse initial decision of the Presiding Officer by filing a notice of appeal and an accompanying appellate brief with the Hearing Clerk and upon all other parties and amicus curiae within twenty (20) days after the initial decision is served upon the parties. The notice of appeal shall set forth alternative findings of fact, alternative conclusions regarding issues of law or discretion, and a proposed order together with relevant references to the record and the initial decision. The appellant's brief shall contain a statement of the issues presented for review, argument on the issues presented, and a short conclusion stating the precise relief sought, together with appropriate references to the record. Within twenty (20) days of the service of notices of appeal and briefs, any other party or amicus curiae may file with the Hearing Clerk a reply brief responding to argument raised by the appellant, together with references to the relevant portions of the record, initial decision, or opposing brief. Reply briefs shall be limited to the scope of the appeal brief.

(b) *Sua sponte review by the Director.* Whenever the Director determines sua sponte to review an initial decision, the Hearing Clerk shall serve notice of such intention on the parties within forty-five (45) days after the initial decision is served upon the parties. The notice shall include a statement of issues to be briefed by the parties and a time schedule for the service and filing of briefs.

(c) *Scope of appeal or review.* The appeal of the initial decision shall be limited to those issues raised by the parties during the course of the proceeding. If the Director determines that issues raised, but not appealed by the parties, should be argued, he shall give the parties or their representatives written notice of such determination to permit preparation of adequate argument. Nothing herein shall prohibit the Director from remanding the case to the Presiding Officer for further proceedings.

(d) *Argument.* The Director may, upon request of a party or sua sponte, assign a time and place for oral argument.

§ 672.23 Final order on appeal.

(a) *Contents of the final order.* When an appeal has been taken or the Director issues a notice of intent to conduct review sua sponte, the Director shall issue a final order as soon as practicable after the filing of all appellate briefs or oral argument. The Director shall adopt, modify or set aside the findings and conclusions contained in the decision or order being reviewed and shall set forth in the final order the reasons for his actions. The Director may, in his discretion, increase or decrease the assessed penalty from the amount recommended in the decision or order being reviewed, except that if the order being reviewed is a default order, the Director may not increase the amount of the penalty.

(b) *Payment of a civil penalty.* The respondent shall pay the full amount of the civil penalty assessed in the final order within sixty (60) days after receipt of the final order unless otherwise agreed by the parties. Payment shall be made by forwarding to the Hearing Clerk a cashier's check or certified check in the amount of the penalty assessed in the final order, payable to the Treasurer, United States of America.

(c) Money due and owing the United States by virtue of an unappealed final decision or settlement order may be collected by referral to the Department of Justice for appropriate civil action against respondent.

§ 672.24 Maximum civil monetary penalties for violations.

(a) For violations occurring prior to August 1, 2016, the maximum civil penalty is $6500 for any violation and $11,000 for knowing violations.

(b) For violations occurring after August 1, 2016, but before January 1, 2017, the maximum civil penalty is adjusted to $16,250 for any violation and $27,500 for knowing violations.

(c) For violations occurring on or after January 1, 2017, the maximum penalty, which may be assessed under part 672 of the title, is the larger of:

(1) The amount for the previous calendar year, or

(2) An amount adjusted for inflation, calculated by multiplying the amount for the previous calendar year by the percentage by which the CPI–U for the month of October preceding the current calendar year exceeds the CPI–U for the month of October of the calendar year two years prior to the current calendar year, adding that amount to the amount for the previous calendar year, and rounding the total to the nearest dollar.

(d) Notice of the maximum penalty which may be assessed under part 672 of this title for calendar years after 2016 will be published by the NSF in the FEDERAL REGISTER on an annual basis on or before January 15 of each calendar year.

[81 FR 41452, June 27, 2016]

PART 673—ANTARCTIC NON-GOVERNMENTAL EXPEDITIONS

Sec.
673.1 Purpose of regulations.
673.2 Scope.
673.3 Definitions.
673.4 Environmental protection information.
673.5 Emergency response plan.

AUTHORITY: 16 U.S.C. 2401 *et. seq.*

SOURCE: 66 FR 42451, Aug. 13, 2001, unless otherwise noted.

§ 673.1 Purpose of regulations.

The purpose of the regulations in this part is to implement the Antarctic Conservation Act of 1978, Public Law 95–541, as amended by the Antarctic Science, Tourism and Conservation Act of 1996, Public Law 104–227, and Article 15 of the Protocol on Environmental Protection to the Antarctic Treaty done at Madrid on October 4, 1991. Specifically, this part requires that all non-governmental expeditions, for which advance notice by the United States is required under the Antarctic Treaty, who use non-flagged vessels ensure that the vessel owner or operator has an appropriate emergency response plan. This part is also designed to ensure that expedition members are informed of their environmental protection obligations under the Antarctic Conservation Act.

(Approved by the Office of Management and Budget under control number 3145–0180)

§ 673.2 Scope.

The requirements in this part apply to non-governmental expeditions to or within Antarctica for which the United States is required to give advance notice under Paragraph (5) of Article VII of the Antarctic Treaty.

§ 673.3 Definitions.

In this part:

Antarctica means the area south of 60 degrees south latitude.

Expedition means an activity undertaken by one or more non-governmental persons organized within or proceeding from the United States to or within Antarctica for which advance notification is required under Paragraph 5 of Article VII of the Antarctic Treaty.

Person has the meaning given that term in section 1 of title 1, United States Code, and includes any person subject to the jurisdiction of the United States except that the term does not include any department, agency, or other instrumentality of the Federal Government.

§ 673.4 Environmental protection information.

(a) Any person who organizes a non-governmental expedition to Antarctica and who does business in the United States shall notify expedition members of the environmental protection obligations of the Antarctic Conservation Act.

(b) The National Science Foundation's Office of Polar Programs may prepare for publication and distribution explanation of the prohibited acts set forth in the Antarctic Conservation Act, as well as other appropriate educational material for tour operators, their clients, and employees. Such material provided to tour operators for distribution to their passengers and crew shall be disseminated prior to or during travel to the Antarctic.

§ 673.5 Emergency response plan.

Any person organizing a non-governmental expedition to or within Antarctica who is transporting passengers aboard a non-U.S. flagged vessel shall ensure that:

(a) The vessel owner's or operator's shipboard oil pollution emergency plan, prepared and maintained according to Regulation 26 of Annex I of the International Convention for the Prevention of Pollution from Ships, 1973, as modified by the Protocol of 1978 relating thereto (MARPOL 73/78), has provisions for prompt and effective response action to such emergencies as might arise in the performance of the vessel's activities in Antarctica. Any emergency response plan which satisfies the requirements contained in 33 CFR 151.26 of the U.S. Coast Guard regulations will also satisfy the requirements of this paragraph. If the vessel owner or operator does not have a shipboard oil pollution emergency plan, a separate plan for prompt and effective response action is required.

(b) The vessel owner or operator agrees to take all reasonable measures to implement the plan for a prompt and effective response action in the event of an emergency, taking into account considerations of risk to human life and safety.

PART 674—ANTARCTIC METEORITES

Sec.
674.1 Purpose of regulations.
674.2 Scope and applicability.
674.3 Definitions.
674.4 Restrictions on collection of meteorites in Antarctica.
674.5 Requirements for collection, handling, documentation and curation of Antarctic meteorites.
674.6 Submission of information to NSF.
674.7 Exception for serendipitous finds.

AUTHORITY: 16 U.S.C. 2401 *et seq.*

SOURCE: 68 FR 15379, Mar. 31, 2003, unless otherwise noted.

§ 674.1 Purpose of regulations.

The purpose of the regulations in this part is to implement the Antarctic Conservation Act of 1978, as amended by the Antarctic Science, Tourism and Conservation Act of 1996, (16 U.S.C 2401 *et seq.*), and Article 7 of the Protocol on Environmental Protection to the Antarctic Treaty done at Madrid on October 4, 1991. Specifically, this part is designed to ensure meteorites in Antarctica will be collected for scientific research purposes only and that U.S. expedition organizers to Antarctica who plan to collect meteorites in Antarctica will ensure that any specimens collected will be properly collected, handled, documented and curated to preserve their scientific value.

§ 674.2 Scope and applicability.

This part applies to any person who collects meteorites in Antarctica. The requirements of § 674.5 apply to any person organizing an expedition to or within Antarctica for which the United States is required to give advance notice under Paragraph (5) of Article VII of the Antarctic Treaty where one of the purposes of the expedition is to collect meteorites in Antarctica. The requirements in this part only apply to the collection of meteorites in Antarctica after April 30, 2003.

§ 674.3 Definitions.

In this part:

Antarctica means the area south of 60 degrees south latitude.

Expedition means an activity undertaken by one or more persons organized within or proceeding from the United States to or within Antarctica for which advance notification is required under Paragraph 5 of Article VII of the Antarctic Treaty.

Incremental cost is the extra cost involved in sharing the samples with other researchers. It does not include the initial cost of collecting the meteorites in Antarctica or the cost of maintaining the samples in a curatorial facility.

Person has the meaning given that term in section 1 of title 1, United States Code, and includes any person subject to the jurisdiction of the United States.

§ 674.4 Restrictions on collection of meteorites in Antarctica.

No person may collect meteorites in Antarctica for other than scientific research purposes.

§ 674.5 Requirements for collection, handling, documentation, and curation of Antarctic meteorites.

(a) Any person organizing an expedition to or within Antarctica, where one of the purposes of the expedition is to collect meteorites in Antarctica, shall ensure that the meteorites will be properly collected, documented, handled, and curated to preserve their scientific value. Curation includes making specimens available to bona fide scientific researchers on a timely basis, in accordance with specified procedures.

(b) Expedition organizers described in paragraph (a) of this section shall develop and implement written procedures for the collection, documentation, and curation of specimens which include the following components:

(1) *Handling requirements.* Handling procedures shall ensure that the specimens are properly labeled and handled to minimize the potential for contamination from the point of collection to the point of curation. At a minimum, handling procedures shall include:

(i) Handling the samples with clean Teflon or polyethylene coated implements or stainless steel implements (or equivalent);

(ii) Double bagging of samples in Teflon or polyethylene (or equivalent) bags;

(iii) A unique sample identifier included with the sample;

(iv) Keeping the samples frozen at or below −15 °C until opened and thawed in a clean laboratory setting at the curation facility; and

(v) Thawing in a clean, dry, non-reactive gas environment, such as nitrogen or argon.

(2) *Sample documentation.* Documentation for each specimen, that includes, at a minimum:

(i) A unique identifier for the sample;
(ii) The date of find;
(iii) The date of collection (if different from date of find);
(iv) The latitude and longitude to within 500 meters of the location of the find and the name of the nearest named geographical feature;
(v) The name, organizational affiliation, and address of the finder or the expedition organizer;
(vi) A physical description of the specimen and of the location of the find; and
(vii) Any observations of the collection activity, such as potential contamination of the specimen.

(3) *Curation.* Make prior arrangements to ensure that any specimens collected in Antarctica will be maintained in a curatorial facility that will:

(i) Preserve the specimens in a manner that precludes chemical or physical degradation;

(ii) Produce an authoritative classification for meteorites that can be shown to belong to a well-established chemical and petrological group, and provide appropriate descriptions for those meteorites that cannot be shown to belong to an established chemical and petrological group;

(iii) Develop and maintain curatorial records associated with the meteorites including collection information, authoritative classification, total known mass, information about handling and sample preparation activities that have been performed on the meteorite, and sub-sample information;

(iv) Submit an appropriate summary of information about the meteorites to the Antarctic Master Directory via the National Antarctic Data Coordination Center as soon as possible, but no later than two years after receipt of samples at the curatorial facility;

(v) Submit information on classification of the meteorite to an internationally recognized meteorite research catalog, such as the "Catalogue of Meteorites" published by the Natural History Museum of London or the "Meteoritical Bulletin" published by the Meteoritical Society;

(vi) Specify procedures by which requests for samples by bonafide scientific researchers will be handled;

(vii) Make samples available to bonafide scientific researchers at no more than incremental cost and within a reasonable period of time; and

(viii) In the event that the initial curatorial facility is no longer in a position to provide curation services for the specimens, or believes that the meteorites no longer merit curation, it shall consult with the National Science Foundation's Office of Polar Programs

National Science Foundation

to identify another appropriate curatorial facility, or to determine another appropriate arrangement.

§ 674.6 Submission of information to NSF.

A copy of the written procedures developed by expedition organizers pursuant to § 674.5(b) shall be furnished to the National Science Foundation's Office of Polar Programs at a minimum of 90 days prior to the planned departure date of the expedition for Antarctica. NSF shall publish a notice of availability of the plan in the FEDERAL REGISTER that provides for a 15 day comment period. NSF shall evaluate the procedures in the plan to determine if they are sufficient to ensure that the meteorites will be properly collected, handled, documented, and curated. NSF shall provide comments on the adequacy of the plan within 45 days of receipt. If NSF advises the expedition organizer that the procedures satisfy the requirements of § 674.5 and the procedures are implemented, the expedition organizer will have satisfied the requirements of this part.

§ 674.7 Exception for serendipitous finds.

A person who makes a serendipitous discovery of a meteorite in Antarctica which could not have been reasonably anticipated, may collect the meteorite for scientific research purposes, provided that the meteorite is collected in the manner most likely to prevent contamination under the circumstances, and provided that the meteorite is otherwise handled, documented and curated in accordance with the requirements of § 674.5.

PART 675—MEDICAL CLEARANCE PROCESS FOR DEPLOYMENT TO ANTARCTICA

Sec.
675.1 Purpose and authority.
675.2 Medical examinations.
675.3 Medical clearance criteria.
675.4 Waiver process.

AUTHORITY: 42 U.S.C. 1870.

SOURCE: 62 FR 31522, June 10, 1997, unless otherwise noted.

§ 675.1 Purpose and authority.

(a) This part sets forth the procedures for medical screening to determine whether candidates for participation in the United States Antarctic Program (USAP) are physically qualified and psychologically adapted for assignment or travel to Antarctica. Medical screening examinations are necessary to determine the presence of any physical or psychological conditions that would threaten the health or safety of the candidate or other USAP participants or that could not be effectively treated by the limited medical care capabilities in Antarctica.

(b) Presidential Memorandum No. 6646 (February 5, 1982) (available from the National Science Foundation, Office of Polar Programs, room 755, 4201 Wilson Blvd., Arlington, VA 22230) sets forth the National Science Foundation's overall management responsibilities for the entire United States national program in Antarctica.

§ 675.2 Medical examinations.

(a) Any individual seeking to travel to Antarctica under sponsorship of the United States Antarctic Program must undergo a medical and dental examination to determine whether the individual is physically qualified for deployment to Antarctica.

(b) The medical and dental examinations may be conducted by a qualified licensed physician or dentist of the candidate's choosing, or designated by the employing organization, following instructions provided by the USAP. The medical examinations shall include a medical history, physical examination and appropriate clinical tests which address major organ systems for medical conditions inconsistent with safe deployment to Antarctica.

(c) The candidate's physician/dentist will submit the required medical information on the appropriate USAP-provided forms to a USAP-designated physician who will determine whether the individual is qualified for deployment to Antarctica based upon Medical Clearance Criteria established by the USAP. All information requested on the forms shall be provided.

(d) Candidates who anticipate spending the austral winter in Antarctica (when evacuation may be impossible) are subject to additional evaluation, including a determination of psychological adaptability for such an isolated assignment. Psychological evaluations of "winter-over" candidates shall be performed by a qualified team of USAP-designated physicians/clinical psychologists.

§ 675.3 Medical clearance criteria.

(a) The USAP shall establish Medical Clearance Criteria for determining eligibility for deployment to Antarctica. (See Medical Standards for Antarctic Deployment available from the National Science Foundation, Office of Polar Programs, room 755.09, 4201 Wilson Blvd., Arlington, VA 22230).

The criteria will include examination of the following major organ systems:

(1) Lungs and chest wall.
(2) Heart and vascular system.
(3) Abdominal organs and gastrointestinal system.
(4) Endocrine or metabolic system.
(5) Genitalia and urinary system.
(6) Musculoskeletal.
(7) Skin and cellular tissues.
(8) Neurological Disorders.
(9) Psychiatric or psychological.
(10) Dental.

(b) The USAP may review and revise the Medical Clearance Criteria periodically as appropriate.

§ 675.4 Waiver process.

(a) If an individual is found not physically qualified for deployment to Antarctica, the USAP's contractor will inform the individual of the determination and of the administrative waiver process, and will provide a waiver application package to the individual upon request.

(b) The waiver applicant should send the completed waiver application package to the USAP's contractor which will forward the package to NSF's Office of Polar Programs for review and a determination on the appropriateness of a waiver. In making the waiver determination, the Office of Polar Programs may consult with other qualified medical personnel and may require waiver applicants to take further medical examinations or to furnish additional medical documentation in support of the waiver application.

(c) The Director, Office of Polar Programs (or designee) will make a final determination, in the exercise of his or her discretion, on the appropriateness of a waiver on a case-by-case basis.

(d) Individuals for whom a waiver is determined to be appropriate are eligible for deployment to Antarctica subject to any necessary limitations/restrictions identified by the Director, Office of Polar Programs, or designee.

PART 680—NATIONAL SCIENCE FOUNDATION RULES OF PRACTICE

Subpart A—Rules of Practice for the National Science Foundation

Sec.
680.10 Definitions; cross-references to employee ethical conduct standards and financial disclosure regulations.
680.11 Staff involvement with NSF proposals and awards.
680.12 One-year NSF post-employment restrictions.
680.13 Purposes for "substitute" requirements.

Subpart B [Reserved]

AUTHORITY: 5 U.S.C. 7301; 42 U.S.C. 1870(a); 5 CFR 2635.105(c)(3).

SOURCE: 47 FR 32131, July 26, 1982, unless otherwise noted.

Subpart A—Rules of Practice for the National Science Foundation

SOURCE: 61 FR 59837, Nov. 25, 1996, unless otherwise noted.

§ 680.10 Definitions; cross-references to employee ethical conduct standards and financial disclosure regulations.

(a) *Definitions.* Under this subpart, unless a provision plainly indicates otherwise:

(1) *Award* means any grant, contract, cooperative agreement, loan, or other arrangement made by the Government.

(2) *Employee* includes, in addition to any individual defined in 5 CFR 2635.102(h), any individual working at NSF under the Intergovernmental Personnel Act. It includes any part-time or intermittent employee, temporary

National Science Foundation § 680.11

consultant; but not a special Government employee, as defined in 18 U.S.C. 202(a).

(3) *Institution* means any university, college, business firm, research institute, professional society, or other organization. It includes all parts of a university or college, including all institutions in a multi-institution State or city system. It includes any university consortium or joint corporation; but not the universities that belong to such a consortium. Those universities shall be considered separate institutions for purposes of this part.

(4) *Proposal* means an application for an award and includes a bid.

(b) *Cross-references to employee ethical conduct standards and financial disclosure regulations.* Members of the National Science Board and other employees of the National Science Foundation (NSF), including special Government employees, should refer to the Standards of Ethical Conduct for Employees of the Executive Branch at 5 CFR part 2635, the National Science Foundation's regulations at 5 CFR part 5301 which supplement the executive branch Standards, and the executive branch financial disclosure regulations at 5 CFR part 2634.

§ 680.11 Staff involvement with NSF proposals and awards.

(a)(1) Many scientists, engineers, and educators interrupt active research and teaching careers to spend a year or two at NSF and then return to research and teaching, usually at the same institution from which they came. Many such visiting scientists, engineers, and educators (and a few permanent employees) who have been principal investigators under NSF awards before coming to NSF, retain some interest or association with the work. If an individual is a principal investigator under an NSF award, the individual is not precluded from retaining ties to the work after becoming an NSF employee. The employee may stay in contact with those who are continuing the work in the employee's laboratory or on his or her project. The employee may continue to supervise graduate students. And the employee may visit and work in the laboratory on his or her own time for these and related purposes.

(2) Before a prospective employee comes to NSF, the prospective employee and the grantee institution must designate, subject to NSF approval, a "substitute principal investigator"—i.e., another scientist who will be responsible for the work and equipment and will represent the institution in any dealings with NSF officials while the prospective employee is at NSF.

(3) Appointment of a substitute principal investigator is unnecessary if all work under an award is to be completely suspended while the employee is at NSF. If the work is to be suspended, the employee and the grantee institution must inform the NSF in writing before the employee's employment begins. Work under the award may be resumed when the employee completes his or her NSF employment, and its term may be extended to account for the time lost during the employee's NSF employment.

(b)(1) NSF will entertain no proposal on which a current NSF employee would be a senior investigator or equivalent, unless it is a proposal for continuation or extension of support for work on which the employee served in that capacity before coming to NSF. Any proposal for continuation of NSF support at essentially the same level (with reasonable allowance for inflation) will normally be considered a proposal for continuation or extension if it would support the work of the same investigator and his or her laboratory or group (if any) in the same general field of science, engineering, or education, notwithstanding that the focus of the work may change in response to research opportunities or educational needs.

(2) Someone other than the current NSF employee must submit any such proposal for continuation or extension of work NSF previously supported and handle all negotiations with NSF, but the capacity in which the current NSF employee will serve should be clearly spelled out in the proposal.

(c) In accordance with 5 CFR 5301.103(a)(1), an NSF employee may not receive, directly or indirectly, any salary, consulting fee, honorarium, or other form of compensation for services, or reimbursement of expenses, from an NSF award.

§ 680.12 One-year NSF post-employment restrictions.

(a) For one year after leaving NSF employment, a former NSF employee, including a special Government employee who has performed work for NSF on more than 60 days in the previous twelve months, shall not represent himself, herself, or any other person in dealings with any NSF official on any proposal, project, or other particular matter.

(b) The one-year restriction contained in paragraph (a) of this section is in addition to any post-employment restriction imposed by statute, including 18 U.S.C. 207 and 41 U.S.C. 423. To the extent that any disqualification required by paragraph (a) of this section is not also required by statute, written exceptions may be granted by the NSF's General Counsel, whose decisions shall be final. Exceptions will be rare and will be granted only where strict application of the rules would result in undue hardship for former short-term employees or for other former employees, and when granting an exception would not result in an unfair advantage to the former employee.

(c)(1) Paragraph (a) of this section applies to particular matters involving specific parties, such as grants, contracts, or other agreements; applications for permits, licenses, or the like; requests for rulings or similar official determinations; claims; investigations or audits; charges or accusations against individuals or firms; adjudicatory hearings; and court cases.

(2) For former employees, other than special Government employees, paragraph (a) of this section also applies to particular matters that do not involve specific parties, such as:

(i) Determinations to establish or dis-establish a particular program or set its budget level for a particular fiscal year;

(ii) Decisions to undertake or terminate a particular project;

(iii) Decisions to open or not open a contract to competitive bidding;

(iv) General policy or rulemaking—including, for example, decisions on particular NSF rules or formal policy, such as adoption or amendment of a resolution by the National Science Board, promulgation or amendment of an NSF regulation or circular, amendment of standard grant or contract terms, or changes to NSF manuals or policy documents; and

(v) Agency positions on particular legislative or regulatory proposals.

(d) Paragraph (a) of this section does not apply to:

(1) Any expression of a former employee's views on policy issues where the circumstances make it obvious that the former employee is only speaking as an informed and interested citizen, not representing any financial or other interests of his or her own or of any other person or institution with which he or she is associated;

(2) Any appearance or communication concerning matters of a personal or individual nature, such as the former employee's taxes, salary, benefits, possible Federal employment, rights as a former employee, or the application of conflict-of-interest rules to something the former employee proposes to do;

(3) Any appearance on the former employee's own behalf in any litigation or administrative proceeding; or

(4) Any presentation of scientific or technical information (at a site visit, for example) or any other communication of scientific or technical information on work being proposed or conducted.

(e) As soon as his or her NSF employment ceases, a former NSF employee (including any former special Government employee described in paragraph (a) of this section) may again be listed as principal investigator on an NSF award, may be listed as principal investigator in any proposal or award, and may sign a proposal as principal investigator. However, the former employee and the grantee institution shall formally designate, subject to NSF approval, a "substitute negotiator" who, though not principally responsible for the work, will represent the former employee and the institution in dealings with NSF officials on any proposal or

National Science Foundation

project for as long as the former employee would be barred from representational contacts with NSF by paragraph (a) of this section or by statute.

§ 680.13 Purposes for "substitute" requirements.

Appointment of a "substitute principal investigator" or "substitute negotiator" ensures against unthinking violation of the restrictions on dealings with NSF officials. It serves this purpose by flagging proposals or awards affected by the restrictions and by identifying someone else with whom NSF officials can properly discuss them or negotiate over them. Designation of a substitute principal investigator while an employee is at NSF has two additional functions: it identifies another person to be responsible for the work and equipment, and it reminds all concerned that during an employee's NSF service his or her attentions should focus on NSF duties.

Subpart B [Reserved]

PART 681—PROGRAM FRAUD CIVIL REMEDIES ACT REGULATIONS

PURPOSE, DEFINITIONS, AND BASIS FOR LIABILITY

Sec.
681.1 Purpose.
681.2 Definitions.
681.3 What is the basis for the imposition of civil penalties and assessments?

PROCEDURES LEADING TO ISSUANCE OF A COMPLAINT

681.4 Who investigates program fraud?
681.5 What happens if program fraud is suspected?
681.6 When may NSF issue a complaint?
681.7 What is contained in a complaint?
681.8 How will the complaint be served?

PROCEDURES FOLLOWING SERVICE OF A COMPLAINT

681.9 How does a defendant respond to the complaint?
681.10 What happens if a defendant fails to file an answer?
681.11 What happens once an answer is filed?

HEARING PROCEDURES

681.12 What kind of hearing is contemplated?
681.13 At the hearing, what rights do the parties have?
681.14 What is the role of the ALJ?
681.15 How are the functions of the ALJ separated from those of the investigating official and the reviewing official?
681.16 Can the reviewing official or the ALJ be disqualified?
681.17 What rights are there to review documents?
681.18 What type of discovery is authorized and how is it conducted?
681.19 Are witness lists exchanged before the hearing?
681.20 Can witnesses be subpoenaed?
681.21 Who pays the costs for a subpoena?
681.22 Are protective orders available?
681.23 How are documents filed and served with the ALJ?
681.24 How is time computed?
681.25 Where is the hearing held?
681.26 How will the hearing be conducted and who has the burden of proof?
681.27 How is evidence presented at the hearing?
681.28 How is witness testimony presented?
681.29 Will the hearing proceedings be recorded?
681.30 Are ex parte communications between a party and the ALJ permitted?
681.31 Are there sanctions for misconduct?
681.32 Are post-hearing briefs required?

DECISIONS AND APPEALS

681.33 How is the case decided?
681.34 How are penalty and assessment amounts determined?
681.35 Can a party request reconsideration of the initial decision?
681.36 When does the initial decision of the ALJ become final?
681.37 What are the procedures for appealing the ALJ decision?
681.38 What happens if an initial decision is appealed?
681.39 Are there any limitations on the right to appeal to the authority head?
681.40 How does the authority head dispose of an appeal?
681.41 What judicial review is available?
681.42 Can the administrative complaint be settled voluntarily?
681.43 How are civil penalties and assessments collected?
681.44 Is there a right to administrative offset?
681.45 What happens to collections?
681.46 What if the investigation indicates criminal misconduct?

SOURCE: 74 FR 26794, June 4, 2009, unless otherwise noted.

PURPOSE, DEFINITIONS, AND BASIS FOR LIABILITY

§ 681.1 Purpose.

This part implements the Program Fraud Civil Remedies Act of 1986, 31

U.S.C. 3801–3812 ("PFCRA"). PFCRA provides NSF, and other Federal agencies, with an administrative remedy to impose civil penalties and assessments against persons who make, submit, or present, or cause to be made, submitted or presented, false, fictitious, or fraudulent claims or written statements to NSF. PFCRA also provides due process protections to all persons who are subject to administrative proceedings under this part.

§ 681.2 Definitions.

For the purposes of this part—

ALJ means an Administrative Law Judge in the authority appointed pursuant to section 3105 of title 5 or detailed to the authority pursuant to section 3344 of title 5.

Authority means the National Science Foundation.

Authority head means the Director of the National Science Foundation or the Director's designee.

Benefit is intended to cover anything of value, including but not limited to, any advantage, preference, privilege, license, permit, favorable decision, ruling, status, or loan guarantee.

Claim is defined in section 3801(a)(3) of title 31 of the United States Code.

Complaint means the administrative complaint served by the reviewing official on the defendant under § 681.8.

Defendant means any person alleged in a complaint under § 681.7 to be liable for a civil penalty or assessment pursuant to PFCRA.

Government means the United States Government.

Individual means a natural person.

Initial decision means the written decision of the ALJ required by § 681.33, and includes a revised initial decision issued following a remand or a motion for reconsideration.

Investigating official means the NSF Inspector General or an employee of the Office of Inspector General designated by the Inspector General.

Knows or *has reason to know* is defined in section 3801(a)(5) of title 31 of the United States Code.

Makes shall include the terms presents, submits, and causes to be made, presented, or submitted. As the context requires, making or made shall likewise include the corresponding forms of such terms.

Person means any individual, partnership, corporation, association, or private organization, and includes the plural of that term.

Representative means an attorney who is in good standing of the bar of any State, Territory, or possession of the United States, or of the District of Columbia, or the Commonwealth of Puerto Rico, or any other individual designated in writing by the defendant.

Reviewing official means the General Counsel of NSF or the General Counsel's designee.

Statement is defined in section 3801(a)(9) of title 5 of the United States Code.

§ 681.3 What is the basis for the imposition of civil penalties and assessments?

(a) *Claims.* (1) Any person shall be subject, in addition to any other remedy that may be prescribed by law, to a civil penalty of not more than $5,000 for each claim if that person makes a claim that the person knows or has reason to know—

(i) Is false, fictitious, or fraudulent;

(ii) Includes or is supported by any written statement which asserts a material fact which is false, fictitious, or fraudulent;

(iii) Includes or is supported by any written statement that—

(A) Omits a material fact;

(B) Is false, fictitious, or fraudulent as a result of such omission; and

(C) Is a statement in which the person making such statement has a duty to include such material fact; or

(iv) Is for payment for the provision of property or services which the person has not provided as claimed.

(2) Each voucher, invoice, claim form, or other individual request or demand for property, services, or money constitutes a separate claim.

(3) A claim shall be considered made to the authority, recipient, or party when such a claim is actually made to an agent, fiscal intermediary, or other entity, including any State or political subdivision of a State, acting for or on behalf of NSF.

(4) Each claim for property, services, or money is subject to a civil penalty

regardless of whether such property, services, or money is actually delivered or paid.

(5) If the Government has made any payment on a claim, a person subject to a civil penalty under paragraph (a)(1) of this section may also be subject to an assessment of not more than twice the amount of such claim or that portion thereof that is determined to be in violation of paragraph (a)(1) of this section. Such assessment shall be in lieu of damages sustained by the Government because of such a claim.

(b) *Statements.* (1) Any person shall be subject, in addition to any other remedy that may be prescribed by law, to a civil penalty of not more than $5,000 for each statement if that person makes a written statement that the person knows or has reason to know—

(i) Asserts a material fact which is false, fictitious, or fraudulent; or

(ii) Is false, fictitious, or fraudulent because it omits a material fact that the person making the statement has a duty to include in such a statement; and

(iii) Contains or is accompanied by an express certification or affirmation of the truthfulness and accuracy of the contents of this statement.

(2) A person will only be subject to a civil penalty under 681.3(b)(1) if the written statement made by the person contains or is accompanied by an express certification or affirmation of the truthfulness and accuracy of the contents of this statement.

(3) Each written representation, certification, or affirmation constitutes a separate statement.

(4) A statement shall be considered made to NSF when it is actually made to an agent, fiscal intermediary, or other entity, including any State or political subdivision of a State, acting for or on behalf of NSF.

(c) No proof of specific intent to defraud is required to establish liability under this section.

(d) In any case in which it is determined that more than one person is liable for making a false, fictitious, or fraudulent claim or statement under this section, each such person may be held liable for a civil penalty and assessment, where appropriate, under this section.

(e) In any case in which it is determined that more than one person is liable for making a claim under this section on which the Government has made payment, an assessment may be imposed against any such person or jointly and severally against any combination of persons.

(f) For claims or statements made on or after August 1, 2016, but before January 1, 2017, the maximum penalty which may be assessed under part 681 of the title is $10,781. For claims or statements made on or after January 1, 2017, the maximum penalty which may be assessed under part 681 of the title is the larger of:

(1) The amount for the previous calendar year, or

(2) An amount adjusted for inflation, calculated by multiplying the amount for the previous calendar year by the percentage by which the CPI-U for the month of October preceding the current calendar year exceeds the CPI-U for the month of October of the calendar year two years prior to the current calendar year, adding that amount to the amount for the previous calendar year, and rounding the total to the nearest dollar.

(g) Notice of the maximum penalty, which may be assessed under part 681 of this title for calendar years after 2016, will be published by NSF in the FEDERAL REGISTER on an annual basis on or before January 15 of each calendar year.

[74 FR 26794, June 4, 2009, as amended at 81 FR 41452, June 27, 2016]

PROCEDURES LEADING TO ISSUANCE OF A COMPLAINT

§ 681.4 Who investigates program fraud?

The Inspector General, or his or her designee, is the investigating official responsible for investigating allegations that a false claim or statement has been made. In this regard, the Inspector General has authority under PFCRA and the Inspector General Act of 1978 (5 U.S.C. App. 3), as amended, to issue administrative subpoenas for the production of records and documents.

§ 681.5 What happens if program fraud is suspected?

(a) If the investigating official concludes that an action under this part is warranted, the investigating official submits a report containing the findings and conclusions of the investigation to the reviewing official. If the reviewing official determines that the report provides adequate evidence that a person made a false, fictitious or fraudulent claim or statement, the reviewing official shall transmit to the Attorney General written notice of an intention to refer the matter for adjudication, with a request for approval of such referral. This notice will include the reviewing official's statements concerning:

(1) The reasons for the referral;

(2) The claims or statements upon which liability would be based;

(3) The evidence that supports liability;

(4) An estimate of the amount of money or the value of property, services, or other benefits requested or demanded in the false claim or statement;

(5) Any exculpatory or mitigating circumstances that may relate to the claims or statements known by the reviewing official or the investigating official; and

(6) A statement that there is a reasonable prospect of collecting an appropriate amount of penalties and assessments.

(b) If, at any time, the Attorney General or his or her designee requests in writing that this administrative process be stayed, the authority head, as identified in § 681.2(c) of this part, must stay the process immediately. The authority head may order the process resumed only upon receipt of the written authorization of the Attorney General.

§ 681.6 When may NSF issue a complaint?

NSF may issue a complaint:

(a) If the Attorney General (or designee) approves the referral of the allegations for adjudication; and

(b) In a case of submission of false claims, if the amount of money or the value of property or services demanded or requested in a false claim, or a group of related claims submitted at the same time, does not exceed $150,000.

§ 681.7 What is contained in a complaint?

(a) A complaint is a written statement giving notice to the person alleged to be liable under 31 U.S.C. 3802 of the specific allegations being referred for adjudication and of the person's right to request a hearing with respect to those allegations.

(b) The complaint will state that NSF seeks to impose civil penalties, assessments, or both, against the defendant and will include:

(1) The allegations of liability against the defendant, including the statutory basis for liability, identification of the claims or statements involved, and the reasons liability allegedly arises from such claims or statements;

(2) The maximum amount of penalties and assessments for which the defendant may be held liable;

(3) A statement that the defendant may request a hearing by filing an answer and may be represented by a representative;

(4) Instructions for filing such an answer; and

(5) A warning that failure to file an answer within 30 days of service of the complaint will result in imposition of the maximum amount of penalties and assessments.

(c) The reviewing official must serve any complaint on the defendant and, if a hearing is requested by the defendant, provide a copy to the ALJ assigned to the case.

§ 681.8 How will the complaint be served?

(a) The complaint must be served on individual defendants directly, a partnership through a general partner, and on corporations or on unincorporated associations through an executive officer or a director, except that service also may be made on any person authorized by appointment or by law to receive process for the defendant.

(b) The complaint may be served either by:

(1) Registered or certified mail; or

(2) Personal delivery by anyone 18 years of age or older.

(c) The date of service is the date of personal delivery or, in the case of service by registered or certified mail, the date of postmark.

(d) When served with the complaint, the defendant should also be served with a copy of this part 681 and 31 U.S.C. 3801–3812.

PROCEDURES FOLLOWING SERVICE OF A COMPLAINT

§ 681.9 How does a defendant respond to the complaint?

(a) A defendant may file an answer with the reviewing official within 30 days of service of the complaint. An answer will be considered a request for an oral hearing.

(b) In the answer, a defendant—

(1) Must admit or deny each of the allegations of liability contained in the complaint (a failure to deny an allegation is considered an admission);

(2) Must state any defense on which the defendant intends to rely;

(3) May state any reasons why he or she believes the penalties, assessments, or both should be less than the statutory maximum; and

(4) Must state the name, address, and telephone number of the person authorized by the defendant to act as the defendant's representative, if any.

(c) If the defendant is unable to file a timely answer which meets the requirements set forth in paragraph (b) of this section, the defendant may file with the reviewing official a general answer denying liability, requesting a hearing, and requesting an extension of time in which to file a complete answer. A general answer must be filed within 30 days of service of the complaint.

(d) If the defendant initially files a general answer requesting an extension of time, the reviewing official must promptly file with the ALJ the complaint, the general answer, and the request for an extension of time.

(e) For good cause shown, the ALJ may grant the defendant up to 30 additional days within which to file an answer meeting the requirements of paragraph (b) of this section. Such answer must be filed with the ALJ and a copy must be served on the reviewing official.

§ 681.10 What happens if a defendant fails to file an answer?

(a) If a defendant does not file any answer within 30 days after service of the complaint, the reviewing official may refer the complaint to the ALJ.

(b) Once the complaint is referred, the ALJ will promptly serve on the defendant a notice that an initial decision will be issued.

(c) The ALJ will assume the facts alleged in the complaint to be true and, if such facts establish liability under the statute, the ALJ will issue an initial decision imposing the maximum amount of penalties and assessments allowed under PFCRA.

(d) Except as otherwise provided in this section, when a defendant fails to file a timely answer, the defendant waives any right to further review of the penalties and assessments imposed in the initial decision.

(e) The initial decision becomes final 30 days after it is issued.

(f) At any time before an initial decision becomes final, a defendant may file a motion with the ALJ asking that the case be reopened. An ALJ may only reopen a case if, in this motion, he or she determines that the defendant set forth extraordinary circumstances that prevented the defendant from filing a timely answer. The initial decision will be stayed until the ALJ makes a decision on the motion. The reviewing official may respond to the motion.

(g) If the ALJ determines that a defendant has demonstrated extraordinary circumstances excusing his failure to file a timely answer, the ALJ will withdraw the initial decision, and grant the defendant an opportunity to answer the complaint.

(h) A decision by the ALJ to deny a defendant's motion to reopen a case is not subject to reconsideration under § 681.35.

(i) The defendant may appeal to the authority head the decision denying a motion to reopen by filing a notice of appeal with the authority head within 15 days after the ALJ denies the motion. The timely filing of a notice of appeal shall stay the initial decision until the authority head decides the issue.

(j) If the defendant files a timely notice of appeal with the authority head, the ALJ shall forward the record of the proceeding to the authority head.

(k) The authority head shall decide expeditiously, based solely on the record before the ALJ, whether extraordinary circumstances excuse the defendant's failure to file a timely answer.

(l) If the authority head decides that extraordinary circumstances excused the defendant's failure to file a timely answer, the authority head shall remand the case to the ALJ with instructions to grant the defendant an opportunity to answer.

(m) If the authority head decides that the defendant's failure to file a timely answer is not excused, the authority head shall reinstate the initial decision of the ALJ, which shall become final and binding upon the parties 30 days after the authority head issues such a decision.

§ 681.11 What happens once an answer is filed?

(a) When the reviewing official receives an answer, he or she must file concurrently, the complaint and the answer with the ALJ, along with a designation of NSF's representative.

(b) When the ALJ receives the complaint and the answer, the ALJ will promptly serve a notice of hearing upon the defendant and the NSF representative, in the same manner as the complaint, which is described in § 681.8. The notice of oral hearing must be served within six years of the date on which the claim or statement is made.

(c) The notice must include:

(1) The tentative date, time, and place of the hearing;

(2) The legal authority and jurisdiction under which the hearing is being held;

(3) The matters of fact and law to be asserted;

(4) A description of the procedures for the conduct of the hearing;

(5) The name, address, and telephone number of the defendant's representative and the representative for NSF; and

(6) Such other matters as the ALJ deems appropriate.

HEARING PROCEDURES

§ 681.12 What kind of hearing is contemplated?

The hearing is a formal proceeding conducted by the ALJ during which a defendant will have the opportunity to cross-examine witnesses, present testimony, and dispute liability.

§ 681.13 At the hearing, what rights do the parties have?

Each party has the right to:

(a) Be represented by a representative;

(b) Request a pre-hearing conference and participate in any conference held by the ALJ;

(c) Conduct discovery;

(d) Agree to stipulations of fact or law which will be made a part of the record;

(e) Present evidence relevant to the issues at the hearing;

(f) Present and cross-examine witnesses;

(g) Present arguments at the hearing as permitted by the ALJ; and

(h) Submit written briefs and proposed findings of fact and conclusions of law after the hearing, as permitted by the ALJ.

§ 681.14 What is the role of the ALJ?

An ALJ retained by NSF serves as the presiding officer at all hearings.

(a) The ALJ shall conduct a fair and impartial hearing, avoid delay, maintain order, and assure that a record of the proceeding is made.

(b) The ALJ has the authority to—

(1) Set and change the date, time, and place of the hearing upon reasonable notice to the parties;

(2) Continue or recess the hearing in whole or in part for a reasonable period of time;

(3) Hold conferences to identify or simplify the issues, or to consider other matters that may aid in the expeditious disposition of the proceeding;

(4) Administer oaths and affirmations;

(5) Issue subpoenas requiring the attendance of witnesses and the production of documents at depositions or at hearings;

(6) Rule on motions and other procedural matters;

(7) Regulate the scope and timing of discovery;

(8) Regulate the course of the hearing and the conduct of representatives and parties;

(9) Examine witnesses;

(10) Receive, rule on, exclude, or limit evidence;

(11) Upon motion of a party, take official notice of facts;

(12) Upon motion of a party, decide cases, in whole or in part, by summary judgment where there is no disputed issue of material fact;

(13) Conduct any conference, argument or hearing on motions in person or by telephone; and

(14) Exercise such other authority as is necessary to carry out the responsibilities of the ALJ under this part.

(c) The ALJ does not have the authority to find Federal statutes or regulations invalid.

§ 681.15 How are the functions of the ALJ separated from those of the investigating official and the reviewing official?

(a) The investigating official, the reviewing official, and any employee or agent of the authority who takes part in investigating, preparing, or presenting a particular case may not, in such case or a factually related case:

(1) Participate in the hearing as the ALJ;

(2) Participate or advise in the review of the initial decision by the authority head; or

(3) Make the collection of penalties and assessment under 31 U.S.C. 3806.

(b) The ALJ shall not be responsible to or subject to the supervision or direction of the investigating official or the reviewing official.

§ 681.16 Can the reviewing official or ALJ be disqualified?

(a) A reviewing official or an ALJ may disqualify himself or herself at any time.

(b) Upon motion of any party, the reviewing official or ALJ may be disqualified as follows:

(1) The motion must be supported by an affidavit containing specific facts establishing that personal bias or other reason for disqualification exists, including the time and circumstances of the discovery of such facts;

(2) The motion must be filed promptly after discovery of the grounds for disqualification or the objection will be deemed waived; and

(3) The party, or representative of record, must certify in writing that the motion is made in good faith.

(c) Once a motion has been filed to disqualify the reviewing official, the ALJ will halt the proceedings until resolving the matter of disqualification. If the ALJ determines that the reviewing official is disqualified, the ALJ will dismiss the complaint without prejudice. If the ALJ disqualifies himself or herself, the case will be promptly reassigned to another ALJ.

§ 681.17 What rights are there to review documents?

(a) Once the ALJ issues a hearing notice pursuant to § 681.11(b), and upon written request to the reviewing official, the defendant may:

(1) Review any relevant and material documents, transcripts, records, and other materials that relate to the allegations set out in the complaint and upon which the findings and conclusions of the investigating official are based, unless such documents are subject to a privilege under Federal law. Upon payment of fees for duplication, the defendant may obtain copies of such documents; and

(2) Obtain a copy of all exculpatory information in the possession of the reviewing official or investigating official relating to the allegations in the complaint, even if it is contained in a document that would otherwise be privileged. If the document would otherwise be privileged, only that portion containing exculpatory information must be disclosed.

(b) The notice sent to the Attorney General from the reviewing official as described in § 681.5(a) is not discoverable under any circumstances.

(c) If the reviewing official does not respond to the defendant's request within 20 days, the defendant may file a motion to compel disclosure of the documents with the ALJ subject to the provisions of this section. Such a motion may only be filed with the ALJ following the filing of an answer pursuant to § 681.9.

§ 681.18 What type of discovery is authorized and how is it conducted?

(a) The following types of discovery are authorized:

(1) Requests for production of documents for inspection and copying;

(2) Requests for admissions of authenticity of any relevant document or of the truth of any relevant fact;

(3) Written interrogatories; and

(4) Depositions.

(b) For the purpose of this section, the term "documents" includes information, documents, reports, answers, records, accounts, papers, and other data and documentary evidence. Nothing contained herein shall be interpreted to require the creation of a document.

(c) Unless mutually agreed to by the parties, discovery is available only as ordered by the ALJ. The ALJ shall regulate the timing of discovery.

(d) *Motions for discovery.* (1) A party seeking discovery may file a motion with the ALJ. Such a motion shall be accompanied by a copy of the requested discovery, or in the case of depositions, a summary of the scope of the proposed deposition.

(2) Within ten days of service, a party may file an opposition to the motion and/or a motion for protective order as provided in § 681.22.

(3) The ALJ may grant a motion for discovery only if he or she finds that the discovery sought—

(i) Is necessary for the expeditious, fair, and reasonable consideration of the issues;

(ii) Is not unduly costly or burdensome;

(iii) Will not unduly delay the proceeding; and

(iv) Does not seek privileged information.

(4) The burden of showing that discovery should be allowed is on the party seeking discovery.

(5) The ALJ may grant discovery subject to a protective order under § 681.22.

(e) *Depositions.* (1) If a motion for deposition is granted, the ALJ shall issue a subpoena for the deponent, which may require the deponent to produce documents. The subpoena shall specify the time and place at which the deposition will be held.

(2) The party seeking to depose shall serve the subpoena in the manner prescribed by § 681.8.

(3) The deponent may file with the ALJ a motion to quash the subpoena or a motion for a protective order within ten days of service.

(4) The party seeking to depose shall provide for the taking of a verbatim transcript of the deposition, which it shall make available to all other parties for inspection and copying.

(f) Each party shall bear its own costs of discovery.

§ 681.19 Are witness lists exchanged before the hearing?

(a) As ordered by the ALJ, the parties must exchange witness lists and copies of proposed hearing exhibits, including copies of any written statements or transcripts of deposition testimony that each party intends to offer in lieu of live testimony.

(b) If a party objects, the ALJ will not admit into evidence the testimony of any witness whose name does not appear on the witness list or any exhibit not provided to an opposing party in advance unless the ALJ finds good cause for the omission or concludes that there is no prejudice to the objecting party.

(c) Unless a party objects within the time set by the ALJ, documents exchanged in accordance with this section are deemed to be authentic for the purpose of admissibility at the hearing.

§ 681.20 Can witnesses be subpoenaed?

(a) A party wishing to procure the appearance and testimony of any individual at the hearing may request that the ALJ issue a subpoena.

(b) A subpoena requiring the attendance and testimony of an individual may also require the individual to produce documents at the hearing.

(c) A party seeking a subpoena shall file a written request not less than 15 days before the date of the hearing unless otherwise allowed by the ALJ for good cause shown. Such request shall specify any documents to be produced and shall designate the witnesses and describe the address and location thereof with sufficient particularity to permit such witnesses to be found.

(d) The subpoena shall specify the time and place at which the witness is to appear and any documents the witness is to produce.

(e) The party seeking the subpoena shall serve it in the manner prescribed in §681.8. A subpoena on a party or upon an individual under the control of a party may be served by first class mail.

(f) A party or the individual to whom the subpoena is directed may file with the ALJ a motion to quash the subpoena within ten days after service or on or before the time specified in the subpoena for compliance if it is less than ten days after service.

§681.21 Who pays the costs for a subpoena?

The party requesting a subpoena shall pay the cost of the fees and mileage of any witness subpoenaed in the amounts that would be payable to a witness in a proceeding in United States District Court. A check for witness fees and mileage shall accompany the subpoena when served, except that when a subpoena is issued on behalf of NSF, a check of fees and mileage need not accompany the subpoena.

§681.22 Are protective orders available?

(a) A party or prospective witness or deponent may file a motion for a protective order with respect to discovery sought by an opposing party or with respect to the hearing, seeking to limit the availability or disclosure of evidence.

(b) In issuing a protective order, the ALJ may make any order which justice requires to protect a party or person from annoyance, embarrassment, oppression, or undue burden or expense, including one or more of the following:

(1) That the discovery not be had;

(2) That the discovery may be had only on specified terms and conditions;

(3) That the discovery may be had only through a method of discovery other than requested;

(4) That certain matters not be inquired into, or that the scope of discovery be limited to certain matters;

(5) That discovery be conducted with no one present except persons designated by the ALJ;

(6) That the contents of the discovery be sealed;

(7) That a deposition after being sealed be opened only by order of the ALJ;

(8) That a trade secret or other confidential research, development, commercial information, or facts pertaining to any criminal investigation, proceeding, or other administrative investigation not be disclosed or be disclosed only in a designated way; or

(9) That the parties simultaneously file specified documents or information enclosed in sealed envelopes to be opened as directed by the ALJ.

§681.23 How are documents filed and served with the ALJ?

(a) Documents filed with the ALJ must include an original and two copies. Every document filed in the proceeding must contain a title (e.g., motion to quash subpoena), a caption setting forth the title of the action, and the case number assigned by the ALJ. Every document must be signed by the person on whose behalf the paper was filed, or his or her representative.

(b) Documents are considered filed when they are mailed. The date of mailing may be established by a certificate from the party or its representative, or by proof that the document was sent by certified or registered mail.

(c) A party filing a document with the ALJ must, at the time of filing, serve a copy of such document on every other party. When a party is represented by a representative, the party's representative must be served in lieu of the party.

(d) A certificate of the individual serving the document constitutes proof of service. The certificate must set forth the manner in which the document was served.

§681.24 How is time computed?

(a) In computing any period of time under this part or in an order issued thereunder, the time begins with the day following the act, event, or default, and includes the last day of the period, unless it is a Saturday, Sunday, or legal holiday observed by the Federal government, in which event it includes the next business day.

(b) When the period of time allowed is less than seven days, intermediate Saturdays, Sundays, and legal holidays observed by the Federal government are excluded from the computation.

(c) Where a document has been served or issued by placing it in the mail, an additional five days will be added to the time permitted for any response.

§ 681.25 Where is the hearing held?

The ALJ will hold the hearing in any judicial district of the United States:

(a) In which the defendant resides or transacts business; or

(b) In which the claim or statement on which liability is based was made to NSF; or

(c) As agreed upon by the defendant and the ALJ.

§ 681.26 How will the hearing be conducted and who has the burden of proof?

(a) The ALJ conducts a hearing in order to determine whether a defendant is liable for a civil penalty, assessment, or both and, if so, the appropriate amount of the penalty and/or assessment. The hearing will be recorded and transcribed, and the transcript of testimony, exhibits admitted at the hearing, and all papers filed in the proceeding constitute the record for a decision by the ALJ.

(b) NSF must prove a defendant's liability and any aggravating factors by a preponderance of the evidence.

(c) A defendant must prove any affirmative defenses and any mitigating factors by a preponderance of the evidence.

§ 681.27 How is evidence presented at the hearing?

(a) The ALJ shall determine the admissibility of evidence.

(b) Except as provided in this part, the ALJ shall not be bound by the Federal Rules of Evidence. However, the ALJ may apply the Federal Rules of Evidence where he or she deems appropriate.

(c) The ALJ shall exclude irrelevant and immaterial evidence.

(d) Although relevant, evidence may be excluded if its probative value is substantially outweighed by the danger of unfair prejudice, confusion of the issues, or by considerations of undue delay or needless presentation of cumulative evidence.

(e) Although relevant, evidence shall be excluded if it is privileged under Federal law.

(f) Evidence concerning offers of compromise or settlement shall be inadmissible to the extent provided in Rule 408 of the Federal Rules of Evidence.

(g) The ALJ shall permit the parties to introduce rebuttal witnesses and evidence.

§ 681.28 How is witness testimony presented?

(a) Except as provided in paragraph (b) of this section, testimony at the hearing shall be given orally by witnesses under oath or affirmation.

(b) At the discretion of the ALJ, testimony may be admitted in the form of a written statement or deposition. Any such statement must be provided to all other parties along with the last known address of such witness, in a manner which allows sufficient time for other parties to subpoena such witness for cross-examination at the hearing. Prior written statements of witnesses proposed to testify at the hearing and deposition transcripts shall be exchanged as provided in § 681.19.

(c) The ALJ shall exercise reasonable control over the mode and order of interrogating witnesses and presenting evidence.

(d) The ALJ shall permit the parties to conduct such cross examination as may be required for a full and true disclosure of the facts.

(e) Upon motion of any party, the ALJ shall order witnesses excluded from the hearing room so that they cannot hear the testimony of other witnesses. This rule does not authorize exclusion of—

(1) A party who is an individual;

(2) In the case of a party that is not an individual, an officer or employee of the party appearing for the entity pro se or designated by the party's representative; or

(3) An individual whose presence is shown by a party to be essential to the presentation of its case, including an individual employed by the Government engaged in assisting the representative for the Government.

§ 681.29 Will the hearing proceedings be recorded?

The hearing will be recorded and transcribed. The transcript of testimony, exhibits and other evidence admitted at the hearing, and all papers and requests filed in the proceeding constitute the record for the decision by the ALJ and the authority head.

§ 681.30 Are ex parte communications between a party and the ALJ permitted?

Ex parte communications between a party and the ALJ are not permitted unless the other party consents to such a communication taking place. This does not prohibit a party from inquiring about the status of a case or asking routine questions concerning administrative functions or procedures.

§ 681.31 Are there sanctions for misconduct?

(a) The ALJ may sanction a person, including any party or representative, for failing to comply with an order, or for engaging in other misconduct that interferes with the speedy, orderly, and fair conduct of a hearing.

(b) Any such sanction shall reasonably relate to the severity and nature of the misconduct.

(c) When a party fails to comply with an order, including an order for taking a deposition, the production of evidence within the party's control, or a request for admission, the ALJ may:

(1) Draw an inference in favor of the requesting party with regard to the information sought;

(2) In the case of requests for admission, deem each matter of which an admission is requested to be admitted;

(3) Prohibit the party failing to comply with such order from introducing evidence concerning, or otherwise relying upon testimony relating to the information sought; and

(4) Strike any part of the pleadings or other submissions of the party failing to comply with such a request.

(d) The ALJ may refuse to consider any motion, request, response, brief or other document which is not filed in a timely fashion.

(e) If a party fails to prosecute or defend an action under this part commenced by service of a notice of hearing, the ALJ may dismiss the action or may issue an initial decision imposing penalties and assessments.

§ 681.32 Are post-hearing briefs required?

Post-hearing briefs are not required, but the ALJ may permit them at his or her discretion.

DECISIONS AND APPEALS

§ 681.33 How is the case decided?

(a) The ALJ will issue an initial decision based only on the record. It will contain findings of fact, conclusions of law, and the amount of any penalties and assessments imposed.

(b) The ALJ will serve the initial decision on all parties within 90 days after the close of the hearing or, if the filing of post-hearing briefs were permitted, within 90 days after the final post-hearing brief was filed.

(c) The findings of fact must include a finding on each of the following issues:

(1) Whether any one or more of the claims or statements identified in the complaint violate this part; and

(2) If the defendant is liable for penalties or assessments, the appropriate amount of any such penalties or assessments, considering any mitigating or aggravating factors.

(d) The initial decision will include a description of the right of a defendant found liable for a civil penalty or assessment to file a motion for reconsideration with the ALJ or a notice of appeal with the authority head.

§ 681.34 How are penalty and assessment amounts determined?

(a) In determining an appropriate amount of civil penalties and assessments, the ALJ and the authority head, upon appeal, should evaluate any circumstances that mitigate or aggravate the violation and should articulate in their opinions the reasons that support the penalties and assessments they impose. Although not exhaustive, the following factors are among those that may influence the ALJ and the authority head in determining the amount of penalties and assessments to impose with respect to the misconduct charged in the complaint:

(1) The number of false, fictitious, or fraudulent claims or statements;
(2) The time period over which such claims or statements were made;
(3) The degree of the defendant's culpability with respect to the misconduct;
(4) The amount of money or the value of the property, services, or benefit falsely claimed;
(5) The value of the Government's actual loss as a result of the misconduct, including foreseeable consequential damages and the cost of the investigation;
(6) The relationship of the amount imposed as civil penalties to the amount of the Government's loss;
(7) The potential or actual impact of the misconduct upon public confidence in the management of Government programs and operations;
(8) Whether the defendant has engaged in a pattern of the same or similar misconduct;
(9) Whether the defendant attempted to conceal the misconduct;
(10) The degree to which the defendant has involved others in the misconduct or in concealing it;
(11) Where the misconduct of employees or agents is imputed to the defendant, the extent to which the defendant's practices fostered or attempted to preclude such misconduct;
(12) Whether the defendant cooperated in or obstructed an investigation of the misconduct;
(13) Whether the defendant assisted in identifying and prosecuting other wrongdoers;
(14) The complexity of the program or transaction, and the degree of the defendant's sophistication with respect to it, including the extent of the defendant's prior participation in the program or in similar transactions;
(15) Whether the defendant has been found, in any criminal, civil, or administrative proceeding to have engaged in similar misconduct or to have dealt dishonestly with the Government of the United States or a state, directly or indirectly; and
(16) The need to deter the defendant and others from engaging in the same or similar misconduct.
(b) Nothing in this section shall be construed to limit the ALJ or the authority head from considering any other factors that in any given case may mitigate or aggravate the offense for which penalties and assessments are imposed.

§ 681.35 Can a party request reconsideration of the initial decision?

(a) Any party may file a motion for reconsideration of the initial decision with the ALJ within 20 days of receipt of the initial decision. If the initial decision was served by mail, there is a rebuttable presumption that the initial decision was received by the party 5 days from the date of mailing.
(b) A motion for reconsideration must be accompanied by a supporting brief and must describe specifically each allegedly erroneous decision.
(c) Any response to a motion for reconsideration will only be allowed if it is requested by the ALJ.
(d) The ALJ will dispose of a motion for reconsideration by denying it or by issuing a revised initial decision.
(e) If the ALJ issues a revised initial decision upon motion of a party, no further motions for reconsideration may be filed by any party.

§ 681.36 When does the initial decision of the ALJ become final?

(a) The initial decision of the ALJ becomes the final decision of NSF, and shall be binding on all parties 30 days after it is issued, unless any party timely files a motion for reconsideration or any defendant adjudged to have submitted a false, fictitious, or fraudulent claim or statement timely appeals to the authority head of NSF, as set forth in § 681.37.
(b) If the ALJ disposes of a motion for reconsideration by denying it or by issuing a revised initial decision, the ALJ's order on the motion for reconsideration becomes the final decision of NSF 30 days after the order is issued, unless a defendant adjudged to have submitted a false, fictitious, fraudulent claim or statement timely appeals to the authority head of NSF, as set forth in § 681.37.

§ 681.37 What are the procedures for appealing the ALJ decision?

(a) Any defendant who submits a timely answer and is found liable for a

National Science Foundation § 681.42

civil penalty or assessment in an initial decision may appeal the decision.

(b) The defendant may file a notice of appeal with the authority head within 30 days following issuance of the initial decision, serving a copy of the notice of appeal on all parties and the ALJ. The authority head may extend this deadline for up to an additional 30 days if an extension request is filed within the initial 30-day period and shows good cause.

(c) The defendant's appeal will not be considered until all timely motions for reconsideration have been resolved.

(d) If a timely motion for reconsideration is denied, a notice of appeal may be filed within 30 days following such denial or issuance of a revised initial decision, whichever applies.

(e) A notice of appeal must be supported by a written brief specifying why the initial decision should be reversed or modified.

(f) The NSF representative may file a brief in opposition to the notice of appeal within 30 days of receiving the defendant's appeal and supporting brief.

(g) If a defendant timely files a notice of appeal, and the time for filing reconsideration motions has expired, the ALJ will forward the record of the proceeding to the authority head.

§ 681.38 What happens if an initial decision is appealed?

(a) An initial decision is stayed automatically pending disposition of a motion for reconsideration or of an appeal to the authority head.

(b) No administrative stay is available following a final decision of the authority head.

§ 681.39 Are there any limitations on the right to appeal to the authority head?

(a) A defendant has no right to appear personally, or through a representative, before the authority head.

(b) There is no right to appeal any interlocutory ruling.

(c) The authority head will not consider any objection or evidence that was not raised before the ALJ unless the defendant demonstrates that the failure to object was caused by extraordinary circumstances. If the defendant demonstrates to the satisfaction of the authority head that extraordinary circumstances prevented the presentation of evidence at the hearing, and that the additional evidence is material, the authority head may remand the matter to the ALJ for consideration of the additional evidence.

§ 681.40 How does the authority head dispose of an appeal?

(a) The authority head may affirm, reduce, reverse, compromise, remand, or settle any penalty or assessment imposed by the ALJ in the initial decision or reconsideration decision.

(b) The authority head will promptly serve each party to the appeal and the ALJ with a copy of his or her decision. This decision must contain a statement describing the right of any person, against whom a penalty or assessment has been made, to seek judicial review.

§ 681.41 What judicial review is available?

31 U.S.C. 3805 authorizes judicial review by the appropriate United States District Court of any final NSF decision imposing penalties or assessments, and specifies the procedures for such review. To obtain judicial review, a defendant must file a petition with the appropriate court in a timely manner.

§ 681.42 Can the administrative complaint be settled voluntarily?

(a) Parties may make offers of compromise or settlement at any time. Any compromise or settlement must be in writing.

(b) The reviewing official has the exclusive authority to compromise or settle the case from the date on which the reviewing official is permitted to issue a complaint until the ALJ issues an initial decision.

(c) The authority head has exclusive authority to compromise or settle the case from the date of the ALJ's initial decision until initiation of any judicial review or any action to collect the penalties and assessments.

(d) The Attorney General has exclusive authority to compromise or settle the case while any judicial review or any action to recover penalties and assessments is pending.

§ 681.43

(e) The investigating official may recommend settlement terms to the reviewing official, the authority head, or the Attorney General, as appropriate.

§ 681.43 How are civil penalties and assessments collected?

Section 3806 and 3808(b) of title 31, United States Code, authorize actions for collection of civil penalties and assessments imposed under this part and specify the procedures for such actions.

§ 681.44 Is there a right to administrative offset?

The amount of any penalty or assessment which has become final, or for which a judgment has been entered, or any amount agreed upon in a compromise or settlement, may be collected by administrative offset under 31 U.S.C. 3716, except that an administrative offset may not be made under this subsection against a refund of an overpayment of Federal taxes, then or later owing by the United States to the defendant.

§ 681.45 What happens to collections?

All amounts collected pursuant to this part shall be deposited as miscellaneous receipts in the Treasury of the United States, except as provided in 31 U.S.C. 3806(g).

§ 681.46 What if the investigation indicates criminal misconduct?

(a) Any investigating official may:

(1) Refer allegations of criminal misconduct directly to the Department of Justice for prosecution or for suit under the False Claims Act or other civil proceeding;

(2) Defer or postpone a report or referral to the reviewing official to avoid interference with a criminal investigation or prosecution; or

(3) Issue subpoenas under any other statutory authority.

(b) Nothing in this part limits the requirement that NSF employees report suspected violations of criminal law to the NSF Office of Inspector General or to the Attorney General.

PART 689—RESEARCH MISCONDUCT

Sec.
689.1 Definitions.
689.2 General policies and responsibilities.
689.3 Actions.
689.4 Role of awardee institutions.
689.5 Initial NSF handling of misconduct matters.
689.6 Investigations.
689.7 Pending proposals and awards.
689.8 Interim administrative actions.
689.9 Dispositions.
689.10 Appeals.

AUTHORITY: 42 U.S.C. 1870(a).

SOURCE: 67 FR 11937, Mar. 18, 2002, unless otherwise noted.

§ 689.1 Definitions.

The following definitions apply to this part:

(a) *Research misconduct* means fabrication, falsification, or plagiarism in proposing or performing research funded by NSF, reviewing research proposals submitted to NSF, or in reporting research results funded by NSF.

(1) *Fabrication* means making up data or results and recording or reporting them.

(2) *Falsification* means manipulating research materials, equipment, or processes, or changing or omitting data or results such that the research is not accurately represented in the research record.

(3) *Plagiarism* means the appropriation of another person's ideas, processes, results or words without giving appropriate credit.

(4) *Research*, for purposes of paragraph (a) of this section, includes proposals submitted to NSF in all fields of science, engineering, mathematics, and education and results from such proposals.

(b) *Research misconduct* does not include honest error or differences of opinion.

§ 689.2 General policies and responsibilities.

(a) NSF will take appropriate action against individuals or institutions upon a finding that research misconduct has occurred. Possible actions are described in § 689.3. NSF may also take interim action during an investigation, as described in § 689.8.

National Science Foundation § 689.3

(b) NSF will find research misconduct only after careful inquiry and investigation by an awardee institution, by another Federal agency, or by NSF. An "inquiry" consists of preliminary information-gathering and preliminary fact-finding to determine whether an allegation or apparent instance of research misconduct has substance and if an investigation is warranted. An investigation must be undertaken if the inquiry determines the allegation or apparent instance of research misconduct has substance. An "investigation" is a formal development, examination and evaluation of a factual record to determine whether research misconduct has taken place, to assess its extent and consequences, and to evaluate appropriate action.

(c) A finding of research misconduct requires that—

(1) There be a significant departure from accepted practices of the relevant research community; and

(2) The research misconduct be committed intentionally, or knowingly, or recklessly; and

(3) The allegation be proven by a preponderance of evidence.

(d) Before NSF makes any final finding of research misconduct or takes any final action on such a finding, NSF will normally afford the accused individual or institution notice, a chance to provide comments and rebuttal, and a chance to appeal. In structuring procedures in individual cases, NSF may take into account procedures already followed by other entities investigating or adjudicating the same allegation of research misconduct.

(e) Debarment or suspension for research misconduct will be imposed only after further procedures described in applicable debarment and suspension regulations, as described in §§ 689.8 and 689.9, respectively. Severe research misconduct, as established under the regulations in this part, is an independent cause for debarment or suspension under the procedures established by the debarment and suspension regulations.

(f) The Office of Inspector General (OIG) oversees investigations of research misconduct and conducts any NSF inquiries and investigations into suspected or alleged research misconduct.

(g) The Deputy Director adjudicates research misconduct proceedings and the Director decides appeals.

(h) Investigative and adjudicative research misconduct records maintained by the agency are exempt from public disclosure under the Freedom of Information Act (5 U.S.C. 552) and the Privacy Act (5 U.S.C. 552a) to the extent permitted by law and regulation.

§ 689.3 Actions.

(a) Possible final actions listed in this paragraph (a) for guidance range from minimal restrictions (Group I) to the most severe and restrictive (Group III). They are not exhaustive and do not include possible criminal sanctions.

(1) *Group I actions.* (i) Send a letter of reprimand to the individual or institution.

(ii) Require as a condition of an award that for a specified period an individual or institution obtain special prior approval of particular activities from NSF.

(iii) Require for a specified period that an institutional official other than those guilty of misconduct certify the accuracy of reports generated under an award or provide assurance of compliance with particular policies, regulations, guidelines, or special terms and conditions.

(2) *Group II actions.* (i) Totally or partially suspend an active award, or restrict for a specified period designated activities or expenditures under an active award.

(ii) Require for a specified period special reviews of all requests for funding from an affected individual or institution to ensure that steps have been taken to prevent repetition of the misconduct.

(iii) Require a correction to the research record.

(3) *Group III actions.* (i) Terminate an active award.

(ii) Prohibit participation of an individual as an NSF reviewer, advisor, or consultant for a specified period.

(iii) Debar or suspend an individual or institution from participation in Federal programs for a specified period

§ 689.4

after further proceedings under applicable regulations.

(b) In deciding what final actions are appropriate when misconduct is found, NSF officials should consider:

(1) How serious the misconduct was;

(2) The degree to which the misconduct was knowing, intentional, or reckless;

(3) Whether it was an isolated event or part of a pattern;

(4) Whether it had a significant impact on the research record, research subjects, other researchers, institutions or the public welfare; and

(5) Other relevant circumstances.

(c) Interim actions may include, but are not limited to:

(1) Totally or partially suspending an existing award;

(2) Suspending eligibility for Federal awards in accordance with debarment-and-suspension regulations;

(3) Proscribing or restricting particular research activities, as, for example, to protect human or animal subjects;

(4) Requiring special certifications, assurances, or other, administrative arrangements to ensure compliance with applicable regulations or terms of the award;

(5) Requiring more prior approvals by NSF;

(6) Deferring funding action on continuing grant increments;

(7) Deferring a pending award;

(8) Restricting or suspending participation as an NSF reviewer, advisor, or consultant.

(d) For those cases governed by the debarment and suspension regulations, the standards of proof contained in the debarment and suspension regulations shall control. Otherwise, NSF will take no final action under this section without a finding of misconduct supported by a preponderance of the relevant evidence.

§ 689.4 Role of awardee institutions.

(a) Awardee institutions bear primary responsibility for prevention and detection of research misconduct and for the inquiry, investigation, and adjudication of alleged research misconduct. In most instances, NSF will rely on awardee institutions to promptly:

(1) Initiate an inquiry into any suspected or alleged research misconduct;

(2) Conduct a subsequent investigation, if warranted;

(3) Take action necessary to ensure the integrity of research, the rights and interests of research subjects and the public, and the observance of legal requirements or responsibilities; and

(4) Provide appropriate safeguards for subjects of allegations as well as informants.

(b) If an institution wishes NSF to defer independent inquiry or investigation, it should:

(1) Complete any inquiry and decide whether an investigation is warranted within 90 days. If completion of an inquiry is delayed, but the institution wishes NSF deferral to continue, NSF may require submission of periodic status reports.

(2) Inform OIG immediately if an initial inquiry supports a formal investigation.

(3) Keep OIG informed during such an investigation.

(4) Complete any investigation and reach a disposition within 180 days. If completion of an investigation is delayed, but the institution wishes NSF deferral to continue, NSF may require submission of periodic status reports.

(5) Provide OIG with the final report from any investigation.

(c) NSF expects institutions to promptly notify OIG should the institution become aware during an inquiry or investigation that:

(1) Public health or safety is at risk;

(2) NSF's resources, reputation, or other interests need protecting;

(3) There is reasonable indication of possible violations of civil or criminal law;

(4) Research activities should be suspended;

(5) Federal action may be needed to protect the interests of a subject of the investigation or of others potentially affected; or

(6) The scientific community or the public should be informed.

(d) Awardee institutions should maintain and effectively communicate to their staffs appropriate policies and procedures relating to research misconduct, which should indicate when NSF should be notified.

§ 689.5 Initial NSF handling of misconduct matters.

(a) NSF staff who learn of alleged misconduct will promptly and discreetly inform OIG or refer informants to OIG.

(b) The identity of informants who wish to remain anonymous will be kept confidential to the extent permitted by law or regulation.

(c) If OIG determines that alleged research misconduct involves potential civil or criminal violations, OIG may refer the matter to the Department of Justice.

(d) Otherwise OIG may:

(1) Inform the awardee institution of the alleged research misconduct and encourage it to undertake an inquiry;

(2) Defer to inquiries or investigations of the awardee institution or of another Federal agency; or

(3) At any time proceed with its own inquiry.

(e) If OIG proceeds with its own inquiry it will normally complete the inquiry no more than 90 days after initiating it.

(f) On the basis of what it learns from an inquiry and in consultation as appropriate with other NSF offices, OIG will decide whether a formal NSF investigation is warranted.

§ 689.6 Investigations.

(a) When an awardee institution or another Federal agency has promptly initiated its own investigation, OIG may defer an NSF inquiry or investigation until it receives the results of that external investigation. If it does not receive the results within 180 days, OIG may proceed with its own investigation.

(b) If OIG decides to initiate an NSF investigation, it must give prompt written notice to the individual or institutions to be investigated, unless notice would prejudice the investigation or unless a criminal investigation is underway or under active consideration. If notice is delayed, it must be given as soon as it will no longer prejudice the investigation or contravene requirements of law or Federal law-enforcement policies.

(c) If a criminal investigation by the Department of Justice, the Federal Bureau of Investigation, or another Federal agency is underway or under active consideration by these agencies or the NSF, OIG will determine what information, if any, may be disclosed to the subject of the investigation or to other NSF employees.

(d) An NSF investigation may include:

(1) Review of award files, reports, and other documents already readily available at NSF or in the public domain;

(2) Review of procedures or methods and inspection of laboratory materials, specimens, and records at awardee institutions;

(3) Interviews with subjects or witnesses;

(4) Review of any documents or other evidence provided by or properly obtainable from parties, witnesses, or other sources;

(5) Cooperation with other Federal agencies; and

(6) Opportunity for the subject of the investigation to be heard.

(e) OIG may invite outside consultants or experts to participate in an NSF investigation. They should be appointed in a manner that ensures the official nature of their involvement and provides them with legal protections available to federal employees.

(f) OIG will make every reasonable effort to complete an NSF investigation and to report its recommendations, if any, to the Deputy Director within 180 days after initiating it.

§ 689.7 Pending proposals and awards.

(a) Upon learning of alleged research misconduct OIG will identify potentially implicated awards or proposals and when appropriate, will ensure that program, grant, and contracting officers handling them are informed (subject to § 689.6(c)).

(b) Neither a suspicion or allegation of research misconduct nor a pending inquiry or investigation will normally delay review of proposals. To avoid influencing reviews, reviewers or panelists will not be informed of allegations or of ongoing inquiries or investigations. However, if allegations, inquiries, or investigations have been rumored or publicized, the responsible Program Director may consult with OIG and, after further consultation

§ 689.8

with the Office of General Counsel, either defer review, inform reviewers to disregard the matter, or inform reviewers of the status of the matter.

§ 689.8 Interim administrative actions.

(a) After an inquiry or during an external or NSF investigation the Deputy Director may order that interim actions (as described in § 689.3(c)) be taken to protect Federal resources or to guard against continuation of any suspected or alleged research misconduct. Such an order will normally be issued on recommendation from OIG and in consultation with the Division of Contracts, Policy, and Oversight or Division of Grants and Agreements, the Office of the General Counsel, the responsible Directorate, and other parts of the Foundation as appropriate.

(b) When suspension is determined to be appropriate, the case will be referred to the suspending official pursuant to 2 CFR part 180, and the suspension procedures of 2 CFR part 180 will be followed, but the suspending official will be either the Deputy Director or an official designated by the Deputy Director.

(c) Such interim actions may be taken whenever information developed during an investigation indicates a need to do so. Any interim action will be reviewed periodically during an investigation by NSF and modified as warranted. An interested party may request a review or modification by the Deputy Director of any interim action.

(d) The Deputy Director will make and OIG will retain a record of interim actions taken and the reasons for taking them.

(e) Interim administrative actions are not final agency actions subject to appeal.

[67 FR 11937, Mar. 18, 2002, as amended at 72 FR 4944, Feb. 2, 2007]

§ 689.9 Dispositions.

(a) After receiving a report from an external investigation by an awardee institution or another Federal agency, OIG will assess the accuracy and completeness of the report and whether the investigating entity followed reasonable procedures. It will either recommend adoption of the findings in whole or in part or, normally within 30 days, initiate a new investigation.

(b) When any satisfactory external investigation or an NSF investigation fails to confirm alleged misconduct—

(1) OIG will notify the subject of the investigation and, if appropriate, those who reported the suspected or alleged misconduct. This notification may include the investigation report.

(2) Any interim administrative restrictions that were imposed will be lifted.

(c) When any satisfactory investigation confirms misconduct—(1) In cases in which debarment is considered by OIG to be an appropriate disposition, the case will be referred to the debarring official pursuant to 2 CFR part 180 and the procedures of 2 CFR part 180 will be followed, but:

(i) The debarring official will be either the Deputy Director, or an official designated by the Deputy Director.

(ii) Except in unusual circumstances, the investigation report and recommended disposition will be included among the materials provided to the subject of the investigation as part of the notice of proposed debarment.

(iii) The notice of the debarring official's decision will include instructions on how to pursue an appeal to the Director.

(2) In all other cases—

(i) Except in unusual circumstances, the investigation report will be provided by OIG to the subject of the investigation, who will be invited to submit comments or rebuttal. Comments or rebuttal submitted within the period allowed, normally 30 days, will receive full consideration and may lead to revision of the report or of a recommended disposition.

(ii) Normally within 45 days after completing an NSF investigation or receiving the report from a satisfactory external investigation, OIG will submit to the Deputy Director the investigation report, any comments or rebuttal from the subject of the investigation, and a recommended disposition. The recommended disposition will propose any final actions to be taken by NSF. Section 689.3 lists possible final actions and considerations to be used in determining them.

(iii) The Deputy Director will review the investigation report and OIG's recommended disposition. Before issuing a disposition the Deputy Director may initiate further hearings or investigation. Normally within 120 days after receiving OIG's recommendations or after completion of any further proceedings, the Deputy Director will send the affected individual or institution a written disposition, specifying actions to be taken. The decision will include instructions on how to pursue an appeal to the Director.

[67 FR 11937, Mar. 18, 2002, as amended at 72 FR 4944, Feb. 2, 2007]

§ 689.10 Appeals.

(a) An affected individual or institution may appeal to the Director in writing within 30 days after receiving the Deputy Director's written decision. The Deputy Director's decision becomes a final administrative action if it is not appealed within the 30 day period.

(b) The Director may appoint an uninvolved NSF officer or employee to review an appeal and make recommendations.

(c) The Director will normally inform the appellant of a final decision within 60 days after receiving the appeal. That decision will be the final administrative action of the Foundation

PART 690—PROTECTION OF HUMAN SUBJECTS (Eff. until 1-19-18)

Sec.
690.101 To what does this policy apply?
690.102 Definitions.
690.103 Assuring compliance with this policy—research conducted or supported by any Federal department or agency.
690.104–690.106 [Reserved]
690.107 IRB membership.
690.108 IRB functions and operations.
690.109 IRB review of research.
690.110 Expedited review procedures for certain kinds of research involving no more than minimal risk, and for minor changes in approved research.
690.111 Criteria for IRB approval of research.
690.112 Review by institution.
690.113 Suspension or termination of IRB approval of research.
690.114 Cooperative research.
690.115 IRB records.
690.116 General requirements for informed consent.
690.117 Documentation of informed consent.
690.118 Applications and proposals lacking definite plans for involvement of human subjects.
690.119 Research undertaken without the intention of involving human subjects.
690.120 Evaluation and disposition of applications and proposals for research to be conducted or supported by a Federal department or agency.
690.121 [Reserved]
690.122 Use of Federal funds.
690.123 Early termination of research support: Evaluation of applications and proposals.
690.124 Conditions.

AUTHORITY: 5 U.S.C. 301; 42 U.S.C. 300v–1(b).

SOURCE: 56 FR 28012, 28022, June 18, 1991, unless otherwise noted.

EFFECTIVE DATE NOTE: At 82 FR 7273, Jan. 19, 2017, part 690 was revised, effective Jan. 1, 2018. For the convenience of the user, the revised text is set forth following this part.

§ 690.101 To what does this policy apply?

(a) Except as provided in paragraph (b) of this section, this policy applies to all research involving human subjects conducted, supported or otherwise subject to regulation by any federal department or agency which takes appropriate administrative action to make the policy applicable to such research. This includes research conducted by federal civilian employees or military personnel, except that each department or agency head may adopt such procedural modifications as may be appropriate from an administrative standpoint. It also includes research conducted, supported, or otherwise subject to regulation by the federal government outside the United States.

(1) Research that is conducted or supported by a federal department or agency, whether or not it is regulated as defined in § 690.102(e), must comply with all sections of this policy.

(2) Research that is neither conducted nor supported by a federal department or agency but is subject to regulation as defined in § 690.102(e) must be reviewed and approved, in compliance with § 690.101, § 690.102, and § 690.107 through § 690.117 of this policy, by an institutional review board (IRB) that operates in accordance with the pertinent requirements of this policy.

§690.101

(b) Unless otherwise required by department or agency heads, research activities in which the only involvement of human subjects will be in one or more of the following categories are exempt from this policy:

(1) Research conducted in established or commonly accepted educational settings, involving normal educational practices, such as (i) research on regular and special education instructional strategies, or (ii) research on the effectiveness of or the comparison among instructional techniques, curricula, or classroom management methods.

(2) Research involving the use of educational tests (cognitive, diagnostic, aptitude, achievement), survey procedures, interview procedures or observation of public behavior, unless:

(i) Information obtained is recorded in such a manner that human subjects can be identified, directly or through identifiers linked to the subjects; and (ii) any disclosure of the human subjects' responses outside the research could reasonably place the subjects at risk of criminal or civil liability or be damaging to the subjects' financial standing, employability, or reputation.

(3) Research involving the use of educational tests (cognitive, diagnostic, aptitude, achievement), survey procedures, interview procedures, or observation of public behavior that is not exempt under paragraph (b)(2) of this section, if:

(i) The human subjects are elected or appointed public officials or candidates for public office; or (ii) federal statute(s) require(s) without exception that the confidentiality of the personally identifiable information will be maintained throughout the research and thereafter.

(4) Research, involving the collection or study of existing data, documents, records, pathological specimens, or diagnostic specimens, if these sources are publicly available or if the information is recorded by the investigator in such a manner that subjects cannot be identified, directly or through identifiers linked to the subjects.

(5) Research and demonstration projects which are conducted by or subject to the approval of department or agency heads, and which are designed to study, evaluate, or otherwise examine:

(i) Public benefit or service programs; (ii) procedures for obtaining benefits or services under those programs; (iii) possible changes in or alternatives to those programs or procedures; or (iv) possible changes in methods or levels of payment for benefits or services under those programs.

(6) Taste and food quality evaluation and consumer acceptance studies, (i) if wholesome foods without additives are consumed or (ii) if a food is consumed that contains a food ingredient at or below the level and for a use found to be safe, or agricultural chemical or environmental contaminant at or below the level found to be safe, by the Food and Drug Administration or approved by the Environmental Protection Agency or the Food Safety and Inspection Service of the U.S. Department of Agriculture.

(c) Department or agency heads retain final judgment as to whether a particular activity is covered by this policy.

(d) Department or agency heads may require that specific research activities or classes of research activities conducted, supported, or otherwise subject to regulation by the department or agency but not otherwise covered by this policy, comply with some or all of the requirements of this policy.

(e) Compliance with this policy requires compliance with pertinent federal laws or regulations which provide additional protections for human subjects.

(f) This policy does not affect any state or local laws or regulations which may otherwise be applicable and which provide additional protections for human subjects.

(g) This policy does not affect any foreign laws or regulations which may otherwise be applicable and which provide additional protections to human subjects of research.

(h) When research covered by this policy takes place in foreign countries, procedures normally followed in the foreign countries to protect human subjects may differ from those set forth in this policy. [An example is a foreign institution which complies with guidelines consistent with the

National Science Foundation § 690.102

World Medical Assembly Declaration (Declaration of Helsinki amended 1989) issued either by sovereign states or by an organization whose function for the protection of human research subjects is internationally recognized.] In these circumstances, if a department or agency head determines that the procedures prescribed by the institution afford protections that are at least equivalent to those provided in this policy, the department or agency head may approve the substitution of the foreign procedures in lieu of the procedural requirements provided in this policy. Except when otherwise required by statute, Executive Order, or the department or agency head, notices of these actions as they occur will be published in the FEDERAL REGISTER or will be otherwise published as provided in department or agency procedures.

(i) Unless otherwise required by law, department or agency heads may waive the applicability of some or all of the provisions of this policy to specific research activities or classes of research activities otherwise covered by this policy. Except when otherwise required by statute or Executive Order, the department or agency head shall forward advance notices of these actions to the Office for Human Research Protections, Department of Health and Human Services (HHS), or any successor office, and shall also publish them in the FEDERAL REGISTER or in such other manner as provided in department or agency procedures.[1]

[56 FR 28012, 28022, June 18, 1991; 56 FR 29756, June 28, 1991, as amended at 70 FR 36328, June 23, 2005]

---

[1] Institutions with HHS-approved assurances on file will abide by provisions of title 45 CFR part 46 subparts A–D. Some of the other Departments and Agencies have incorporated all provisions of title 45 CFR part 46 into their policies and procedures as well. However, the exemptions at 45 CFR 46.101(b) do not apply to research involving prisoners, subpart C. The exemption at 45 CFR 46.101(b)(2), for research involving survey or interview procedures or observation of public behavior, does not apply to research with children, subpart D, except for research involving observations of public behavior when the investigator(s) do not participate in the activities being observed.

§ 690.102 Definitions.

(a) *Department or agency head* means the head of any federal department or agency and any other officer or employee of any department or agency to whom authority has been delegated.

(b) *Institution* means any public or private entity or agency (including federal, state, and other agencies).

(c) *Legally authorized representative* means an individual or judicial or other body authorized under applicable law to consent on behalf of a prospective subject to the subject's participation in the procedure(s) involved in the research.

(d) *Research* means a systematic investigation, including research development, testing and evaluation, designed to develop or contribute to generalizable knowledge. Activities which meet this definition constitute research for purposes of this policy, whether or not they are conducted or supported under a program which is considered research for other purposes. For example, some demonstration and service programs may include research activities.

(e) *Research subject to regulation,* and similar terms are intended to encompass those research activities for which a federal department or agency has specific responsibility for regulating as a research activity, (for example, Investigational New Drug requirements administered by the Food and Drug Administration). It does not include research activities which are incidentally regulated by a federal department or agency solely as part of the department's or agency's broader responsibility to regulate certain types of activities whether research or non-research in nature (for example, Wage and Hour requirements administered by the Department of Labor).

(f) *Human subject* means a living individual about whom an investigator (whether professional or student) conducting research obtains

(1) Data through intervention or interaction with the individual, or

(2) Identifiable private information.

Intervention includes both physical procedures by which data are gathered (for

225

example, venipuncture) and manipulations of the subject or the subject's environment that are performed for research purposes. Interaction includes communication or interpersonal contact between investigator and subject. "Private information" includes information about behavior that occurs in a context in which an individual can reasonably expect that no observation or recording is taking place, and information which has been provided for specific purposes by an individual and which the individual can reasonably expect will not be made public (for example, a medical record). Private information must be individually identifiable (i.e., the identity of the subject is or may readily be ascertained by the investigator or associated with the information) in order for obtaining the information to constitute research involving human subjects.

(g) *IRB* means an institutional review board established in accord with and for the purposes expressed in this policy.

(h) *IRB approval* means the determination of the IRB that the research has been reviewed and may be conducted at an institution within the constraints set forth by the IRB and by other institutional and federal requirements.

(i) *Minimal risk* means that the probability and magnitude of harm or discomfort anticipated in the research are not greater in and of themselves than those ordinarily encountered in daily life or during the performance of routine physical or psychological examinations or tests.

(j) *Certification* means the official notification by the institution to the supporting department or agency, in accordance with the requirements of this policy, that a research project or activity involving human subjects has been reviewed and approved by an IRB in accordance with an approved assurance.

§ 690.103 **Assuring compliance with this policy—research conducted or supported by any Federal department or agency.**

(a) Each institution engaged in research which is covered by this policy and which is conducted or supported by a federal department or agency shall provide written assurance satisfactory to the department or agency head that it will comply with the requirements set forth in this policy. In lieu of requiring submission of an assurance, individual department or agency heads shall accept the existence of a current assurance, appropriate for the research in question, on file with the Office for Human Research Protections, HHS, or any successor office, and approved for federalwide use by that office. When the existence of an HHS-approved assurance is accepted in lieu of requiring submission of an assurance, reports (except certification) required by this policy to be made to department and agency heads shall also be made to the Office for Human Research Protections, HHS, or any successor office.

(b) Departments and agencies will conduct or support research covered by this policy only if the institution has an assurance approved as provided in this section, and only if the institution has certified to the department or agency head that the research has been reviewed and approved by an IRB provided for in the assurance, and will be subject to continuing review by the IRB. Assurances applicable to federally supported or conducted research shall at a minimum include:

(1) A statement of principles governing the institution in the discharge of its responsibilities for protecting the rights and welfare of human subjects of research conducted at or sponsored by the institution, regardless of whether the research is subject to federal regulation. This may include an appropriate existing code, declaration, or statement of ethical principles, or a statement formulated by the institution itself. This requirement does not preempt provisions of this policy applicable to department- or agency-supported or regulated research and need not be applicable to any research exempted or waived under § 690.101 (b) or (i).

(2) Designation of one or more IRBs established in accordance with the requirements of this policy, and for which provisions are made for meeting space and sufficient staff to support the IRB's review and recordkeeping duties.

National Science Foundation § 690.103

(3) A list of IRB members identified by name; earned degrees; representative capacity; indications of experience such as board certifications, licenses, etc., sufficient to describe each member's chief anticipated contributions to IRB deliberations; and any employment or other relationship between each member and the institution; for example: full-time employee, part-time employee, member of governing panel or board, stockholder, paid or unpaid consultant. Changes in IRB membership shall be reported to the department or agency head, unless in accord with § 690.103(a) of this policy, the existence of an HHS-approved assurance is accepted. In this case, change in IRB membership shall be reported to the Office for Human Research Protections, HHS, or any successor office.

(4) Written procedures which the IRB will follow (i) for conducting its initial and continuing review of research and for reporting its findings and actions to the investigator and the institution; (ii) for determining which projects require review more often than annually and which projects need verification from sources other than the investigators that no material changes have occurred since previous IRB review; and (iii) for ensuring prompt reporting to the IRB of proposed changes in a research activity, and for ensuring that such changes in approved research, during the period for which IRB approval has already been given, may not be initiated without IRB review and approval except when necessary to eliminate apparent immediate hazards to the subject.

(5) Written procedures for ensuring prompt reporting to the IRB, appropriate institutional officials, and the department or agency head of (i) any unanticipated problems involving risks to subjects or others or any serious or continuing noncompliance with this policy or the requirements or determinations of the IRB and (ii) any suspension or termination of IRB approval.

(c) The assurance shall be executed by an individual authorized to act for the institution and to assume on behalf of the institution the obligations imposed by this policy and shall be filed in such form and manner as the department or agency head prescribes.

(d) The department or agency head will evaluate all assurances submitted in accordance with this policy through such officers and employees of the department or agency and such experts or consultants engaged for this purpose as the department or agency head determines to be appropriate. The department or agency head's evaluation will take into consideration the adequacy of the proposed IRB in light of the anticipated scope of the institution's research activities and the types of subject populations likely to be involved, the appropriateness of the proposed initial and continuing review procedures in light of the probable risks, and the size and complexity of the institution.

(e) On the basis of this evaluation, the department or agency head may approve or disapprove the assurance, or enter into negotiations to develop an approvable one. The department or agency head may limit the period during which any particular approved assurance or class of approved assurances shall remain effective or otherwise condition or restrict approval.

(f) Certification is required when the research is supported by a federal department or agency and not otherwise exempted or waived under § 690.101 (b) or (i). An institution with an approved assurance shall certify that each application or proposal for research covered by the assurance and by § 690.103 of this Policy has been reviewed and approved by the IRB. Such certification must be submitted with the application or proposal or by such later date as may be prescribed by the department or agency to which the application or proposal is submitted. Under no condition shall research covered by § 690.103 of the Policy be supported prior to receipt of the certification that the research has been reviewed and approved by the IRB. Institutions without an approved assurance covering the research shall certify within 30 days after receipt of a request for such a certification from the department or agency, that the application or proposal has been approved by the IRB. If the certification is not submitted within these time limits, the application or proposal may be returned to the institution.

(Approved by the Office of Management and Budget under Control Number 0990–0260)

[56 FR 28012, 28022, June 18, 1991; 56 FR 29756, June 28, 1991, as amended at 70 FR 36328, June 23, 2005]

§§ 690.104–690.106 [Reserved]

§ 690.107 IRB membership.

(a) Each IRB shall have at least five members, with varying backgrounds to promote complete and adequate review of research activities commonly conducted by the institution. The IRB shall be sufficiently qualified through the experience and expertise of its members, and the diversity of the members, including consideration of race, gender, and cultural backgrounds and sensitivity to such issues as community attitudes, to promote respect for its advice and counsel in safeguarding the rights and welfare of human subjects. In addition to possessing the professional competence necessary to review specific research activities, the IRB shall be able to ascertain the acceptability of proposed research in terms of institutional commitments and regulations, applicable law, and standards of professional conduct and practice. The IRB shall therefore include persons knowledgeable in these areas. If an IRB regularly reviews research that involves a vulnerable category of subjects, such as children, prisoners, pregnant women, or handicapped or mentally disabled persons, consideration shall be given to the inclusion of one or more individuals who are knowledgeable about and experienced in working with these subjects.

(b) Every nondiscriminatory effort will be made to ensure that no IRB consists entirely of men or entirely of women, including the institution's consideration of qualified persons of both sexes, so long as no selection is made to the IRB on the basis of gender. No IRB may consist entirely of members of one profession.

(c) Each IRB shall include at least one member whose primary concerns are in scientific areas and at least one member whose primary concerns are in nonscientific areas.

(d) Each IRB shall include at least one member who is not otherwise affiliated with the institution and who is not part of the immediate family of a person who is affiliated with the institution.

(e) No IRB may have a member participate in the IRB's initial or continuing review of any project in which the member has a conflicting interest, except to provide information requested by the IRB.

(f) An IRB may, in its discretion, invite individuals with competence in special areas to assist in the review of issues which require expertise beyond or in addition to that available on the IRB. These individuals may not vote with the IRB.

§ 690.108 IRB functions and operations.

In order to fulfill the requirements of this policy each IRB shall:

(a) Follow written procedures in the same detail as described in § 690.103(b)(4) and, to the extent required by, § 690.103(b)(5).

(b) Except when an expedited review procedure is used (see § 690.110), review proposed research at convened meetings at which a majority of the members of the IRB are present, including at least one member whose primary concerns are in nonscientific areas. In order for the research to be approved, it shall receive the approval of a majority of those members present at the meeting.

§ 690.109 IRB review of research.

(a) An IRB shall review and have authority to approve, require modifications in (to secure approval), or disapprove all research activities covered by this policy.

(b) An IRB shall require that information given to subjects as part of informed consent is in accordance with § 690.116. The IRB may require that information, in addition to that specifically mentioned in § 690.116, be given to the subjects when in the IRB's judgment the information would meaningfully add to the protection of the rights and welfare of subjects.

(c) An IRB shall require documentation of informed consent or may waive documentation in accordance with § 690.117.

(d) An IRB shall notify investigators and the institution in writing of its decision to approve or disapprove the proposed research activity, or of modifications required to secure IRB approval of the research activity. If the IRB decides to disapprove a research activity, it shall include in its written notification a statement of the reasons for its decision and give the investigator an opportunity to respond in person or in writing.

(e) An IRB shall conduct continuing review of research covered by this policy at intervals appropriate to the degree of risk, but not less than once per year, and shall have authority to observe or have a third party observe the consent process and the research.

(Approved by the Office of Management and Budget under Control Number 0990–0260)

[56 FR 28012, 28022, June 18, 1991, as amended at 70 FR 36328, June 23, 2005]

§ 690.110 Expedited review procedures for certain kinds of research involving no more than minimal risk, and for minor changes in approved research.

(a) The Secretary, HHS, has established, and published as a Notice in the FEDERAL REGISTER, a list of categories of research that may be reviewed by the IRB through an expedited review procedure. The list will be amended, as appropriate after consultation with other departments and agencies, through periodic republication by the Secretary, HHS, in the FEDERAL REGISTER. A copy of the list is available from the Office for Human Research Protections, HHS, or any successor office.

(b) An IRB may use the expedited review procedure to review either or both of the following:

(1) Some or all of the research appearing on the list and found by the reviewer(s) to involve no more than minimal risk,

(2) Minor changes in previously approved research during the period (of one year or less) for which approval is authorized.

Under an expedited review procedure, the review may be carried out by the IRB chairperson or by one or more experienced reviewers designated by the chairperson from among members of the IRB. In reviewing the research, the reviewers may exercise all of the authorities of the IRB except that the reviewers may not disapprove the research. A research activity may be disapproved only after review in accordance with the non-expedited procedure set forth in § 690.108(b).

(c) Each IRB which uses an expedited review procedure shall adopt a method for keeping all members advised of research proposals which have been approved under the procedure.

(d) The department or agency head may restrict, suspend, terminate, or choose not to authorize an institution's or IRB's use of the expedited review procedure.

[56 FR 28012, 28022, June 18, 1991, as amended at 70 FR 36328, June 23, 2005]

§ 690.111 Criteria for IRB approval of research.

(a) In order to approve research covered by this policy the IRB shall determine that all of the following requirements are satisfied:

(1) Risks to subjects are minimized: (i) By using procedures which are consistent with sound research design and which do not unnecessarily expose subjects to risk, and (ii) whenever appropriate, by using procedures already being performed on the subjects for diagnostic or treatment purposes.

(2) Risks to subjects are reasonable in relation to anticipated benefits, if any, to subjects, and the importance of the knowledge that may reasonably be expected to result. In evaluating risks and benefits, the IRB should consider only those risks and benefits that may result from the research (as distinguished from risks and benefits of therapies subjects would receive even if not participating in the research). The IRB should not consider possible long-range effects of applying knowledge gained in the research (for example, the possible effects of the research on public policy) as among those research risks that fall within the purview of its responsibility.

(3) Selection of subjects is equitable. In making this assessment the IRB should take into account the purposes of the research and the setting in

which the research will be conducted and should be particularly cognizant of the special problems of research involving vulnerable populations, such as children, prisoners, pregnant women, mentally disabled persons, or economically or educationally disadvantaged persons.

(4) Informed consent will be sought from each prospective subject or the subject's legally authorized representative, in accordance with, and to the extent required by §690.116.

(5) Informed consent will be appropriately documented, in accordance with, and to the extent required by §690.117.

(6) When appropriate, the research plan makes adequate provision for monitoring the data collected to ensure the safety of subjects.

(7) When appropriate, there are adequate provisions to protect the privacy of subjects and to maintain the confidentiality of data.

(b) When some or all of the subjects are likely to be vulnerable to coercion or undue influence, such as children, prisoners, pregnant women, mentally disabled persons, or economically or educationally disadvantaged persons, additional safeguards have been included in the study to protect the rights and welfare of these subjects.

§690.112 Review by institution.

Research covered by this policy that has been approved by an IRB may be subject to further appropriate review and approval or disapproval by officials of the institution. However, those officials may not approve the research if it has not been approved by an IRB.

§690.113 Suspension or termination of IRB approval of research.

An IRB shall have authority to suspend or terminate approval of research that is not being conducted in accordance with the IRB's requirements or that has been associated with unexpected serious harm to subjects. Any suspension or termination of approval shall include a statement of the reasons for the IRB's action and shall be reported promptly to the investigator, appropriate institutional officials, and the department or agency head.

(Approved by the Office of Management and Budget under Control Number 0990–0260)

[56 FR 28012, 28022, June 18, 1991, as amended at 70 FR 36328, June 23, 2005]

§690.114 Cooperative research.

Cooperative research projects are those projects covered by this policy which involve more than one institution. In the conduct of cooperative research projects, each institution is responsible for safeguarding the rights and welfare of human subjects and for complying with this policy. With the approval of the department or agency head, an institution participating in a cooperative project may enter into a joint review arrangement, rely upon the review of another qualified IRB, or make similar arrangements for avoiding duplication of effort.

§690.115 IRB records.

(a) An institution, or when appropriate an IRB, shall prepare and maintain adequate documentation of IRB activities, including the following:

(1) Copies of all research proposals reviewed, scientific evaluations, if any, that accompany the proposals, approved sample consent documents, progress reports submitted by investigators, and reports of injuries to subjects.

(2) Minutes of IRB meetings which shall be in sufficient detail to show attendance at the meetings; actions taken by the IRB; the vote on these actions including the number of members voting for, against, and abstaining; the basis for requiring changes in or disapproving research; and a written summary of the discussion of controverted issues and their resolution.

(3) Records of continuing review activities.

(4) Copies of all correspondence between the IRB and the investigators.

(5) A list of IRB members in the same detail as described is §690.103(b)(3).

(6) Written procedures for the IRB in the same detail as described in §690.103(b)(4) and §690.103(b)(5).

(7) Statements of significant new findings provided to subjects, as required by §690.116(b)(5).

National Science Foundation § 690.116

(b) The records required by this policy shall be retained for at least 3 years, and records relating to research which is conducted shall be retained for at least 3 years after completion of the research. All records shall be accessible for inspection and copying by authorized representatives of the department or agency at reasonable times and in a reasonable manner.

(Approved by the Office of Management and Budget under Control Number 0990–0260)

[56 FR 28012, 28022, June 18, 1991, as amended at 70 FR 36328, June 23, 2005]

§ 690.116 General requirements for informed consent.

Except as provided elsewhere in this policy, no investigator may involve a human being as a subject in research covered by this policy unless the investigator has obtained the legally effective informed consent of the subject or the subject's legally authorized representative. An investigator shall seek such consent only under circumstances that provide the prospective subject or the representative sufficient opportunity to consider whether or not to participate and that minimize the possibility of coercion or undue influence. The information that is given to the subject or the representative shall be in language understandable to the subject or the representative. No informed consent, whether oral or written, may include any exculpatory language through which the subject or the representative is made to waive or appear to waive any of the subject's legal rights, or releases or appears to release the investigator, the sponsor, the institution or its agents from liability for negligence.

(a) Basic elements of informed consent. Except as provided in paragraph (c) or (d) of this section, in seeking informed consent the following information shall be provided to each subject:

(1) A statement that the study involves research, an explanation of the purposes of the research and the expected duration of the subject's participation, a description of the procedures to be followed, and identification of any procedures which are experimental;

(2) A description of any reasonably foreseeable risks or discomforts to the subject;

(3) A description of any benefits to the subject or to others which may reasonably be expected from the research;

(4) A disclosure of appropriate alternative procedures or courses of treatment, if any, that might be advantageous to the subject;

(5) A statement describing the extent, if any, to which confidentiality of records identifying the subject will be maintained;

(6) For research involving more than minimal risk, an explanation as to whether any compensation and an explanation as to whether any medical treatments are available if injury occurs and, if so, what they consist of, or where further information may be obtained;

(7) An explanation of whom to contact for answers to pertinent questions about the research and research subjects' rights, and whom to contact in the event of a research-related injury to the subject; and

(8) A statement that participation is voluntary, refusal to participate will involve no penalty or loss of benefits to which the subject is otherwise entitled, and the subject may discontinue participation at any time without penalty or loss of benefits to which the subject is otherwise entitled.

(b) Additional elements of informed consent. When appropriate, one or more of the following elements of information shall also be provided to each subject:

(1) A statement that the particular treatment or procedure may involve risks to the subject (or to the embryo or fetus, if the subject is or may become pregnant) which are currently unforeseeable;

(2) Anticipated circumstances under which the subject's participation may be terminated by the investigator without regard to the subject's consent;

(3) Any additional costs to the subject that may result from participation in the research;

(4) The consequences of a subject's decision to withdraw from the research and procedures for orderly termination of participation by the subject;

(5) A statement that significant new findings developed during the course of the research which may relate to the subject's willingness to continue participation will be provided to the subject; and

(6) The approximate number of subjects involved in the study.

(c) An IRB may approve a consent procedure which does not include, or which alters, some or all of the elements of informed consent set forth above, or waive the requirement to obtain informed consent provided the IRB finds and documents that:

(1) The research or demonstration project is to be conducted by or subject to the approval of state or local government officials and is designed to study, evaluate, or otherwise examine: (i) Public benefit of service programs; (ii) procedures for obtaining benefits or services under those programs; (iii) possible changes in or alternatives to those programs or procedures; or (iv) possible changes in methods or levels of payment for benefits or services under those programs; and

(2) The research could not practicably be carried out without the waiver or alteration.

(d) An IRB may approve a consent procedure which does not include, or which alters, some or all of the elements of informed consent set forth in this section, or waive the requirements to obtain informed consent provided the IRB finds and documents that:

(1) The research involves no more than minimal risk to the subjects;

(2) The waiver or alteration will not adversely affect the rights and welfare of the subjects;

(3) The research could not practicably be carried out without the waiver or alteration; and

(4) Whenever appropriate, the subjects will be provided with additional pertinent information after participation.

(e) The informed consent requirements in this policy are not intended to preempt any applicable federal, state, or local laws which require additional information to be disclosed in order for informed consent to be legally effective.

(f) Nothing in this policy is intended to limit the authority of a physician to provide emergency medical care, to the extent the physician is permitted to do so under applicable federal, state, or local law.

(Approved by the Office of Management and Budget under Control Number 0990–0260)

[56 FR 28012, 28022, June 18, 1991, as amended at 70 FR 36328, June 23, 2005]

§ 690.117 Documentation of informed consent.

(a) Except as provided in paragraph (c) of this section, informed consent shall be documented by the use of a written consent form approved by the IRB and signed by the subject or the subject's legally authorized representative. A copy shall be given to the person signing the form.

(b) Except as provided in paragraph (c) of this section, the consent form may be either of the following:

(1) A written consent document that embodies the elements of informed consent required by § 690.116. This form may be read to the subject or the subject's legally authorized representative, but in any event, the investigator shall give either the subject or the representative adequate opportunity to read it before it is signed; or

(2) A short form written consent document stating that the elements of informed consent required by § 690.116 have been presented orally to the subject or the subject's legally authorized representative. When this method is used, there shall be a witness to the oral presentation. Also, the IRB shall approve a written summary of what is to be said to the subject or the representative. Only the short form itself is to be signed by the subject or the representative. However, the witness shall sign both the short form and a copy of the summary, and the person actually obtaining consent shall sign a copy of the summary. A copy of the summary shall be given to the subject or the representative, in addition to a copy of the short form.

(c) An IRB may waive the requirement for the investigator to obtain a signed consent form for some or all subjects if it finds either:

(1) That the only record linking the subject and the research would be the consent document and the principal risk would be potential harm resulting

from a breach of confidentiality. Each subject will be asked whether the subject wants documentation linking the subject with the research, and the subject's wishes will govern; or

(2) That the research presents no more than minimal risk of harm to subjects and involves no procedures for which written consent is normally required outside of the research context.

In cases in which the documentation requirement is waived, the IRB may require the investigator to provide subjects with a written statement regarding the research.

(Approved by the Office of Management and Budget under Control Number 0990–0260)

[56 FR 28012, 28022, June 18, 1991, as amended at 70 FR 36328, June 23, 2005]

§ 690.118 Applications and proposals lacking definite plans for involvement of human subjects.

Certain types of applications for grants, cooperative agreements, or contracts are submitted to departments or agencies with the knowledge that subjects may be involved within the period of support, but definite plans would not normally be set forth in the application or proposal. These include activities such as institutional type grants when selection of specific projects is the institution's responsibility; research training grants in which the activities involving subjects remain to be selected; and projects in which human subjects' involvement will depend upon completion of instruments, prior animal studies, or purification of compounds. These applications need not be reviewed by an IRB before an award may be made. However, except for research exempted or waived under § 690.101 (b) or (i), no human subjects may be involved in any project supported by these awards until the project has been reviewed and approved by the IRB, as provided in this policy, and certification submitted, by the institution, to the department or agency.

§ 690.119 Research undertaken without the intention of involving human subjects.

In the event research is undertaken without the intention of involving human subjects, but it is later proposed to involve human subjects in the research, the research shall first be reviewed and approved by an IRB, as provided in this policy, a certification submitted, by the institution, to the department or agency, and final approval given to the proposed change by the department or agency.

§ 690.120 Evaluation and disposition of applications and proposals for research to be conducted or supported by a Federal department or agency.

The department or agency head will evaluate all applications and proposals involving human subjects submitted to the department or agency through such officers and employees of the department or agency and such experts and consultants as the department or agency head determines to be appropriate. This evaluation will take into consideration the risks to the subjects, the adequacy of protection against these risks, the potential benefits of the research to the subjects and others, and the importance of the knowledge gained or to be gained.

(b) On the basis of this evaluation, the department or agency head may approve or disapprove the application or proposal, or enter into negotiations to develop an approvable one.

§ 690.121 [Reserved]

§ 690.122 Use of Federal funds.

Federal funds administered by a department or agency may not be expended for research involving human subjects unless the requirements of this policy have been satisfied.

§ 690.123 Early termination of research support: Evaluation of applications and proposals.

(a) The department or agency head may require that department or agency support for any project be terminated or suspended in the manner prescribed in applicable program requirements, when the department or agency head finds an institution has materially failed to comply with the terms of this policy.

(b) In making decisions about supporting or approving applications or proposals covered by this policy the department or agency head may take into account, in addition to all other

§ 690.124

eligibility requirements and program criteria, factors such as whether the applicant has been subject to a termination or suspension under paragarph (a) of this section and whether the applicant or the person or persons who would direct or has have directed the scientific and technical aspects of an activity has have, in the judgment of the department or agency head, materially failed to discharge responsibility for the protection of the rights and welfare of human subjects (whether or not the research was subject to federal regulation).

§ 690.124 Conditions.

With respect to any research project or any class of research projects the department or agency head may impose additional conditions prior to or at the time of approval when in the judgment of the department or agency head additional conditions are necessary for the protection of human subjects.

EFFECTIVE DATE NOTE: At 82 FR 7273, Jan. 19, 2017, part 690 was revised, effective Jan. 19, 2018. For the convenience of the user, the revised text is set forth as follows:

PART 690—PROTECTION OF HUMAN SUBJECTS (Eff. 1-19-18)

Sec.
690.101 To what does this policy apply?
690.102 Definitions for purposes of this policy.
690.103 Assuring compliance with this policy—research conducted or supported by any Federal department or agency.
690.104 Exempt research.
690.105 [Reserved]
690.106 [Reserved]
690.107 IRB membership.
690.108 IRB functions and operations.
690.109 IRB review of research.
690.110 Expedited review procedures for certain kinds of research involving no more than minimal risk, and for minor changes in approved research.
690.111 Criteria for IRB approval of research.
690.112 Review by institution.
690.113 Suspension or termination of IRB approval of research.
690.114 Cooperative research.
690.115 IRB records.
690.116 General requirements for informed consent.
690.117 Documentation of informed consent.
690.118 Applications and proposals lacking definite plans for involvement of human subjects.
690.119 Research undertaken without the intention of involving human subjects.
690.120 Evaluation and disposition of applications and proposals for research to be conducted or supported by a Federal department or agency.
690.121 [Reserved]
690.122 Use of Federal funds.
690.123 Early termination of research support: Evaluation of applications and proposals.
690.124 Conditions.

AUTHORITY: 5 U.S.C. 301; 42 U.S.C. 300v-1(b).

§ 690.101 To what does this policy apply?

(a) Except as detailed in § 690.104, this policy applies to all research involving human subjects conducted, supported, or otherwise subject to regulation by any Federal department or agency that takes appropriate administrative action to make the policy applicable to such research. This includes research conducted by Federal civilian employees or military personnel, except that each department or agency head may adopt such procedural modifications as may be appropriate from an administrative standpoint. It also includes research conducted, supported, or otherwise subject to regulation by the Federal Government outside the United States. Institutions that are engaged in research described in this paragraph and institutional review boards (IRBs) reviewing research that is subject to this policy must comply with this policy.

(b) [Reserved]

(c) Department or agency heads retain final judgment as to whether a particular activity is covered by this policy and this judgment shall be exercised consistent with the ethical principles of the Belmont Report.[62]

(d) Department or agency heads may require that specific research activities or classes of research activities conducted, supported, or otherwise subject to regulation by the Federal department or agency but not otherwise covered by this policy comply with some or all of the requirements of this policy.

(e) Compliance with this policy requires compliance with pertinent federal laws or regulations that provide additional protections for human subjects.

(f) This policy does not affect any state or local laws or regulations (including tribal law passed by the official governing body of an American Indian or Alaska Native tribe) that may otherwise be applicable and that provide additional protections for human subjects.

---

[62] The National Commission for the Protection of Human Subjects of Biomedical and Behavioral Research.- Belmont Report. Washington, DC: U.S. Department of Health and Human Services. 1979.

National Science Foundation

(g) This policy does not affect any foreign laws or regulations that may otherwise be applicable and that provide additional protections to human subjects of research.

(h) When research covered by this policy takes place in foreign countries, procedures normally followed in the foreign countries to protect human subjects may differ from those set forth in this policy. In these circumstances, if a department or agency head determines that the procedures prescribed by the institution afford protections that are at least equivalent to those provided in this policy, the department or agency head may approve the substitution of the foreign procedures in lieu of the procedural requirements provided in this policy. Except when otherwise required by statute, Executive Order, or the department or agency head, notices of these actions as they occur will be published in the FEDERAL REGISTER or will be otherwise published as provided in department or agency procedures.

(i) Unless otherwise required by law, department or agency heads may waive the applicability of some or all of the provisions of this policy to specific research activities or classes of research activities otherwise covered by this policy, provided the alternative procedures to be followed are consistent with the principles of the Belmont Report.[63] Except when otherwise required by statute or Executive Order, the department or agency head shall forward advance notices of these actions to the Office for Human Research Protections, Department of Health and Human Services (HHS), or any successor office, or to the equivalent office within the appropriate Federal department or agency, and shall also publish them in the FEDERAL REGISTER or in such other manner as provided in department or agency procedures. The waiver notice must include a statement that identifies the conditions under which the waiver will be applied and a justification as to why the waiver is appropriate for the research, including how the decision is consistent with the principles of the Belmont Report.

(j) Federal guidance on the requirements of this policy shall be issued only after consultation, for the purpose of harmonization (to the extent appropriate), with other Federal departments and agencies that have adopted this policy, unless such consultation is not feasible.

(k) [Reserved]

(l) Compliance dates and transition provisions:

(1) For purposes of this section, the *pre-2018 Requirements* means this subpart as published in the 2016 edition of the Code of Federal Regulations.

(2) For purposes of this section, the *2018 Requirements* means the Federal Policy for the Protection of Human Subjects requirements contained in this subpart. The compliance date for §690.114(b) (cooperative research) of the 2018 Requirements is January 20, 2020.

(3) Research initially approved by an IRB, for which such review was waived pursuant to §690.101(i), or for which a determination was made that the research was exempt before January 19, 2018, shall comply with the pre-2018 Requirements, except that an institution engaged in such research on or after January 19, 2018, may instead comply with the 2018 Requirements if the institution determines that such ongoing research will comply with the 2018 Requirements and an IRB documents such determination.

(4) Research initially approved by an IRB, for which such review was waived pursuant to §690.101(i), or for which a determination was made that the research was exempt on or after January 19, 2018, shall comply with the 2018 Requirements.

(m) Severability: Any provision of this part held to be invalid or unenforceable by its terms, or as applied to any person or circumstance, shall be construed so as to continue to give maximum effect to the provision permitted by law, unless such holding shall be one of utter invalidity or unenforceability, in which event the provision shall be severable from this part and shall not affect the remainder thereof or the application of the provision to other persons not similarly situated or to other dissimilar circumstances.

§690.102 Definitions for purposes of this policy.

(a) *Certification* means the official notification by the institution to the supporting Federal department or agency component, in accordance with the requirements of this policy, that a research project or activity involving human subjects has been reviewed and approved by an IRB in accordance with an approved assurance.

(b) *Clinical trial* means a research study in which one or more human subjects are prospectively assigned to one or more interventions (which may include placebo or other control) to evaluate the effects of the interventions on biomedical or behavioral health-related outcomes.

(c) *Department or agency head* means the head of any Federal department or agency, for example, the Secretary of HHS, and any other officer or employee of any Federal department or agency to whom the authority provided by these regulations to the department or agency head has been delegated.

(d) *Federal department or agency* refers to a federal department or agency (the department or agency itself rather than its bureaus, offices or divisions) that takes appropriate administrative action to make this

---

[63] *Id.*

policy applicable to the research involving human subjects it conducts, supports, or otherwise regulates (*e.g.*, the U.S. Department of Health and Human Services, the U.S. Department of Defense, or the Central Intelligence Agency).

(e)(1) *Human subject* means a living individual about whom an investigator (whether professional or student) conducting research:

(i) Obtains information or biospecimens through intervention or interaction with the individual, and uses, studies, or analyzes the information or biospecimens; or

(ii) Obtains, uses, studies, analyzes, or generates identifiable private information or identifiable biospecimens.

(2) *Intervention* includes both physical procedures by which information or biospecimens are gathered (*e.g.*, venipuncture) and manipulations of the subject or the subject's environment that are performed for research purposes.

(3) *Interaction* includes communication or interpersonal contact between investigator and subject.

(4) *Private information* includes information about behavior that occurs in a context in which an individual can reasonably expect that no observation or recording is taking place, and information that has been provided for specific purposes by an individual and that the individual can reasonably expect will not be made public (*e.g.*, a medical record).

(5) *Identifiable private information* is private information for which the identity of the subject is or may readily be ascertained by the investigator or associated with the information.

(6) *An identifiable biospecimen* is a biospecimen for which the identity of the subject is or may readily be ascertained by the investigator or associated with the biospecimen.

(7) Federal departments or agencies implementing this policy shall:

(i) Upon consultation with appropriate experts (including experts in data matching and re-identification), reexamine the meaning of "identifiable private information," as defined in paragraph (e)(5) of this section, and "identifiable biospecimen," as defined in paragraph (e)(6) of this section. This reexamination shall take place within 1 year and regularly thereafter (at least every 4 years). This process will be conducted by collaboration among the Federal departments and agencies implementing this policy. If appropriate and permitted by law, such Federal departments and agencies may alter the interpretation of these terms, including through the use of guidance.

(ii) Upon consultation with appropriate experts, assess whether there are analytic technologies or techniques that should be considered by investigators to generate "identifiable private information," as defined in paragraph (e)(5) of this section, or an "identifiable biospecimen," as defined in paragraph (e)(6) of this section. This assessment shall take place within 1 year and regularly thereafter (at least every 4 years). This process will be conducted by collaboration among the Federal departments and agencies implementing this policy. Any such technologies or techniques will be included on a list of technologies or techniques that produce identifiable private information or identifiable biospecimens. This list will be published in the FEDERAL REGISTER after notice and an opportunity for public comment. The Secretary, HHS, shall maintain the list on a publicly accessible Web site.

(f) *Institution* means any public or private entity, or department or agency (including federal, state, and other agencies).

(g) *IRB* means an institutional review board established in accord with and for the purposes expressed in this policy.

(h) *IRB approval* means the determination of the IRB that the research has been reviewed and may be conducted at an institution within the constraints set forth by the IRB and by other institutional and federal requirements.

(i) *Legally authorized representative* means an individual or judicial or other body authorized under applicable law to consent on behalf of a prospective subject to the subject's participation in the procedure(s) involved in the research. If there is no applicable law addressing this issue, *legally authorized representative* means an individual recognized by institutional policy as acceptable for providing consent in the nonresearch context on behalf of the prospective subject to the subject's participation in the procedure(s) involved in the research.

(j) *Minimal risk* means that the probability and magnitude of harm or discomfort anticipated in the research are not greater in and of themselves than those ordinarily encountered in daily life or during the performance of routine physical or psychological examinations or tests.

(k) *Public health authority* means an agency or authority of the United States, a state, a territory, a political subdivision of a state or territory, an Indian tribe, or a foreign government, or a person or entity acting under a grant of authority from or contract with such public agency, including the employees or agents of such public agency or its contractors or persons or entities to whom it has granted authority, that is responsible for public health matters as part of its official mandate.

(l) *Research* means a systematic investigation, including research development, testing, and evaluation, designed to develop or contribute to generalizable knowledge. Activities that meet this definition constitute research for purposes of this policy, whether or not they are conducted or supported under a program that is considered research for

National Science Foundation Pt. 690, Nt.

other purposes. For example, some demonstration and service programs may include research activities. For purposes of this part, the following activities are deemed not to be research:

(1) Scholarly and journalistic activities (*e.g.*, oral history, journalism, biography, literary criticism, legal research, and historical scholarship), including the collection and use of information, that focus directly on the specific individuals about whom the information is collected.

(2) Public health surveillance activities, including the collection and testing of information or biospecimens, conducted, supported, requested, ordered, required, or authorized by a public health authority. Such activities are limited to those necessary to allow a public health authority to identify, monitor, assess, or investigate potential public health signals, onsets of disease outbreaks, or conditions of public health importance (including trends, signals, risk factors, patterns in diseases, or increases in injuries from using consumer products). Such activities include those associated with providing timely situational awareness and priority setting during the course of an event or crisis that threatens public health (including natural or man-made disasters).

(3) Collection and analysis of information, biospecimens, or records by or for a criminal justice agency for activities authorized by law or court order solely for criminal justice or criminal investigative purposes.

(4) Authorized operational activities (as determined by each agency) in support of intelligence, homeland security, defense, or other national security missions.

(m) *Written*, or *in writing*, for purposes of this part, refers to writing on a tangible medium (*e.g.*, paper) or in an electronic format.

§ 690.103 Assuring compliance with this policy—research conducted or supported by any Federal department or agency.

(a) Each institution engaged in research that is covered by this policy, with the exception of research eligible for exemption under § 690.104, and that is conducted or supported by a Federal department or agency, shall provide written assurance satisfactory to the department or agency head that it will comply with the requirements of this policy. In lieu of requiring submission of an assurance, individual department or agency heads shall accept the existence of a current assurance, appropriate for the research in question, on file with the Office for Human Research Protections, HHS, or any successor office, and approved for Federal-wide use by that office. When the existence of an HHS-approved assurance is accepted in lieu of requiring submission of an assurance, reports (except certification) required by this policy to be made to department and agency heads shall also be made to the Office for Human Research Protections, HHS, or any successor office. Federal departments and agencies will conduct or support research covered by this policy only if the institution has provided an assurance that it will comply with the requirements of this policy, as provided in this section, and only if the institution has certified to the department or agency head that the research has been reviewed and approved by an IRB (if such certification is required by § 690.103(d)).

(b) The assurance shall be executed by an individual authorized to act for the institution and to assume on behalf of the institution the obligations imposed by this policy and shall be filed in such form and manner as the department or agency head prescribes.

(c) The department or agency head may limit the period during which any assurance shall remain effective or otherwise condition or restrict the assurance.

(d) Certification is required when the research is supported by a Federal department or agency and not otherwise waived under § 690.101(i) or exempted under § 690.104. For such research, institutions shall certify that each proposed research study covered by the assurance and this section has been reviewed and approved by the IRB. Such certification must be submitted as prescribed by the Federal department or agency component supporting the research. Under no condition shall research covered by this section be initiated prior to receipt of the certification that the research has been reviewed and approved by the IRB.

(e) For nonexempt research involving human subjects covered by this policy (or exempt research for which limited IRB review takes place pursuant to § 690.104(d)(2)(iii), (d)(3)(i)(C), or (d)(7) or (8)) that takes place at an institution in which IRB oversight is conducted by an IRB that is not operated by the institution, the institution and the organization operating the IRB shall document the institution's reliance on the IRB for oversight of the research and the responsibilities that each entity will undertake to ensure compliance with the requirements of this policy (*e.g.*, in a written agreement between the institution and the IRB, by implementation of an institution-wide policy directive providing the allocation of responsibilities between the institution and an IRB that is not affiliated with the institution, or as set forth in a research protocol).

(Approved by the Office of Management and Budget under Control Number 0990–0260)

§ 690.104 Exempt research.

(a) Unless otherwise required by law or by department or agency heads, research activities in which the only involvement of human subjects will be in one or more of the categories in paragraph (d) of this section are exempt from the requirements of this policy, except that such activities must comply with the requirements of this section and as specified in each category.

(b) Use of the exemption categories for research subject to the requirements of subparts B, C, and D: Application of the exemption categories to research subject to the requirements of 45 CFR part 46, subparts B, C, and D, is as follows:

(1) *Subpart B.* Each of the exemptions at this section may be applied to research subject to subpart B if the conditions of the exemption are met.

(2) *Subpart C.* The exemptions at this section do not apply to research subject to subpart C, except for research aimed at involving a broader subject population that only incidentally includes prisoners.

(3) *Subpart D.* The exemptions at paragraphs (d)(1), (4), (5), (6), (7), and (8) of this section may be applied to research subject to subpart D if the conditions of the exemption are met. Paragraphs (d)(2)(i) and (ii) of this section only may apply to research subject to subpart D involving educational tests or the observation of public behavior when the investigator(s) do not participate in the activities being observed. Paragraph (d)(2)(iii) of this section may not be applied to research subject to subpart D.

(c) [Reserved]

(d) Except as described in paragraph (a) of this section, the following categories of human subjects research are exempt from this policy:

(1) Research, conducted in established or commonly accepted educational settings, that specifically involves normal educational practices that are not likely to adversely impact students' opportunity to learn required educational content or the assessment of educators who provide instruction. This includes most research on regular and special education instructional strategies, and research on the effectiveness of or the comparison among instructional techniques, curricula, or classroom management methods.

(2) Research that only includes interactions involving educational tests (cognitive, diagnostic, aptitude, achievement), survey procedures, interview procedures, or observation of public behavior (including visual or auditory recording) if at least one of the following criteria is met:

(i) The information obtained is recorded by the investigator in such a manner that the identity of the human subjects cannot readily be ascertained, directly or through identifiers linked to the subjects;

(ii) Any disclosure of the human subjects' responses outside the research would not reasonably place the subjects at risk of criminal or civil liability or be damaging to the subjects' financial standing, employability, educational advancement, or reputation; or

(iii) The information obtained is recorded by the investigator in such a manner that the identity of the human subjects can readily be ascertained, directly or through identifiers linked to the subjects, and an IRB conducts a limited IRB review to make the determination required by §690.111(a)(7).

(3)(i) Research involving benign behavioral interventions in conjunction with the collection of information from an adult subject through verbal or written responses (including data entry) or audiovisual recording if the subject prospectively agrees to the intervention and information collection and at least one of the following criteria is met:

(A) The information obtained is recorded by the investigator in such a manner that the identity of the human subjects cannot readily be ascertained, directly or through identifiers linked to the subjects;

(B) Any disclosure of the human subjects' responses outside the research would not reasonably place the subjects at risk of criminal or civil liability or be damaging to the subjects' financial standing, employability, educational advancement, or reputation; or

(C) The information obtained is recorded by the investigator in such a manner that the identity of the human subjects can readily be ascertained, directly or through identifiers linked to the subjects, and an IRB conducts a limited IRB review to make the determination required by §690.111(a)(7).

(ii) For the purpose of this provision, benign behavioral interventions are brief in duration, harmless, painless, not physically invasive, not likely to have a significant adverse lasting impact on the subjects, and the investigator has no reason to think the subjects will find the interventions offensive or embarrassing. Provided all such criteria are met, examples of such benign behavioral interventions would include having the subjects play an online game, having them solve puzzles under various noise conditions, or having them decide how to allocate a nominal amount of received cash between themselves and someone else.

(iii) If the research involves deceiving the subjects regarding the nature or purposes of the research, this exemption is not applicable unless the subject authorizes the deception through a prospective agreement to participate in research in circumstances in which the subject is informed that he or she will be unaware of or misled regarding the nature or purposes of the research.

(4) Secondary research for which consent is not required: Secondary research uses of identifiable private information or identifiable biospecimens, if at least one of the following criteria is met:

(i) The identifiable private information or identifiable biospecimens are publicly available;

(ii) Information, which may include information about biospecimens, is recorded by the investigator in such a manner that the identity of the human subjects cannot readily be ascertained directly or through identifiers linked to the subjects, the investigator does not contact the subjects, and the investigator will not re-identify subjects;

(iii) The research involves only information collection and analysis involving the investigator's use of identifiable health information when that use is regulated under 45 CFR parts 160 and 164, subparts A and E, for the purposes of "health care operations" or "research" as those terms are defined at 45 CFR 164.501 or for "public health activities and purposes" as described under 45 CFR 164.512(b); or

(iv) The research is conducted by, or on behalf of, a Federal department or agency using government-generated or government-collected information obtained for nonresearch activities, if the research generates identifiable private information that is or will be maintained on information technology that is subject to and in compliance with section 208(b) of the E-Government Act of 2002, 44 U.S.C. 3501 note, if all of the identifiable private information collected, used, or generated as part of the activity will be maintained in systems of records subject to the Privacy Act of 1974, 5 U.S.C. 552a, and, if applicable, the information used in the research was collected subject to the Paperwork Reduction Act of 1995, 44 U.S.C. 3501 *et seq.*

(5) Research and demonstration projects that are conducted or supported by a Federal department or agency, or otherwise subject to the approval of department or agency heads (or the approval of the heads of bureaus or other subordinate agencies that have been delegated authority to conduct the research and demonstration projects), and that are designed to study, evaluate, improve, or otherwise examine public benefit or service programs, including procedures for obtaining benefits or services under those programs, possible changes in or alternatives to those programs or procedures, or possible changes in methods or levels of payment for benefits or services under those programs. Such projects include, but are not limited to, internal studies by Federal employees, and studies under contracts or consulting arrangements, cooperative agreements, or grants. Exempt projects also include waivers of otherwise mandatory requirements using authorities such as sections 1115 and 1115A of the Social Security Act, as amended.

(i) Each Federal department or agency conducting or supporting the research and demonstration projects must establish, on a publicly accessible Federal Web site or in such other manner as the department or agency head may determine, a list of the research and demonstration projects that the Federal department or agency conducts or supports under this provision. The research or demonstration project must be published on this list prior to commencing the research involving human subjects.

(ii) [Reserved]

(6) Taste and food quality evaluation and consumer acceptance studies:

(i) If wholesome foods without additives are consumed, or

(ii) If a food is consumed that contains a food ingredient at or below the level and for a use found to be safe, or agricultural chemical or environmental contaminant at or below the level found to be safe, by the Food and Drug Administration or approved by the Environmental Protection Agency or the Food Safety and Inspection Service of the U.S. Department of Agriculture.

(7) Storage or maintenance for secondary research for which broad consent is required: Storage or maintenance of identifiable private information or identifiable biospecimens for potential secondary research use if an IRB conducts a limited IRB review and makes the determinations required by §690.111(a)(8).

(8) Secondary research for which broad consent is required: Research involving the use of identifiable private information or identifiable biospecimens for secondary research use, if the following criteria are met:

(i) Broad consent for the storage, maintenance, and secondary research use of the identifiable private information or identifiable biospecimens was obtained in accordance with §690.116(a)(1) through (4), (a)(6), and (d);

(ii) Documentation of informed consent or waiver of documentation of consent was obtained in accordance with §690.117;

(iii) An IRB conducts a limited IRB review and makes the determination required by §690.111(a)(7) and makes the determination that the research to be conducted is within the scope of the broad consent referenced in paragraph (d)(8)(i) of this section; and (iv) The investigator does not include returning individual research results to subjects as part of the study plan. This provision does not prevent an investigator from abiding by any legal requirements to return individual research results.

(Approved by the Office of Management and Budget under Control Number 0990–0260)

§§ 690.105—690.106 [Reserved]

§ 690.107 IRB membership.

(a) Each IRB shall have at least five members, with varying backgrounds to promote complete and adequate review of research activities commonly conducted by the institution. The IRB shall be sufficiently qualified through the experience and expertise of its members (professional competence), and the diversity of its members, including race, gender, and cultural backgrounds and sensitivity to such issues as community attitudes, to promote respect for its advice and counsel in safeguarding the rights and welfare of human subjects. The IRB shall be able to ascertain the acceptability of proposed research in terms of institutional commitments (including policies and resources) and regulations, applicable law, and standards of professional conduct and practice. The IRB shall therefore include persons knowledgeable in these areas. If an IRB regularly reviews research that involves a category of subjects that is vulnerable to coercion or undue influence, such as children, prisoners, individuals with impaired decision-making capacity, or economically or educationally disadvantaged persons, consideration shall be given to the inclusion of one or more individuals who are knowledgeable about and experienced in working with these categories of subjects.

(b) Each IRB shall include at least one member whose primary concerns are in scientific areas and at least one member whose primary concerns are in nonscientific areas.

(c) Each IRB shall include at least one member who is not otherwise affiliated with the institution and who is not part of the immediate family of a person who is affiliated with the institution.

(d) No IRB may have a member participate in the IRB's initial or continuing review of any project in which the member has a conflicting interest, except to provide information requested by the IRB.

(e) An IRB may, in its discretion, invite individuals with competence in special areas to assist in the review of issues that require expertise beyond or in addition to that available on the IRB. These individuals may not vote with the IRB.

§ 690.108 IRB functions and operations.

(a) In order to fulfill the requirements of this policy each IRB shall:

(1) Have access to meeting space and sufficient staff to support the IRB's review and recordkeeping duties;

(2) Prepare and maintain a current list of the IRB members identified by name; earned degrees; representative capacity; indications of experience such as board certifications or licenses sufficient to describe each member's chief anticipated contributions to IRB deliberations; and any employment or other relationship between each member and the institution, for example, full-time employee, part-time employee, member of governing panel or board, stockholder, paid or unpaid consultant;

(3) Establish and follow written procedures for:

(i) Conducting its initial and continuing review of research and for reporting its findings and actions to the investigator and the institution;

(ii) Determining which projects require review more often than annually and which projects need verification from sources other than the investigators that no material changes have occurred since previous IRB review; and

(iii) Ensuring prompt reporting to the IRB of proposed changes in a research activity, and for ensuring that investigators will conduct the research activity in accordance with the terms of the IRB approval until any proposed changes have been reviewed and approved by the IRB, except when necessary to eliminate apparent immediate hazards to the subject.

(4) Establish and follow written procedures for ensuring prompt reporting to the IRB; appropriate institutional officials; the department or agency head; and the Office for Human Research Protections, HHS, or any successor office, or the equivalent office within the appropriate Federal department or agency of

(i) Any unanticipated problems involving risks to subjects or others or any serious or continuing noncompliance with this policy or the requirements or determinations of the IRB; and

(ii) Any suspension or termination of IRB approval.

(b) Except when an expedited review procedure is used (as described in § 690.110), an IRB must review proposed research at convened meetings at which a majority of the members of the IRB are present, including at least one member whose primary concerns are in nonscientific areas. In order for the research to be approved, it shall receive the approval of a majority of those members present at the meeting.

(Approved by the Office of Management and Budget under Control Number 0990–0260)

§ 690.109 IRB review of research.

(a) An IRB shall review and have authority to approve, require modifications in (to secure approval), or disapprove all research activities covered by this policy, including exempt research activities under § 690.104 for which limited IRB review is a condition of exemption (under § 690.104(d)(2)(iii), (d)(3)(i)(C), and (d)(7), and (8)).

(b) An IRB shall require that information given to subjects (or legally authorized representatives, when appropriate) as part of informed consent is in accordance with § 690.116. The IRB may require that information, in addition to that specifically mentioned in § 690.116, be given to the subjects when in the IRB's judgment the information would meaningfully add to the protection of the rights and welfare of subjects.

(c) An IRB shall require documentation of informed consent or may waive documentation in accordance with § 690.117.

National Science Foundation

(d) An IRB shall notify investigators and the institution in writing of its decision to approve or disapprove the proposed research activity, or of modifications required to secure IRB approval of the research activity. If the IRB decides to disapprove a research activity, it shall include in its written notification a statement of the reasons for its decision and give the investigator an opportunity to respond in person or in writing.

(e) An IRB shall conduct continuing review of research requiring review by the convened IRB at intervals appropriate to the degree of risk, not less than once per year, except as described in § 690.109(f).

(f)(1) Unless an IRB determines otherwise, continuing review of research is not required in the following circumstances:

(i) Research eligible for expedited review in accordance with § 690.110;

(ii) Research reviewed by the IRB in accordance with the limited IRB review described in § 690.104(d)(2)(iii), (d)(3)(i)(C), or (d)(7) or (8);

(iii) Research that has progressed to the point that it involves only one or both of the following, which are part of the IRB-approved study:

(A) Data analysis, including analysis of identifiable private information or identifiable biospecimens, or

(B) Accessing follow-up clinical data from procedures that subjects would undergo as part of clinical care.

(2) [Reserved]

(g) An IRB shall have authority to observe or have a third party observe the consent process and the research.

(Approved by the Office of Management and Budget under Control Number 0990–0260)

§ 690.110 Expedited review procedures for certain kinds of research involving no more than minimal risk, and for minor changes in approved research.

(a) The Secretary of HHS has established, and published as a Notice in the FEDERAL REGISTER, a list of categories of research that may be reviewed by the IRB through an expedited review procedure. The Secretary will evaluate the list at least every 8 years and amend it, as appropriate, after consultation with other federal departments and agencies and after publication in the FEDERAL REGISTER for public comment. A copy of the list is available from the Office for Human Research Protections, HHS, or any successor office.

(b)(1) An IRB may use the expedited review procedure to review the following:

(i) Some or all of the research appearing on the list described in paragraph (a) of this section, unless the reviewer determines that the study involves more than minimal risk;

(ii) Minor changes in previously approved research during the period for which approval is authorized; or

(iii) Research for which limited IRB review is a condition of exemption under § 690.104(d)(2)(iii), (d)(3)(i)(C), and (d)(7) and (8).

(2) Under an expedited review procedure, the review may be carried out by the IRB chairperson or by one or more experienced reviewers designated by the chairperson from among members of the IRB. In reviewing the research, the reviewers may exercise all of the authorities of the IRB except that the reviewers may not disapprove the research. A research activity may be disapproved only after review in accordance with the nonexpedited procedure set forth in § 690.108(b).

(c) Each IRB that uses an expedited review procedure shall adopt a method for keeping all members advised of research proposals that have been approved under the procedure.

(d) The department or agency head may restrict, suspend, terminate, or choose not to authorize an institution's or IRB's use of the expedited review procedure.

§ 690.111 Criteria for IRB approval of research.

(a) In order to approve research covered by this policy the IRB shall determine that all of the following requirements are satisfied:

(1) Risks to subjects are minimized:

(i) By using procedures that are consistent with sound research design and that do not unnecessarily expose subjects to risk, and

(ii) Whenever appropriate, by using procedures already being performed on the subjects for diagnostic or treatment purposes.

(2) Risks to subjects are reasonable in relation to anticipated benefits, if any, to subjects, and the importance of the knowledge that may reasonably be expected to result. In evaluating risks and benefits, the IRB should consider only those risks and benefits that may result from the research (as distinguished from risks and benefits of therapies subjects would receive even if not participating in the research). The IRB should not consider possible long-range effects of applying knowledge gained in the research (e.g., the possible effects of the research on public policy) as among those research risks that fall within the purview of its responsibility.

(3) Selection of subjects is equitable. In making this assessment the IRB should take into account the purposes of the research and the setting in which the research will be conducted. The IRB should be particularly cognizant of the special problems of research that involves a category of subjects who are vulnerable to coercion or undue influence, such as children, prisoners, individuals with impaired decision-making capacity, or economically or educationally disadvantaged persons.

(4) Informed consent will be sought from each prospective subject or the subject's legally authorized representative, in accordance with, and to the extent required by, § 690.116.

(5) Informed consent will be appropriately documented or appropriately waived in accordance with § 690.117.

(6) When appropriate, the research plan makes adequate provision for monitoring the data collected to ensure the safety of subjects.

(7) When appropriate, there are adequate provisions to protect the privacy of subjects and to maintain the confidentiality of data.

(i) The Secretary of HHS will, after consultation with the Office of Management and Budget's privacy office and other Federal departments and agencies that have adopted this policy, issue guidance to assist IRBs in assessing what provisions are adequate to protect the privacy of subjects and to maintain the confidentiality of data.

(ii) [Reserved]

(8) For purposes of conducting the limited IRB review required by § 690.104(d)(7), the IRB need not make the determinations at paragraphs (a)(1) through (7) of this section, and shall make the following determinations:

(i) Broad consent for storage, maintenance, and secondary research use of identifiable private information or identifiable biospecimens is obtained in accordance with the requirements of § 690.116(a)(1)–(4), (a)(6), and (d);

(ii) Broad consent is appropriately documented or waiver of documentation is appropriate, in accordance with § 690.117; and

(iii) If there is a change made for research purposes in the way the identifiable private information or identifiable biospecimens are stored or maintained, there are adequate provisions to protect the privacy of subjects and to maintain the confidentiality of data.

(b) When some or all of the subjects are likely to be vulnerable to coercion or undue influence, such as children, prisoners, individuals with impaired decision-making capacity, or economically or educationally disadvantaged persons, additional safeguards have been included in the study to protect the rights and welfare of these subjects.

§ 690.112 Review by institution.

Research covered by this policy that has been approved by an IRB may be subject to further appropriate review and approval or disapproval by officials of the institution. However, those officials may not approve the research if it has not been approved by an IRB.

§ 690.113 Suspension or termination of IRB approval of research.

An IRB shall have authority to suspend or terminate approval of research that is not being conducted in accordance with the IRB's requirements or that has been associated with unexpected serious harm to subjects. Any suspension or termination of approval shall include a statement of the reasons for the IRB's action and shall be reported promptly to the investigator, appropriate institutional officials, and the department or agency head.

(Approved by the Office of Management and Budget under Control Number 0990–0260)

§ 690.114 Cooperative research.

(a) Cooperative research projects are those projects covered by this policy that involve more than one institution. In the conduct of cooperative research projects, each institution is responsible for safeguarding the rights and welfare of human subjects and for complying with this policy.

(b)(1) Any institution located in the United States that is engaged in cooperative research must rely upon approval by a single IRB for that portion of the research that is conducted in the United States. The reviewing IRB will be identified by the Federal department or agency supporting or conducting the research or proposed by the lead institution subject to the acceptance of the Federal department or agency supporting the research.

(2) The following research is not subject to this provision:

(i) Cooperative research for which more than single IRB review is required by law (including tribal law passed by the official governing body of an American Indian or Alaska Native tribe); or

(ii) Research for which any Federal department or agency supporting or conducting the research determines and documents that the use of a single IRB is not appropriate for the particular context.

(c) For research not subject to paragraph (b) of this section, an institution participating in a cooperative project may enter into a joint review arrangement, rely on the review of another IRB, or make similar arrangements for avoiding duplication of effort.

§ 690.115 IRB records.

(a) An institution, or when appropriate an IRB, shall prepare and maintain adequate documentation of IRB activities, including the following:

(1) Copies of all research proposals reviewed, scientific evaluations, if any, that accompany the proposals, approved sample consent forms, progress reports submitted by investigators, and reports of injuries to subjects.

(2) Minutes of IRB meetings, which shall be in sufficient detail to show attendance at the meetings; actions taken by the IRB; the vote on these actions including the number of

members voting for, against, and abstaining; the basis for requiring changes in or disapproving research; and a written summary of the discussion of controverted issues and their resolution.

(3) Records of continuing review activities, including the rationale for conducting continuing review of research that otherwise would not require continuing review as described in §690.109(f)(1).

(4) Copies of all correspondence between the IRB and the investigators.

(5) A list of IRB members in the same detail as described in §690.108(a)(2).

(6) Written procedures for the IRB in the same detail as described in §690.108(a)(3) and (4).

(7) Statements of significant new findings provided to subjects, as required by §690.116(c)(5).

(8) The rationale for an expedited reviewer's determination under §690.110(b)(1)(i) that research appearing on the expedited review list described in §690.110(a) is more than minimal risk.

(9) Documentation specifying the responsibilities that an institution and an organization operating an IRB each will undertake to ensure compliance with the requirements of this policy, as described in §690.103(e).

(b) The records required by this policy shall be retained for at least 3 years, and records relating to research that is conducted shall be retained for at least 3 years after completion of the research. The institution or IRB may maintain the records in printed form, or electronically. All records shall be accessible for inspection and copying by authorized representatives of the Federal department or agency at reasonable times and in a reasonable manner.

(Approved by the Office of Management and Budget under Control Number 0990–0260)

§690.116 General Requirements for informed consent.

(a) *General.* General requirements for informed consent, whether written or oral, are set forth in this paragraph and apply to consent obtained in accordance with the requirements set forth in paragraphs (b) through (d) of this section. Broad consent may be obtained in lieu of informed consent obtained in accordance with paragraphs (b) and (c) of this section only with respect to the storage, maintenance, and secondary research uses of identifiable private information and identifiable biospecimens. Waiver or alteration of consent in research involving public benefit and service programs conducted by or subject to the approval of state or local officials is described in paragraph (e) of this section. General waiver or alteration of informed consent is described in paragraph (f) of this section. Except as provided elsewhere in this policy:

(1) Before involving a human subject in research covered by this policy, an investigator shall obtain the legally effective informed consent of the subject or the subject's legally authorized representative.

(2) An investigator shall seek informed consent only under circumstances that provide the prospective subject or the legally authorized representative sufficient opportunity to discuss and consider whether or not to participate and that minimize the possibility of coercion or undue influence.

(3) The information that is given to the subject or the legally authorized representative shall be in language understandable to the subject or the legally authorized representative.

(4) The prospective subject or the legally authorized representative must be provided with the information that a reasonable person would want to have in order to make an informed decision about whether to participate, and an opportunity to discuss that information.

(5) Except for broad consent obtained in accordance with paragraph (d) of this section:

(i) Informed consent must begin with a concise and focused presentation of the key information that is most likely to assist a prospective subject or legally authorized representative in understanding the reasons why one might or might not want to participate in the research. This part of the informed consent must be organized and presented in a way that facilitates comprehension.

(ii) Informed consent as a whole must present information in sufficient detail relating to the research, and must be organized and presented in a way that does not merely provide lists of isolated facts, but rather facilitates the prospective subject's or legally authorized representative's understanding of the reasons why one might or might not want to participate.

(6) No informed consent may include any exculpatory language through which the subject or the legally authorized representative is made to waive or appear to waive any of the subject's legal rights, or releases or appears to release the investigator, the sponsor, the institution, or its agents from liability for negligence.

(b) *Basic elements of informed consent.* Except as provided in paragraph (d), (e), or (f) of this section, in seeking informed consent the following information shall be provided to each subject or the legally authorized representative:

(1) A statement that the study involves research, an explanation of the purposes of the research and the expected duration of the subject's participation, a description of the procedures to be followed, and identification of any procedures that are experimental;

(2) A description of any reasonably foreseeable risks or discomforts to the subject;

(3) A description of any benefits to the subject or to others that may reasonably be expected from the research;

(4) A disclosure of appropriate alternative procedures or courses of treatment, if any, that might be advantageous to the subject;

(5) A statement describing the extent, if any, to which confidentiality of records identifying the subject will be maintained;

(6) For research involving more than minimal risk, an explanation as to whether any compensation and an explanation as to whether any medical treatments are available if injury occurs and, if so, what they consist of, or where further information may be obtained;

(7) An explanation of whom to contact for answers to pertinent questions about the research and research subjects' rights, and whom to contact in the event of a research-related injury to the subject;

(8) A statement that participation is voluntary, refusal to participate will involve no penalty or loss of benefits to which the subject is otherwise entitled, and the subject may discontinue participation at any time without penalty or loss of benefits to which the subject is otherwise entitled; and

(9) One of the following statements about any research that involves the collection of identifiable private information or identifiable biospecimens:

(i) A statement that identifiers might be removed from the identifiable private information or identifiable biospecimens and that, after such removal, the information or biospecimens could be used for future research studies or distributed to another investigator for future research studies without additional informed consent from the subject or the legally authorized representative, if this might be a possibility; or

(ii) A statement that the subject's information or biospecimens collected as part of the research, even if identifiers are removed, will not be used or distributed for future research studies.

(c) *Additional elements of informed consent.* Except as provided in paragraph (d), (e), or (f) of this section, one or more of the following elements of information, when appropriate, shall also be provided to each subject or the legally authorized representative:

(1) A statement that the particular treatment or procedure may involve risks to the subject (or to the embryo or fetus, if the subject is or may become pregnant) that are currently unforeseeable;

(2) Anticipated circumstances under which the subject's participation may be terminated by the investigator without regard to the subject's or the legally authorized representative's consent;

(3) Any additional costs to the subject that may result from participation in the research;

(4) The consequences of a subject's decision to withdraw from the research and procedures for orderly termination of participation by the subject;

(5) A statement that significant new findings developed during the course of the research that may relate to the subject's willingness to continue participation will be provided to the subject;

(6) The approximate number of subjects involved in the study;

(7) A statement that the subject's biospecimens (even if identifiers are removed) may be used for commercial profit and whether the subject will or will not share in this commercial profit;

(8) A statement regarding whether clinically relevant research results, including individual research results, will be disclosed to subjects, and if so, under what conditions; and

(9) For research involving biospecimens, whether the research will (if known) or might include whole genome sequencing (*i.e.,* sequencing of a human germline or somatic specimen with the intent to generate the genome or exome sequence of that specimen).

(d) *Elements of broad consent for the storage, maintenance, and secondary research use of identifiable private information or identifiable biospecimens.* Broad consent for the storage, maintenance, and secondary research use of identifiable private information or identifiable biospecimens (collected for either research studies other than the proposed research or nonresearch purposes) is permitted as an alternative to the informed consent requirements in paragraphs (b) and (c) of this section. If the subject or the legally authorized representative is asked to provide broad consent, the following shall be provided to each subject or the subject's legally authorized representative:

(1) The information required in paragraphs (b)(2), (b)(3), (b)(5), and (b)(8) and, when appropriate, (c)(7) and (9) of this section;

(2) A general description of the types of research that may be conducted with the identifiable private information or identifiable biospecimens. This description must include sufficient information such that a reasonable person would expect that the broad consent would permit the types of research conducted;

(3) A description of the identifiable private information or identifiable biospecimens that might be used in research, whether sharing of identifiable private information or identifiable biospecimens might occur, and the types of institutions or researchers that might conduct research with the identifiable private information or identifiable biospecimens;

(4) A description of the period of time that the identifiable private information or identifiable biospecimens may be stored and maintained (which period of time could be

indefinite), and a description of the period of time that the identifiable private information or identifiable biospecimens may be used for research purposes (which period of time could be indefinite);

(5) Unless the subject or legally authorized representative will be provided details about specific research studies, a statement that they will not be informed of the details of any specific research studies that might be conducted using the subject's identifiable private information or identifiable biospecimens, including the purposes of the research, and that they might have chosen not to consent to some of those specific research studies;

(6) Unless it is known that clinically relevant research results, including individual research results, will be disclosed to the subject in all circumstances, a statement that such results may not be disclosed to the subject; and

(7) An explanation of whom to contact for answers to questions about the subject's rights and about storage and use of the subject's identifiable private information or identifiable biospecimens, and whom to contact in the event of a research-related harm.

(e) *Waiver or alteration of consent in research involving public benefit and service programs conducted by or subject to the approval of state or local officials*—(1) *Waiver.* An IRB may waive the requirement to obtain informed consent for research under paragraphs (a) through (c) of this section, provided the IRB satisfies the requirements of paragraph (e)(3) of this section. If an individual was asked to provide broad consent for the storage, maintenance, and secondary research use of identifiable private information or identifiable biospecimens in accordance with the requirements at paragraph (d) of this section, and refused to consent, an IRB cannot waive consent for the storage, maintenance, or secondary research use of the identifiable private information or identifiable biospecimens.

(2) *Alteration.* An IRB may approve a consent procedure that omits some, or alters some or all, of the elements of informed consent set forth in paragraphs (b) and (c) of this section provided the IRB satisfies the requirements of paragraph (e)(3) of this section. An IRB may not omit or alter any of the requirements described in paragraph (a) of this section. If a broad consent procedure is used, an IRB may not omit or alter any of the elements required under paragraph (d) of this section.

(3) *Requirements for waiver and alteration.* In order for an IRB to waive or alter consent as described in this subsection, the IRB must find and document that:

(i) The research or demonstration project is to be conducted by or subject to the approval of state or local government officials and is designed to study, evaluate, or otherwise examine:

(A) Public benefit or service programs;

(B) Procedures for obtaining benefits or services under those programs;

(C) Possible changes in or alternatives to those programs or procedures; or

(D) Possible changes in methods or levels of payment for benefits or services under those programs; and

(ii) The research could not practicably be carried out without the waiver or alteration.

(f) *General waiver or alteration of consent—*(1) *Waiver.* An IRB may waive the requirement to obtain informed consent for research under paragraphs (a) through (c) of this section, provided the IRB satisfies the requirements of paragraph (f)(3) of this section. If an individual was asked to provide broad consent for the storage, maintenance, and secondary research use of identifiable private information or identifiable biospecimens in accordance with the requirements at paragraph (d) of this section, and refused to consent, an IRB cannot waive consent for the storage, maintenance, or secondary research use of the identifiable private information or identifiable biospecimens.

(2) *Alteration.* An IRB may approve a consent procedure that omits some, or alters some or all, of the elements of informed consent set forth in paragraphs (b) and (c) of this section provided the IRB satisfies the requirements of paragraph (f)(3) of this section. An IRB may not omit or alter any of the requirements described in paragraph (a) of this section. If a broad consent procedure is used, an IRB may not omit or alter any of the elements required under paragraph (d) of this section.

(3) *Requirements for waiver and alteration.* In order for an IRB to waive or alter consent as described in this subsection, the IRB must find and document that:

(i) The research involves no more than minimal risk to the subjects;

(ii) The research could not practicably be carried out without the requested waiver or alteration;

(iii) If the research involves using identifiable private information or identifiable biospecimens, the research could not practicably be carried out without using such information or biospecimens in an identifiable format;

(iv) The waiver or alteration will not adversely affect the rights and welfare of the subjects; and

(v) Whenever appropriate, the subjects or legally authorized representatives will be provided with additional pertinent information after participation.

(g) *Screening, recruiting, or determining eligibility.* An IRB may approve a research proposal in which an investigator will obtain information or biospecimens for the purpose of screening, recruiting, or determining the eligibility of prospective subjects without the informed consent of the prospective subject or the subject's legally authorized representative, if either of the following conditions are met:

(1) The investigator will obtain information through oral or written communication with the prospective subject or legally authorized representative, or

(2) The investigator will obtain identifiable private information or identifiable biospecimens by accessing records or stored identifiable biospecimens.

(h) *Posting of clinical trial consent form.* (1) For each clinical trial conducted or supported by a Federal department or agency, one IRB-approved informed consent form used to enroll subjects must be posted by the awardee or the Federal department or agency component conducting the trial on a publicly available Federal Web site that will be established as a repository for such informed consent forms.

(2) If the Federal department or agency supporting or conducting the clinical trial determines that certain information should not be made publicly available on a Federal Web site (*e.g.* confidential commercial information), such Federal department or agency may permit or require redactions to the information posted.

(3) The informed consent form must be posted on the Federal Web site after the clinical trial is closed to recruitment, and no later than 60 days after the last study visit by any subject, as required by the protocol.

(i) *Preemption.* The informed consent requirements in this policy are not intended to preempt any applicable Federal, state, or local laws (including tribal laws passed by the official governing body of an American Indian or Alaska Native tribe) that require additional information to be disclosed in order for informed consent to be legally effective.

(j) *Emergency medical care.* Nothing in this policy is intended to limit the authority of a physician to provide emergency medical care, to the extent the physician is permitted to do so under applicable Federal, state, or local law (including tribal law passed by the official governing body of an American Indian or Alaska Native tribe).

(Approved by the Office of Management and Budget under Control Number 0990–0260)

§ 690.117 **Documentation of informed consent.**

(a) Except as provided in paragraph (c) of this section, informed consent shall be documented by the use of a written informed consent form approved by the IRB and signed (including in an electronic format) by the subject or the subject's legally authorized representative. A written copy shall be given to the person signing the informed consent form.

(b) Except as provided in paragraph (c) of this section, the informed consent form may be either of the following:

(1) A written informed consent form that meets the requirements of § 690.116. The investigator shall give either the subject or the subject's legally authorized representative adequate opportunity to read the informed consent form before it is signed; alternatively, this form may be read to the subject or the subject's legally authorized representative.

(2) A short form written informed consent form stating that the elements of informed consent required by § 690.116 have been presented orally to the subject or the subject's legally authorized representative, and that the key information required by § 690.116(a)(5)(i) was presented first to the subject, before other information, if any, was provided. The IRB shall approve a written summary of what is to be said to the subject or the legally authorized representative. When this method is used, there shall be a witness to the oral presentation. Only the short form itself is to be signed by the subject or the subject's legally authorized representative. However, the witness shall sign both the short form and a copy of the summary, and the person actually obtaining consent shall sign a copy of the summary. A copy of the summary shall be given to the subject or the subject's legally authorized representative, in addition to a copy of the short form.

(c)(1) An IRB may waive the requirement for the investigator to obtain a signed informed consent form for some or all subjects if it finds any of the following:

(i) That the only record linking the subject and the research would be the informed consent form and the principal risk would be potential harm resulting from a breach of confidentiality. Each subject (or legally authorized representative) will be asked whether the subject wants documentation linking the subject with the research, and the subject's wishes will govern;

(ii) That the research presents no more than minimal risk of harm to subjects and involves no procedures for which written consent is normally required outside of the research context; or

(iii) If the subjects or legally authorized representatives are members of a distinct cultural group or community in which signing forms is not the norm, that the research presents no more than minimal risk of harm to subjects and provided there is an appropriate alternative mechanism for documenting that informed consent was obtained.

(2) In cases in which the documentation requirement is waived, the IRB may require

the investigator to provide subjects or legally authorized representatives with a written statement regarding the research.

(Approved by the Office of Management and Budget under Control Number 0990–0260)

§ 690.118 Applications and proposals lacking definite plans for involvement of human subjects.

Certain types of applications for grants, cooperative agreements, or contracts are submitted to Federal departments or agencies with the knowledge that subjects may be involved within the period of support, but definite plans would not normally be set forth in the application or proposal. These include activities such as institutional type grants when selection of specific projects is the institution's responsibility; research training grants in which the activities involving subjects remain to be selected; and projects in which human subjects' involvement will depend upon completion of instruments, prior animal studies, or purification of compounds. Except for research waived under § 690.101(i) or exempted under § 690.104, no human subjects may be involved in any project supported by these awards until the project has been reviewed and approved by the IRB, as provided in this policy, and certification submitted, by the institution, to the Federal department or agency component supporting the research.

§ 690.119 Research undertaken without the intention of involving human subjects.

Except for research waived under § 690.101(i) or exempted under § 690.104, in the event research is undertaken without the intention of involving human subjects, but it is later proposed to involve human subjects in the research, the research shall first be reviewed and approved by an IRB, as provided in this policy, a certification submitted by the institution to the Federal department or agency component supporting the research, and final approval given to the proposed change by the Federal department or agency component.

§ 690.120 Evaluation and disposition of applications and proposals for research to be conducted or supported by a Federal department or agency.

(a) The department or agency head will evaluate all applications and proposals involving human subjects submitted to the Federal department or agency through such officers and employees of the Federal department or agency and such experts and consultants as the department or agency head determines to be appropriate. This evaluation will take into consideration the risks to the subjects, the adequacy of protection against these risks, the potential benefits of the research to the subjects and others, and the importance of the knowledge gained or to be gained.

(b) On the basis of this evaluation, the department or agency head may approve or disapprove the application or proposal, or enter into negotiations to develop an approvable one.

§ 690.121 [Reserved]

§ 690.122 Use of Federal funds.

Federal funds administered by a Federal department or agency may not be expended for research involving human subjects unless the requirements of this policy have been satisfied.

§ 690.123 Early termination of research support: Evaluation of applications and proposals.

(a) The department or agency head may require that Federal department or agency support for any project be terminated or suspended in the manner prescribed in applicable program requirements, when the department or agency head finds an institution has materially failed to comply with the terms of this policy.

(b) In making decisions about supporting or approving applications or proposals covered by this policy the department or agency head may take into account, in addition to all other eligibility requirements and program criteria, factors such as whether the applicant has been subject to a termination or suspension under paragraph (a) of this section and whether the applicant or the person or persons who would direct or has/have directed the scientific and technical aspects of an activity has/have, in the judgment of the department or agency head, materially failed to discharge responsibility for the protection of the rights and welfare of human subjects (whether or not the research was subject to federal regulation).

§ 690.124 Conditions.

With respect to any research project or any class of research projects the department or agency head of either the conducting or the supporting Federal department or agency may impose additional conditions prior to or at the time of approval when in the judgment of the department or agency head additional conditions are necessary for the protection of human subjects.

PARTS 691–699 [RESERVED]

CHAPTER VII—COMMISSION ON CIVIL RIGHTS

Part		Page
700	[Reserved]	
701	Organization and functions of the Commission	251
702	Rules on hearings, reports, and meetings of the Commission	254
703	Operations and functions of State Advisory Committees	263
704	Information disclosure and communications	266
705	Materials available pursuant to 5 U.S.C. 552a	273
706	Employee responsibilities and conduct	278
707	Enforcement of nondiscrimination on the basis of disability in programs or activities conducted by U.S. Commission on Civil Rights	279
708	Collection by salary offset from indebted current and former employees	285
709–799	[Reserved]	

PART 700 [RESERVED]

PART 701—ORGANIZATION AND FUNCTIONS OF THE COMMISSION

Subpart A—Organizations and Functions

Sec.
701.1 Establishment.
701.2 Responsibilities.

Subpart B—Organization Statement

701.10 Membership of the Commission.
701.11 Commission meetings—duties of the Chairperson.
701.12 Staff Director.
701.13 Staff organization and functions.

AUTHORITY: 42 U.S.C. 1975, 1975a, 1975b.

SOURCE: 67 FR 70482, Nov. 22, 2002, unless otherwise noted.

Subpart A—Organizations and Functions

§ 701.1 Establishment.

The United States Commission on Civil Rights (hereinafter referred to as the "Commission") is a bipartisan agency of the executive branch of the Government. The predecessor agency to the present Commission was established by the Civil Rights Act of 1957, 71 Stat. 634. This Act was amended by the Civil Rights Act of 1960, 74 Stat. 86; the Civil Rights Act of 1964, 78 Stat. 241; by 81 Stat. 582 (1967); by 84 Stat. 1356 (1970); by 86 Stat. 813 (1972); and by the Civil Rights Act of 1978, 92 Stat. 1067. The present Commission was established by the United States Commission on Civil Rights Act of 1983, 97 Stat. 1301, as amended by the Civil Rights Commission Amendments Act of 1994, 108 Stat. 4339. The statutes are codified in 42 U.S.C. 1975 through 1975d. (Hereinafter, the 1994 Act will be referred to as "the Act.")

§ 701.2 Responsibilities.

(a) The Commission's authority under 42 U.S.C. 1975a(a) may be summarized as follows:

(1) To investigate allegations in writing under oath or affirmation that citizens of the United States are being deprived of their right to vote and have that vote counted by reason of color, race, religion, sex, age, disability, or national origin;

(2) To study and collect information relating to discrimination or a denial of equal protection of the laws under the Constitution because of color, race, religion, sex, age, disability or national origin or in the administration of justice;

(3) To appraise the laws and policies of the Federal Government relating to discrimination or denials of equal protection of the laws under the Constitution because of, color, race, religion, sex, age, disability, or national origin or in the administration of justice;

(4) To serve as a national clearinghouse for information relating to discrimination or denials of equal protection of the laws because of color, race, religion, sex, age, disability, or national origin;

(5) To prepare public service announcements and advertising campaigns to discourage discrimination or denials of equal protection of the laws because of color, race, religion, sex, age, disability, or national origin.

(b) Under 42 U.S.C. 1975a(c), the Commission is required to submit at least one report annually that monitors Federal civil rights enforcement efforts in the United States and other such reports to the President and to the Congress at such times as the Commission, the Congress, or the President shall deem appropriate.

(c) In fulfilling these responsibilities the Commission is authorized by the Act to hold hearings and to issue subpoenas for the attendance of witnesses; to consult with governors, attorneys general; and other representatives of State and local governments, and private organizations; and is required to establish an advisory committee in each State. The Act also provides that all Federal agencies shall cooperate fully with the Commission so that it may effectively carry out its functions and duties.

Subpart B—Organization Statement

§ 701.10 Membership of the Commission.

(a) The Commission is composed of eight members (or "Commissioners"), not more than four of whom may be of the same political party. The President shall appoint four members, the President pro tempore of the Senate shall appoint two, and the Speaker of the House of Representatives shall appoint two.

(b) The Chairperson and Vice Chairperson of the Commission are designated by the President with the concurrence of a majority of the Commissioners. The Vice Chairperson acts as Chairperson in the absence or disability of the Chairperson or in the event of a vacancy in that office.

(c) No vacancy in the Commission affects its powers and any vacancy is filled in the same manner and is subject to the same limitations with respect to party affiliations as previous appointments.

(d) Five members of the Commission constitute a quorum.

§ 701.11 Commission meetings—duties of the Chairperson.

(a) At a meeting of the Commission in each calendar year, the Commission shall, by vote of the majority, adopt a schedule of Commission meetings for the following calendar year.

(b) In addition to the regularly scheduled meetings, it is the responsibility of the Chairperson to call the Commission to meet in a special open meeting at such time and place as he or she shall deem appropriate; provided however, that upon the motion of a member, and a favorable vote by a majority of Commission members, a special meeting of the Commission may be held in the absence of a call by the Chairperson.

(c) The Chairperson, after consulting with the Staff Director, shall establish the agenda for each meeting. The agenda at the meeting of the Commission may be modified by the addition or deletion of specific items upon the motion of a Commissioner and a favorable vote by a majority of the members.

(d) In the event that after consulting with the members of the Commission and consideration of the views of the members the Chairperson determines that there are insufficient substantive items on a proposed meeting agenda to warrant holding a scheduled meeting, the Chairperson may cancel such meeting.

§ 701.12 Staff Director.

A Staff Director for the Commission is appointed by the President with the concurrence of a majority of the Commissioners. The Staff Director is the administrative head of the agency.

§ 701.13 Staff organization and functions.

The Commission staff organization and function are as follows:

(a) *Office of the Staff Director.* Under the direction of the Staff Director, this Office defines and disseminates to staff the policies established by the Commissioners; develops program plans for presentation to the Commissioners; evaluates program results; supervises and coordinates the work of other agency offices; manages the administrative affairs of the agency; appoints an Equal Employment Opportunity Officer for the agency's in-house Equal Employment Opportunity Program; and conducts agency liaison with the Executive Office of the President, the Congress, and other Federal agencies.

(b) *Office of the Deputy Staff Director.* Under the direction of the Deputy Staff Director, this Office is responsible for the day-to-day administration of the agency; evaluation of quantity and quality of program efforts; personnel administration; and the supervision of Office Directors who do not report directly to the Staff Director.

(c) *Office of the General Counsel.* Under the direction of the General Counsel, who reports directly to the Staff Director, this office serves as legal counsel to the Commissioners and to the agency; legal aspects of agency-related personnel actions, employment issues, and labor relations issues; plans and conducts hearings and consultations for the Commission; conducts legal studies; prepares reports of legal studies and hearings; drafts or reviews proposals for legislative and executive action; receives and responds to requests for material under the Freedom of Information Act, Federal Advisory Committee Act, Administrative Procedures Act, and the Sunshine Act; serves as the agency's ethics office and responds to requests for advice and guidance on questions of ethical conduct, conflicts of interest, and reporting financial interest; and reviews all agency publications and congressional testimony for legal sufficiency.

(d) *Office of Management.* This Office is responsible for all administrative, management, and facilitative services necessary for the operation of the agency, including financial management, personnel, publications, and the National Clearinghouse Library. This office consists of three divisions reporting directly to the Staff Director.

(1) *Administrative Services and Clearinghouse Division.* Under the direction of the Chief of Administrative Services, this Division is responsible for the identification and acquisition of Commission hearing facilities; oversight of the Rankin Library and the distribution of publications; procurement; information and resources management; security; telecommunications; transportation; space management; repair and maintenance services; supplies; central mailing lists; and assorted other administrative duties and functions;

(2) *Budget and Finance Division.* Under the direction of the Chief of Budget and Finance, this Division is responsible for budget preparation, formulation, justification, and execution; financial management; and accounting, including travel for Commissioners and staff; and

(3) *Human Resources Division.* Under the direction of the Director of Human Resources, this Division is responsible for human resources development, including career staffing, classification, benefits, time and attendance, training, and compensation.

(e) *Office of Federal Civil Rights Evaluation.* Under the direction of an Assistant Staff Director, this Office is responsible for monitoring, evaluating and reporting on the civil rights enforcement effort of the Federal Government; developing concepts for programs, projects, and policies directed toward the achievement of Commission goals; preparing documents that articulate the Commission's views and concerns regarding Federal civil rights to Federal agencies having appropriate jurisdiction; and receiving complaints alleging denial of civil rights because of color, race, religion, sex, age, disability, or national origin and referring these complaints to the appropriate government agency for investigation and resolution.

(f) *Congressional Affairs Unit.* This Unit is responsible for liaison with committees and members of Congress or their staffs, monitoring legislative activities relating to civil rights, and preparing testimony for presentation before committees of Congress when such testimony has been requested by a committee.

(g) *Public Affairs Unit.* Under the direction of the Chief of Public Affairs, this Unit is responsible for planning and managing briefings at which the Commission receives information regarding civil rights issues; developing plans for community outreach activities; managing the Commission's public service announcements; media releases and press conferences; preparing for publication periodic updates of Commission activities and a Commission civil rights magazine; and keeping the Commission and Commission staff apprised of civil rights conferences and activities.

(h) *Regional Programs Coordination Unit.* Under the direction of the Chief of the Regional Programs Coordination Unit, this Unit is responsible for directing and coordinating the programs and work of the regional offices and 51 State Advisory Committees to the Commission and maintaining liaison between the regional offices and the various headquarters' offices of the Commission.

(i) *Regional Offices.* The Commission has six regional offices, each headed by a Director, that coordinate studies and fact-finding activities on a variety of civil rights issues addressed by the State Advisory Committees (SAC) in their regions and approved by the Staff Director; report to the Commission on the results of SAC activities; submit SAC reports to the Commission for action; and assist with follow-up on recommendations included in SAC or Commission reports. The name of the Director, the address, and telephone and facsimile numbers for each regional office are published annually in the "United States Government Manual". The regions and the SACs that they serve are:

Region I: Eastern Regional Office, Washington, DC

Connecticut, Delaware, District of Columbia, Maine, Maryland, Massachusetts, New Hampshire, New Jersey, New York, Pennsylvania, Rhode Island, and Vermont, Virginia, West Virginia.

Region II: Southern Regional Office, Atlanta, Georgia

Florida, Georgia, Kentucky, North Carolina, South Carolina, and Tennessee.

Region III: Midwestern Regional Office, Chicago, Illinois

Illinois, Indiana, Michigan, Minnesota, Ohio, and Wisconsin.

Region IV: Central Regional Office, Kansas City, Kansas

Alabama, Arkansas, Iowa, Kansas, Louisiana, Mississippi, Missouri, Nebraska, and Oklahoma.

Region V: Rocky Mountain Regional Office, Denver, Colorado

Colorado, Montana, New Mexico, North Dakota, South Dakota, Utah, and Wyoming.

Region VI: Western Regional Office, Los Angeles, California

Alaska, Arizona, California, Hawaii, Idaho, Nevada, Oregon, Texas, and Washington.

PART 702—RULES ON HEARINGS, REPORTS, AND MEETINGS OF THE COMMISSION

Subpart A—Hearings and Reports

Sec.
702.1 Definitions.
702.2 Authorization for hearing.
702.3 Notice of hearing.
702.4 Subpoenas.
702.5 Conduct of proceedings.
702.6 Executive session.
702.7 Counsel.
702.8 Evidence at Commission proceedings.
702.9 Cross-examination at public session.
702.10 Voluntary witnesses at public session of a hearing.
702.11 Special executive session.
702.12 Contempt of the Commission.
702.13 Intimidation of witnesses.
702.14 Transcript of Commission proceedings.
702.15 Witness fees.
702.16 Attendance of news media at public sessions.
702.17 Communications with respect to Commission proceedings.
702.18 Commission reports.

Subpart B—Meetings

702.50 Purpose and scope.
702.51 Definitions.
702.52 Open meeting requirements.
702.53 Closed meetings.
702.54 Closed meeting procedures.
702.55 Public announcement of meetings.
702.56 Records.
702.57 Administrative review.

AUTHORITY: 42 U.S.C. 1975, 1975a, 1975b.

SOURCE: 67 FR 70482, Nov. 22, 2002, unless otherwise noted.

Subpart A—Hearings and Reports

§ 702.1 Definitions.

For purposes of this part, the following definitions shall apply unless otherwise provided:

(a) *The Act* means the United States Commission on Civil Rights Act of 1983, 97 Stat. 1301, as amended by the Civil Rights Commission Amendments Act of 1994, 108 Stat. 4339, codified in 42 U.S.C. 1975 through 1975d.

(b) *The Commission* means the United States Commission on Civil Rights or, as provided in § 702.2, to any authorized subcommittee thereof.

(c) *The Chairperson* means the Chairperson of the Commission or authorized subcommittee thereof or to any acting Chairperson of the Commission or of such subcommittee.

(d) *Proceeding* means collectively to any public session of the Commission and executive session held in connection therewith.

(e) *Hearing* means collectively to a public session of the Commission and any executive session held in connection therewith, including the attendance of witnesses or the production of written or other matters for which subpoenas have been issued.

(f) *Witnesses* are persons subpoenaed to attend and testify or produce written or other matter.

(g) *The rules in this part* means the Rules on Hearings of the Commission.

(h) *Report* means statutory reports or portions thereof issued pursuant to 42 U.S.C. 1975a(c).

(i) *Verified answer* means an answer the truth of which is substantiated by

Commission on Civil Rights

oath or affirmation attested to by a notary public or other person who has legal authority to administer oaths.

§ 702.2 Authorization for hearing.

Under 42 U.S.C. 1975a(e)(1) the Commission or, on the authorization of the Commission, any subcommittee of two or more members, at least one of whom shall be of each major political party, may, for the purpose of carrying out the provisions of the Act, hold such hearings and act at such times and locations as the Commission or such authorized subcommittee may deem advisable. The holding of hearings by the Commission or the appointment of a subcommittee to hold hearings pursuant to this section must be approved by a majority of the Commission or by a majority of the members present at a meeting at which at least a quorum of five members is present.

§ 702.3 Notice of hearing.

At least 30 days prior to the commencement of any hearing, the Commission shall publish in the FEDERAL REGISTER notice of the date on which such hearing is to commence, the location at which it is to be held, and the subject of the hearing.

§ 702.4 Subpoenas.

(a) Subpoenas for the attendance and testimony of witnesses or the production of written or other matter may be issued by the Commission over the signature of the Chairperson and may be served by any person designated by the Chairperson.

(b) A witness compelled to appear before the Commission or required to produce written or other matter shall be served with a copy of the rules in this part at the time of service of the subpoena.

(c) The Commission may issue subpoenas for the attendance and testimony of witnesses or for the production of written or other matter. Such a subpoena may not require the presence of a witness more than 100 miles outside the location wherein the witness is found or resides or is domiciled or transacts business or has appointed an agent for receipt of service of process.

(d) The Chairperson shall receive and the Commission shall dispose of requests to subpoena additional witnesses except as otherwise provided in § 702.6(e).

(e) Requests for subpoenas shall be in writing, supported by a showing of the general relevance and materiality of the evidence sought. Witness fees and mileage shall be computed and paid pursuant to § 702.15.

(f) Subpoenas shall be issued at a reasonably sufficient time in advance of their scheduled return, in order to give subpoenaed persons an opportunity to prepare for their appearance and to employ counsel, should they so desire.

(g) No subpoenaed document or information contained therein shall be made public unless it is introduced into and received as part of the official record of the hearing.

§ 702.5 Conduct of proceedings.

(a) The Chairperson shall announce in an opening statement the subject of the proceedings.

(b) Following the opening statement, the Commission shall first convene in executive session if one is required pursuant to the provisions of § 702.6.

(c) The Chairperson, subject to the approval of the Commission, shall:

(1) Set the order of presentation of evidence and appearance of witnesses;

(2) Rule on objections and motions;

(3) Administer oaths and affirmations;

(4) Make all rulings with respect to the introduction into or exclusion from the record of documentary or other evidence;

(5) Regulate the course and decorum of the proceedings and the conduct of the parties and their counsel to ensure that the proceedings are conducted in a fair and impartial manner.

(d) Proceedings shall be conducted with reasonable dispatch and due regard shall be had for the convenience and necessity of witnesses.

(e) The questioning of witnesses shall be conducted only by Members of the Commission, by authorized Commission staff personnel, or by counsel to the extent provided in § 702.7.

(f) In addition to persons served with a copy of the rules in this part pursuant to §§ 702.4 and 702.6, a copy of the rules in this part will be made available to all witnesses.

(g) The Chairperson may punish breaches of order and decorum by censure and exclusion from the proceedings.

§ 702.6 Executive session.

(a) If the Commission determines that evidence or testimony at any hearing may tend to defame, degrade, or incriminate any person, it shall receive such evidence or testimony or summary of such evidence or testimony in executive session.

(b) The Commission shall afford any persons defamed, degraded, or incriminated by such evidence or testimony an opportunity to appear and be heard in executive session, with a reasonable number of additional witnesses requested by them, before deciding to use such evidence or testimony.

(1) Such person shall be served with notice, in writing, at least 10 days prior to the date, time, and location for the appearance of witnesses at executive session or where service is by mail at least 14 days prior to such date. This notice shall be accompanied by a copy of the rules in this part and by a brief summary of the information that the Commission has determined may tend to defame, degrade, or incriminate such person;

(2) The notice, summary, and rules in this part shall be served by certified mail or by leaving a copy thereof at the last known residence or business address of such person; and

(3) The date of service, for purposes of this section, shall be the day when the material is deposited in the mail or is delivered in person, whichever is applicable. When service is made by mail, the return post office receipt shall be proof of service; in all other cases, the acknowledgment of the party served or the verified return of the one making service shall be proof of the same.

(c) If a person receiving notice under this section notifies the Commission within five days of service of such notice or where service is by mail within eight days of service of such notice that the scheduled appearance constitutes a hardship, the Commission may, in its discretion, set a new date or time for such person's appearance at the executive session.

(d) In the event such persons fail to appear at executive session at the time and location scheduled under paragraph (b) or (c) of this section, they shall not be entitled to another opportunity to appear at executive session, except as provided in § 702.11.

(e) If such persons intend to submit sworn statements of themselves or others, or if they intend that witnesses appear in their behalf at executive session, they shall, no later than 48 hours prior to the time set under paragraph (b) or (c) of this section, submit to the Commission all such statements and a list of all witnesses. The Commission will inform such persons whether the number of witnesses requested is reasonable within the meaning of paragraph (b) of this section. In addition, the Commission will receive and dispose of requests from such persons to subpoena other witnesses. Requests for subpoenas shall be made sufficiently in advance of the scheduled executive session to afford subpoenaed persons reasonable notice of their obligation to appear at that session. Subpoenas returnable at executive session shall be governed by the provisions of § 702.4.

(f) Persons for whom an executive session has been scheduled, and persons compelled to appear at such session, may be represented by counsel at such session to the extent provided by § 702.7.

(g) Attendance at executive session shall be limited to Commissioners; authorized Commission staff personnel; witnesses, and their counsel at the time scheduled for their appearance; and such other persons whose presence is requested or consented to by the Commission.

(h) In the event the Commission determines to release or to use evidence or testimony that it has determined may tend to defame, degrade, or incriminate any persons in such a manner as to reveal publicly their identity, such evidence or testimony, prior to such public release or use, will be presented at a public session, and the Commission will afford them an opportunity to appear as voluntary witnesses or to file a sworn statement in their own behalf and to submit brief and pertinent sworn statements of others.

Commission on Civil Rights § 702.12

§ 702.7 Counsel.

(a) Persons compelled to appear in person before the Commission and any witness appearing at a public session of the Commission will be accorded the right to be accompanied and advised by counsel, who will have the right to subject their clients to reasonable examination, make objections on the record, and briefly argue the basis for such objections.

(b) For the purpose of this section, counsel shall mean an attorney at law admitted to practice before the Supreme Court of the United States or the highest court of any State or Territory of the United States.

(c) Failure of any persons to obtain counsel shall not excuse them from attendance in response to a subpoena, nor shall any persons be excused in the event their counsel is excluded from the proceeding pursuant to § 702.6(g). In the latter case, however, such persons shall be afforded a reasonable time to obtain other counsel, said time to be determined by the Commission.

§ 702.8 Evidence at Commission proceedings.

(a) The rules of evidence prevailing in courts of law or equity shall not control proceedings of the Commission.

(b) Where a witness testifying at a public session of a hearing or a session for return of subpoenaed documents offers the sworn statements of other persons, such statements, in the discretion of the Commission, may be included in the record, provided they are received by the Commission 24 hours in advance of the witness' appearance.

(c) The prepared statement of a witness testifying at a public session of a hearing, in the discretion of the Commission, may be placed into the record, provided that such statement is received by the Commission 24 hours in advance of the witness' appearance.

(d) In the discretion of the Commission, evidence may be included in the record after the close of a public session of a hearing provided the Commission determines that such evidence does not tend to defame, degrade, or incriminate any person.

(e) The Commission will determine the pertinence of testimony and evidence adduced at its proceedings and may refuse to include in the record of a proceeding or may strike from the record any evidence it considers to be cumulative, immaterial, or not pertinent.

§ 702.9 Cross-examination at public session.

If the Commission determines that oral testimony of a witness at a public session tends to defame, degrade, or incriminate any person, such person, or through counsel, shall be permitted to submit questions to the Commission in writing, which, in the discretion of the Commission, may be put to such witness by the Chairperson or by authorized Commission staff personnel.

§ 702.10 Voluntary witnesses at public session of a hearing.

A person who has not been subpoenaed and who has not been afforded an opportunity to appear pursuant to § 702.6 may be permitted, in the discretion of the Commission, to make an oral or written statement at a public session of a hearing. Such person may be questioned to the same extent and in the same manner as other witnesses before the Commission.

§ 702.11 Special executive session.

If, during the course of a public session, evidence is submitted that was not previously presented at executive session and that the Commission determines may defame, degrade, or incriminate any person, the provisions of § 702.6 shall apply and such extensions, recesses or continuances of the public session shall be ordered by the Commission, as it deems necessary. The time and notice requirements of § 702.6 may be modified by the Commission provided reasonable notice of a scheduled executive session is afforded such person; the Commission may, in its discretion, strike such evidence from the record, in which case the provisions of § 702.6 shall not apply.

§ 702.12 Contempt of the Commission.

Proceedings and process of the Commission are governed by 42 U.S.C. 1975a(e)(2), which provides that in case of contumacy or refusal to obey a subpoena, the Attorney General may in a

§ 702.13 Intimidation of witnesses.

Witnesses at Commission proceedings are protected by the provisions of 18 U.S.C. 1505, which provide that whoever, with intent to avoid, evade, prevent, or obstruct compliance, in whole or in part, with any civil investigative demand duly and properly made under the Antitrust Civil Process Act, willfully withholds, misrepresents, removes from any place, conceals, covers up, destroys, mutilates, alters, or by other means falsifies any documentary material, answers to written interrogatories, or oral testimony, which is the subject of such demand; or attempts to do so or solicits another to do so; or whoever corruptly, or by threats or force, or by any threatening letter or communication influences, obstructs, or impedes or endeavors to influence, obstruct, or impede the due and proper administration of the law under which any pending proceeding is being had before any department or agency of the United States, or the due and proper exercise of the power of inquiry under which any inquiry or investigation is being had by either House, or any committee of either House or any joint committee of the Congress shall be fined under this title or imprisoned not more than five years, or both.

§ 702.14 Transcript of Commission proceedings.

(a) An accurate transcript shall be made of the testimony of all witnesses at all proceedings of the Commission. Transcripts shall be recorded solely by the official reporter or by any other person or means designated by the Commission.

(b) Every person who submits data or evidence shall be entitled to retain or, on payment of lawfully prescribed costs, procure a copy or transcript thereof, except that witnesses in a hearing held in executive session may be limited, for good cause, to inspection of the official transcript of their testimony. Transcript copies of public sessions may be obtained by the public upon the payment of the cost thereof.

(c) Persons who have presented testimony at a proceeding may ask within 60 days after the close of the proceeding to correct errors in the transcript of their testimony. Such requests shall be granted only to make the transcript conform to their testimony as presented at the proceeding.

§ 702.15 Witness fees.

A witness attending any session of the Commission shall be paid the same fees and mileage that are paid witnesses in the courts of the United States. Mileage payments must be tendered at the witness' request upon service of a subpoena issued on behalf of the Commission or any subcommittee thereof.

§ 702.16 Attendance of news media at public sessions.

Reasonable access for coverage of public sessions shall be provided to the various communications media, including newspapers, magazines, radio, newsreels, and television, subject to the physical limitations of the room in which the session is held and consideration of the physical comfort of Commission members, staff, and witnesses. However, no witnesses shall be televised, filmed, or photographed during the session nor shall the testimony of any witness be broadcast or recorded for broadcasting if the witness objects.

§ 702.17 Communications with respect to Commission proceedings.

During any proceeding held outside Washington, DC, communications to the Commission with respect to such proceeding must be made to the Chairperson or authorized Commission staff personnel in attendance. All requests for subpoenas returnable at a hearing, requests for appearance of witnesses at a hearing, and statements or other documents for inclusion in the record of a proceeding, required to be submitted in advance, must be submitted to the Chairperson, or such authorized person as the Chairperson may appoint, at an office located in the community where such hearing or proceeding is scheduled to be held. The location of such office will be set forth in all subpoenas issued under the rules in this part and in all notices prepared pursuant to § 706.2.

§ 702.18 Commission reports.

(a) If a Commission report tends to defame, degrade, or incriminate any person, the report or relevant portions thereof shall be delivered to such person at least 30 days before the report is made public to allow such person to make a timely verified answer to the report. The Commission shall afford such person an opportunity to file with the Commission a verified answer to the report or relevant portions thereof not later than 20 days after service as provided by the regulations in this part.

(1) Such person shall be served with a copy of the report or relevant portions thereof, with an indication of the section(s) that the Commission has determined tend to defame, degrade, or incriminate such person, a copy of the Act, and a copy of the regulations in this part.

(2) The report or relevant portions thereof, the Act, and regulations in this part shall be served by certified mail, return receipt requested, or by leaving a copy thereof at the last known residence or business address or the agent of such person.

(3) The date of service for the purposes of this section shall be the day the material is delivered either by the post office or otherwise, to such person or the agent of such person or at the last known residence or business address of such person. The acknowledgement of the party served or the verified return of the one making service shall be proof of service except that when service is made by mail, the return post office receipt shall also constitute proof of same.

(b) If a person receiving a Commission report or relevant portions thereof under this part requests an extension of time from the Commission within seven days of service of such report, the Commission may, upon a showing of good cause, grant the person additional time within which to file a verified answer.

(c) A verified answer shall plainly and concisely state the facts and law constituting the person's reply or defense to the charges or allegations contained in the report.

(d) Such verified answer shall be published as an appendix to the report; however, the Commission may except from the answer such matter as it determines to be scandalous, prejudicial, or unnecessary.

Subpart B—Meetings

§ 702.50 Purpose and scope.

This subpart contains the regulations of the United States Commission on Civil Rights implementing sections (a)–(f) of 5 U.S.C. 552b, the "Government in the Sunshine Act." They are adopted to further the principle that the public is entitled to the fullest practicable information regarding the decision-making processes of the Commission. They open meetings of the Commission to public observation except where the rights of individuals are involved or the ability of the Commission to carry out its responsibilities requires confidentiality.

§ 702.51 Definitions.

(a) *Commission* means the United States Commission on Civil Rights and any subcommittee of the Commission authorized under the United States Commission on Civil Rights Act of 1983, 97 Stat. 1301, as amended by the Civil Rights Commission Amendments Act of 1994, 108 Stat. 4339. The statutes are codified in 42 U.S.C. 1975 through 1975d.

(b) *Commissioner* means a member of the U.S. Commission on Civil Rights appointed by the President, the President pro tempore of the Senate, or the Speaker of the House of Representatives, as provided in 42 U.S.C. 1975.

(c) *Meeting* means the deliberations of at least the number of Commissioners required to take action on behalf of the Commission where such deliberations determine or result in the joint conduct or disposition of official Commission business.

(1) The number of Commissioners required to take action on behalf of the Commission is four, except that such number is two when the Commissioners are a subcommittee of the Commission authorized under 42 U.S.C. 1975a(e)(1).

(2) Deliberations among Commissioners regarding the setting of the time, location, or subject matter of a meeting, whether the meeting is open or closed, whether to withhold information discussed at a closed meeting,

and any other deliberations required or permitted by 5 U.S.C. 552b (d) and (e) and §702.54 and §702.55 of this subpart, are not meetings for the purposes of this subpart.

(3) The consideration by Commissioners of Commission business that is not discussed through conference calls or a series of two party calls by the number of Commissioners required to take action on behalf of the Commission is not a meeting for the purposes of this subpart.

(d) *Public announcement or publicly announce* means the use of reasonable methods, such as the posting on the Commission's website or public notice bulletin boards and the issuing of press releases, to communicate information to the public regarding Commission meetings.

(e) *Staff Director* means the Staff Director of the Commission.

§702.52 Open meeting requirements.

(a) Every portion of every Commission meeting shall be open to public observation, except as provided in §702.53 of this subpart. Commissioners shall not jointly conduct or dispose of agency business other than in accordance with this subpart.

(b) This subpart gives the public the right to attend and observe Commission open meetings; it confers no right to participate in any way in such meetings.

(c) The Staff Director shall be responsible for making physical arrangements for Commission open meetings that provide ample space, sufficient visibility, and adequate acoustics for public observation.

(d) The presiding Commissioner at an open meeting may exclude persons from a meeting and shall take all steps necessary to preserve order and decorum.

§702.53 Closed meetings.

(a) The Commission may close a portion or portions of a meeting and withhold information pertaining to such meeting when it determines that the public interest does not require otherwise and when such portion or portions of a meeting or the disclosure of such information is likely to:

(1) Disclose matters that are:

(i) Specifically authorized under criteria established by an Executive Order to be kept secret in the interests of national defense or foreign policy and

(ii) In fact properly classified pursuant to such Executive Order;

(2) Disclose information relating solely to the internal personnel rules and practices of the Commission;

(3) Disclose matters specifically exempted from disclosure by statute (other than 5 U.S.C. 552b), provided that such statute:

(i) Requires that the matters be withheld from the public in such a manner as to leave no discretion on the issue, or

(ii) Establishes particular criteria for withholding or refers to particular types of matters to be withheld;

(4) Disclose trade secrets and commercial or financial information obtained from a person and is privileged or confidential;

(5) Involve accusing any person of a crime or formally censuring any person;

(6) Disclose information of a personal nature where disclosure would constitute a clearly unwarranted invasion of personal privacy;

(7) Disclose investigatory records compiled for law enforcement purposes, or information that if written would be contained in such records, but only to the extent that the production of such records or information would:

(i) Interfere with enforcement proceedings,

(ii) Deprive a person of a right to a fair trial or an impartial adjudication,

(iii) Constitute an unwarranted invasion of personal privacy,

(iv) Disclose the identity of a confidential source and, in the case of a record received by the Commission from a criminal law enforcement authority in the course of a criminal investigation or by an agency conducting a lawful national security intelligence investigation, confidential information furnished only by the confidential source,

(v) Disclose investigative techniques and procedures, or

(vi) Endanger the life or physical safety of law enforcement personnel;

(8) Disclose information received by the Commission and contained in or related to examination, operating, or condition reports prepared by, on behalf of, or for the use of an agency responsible for the regulation or supervision of financial institutions;

(9) Disclose information the premature disclosure of that would:

(i) In the case of information received by the Commission from an agency that regulates currencies, securities, commodities, or financial institutions, be likely to:

(A) Lead to significant financial speculation in currencies, securities, or commodities, or

(B) Significantly endanger the stability of any financial institution; or

(ii) Be likely to significantly frustrate implementation of a proposed action, except that this paragraph shall not apply in any instance where the Commission has already disclosed to the public the content or nature of its proposed action or where the Commission is required by law to make such disclosure on its own initiative prior to taking final agency action on such proposal; or

(10) Specifically concern the Commission's issuance of a subpoena or the Commission's participation in a civil action or proceeding, an action in a foreign court or international tribunal, or an arbitration.

(b) [Reserved]

§ 702.54 Closed meeting procedures.

(a) A meeting or portion thereof will be closed, and information pertaining to a closed meeting will be withheld, only after four Commissioners when no Commissioner's position is vacant, three Commissioners when there is a vacancy, or two Commissioners on a subcommittee authorized under 42 U.S.C. 1975a(e)(1), vote to take such action.

(b)(1) A separate vote shall be taken with respect to each meeting, a portion or portions of which are proposed to be closed to the public under § 702.53, and with respect to any information to be withheld under § 702.53.

(2) A single vote may be taken with respect to a series of meetings, a portion or portions of which are proposed to be closed to the public, or with respect to any information concerning such series of meetings, so long as:

(i) Each meeting in such series involves the same particular matters, and

(ii) Is scheduled to be held no more than thirty (30) days after the initial meeting in such series.

(c) The Commission will vote on the question of closing a meeting or portion thereof and withholding information under paragraph (b) of this section if one Commissioner calls for such a vote. The vote of each Commissioner participating in a vote to close a meeting shall be recorded and no proxies shall be allowed.

(1) If such vote is against closing a meeting and withholding information, the Staff Director, within one working day of such vote, shall make publicly available by putting in a place easily accessible to the public a written copy of such vote reflecting the vote of each Commissioner.

(2) If such vote is for closing a meeting and withholding information, the Staff Director, within one working day of such vote, shall make publicly available by putting in a place easily accessible to the public a written copy of such vote reflecting the vote of each Commissioner, and:

(i) A full written explanation of the decision to close the meeting or portions thereof (such explanation will be as detailed as possible without revealing the exempt information);

(ii) A list of all persons other than staff members expected to attend the meeting and their affiliation (the identity of persons expected to attend such meeting will be withheld only if revealing their identity would reveal the exempt information that is the subject of the closed meeting).

(d) Prior to any vote to close a meeting or portion thereof under paragraph (c) of this section, the Commissioners shall obtain from the General Counsel an opinion as to whether the closing of a meeting or portions thereof is in accordance with paragraphs (a)(1) through (10) of § 702.53.

(1) For every meeting closed in accordance with paragraphs (a)(1) through (10) of § 702.53, the General Counsel shall publicly certify in writing that, in his or her opinion, the

§ 702.55

meeting may be closed to the public and shall cite each relevant exemptive provision.

(2) A copy of certification by the General Counsel together with a statement from the presiding officer of the closed meeting setting forth the time and location of the meeting and the persons present, shall be retained by the Commission.

(e) For all meetings closed to the public, the Commission shall maintain a complete verbatim transcript or electronic recording adequate to record fully the proceedings of each meeting or portion of a meeting, which sets forth the time and location of the meeting and the persons present. In the case of a meeting or a portion of a meeting closed to the public pursuant to paragraphs (a)(8), (9)(i)(A), or (10) of § 702.53, the Commission may retain a set of minutes and such minutes shall fully and clearly describe all matters discussed and provide a full and accurate summary of any actions taken, and the reasons therefor, including a description of each of the views expressed on any item and the record of any roll call vote (reflecting the vote of each member on the question). All documents considered in connection with any action shall be identified in such minutes.

(f) Any person whose interests may be directly affected by a portion of a meeting may request that such portion be closed to the public under § 702.53 or that it be open to the public if the Commission has voted to close the meeting pursuant to § 702.53(a)(5), (6) or (7). The Commission will vote on the request if one Commissioner asks that a vote be taken. Such requests shall be made to the Staff Director within a reasonable amount of time after the meeting or vote in question is publicly announced.

§ 702.55 Public announcement of meetings.

(a) *Agenda.* The Staff Director shall set as early as possible but in any event at least eight calendar days before a meeting, the time, location, and subject matter for the meeting. Agenda items will be identified in adequate detail to inform the general public of the specific business to be discussed at the meeting.

(b) *Notice.* The Staff Director, at least eight calendar days before a meeting, shall make public announcement of:

(1) The time of the meeting;
(2) Its location;
(3) Its subject matter;
(4) Whether it is open or closed to the public; and
(5) The name and phone number of a Commission staff member who will respond to requests for information about the meeting.

(c) *Changes.* (1) The time of day or location of a meeting may be changed following the public announcement required by paragraph (b) of this section, if the Staff Director publicly announces such change at the earliest practicable time subsequent to the decision to change the time of day or location of the meeting.

(2) The date of a meeting may be changed following the public announcement required by paragraph (b) of this section, or a meeting may be scheduled less than eight calendar days in advance, if:

(i) Four Commissioners when no Commissioner's position is vacant, three Commissioners when there is such a vacancy, or two Commissioners on a subcommittee authorized under 42 U.S.C. 1975a(d), determine by recorded vote that Commission business requires such a meeting at an earlier date; and

(ii) The Staff Director, at the earliest practicable time following such vote, makes public announcement of the time, location, and subject matter of such meeting and whether it is open or closed to the public.

(3) The subject matter of a meeting or the determination to open or close a meeting or a portion of a meeting to the public may be changed following the public announcement required by paragraph (b) of this section if:

(i) Four Commissioners when no Commissioner's position is vacant, three Commissioners when there is such a vacancy, or two Commissioners on a subcommittee authorized under 42 U.S.C. 1975a(e)(1) determine by recorded vote that Commission business so requires; and

(ii) The Staff Director publicly announces such change and the vote of each Commissioner upon such change at the earliest practicable time subsequent to the decision to make such change.

(d)(1) FEDERAL REGISTER. Immediately following all public announcements required by paragraphs (b) and (c) of this section, notice of the time, location, and subject matter of a meeting, whether the meeting is open or closed to the public, any change in one of the preceding, and the name and phone number of the official designated by the Commission to respond to requests for information about meeting, shall be submitted for publication in the FEDERAL REGISTER.

(2) Notice of a meeting will be published in the FEDERAL REGISTER even after the meeting that is the subject of the notice has occurred in order to provide a public record of all Commission meetings.

§ 702.56 Records.

(a) The Commission shall promptly make available to the public in an easily accessible place at Commission headquarters the following materials:

(1) A copy of the certification by the General Counsel required by § 702.54(e)(1).

(2) A copy of all recorded votes required to be taken by these rules.

(3) A copy of all announcements published in the FEDERAL REGISTER pursuant to this subpart.

(4) Transcripts, electronic recordings, and minutes of closed meetings determined not to contain items of discussion or information that may be withheld under § 702.53. Copies of such material will be furnished to any person at the actual cost of transcription or duplication.

(b)(1) Requests to review or obtain copies of records compiled under this Act, other than transcripts, electronic recordings, or minutes of a closed meeting, will be processed under the Freedom of Information Act and, where applicable, the Privacy Act regulations of the Commission (parts 704 and 705, respectively, of this title). Nothing in this subpart expands or limits the present rights of any person under the rules in this part with respect to such requests.

(2) Requests to review or obtain copies of transcripts, electronic recordings, or minutes of a closed meeting maintained under § 702.54(e) and not released under paragraph (a)(4) of this section shall be directed to the Staff Director who shall respond to such requests within ten (10) working days.

(c) The Commission shall maintain a complete verbatim copy of the transcript, a complete copy of minutes, or a complete electronic recording of each meeting, or portion of a meeting, closed to the public, for a period of two years after such meeting or until one year after the conclusion of any agency proceeding with respect to which the meeting or portion was held, whichever occurs later.

§ 702.57 Administrative review.

Any person who believes a Commission action governed by this subpart to be contrary to the provisions of this subpart shall file an objection in writing with the Staff Director specifying the violation and suggesting corrective action. Whenever possible, the Staff Director shall respond within ten (10) working days of the receipt of such objections.

PART 703—OPERATIONS AND FUNCTIONS OF STATE ADVISORY COMMITTEES

Sec.
703.1 Name and establishment.
703.2 Functions.
703.3 Scope of subject matter.
703.4 Advisory Committee Management Officer.
703.5 Membership.
703.6 Officers.
703.7 Subcommittees—Special assignments.
703.8 Meetings.
703.9 Reimbursement of members.
703.10 Public availability of documents and other materials.

AUTHORITY: 42 U.S.C. 1975a(d).

SOURCE: 67 FR 70482, Nov. 22, 2002, unless otherwise noted.

§ 703.1 Name and establishment.

Pursuant to 42 U.S.C. 1975a(d), the Commission has chartered and maintains Advisory Committees to the

§ 703.2

Commission in each State, and the District of Columbia. All relevant provisions of the Federal Advisory Committee Act of 1972 (Public Law 92–463, as amended) are applicable to the management, membership, and operations of such committees and subcommittees thereof.

§ 703.2 Functions.

Under the Commission's charter each Advisory Committee shall:

(a) Advise the Commission in writing of any knowledge or information it has of any alleged deprivation of the right to vote and to have the vote counted by reason of color, race, religion, sex, age, disability, or national origin, or that citizens are being accorded or denied the right to vote in Federal elections as a result of patterns or practices of fraud or discrimination;

(b) Advise the Commission concerning matters related to discrimination or a denial of equal protection of the laws under the Constitution and the effect of the laws and policies of the Federal Government with respect to equal protection of the laws;

(c) Advise the Commission upon matters of mutual concern in the preparation of reports of the Commission to the President and the Congress;

(d) Receive reports, suggestions, and recommendations from individuals, public and private organizations, and public officials upon matters pertinent to inquiries conducted by the Advisory Committee;

(e) Initiate and forward advice and recommendations to the Commission upon matters that the Advisory Committee has studied;

(f) Assist the Commission in the exercise of its clearinghouse function and with respect to other matters that the Advisory Committee has studied;

(g) Attend, as observers, any open hearing or conference that the Commission may hold within the State.

§ 703.3 Scope of subject matter.

The scope of the subject matter to be dealt with by Advisory Committees shall be those subjects of inquiry or study with which the Commission itself is authorized to investigate, pursuant to 42 U.S.C. 1975(a). Each Advisory Committee shall confine its studies to the State covered by its charter. It may, however, subject to the requirements of § 703.4, undertake to study, within the limitations of the Act, subjects other than those chosen by the Commission for study.

§ 703.4 Advisory Committee Management Officer.

(a) The Chief of the Regional Programs Coordination Unit is designated as Advisory Committee Management Officer pursuant to the requirements of the Federal Advisory Committee Act of 1972 (Public Law 92–463, as amended).

(b) Such Officer shall carry out the functions specified in section 8(b) of the Federal Advisory Committee Act.

(c) Such Officer shall, for each Advisory Committee, appoint a Commission employee to provide services to the Committee and to be responsible for supervising the activity of the Committee pursuant to section 8 of the Federal Advisory Committee Act. The employee is subject to the supervision of the Regional Director of the Commission responsible for the State within which said Committee is chartered.

§ 703.5 Membership.

(a) Subject to exceptions made from time to time by the Commission to fit special circumstances, each Advisory Committee shall consist of at least 11 members appointed by the Commission. Members of the Advisory Committees shall serve for a fixed term to be set by the Commission upon the appointment of a member subject to the duration of Advisory Committees as prescribed by the charter, provided that members of the Advisory Committee may, at any time, be removed by the Commission.

(b) No person is to be denied an opportunity to serve on a State Advisory Committee because of race, age, sex, religion, national origin, or disability. The Commission shall encourage membership on the State Advisory Committee to be broadly diverse.

[71 FR 8485, Feb. 17, 2006]

§ 703.6 Officers.

(a) The officers of each Advisory Committee shall be a Chairperson, Vice Chairperson, and such other officers as may be deemed advisable.

(b) The Chairperson shall be appointed by the Commission.

(c) The Vice Chairperson and other officers shall be elected by the majority vote of the full membership of the Committee.

(d) The Chairperson, or in his or her absence the Vice Chairperson, under the direction of the Commission staff member appointed pursuant to §703.4(b) shall:

(1) Call meetings of the Committee;

(2) Preside over meetings of the Committee;

(3) Appoint all subcommittees of the Committee;

(4) Certify for accuracy the minutes of Committee meetings prepared by the assigned Commission staff member; and

(5) Perform such other functions as the Committee may authorize or the Commission may request.

§ 703.7 Subcommittees—Special assignments.

Subject to the approval of the designated Commission employee, an Advisory Committee may:

(a) Establish subcommittees, composed of members of the Committee, to study and report upon matters under consideration and authorize such subcommittees to take specific action within the competence of the Committee; and

(b) Designate individual members of the Committee to perform special projects involving research or study on matters under consideration by the Committee.

§ 703.8 Meetings.

(a) Meetings of a Committee shall be convened by the designated Commission employee or subject to his or her approval by the Chairperson or a majority of the Advisory Committee members. The agenda for such Committee or subcommittee meeting shall be approved by the designated Commission employee.

(b) A quorum shall consist of one-half or more of the members of the Committee, or five members, whichever is the lesser, except that with respect to the conduct of fact-finding meetings as authorized in paragraph (e) of this section, a quorum shall consist of three members.

(c) Notice of all meetings of an Advisory Committee shall be given to the public.

(1) Notice shall be published in the FEDERAL REGISTER at least 15 days prior to the meetings, provided that in emergencies such requirement may be waived.

(2) Notice of meetings shall be provided to the public by press releases and other appropriate means.

(3) Each notice shall contain a statement of the purpose of the meeting, a summary of the agenda, and the date, time, and location of such meeting.

(d) Except as provided for in paragraph (d)(1) of this section, all meetings of Advisory Committees or subcommittees shall be open to the public.

(1) The Chief of the Regional Programs Coordination Unit may authorize a Committee or subcommittee to hold a meeting closed to the public if he or she determines that the closing of such meeting is in the public interest provided that prior to authorizing the holding of a closed meeting the Chief of the Regional Programs Coordination Unit has requested and received the opinion of the General Counsel with respect to whether the meeting may be closed under one or more of the exemptions provided in the Government in the Sunshine Act, 5 U.S.C. 552b(c).

(2) In the event that any meeting or portion thereof is closed to the public, the Committee shall publish, at least annually, in summary form a report of the activities conducted in meetings not open to the public.

(e) Advisory Committees and subcommittees may hold fact-finding meetings for the purpose of inviting the attendance of and soliciting information and views from government officials and private persons respecting subject matters within the jurisdiction of the Committee or subcommittee.

(f) Any person may submit a written statement at any business or fact-finding meeting of an Advisory Committee or subcommittee.

(g) At the discretion of the designated Commission employee or his or her designee, any person may make an oral presentation at any business or fact-finding meeting, provided that such presentation will not defame, degrade, or incriminate any other person as prohibited by the Act.

§ 703.9 Reimbursement of members.

(a) Advisory Committee members may be reimbursed by the Commission by a per diem subsistence allowance and for travel expenses at rates not to exceed those prescribed by Congress for Government employees, for the following activities only:

(1) Attendance at meetings, as provided for in § 703.8; and

(2) Any activity specifically requested and authorized by the Commission to be reimbursed.

(b) Members will be reimbursed for the expense of travel by private automobile on a mileage basis only to the extent such expense is no more than that of suitable public transportation for the same trip unless special circumstances justify the additional expense of travel by private automobile.

§ 703.10 Public availability of documents and other materials.

Part 704 of this chapter shall be applicable to reports, publications, and other materials prepared by or for Advisory Committees.

PART 704—INFORMATION DISCLOSURE AND COMMUNICATIONS

Sec.
704.1 Material available pursuant to 5 U.S.C. 552.
704.2 Complaints.
704.3 Other requests and communications.
704.4 Restrictions on disclosure of information.

AUTHORITY: 5 U.S.C. 552, 552a, 552b.

SOURCE: 67 FR 70482, Nov. 22, 2002, unless otherwise noted.

§ 704.1 Material available pursuant to 5 U.S.C. 552.

(a) *Purpose, scope, and definitions.* (1) This section contains the regulations of the United States Commission on Civil Rights implementing the Freedom of Information Act, 5 U.S.C. 552. These regulations inform the public with respect to where and how records and information may be obtained from the Commission. Officers and employees of the Commission shall make Commission records available under 5 U.S.C. 552 only as prescribed in this section. Nothing contained in this section, however, shall be construed to prohibit officers or employees of the Commission from routinely furnishing information or records that are customarily furnished in the regular performance of their duties.

(2) For the purposes of this part the following terms are defined as indicated:

Commission means the United States Commission on Civil Rights;

FOIA means Freedom of Information Act, 5 U.S.C. 552;

FOIA Request means a request in writing, for records pursuant to 5 U.S.C. 552, which meets the requirements of paragraph (d) of this part. This part does not apply to telephone or other oral communications or requests not complying with paragraph (d)(1)(i) of this section.

Office of the General Counsel means the General Counsel of the Commission or his or her designee;

Staff Director means the Staff Director of the Commission.

(b) *General policy.* In order to foster the maximum participation of an informed public in the affairs of Government, the Commission will make the fullest possible disclosure of its identifiable records and information consistent with such considerations as those provided in the exemptions of 5 U.S.C. 552 that are set forth in paragraph (f) of this section.

(c) *Material maintained on file pursuant to 5 U.S.C. 552(a)(2).* Material maintained on file pursuant to 5 U.S.C. 552(a)(2) shall be available for inspection during regular business hours at the offices of the Commission at 624 9th Street, NW., Washington, DC 20425. Copies of such material shall be available upon written request, specifying the material desired, addressed to the Office of the General Counsel, U.S. Commission on Civil Rights, 624 9th Street, NW., Washington, DC 20425, and upon the payment of fees, if any, determined in accordance with paragraph (e) of this section.

(1) *Current index.* Included in the material available pursuant to 5 U.S.C. 552(a)(2) shall be an index of:

(i) All other material maintained on file pursuant to 5 U.S.C. 552(a)(2); and

(ii) All material published by the Commission in the FEDERAL REGISTER and currently in effect.

(2) *Deletion of identifying details.* Wherever deletions from material maintained on file pursuant to 5 U.S.C. 552(a)(2) are required in order to prevent a clearly unwarranted invasion of privacy, justification for the deletions shall be placed as a preamble to documents from which such deletions are made.

(d) *Materials available pursuant to 5 U.S.C. 552(a)(3)*—(1) *Request procedures.* (i) Each request for records pursuant to this section shall be in writing over the signature of the requester, addressed to the Office of the General Counsel, U.S. Commission on Civil Rights, 624 9th Street, NW., Washington, DC 20425 and:

(A) Shall clearly and prominently be identified as a request for information under the Freedom of Information Act (if submitted by mail or otherwise submitted in an envelope or other cover, be clearly and prominently identified as such on the envelope or other cover—*e.g.*, FOIA); and

(B) Shall contain a sufficiently specific description of the record requested with respect to names, dates, and subject matter to permit such record to be identified and located; and

(C) Shall contain a statement that whatever costs involved pursuant to paragraph (e) of this section will be paid, that such costs will be paid up to a specified amount, or that waiver or reduction of fees is requested pursuant to paragraph (e) of this section.

(ii) If the information submitted pursuant to paragraph (d)(1)(i)(B) of this section is insufficient to enable identification and location of the records, the General Counsel shall as soon as possible notify the requester in writing indicating the additional information needed. Every reasonable effort shall be made to assist in the identification and location of the record sought. Time requirements under the regulations in this part are tolled from the date notification under this section is sent to the requester until an answer in writing to such notification is received from requester.

(iii) A request for records that is not in writing or does not comply with paragraph (d)(1)(i) of this section is not a request under the Freedom of Information Act and the 10 day time limit for agency response under the Act will not be deemed applicable.

(iv) Except as otherwise provided in this section, the General Counsel shall immediately notify the requester of noncompliance with paragraphs (d)(1)(i)(C) and (e) of this section.

(2) *Agency determinations.* (i) Responses to all requests pursuant to 5 U.S.C. 552(a)(3) shall be made by the General Counsel in writing to the requester within 10 working days after receipt by the General Counsel of such request except as specifically exempted under paragraphs (d)(1) (ii), (iii) and (iv) of this section, and shall state:

(A) Whether and to what extent the Commission will comply with the request;

(B) The probable availability of the records or that the records may be furnished with deletions or that records will be denied as exempt pursuant to 5 U.S.C. 552(b)(1) through (9);

(C) The estimated costs, determined in accordance with paragraph (e) of this section, including waiver or reduction of fee as appropriate and any deposit or prepayment requirement; and

(D) When records are to be provided, the time and place at which records or copies will be available determined in accordance with the terms of the request and with paragraph (d)(3) of this section. Such response shall be termed a determination notice.

(ii) In the case of denial of requests in whole or part the determination notice shall state:

(A) Specifically what records are being denied;

(B) The reasons for such denials;

(C) The specific statutory exemption(s) upon which such denial is based;

(D) The names and titles or positions of every person responsible for the denial of such request; and

(E) The right of appeal to the Staff Director of the Commission and procedures for such appeal as provided under paragraph (g) of this section.

(iii) Each request received by the Office of the General Counsel for records pursuant to the regulations in this part shall be recorded immediately. The record of each request shall be kept current, stating the date and time the request is received, the name and address of the person making the request, any amendments to such request, the nature of the records requested, the action taken regarding the request, including waiver of fees, extensions of time pursuant to 5 U.S.C. 552(a)(6)(B), and appeals. The date and subject of any letters pursuant to paragraph (d)(1) of this section or agency determinations pursuant to paragraph (d)(2)(i) of this section, the date(s) any records are subsequently furnished, and the payment requested and received.

(3) *Time limitations.* (i) Time limitations for agency response to a request for records established by the regulations in this part shall begin when the request is recorded pursuant to paragraph (d)(2)(iii) of this section. A written request pursuant to FOIA but sent to an office of the Commission other than the Office of the General Counsel shall be date stamped, initialed, and redirected immediately to the Office of the General Counsel. The required period for agency determination shall begin when it is received by the Office of the General Counsel in accordance with paragraph (d)(2)(iii) of this section.

(ii) In unusual circumstances, pursuant to 5 U.S.C. 552(a)(6)(B), the General Counsel may, in the case of initial determinations under the regulations in this part, extend the 10 working day time limit in which the agency is required to make its determination notification. Such extension shall be communicated in writing to the requesting party setting forth with particularity the reasons for such extension and the date on which a determination is expected to be transmitted. Such extensions may not exceed 10 working days for any request and may only be used to the extent necessary to properly process a particular request. Such extension is permissible only where there is a demonstrated need:

(A) To search for and collect the requested records from field facilities or other establishments that are separate from the Office of the General Counsel;

(B) To search for, collect, and appropriately examine a voluminous amount of separate and distinct records that are demanded in a single request; or

(C) For consultation, which shall be conducted with all practicable speed, with another agency having a substantial interest in the determination of the request or among two or more components of the same agency having substantial subject matter interest therein.

(e) *Fees*—(1) *Definitions.* The following definitions apply to the terms when used in this section:

(i) *Direct costs* means those expenditures that the Commission actually incurs in searching for and duplicating (and in the case of commercial requesters, reviewing) documents to respond to a request made under paragraph (d) of this section. Direct costs include, for example, the salary of the employee(s) performing the work (the basic rate of pay for the employee(s) plus 16 percent of that rate to cover benefits) and the cost of operating duplicating machinery. Not included in direct costs are overhead expenses such as costs of space and heating or lighting the facility in which the records are stored.

(ii) *Search* means all time spent looking for material that is responsive to a request, including page-by-page or line-by-line identification within documents. However, an entire document will be duplicated if this would prove to be a more efficient and less expensive method of complying with a request than a more detailed manner of searching. Search is distinguished from review of material in order to determine whether the material is exempt from disclosure.

(iii) *Duplication* means the process of making a copy of a document necessary to respond to a request for disclosure of records. Such copies can take the form of paper or machine readable documentation (*e.g.*, magnetic tape or disk), among others.

(iv) *Review* means the process of examining documents located in response to an information request to determine whether any portion of any document is permitted to be withheld. It also includes processing any documents for disclosure, *e.g.*, doing all that is necessary to prepare them for release. Review does not include time spent resolving general legal or policy issues regarding the application of exemptions.

(v) *Commercial use request* means a request from or on behalf of one who seeks information for a use or purpose that furthers the commercial, trade, or profit interests of the requester or the person on whose behalf the request is made. In deciding whether a requester properly belongs in this category, the General Counsel will determine the use to which a requester will put the documents requested. When the General Counsel has reasonable cause to doubt such intended use, or where such use is not clear from the request itself, the General Counsel will seek additional clarification before assigning the request to a specific category.

(vi) *Educational institution* means a school, an institution of higher education, an institution of professional education, or an institution of vocational education that operates a program or programs of scholarly research.

(vii) *Noncommercial scientific institution* means an institution that is not operated on a commercial basis and that is operated solely for the purpose of conducting scientific research the results of which are not intended to promote any particular product or industry.

(viii) *Representative of the news media* means any person actively gathering news for an entity that is organized and operated to publish or broadcast news to the public. The term news means information that is about current events or that would be of current interest to the public. News media entities include television or radio stations broadcasting to the public at large, and publishers of periodicals (but only in those instances when they can qualify as disseminators of news) who make their products available for purchase or subscription by the general public. Freelance journalists may be regarded as working for a news organization if they can demonstrate a solid basis for expecting publication through that organization, even though not actually employed by it.

(2) *Costs to be included in fees.* The direct costs included in fees will vary according to the following categories of requests:

(i) *Commercial use requests.* Fees will include the Commission's direct costs for searching for, reviewing, and duplicating the requested records.

(ii) *Educational and noncommercial scientific institution requests.* The Commission will provide documents to requesters in this category for the cost of duplication alone, excluding charges for the first 100 pages. To be eligible for inclusion in this category, requesters must show that the request is being made under the auspices of a qualifying institution and that the records are sought in furtherance of scholarly (if the request is from an educational institution) or scientific (if the request is from a noncommercial scientific institution) research.

(iii) *Requests from representatives of the news media.* The Commission will provide documents to requesters in this category for the cost of duplication alone, excluding charges for the first 100 pages. To be eligible for inclusion in this category a requester must meet the criteria in paragraph (e)(1)(viii) of this section.

(iv) *All other requests.* The Commission will charge requesters who do not fit into any of the categories in paragraphs (e)(2)(i) through (iii) of this section fees that cover the direct costs of searching for and duplicating records that are responsive to the requests, except for the first two hours of search time and the first 100 pages duplicated. However, requests from persons for records about themselves will continue to be treated under the fee provisions of the Privacy Act of 1974 and §705.10 of this chapter.

(3) *Fee calculation.* Fees will be calculated as follows:

(i) *Manual search.* At the salary rate (basic pay plus 16 percent) of the employee(s) making the search.

(ii) *Computer search.* At the actual direct cost of providing the search, including computer search time directly attributable to search for records responsive to the request, runs, and operator salary apportionable to the search.

(iii) *Review* (commercial use requests only). At the salary rate (basic pay plus 16 percent) of the employee(s) conducting the review. Only the review necessary at the initial administrative

§ 704.1

level to determine the applicability of any exemption, and not review at the administrative appeal level, will be included in the fee.

(iv) *Duplication.* At 20 cents per page for paper copy. For copies of records prepared by computer (such as tapes or printouts), the actual cost of production, including operator time, will be charged.

(v) *Additional services; certification.* Express mail and other additional services that may be arranged by the requester will be charged at actual cost. The fee for certification or authentication of copies shall be $3.00 per document.

(vi) *Assessment of interest.* The Commission may begin assessing interest charges on the 31st day following the day the fee bill is sent. Interest will be at the rate prescribed in 31 U.S.C. 3717 and will accrue from the date of billing.

(vii) No fee shall be charged if the total billable cost calculated under paragraphs (e)(2) and (3) of this section is less than $10.00.

(4) *Waiver or reduction of fees.* (i) Documents will be furnished without charge, or at a reduced charge, where disclosure of the information is in the public interest because it is likely to contribute significantly to public understanding of the operations or activities of the government and is not primarily in the commercial interest of the requester.

(ii) Whenever a waiver or reduction of fees is granted, only one copy of the record will be furnished.

(iii) The decision of the General Counsel on any fee waiver or reduction request shall be final and unappealable.

(5) *Payment procedures*—(i) *Fee payment.* Payment of fees shall be made by cash (if delivered in person), check, or money order payable to the United States Commission on Civil Rights.

(ii) *Notification of fees.* No work shall be done that will result in fees in excess of $25.00 without written authorization from the requester. Where it is anticipated that fees will exceed $25.00, and the requester has not indicated in advance a willingness to pay fees as high as are anticipated, the requester will be notified of the amount of the projected fees. The notification shall offer the requester an opportunity to confer with the General Counsel in an attempt to reformulate the request so as to meet the requester's needs at a lower cost. The administrative time limits prescribed in 5 U.S.C. 552(a)(6) will not begin until after the requester agrees in writing to accept the prospective charges.

(6) *Advance payment of fees.* When fees are projected to exceed $250.00, the requester may be required to make an advance payment of all or part of the fee before the request is processed. If a requester has previously failed to pay a fee in a timely fashion (*i.e.*, within 30 days of the billing date), the requester will be required to pay the full amount owed plus any applicable interest, and to make an advance payment of the full amount of the estimated fee before a new or pending request is processed from that requester. The administrative time limits prescribed in 5 U.S.C. 552(a)(6) will not begin until after the requester has complied with this provision.

(7) *Other provisions*—(i) *Charges for unsuccessful search.* Charges may be assessed for time spent searching for requested records, even if the search fails to locate responsive records or the records are determined, after review, to be exempt from disclosure.

(ii) *Aggregating requests to avoid fees.* Multiple requests shall be aggregated when the General Counsel reasonably determines that a requester or group of requesters is attempting to break down a request into a series of requests to evade fees.

(iii) *Debt Collection Improvement Act of 1996.* The Debt Collection Improvement Act of 1996 (Pub. L. 104–134), including disclosure to consumer reporting agencies and use of collection agencies, will be used to encourage payment where appropriate.

(f) *Exemptions* (5 U.S.C. 552(b))–(1) *General.* The Commission may exempt from disclosure matters that are:

(i)(A) Specifically authorized under criteria established by an Executive Order to be kept secret in the interest of national defense or foreign policy and

(B) Are in fact properly classified pursuant to such Executive Order.

Commission on Civil Rights § 704.1

(ii) Related solely to the internal personnel rules and practices of an agency;

(iii) Specifically exempted from disclosure by statute;

(iv) Trade secrets and commercial or financial information obtained from a person and privileged or confidential;

(v) Interagency or intra-agency memoranda or letters that would not be available by law to a party other than an agency in litigation with the agency;

(vi) Personnel and medical files and similar files the disclosure of which would constitute a clearly unwarranted invasion of personal privacy;

(vii) Records or information compiled for law enforcement purposes, but only to the extent that the production of such law enforcement records or information:

(A) Could reasonably be expected to interfere with enforcement proceedings;

(B) Could deprive a person of a right to a fair trial or an impartial adjudication;

(C) Could reasonably be expected to constitute an unwarranted invasion of personal privacy;

(D) Could reasonably be expected to disclose the identity of a confidential source, including a State, local, or foreign agency or authority or any private institution that furnished information on a confidential basis;

(E) Could disclose techniques and procedures for all enforcement investigations or prosecutions, or could disclose guidelines for law enforcement investigations or prosecutions if such disclosure could reasonably be expected to risk circumvention of the law; or

(F) Could reasonably be expected to endanger the life or physical safety of any individual;

(viii) Contained in or related to examination, operating, or condition reports prepared by, on behalf of, or for the use of an agency responsible for the regulation or supervision of financial institutions; and

(ix) Geological and geophysical information and data, including maps, concerning wells.

(2) Investigatory records or information. (5 U.S.C. 552(b)(7)).

(i) Among the documents exempt from disclosure pursuant to paragraph (f)(1)(vii) of this section shall be records or information reflecting investigations that either are conducted for the purpose of determining whether a violation(s) of legal right has taken place, or have disclosed that a violation(s) of legal right has taken place, but only to the extent that production of such records or information would fall within the classifications established in paragraphs (f)(1)(vii)(B) through (F) of this section.

(ii) Among the documents exempt from disclosure under paragraphs(f)(1)(vii)(D) and (f)(2)(i) of this section concerning confidential sources shall be documents that disclose the fact or the substance of a communication made to the Commission in confidence relating to an allegation or support of an allegation of wrongdoing by certain persons. It is sufficient under this section to indicate the confidentiality of the source if the substance of the communication or the circumstances of the communication indicate that investigative effectiveness could reasonably be expected to be inhibited by disclosure.

(iii) Whenever a request is made that involves access to records described in paragraph (f)(1)(vii)(A) of this section and the investigation or proceeding involves a possible violation of criminal law and there is reason to believe that the subject of the investigation or proceeding is not aware of its pendency and disclosure of the existence of the records could reasonably be expected to interfere with enforcement proceedings, the Commission may, during only such time as that circumstance continues, treat the records as not subject to the requirements of 5 U.S.C. 552 and this section.

(3) Any reasonably segregable portion of a record shall be provided to any person requesting such record after deletion of the portions that are exempt under this section.

(g) *Administrative appeals.* (1) These procedures apply whenever a requester is denied records under paragraph (d)(2)(i) of this section.

(2) Parties may appeal decisions under paragraph (d)(2)(i) of this section

§ 704.2

within 90 days of the date of such decision by filing a written request for review addressed to the Staff Director, U.S. Commission on Civil Rights, 624 9th Street, NW., Washington, DC 20425, by certified mail, including a copy of the written denial, and may include a statement of the circumstances, reasons or arguments advanced in support of disclosure. Review will be made by the Staff Director on the basis of the written record.

(3) The decision on review of any appeal filed under this section shall be in writing over the signature of the Staff Director will be promptly communicated to the person requesting review and will constitute the final action of the Commission.

(4) Determinations of appeals filed under this section shall be made within 20 working days after the receipt of such appeal. If, on appeal, denial of records is in whole or part upheld, the Staff Director shall notify the persons making such request of the provisions for judicial review of that determination under 5 U.S.C. 552(a)(6).

(5) An extension of time may be granted under this section pursuant to criteria established in paragraph (d)(3)(ii) (A) through (C) of this section, except that such extension together with any extension, which may have been granted pursuant to paragraph (d)(3)(ii) of this section, may not exceed a total of 10 working days.

§ 704.2 Complaints.

Any person may bring to the attention of the Commission a grievance that he or she believes falls within the jurisdiction of the Commission, as set forth in section 3 of the Act. This shall be done by submitting a complaint in writing to the Office of Civil Rights Evaluation, U.S. Commission on Civil Rights, 9th Street, NW., Washington, DC 20425. Allegations falling under section 3(a)(1) of the Act must be under oath or affirmation. All complaints should set forth the pertinent facts upon which the complaint is based, including but not limited to specification of:

(a) Names and titles of officials or other persons involved in acts forming the basis for the complaint;

(b) Accurate designations of place locations involved;

(c) Dates of events described in the complaint.

§ 704.3 Other requests and communications.

Requests for information should be addressed to the Public Affairs Unit and requests for Commission literature should be directed to National Clearinghouse Library, U.S. Commission on Civil Rights, 624 9th Street, NW., Washington DC 20425. Communications with respect to Commission proceedings should be made pursuant to § 702.17 of this chapter. All other communications should be directed to Office of Staff Director, U.S. Commission on Civil Rights, 624 9th Street, Washington, DC 20425.

§ 704.4 Restrictions on disclosure of information.

(a) By the provisions of the Act, no evidence or testimony or summary of evidence or testimony taken in executive session may be released or used in public sessions without the consent of the Commission, and any person who releases or uses in public without the consent of the Commission such evidence or testimony taken in executive session shall be fined not more than $1,000 or imprisoned for not more than 1 year.

(b) Unless a matter of public record, all information or documents obtained or prepared by any Commissioner, officer, or employee of the Commission, including members of Advisory Committees, in the course of his or official duties, or by virtue of his or her official status, shall not be disclosed or used by such person for any purpose except in the performance of his or her official duties.

(c) Any Commissioner, officer, or employee of the Commission, including members of Advisory Committees, who is served with a subpoena, order, or other demand requiring the disclosure of such information or the production of such documents shall appear in response to such subpoena, order, or other demand and, unless otherwise directed by the Commission, shall respectfully decline to disclose the information or produce the documents called for, basing his or her refusal upon this section. Any such person who is served with such a subpoena, order, or other demand shall promptly advise the Commission of the service of such subpoena, order, or other demand, the nature of the information or documents sought, and any circumstances that may bear upon the desirability of making available such information or documents.

PART 705—MATERIALS AVAILABLE PURSUANT TO 5 U.S.C. 552a

Sec.
705.1 Purpose and scope.
705.2 Definitions.
705.3 Procedures for requests pertaining to individual records in a system of records.
705.4 Times, places, and requirements for identification of individuals making requests and identification of records requested.
705.5 Disclosure of requested information to individuals.
705.6 Request for correction or amendment to record.
705.7 Agency review of request for correction or amendment of the record.
705.8 Appeal of an initial adverse agency determination.
705.9 Disclosure of records to a person other than the individual to whom the record pertains.
705.10 Fees.
705.11 Penalties.
705.12 Special procedures: Information furnished by other agencies.
705.13 Exemptions.
705.95 Accounting of the disclosures of records.

AUTHORITY: 5 U.S.C. 552a.

SOURCE: 67 FR 70482, Nov. 22, 2002, unless otherwise noted.

§ 705.1 Purpose and scope.

(a) The purpose of this part is to set forth rules to inform the public regarding information maintained by the United States Commission on Civil Rights about identifiable individuals and to inform those individuals how they may gain access to and correct or amend information about themselves.

(b) The rules in this part carry out the requirements of the Privacy Act of 1974 (Public Law 93–579) and in particular 5 U.S.C. 552a as added by that Act.

(c) The rules in this part apply only to records disclosed or requested under the Privacy Act of 1974, and not to requests for information made pursuant to the Freedom of Information Act, 5 U.S.C. 552.

§ 705.2 Definitions.

For the purpose of this part:

(a) *Commission* and *agency* mean the U.S. Commission on Civil Rights;

(b) *Individual* means a citizen of the United States or an alien lawfully admitted for permanent residence;

(c) *Maintain* includes maintain, collect, use, or disseminate;

(d) *Record* means any item, collection, or grouping of information about an individual that is maintained by the Commission, including, but not limited to, his or her education, financial transactions, medical history, and criminal or employment history and that contains his or her name, or the identifying number, symbol, or other identifying particular assigned to the individual;

(e) *System record* means a group of any records under the control of the Commission from which information may be retrieved by the name of the individual or by some identifying number, symbol, or other identifying particular assigned to that individual;

(f) *Statistical record* means a record in a system of records maintained for statistical research or reporting purposes only and not used in whole or in part in making any determination about an identifiable individual, except as provided in 13 U.S.C. 8;

(g) *Routine use* means, with respect to the disclosure of a record, the use of such record for a purpose that is compatible with the purpose for which it was collected;

(h) *Confidential source* means a source who furnished information to the Government under an express promise that the identity of the source would remain confidential, or, prior to September 27, 1975, under an implied promise that the identity of the source would be held in confidence; and

(i) *Act* means the Privacy Act of 1974, Public Law 93–579.

§ 705.3 Procedures for requests pertaining to individual records in a system of records.

(a) An individual seeking notification of whether a system of records contains a record pertaining to him or her or an individual seeking access to information or records pertaining to him or her, that are available under the Privacy Act of 1974, shall present his or her request in person or in writing to the General Counsel of the Commission.

(b) In addition to meeting the requirements set forth in § 705.4(c) or (d), any person who requests information under the regulations in this part shall provide a reasonably specific description of the information sought so that it may be located without undue search or inquiry. If possible, that description should include the nature of the records sought, the approximate dates covered by the record, and, if known by the requester, the system in which the record is thought to be included. Requested information that is not identified by a reasonably specific description is not an identifiable record, and the request for that information cannot be treated as a formal request.

(c) If the description is insufficient, the agency will notify the requester and, to the extent possible, indicate the additional information required. Every reasonable effort shall be made to assist a requester in the identification and location of the record or records sought.

§ 705.4 Times, places, and requirements for identification of individuals making requests and identification of records requested.

(a) The General Counsel is the designated Privacy Act Officer for the Commission.

(b) An individual making a request to the General Counsel in person may do so at the Commission's headquarters office, 624 9th Street, N.W., Washington, D.C. 20425, on any business day during business hours. Persons may also appear for purposes of identification only, at any of the regional offices of the Commission on any business day during business hours. Regional offices are located as follows:

Region I: Eastern Regional Office, Washington, DC

Connecticut, Delaware, District of Columbia, Maine, Maryland, Massachusetts, New Hampshire, New Jersey, New York, Pennsylvania, Rhode Island, Vermont, Virginia, and West Virginia.

Region II: Southern Regional Office, Atlanta, Georgia

Florida, Georgia, Kentucky, North Carolina, South Carolina, and Tennessee.

Region III: Midwestern Regional Office, Chicago, Illinois

Illinois, Indiana, Michigan, Minnesota, Ohio, and Wisconsin.

Region IV: Central Regional Office, Kansas City, Kansas

Alabama, Arkansas, Iowa, Kansas, Louisiana, Mississippi, Missouri, Nebraska, and Oklahoma.

Region V: Rocky Mountain Regional Office, Denver, Colorado

Colorado, Montana, New Mexico, North Dakota, South Dakota, Utah, and Wyoming.

Region VI: Western Regional Office, Los Angeles, California

Alaska, Arizona, California, Hawaii, Idaho, Nevada, Oregon, Texas, and Washington.

(c) An individual seeking access to records in person may establish his or her identity by the presentation of one document bearing a photograph (such as a driver's license, passport, or identification card or badge) or by the presentation of two items of identification that do not bear a photograph, but do bear both a name and address (such as a credit card). When identification is made without photographic identification, the Commission will request a signature comparison to the signature appearing on the items offered for identification, whenever possible and practical.

(d) An individual seeking access to records by mail shall establish his or her identity by a signature, address, date of birth, and one other identification, such as a copy of a driver's license, passport, identification card or badge, credit card, or other document. The words *Privacy Act Request* should be placed in capital letters on the face of the envelope in order to facilitate requests by mail.

(e) An individual seeking access in person or by mail who cannot provide the required documentation of identification may provide a notarized statement, swearing or affirming to his or her identity and to the fact that he or she understands that there are criminal penalties for the making of false statements.

(f) The parent or guardian of a minor or a person judicially determined to be incompetent, in addition to establishing the identity of the minor or incompetent person he or she represents as required by paragraphs (a) through (c) of this section, shall establish his or her own parentage or guardianship by furnishing a copy of a birth certificate showing parentage or court order establishing guardianship.

(g) An individual seeking to review information about himself or herself may be accompanied by another person of his or her own choosing. In all such cases, the individual seeking access shall be required to furnish a written statement authorizing the discussion of his or her record in the presence of the accompanying person.

§ 705.5 Disclosure of requested information to individuals.

The General Counsel, or one or more assistants designated by him or her, upon receiving a request for notification of the existence of a record or for access to a record shall:

(a) Determine whether such record exists;

(b) Determine whether access is available under the Privacy Act;

(c) Notify the requesting person of those determinations within 10 (ten) working days (excluding Saturdays, Sundays, and legal public holidays); and

(d) Provide access to information pertaining to that person that has been determined to be available.

§ 705.6 Request for correction or amendment to record.

(a) Any individual who has reviewed a record pertaining to him or her that was furnished to him or her under this part may request the agency to correct or amend all or part of that record.

(b) Each individual requesting a correction or amendment shall send the request to the General Counsel.

(c) Each request for a correction or amendment of a record shall contain the following information:

(1) The name of the individual requesting the correction or amendment.

(2) The name of the system of records in which the record sought to be amended is maintained.

(3) The location of the record system from which the record was obtained.

(4) A copy of the record sought to be amended or a description of that record.

(5) A statement of the material in the record that should be corrected or amended.

(6) A statement of the specific wording of the correction or amendment sought.

(7) A statement of the basis for the requested correction or amendment, including any material that the individual can furnish to substantiate the reasons for the amendment sought.

§ 705.7 Agency review of request for correction or amendment of the record.

Within ten (10) working days (excluding Saturdays, Sundays and legal public holidays) of the receipt of the request for the correction or amendment of a record, the General Counsel shall acknowledge receipt of the request and inform the individual that his or her request has been received and inform the individual whether further information is required before the correction or amendment can be considered. Further, the General Counsel shall promptly and, under normal circumstances, not later than thirty (30) working days after receipt of the request, make the requested correction or amendment or notify the individual of his or her refusal to do so, including in the notification the reasons for the refusal and the procedures established by the Commission by which the individual may initiate a review of that refusal. In the event of correction or amendment, an individual shall be provided with one copy of each record or portion thereof corrected or amended pursuant to his or her request without charge as evidence of the correction or amendment. The Commission shall also provide to all prior recipients of such a record, the corrected or amended information to the extent that it is relevant to the information previously furnished to a recipient pursuant to the Privacy Act.

§ 705.8 Appeal of an initial adverse agency determination.

(a) Any individual whose request for access or for a correction or amendment that has been denied, in whole or in part, by the General Counsel may appeal that decision to the Staff Director of the Commission, 624 9th Street, NW., Washington, DC 20425, or to a designee of the Staff Director.

(b) The appeal shall be in writing and shall:

(1) Name the individual making the appeal;

(2) Identify the record sought to be amended or corrected;

(3) Name the record system in which that record is contained;

(4) Contain a short statement describing the amendment or correction sought; and

(5) State the name of the person who initially denied the correction or amendment.

(c) Not later than thirty (30) working days (excluding Saturdays, Sundays, and legal public holidays) after the date on which the agency received the appeal, the Staff Director shall complete his or her review of the appeal and make a final decision thereon, unless, for good cause shown, the Staff Director extends the appeal period beyond the initial thirty (30) day appeal period. In the event of such an extension, the Staff Director shall promptly notify the individual making the appeal that the period for a final decision has been extended.

(d) After review of an appeal request, the Staff Director will send a written notice to the requester containing the following information:

(1) The decision; and if the denial is upheld, the reasons for the decision;

(2) The right of the requester to institute a civil action in a Federal District Court for judicial review of the decision if the appeal is denied; and

(3) The right of the requester to file with the Commission a concise statement setting forth the reasons for his or her disagreement with the Commission's decision denying the request. The Commission shall make this statement available to any person to whom the record is later disclosed together with a brief statement, if the Commission considers it appropriate, of the agency's reasons for denying the requested correction or amendment. These statements shall also be provided to all prior recipients of the record to the extent that it is relevant to the information previously furnished to a recipient pursuant to the Privacy Act.

§ 705.9 Disclosure of records to a person other than the individual to whom the record pertains.

(a) Any individual who desires to have his or her record disclosed to or mailed to a third person may authorize that person to act as his or her agent for that specific purpose. The authorization shall be in writing, signed by the individual, and notarized. The agent shall also submit proof of his or her own identity as provided in § 705.4.

(b) The parent of any minor individual or the legal guardian of any individual who has been declared by a court to be incompetent, due to physical or mental incapacity, may act on behalf of that individual in any matter covered by this part. A parent or guardian who desires to act on behalf of such an individual shall present suitable evidence of parentage or guardianship by birth certificate, copy of a court order or similar documents, and proof of the individual's identity as provided in § 705.4.

(c) An individual to whom a record is to be disclosed, in person, pursuant to this part may have a person of his or her own choosing accompany the individual when the record is disclosed.

§ 705.10 Fees.

If an individual requests copies of his or her records the charge shall be three (3) cents per page; however, the Commission shall not charge for copies furnished to an individual as a necessary part of the process of disclosing the record to an individual. Fees may be waived or reduced in accordance with § 704.1(e) of this chapter because of

Commission on Civil Rights § 705.13

indigency, where the cost is nominal, when it is in the public interest not to charge, or when waiver would not constitute an unreasonable expense to the Commission.

§ 705.11 Penalties.

Any person who makes a false statement in connection with any request for a record, or in any request for an amendment to a record under this part, is subject to the penalties prescribed in 18 U.S.C. 494 and 495.

§ 705.12 Special procedures: Information furnished by other agencies.

When records or information sought from the Commission include information furnished by other Federal agencies, the General Counsel shall consult with the appropriate agency prior to making a decision to disclose or to refuse to disclose the record, but the decision whether or not to disclose the record shall be made by the General Counsel.

§ 705.13 Exemptions.

(a) Under the provision of 5 U.S.C. 552a(k), it has been determined by the agency that the following exemptions are necessary and proper and may be asserted by the agency:

(1) *Exemption (k)(2) of the Act.* Investigatory material compiled for law enforcement purposes, other than material within the scope of subsection (j)(2) of the Privacy Act: *Provided, however,* That if any individual is denied any right, privilege, or benefit that he or she would otherwise be eligible for, as a result of the maintenance of such material, such material shall be provided to such individual, except to the extent that the disclosure of such material would reveal the identify of a source who furnished information to the Government under an express promise that the identity of the source would be held in confidence, or, prior to [the effective date of this section], under an implied promise that the identity of the source would be held in confidence.

(2) *Exemption (k)(4) of the Act.* Statistical personnel records that are used only to generate aggregate data or for other evaluative or analytical purposes and that are not used to make decisions on the rights, benefits, or entitlements of individuals.

(3) *Exemption (k)(5) of the Act.* Investigatory material maintained solely for the purposes of determining an individual's qualifications, eligibility, or suitability for employment in the Federal civilian service, Federal contracts, or access to classified information, but only to the extent that disclosure of such material would reveal the identity of the source who furnished information to the Government under an express promise that the identity of the source would be held in confidence, or prior to September 27, 1975, under an implied promise that the identity of the source would be held in confidence.

(4) *Exemption (k)(6) of the Act.* Testing or examination material used solely to determine individual qualifications for promotion or appointment in the Federal service the disclosure of which would compromise the objectivity or fairness of the testing or examination process.

(b) Following are Commission systems of records that are partially exempt under 5 U.S.C. 552a(k)(2), (4), (5), and (6) and the reasons for such exemptions:

(1) Appeals, Grievances, and Complaints (staff)—Commission Project, CRC–001. Exempt partially under 5 U.S.C. 552a(k)(2). The reasons for possibly asserting the exemptions are to prevent subjects of investigation from frustrating the investigatory process, to prevent disclosure of investigative techniques, to maintain the ability to obtain necessary information, to fulfill commitments made to sources to protect their identities and the confidentiality of information and to avoid endangering these sources.

(2) Complaints, CRC–003—Exempt partially under 5 U.S.C. 552a(k)(2). The reasons for possibly asserting the exemptions are to prevent subjects of investigation from frustrating the investigatory process, to prevent disclosure of investigative techniques, to maintain the ability to obtain necessary information, to fulfill commitments made to sources to protect their identities and the confidentiality of information and to avoid endangering these sources.

§ 705.95

(3) Commission projects, CRC–004—Partially exempt under 5 U.S.C. 552a(k)(2). The reasons for asserting the exemptions are to prevent subjects of investigation from frustrating the investigatory process, to prevent disclosure of investigative techniques, to maintain the ability to obtain necessary information, to fulfill commitments made to sources to protect their identities and the confidentiality of information and to avoid endangering these sources.

(4) Other Employee Programs: EEO, Troubled Employee, and Upward Mobility, CRC–006—Partially exempt under 5 U.S.C. 552a(k)(4), (5), and (6). The reasons for asserting the exemptions are to maintain the ability to obtain candid and necessary information, to fulfill commitments made to sources to protect the confidentiality of information, to avoid endangering these sources and, primarily, to facilitate proper selection or continuance of the best applicants or persons for a given position.

(5) State Advisory Committees Projects, CRC–009—Partially exempt under 5 U.S.C. 552a(k)(2). The reasons for possibly asserting the exemptions are to prevent subjects of investigation from frustrating the investigatory process, to prevent disclosure of investigative techniques, to maintain the ability to obtain necessary information, to fulfill commitments made to sources to protect their identities and the confidentiality of information and to avoid endangering these sources.

§ 705.95 Accounting of the disclosures of records.

(a) All disclosures of records covered by this part, except for the exemptions listed in paragraph (b) of this section, shall be accounted for by keeping a written record of the particular record disclosed, the name and address of the person or agency to whom or to which disclosed, and the date, nature, and purpose of the disclosure.

(b) No accounting is required for disclosures of records to those officials and employees of the Commission who have a need for the record in the performance of their duties or if disclosure would be required under the Freedom of Information Act. 5 U.S.C. 552.

(c) The accounting shall be maintained for 5 years or until the record is destroyed or transferred to the National Archives and Records Administrator for storage, in which event, the accounting pertaining to those records, unless maintained separately, shall be transferred with the records themselves.

(d) The accounting of disclosures may be recorded in any system the Commission determines is sufficient for this purpose, however, the Commission must be able to construct from its system a listing of all disclosures. The system of accounting of disclosures is not a system of records under the definition in § 705.2(e) and no accounting need be maintained for disclosure of the accounting of disclosures.

(e) Upon request of an individual to whom a record pertains, the accounting of the disclosures of that record shall be made available to the requester, provided that he or she has complied with § 705.3(a) and with § 705.4(c) or (d).

PART 706—EMPLOYEE RESPONSIBILITIES AND CONDUCT

AUTHORITY: 5 U.S.C. 7301; 42 U.S.C. 1975b(d).

§ 706.1 Cross-references to employee ethical conduct standards, financial disclosure and financial interests regulations and other conduct rules.

Employees of the United States Commission on Civil Rights are subject to the executive branch standards of ethical conduct contained in 5 CFR part 2635, the Commission regulations at 5 CFR part 7801 which supplement the executive branchwide standards, the executive branch financial disclosure regulations contained in 5 CFR part 2634, and the executive branch financial interests regulations contained in 5 CFR part 2640, as well as the executive branch employee responsibilities and conduct regulations contained in 5 CFR part 735.

[73 FR 33727, June 13, 2008]

PART 707—ENFORCEMENT OF NONDISCRIMINATION ON THE BASIS OF DISABILITY IN PROGRAMS OR ACTIVITIES CONDUCTED BY U.S. COMMISSION ON CIVIL RIGHTS

Sec.
707.1 Purpose.
707.2 Application.
707.3 Definitions.
707.4 Self-evaluation and remedial measures.
707.5 Notice.
707.6 General prohibitions against discrimination.
707.7 Employment.
707.8 Physical access.
707.9 Access to communications.
707.10 Auxiliary aids.
707.11 Eliminating discriminatory qualifications and selection criteria.
707.12 Compliance procedures.

AUTHORITY: 29 U.S.C. 791 et seq.

SOURCE: 67 FR 70482, Nov. 22, 2002, unless otherwise noted.

§ 707.1 Purpose.

The purpose of this part is to effectuate section 119 of the Rehabilitation, Comprehensive Services, and Developmental Disabilities Amendments of 1978, which amended section 504 of the Rehabilitation Act of 1973, to prohibit discrimination on the basis of disability in programs or activities conducted by Executive agencies or the United States Postal Service.

§ 707.2 Application.

This part applies to all programs and activities, including employment, conducted by the Agency.

§ 707.3 Definitions.

For the purposes of this part, the term—

(a) *Agency* means the U.S. Commission on Civil Rights and its State Advisory Committees.

(b) *Auxiliary aids* means services or devices that enable persons with impaired sensory, manual, or speaking skills to have an equal opportunity to participate in, and enjoy the benefits of, programs or activities conducted by the Agency. For example, auxiliary aids useful for persons with impaired vision include readers, Braille materials, audio recordings, and other similar services and devices. Auxiliary aids useful for persons with impaired hearing include telephone handset amplifiers, telephones compatible with hearing aids, telecommunication devices for deaf persons (TDD's), interpreters, note takers, written materials, and other similar services and devices.

(c) *Complete complaint* means a written statement that contains the complainant's name and address and describes the Agency's alleged discriminatory action in sufficient detail to inform the Agency of the nature and date of the alleged violation of section 504. It shall be signed by the complainant or by someone authorized to do so on his or her behalf. Complaints filed on behalf of classes or third parties shall describe or identify (by name, if possible) the alleged victims of discrimination.

(d) *Facility* means all or any portion of buildings, structures, equipment, roads, walks, parking lots, vehicles, or other real or personal property.

(e) *Individual with disabilities* means any person who has a physical or mental impairment that substantially limits one or more major life activities, has a record of such an impairment, or is regarded as having such an impairment. As used in this definition, the phrase:

(1) Physical or mental impairment includes—

(i) Any physiological disorder or condition, cosmetic disfigurement, or anatomical loss affecting one or more of the following body systems: Neurological, musculoskeletal; special sense organs; respiratory, including speech organs; cardiovascular; reproductive; digestive; genitourinary; hemic and lymphatic; skin; and endocrine; or

(ii) Any mental or psychological disorder, such as mental retardation, organic brain syndrome, emotional or mental illness, and specific learning disabilities. The term physical or mental impairment includes, but is not limited to, such diseases and conditions as orthopedic, visual, speech and hearing impairments, cerebral palsy, epilepsy, muscular dystrophy, multiple sclerosis, cancer, heart disease, diabetes, mental retardation, emotional illness, drug addiction, and alcoholism.

§ 707.4

(2) *Major life activities* includes functions such as caring for one's self, performing manual tasks, walking, seeing, hearing, speaking, breathing, learning, and working.

(3) *Has a record of such an impairment* means has a history of, or has been misclassified as having, a mental or physical impairment that substantially limits one or more major life activities.

(4) *Is regarded as having an impairment* means—

(i) Has a physical or mental impairment that does not substantially limit major life activities but is treated by the Agency as constituting such a limitation;

(ii) Has a physical or mental impairment that substantially limits major life activities only as a result of the attitudes of others toward such impairment; or

(iii) Has none of the impairments defined in paragraph (e)(1) of this definition but is treated by the Agency as having such an impairment.

(f) *Qualified individual with disabilities* means—

(1) With respect to any Agency program or activity under which a person is required to perform services or to achieve a level of accomplishment, an individual with disabilities who meets the essential eligibility requirements and who can achieve the purpose of the program or activity without modifications in the program or activity that the Agency can demonstrate would result in a fundamental alteration in its nature; and

(2) With respect to employment, an individual with disabilities who meets the definition set forth in 29 CFR 1614.203, which is made applicable to this part by § 707.7.

(3) With respect to any other Agency program or activity, an individual with disabilities who meets the essential eligibility requirements for participation in, or receipt of benefits from, that program or activity.

(g) *Section 504* means section 504 of the Rehabilitation Act of 1973 (Public Law 93–112, 87 Stat. 394 (29 U.S.C. 794), as amended through 1998. As used in this part, section 504 applies only to programs or activities conducted by the Agency. The Agency does not operate any programs of Federal financial assistance to other entities.

§ 707.4 Self-evaluation and remedial measures.

(a) The Agency shall, before February 16, 1991 evaluate its current policies and practices, and the effects thereof, that do not or may not meet the requirements of this part, and, to the extent modification of any such policies and practices is required, the Agency shall proceed to make the necessary modifications.

(b) The Agency shall provide an opportunity to interested persons, including individuals with disabilities and organizations representing individuals with disabilities, to participate in the self-evaluation process by submitting comments (both oral and written).

(c) The Agency shall, for at least three years following completion of the evaluation required under paragraph (a) of this section, maintain on file and make available for public inspection:

(1) A description of areas examined and any problems identified; and

(2) A description of any modifications made.

§ 707.5 Notice.

(a) The Agency shall make available to all employees, applicants, and other interested persons, as appropriate, information regarding the provisions of this part and its applicability to the programs or activities conducted by the Agency, and such information shall be made available to the extent the Staff Director finds necessary to apprise such persons of the protections against discrimination assured them by section 504 and this part.

(b) The Agency shall ensure that interested persons, including persons with impaired vision or hearing, can obtain information as to the existence and location of accessible services, activities, and facilities.

(c) The Agency shall take appropriate steps to provide individuals with disabilities with information regarding their section 504 rights under the Agency's programs or activities.

§ 707.6 General prohibitions against discrimination.

(a) No qualified individual with disabilities shall, on the basis of disability, be excluded from participation in, be denied the benefits of, or otherwise be subjected to discrimination under any program or activity conducted by the Agency.

(b)(1) The Agency, in providing any aid, benefit, or service, shall not, directly or through contractual, licensing, or other arrangements, on the basis of disability—

(i) Deny a qualified individual with disabilities the opportunity to participate in or benefit from the aid, benefit(s), or service(s);

(ii) Afford a qualified individual with disabilities an opportunity to participate in or benefit from the aid, benefit(s), or service(s) that are not equal to that afforded others;

(iii) Provide a qualified individual with disabilities with an aid, benefit(s), or service(s) that are not as effective in affording equal opportunity to obtain the same result, to gain the same benefit, or to reach the same level of achievement as that provided to others;

(iv) Provide different or separate aid, benefits, or services to individuals with disabilities or to any class of individuals with disabilities than are provided to others unless such action is necessary to provide qualified individuals with disabilities with aid, benefits, or services that are as effective as those provided to others;

(v) Deny a qualified individual with disabilities the opportunity to participate as a member of planning or advisory boards or committees; or

(vi) Otherwise limit a qualified individual with disabilities in the enjoyment of any right, privilege, advantage, or opportunity enjoyed by others receiving the aid, benefit(s), or service(s).

(2) The Agency shall not deny a qualified individual with disabilities the opportunity to participate in programs or activities that are not separate or different, despite the existence of permissibly separate or different programs or activities.

(3) The Agency shall not, directly or through contractual or other arrangements, utilize criteria or methods of administration the purpose or effect of which would—

(i) Subject qualified individuals with disabilities to discrimination on the basis of disability; or

(ii) Defeat or substantially impair accomplishment of the objectives of a program or activity with respect to individuals with disabilities.

(4) The Agency shall not in determining the site or location of a facility or activity make selections the purpose or effect of which would—

(i) Exclude individuals with disabilities from, deny them the benefits of, or otherwise subject them to discrimination under any program or activity conducted by the Agency; or

(ii) Defeat or substantially impair the accomplishment of the objectives of a program or activity with respect to individuals with disabilities.

(5) The Agency, in the selection of procurement contractors, shall not use criteria that subject qualified individuals with disabilities to discrimination on the basis of disability.

(c) The exclusion of non-disabled persons from the benefits of a program limited by Federal statute or Executive order to individuals with disabilities or the exclusion of a specific class of individuals with disabilities from a program limited by Federal statute or Executive order to a different class of individuals with disabilities is not prohibited by this part.

(d) The Agency shall administer programs and activities in the most integrated setting appropriate to the needs of qualified individuals with disabilities.

§ 707.7 Employment.

No qualified individual with disabilities shall, on the basis of disability, be subjected to discrimination in employment under any program or activity conducted by the Agency. The definitions, requirements, and procedures of section 501 of the Rehabilitation Act of 1973 (29 U.S.C. 791), as established by the Equal Employment Opportunity Commission in 29 CFR 1614.101 through 1614.110, shall apply to employment in programs or activities conducted by the Agency.

§ 707.8 Physical access.

(a) *Discrimination prohibited.* Except as otherwise provided in this section, no qualified individual with disabilities shall, because the Agency's facilities are inaccessible to or unusable by individuals with disabilities, be denied the benefits of, be excluded from participation in, or otherwise be subjected to discrimination under any program or activity conducted by the Agency.

(b) *Existing facilities-program access—* (1) *Existing facilities defined.* For the purpose of this section, existing facilities means those facilities owned, leased or used through some other arrangement by the Agency on March 28, 1990.

(2) *General.* The Agency shall operate each program or activity conducted in an existing facility so that the program or activity, when viewed in its entirety, is readily accessible to and usable by individuals with disabilities. This paragraph does not—

(i) Necessarily require the Agency to make each of its existing facilities accessible to and usable by individuals with disabilities

(ii) Require the Agency to take any action that it can demonstrate would result in a fundamental alteration in the nature of a program or activity or in undue financial and administrative burdens. In those circumstances where Agency personnel believe that the proposed action would fundamentally alter the program or activity or would result in undue financial and administrative burdens, the Agency has the burden of proving that compliance with this paragraph would result in such alteration or burdens. The decision that compliance would result in such alteration or burdens must be made by the Staff Director or his or her designee after considering all Agency resources available for use in the funding and operation of the conducted program or activity, and must be accompanied by a written statement of the reasons for reaching that conclusion. If an action would result in such an alteration or such burdens, the Agency shall take any other action that would not result in such an alteration or such burdens but would nevertheless ensure that individuals with disabilities receive the benefits and services of the program or activity.

(3) *Methods.* (i) The Agency may comply with the requirements of this section through such means as redesign of equipment, reassignment of services to accessible buildings, assignment of aides to individuals with disabilities, delivery of services at alternative accessible sites, alteration of existing facilities and construction of new facilities, use of accessible vehicles, or any other methods that result in making its program or activities readily accessible to and usable by individuals with disabilities.

(ii) The Agency is not required to make structural changes in existing facilities where other methods are effective in achieving compliance with paragraph (b)(2) of this section. The Agency, in making alterations to existing buildings to achieve program accessibility, shall meet accessibility requirements imposed by the Architectural Barriers Act of 1968, 42 U.S.C. 4151 through 4157,

(iii) In choosing among available methods for meeting the requirements of this section, the Agency shall give priority to those methods that offer programs and activities to qualified individuals with disabilities in the most integrated setting appropriate to the needs of qualified individuals with disabilities.

(4) *Time period for compliance.* The Agency shall comply with the obligations established under this section before April 17, 1990, except that where structural changes in facilities are undertaken, such changes shall be made before February 16, 1993, but in any event as expeditiously as possible.

(5) *Transition plan.* In the event that structural changes to facilities will be undertaken to achieve program accessibility, the Agency shall develop, before August 16, 1990, a transition plan setting forth the steps necessary to complete such changes. The Agency shall provide an opportunity to interested persons, including individuals with disabilities and organizations representing individuals with disabilities, to participate in the development of the transition plan by submitting comments (both oral and written). A copy of the transition plan shall be made

available for public inspection. The plan shall, at a minimum—

(i) Identify physical obstacles in the Agency's facilities that limit the accessibility of its programs or activities to individuals with disabilities;

(ii) Describe in detail the methods that will be used to make the facilities accessible;

(iii) Specify the schedule for taking the steps necessary to achieve compliance with this paragraph and, if the time period of the transition plan is longer than 1 year, identify steps that will be taken during each year of the transition period; and

(iv) Indicate the official response for implementation of the plan.

(6) The Agency shall provide signs at a primary entrance to each of its inaccessible facilities, directing users to a location at which they can obtain information about accessible facilities. The international symbol for accessibility shall be used at each primary entrance of an accessible facility.

(c) *New purchases, leases, or other arrangements.* (1) Any building or facility acquired after March 28, 1990, whether by purchase, lease (other than lease renewal), or any other arrangement, shall be readily accessible to and usable by individuals with disabilities.

(2) Nothing in this paragraph requires the Agency to take any action that it can demonstrate would result in a fundamental alteration in the nature of a program or activity or in undue financial and administrative burdens. In those circumstances where Agency personnel believe that the proposed action would fundamentally alter the program or activity or would result in undue financial and administrative burdens, the Agency has the burden of proving that compliance with this paragraph would result in such alteration or burdens. The decision that compliance would result in such alteration or burdens must be made by the Staff Director or his or her designee after considering all Agency resources available for use in the funding and operation of the conducted program or activity, and must be accompanied by a written statement of the reasons for reaching that conclusion. If an action would result in such an alteration or such burdens, the Agency shall take any other action that would not result in such an alteration or such burdens but would nevertheless ensure that individuals with disabilities receive the benefits and services of the program or activity.

(d) New construction and alterations. Each building or part of a building that is constructed or altered by, on behalf of, or for the use of the Agency shall be designed, constructed, or altered so as to be readily accessible to and usable by individuals with disabilities in accordance with the requirements imposed by the Architectural Barriers Act of 1968, 42 U.S.C. 4151 through 4157.

§ 707.9 **Access to communications.**

(a) Discrimination prohibited. Except as otherwise provided in this section, no qualified individual with disabilities shall, because the Agency's communications are inaccessible to or unusable by individuals with disabilities, be denied the benefits of, be excluded from participation in, or otherwise be subjected to discrimination under any program or activity conducted by the Agency.

(b) The Agency shall take appropriate steps to ensure effective communication with applicants, participants, personnel of other Federal entities, and members of the public.

(c) Specific requirements regarding oral communications—(1) Telecommunications devices for deaf persons. (i) The Agency headquarters and each regional office shall maintain and reliably answer at least one telecommunications device for deaf persons (TDD) or equally effective telecommunications device.

(ii) The Agency shall ensure that all Agency letterhead, forms, and other documents listing any Agency telephone number list the appropriate TDD numbers.

(2) Interpreter service. (i) The Agency shall establish a reliable system for the provision of qualified interpreters to individuals with disabilities for Agency programs or activities. This provision does not require the Agency to have an interpreter on staff, but does require the Agency to be able to provide a qualified interpreter on reasonable notice.

(ii) Notice of the availability of interpreter service shall be included in all announcements notifying the public of Agency activities to which the public is invited or which it is permitted to attend, including but not limited to the Commission's meetings, consultations, hearings, press conferences, and State Advisory Committee conferences and meetings. This notice shall designate the Agency official(s) and the address, telephone and TDD number to call to request interpreter services.

(d) Specific requirements for printed communications. (1) The Agency shall establish a system to provide to individuals with disabilities appropriate reader or taping service for all Agency publications that are available to the public. This provision does not require the Agency to have a reader or taper on staff, but does require the Agency to be able to provide appropriate reader or taping service within a reasonable time and on reasonable notice. The Agency shall effectively notify qualified individuals with disabilities of the availability of reader or taping services.

(2) Notice of the availability of reader or taping service shall be included in all publications that are available to the public. This notice shall designate the Agency official(s) and the address, telephone, and TDD number to call to request interpreter services.

(e) Nothing in this section or §707.10 requires the Agency to take any action that it can demonstrate would result in a fundamental alteration in the nature of a program or activity or in undue financial and administrative burdens. In those circumstances where Agency personnel believe that the proposed action would fundamentally alter the program or activity or would result in undue financial and administrative burdens, the Agency has the burden of proving that compliance with this section or §707.10 would result in such alteration or burdens. The decision that compliance would result in such alteration or burdens must be made by the Staff Director or his or her designee after considering all Agency resources available for use in the funding and operation of the conducted program or activity and must be accompanied by a written statement of the reasons for reaching that conclusion. If an action required to comply with this paragraph would result in such an alteration or such burdens, the Agency shall take any other action that would not result in such an alteration or such burdens but would nevertheless ensure that, to the maximum extent possible, individuals with disabilities receive the benefits and services of the program or activity.

§ 707.10 Auxiliary aids.

(a) The Agency shall furnish appropriate auxiliary aids where necessary to afford an individual with disabilities an equal opportunity to participate in, and enjoy the benefits of, a program or activity conducted by the Agency.

(b) In determining what type of auxiliary aid is necessary, the Agency shall give primary consideration to the requests of the individual with disabilities.

(c) The Agency need not provide individually prescribed devices, readers for personal use or study, or other devices of a personal nature.

§ 707.11 Eliminating discriminatory qualifications and selection criteria.

The Agency shall not make use of any qualification standard, eligibility requirement, or selection criterion that excludes particular classes of individuals with disabilities from an Agency program or activity merely because the persons are disabled, without regard to an individual's actual ability to participate. An irrebuttable presumption of inability to participate based upon a disability shall be permissible only if the condition would, in all instances, prevent an individual from meeting the essential eligibility requirements for participating in, or receiving the benefits of, the particular program or activity.

§ 707.12 Compliance procedures.

(a) Except as provided in paragraph (b) of this section, this section applies to all allegations of discrimination on the basis of disability in programs or activities conducted by the Agency.

(b) The Agency shall process complaints alleging violations of section 504 with respect to employment according to the procedures established in 29 U.S.C. 791 by the Equal Employment Opportunity Commission in 29 CFR part 1613 pursuant to section 501 of the

Commission on Civil Rights

§ 708.1

Rehabilitation Act of 1973 (29 U.S.C. 791).

(c) Responsibility for implementation and operation of this section shall be vested in the Office of General Counsel.

(d) The Agency shall accept and investigate all complete complaints for which it has jurisdiction. All complete complaints must be filed within 180 days of the alleged act of discrimination. The Agency may extend this time period for good cause.

(e) If the Agency receives a complaint over which it does not have jurisdiction, it shall promptly notify the complainant and shall make reasonable efforts to refer the complaint to the appropriate Government entity.

(f) The Agency shall notify the Architectural and Transportation Barriers Compliance Board upon receipt of any complaint alleging that a building or facility that is subject to the Architectural Barriers Act of 1968, 42 U.S.C. 4151 through 4157, is not readily accessible to and usable by individuals with disabilities.

(g) Within 180 days of the receipt of a complete complaint for which it has jurisdiction, the Agency shall notify the complainant of the results of the investigation in a letter containing—

(1) Findings of fact and conclusions of law;

(2) A description of a remedy for each violation found; and

(3) A notice of the right to appeal.

(h) Appeals of the findings of fact and conclusions of law or remedies must be filed by the complainant within 90 days of receipt from the Agency of the letter required by paragraph (g) of this section. The Staff Director may extend this time for good cause.

(i) Timely appeals shall be accepted and processed by the Staff Director or the Staff Director's designee.

(j) The Agency shall notify the complainant in writing of the results of the appeal within 60 days of the receipt of the request. If the head of the Agency determines that additional information is needed from the complainant, it shall have 60 days from the date it receives the additional information to make its determination on the appeal.

(k) The time limits cited in paragraphs (d), (g), (h), and (j) of this section may be extended for an individual case when the Staff Director determines that there is good cause, based on the particular circumstances of that case, for the extension.

(l) The Agency may delegate its authority for conducting complaint investigations to other Federal agencies; however, the authority for making the final determination may not be delegated to another Agency.

PART 708—COLLECTION BY SALARY OFFSET FROM INDEBTED CURRENT AND FORMER EMPLOYEES

Sec.
708.1 Purpose and scope.
708.2 Policy.
708.3 Definitions.
708.4 Applicability.
708.5 Notice.
708.6 Petitions for hearing.
708.7 Hearing procedures.
708.8 Written decision.
708.9 Coordinating offset with another Federal agency.
708.10 Procedures for salary offset.
708.11 Refunds.
708.12 Statute of limitations.
708.13 Non-waiver of rights by payments.
708.14 Interest, penalties, and administrative costs.

AUTHORITY: 5 U.S.C. 5514.

SOURCE: 67 FR 70482, Nov. 22, 2002, unless otherwise noted.

§ 708.1 Purpose and scope.

(a) The regulations in this part provide the procedure pursuant to 5 U.S.C. 5514 and 5 CFR 550.1101 through 550.1110 for the collection by administrative offset of a Federal employee's salary without his or her consent to satisfy certain debts owed to the Federal government. This procedure applies to all Federal employees who owe debts to the U.S. Commission on Civil Rights (Commission). This provision does not apply when the employee consents to recovery from his or her current pay account.

(b) This procedure does not apply to debts or claims arising under:

(1) The Internal Revenue Code (26 U.S.C. 1 et seq.);

(2) The Social Security Act (42 U.S.C. 301 et seq.);

§ 708.2

(3) The tariff laws of the United States; or

(4) To any case where collection of a debt by salary offset is explicitly provided for or prohibited by another statute (*e.g.*, travel advances in 5 U.S.C. 5705 and employee training expenses in 5 U.S.C. 4108).

(c) The Commission shall except from salary offset provisions any adjustments to pay arising out of an employee's election of coverage or a change in coverage under a Federal benefits programs requiring periodic payroll deductions from pay, if the amount to be recovered was accumulated over four pay periods or less.

(d) These procedures do not preclude an employee or former employee from requesting a waiver of a salary overpayment under 5 U.S.C. 5584 or 10 U.S.C. 2774 or in any way questioning the amount or validity of the debt by submitting a subsequent claim to the General Accounting Office (GAO) in accordance with procedures prescribed by the GAO. In addition, this procedure does not preclude an employee from requesting a waiver pursuant to other statutory provisions applicable to the particular debt being collected.

§ 708.2 Policy.

It is the policy of the Commission to apply the procedures in the regulations in this part uniformly and consistently in the collection of internal debts from its current and former employees.

§ 708.3 Definitions.

For the purposes of the regulations in this part the following definitions apply:

(a) *Agency* means:

(1) An Executive agency as defined in 5 U.S.C. 105, including the U.S. Postal Service and the U.S. Postal Rate Commission;

(2) A military department as defined in 5 U.S.C. 102;

(3) An agency or court in the judicial branch, including a court as defined in 28 U.S.C. 610, the District Court for the Northern Mariana Islands, and the Judicial panel on Multidistrict Litigation;

(4) An agency of the legislative branch, including the U.S. Senate and the U.S. House of Representatives; and

(5) Other independent establishments that are entities of the Federal Government.

(b) *Creditor agency* means the agency to which the debt is owed.

(c) *Debt* means an amount owed to the United States from sources, which include loans insured or guaranteed by the United States and amounts due the United States from fees, leases, rents, royalties, services, sales of real or personal property, overpayments, penalties, damages, interest, fines and forfeitures (except those arising under the Uniform Code of Military Justice), and all other similar sources.

(d) *Deputy Staff Director* means the Deputy Staff Director of the Commission or in his or her absence, or in the event of a vacancy in the position or its elimination, the Director of Human Resources.

(e) *Disposable pay* means that part of current basic pay, special pay, incentive pay, retired pay, retainer pay, or in the case of an employee not entitled to basic pay, other authorized pay remaining from an employee's Federal pay after required deductions for social security, Federal, state or local income tax, health insurance premiums, retirement contributions, life insurance premiums, Federal employment taxes, and any other deductions that are required to be withheld by law.

(f) *Employee* means a current employee of an agency, including a current member of the Armed Forces or a Reserve of the Armed Forces (Reserves).

(g) *Former employee* means an employee who is no longer employed with the Commission but is currently employed with another Federal agency.

(h) *FCCS* means the Federal Claims Collection Standards jointly published by the Department of Justice and the General Accounting Office at 4 CFR chapter I.

(i) *Hearing official* means an individual responsible for conducting any hearing with respect to the existence or amount of a debt claimed, and who renders a decision on the basis of such hearing. A hearing official may not be under the supervision or control of the Deputy Staff Director of the Commission.

(j) *Paying agency* means the agency employing the individual who owes the debt and is responsible for authorizing the payment of his or her current pay.

(k) *Pay interval* will normally be the biweekly pay period but may be some regularly recurring period of time in which pay is received.

(l) *Retainer pay* means the pay above the maximum rate of an employee's grade that he or she is allowed to keep in special situations rather than having the employee's rate of basic pay reduced.

(m) *Salary offset* means an administrative offset to collect a debt under 5 U.S.C. 5514 by deduction(s) at one or more officially established pay intervals from the current pay account of an employee without his or her consent.

(n) *Waiver* means the cancellation, remission, forgiveness, or non-recovery of a debt allegedly owed by an employee to an agency as permitted or required by 5 U.S.C. 5584, 10 U.S.C. 2774, or 5 U.S.C. 8346(b), or any other law.

§ 708.4 Applicability.

The regulations in this part are to be followed when:

(a) The Commission is owed a debt by an individual who is a current employee of the Commission; or

(b) The Commission is owed a debt by an individual currently employed by another Federal agency; or

(c) The Commission employs an individual who owes a debt to another Federal agency.

§ 708.5 Notice.

(a) Deductions shall not be made unless the employee who owes the debt has been provided with written notice signed by the Deputy Staff Director or in his or her absence, or in the event of a vacancy in that position or its elimination, the Director of Human Resources (or the U.S. Department of Agriculture, National Finance Center acting on behalf of the Commission) of the debt at least 30 days before salary offset commences.

(b) The written notice from the Deputy Staff Director, acting on behalf of the Commission, as the creditor agency, shall contain:

(1) A statement that the debt is owed and an explanation of its origin, nature, and amount;

(2) The agency's intention to collect the debt by deducting from the employee's current disposable pay account;

(3) The amount, frequency, proposed beginning date, and duration of the intended deduction(s);

(4) An explanation of the requirements concerning the current interest rate, penalties, and administrative costs, including a statement that such charges will be assessed unless excused in accordance with the Federal Claims Collections Standards (4 CFR chapter I);

(5) The employee's right to inspect, request, or receive a copy of the government records relating to the debt;

(6) The employee's right to enter into a written repayment schedule for the voluntary repayment of the debt in lieu of offset;

(7) The right to a hearing conducted by an impartial hearing official (either an administrative law judge or an official who is not under the control of the Commission);

(8) The method and time period for petitioning for a hearing;

(9) A statement that the timely filing (*i.e.*, within 15 calendar days) of a petition for a hearing will stay the commencement of collection proceedings;

(10) A statement that a final decision on the hearing (if one is requested) will be issued at the earliest practical date but not later than 60 days after the filing of the petition requesting the hearing unless the employee requests and the hearing official grants a delay in the proceedings.

(11) A statement that an employee knowingly submitting false or frivolous statements (5 CFR 550.1101), representations, or evidence may subject the employee to disciplinary procedures under 5 U.S.C. 7501 *et seq.* and 5 CFR part 752; penalties under the False Claims Act, 31 U.S.C. 3729–3731; or criminal penalties under 18 U.S.C. 286, 287, 1001, and 1002;

(12) A statement of other rights and remedies available to the employee under statutes or regulations governing the program for which the collection is being made;

(13) A statement that an employee will be promptly refunded any amount paid or deducted for a debt that is later waived or found not valid unless there are applicable contractual or statutory provisions to the contrary; and

(14) The name, address, and phone number of an official who can be contacted concerning the indebtedness.

§ 708.6 Petitions for hearing.

(a) Except as provided in paragraph (d) of this section, an employee who wants a hearing must file a written petition for a hearing to be received by the Deputy Staff Director not later than 15 calendar days from the date of receipt of the Notice of Offset. The petition must state why the employee believes the determination of the Commission concerning the existence or amount of the debt is in error.

(b) The petition must be signed by the employee and should identify and explain with reasonable specificity and brevity the facts, evidence, and witnesses that the employee believes support his or her position.

(c) If the employee objects to the percentage of disposable pay to be deducted from each check, the petition should state the objection and the reasons for it.

(d) If the employee files a petition for a hearing later than the 15 calendar days from the date of receipt of the Notice of Offset, as described in paragraph (a) of this section, the hearing official may accept the request if the employee can show that there was good cause (such as due to circumstances beyond his or her control or because he or she was not informed or aware of the time limit) for failing to meet the deadline date.

(e) An employee will not be granted a hearing and will have his or her disposable pay offset in accordance with the Deputy Staff Director's offset schedule if he or she fails to show good cause why he or she failed to file the petition for a hearing within the stated time limits.

§ 708.7 Hearing procedures.

(a) If an employee timely files a petition for a hearing under § 708.6, the Deputy Staff Director shall select the time, date, and location for the hearing.

(b) The hearing shall be conducted by an impartial hearing official.

(c) The Commission, as the creditor agency, will have the burden of proving the existence of the debt.

(d) The employee requesting the hearing shall have the burden of proof to demonstrate that the existence or amount of the debt is in error.

§ 708.8 Written decision.

(a) The hearing official shall issue a written opinion no later than sixty (60) days after the filing of the petition for hearing; or no longer than sixty (60) days from the proceedings if an extension has been granted pursuant to § 708.5(b)(10).

(b) The written opinion will include: A statement of the facts presented to demonstrate the nature and origin of the alleged debt; the hearing official's analysis, findings, and conclusions; the amount and validity of the debt; and, if applicable, the repayment schedule.

§ 708.9 Coordinating offset with another Federal agency.

(a) The Commission is the creditor agency when the Deputy Staff Director determines that an employee of another Federal agency owes a delinquent debt to the Commission. The Deputy Staff Director shall, as appropriate:

(1) Arrange for a hearing upon the proper petitioning by the employee;

(2) Certify in writing that the employee of the paying agency owes the debt, the amount, and basis of the debt, the date on which payment is due, the date the Government's right to collect the debt first accrued, and that the Commission's regulations for salary offset have been approved by the Office of Personnel Management;

(3) If the collection must be made in installments, the Commission, as the creditor agency, will advise the paying agency of the amount or percentage of disposable pay to be collected in each installment and the number and the commencement date of the installments;

(4) Advise the paying agency of the actions taken under 5 U.S.C. 5514(a) and provide the dates on which action was taken, unless the employee has

consented to salary offset in writing or signed a statement acknowledging receipt of procedures required by law. The written consent or acknowledgement must be sent to the paying agency;

(5) If the employee is in the process of separating, the Commission will submit its debt claim to the paying agency as provided in this part. The paying agency must certify any amounts already collected, notify the employee, and send a copy of the certification of the monies already collected and notice of the employee's separation to the Commission. If the paying agency is aware that the employee is entitled to Civil Service or Foreign Service Retirement and Disability Fund or similar payments, it must provide written notification to the agency has been rendered in favor of the Commission.

(6) If the employee has already separated and all payments due from the paying agency have been paid, the Assistant Staff Director for Management may request, unless otherwise prohibited, that money payable to the employee from the Civil Service Retirement and Disability Fund or other similar funds be collected by administrative offset. The Commission will provide the agency responsible for these payments with a properly certified claim.

(b) The Commission is the paying agency when an employee of this agency owes a debt to another Federal agency that is the creditor agency.

(1) Upon receipt of a properly certified debt claim from a creditor agency, deductions will be scheduled to begin at the next established pay interval.

(2) The Commission must give the employee written notice that it has received a certified debt claim from a creditor agency (including the amount), and the date that deductions will be scheduled to begin and the amount of the deduction.

(3) The Commission shall not review the merits of the creditor agency's determination of the amount of the certified claim or of its validity.

(4) If the employee transfers to another paying agency after the creditor agency has submitted its debt claim but before the debt is collected completely, the Commission must certify the total amount collected to the creditor agency with notice of the employee's transfer. One copy of this certification must be furnished to the employee. The creditor agency will submit a properly certified claim to the new paying agency before collection can be resumed.

(5) When the Commission, as a paying agency, receives an incomplete debt claim from a creditor agency, it must return the debt claim with a notice that procedures under 5 U.S.C. 5514 and this subpart must be provided and a properly certified debt claim received before action will be taken to collect from the employee's current pay account.

§ 708.10 Procedures for salary offset.

(a) Deductions to liquidate an employee's debt will be by the method and in the amount stated in the Assistant Staff Director for Management's written notice of intent to collect from the employee's current pay, unless alternative arrangements for repayment are made.

(b) If the employee filed a petition for a hearing with the Assistant Staff Director for Management before the expiration of the period provided, then deductions will begin after the hearing official has provided the employee with a hearing, and a final written decision has been rendered in favor of the Commission.

(c) A debt will be collected in a lump-sum if possible.

(d) If an employee is financially unable to pay in one lump sum or the amount of the debt exceeds 15 percent of disposable pay for an officially established pay interval, collection must be made in installments. The size of the installment deduction(s) will bear a reasonable relationship to the size of the debt and the deduction will be established for a period not greater than the anticipated period of employment. The deduction for the pay intervals for any period must not exceed 15% of disposable pay unless the employee has agreed in writing to a deduction of a greater amount. If possible, the installment payment will be sufficient in size and frequency to liquidate the debt in no more than three years.

(e) Installment payments may be less than 15 percent of disposable pay if the Assistant Staff Director for Management determines that the 15 percent deduction would create an extreme financial hardship.

(f) Installment payments of less than $25.00 per pay period or $50.00 per month, will only be accepted in the most unusual circumstances.

(g) Unliquidated debts may be offset by the paying agency under 31 U.S.C. 3716 against any financial payment due to a separating employee including but not limited to final salary payment, retired pay, or lump sum leave, etc. as of the date of separation to the extent necessary to liquidate the debt.

(h) If the debt cannot be liquidated by offset from any final payment due a separated employee it may be recovered by the offset in accordance with 31 U.S.C. 3716 from any later payments due the former employee from the United States.

§ 708.11 Refunds.

(a) The Commission will refund promptly any amounts deducted to satisfy debts owned to the Commission when the debt is waived, found not owed to the Commission, or when directed by an administrative or judicial order; or the creditor agency will promptly return any amounts deducted and forwarded by the Commission to satisfy debts owed to the creditor agency when the debt is waived, found not owed, or when directed by an administrative or judicial order.

(b) Upon receipt of monies returned in accordance with paragraph (a) of this section, the Commission will refund the amount to the current or former employee.

(c) Unless required by law, refunds under this section shall not bear interest nor shall liability be conferred to the Commission for debt or refunds owed by other creditor agencies.

§ 708.12 Statute of limitations.

If a debt has been outstanding for more than 10 years after the agency's right to collect the debt first accrued, the agency may not collect by salary offset unless facts material to the government's right to collect were not known and could not reasonably have been known by the official or officials who were charged with the responsibility for discovery and collection of such debts.

§ 708.13 Non-waiver of rights by payments.

An employee's involuntary payment of all or any part of a debt collected under the regulations in this part will not be construed as a waiver of any rights that employee may have under 5 U.S.C. 5514 or any other provision of contract or law unless there are statutory or contractual provisions to the contrary.

§ 708.14 Interest, penalties, and administrative costs.

Charges may be assessed for interest, penalties, and administrative costs.

PARTS 709–799 [RESERVED]

CHAPTER VIII—OFFICE OF PERSONNEL MANAGEMENT

Part		Page
800	Multi-State Plan Program	293
801–899	[Reserved]	

PART 800—MULTI-STATE PLAN PROGRAM

Subpart A—General Provisions and Definitions

Sec.
800.10 Basis and scope.
800.20 Definitions.

Subpart B—Multi-State Plan Program Issuer Requirements

800.101 General requirements.
800.102 Compliance with Federal law.
800.103 Authority to contract with issuers.
800.104 Phased expansion, etc.
800.105 Benefits.
800.106 Cost-sharing limits, advance payments of premium tax credits, and cost-sharing reductions.
800.107 Levels of coverage.
800.108 Assessments and user fees.
800.109 Network adequacy.
800.110 Service area.
800.111 Accreditation requirement.
800.112 Reporting requirements.
800.113 Benefit plan material or information.
800.114 Compliance with applicable State law.
800.115 Level playing field.
800.116 Process for dispute resolution.

Subpart C—Premiums, Rating Factors, Medical Loss Ratios, and Risk Adjustment

800.201 General requirements.
800.202 Rating factors.
800.203 Medical loss ratio.
800.204 Reinsurance, risk corridors, and risk adjustment.

Subpart D—Application and Contracting Procedures

800.301 Application process.
800.302 Review of applications.
800.303 MSP Program contracting.
800.304 Term of the contract.
800.305 Contract renewal process.
800.306 Nonrenewal.

Subpart E—Compliance

800.401 Contract performance.
800.402 Contract quality assurance.
800.403 Fraud and abuse.
800.404 Compliance actions.
800.405 Reconsideration of compliance actions.

Subpart F—Appeals by Enrollees of Denials of Claims for Payment or Service

800.501 General requirements.
800.502 MSP issuer internal claims and appeals.
800.503 External review.
800.504 Judicial review.

Subpart G—Miscellaneous

800.601 Reservation of authority.
800.602 Consumer choice with respect to certain services.
800.603 Disclosure of information.

AUTHORITY: Sec. 1334 of Pub. L. 111–148, 124 Stat. 119; Pub. L. 111–152, 124 Stat. 1029 (42 U.S.C. 18054).

SOURCE: 80 FR 9655, Feb. 24, 2015; 80 FR 16577, Mar. 30, 2015, unless otherwise noted.

Subpart A—General Provisions and Definitions

§ 800.10 Basis and scope.

(a) *Basis.* This part is based on the following sections of title I of the Affordable Care Act:

(1) *1001.* Amendments to the Public Health Service Act.

(2) *1302.* Essential Health Benefits Requirements.

(3) *1311.* Affordable Choices of Health Benefit Plans.

(4) *1324.* Level Playing Field.

(5) *1334.* Multi-State Plans.

(6) *1341.* Transitional Reinsurance Program for Individual Market in Each State.

(7) *1342.* Establishment of Risk Corridors for Plans in Individual and Small Group Markets.

(8) *1343.* Risk Adjustment.

(b) *Scope.* This part establishes standards for health insurance issuers to contract with the United States Office of Personnel Management (OPM) to offer Multi-State Plan (MSP) options to provide health insurance coverage on Exchanges for each State. It also establishes standards for appeal of a decision by OPM affecting the issuer's participation in the MSP Program and standards for an enrollee in an MSP option to appeal denials of payment or services by an MSP issuer.

§ 800.20 Definitions.

For purposes of this part:

Actuarial value (AV) has the meaning given that term in 45 CFR 156.20.

Affordable Care Act means the Patient Protection and Affordable Care Act (Pub. L. 111–148), as amended by the

§ 800.20

Health Care and Education Reconciliation Act of 2010 (Pub. L. 111–152).

Applicant means an issuer or group of issuers that has submitted an application to OPM to be considered for participation in the Multi-State Plan Program.

Benefit plan material or information means explanations or descriptions, whether printed or electronic, that describe a health insurance issuer's products. The term does not include a policy or contract for health insurance coverage.

Cost sharing has the meaning given that term in 45 CFR 155.20.

Director means the Director of the United States Office of Personnel Management.

EHB-benchmark plan has the meaning given that term in 45 CFR 156.20.

Exchange means a governmental agency or non-profit entity that meets the applicable requirements of 45 CFR part 155 and makes qualified health plans (QHPs) and MSP options available to qualified individuals and qualified employers. Unless otherwise identified, this term refers to State Exchanges, regional Exchanges, subsidiary Exchanges, and a Federally-facilitated Exchange.

Federal Employees Health Benefits Program or *FEHB Program* means the health benefits program administered by the United States Office of Personnel Management pursuant to chapter 89 of title 5, United States Code.

Group of issuers means:

(1) A group of health insurance issuers that are affiliated either by common ownership and control or by common use of a nationally licensed service mark (as defined in this section); or

(2) An affiliation of health insurance issuers and an entity that is not an issuer but that owns a nationally licensed service mark (as defined in this section).

Health insurance coverage means benefits consisting of medical care (provided directly, through insurance or reimbursement, or otherwise) under any hospital or medical service policy or certificate, hospital or medical service plan contract, or health maintenance organization contract offered by a health insurance issuer. Health insurance coverage includes group health insurance coverage, individual health insurance coverage, and short-term, limited duration insurance.

Health insurance issuer or *issuer* means an insurance company, insurance service, or insurance organization (including a health maintenance organization) that is required to be licensed to engage in the business of insurance in a State and that is subject to State law that regulates insurance (within the meaning of section 514(b)(2) of the Employee Retirement Income Security Act (ERISA)). This term does not include a group health plan as defined in 45 CFR 146.145(a).

HHS means the United States Department of Health and Human Services.

Level of coverage means one of four standardized actuarial values of plan coverage as defined by section 1302(d)(1) of the Affordable Care Act.

Licensure means the authorization obtained from the appropriate State official or regulatory authority to offer health insurance coverage in the State.

Multi-State Plan option or *MSP option* means a discrete pairing of a package of benefits with particular cost sharing (which does not include premium rates or premium rate quotes) that is offered pursuant to a contract with OPM pursuant to section 1334 of the Affordable Care Act and meets the requirements of 45 CFR part 800.

Multi-State Plan Program or *MSP Program* means the program administered by OPM pursuant to section 1334 of the Affordable Care Act.

Multi-State Plan Program issuer or *MSP issuer* means a health insurance issuer or group of issuers (as defined in this section) that has a contract with OPM to offer health plans pursuant to section 1334 of the Affordable Care Act and meets the requirements of this part.

Nationally licensed service mark means a word, name, symbol, or device, or any combination thereof, that an issuer or group of issuers uses consistently nationwide to identify itself.

Non-profit entity means:

(1) An organization that is incorporated under State law as a non-profit entity and licensed under State law as a health insurance issuer; or

Office of Personnel Management § 800.101

(2) A group of health insurance issuers licensed under State law, a substantial portion of which are incorporated under State law as non-profit entities.

OPM means the United States Office of Personnel Management.

Percentage of total allowed cost of benefits has the meaning given that term in 45 CFR 156.20.

Plan year means a consecutive 12-month period during which a health plan provides coverage for health benefits. A plan year may be a calendar year or otherwise.

Prompt payment means a requirement imposed on a health insurance issuer to pay a provider or enrollee for a claimed benefit or service within a defined time period, including the penalty or consequence imposed on the issuer for failure to meet the requirement.

Qualified Health Plan or *QHP* means a health plan that has in effect a certification that it meets the standards described in subpart C of 45 CFR part 156 issued or recognized by each Exchange through which such plan is offered pursuant to the process described in subpart K of 45 CFR part 155.

Rating means the process, including rating factors, numbers, formulas, methodologies, and actuarial assumptions, used to set premiums for a health plan.

Secretary means the Secretary of the Department of Health and Human Services.

SHOP means a Small Business Health Options Program operated by an Exchange through which a qualified employer can provide its employees and their dependents with access to one or more qualified health plans (QHPs).

Silver plan variation has the meaning given that term in 45 CFR 156.400.

Small employer means, in connection with a group health plan with respect to a calendar year and a plan year, an employer who employed an average of at least one but not more than 100 employees on business days during the preceding calendar year and who employs at least one employee on the first day of the plan year. In the case of plan years beginning before January 1, 2016, a State may elect to define *small employer* by substituting "50 employees" for "100 employees."

Standard plan has the meaning given that term in 45 CFR 156.400.

State means each of the 50 States or the District of Columbia.

State Insurance Commissioner means the commissioner or other chief insurance regulatory official of a State.

State-level issuer means a health insurance issuer designated by the Multi-State Plan (MSP) issuer to offer an MSP option or MSP options. The State-level issuer may offer health insurance coverage through an MSP option in all or part of one or more States.

Subpart B—Multi-State Plan Program Issuer Requirements

§ 800.101 General requirements.

An MSP issuer must:

(a) *Licensed.* Be licensed as a health insurance issuer in each State where it offers health insurance coverage;

(b) *Contract with OPM.* Have a contract with OPM pursuant to this part;

(c) *Required levels of coverage.* Offer levels of coverage as required by § 800.107 of this part;

(d) *Eligibility and enrollment.* MSP options and MSP issuers must meet the same requirements for eligibility, enrollment, and termination of coverage as those that apply to QHPs and QHP issuers pursuant to 45 CFR part 155, subparts D, E, and H, and 45 CFR 156.250, 156.260, 156.265, 156.270, and 156.285;

(e) *Applicable to each MSP issuer.* Ensure that each of its MSP options meets the requirements of this part;

(f) *Compliance.* Comply with all standards set forth in this part;

(g) *OPM direction and other legal requirements.* Timely comply with OPM instructions and directions and with other applicable law; and

(h) *Other requirements.* Meet such other requirements as determined appropriate by OPM, in consultation with HHS, pursuant to section 1334(b)(4) of the Affordable Care Act.

(i) *Non-discrimination.* MSP options and MSP issuers must comply with applicable Federal and State non-discrimination laws, including the standards set forth in 45 CFR 156.125 and 156.200(e).

§ 800.102 Compliance with Federal law.

(a) *Public Health Service Act.* As a condition of participation in the MSP Program, an MSP issuer must comply with applicable provisions of part A of title XXVII of the PHS Act. Compliance shall be determined by the Director.

(b) *Affordable Care Act.* As a condition of participation in the MSP Program, an MSP issuer must comply with applicable provisions of title I of the Affordable Care Act. Compliance shall be determined by the Director.

§ 800.103 Authority to contract with issuers.

(a) *General.* OPM may enter into contracts with health insurance issuers to offer at least two MSP options on Exchanges and SHOPs in each State, without regard to any statutes that would otherwise require competitive bidding.

(b) *Non-profit entity.* In entering into contracts with health insurance issuers to offer MSP options, OPM will enter into a contract with at least one non-profit entity as defined in § 800.20 of this part.

(c) *Group of issuers.* Any contract to offer MSP options may be with a group of issuers as defined in § 800.20 of this part.

(d) *Individual and group coverage.* The contracts will provide for individual health insurance coverage and for group health insurance coverage for small employers.

§ 800.104 Phased expansion, etc.

(a) *Phase-in.* OPM may enter into a contract with a health insurance issuer to offer MSP options if the health insurance issuer agrees that:

(1) With respect to the first year for which the health insurance issuer offers MSP options, the health insurance issuer will offer MSP options in at least 60 percent of the States;

(2) With respect to the second such year, the health insurance issuer will offer the MSP options in at least 70 percent of the States;

(3) With respect to the third such year, the health insurance issuer will offer the MSP options in at least 85 percent of the States; and

(4) With respect to each subsequent year, the health insurance issuer will offer the MSP options in all States.

(b) *Partial coverage within a State.* (1) OPM may enter into a contract with an MSP issuer even if the MSP issuer's MSP options for a State cover fewer than all the service areas specified for that State pursuant to § 800.110 of this part.

(2) If an issuer offers both an MSP option and QHP on the same Exchange, an MSP issuer must offer MSP coverage in a service area or areas that is equal to the greater of:

(i) The QHP service area defined by the issuer or,

(ii) The service area specified for that State pursuant to § 800.110 of this part covered by the issuer's QHP.

(c) *Participation in SHOPs.* (1) An MSP issuer's participation in a Federally-facilitated SHOP must be consistent with the requirements for QHP issuers specified in 45 CFR 156.200(g).

(2) An MSP issuer must comply with State standards governing participation in a State-based SHOP, consistent with § 800.114. For these State-based SHOP standards, OPM retains discretion to allow an MSP issuer to phase-in SHOP participation in States pursuant to section 1334(e) of the Affordable Care Act.

(d) *Licensed where offered.* OPM may enter into a contract with an MSP issuer who is not licensed in every State, provided that the issuer is licensed in every State where it offers MSP coverage through any Exchanges in that State and demonstrates to OPM that it is making a good faith effort to become licensed in every State consistent with the timeframe in paragraph (a) of this section.

§ 800.105 Benefits.

(a) *Package of benefits.* (1) An MSP issuer must offer a package of benefits that includes the essential health benefits (EHB) described in section 1302 of the Affordable Care Act for each MSP option within a State.

(2) The package of benefits referred to in paragraph (a)(1) of this section must comply with section 1302 of the Affordable Care Act, as well as any applicable standards set by OPM and any applicable standards set by HHS.

(b) *Package of benefits options.* (1) An MSP issuer must offer at least one uniform package of benefits in each State that is substantially equal to:

(i) The EHB-benchmark plan in each State in which it operates; or

(ii) Any EHB-benchmark plan selected by OPM under paragraph (c) of this section.

(2) An issuer applying to participate in the MSP Program may select either or both of the package of benefits options described in paragraph (b)(1) of this section in its application. In each State, the issuer may choose one EHB-benchmark for each product it offers.

(3) An MSP issuer must comply with any State standards relating to substitution of benchmark benefits or standard benefit designs.

(c) *OPM selection of benchmark plans.* (1) The OPM-selected EHB-benchmark plans are the three largest Federal Employees Health Benefits (FEHB) Program plan options, as identified by HHS pursuant to section 1302(b) of the Affordable Care Act, and as supplemented pursuant to paragraphs (c)(2) through (5) of this section.

(2) Any EHB-benchmark plan selected by OPM under paragraph (c)(1) lacking coverage of pediatric oral services or pediatric vision services must be supplemented by the addition of the entire category of benefits from the largest Federal Employee Dental and Vision Insurance Program (FEDVIP) dental or vision plan options, respectively, pursuant to 45 CFR 156.110(b) and section 1302(b) of the Affordable Care Act.

(3) In all States where an MSP issuer uses the OPM-selected EHB-benchmark plan, the MSP issuer may manage formularies around the needs of anticipated or actual users, subject to approval by OPM.

(4) An MSP issuer must follow the definition of habilitative services and devices as follows:

(i) An MSP issuer must follow the Federal definitions where HHS specifically defines habilitative services and devices if the State does not define the term, if the State defines the term in a conflicting way, or if the State definition is less stringent than the Federal definition.

(ii) An MSP issuer must follow State definitions where the State specifically defines the habilitative services and devices category pursuant to 45 CFR 156.110(f) and the State definition is not in conflict with the Federal definition or goes above the standards set in the Federal definition.

(iii) In the case of any State that does not define this category and absent a clearly applicable Federal definition, if any OPM-selected EHB-benchmark plan lacks coverage of habilitative services and devices, OPM may determine what habilitative services and devices are to be included in that EHB-benchmark plan.

(5) Any EHB-benchmark plan selected by OPM under paragraph (c)(1) of this section must include, for each State, any State-required benefits enacted before December 31, 2011, that are included in the State's EHB-benchmark plan as described in paragraph (b)(1)(i) of this section, or specific to the market in which the plan is offered.

(d) *OPM approval.* An MSP issuer's package of benefits, including its formulary, must be submitted for approval by OPM, which will review a package of benefits proposed by an MSP issuer and determine if it is substantially equal to an EHB-benchmark plan described in paragraph (b)(1) of this section, pursuant to standards set forth by OPM and any applicable standards set forth by HHS, including 45 CFR 156.115, 156.122, and 156.125.

(e) *State payments for additional State-required benefits.* If a State requires that benefits in addition to the benchmark package be offered to MSP enrollees in that State, then pursuant to section 1334(c)(2) of the Affordable Care Act, the State must defray the cost of such additional benefits by making payments either to the enrollee or to the MSP issuer on behalf of the enrollee.

§ 800.106 Cost-sharing limits, advance payments of premium tax credits, and cost-sharing reductions.

(a) *Cost-sharing limits.* For each MSP option it offers, an MSP issuer must ensure that the cost-sharing provisions of the MSP option comply with section 1302(c) of the Affordable Care Act, as

§ 800.107

well as any applicable standards set by OPM or HHS.

(b) *Advance payments of premium tax credits and cost-sharing reductions.* For each MSP option it offers, an MSP issuer must ensure that an eligible individual receives the benefit of advance payments of premium tax credits under section 36B of the Internal Revenue Code and the cost-sharing reductions under section 1402 of the Affordable Care Act. An MSP issuer must also comply with any applicable standards set by OPM or HHS.

§ 800.107 Levels of coverage.

(a) *Silver and gold levels of coverage required.* An MSP issuer must offer at least one MSP option at the silver level of coverage and at least one MSP option at the gold level of coverage on each Exchange in which the issuer is certified to offer an MSP option pursuant to a contract with OPM.

(b) *Bronze or platinum metal levels of coverage permitted.* Pursuant to a contract with OPM, an MSP issuer may offer one or more MSP options at the bronze level of coverage or the platinum level of coverage, or both, on any Exchange or SHOP in any State.

(c) *Child-only plans.* For each level of coverage, the MSP issuer must offer a child-only MSP option at the same level of coverage as any health insurance coverage offered to individuals who, as of the beginning of the plan year, have not attained the age of 21.

(d) *Plan variations for the reduction or elimination of cost-sharing.* An MSP issuer must comply with section 1402 of the Affordable Care Act, as well as any applicable standards set by OPM or HHS.

(e) *OPM approval.* An MSP issuer must submit the levels of coverage plans and plan variations to OPM for review and approval by OPM.

§ 800.108 Assessments and user fees.

(a) *Discretion to charge assessment and user fees.* Beginning in plan year 2015, OPM may require an MSP issuer to pay an assessment or user fee as a condition of participating in the MSP Program.

(b) *Determination of amount.* The amount of the assessment or user fee charged by OPM for a plan year is the amount determined necessary by OPM to meet the costs of OPM's functions under the Affordable Care Act for a plan year, including but not limited to such functions as entering into contracts with, certifying, recertifying, decertifying, and overseeing MSP options and MSP issuers for that plan year. The amount of the assessment or user fee charged by OPM will be offset against the assessment or user fee amount required by any State-based Exchange or federally-facilitated Exchange such that the total of all assessments and user fees paid by the MSP issuer for the year for the MSP option shall be no greater than nor less than the amount of the assessment or user fee paid by QHP issuers in that State-based Exchange or federally-facilitated Exchange for that year.

(c) *Process for collecting MSP assessment or user fees.* OPM may require an MSP issuer to make payment of the MSP Program assessment or user fee amount directly to OPM, or may establish other mechanisms for the collection process.

§ 800.109 Network adequacy.

(a) *General requirement.* An MSP issuer must ensure that the provider network of each of its MSP options, as available to all enrollees, meets the following standards:

(1) Maintains a network that is sufficient in number and types of providers to assure that all services will be accessible without unreasonable delay;

(2) Is consistent with the network adequacy provisions of section 2702(c) of the Public Health Service Act; and

(3) Includes essential community providers in compliance with 45 CFR 156.235.

(b) *Provider directory.* An MSP issuer must make its provider directory for an MSP option available to the Exchange for publication online pursuant to guidance from the Exchange and to potential enrollees in hard copy, upon request. In the provider directory, an MSP issuer must identify providers that are not accepting new patients.

(c) *OPM guidance.* OPM will issue guidance containing the criteria and standards that it will use to determine the adequacy of a provider network.

Office of Personnel Management § 800.113

§ 800.110 Service area.

An MSP issuer must offer an MSP option within one or more service areas in a State defined by each Exchange pursuant to 45 CFR 155.1055. If an Exchange permits issuers to define their service areas, an MSP issuer must obtain OPM's approval for its proposed service areas. Pursuant to § 800.104 of this part, OPM may enter into a contract with an MSP issuer even if the MSP issuer's MSP options for a State cover fewer than all the service areas specified for that State. MSP options will follow the same standards for service areas for QHPs pursuant to 45 CFR 155.1055.

§ 800.111 Accreditation requirement.

(a) *General requirement.* An MSP issuer must be or become accredited consistent with the requirements for QHP issuers specified in section 1311 of the Affordable Care Act and 45 CFR 156.275(a)(1).

(b) *Release of survey.* An MSP issuer must authorize the accrediting entity that accredits the MSP issuer to release to OPM and to the Exchange a copy of its most recent accreditation survey, together with any survey-related information that OPM or an Exchange may require, such as corrective action plans and summaries of findings.

(c) *Timeframe for accreditation.* An MSP issuer that is not accredited as of the date that it enters into a contract with OPM must become accredited within the timeframe established by OPM as authorized by 45 CFR 155.1045.

§ 800.112 Reporting requirements.

(a) *OPM specification of reporting requirements.* OPM will specify the data and information that must be reported by an MSP issuer, including data permitted or required by the Affordable Care Act and such other data as OPM may determine necessary for the oversight and administration of the MSP Program. OPM will also specify the form, manner, processes, and frequency for the reporting of data and information. The Director may require that MSP issuers submit claims payment and enrollment data to facilitate OPM's oversight and administration of the MSP Program in a manner similar to the FEHB Program.

(b) *Quality and quality improvement standards.* An MSP issuer must comply with any standards required by OPM for reporting quality and quality improvement activities, including but not limited to implementation of a quality improvement strategy, disclosure of quality measures to enrollees and prospective enrollees, reporting of pediatric quality measures, and implementation of rating and enrollee satisfaction surveys, which will be similar to standards under section 1311(c)(1)(E), (H), and (I), (c)(3), and (c)(4) of the Affordable Care Act.

§ 800.113 Benefit plan material or information.

(a) *Compliance with Federal and State law.* An MSP issuer must comply with Federal and State laws relating to benefit plan material or information, including the provisions of this section and guidance issued by OPM specifying its standards, process, and timeline for approval of benefit plan material or information.

(b) *General standards for MSP applications and notices.* An MSP issuer must provide all applications and notices to enrollees in accordance with the standards described in 45 CFR 155.205(c). OPM may establish additional standards to meet the needs of MSP enrollees.

(1) *Accuracy.* An MSP issuer is responsible for the accuracy of its benefit plan material or information.

(2) *Truthful, not misleading, no material omissions, and plain language.* All benefit plan material or information must be:

(i) Truthful, not misleading, and without material omissions; and

(ii) Written in plain language, as defined in section 1311(e)(3)(B) of the Affordable Care Act.

(3) *Uniform explanation of coverage documents and standardized definitions.* An MSP issuer must comply with the provisions of section 2715 of the PHS Act and regulations issued to implement that section.

(4) *OPM review and approval of benefit plan material or information.* OPM may request an MSP issuer to submit to

§ 800.114

OPM benefit plan material or information, as defined in § 800.20. OPM reserves the right to review and approve benefit plan material or information to ensure that an MSP issuer complies with Federal and State laws, and the standards prescribed by OPM with respect to benefit plan material or information.

(5) *Statement on certification by OPM.* An MSP issuer may include a statement in its benefit plan material or information that:

(i) OPM has certified the MSP option as eligible to be offered on the Exchange; and

(ii) OPM monitors the MSP option for compliance with all applicable law.

§ 800.114 Compliance with applicable State law.

(a) *Compliance with State law.* An MSP issuer must, with respect to each of its MSP options, generally comply with State law pursuant to section 1334(b)(2) of the Affordable Care Act. However, the MSP options and MSP issuers are not subject to State laws that:

(1) Are inconsistent with section 1334 of the Affordable Care Act or this part;

(2) Prevent the application of a requirement of part A of title XXVII of the PHS Act; or

(3) Prevent the application of a requirement of title I of the Affordable Care Act.

(b) *Determination of inconsistency.* After consultation with the State and HHS, OPM reserves the right to determine, in its judgment, as effectuated through an MSP Program contract, these regulations, or OPM guidance, whether the standards set forth in paragraph (a) of this section are satisfied with respect to particular State laws.

§ 800.115 Level playing field.

An MSP issuer must, with respect to each of its MSP options, meet the following requirements in order to ensure a level playing field, subject to § 800.114:

(a) *Guaranteed renewal.* Guarantee that an enrollee can renew enrollment in an MSP option in compliance with sections 2703 and 2742 of the PHS Act;

(b) *Rating.* In proposing premiums for OPM approval, use only the rating factors permitted under section 2701 of the PHS Act and State law;

(c) *Preexisting conditions.* Not impose any preexisting condition exclusion and comply with section 2704 of the PHS Act;

(d) *Non-discrimination.* Comply with section 2705 of the PHS Act;

(e) *Quality improvement and reporting.* Comply with all Federal and State quality improvement and reporting requirements. Quality improvement and reporting means quality improvement as defined in section 1311(h) of the Affordable Care Act and quality improvement plans or strategies required under State law, and quality reporting as defined in section 2717 of the PHS Act and section 1311(g) of the Affordable Care Act. Quality improvement also includes activities such as, but not limited to, implementation of a quality improvement strategy, disclosure of quality measures to enrollees and prospective enrollees, and reporting of pediatric quality measures, which will be similar to standards under section 1311(c)(1)(E), (H), and (I) of the Affordable Care Act;

(f) *Fraud and abuse.* Comply with all Federal and State fraud and abuse laws;

(g) *Licensure.* Be licensed in every State in which it offers an MSP option;

(h) *Solvency and financial requirements.* Comply with the solvency standards set by each State in which it offers an MSP option;

(i) *Market conduct.* Comply with the market conduct standards of each State in which it offers an MSP option;

(j) *Prompt payment.* Comply with applicable State law in negotiating the terms of payment in contracts with its providers and in making payments to claimants and providers;

(k) *Appeals and grievances.* Comply with Federal standards under section 2719 of the PHS Act for appeals and grievances relating to adverse benefit determinations, as described in subpart F of this part;

(l) *Privacy and confidentiality.* Comply with all Federal and State privacy and security laws and requirements, including any standards required by OPM in guidance or contract, which will be similar to the standards contained in

Office of Personnel Management

45 CFR part 164 and applicable State law; and

(m) *Benefit plan material or information.* Comply with Federal and State law, including § 800.113 of this part.

§ 800.116 Process for dispute resolution.

(a) *Determinations about applicability of State law under section 1334(b)(2) of the Affordable Care Act.* In the event of a dispute about the applicability to an MSP option or MSP issuer of a State law, the State may request that OPM reconsider a determination that an MSP option or MSP issuer is not subject to such State law.

(b) *Required demonstration.* A State making a request under paragraph (a) of this section must demonstrate that the State law at issue:

(1) Is not inconsistent with section 1334 of the Affordable Care Act or this part;

(2) Does not prevent the application of a requirement of part A of title XXVII of the PHS Act; and

(3) Does not prevent the application of a requirement of title I of the Affordable Care Act.

(c) *Request for review.* The request must be in writing and include contact information, including the name, telephone number, email address, and mailing address of the person or persons whom OPM may contact regarding the request for review. The request must be in such form, contain such information, and be submitted in such manner and within such timeframe as OPM may prescribe.

(1) The requester may submit to OPM any relevant information to support its request.

(2) OPM may obtain additional information relevant to the request from any source as it may, in its judgment, deem necessary. OPM will provide the requester with a copy of any additional information it obtains and provide an opportunity for the requester to respond (including by submission of additional information or explanation).

(3) OPM will issue a written decision within 60 calendar days after receiving the written request, or after the due date for a response under paragraph (c)(2) of this section, whichever is later,

§ 800.201

unless a different timeframe is agreed upon.

(4) OPM's written decision will constitute final agency action that is subject to review under the Administrative Procedure Act in the appropriate U.S. district court. Such review is limited to the record that was before OPM when OPM made its decision.

Subpart C—Premiums, Rating Factors, Medical Loss Ratios, and Risk Adjustment

§ 800.201 General requirements.

(a) *Premium negotiation.* OPM will negotiate annually with an MSP issuer, on a State by State basis, the premiums for each MSP option offered by that issuer in that State. Such negotiations may include negotiations about the cost-sharing provisions of an MSP option.

(b) *Duration.* Premiums will remain in effect for the plan year.

(c) *Guidance on rate development.* OPM will issue guidance addressing methods for the development of premiums for the MSP Program. That guidance will follow State rating standards generally applicable in a State, to the greatest extent practicable.

(d) *Calculation of actuarial value.* An MSP issuer must calculate actuarial value in the same manner as QHP issuers under section 1302(d) of the Affordable Care Act, as well as any applicable standards set by OPM or HHS.

(e) *OPM rate review process.* An MSP issuer must participate in the rate review process established by OPM to negotiate rates for MSP options. The rate review process established by OPM will be similar to the process established by HHS pursuant to section 2794 of the PHS Act and disclosure and review standards established under 45 CFR part 154.

(f) *State effective rate review.* With respect to its MSP options, an MSP issuer is subject to a State's rate review process, including a State's Effective Rate Review Program established by HHS pursuant to section 2794 of the PHS Act and 45 CFR part 154. In the event HHS is reviewing rates for a State pursuant to section 2794 of the PHS Act, HHS will defer to OPM's judgment regarding the MSP options'

§ 800.202

proposed rate increase. If a State withholds approval of an MSP option and OPM determines, in its discretion, that the State's action would prevent OPM from administrating the MSP Program, OPM retains authority to make the final decision to approve rates for participation in the MSP Program, notwithstanding the absence of State approval.

(g) *Single risk pool.* An MSP issuer must consider all enrollees in an MSP option to be in the same risk pool as all enrollees in all other health plans in the individual market or the small group market, respectively, in compliance with section 1312(c) of the Affordable Care Act, 45 CFR 156.80, and any applicable Federal or State laws and regulations implementing that section.

§ 800.202 Rating factors.

(a) *Permissible rating factors.* In proposing premiums for each MSP option, an MSP issuer must use only the rating factors permitted under section 2701 of the PHS Act.

(b) *Application of variations based on age or tobacco use.* Rating variations permitted under section 2701 of the PHS Act must be applied by an MSP issuer based on the portion of the premium attributable to each family member covered under the coverage in accordance with any applicable Federal or State laws and regulations implementing section 2701(a) of the PHS Act.

(c) *Age rating.* For age rating, an MSP issuer must use the ratio established by the State in which the MSP option is offered, if it is less than 3:1.

(1) *Age bands.* An MSP issuer must use the uniform age bands established under HHS regulations implementing section 2701(a) of the PHS Act.

(2) *Age curves.* An MSP issuer must use the age curves established under HHS regulations implementing section 2701(a) of the PHS Act, or age curves established by a State pursuant to HHS regulations.

(d) *Rating areas.* An MSP issuer must use the rating areas appropriate to the State in which the MSP option is offered and established under HHS regulations implementing section 2701(a) of the PHS Act.

(e) *Tobacco rating.* An MSP issuer must apply tobacco use as a rating factor in accordance with any applicable Federal or State laws and regulations implementing section 2701(a) of the PHS Act.

(f) *Wellness programs.* An MSP issuer must comply with any applicable Federal or State laws and regulations implementing section 2705 of the PHS Act.

§ 800.203 Medical loss ratio.

(a) *Required medical loss ratio.* An MSP issuer must attain:

(1) The medical loss ratio (MLR) required under section 2718 of the PHS Act and regulations promulgated by HHS; and

(2) Any MSP-specific MLR that OPM may set in the best interests of MSP enrollees or that is necessary to be consistent with a State's requirements with respect to MLR.

(b) *Consequences of not attaining required medical loss ratio.* If an MSP issuer fails to attain an MLR set forth in paragraph (a) of this section, OPM may take any appropriate action, including but not limited to intermediate sanctions, such as suspension of marketing, decertifying an MSP option in one or more States, or terminating an MSP issuer's contract pursuant to § 800.404 of this part.

§ 800.204 Reinsurance, risk corridors, and risk adjustment.

(a) *Transitional reinsurance program.* An MSP issuer must comply with section 1341 of the Affordable Care Act, 45 CFR part 153, and any applicable Federal or State regulations under section 1341 that set forth requirements to implement the transitional reinsurance program for the individual market.

(b) *Temporary risk corridors program.* An MSP issuer must comply with section 1342 of the Affordable Care Act, 45 CFR part 153, and any applicable Federal regulations under section 1342 that set forth requirements to implement the risk corridor program.

(c) *Risk adjustment program.* An MSP issuer must comply with section 1343 of the Affordable Care Act, 45 CFR part 153, and any applicable Federal or State regulations under section 1343 that set forth requirements to implement the risk adjustment program.

Subpart D—Application and Contracting Procedures

§ 800.301 Application process.

(a) *Acceptance of applications.* Without regard to 41 U.S.C. 6101(b)–(d), or any other statute requiring competitive bidding, OPM may consider annual applications from health insurance issuers, including groups of health insurance issuers as defined in § 800.20, to participate in the MSP Program. If OPM determines that it is not beneficial for the MSP Program to consider new issuer applications for an upcoming year, OPM will issue a notice to that effect. Each existing MSP issuer may complete a renewal application annually.

(b) *Form and manner of applications.* An applicant must submit to OPM, in the form and manner and in accordance with the timeline specified by OPM, the information requested by OPM for determining whether an applicant meets the requirements of this part.

§ 800.302 Review of applications.

(a) *Determinations.* OPM will determine if an applicant meets the requirements of this part. If OPM determines that an applicant meets the requirements of this part, OPM may accept the applicant to enter into contract negotiations with OPM to participate in the MSP Program.

(b) *Requests for additional information.* OPM may request additional information from an applicant before making a decision about whether to enter into contract negotiations with that applicant to participate in the MSP Program.

(c) *Declination of application.* If, after reviewing an application to participate in the MSP Program, OPM declines to enter into contract negotiations with the applicant, OPM will inform the applicant in writing of the reasons for that decision.

(d) *Discretion.* The decision whether to enter into contract negotiations with a health insurance issuer who has applied to participate in the MSP Program is committed to OPM's discretion.

(e) *Impact on future applications.* OPM's declination of an application to participate in the MSP Program will not preclude the applicant from submitting an application for a subsequent year to participate in the MSP Program.

§ 800.303 MSP Program contracting.

(a) *Participation in MSP Program.* To become an MSP issuer, the applicant and the Director or the Director's designee must sign a contract that meets the requirements of this part.

(b) *Standard contract.* OPM will establish a standard contract for the MSP Program.

(c) *Premiums.* OPM and the applicant will negotiate the premiums for an MSP option for each plan year in accordance with the provisions of subpart C of this part.

(d) *Package of benefits.* OPM must approve the applicant's package of benefits for its MSP option.

(e) *Additional terms and conditions.* OPM may elect to negotiate with an applicant such additional terms, conditions, and requirements that:

(1) Are in the interests of MSP enrollees; or

(2) OPM determines to be appropriate.

(f) *Certification to offer health insurance coverage.*

(1) For each plan year, an MSP Program contract will specify MSP options that OPM has certified, the specific package(s) of benefits authorized to be offered on each Exchange, and the premiums to be charged for each package of benefits on each Exchange.

(2) An MSP issuer may not offer an MSP option on an Exchange unless its MSP Program contract with OPM includes a certification authorizing the MSP issuer to offer the MSP option on that Exchange in accordance with paragraph (f)(1) of this section.

§ 800.304 Term of the contract.

(a) *Term of a contract.* The term of the contract will be specified in the MSP Program contract and must be for a period of at least the 12 consecutive months defined as the plan year.

(b) *Plan year.* The plan year is a consecutive 12-month period during which an MSP option provides coverage for health benefits. A plan year may be a calendar year or otherwise.

§ 800.305 Contract renewal process.

(a) *Renewal.* To continue participating in the MSP Program, an MSP issuer must provide to OPM, in the form and manner and in accordance with the timeline prescribed by OPM, the information requested by OPM for determining whether the MSP issuer continues to meet the requirements of this part.

(b) *OPM decision.* Subject to paragraph (c) of this section, OPM will renew the MSP Program contract of an MSP issuer who timely submits the information described in paragraph (a).

(c) *OPM discretion not to renew.* OPM may decline to renew the contract of an MSP issuer if:

(1) OPM and the MSP issuer fail to agree on premiums and benefits for an MSP option for the subsequent plan year;

(2) The MSP issuer has engaged in conduct described in § 800.404(a) of this part; or

(3) OPM determines that the MSP issuer will be unable to comply with a material provision of section 1334 of the Affordable Care Act or this part.

(d) *Failure to agree on premiums and benefits.* Except as otherwise provided in this part, if an MSP issuer has complied with paragraph (a) of this section and OPM and the MSP issuer fail to agree on premiums and benefits for an MSP option on one or more Exchanges for the subsequent plan year by the date required by OPM, either party may provide notice of nonrenewal pursuant to § 800.306 of this part, or OPM may in its discretion withdraw the certification of that MSP option on the Exchange or Exchanges for that plan year. In addition, if OPM and the MSP issuer fail to agree on benefits and premiums for an MSP option on one or more Exchanges by the date set by OPM and in the event of no action (no notice of nonrenewal or renewal) by either party, the MSP Program contract will be renewed and the existing premiums and benefits for that MSP option on that Exchange or Exchanges will remain in effect for the subsequent plan year.

§ 800.306 Nonrenewal.

(a) *Nonrenewal.* Nonrenewal may pertain to the MSP issuer or the State-level issuer. The circumstances under which nonrenewal may occur are:

(1) *Nonrenewal of contract.* As used in this subpart and subpart E of this part, "nonrenewal of contract" means a decision by either OPM or an MSP issuer not to renew an MSP Program contract.

(2) *Nonrenewal of participation.* As used in this subpart and subpart E of this part, "nonrenewal of participation" means a decision by OPM, an MSP issuer, or a State-level issuer not to renew a State-level issuer's participation in a MSP Program contract.

(b) *Notice required.* Either OPM or an MSP issuer may decline to renew an MSP Program contract by providing a written notice of nonrenewal to the other party.

(c) *MSP issuer responsibilities.* The MSP issuer's written notice of nonrenewal must be made in accordance with its MSP Program contract with OPM. The MSP issuer also must comply with any requirements regarding the termination of a plan that are applicable to a QHP offered on an Exchange on which the MSP option was offered, including a requirement to provide advance written notice of termination to enrollees. MSP issuers shall provide written notice to enrollees in accordance with § 800.404(d).

Subpart E—Compliance

§ 800.401 Contract performance.

(a) *General.* An MSP issuer must perform an MSP Program contract with OPM in accordance with the requirements of section 1334 of the Affordable Care Act and this part. The MSP issuer must continue to meet such requirements while under an MSP Program contract with OPM.

(b) *Specific requirements for issuers.* In addition to the requirements described in paragraph (a) of this section, each MSP issuer must:

(1) Have, in the judgment of OPM, the financial resources to carry out its obligations under the MSP Program;

(2) Keep such reasonable financial and statistical records, and furnish to OPM such reasonable financial and statistical reports with respect to the MSP option or the MSP issuer, as may be requested by OPM;

Office of Personnel Management § 800.401

(3) Permit representatives of OPM (including the OPM Office of Inspector General), the U.S. Government Accountability Office, and any other applicable Federal Government auditing entities to audit and examine its records and accounts that pertain, directly or indirectly, to the MSP option at such reasonable times and places as may be designated by OPM or the U.S. Government Accountability Office;

(4) Timely submit to OPM a properly completed and signed novation or change-of-name agreement in accordance with subpart 42.12 of 48 CFR part 42;

(5) Perform the MSP Program contract in accordance with prudent business practices, as described in paragraph (c) of this section; and

(6) Not perform the MSP Program contract in accordance with poor business practices, as described in paragraph (d) of this section.

(c) *Prudent business practices.* OPM will consider an MSP issuer's specific circumstances and facts in using its discretion to determine compliance with paragraph (b)(5) of this section. For purposes of paragraph (b)(5) of this section, prudent business practices include, but are not limited to, the following:

(1) Timely compliance with OPM instructions and directives;

(2) Legal and ethical business and health care practices;

(3) Compliance with the terms of the MSP Program contract, regulations, and statutes;

(4) Timely and accurate adjudication of claims or rendering of medical services;

(5) Operating a system for accounting for costs incurred under the MSP Program contract, which includes segregating and pricing MSP option medical utilization and allocating indirect and administrative costs in a reasonable and equitable manner;

(6) Maintaining accurate accounting reports of costs incurred in the administration of the MSP Program contract;

(7) Applying performance standards for assuring contract quality as outlined at § 800.402; and

(8) Establishing and maintaining a system of internal controls that provides reasonable assurance that:

(i) The provision and payments of benefits and other expenses comply with legal, regulatory, and contractual guidelines;

(ii) MSP funds, property, and other assets are safeguarded against waste, loss, unauthorized use, or misappropriation; and

(iii) Data is accurately and fairly disclosed in all reports required by OPM.

(d) *Poor business practices.* OPM will consider an MSP issuer's specific circumstances and facts in using its discretion to determine compliance with paragraph (b)(6) of this section. For purposes of paragraph (b)(6) of this section, poor business practices include, but are not limited to, the following:

(1) Using fraudulent or unethical business or health care practices or otherwise displaying a lack of business integrity or honesty;

(2) Repeatedly or knowingly providing false or misleading information in the rate setting process;

(3) Failing to comply with OPM instructions and directives;

(4) Having an accounting system that is incapable of separately accounting for costs incurred under the contract and/or that lacks the internal controls necessary to fulfill the terms of the contract;

(5) Failing to ensure that the MSP issuer properly pays or denies claims, or, if applicable, provides medical services that are inconsistent with standards of good medical practice; and

(6) Entering into contracts or employment agreements with providers, provider groups, or health care workers that include provisions or financial incentives that directly or indirectly create an inducement to limit or restrict communication about medically necessary services to any individual covered under the MSP Program. Financial incentives are defined as bonuses, withholds, commissions, profit sharing or other similar adjustments to basic compensation (*e.g.*, service fee, capitation, salary) which have the effect of limiting or reducing communication about appropriate medically necessary services.

§ 800.402

(e) *Performance escrow account.* OPM may require MSP issuers to pay an assessment into an escrow account to ensure contract compliance and benefit MSP enrollees.

§ 800.402 Contract quality assurance.

(a) *General.* This section prescribes general policies and procedures to ensure that services acquired under MSP Program contracts conform to the contract's quality requirements.

(b) *Internal controls.* OPM may periodically evaluate the contractor's system of internal controls under the quality assurance program required by the contract and will acknowledge in writing if the system is inconsistent with the requirements set forth in the contract. OPM's reviews do not diminish the contractor's obligation to implement and maintain an effective and efficient system to apply the internal controls.

(c) *Performance standards.* (1) OPM will issue specific performance standards for MSP Program contracts and will inform MSP issuers of the applicable performance standards prior to negotiations for the contract year. OPM may benchmark its standards against standards generally accepted in the insurance industry. OPM may authorize nationally recognized standards to be used to fulfill this requirement.

(2) MSP issuers must comply with the performance standards issued pursuant to this section.

§ 800.403 Fraud and abuse.

(a) *Program required.* An MSP issuer must conduct a program to assess its vulnerability to fraud and abuse as well as to address such vulnerabilities.

(b) *Fraud detection system.* An MSP issuer must operate a system designed to detect and eliminate fraud and abuse by employees and subcontractors of the MSP issuer, by providers furnishing goods or services to MSP enrollees, and by MSP enrollees.

(c) *Submission of information.* An MSP issuer must provide to OPM such information or assistance as may be necessary for the agency to carry out the duties and responsibilities, including those of the Office of Inspector General as specified in sections 4 and 6 of the Inspector General Act of 1978 (5 U.S.C. App.). An MSP issuer must provide any requested information in the form, manner, and timeline prescribed by OPM.

§ 800.404 Compliance actions.

(a) *Causes for OPM compliance actions.* The following constitute cause for OPM to impose a compliance action described in paragraph (b) of this section against an MSP issuer:

(1) Failure by the MSP issuer to meet the requirements set forth in § 800.401(a) and (b);

(2) An MSP issuer's sustained failure to perform the MSP Program contract in accordance with prudent business practices, as described in § 800.401(c);

(3) A pattern of poor conduct or evidence of poor business practices such as those described in § 800.401(d); or

(4) Such other violations of law or regulation as OPM may determine, including pursuant to its authority under §§ 800.102 and 800.114.

(b) *Compliance actions.* (1) OPM may impose a compliance action against an MSP issuer at any time during the contract term if it determines that the MSP issuer is not in compliance with applicable law, this part, or the terms of its contract with OPM.

(2) Compliance actions may include, but are not limited to:

(i) Establishment and implementation of a corrective action plan;

(ii) Imposition of intermediate sanctions, such as suspension of marketing;

(iii) Performance incentives;

(iv) Reduction of service area or areas;

(v) Withdrawal of the certification of the MSP option or options offered on one or more Exchanges;

(vi) Nonrenewal of participation

(vii) Nonrenewal of contract; and

(viii) Withdrawal of approval or termination of the MSP Program contract.

(c) *Notice of compliance action.* (1) OPM must notify an MSP issuer in writing of a compliance action under this section. Such notice must indicate the specific compliance action undertaken and the reason for the compliance action.

(2) For compliance actions listed in § 800.404(b)(2)(v) through (viii), such notice must include a statement that the

Office of Personnel Management § 800.405

MSP issuer is entitled to request a reconsideration of OPM's determination to impose a compliance action pursuant to § 800.405.

(3) Upon imposition of a compliance action listed in paragraphs (b)(2)(iv) through (vii) of this section, OPM must notify the State Insurance Commissioner(s) and Exchange officials in the State or States in which the compliance action is effective.

(d) *Notice to enrollees.* If the contract is terminated, if OPM withdraws certification of an MSP option, or if a State-level issuer's participation in the MSP Program contract is not renewed, as described in §§ 800.306 and 800.404(b)(2), or in any situation in which an MSP option is no longer available to enrollees, the MSP issuer must comply with any State or Exchange requirements regarding discontinuing a particular type of coverage that are applicable to a QHP offered on the Exchange on which the MSP option was offered, including a requirement to provide advance written notice before the coverage will be discontinued. If a State or Exchange does not have requirements about advance notice to enrollees, the MSP issuer must inform current MSP enrollees in writing of the discontinuance of the MSP option no later than 90 days prior to discontinuing the MSP option, unless OPM determines that there is good cause for less than 90 days' notice.

(e) *Definition.* As used in this subpart, "termination" means a decision by OPM to cancel an MSP Program contract prior to the end of its contract term. The term includes OPM's withdrawal of approval of an MSP Program contract.

§ 800.405 Reconsideration of compliance actions.

(a) *Right to request reconsideration.* An MSP issuer may request that OPM reconsider a determination to impose one of the following compliance actions:

(1) Withdrawal of the certification of the MSP option or options offered on one or more Exchanges;

(2) Nonrenewal of participation

(3) Nonrenewal of contract; or

(4) Termination of the MSP Program contract.

(b) *Request for reconsideration and/or hearing.* (1) An MSP issuer with a right to request reconsideration specified in paragraph (a) of this section may request a hearing in which OPM will reconsider its determination to impose a compliance action.

(2) A request under this section must be in writing and contain contact information, including the name, telephone number, email address, and mailing address of the person or persons whom OPM may contact regarding a request for a hearing with respect to the reconsideration. The request must be in such form, contain such information, and be submitted in such manner as OPM may prescribe.

(3) The request must be received by OPM within 15 calendar days after the date of the MSP issuer's receipt of the notice of compliance action. The MSP issuer may request that OPM's reconsideration allow a representative of the MSP issuer to appear personally before OPM.

(4) A request under this section must include a detailed statement of the reasons that the MSP issuer disagrees with OPM's imposition of the compliance action, and may include any additional information that will assist OPM in rendering a final decision under this section.

(5) OPM may obtain additional information relevant to the request from any source as it may, in its judgment, deem necessary. OPM will provide the MSP issuer with a copy of any additional information it obtains and provide an opportunity for the MSP issuer to respond (including by submitting additional information or explanation).

(6) OPM's reconsideration and hearing, if requested, may be conducted by the Director or a representative designated by the Director who did not participate in the initial decision that is the subject of the request for review.

(c) *Notice of final decision.* OPM will notify the MSP issuer, in writing, of OPM's final decision on the MSP issuer's request for reconsideration and the specific reasons for that final decision. OPM's written decision will constitute final agency action that is subject to review under the Administrative Procedure Act in the appropriate

§ 800.501

U.S. district court. Such review is limited to the record that was before OPM when it made its decision.

Subpart F—Appeals by Enrollees of Denials of Claims for Payment or Service

§ 800.501 General requirements.

(a) *Definitions.* For purposes of this subpart:

(1) *Adverse benefit determination* has the meaning given that term in 45 CFR 147.136(a)(2)(i).

(2) *Claim* means a request for:

(i) Payment of a health-related bill; or

(ii) Provision of a health-related service or supply.

(b) *Applicability.* This subpart applies to enrollees and to other individuals or entities who are acting on behalf of an enrollee and who have the enrollee's specific written consent to pursue a remedy of an adverse benefit determination.

§ 800.502 MSP issuer internal claims and appeals.

(a) *Processes.* MSP issuers must comply with the internal claims and appeals processes applicable to group health plans and health insurance issuers under 45 CFR 147.136(b).

(b) *Timeframes and notice of determination.* An MSP issuer must provide written notice to an enrollee of its determination on a claim brought under paragraph (a) of this section according to the timeframes and notification rules under 45 CFR 147.136(b) and (e), including the timeframes for urgent claims. If the MSP issuer denies a claim (or a portion of the claim), the enrollee may appeal the adverse benefit determination to the MSP issuer in accordance with 45 CFR 147.136(b).

§ 800.503 External review.

(a) *External review by OPM.* OPM will conduct external review of adverse benefit determinations using a process similar to OPM review of disputed claims under 5 CFR 890.105(e), subject to the standards and timeframes set forth in 45 CFR 147.136(d).

(b) *Notice.* Notices to MSP enrollees regarding external review under paragraph (a) of this section must comply with 45 CFR 147.136(e), and are subject to review and approval by OPM.

(c) *Issuer obligation.* An MSP issuer must pay a claim or provide a health-related service or supply pursuant to OPM's final decision or the final decision of an independent review organization without delay, regardless of whether the plan or issuer intends to seek judicial review of the external review decision and unless or until there is a judicial decision otherwise.

§ 800.504 Judicial review.

(a) OPM's written decision under the external review process established under § 800.503(a) of this part will constitute final agency action that is subject to review under the Administrative Procedure Act in the appropriate U.S. district court. A decision made by an independent review organization under the process established under § 800.503(a) is not within OPM's discretion and therefore is not final agency action.

(b) Judicial review under paragraph (a) of this section is limited to the record that was before OPM when OPM made its decision.

Subpart G—Miscellaneous

§ 800.601 Reservation of authority.

OPM reserves the right to implement and supplement these regulations with written operational guidelines.

§ 800.602 Consumer choice with respect to certain services.

(a) *Assured availability of varied coverage.* Consistent with § 800.104 of this part, OPM will ensure that at least one of the MSP issuers on each Exchange in each State offers at least one MSP option that does not provide coverage of services described in section 1303(b)(1)(B)(i) of the Affordable Care Act.

(b) *State opt-out.* An MSP issuer may not offer abortion coverage in any State where such coverage of abortion services is prohibited by State law.

(c) *Notice to Enrollees*—(1) *Notice of exclusion.* The MSP issuer must provide notice to consumers prior to enrollment that non-excepted abortion services are not a covered benefit in the

Office of Personnel Management

form, manner, and timeline prescribed by OPM.

(2) *Notice of coverage.* If an MSP issuer chooses to offer an MSP option that covers non-excepted abortion services, in addition to an MSP option that does not cover non-excepted abortion services, the MSP issuer must provide notice to consumers prior to enrollment that non-excepted abortion services are a covered benefit. An MSP issuer must provide notice in a manner consistent with 45 CFR 147.200(a)(3), to meet the requirements of 45 CFR 156.280(f). OPM may provide guidance on the form, manner, and timeline for this notice.

(3) *OPM review and approval of notices.* OPM may require an MSP issuer to submit to OPM such notices. OPM reserves the right to review and approve these consumer notices to ensure that an MSP issuer complies with Federal and State laws, and the standards prescribed by OPM with respect to § 800.602.

§ 800.603 Disclosure of information.

(a) *Disclosure to certain entities.* OPM may provide information relating to the activities of MSP issuers or State-level issuers to a State Insurance Commissioner or Director of a State-based Exchange.

(b) *Conditions of when to disclose.* OPM shall only make a disclosure described in this section to the extent that such disclosure is:

(1) Necessary or appropriate to permit OPM's Director, a State Insurance Commissioner, or Director of a State-based Exchange to administer and enforce laws applicable to an MSP issuer or State-level issuer over which it has jurisdiction, or

(2) Otherwise in the best interests of enrollees or potential enrollees in MSP options.

(c) *Confidentiality of information.* OPM will take appropriate steps to cause the recipient of this information to preserve the information as confidential.

PARTS 801–899 [RESERVED]

CHAPTER IX—DENALI COMMISSION

Part		Page
900	National Environmental Policy Act implementing procedures	313
901–999	[Reserved]	

PART 900—NATIONAL ENVIRONMENTAL POLICY ACT IMPLEMENTING PROCEDURES

Subpart A—General

Sec.
900.101 Purpose.
900.102 Environmental policy.
900.103 Terms and abbreviations.
900.104 Federal and intergovernmental relationships.
900.105 Applicant responsibility.
900.106 Denali Commission responsibility.
900.107 Role of lead and cooperating agencies.
900.108 Public involvement.

Subpart B—Environmental Review Procedures

900.201 Environmental review process.
900.202 Emergency actions.
900.203 Determination of federal actions.
900.204 Categorical exclusions.
900.205 Environmental assessment.
900.206 Environmental impact statement.
900.207 Programmatic environmental reviews.

Subpart C—Environmental Assessments

900.301 Content.
900.302 General considerations in preparing environmental assessments.
900.303 Public involvement.
900.304 Actions resulting from assessment.
900.305 Findings of no significant impact.
900.306 Proposals normally requiring an EA.

Subpart D—Environmental Impact Statements

900.401 Notice of intent and scoping.
900.402 Preparation and filing of draft and final EISs.
900.403 Supplemental EIS.
900.404 Adoption.
900.405 Proposals normally requiring an EIS.

APPENDIX A TO PART 900—CATEGORICAL EXCLUSIONS

AUTHORITY: 42 U.S.C. 3121, 4321; 40 CFR parts 1500 through 1508.

SOURCE: 81 FR 53033, Aug. 11, 2016, unless otherwise noted.

Subpart A—General

§ 900.101 Purpose.

This regulation prescribes the policies and procedures of the Denali Commission (Commission) for implementing the National Environmental Policy Act of 1969 (NEPA) as amended (42 U.S.C. 4321–4347) and the Council on Environmental Quality (CEQ) Regulations for Implementing the Procedural Provisions of NEPA (40 CFR parts 1500 through 1508). This regulation also addresses other related federal environmental laws, statutes, regulations, and Executive Orders that apply to Commission actions. This part adopts, supplements, and is to be used in conjunction with, 40 CFR parts 1500 through 1508, consistent with 40 CFR 1507.3.

§ 900.102 Environmental policy.

It is the policy of the Commission to:

(a) Comply with the procedures and policies of NEPA and other related environmental laws, regulations, and orders applicable to Commission actions;

(b) Provide guidance to applicants responsible for ensuring that proposals comply with all appropriate Commission requirements;

(c) Integrate NEPA requirements and other planning and environmental review procedures required by law or Commission practice so that all such procedures run concurrently rather than consecutively;

(d) Encourage and facilitate public involvement in Commission decisions that affect the quality of the human environment;

(e) Use the NEPA process to identify and assess reasonable alternatives to proposed Commission actions to avoid or minimize adverse effects upon the quality of the human environment;

(f) Use all practicable means consistent with NEPA and other essential considerations of national policy to restore or enhance the quality of the human environment and avoid, minimize, or otherwise mitigate any possible adverse effects of the Commission's actions upon the quality of the human environment; and

(g) Consider and give important weight to factors including customary and traditional uses of resources, recreation, and the objectives of Federal, regional, State, local and tribal land use plans, policies, and controls for the area concerned in developing proposals and making decisions in order to achieve a proper balance between the development and utilization of natural, cultural and human resources and the

§ 900.103

protection and enhancement of environmental quality (see NEPA section 101 and 40 CFR 1508.14). In particular the Commission will consider potential effects on subsistence activities, which are critically important to the daily existence of Alaska Native villages.

§ 900.103 Terms and abbreviations.

(a) For the purposes of this part, the definitions in the CEQ Regulations, 40 CFR parts 1500 through 1508, are adopted and supplemented as set out in paragraphs (a)(1) through (5) of this section. In the event of a conflict the CEQ Regulations apply.

(1) *Action.* Action and Federal action as defined in 40 CFR 1508.18, include projects, programs, plans, or policies, subject to the Commission's control and responsibility.

(2) *Applicant.* The federal, state, local government or non-governmental partner or organization applying to the Commission for financial assistance or other approval. An applicant may also be a partner organization in receipt of award funds.

(3) *Approving Official.* The Denali Commission staff member designated by the Federal Co-Chair or his/her designee to fulfill the responsibilities defined in § 900.106, including overseeing development of and approval of the NEPA document.

(4) *Commission proposal (or proposal).* A proposal, as defined at 40 CFR 1508.23, is a Commission proposal whether initiated by the Commission, another federal agency, or an applicant.

(5) *Federal Co-Chair.* One of the seven members of the Commission, appointed by the Secretary of Commerce, as defined in the Denali Commission Act of 1998, 42 U.S.C. 3121, Public Law 105–277.

(b) The following abbreviations are used throughout this part:

(1) CATEX—Categorical exclusions;
(2) CEQ—Council on Environmental Quality;
(3) EA—Environmental assessment;
(4) EIS—Environmental impact statement;
(5) FONSI—Finding of no significant impact;
(6) NEPA—National Environmental Policy Act of 1969, as amended;
(7) NOI—Notice of intent; and
(8) ROD—Record of decision.

§ 900.104 Federal and intergovernmental relationships.

The Denali Commission was created to deliver the services of the federal government in the most cost-effective manner practicable. In order to reduce administrative and overhead costs, the Commission partners with federal, state and local agencies and Alaska Native villages and commonly depends on these governmental agencies for project management. Consequently, the Commission generally relies on the expertise and processes already in use by partnering agencies to help prepare Commission NEPA analyses and documents.

(a) With federal partners, the Commission will work as either a joint lead agency (40 CFR 1501.5 and 1508.16) or co-operating agency (40 CFR 1501.6 and 1508.5). The Commission may invite other Federal agencies to serve as the lead agency, a joint lead agency, or as a cooperating agency.

(b) Consistent with 40 CFR 1508.5, the Commission will typically invite Alaska Native villages and state and local government partners to serve as co-operating agencies.

(c) Requests for the Commission to serve as a lead agency (40 CFR 1501.5(d)), for CEQ to determine which Federal agency shall be the lead agency (40 CFR 1501.5(e)), or for the Commission to serve as a cooperating agency (40 CFR 1501.6(a)(1)) shall be mailed to the Commission office.

§ 900.105 Applicant responsibility.

(a) Applicants shall work under Commission direction provided by the Approving Official, and assist the Commission in fulfilling its NEPA obligations by preparing NEPA analyses and documents that comply with the provisions of NEPA (42 U.S.C. 4321–4347), the CEQ Regulations (40 CFR parts 1500 through 1508), and the requirements set forth in this part.

(b) Applicants shall follow Commission direction when they assist the Commission with the following responsibilities, among others:

(1) Prepare and disseminate applicable environmental documentation concurrent with a proposal's engineering, planning, and design;

(2) Create and distribute public notices;

(3) Coordinate public hearings and meetings as required;

(4) Submit all environmental documents created pursuant to this part to the Commission for review and approval before public distribution;

(5) Participate in all Commission-conducted hearings or meetings;

(6) Consult with the Commission prior to obtaining the services of an environmental consultant; in the case that an EIS is required, the consultant or contractor will be selected by the Commission; and

(7) Implement mitigation measures included as voluntary commitments by the applicant or as requirements of the applicant in environmental documents.

§ 900.106 Denali Commission responsibility.

(a) The Federal Co-Chair or his/her designee shall designate an Approving Official for each Commission proposal, and shall provide environmental guidance to the Approving Official;

(b) The Approving Official shall provide direction and guidance to the applicant as well as identification and development of required analyses and documentation;

(c) The Approving Official shall make an independent evaluation of the environmental issues, take responsibility for the scope and content of the environmental document (EA or EIS), and make the environmental finding;

(d) The Approving Official shall ensure mitigation measures included in environmental documents are implemented; and

(e) The Approving official shall be responsible for coordinating communications with cooperating agencies and other federal agencies.

§ 900.107 Role of lead and cooperating agencies.

In accordance with § 900.104, the Commission may defer the lead agency role to other federal agencies in accordance with 40 CFR 1501.5, and the Commission will then exercise its role as either a joint lead or a cooperating agency in accordance with 40 CFR 1501.6.

§ 900.108 Public involvement.

(a) When public involvement is required pursuant to subparts C and D of this part, interested persons and the affected public shall be provided notice of the availability of environmental documents, NEPA-related hearings, and public meetings. Such notice will be made on the Commission Web site and other means such that the community is notified (e.g., community postings, newspaper, radio or television).

(b) Applicants shall assist the Commission in providing the opportunity for public participation and considering the public comments on the proposal as described in subparts C and D of this part.

(c) Interested persons can obtain information or status reports on EISs and other elements of the NEPA process from the Commission's office at 510 L Street, Suite 410; Anchorage, Alaska 99501; or on the Commission Web site at *http://www.denali.gov*. Telephone: (907) 271–1414. The Commission will provide hard copies of NEPA documents to governmental and/or tribal entities in the affected communities.

(d) In the interests of national security or the public health, safety, or welfare, the Commission may reduce any time periods that the Commission has established and that are not required by the CEQ Regulations. The Commission shall publish a notice on the Web site at *http://www.denali.gov* and notify interested parties (see 40 CFR 1506.6) specifying the revised time periods for the proposed action and the rationale for the reduction.

Subpart B—Environmental Review Procedures

§ 900.201 Environmental review process.

(a) *General.* The environmental review process is the investigation of potential environmental impacts to determine the environmental process to be followed and to assist in the preparation of the environmental document.

(b) *Early coordination.* Applicants will contact the Commission and work with the Approving Official to begin the environmental review process as soon as

§ 900.202

Denali Commission assistance is projected. Environmental issues shall be identified and considered early in the proposal planning process. A systematic, interdisciplinary approach that includes community involvement and intergovernmental coordination to expand the potential sources of information and identify areas of concern will be used. Environmental permits and other forms of approval, concurrence, or consultation may be required. The planning process shall include permitting and other review processes to ensure that necessary information will be collected and provided to permitting and reviewing agencies in a timely manner.

§ 900.202 Emergency actions.

(a) *General.* Emergency circumstances may require immediate actions that preclude following standard NEPA processes. The Council shall limit alternative arrangements to those actions that are necessary to control the immediate impacts of the emergency. In the event of emergency circumstances, the Approving Official should coordinate with the Federal Co-Chair as soon as practicable. Immediate emergency actions necessary to protect the lives and safety of the public or prevent adverse impacts to ecological resources and functions should never be delayed in order to comply with these NEPA procedures. Alternative arrangements for NEPA compliance are permitted for emergency actions pursuant to paragraphs (b) through (d) of this section.

(b) *Categorical exclusion (CATEX).* When emergency circumstances make it necessary to determine whether an extraordinary circumstance would preclude the use of a CATEX, the Approving Official shall make the determination as soon as practicable. If an extraordinary circumstance exists, the Approving Official shall comply with paragraphs (c) and (d) of this section, as applicable.

(c) *Environmental assessment (EA).* When emergency circumstances make it necessary to take an action that requires an EA before the EA can be completed, the Approving Official will consult with the Federal Co-Chair to develop alternative arrangements to meet the requirements of these NEPA implementing procedures and CEQ Regulations pertaining to EAs. Alternative arrangements should focus on minimizing adverse environmental impacts of the proposed action and the emergency. To the maximum extent practicable, these alternative arrangements should include the content, interagency coordination, and public notification and involvement that would normally be undertaken for an EA for the action at issue and cannot alter the requirements of the CEQ Regulations at 40 CFR 1508.9(a)(1) and (b). The Federal Co-Chair may grant an alternative arrangement. Any alternative arrangement shall be documented. The Federal Co-Chair will inform CEQ of the alternative arrangements at the earliest opportunity.

(d) *Environmental Impact Statement (EIS).* Where emergency circumstances make it necessary to take actions with significant environmental impacts without observing other provisions of these NEPA implementing procedures and the CEQ Regulations (see 40 CFR 1506.11) the Federal Co-Chair may consult with CEQ about alternative arrangements for implementation of NEPA. In these situations, the Commission may reduce processing times or, if the emergency situation warrants, abbreviate its preparation and processing of EISs. Any request for alternative arrangements must be submitted by the Federal Co-Chair to CEQ and notice of a potential request should be provided to CEQ at the earliest opportunity. For projects undertaken by an applicant, the Approving Official will inform the Federal Co-Chair about the emergency. The Federal Co-Chair will consult CEQ requesting the alternative arrangements for complying with NEPA.

§ 900.203 Determination of federal actions.

(a) The Commission shall determine whether any Commission proposal:

(1) Is categorically excluded from preparation of either an EA or an EIS;

(2) Requires preparation of an EA; or

(3) Requires preparation of an EIS.

(b) Notwithstanding any other provision of this part, the Commission may prepare a NEPA document to assist

Denali Commission § 900.204

any Commission action at any time in order to further the purposes of NEPA. This NEPA document may be done to analyze the consequences of ongoing Commission activities, to support Commission planning, to assess the need for mitigation, to disclose fully the potential environmental consequences of Commission actions, or for any other reason. Documents prepared under this paragraph shall be prepared in the same manner as Commission documents prepared under this part.

§ 900.204 Categorical exclusions.

(a) *General.* A categorical exclusion (CATEX) is defined in 40 CFR 1508.4 as a category of actions which do not individually or cumulatively have a significant effect on the human environment and, for which in the absence of extraordinary circumstances or sensitive resources, neither an EA nor an EIS is required. Actions that meet the conditions in paragraph (b) of this section and are listed in section A of appendix A of this part can be categorically excluded from further analysis and documentation in an EA or EIS. Actions that meet the screening conditions in paragraph (b) of this section and are listed in section B of appendix A require satisfactory completion of a Denali Commission CATEX checklist in order to be categorically excluded from further analysis and documentation in an EA or EIS.

(b) *Conditions.* The following three conditions must be met for an action to be categorically excluded from further analysis in an EA or EIS.

(1) The action has not been segmented (too narrowly defined or broken down into small parts in order minimize its potential effects and avoid a higher level of NEPA review) and its scope includes the consideration of connected actions and, when evaluating extraordinary circumstances, cumulative impacts.

(2) No extraordinary circumstances described in paragraph (c) of this section exist, unless resolved through other regulatory means.

(3) One categorical exclusion described in either section of appendix A of this part encompasses the proposed action.

(c) *Extraordinary circumstances.* Any action that normally would be classified as a CATEX but could involve extraordinary circumstances will require appropriate environmental review documented in a Denali Commission CATEX checklist to determine if the CATEX classification is proper or if an EA or EIS should be prepared. Extraordinary circumstances to be considered include those likely to:

(1) Have a reasonable likelihood of significant impacts on public health, public safety, or the environment;

(2) Have effects on the environment that are likely to be highly controversial or involve unresolved conflicts concerning alternative uses of available resources;

(3) Have possible effects on the human environment that are highly uncertain, involve unique or unknown risks, or are scientifically controversial;

(4) Establish a precedent for future action or represent a decision in principle about future actions with potentially significant environmental effects;

(5) Relate to other actions with individually insignificant but cumulatively significant environmental effects;

(6) Have a greater scope or size than is normal for the category of action;

(7) Have the potential to degrade already existing poor environmental conditions or to initiate a degrading influence, activity, or effect in areas not already significantly modified from their natural condition;

(8) Have a disproportionately high and adverse effect on low income or minority populations (see Executive Order 12898);

(9) Limit access to and ceremonial use of Indian sacred sites on federal lands by Indian religious practitioners or adversely affect the physical integrity of such sacred sites (see Executive Order 13007);

(10) Threaten a violation of a federal, tribal, state or local law or requirement imposed for the protection of the environment;

(11) Have a reasonable likelihood of significant impact to subsistence activities; or

§ 900.205

(12) Have a reasonable likelihood of significant impacts on environmentally sensitive resources, such as:

(i) Properties listed, or eligible for listing, in the National Register of Historic Places;

(ii) Species listed, or proposed to be listed, on the List of Endangered or Threatened Species, or their habitat; or

(iii) Natural resources and unique geographic characteristics such as historic or cultural resources; park, recreation or refuge lands; wilderness areas; wild or scenic rivers; national natural landmarks; sole or principal drinking water aquifers; prime farmlands; special aquatic sites (defined under Section 404 of the Clean Water Act); floodplains; national monuments; and other ecologically significant or critical areas.

§ 900.205 Environmental assessment.

(a) An EA is required for all proposals, except those exempt from NEPA or categorically excluded under this part, and those requiring or determined to require an EIS. EAs provide sufficient evidence and analysis to determine whether to prepare an EIS or a finding of no significant impact (FONSI).

(b) In addition, an EA may be prepared on any action at any time in order to assist in planning and decision making, to aid in the Commission's compliance with NEPA when no EIS is necessary, or to facilitate EIS preparation.

(c) EAs shall be prepared in accordance with subpart C of this part and shall contain analyses to support conclusions regarding environmental impacts. If a FONSI is proposed, it shall be prepared in accordance with § 900.305.

§ 900.206 Environmental impact statement.

An EIS is required when the project is determined to have a potentially significant impact on the human environment. EISs shall be prepared in accordance with subpart D of this part.

§ 900.207 Programmatic environmental reviews.

(a) A programmatic NEPA review is used to assess the environmental impacts of a proposed action that is broad in reach, such as a program, plan, or policy (see 40 CFR 1502.4). Analyses of subsequent actions that fall within the program, plan, or policy may be tiered to the programmatic review, as described in 40 CFR 1502.20 and 1508.28.

(b) Programmatic NEPA reviews may take the form of a programmatic EA or a programmatic EIS.

(c) A programmatic EA shall meet all of the requirements for EAs in subpart C of this part, including those for content and public involvement. In order to adopt a programmatic EA prepared by another agency that did not provide the same public involvement opportunities as the Commission, the Commission shall provide notice of the availability of the programmatic EA and make it available for public comment consistent with § 900.303(b) and (c) before adopting it.

(d) A programmatic EIS shall meet all of the requirements for EISs in subpart D of this part and in 40 CFR parts 1500 through 1508.

Subpart C—Environmental Assessments

§ 900.301 Content.

(a) An EA shall include brief discussions of the need for the proposal; of alternatives to the proposal as required by NEPA section 102(2)(E); and of the environmental impacts of the proposal and alternatives. The EA shall also include a listing of agencies and persons consulted in the preparation of the EA.

(b) An EA may describe a broad range of alternatives and proposed mitigation measures to facilitate planning and decisionmaking.

(c) The EA should also document compliance, to the extent possible, with all applicable environmental laws and Executive Orders, or provide reasonable assurance that those requirements can be met.

(d) The EA should be a concise public document. The level of detail and depth of impact analysis will normally be limited to the minimum needed to

Denali Commission

determine the significance of potential environmental effects.

§ 900.302 General considerations in preparing environmental assessments.

(a) *Adoption of an EA.* The Commission may adopt an EA prepared for a proposal before the Commission by another agency or an applicant when the EA, or a portion thereof, addresses the proposed Commission action and meets the standards for an adequate analysis under this part and relevant provisions of 40 CFR parts 1500 through 1508, provided that the Commission makes its own evaluation of the environmental issues and takes responsibility for the scope and content of the EA in accordance with 40 CFR 1506.5(b).

(b) *Incorporation by reference into the EA.* Any document may be incorporated by reference in accordance with 40 CFR 1502.21 and used in preparing an EA in accordance with 40 CFR 1501.4(e) and 1506.5(a), provided that the Commission makes its own evaluation of the environmental issues and takes responsibility for the scope and content of the EA in accordance with 40 CFR 1506.5(b).

§ 900.303 Public involvement.

(a) Commission approval is required before an EA is made available to the public and the notice of availability is published.

(b) The public shall be provided notice of the availability of EAs and draft FONSIs in accordance with 40 CFR 1506.6 and § 900.108(a) by the Approving Official. The Approving Official is responsible for making the EA available for public inspection and will provide hard copies on request to the affected units of Alaska Native/American Indian tribal organizations and/or local government.

(c) EAs and draft FONSIs will be available for public comment for not less than 15 calendar days but may be published for a longer period of time as determined by the Approving Official.

(d) Final Commission action will be taken after public comments received on an EA and draft FONSI are reviewed and considered.

§ 900.304 Actions resulting from assessment.

(a) *Accepted without modification.* The Commission may accept a proposal without modifications if the EA indicates that the proposal does not have significant environmental impacts and a FONSI is prepared in accordance with § 900.305.

(b) *Accepted with modification.* If an EA identifies potentially significant environmental impacts, the proposal may be modified to eliminate such impacts. Proposals so modified may be accepted by the Commission if the proposed changes are evaluated in an EA and a FONSI is prepared in accordance with § 900.305.

(c) *Mitigated FONSI.* If mitigation is required to reduce the impacts below significant the FONSI shall identify the mitigation and describe applicable monitoring and enforcement measures intended to ensure the implementation of the mitigation measures.

(d) *Prepare an EIS.* The Commission shall require that the proposal be evaluated in an EIS, prepared in accordance with subpart D to this part, if the EA indicates significant environmental impacts that cannot be mitigated below a specified level of significance.

(e) *Rejected.* The Commission may always elect to reject a proposal.

§ 900.305 Findings of no significant impact.

(a) *Definition.* Finding of no significant impact (FONSI) means a document by the Commission briefly presenting the reasons why an action, not otherwise excluded as provided in § 900.204, will not have a significant impact on the human environment and for which an EIS will not be prepared.

(b) *Applicant responsibility.* The applicant shall assist the Commission with preparing the EA. The Commission remains responsible for compiling the public hearing summary or minutes, where applicable; and copies of any written comments received and responses thereto.

(c) *Content.* A FONSI shall include the EA or a summary of it and shall note any other environmental documents related to it (40 CFR 1501.7(a)(5)).

If the assessment is included, the finding need not repeat any of the discussion in the assessment but may incorporate it by reference.

(d) *Publication.* The Commission shall make the final FONSI available to the public on the Commission Web site.

(e) *Special circumstances.* The FONSI notice of availability will be made available for public review (including State and areawide clearinghouses) for 30 days before the Commission makes its final determination whether to prepare an environmental impact statement and before the action may begin (40 CFR 1501.4(e)(2)) where:

(1) The proposed action is, or is closely similar to, one which normally requires the preparation of an environmental impact statement under §900.405; or

(2) The nature of the proposed action is one without precedent.

§900.306 Proposals normally requiring an EA.

Proposals that normally require preparation of an EA include the following:

(a) Initial field demonstration of a new technology; and

(b) Field trials of a new product or new uses of an existing technology.

Subpart D—Environmental Impact Statements

§900.401 Notice of intent and scoping.

(a) The Commission shall publish a NOI, as described in 40 CFR 1508.22, in the FEDERAL REGISTER as soon as practicable after a decision is made to prepare an EIS, in accordance with 40 CFR 1501.7. If there will be a lengthy period of time between the Commission's decision to prepare an EIS and its actual preparation, the Commission may defer publication of the NOI until a reasonable time before preparing the EIS, provided that the Commission allows a reasonable opportunity for interested parties to participate in the EIS process. Consistent with §900.201(b), the Commission and the applicant will coordinate during the time period prior to the publication of the NOI to identify: the scope of the action, potential modifications to the proposal, potential alternatives, environmental constraints, potential timeframes for the environmental review, and federal, state, or tribal entities that could be interested in the project, including those with the potential to become cooperating agencies. Through the NOI, the Commission shall invite comments and suggestions on the scope of the EIS.

(b) Publication of the NOI in the FEDERAL REGISTER shall begin the public scoping process. The public scoping process for a Commission EIS shall allow a minimum of 30 days for the receipt of public comments.

§900.402 Preparation and filing of draft and final EISs.

(a) *General.* Except for proposals for legislation as provided for in 40 CFR 1506.8, EISs shall be prepared in two stages and may be supplemented.

(b) *Format.* The EIS format recommended by 40 CFR 1502.10 shall be used unless a determination is made on a particular project that there is a compelling reason to do otherwise. In such a case, the EIS format must meet the minimum requirements prescribed in 40 CFR 1502.10, as further described in 40 CFR 1502.11 through 1502.18.

(c) *Applicant role.* The draft or final EIS shall be prepared by the Commission with assistance from the applicant under appropriate guidance and direction from the Approving Official.

(d) *Third-party consultants.* A third-party consultant selected by the Commission or in cooperation with a cooperating agency may prepare the draft or final EIS.

(e) *Commission responsibility.* The Commission shall provide a schedule with time limits, guidance, participate in the preparation, independently evaluate, and take responsibility for the content of the draft and final EIS.

(f) *Filing.* After a draft or final EIS has been prepared, the Commission shall file the EIS with the Environmental Protection Agency (EPA). The EPA will publish a notice of availability in accordance with 40 CFR 1506.9 and 1506.10.

(g) *Draft to final EIS.* When a final EIS does not require substantial changes from the draft EIS, the Commission may document required changes in errata sheets, insertion pages, and revised sections. The Commission will then circulate such changes together with comments on the draft EIS, responses to comments, and other appropriate information as its final EIS. The Commission will not circulate the draft EIS again; however, the Commission will post the EIS on its Web site and provide the draft EIS if requested.

(h) *Record of decision.* A record of decision (ROD) will be prepared in accordance with 40 CFR 1505.2.

§ 900.403 Supplemental EIS.

(a) Supplements to either draft or final EISs shall be prepared, as prescribed in 40 CFR 1502.9, when the Commission finds that there are substantial changes are proposed in a project that are relevant to environmental concerns; or when there are significant new circumstances or information relevant to environmental concerns and bearing on the proposed action or its impacts.

(b) Where Commission action remains to be taken and the EIS is more than three years old, the Commission will review the EIS to determine whether it is adequate or requires supplementation.

(c) The Commission shall prepare, circulate and file a supplement to an EIS in the same fashion (exclusive of scoping) as a draft and final EIS. In addition, the supplement and accompanying administrative record shall be included in the administrative record for the proposal. When an applicant is involved, the applicant shall, under the direction of the approving official, provide assistance.

(d) An NOI to prepare a supplement to a final EIS will be published in those cases where a ROD has already been issued.

§ 900.404 Adoption.

(a) The Commission may adopt a draft or final EIS or portion thereof (see 40 CFR 1506.3), including a programmatic EIS, prepared by another agency.

(b) If the actions covered by the original EIS and the proposal are substantially the same, the Commission shall recirculate it as a final statement. Otherwise, the Commission shall treat the statement as a draft and recirculate it except as provided in paragraph (c) of this section.

(c) Where the Commission is a cooperating agency, it may adopt the EIS of the lead agency without recirculating it when, after an independent review of the EIS, the Commission concludes that its comments and suggestions have been satisfied.

(d) When the Commission adopts an EIS which is not final within the agency that prepared it, or when the action it assesses is the subject of a referral under 40 CFR part 1504, or when the EIS's adequacy is the subject of a judicial action which is not final, the Commission shall so specify.

§ 900.405 Proposals normally requiring an EIS.

An EIS will normally be required for:

(a) Large scale infrastructure construction efforts such as the relocation of an entire community;

(b) A project that requires a formal consultation under Section 7 of the Endangered Species Act; or

(c) Where implementation of the proposal may directly cause or induce changes that significantly:

(1) Displace population;

(2) Alter the character of existing residential areas; or

(3) Adversely affect a floodplain.

APPENDIX A TO PART 900—CATEGORICAL EXCLUSIONS

A. General Categorical Exclusions

Actions consistent with any of the following categories are, in the absence of extraordinary circumstances, categorically excluded from further analysis in an EA or EIS:

A1. Routine administrative and management activities including, but not limited to, those activities related to budgeting, finance, personnel actions, procurement activities, compliance with applicable executive orders and procedures for sustainable or "greened" procurement, retaining legal counsel, public affairs activities (e.g., issuing press releases, newsletters and notices of funding availability), internal and external program evaluation and monitoring (e.g., site visits), database development and maintenance, and computer systems administration.

A2. Routine activities that the Commission does to support its program partners and stakeholders, such as serving on task forces, ad hoc committees or representing Commission interests in other forums.

A3. Approving and issuing grants for administrative overhead support.

A4. Approving and issuing grants for social services, education and training programs, including but not limited to support for Head Start, senior citizen programs, drug treatment programs, and funding internships, except for projects involving construction, renovation, or changes in land use.

A5. Approving and issuing grants for facility planning and design.

A6. Nondestructive data collection, inventory, study, research, and monitoring activities (e.g., field, aerial and satellite surveying and mapping).

A7. Research, planning grants and technical assistance projects that are not reasonably expected to commit the federal government to a course of action, to result in legislative proposals, or to result in direct development.

A8. Acquisition and installation of equipment including, but not limited to, EMS, emergency and non-expendable medical equipment (e.g., digital imaging devices and dental equipment), and communications equipment (e.g., computer upgrades).

B. Program Categorical Exclusions

Actions consistent with any of the following categories are, in the absence of extraordinary circumstances, categorically excluded from further analysis and documentation in an EA or EIS upon completion of the Denali Commission CATEX checklist:

B1. Upgrade, repair, maintenance, replacement, or minor renovations and additions to buildings, roads, harbors and other maritime facilities, grounds, equipment, and other facilities, including but not limited to, roof replacement, foundation repair, ADA access ramp and door improvements, weatherization and energy efficiency related improvements, HVAC renovations, painting, floor system replacement, repaving parking lots and ground maintenance, that do not result in a change in the functional use of the real property.

B2. Engineering studies and investigations that do not permanently change the environment.

B3. Construction or lease of new infrastructure including, but not limited to, health care facilities, community buildings, housing, and bulk fuel storage and power generation plants, where such lease or construction:

(a) Is at the site of existing infrastructure and capacity is not substantially increased; or

(b) Is for infrastructure of less than 12,000 square feet of useable space when less than two aces of surface land area are involved at a new site.

B4. Construction or modification of electric power stations or interconnection facilities (including, but not limited to, switching stations and support facilities).

B5. Construction of electric powerlines approximately ten miles in length or less, or approximately 20 miles in length or less within previously disturbed or developed powerline or pipeline rights-of-way.

B6. Upgrading or rebuilding approximately twenty miles in length or less of existing electric powerlines, which may involve minor relocations of small segments or the powerlines.

B7. Demolition, disposal, or improvements involving buildings or structures when done in accordance with applicable regulations, including those regulations applying to removal of asbestos, polychlorinated biphenyls (PCBs), and other hazardous materials.

PARTS 901–999 [RESERVED]

CHAPTER X—OFFICE OF COMMUNITY SERVICES, ADMINISTRATION FOR CHILDREN AND FAMILIES, DEPARTMENT OF HEALTH AND HUMAN SERVICES

Part		Page
1000	Individual development account reserve funds established pursuant to Grants for Assets for Independence	325
1050	Charitable choice under the Community Services Block Grant Act programs	325
1080	Emergency Community Services Homeless Grant Program	327
1081–1099	[Reserved]	

PART 1000—INDIVIDUAL DEVELOPMENT ACCOUNT RESERVE FUNDS ESTABLISHED PURSUANT TO GRANTS FOR ASSETS FOR INDEPENDENCE

Sec.
1000.1 Scope.
1000.2 Definitions.
1000.3 Requirements.

AUTHORITY: 42 U.S.C. 604 nt.

SOURCE: 66 FR 48972, Sept. 25, 2001, unless otherwise noted.

§ 1000.1 Scope.

This part applies to the Office of Community Services' Assets for Independence Program.

§ 1000.2 Definitions.

Individual Development Account means a trust or custodial account created or organized in the United States exclusively for the purpose of paying the qualified expenses of an eligible individual, as defined in section 404(2) of Pub. L. 105–285, or enabling the eligible individual to make an emergency withdrawal as defined in section 404(3) of Pub. L. 105–385. The written governing instrument creating the trust or custodial account must meet the requirements of Section 404(5) of Pub. L. 105–285, and of the Project Eligibility Requirements set forth in Program Announcements.

Qualified Entity means one or more not-for-profit organizations described in section 501(c)(3) of the Internal Revenue Code of 1986 and exempt from taxation under section 501(a) of such Code; or a State or local government agency; or a tribal government which has submitted an application under section 405 of Pub. L. 105–285 jointly with a 501(c)(3) organization that is exempt from taxation under 501(a) of the Internal Revenue Code of 1986; or an entity that is a credit union designated as a low-income credit union by the National Credit Union Administration (NCUA), or an organization designated as a community development financial institution by the Secretary of the Treasury (or Community Development Financial Institutions Fund), and can demonstrate a collaborative relationship with a local community-based organization whose activities are designed to address poverty in the community and the needs of community members for economic independence and stability.

Reserve Fund means a fund, established by a qualified entity, that shall include all funds provided to the qualified entity from any public or private source in connection with the demonstration project and the proceeds from any investment made with such funds. The fund shall be maintained in accordance with section 407(c)(3), as amended. No less than 85 percent of the Federal grant funds in the Reserve Fund shall be used as matching contributions for Individual Development Accounts.

[66 FR 48972, Sept. 25, 2001, as amended at 67 FR 19518, Apr. 22, 2002]

§ 1000.3 Requirements.

(a) A qualified entity, other than a State or local government agency or tribal government, shall establish a Reserve Fund for use in the Assets for Independence program. Each reserve fund established by a qualified entity, other than a State or local government agency or tribal government, is subject to the Department of Health and Human Services' uniform administrative requirements under 45 CFR part 75.

(b) Any reserve fund established by a qualified entity that is a State or local government agency or tribal government is subject to the Department of Health and Human Services' uniform administrative requirements under 45 CFR part 75.

[66 FR 48972, Sept. 25, 2001, as amended at 81 FR 3021, Jan. 20, 2016]

PART 1050—CHARITABLE CHOICE UNDER THE COMMUNITY SERVICES BLOCK GRANT ACT PROGRAMS

Sec.
1050.1 Scope.
1050.2 Definitions.
1050.3 What conditions apply to the Charitable Choice provisions of the CSBG Act?

AUTHORITY: 42 U.S.C. 9901 *et seq.*

SOURCE: 68 FR 56469, Sept. 30, 2003, unless otherwise noted.

§ 1050.1 Scope.

This part applies to programs authorized under the Community Services Block Grant Act (CSBG Act). Title 42 U.S.C. 9901, 9913, 9920, 9921, 9922, 9923.

§ 1050.2 Definitions.

Applicable program means any program authorized under Title II of the Community Opportunities, Accountability, and Training and Education Act of 1998, 42 U.S.C. 9901, *et seq.*

Direct funding, directly funded or funding provided directly means funding that is provided to an organization directly by a governmental entity or an intermediate organization that has the same duties as a governmental entity, as opposed to funding that an organization receives as a result of the genuine and independent private choice of a beneficiary.

Intermediate organization means an organization that is authorized by the terms of a contract, grant or other agreement with the Federal Government, or a State or local government, to select other non-governmental organizations to provide assistance under an applicable program. For example, when a State uses CSBG Act funds to pay for technical assistance services provided by a private entity and also authorizes that entity to subcontract for a portion of the technical assistance effort, the private entity is an intermediate organization.

Program beneficiary or recipient means an individual who receives services under a program funded in whole or part by an applicable program.

Program participant means a public or private entity that has received financial assistance under an applicable program.

§ 1050.3 What conditions apply to the Charitable Choice provisions of the CSBG Act?

These Charitable Choice provisions apply whenever the Federal government, or a State or local government, uses funds under the CSBG Act to provide awards, contracts, or other assistance under any program authorized in the Community Services Block Grant, 42 U.S.C. 9901, *et seq.* Additionally, these provisions apply whenever an intermediate organization acting under a contract, grant, or other agreement with a Federal, State, or local government entity selects nongovernmental organizations to provide assistance under any of the programs authorized under the Community Services Block Grant Act.

(a)(1) Religious organizations are eligible, on the same basis as any other organization, to participate in the applicable programs as long as they use program funds consistent with the Establishment Clause and the Free Exercise Clause of the First Amendment to the United States Constitution.

(2) Neither the Federal government nor a State or local government receiving funds under an applicable program shall discriminate against an organization that applies to provide, or provides, services or benefits on the basis of the organization's religious character or affiliation.

(b) No program participant that receives direct funding under an applicable program may expend the program funds for inherently religious activities, such as worship, religious instruction, or proselytization. If an organization conducts such activities, it must offer them separately, in time or location, from the programs or services directly funded under any applicable program, and participation must be voluntary for program beneficiaries.

(c) A religious organization that participates in an applicable program will retain its independence from Federal, State, and local governments and may continue to carry out its mission, including the definition, practice and expression of its religious beliefs, provided that it does not expend any direct funding under the applicable program to support any inherently religious activities, such as worship, religious instruction, or proselytization. Among other things, religious organizations may use space in their facilities to provide services funded under an applicable program without removing religious art, icons, scriptures, or other symbols. In addition, such a religious organization retains the authority over its internal governance, and it may retain religious terms in its organization's name, select its board members on a religious basis, and include religious references in its organization's mission statements and other governing documents.

(d) The participation of a religious organization in, or its receipt of funds from, an applicable program does not affect that organization's exemption provided under 42 U.S.C. 2000e–1 regarding employment practices.

(e) A religious organization that receives funds under an applicable program, shall not, in providing program services or benefits, discriminate against a program beneficiary or prospective program beneficiary on the basis of religion or a religious belief.

(f) Religious organizations that receive funds under an applicable program are subject to the same regulations as other nongovernmental organizations to account, in accordance with generally accepted auditing and accounting principles, for the use of such funds. In addition, religious organizations are required to keep any Federal funds they receive for services segregated in a separate account from non-Federal funds. Only the segregated government funds are subject to audit by the government under the applicable program.

(g) If a State or local government contributes its own funds to supplement CSBG Act funded activities, the State or local government has the option to segregate the Federal funds or commingle them. However, if the funds are commingled, the Charitable Choice provisions apply to all of the commingled funds.

(h) If a nongovernmental passthrough entity, acting under a grant, contract, or other agreement with the Federal, State or local government, is given the authority to select nongovernmental organizations to provide services under an applicable program, then the intermediate organization must ensure that the service provider complies with these Charitable Choice provisions and 45 CFR 87.1 and 87.3(i) through (l). The pass-through entity retains all other rights of a nongovernmental organization under the Charitable Choice provisions.

[68 FR 56469, Sept. 30, 2003, as amended at 81 FR 19428, Apr. 4, 2016]

PART 1080—EMERGENCY COMMUNITY SERVICES HOMELESS GRANT PROGRAM

Sec.
1080.1 Scope.
1080.2 Definitions.
1080.3 Allocation of funds.
1080.4 Eligible use of funds.
1080.5 Application procedures for States.
1080.6 Funding of alternative organizations.
1080.7 Funding of Indian tribes.
1080.8 Reporting requirements.
1080.9 Other requirements.

AUTHORITY: 42 U.S.C. 11302 (101 Stat. 485); 42 U.S.C. 11461–11464, 11472 (101 Stat. 532–533), as amended.

SOURCE: 54 FR 6372, Feb. 9, 1989, unless otherwise noted.

§ 1080.1 Scope.

This part applies to the Emergency Community Services Homeless Grant Program.

§ 1080.2 Definitions.

(a) *Homeless* or *homeless individual* includes:

(1) An individual who lacks a fixed, regular, and adequate nighttime residence; and

(2) An individual who has a primary nighttime residence that is:

(i) A supervised publicly or privately operated shelter designed to provide temporary living accommodations (including welfare hotels, congregate shelters, and transitional housing for the mentally ill);

(ii) An institution that provides a temporary residence for individuals intended to be institutionalized; or

(iii) A public or private place not designed for, or ordinarily used as, a regular sleeping accommodation for human beings.

The term *homeless* or *homeless individual* does not include any individual imprisoned or otherwise detained pursuant to an Act of the Congress or a State law.

(b) *Indian tribe* means any tribe, band, nation, or other organized group or community of Indians, including any Alaska Native village or regional or village corporation (as defined in, or established pursuant to, the Alaska Native Claims Settlement Act), that is recognized by the Federal Government as eligible for special programs and

§ 1080.3

services provided to Indians because of their status as Indians.

(c) *State* includes the 50 States, the District of Columbia, the Commonwealth of Puerto Rico, the Virgin Islands, Guam, American Samoa, the Commonwealth of the Northern Mariana Islands, and the Republic of Palau.

§ 1080.3 Allocation of funds.

From the amounts made available under the Emergency Community Services Homeless Grant Program, the Secretary shall make grants to States that administer programs under the Community Services Block Grant Act (42 U.S.C. 9901 *et seq.*), after taking into account the amount set aside for Indian tribes in § 1080.7(a) of this chapter. Such grants shall be allocated to the States in accordance with the formula set forth in subsections (a) and (b) of section 674 of such Act (42 U.S.C. 9903 (a) and (b)). No funds shall be allocated under subsection (c) of section 674 of such Act (42 U.S.C. 9903(c)).

§ 1080.4 Eligible use of funds.

Amounts awarded under the Emergency Community Services Homeless Grant Program may be used only for the following purposes:

(a) Expansion of comprehensive services to homeless individuals to provide follow-up and long-term services to help them make the transition out of poverty;

(b) Renovation of buildings to be used to provide such services, except that not more than 50 percent of such amounts may be used for such purpose, and provided that all procedures required under the National Historic Preservation Act are followed;

(c) Provision of assistance in obtaining social and maintenance services and income support services for homeless individuals;

(d) Promotion of private sector and other assistance to homeless individuals; and

(e) After October 1, 1988, provision of assistance to any individual who has received a notice of foreclosure, eviction, or termination of utility services, if—

(1) The inability of the individual to make mortgage, rental, or utility payments is due to a sudden reduction in income;

(2) The assistance is necessary to avoid the foreclosure, eviction, or termination of utility services; and

(3) There is a reasonable prospect that the individual will be able to resume the payments within a reasonable period of time.

(f) Provision of, or referral to, violence counseling for homeless children and individuals, and the provision of violence counseling training to individuals who work with homeless children and individuals; and,

(g) Not more than 5 percent of the amount received will be used to defray State administrative costs.

[54 FR 6372, Feb. 9, 1989, as amended at 57 FR 27946, June 23, 1992]

§ 1080.5 Application procedures for States.

(a) Each State requesting funds under the Emergency Community Services Homeless Grant Program shall submit to the Office of Community Services an application for funds for each fiscal year, at a time established by the Secretary. Approval must be requested of and received from the Office of Community Services before a State may implement changes to the information requested by paragraph (b) of this section after an application has been approved.

(b) The application may be in any format, but must include a description of the agencies, organizations, and activities that the State intends to support with the amounts received. In addition, the application must include the following assurances, signed by the Governor or his/her designee:

(1) The State will award not less than 95 percent of the amounts it receives to:

(i) Community action agencies and other organizations that are eligible to receive amounts under section 675(c)(2)(A) of the Community Services Block Grant Act (42 U.S.C. 9904(c)(2)(A));

(ii) Organizations serving migrant and seasonal farmworkers; and

(iii) Any organization to which a State, that applied for and received a waiver from the Secretary under Public Law 98–139, made a grant under the

Community Services Block Grant Act (42 U.S.C. 9901 et seq.) for fiscal year 1984;

(2) No amount received will be used to supplant other programs for homeless individuals administered by the State;

(3) Not more than 5 percent of the amount received will be used to defray State administrative costs;

(4) Every effort will be made to award the funds within 60 days of their receipt;

(5) Not more than 25 percent of the amounts received will be used for the purpose described in § 1080.4(e) of these regulations; and

(6) The State will have mechanisms in place to assure coordination among State and local agencies serving the homeless. This will include coordination at the State level with the agency responsible for developing the Comprehensive Homeless Assistance Plan or the Comprehensive Housing Affordability Strategy as required by section 401 of such Act (42 U.S.C. 11361), as amended by section 836 of the Cranston-Gonzalez National Affordable Housing Act.

(7) The State will have procedures in place to assure compliance with the provisions of the National Historic Preservation Act prior to the awarding of any amounts to be used for renovating any properties that are listed on, or eligible for inclusion on, the National Register of Historic Places.

(Information collection requirements are approved by the Office of Management and Budget under control number 0970–0088)

[54 FR 6372, Feb. 9, 1989, as amended at 57 FR 27946, June 23, 1992]

§ 1080.6 Funding of alternative organizations.

(a) If a State does not apply for or submits an approvable application for a grant under the Emergency Community Services Homeless Grant Program, the Secretary shall use the amounts that would have been allocated to that State to make grants to agencies and organizations in the State that meet the requirements of § 1080.5(b)(1).

(b) The amounts allocated under this section in any fiscal year shall be awarded to eligible agencies and organizations in the same proportion as funds distributed to those agencies and organizations by the State for the previous fiscal year under the Community Services Block Grant Program (42 U.S.C. 9904(c)(2)(A)).

(c) Agencies and organizations eligible to be funded under this section shall submit an application meeting the requirements of §§ 1080.5(a) and 1080.5(b)(2), (3), (5), (6) and (7), at a time specified by the Secretary. If such an agency or organization does not apply for or submit an approvable application under this section, the funds that would have been allocated to them shall be reallocated by the Secretary to the remaining eligible agencies and organizations on a pro rata basis.

[54 FR 6372, Feb. 9, 1989, as amended at 57 FR 27946, June 23, 1992]

§ 1080.7 Funding of Indian tribes.

(a) Not less than 1.5 percent of the funds provided in each fiscal year for the Emergency Community Services Homeless Grant Program shall be allocated by the Secretary directly to Indian tribes that have applied for and received a direct grant award under section 674(c) of the Community Services Block Grant Act (41 U.S.C. 9903(c)) for that fiscal year.

(b) An Indian tribe funded under this section is not required to submit an application for Emergency Community Services Homeless Grant Program funds. A tribe's application for a direct grant award under section 674(c) of the Community Services Block Grant Act (42 U.S.C. 9903(c)) that is submitted by September 1 for the succeeding fiscal year will be considered as an application for Emergency Community Services Homeless Grant Program funds for that fiscal year. Acceptance of the Community Services Block Grant application by the Office of Community Services will constitute approval of an award of funds under this section.

(c) Funds allocated under this section shall be allotted to an Indian tribe in an amount that bears the same ratio to all the funds allocated under this section as the tribe's poverty population bears to the total poverty population of all tribes funded under this section, except that no tribe shall receive an amount of less than:

§ 1080.8

(1) $500, for those tribes whose allocation under this section would otherwise be at least $1 but no more than $500; or

(2) $1000, for those tribes whose allocation under this section would otherwise be at least $501 but less than $1000.

(d) For purposes of this section, an Indian tribe's poverty population shall be calculated by multiplying the tribe's overall population by the Indian rural poverty rate for the State in which it is located, using the population and rural poverty rate figures established for the purposes of making direct grants under section 674(c) of the Community Services Block Grant Act (42 U.S.C. 9903(c)).

§ 1080.8 Reporting requirements.

Each recipient of funds under the Emergency Community Services Homeless Grant Program shall submit an annual report to the Secretary, within 6 months of the end of the period covered by the report, on the expenditure of funds and the implementation of the program for that fiscal year.

(a) The report is to state the types of activities funded, any efforts undertaken by the grantee and its subgrantees to coordinate homeless activities funded under this program with other homeless assistance activities in the State and communities, the number of individuals served and any impediments, including statutory and regulatory restrictions to homeless individuals' use of the program and to their obtaining services or benefits under the program.

(b) Such annual report shall provide information on the use of funds to defray State administrative costs, including the types of activities which specifically address services to the homeless and also those activities that are related to the administrative costs associated with the coordination and integration of services to the homeless.

(c) States shall also provide information in the annual report which details programs, progress, and activities that are specifically related to expenditures for renovation, including the effects of such activities on historic properties, and the provision of, or referral to, services for domestic violence.

(Information collection requirements are approved by the Office of Management and Budget under control number 0970–0088)

[57 FR 27946, June 23, 1992]

§ 1080.9 Other requirements.

All recipients of grants under the Emergency Community Services Homeless Grant Program shall be subject to the following regulations applicable to the block grant programs in the Department of Health and Human Services:

(a) 45 CFR part 96, subpart B, § 96.12—Grant Payment, concerning the timing and method of disbursing grant awards;

(b) 45 CFR part 96, subpart B, § 96.14—Time Period for Obligation and Expenditure of Grant Funds, as amended, concerning the availability of grant funds;

(c) 45 CFR part 96, subpart C—Financial Management, as amended, concerning financial management and audit requirements;

(d) 45 CFR part 96, subpart E—Enforcement, as amended, concerning enforcement and complaint procedures; and

(e) 45 CFR part 96, subpart F—Hearing Procedures, concerning hearing procedures.

PARTS 1081–1099 [RESERVED]

CHAPTER XI—NATIONAL FOUNDATION ON THE ARTS AND THE HUMANITIES

EDITORIAL NOTE: Nomenclature changes to chapter XI appear at 66 FR 47096, Sept. 11, 2001.

SUBCHAPTER A—GENERAL

Part		Page
1100	Statement for the guidance of the public—Organization, procedure and availability of information	333
1105	Standards of conduct for employees	337
1110	Nondiscrimination in federally assisted programs	337
1115	Privacy Act regulations	348

SUBCHAPTER B—NATIONAL ENDOWMENT FOR THE ARTS

1116–1148	[Reserved]	
1149	Program Fraud Civil Remedies Act regulations	353
1150	Collection of claims	370
1151	Nondiscrimination on the basis of handicap	382
1152	Intergovernmental review of National Endowment for the Arts programs and activities	391
1153	Enforcement of nondiscrimination on the basis of handicap in programs or activities conducted by the National Endowment for the Arts	394
1156	Nondiscrimination on the basis of age	401
1157	[Reserved]	
1158	New restrictions on lobbying	407
1159	Implementation of the Privacy Act of 1974	419

SUBCHAPTER C—FEDERAL COUNCIL ON THE ARTS AND THE HUMANITIES

1160	Indemnities under the Arts and Artifacts Indemnity Act	428

SUBCHAPTER D—NATIONAL ENDOWMENT FOR THE HUMANITIES

1168	New restrictions on lobbying	433
1170	Nondiscrimination on the basis of handicap in federally assisted programs or activities	444

Part		Page
1171	Public access to NEH records under the Freedom of Information Act	456
1172	Nondiscrimination on the basis of age in federally assisted programs or activities	466
1174	[Reserved]	
1175	Enforcement of nondiscrimination on the basis of handicap in programs or activities conducted by the National Endowment for the Humanities	473
1176	Part-time career employment	478
1177	Claims collection	480
1178	Use of penalty mail in the location and recovery of missing children	483
1179	Salary offset	484

SUBCHAPTER E—INSTITUTE OF MUSEUM AND LIBRARY SERVICES

1180	[Reserved]	
1181	Enforcement of nondiscrimination on the basis of handicap in programs or activities conducted by the Institute of Museum and Library Services	488
1182	Implementation of the Privacy Act of 1974	493
1183	[Reserved]	
1184	Implementation of the Freedom of Information Act	501
1185–1199	[Reserved]	

SUBCHAPTER A—GENERAL

PART 1100—STATEMENT FOR THE GUIDANCE OF THE PUBLIC—ORGANIZATION, PROCEDURE AND AVAILABILITY OF INFORMATION

Sec.
1100.1 Definitions.
1100.2 Organization.
1100.3 Availability of information to the public.
1100.4 Current index.
1100.5 Agency procedures for handling requests for documents.
1100.6 Fees.
1100.7 Foundation report of actions.

AUTHORITY: 5 U.S.C. 552, as amended by Pub. L. 99–570, 100 Stat. 3207.

SOURCE: 52 FR 48266, Dec. 21, 1987, unless otherwise noted.

§ 1100.1 Definitions.

(a) *Agency* means the National Endowment for the Arts.

(b) *Commercial use request* means a request by or on behalf of anyone who seeks information for a use or purpose that furthers the commercial trade or profit interests of the requestor (or the person on whose behalf the request is made.) The agency must determined the use to which a requestor will put the document. Where the agency has reasonable cause to doubt the use to which a requestor will put the records sought or the use is not clear from the request, the agency may seek additional clarification. The requestor fears the burden of demonstrating the use or purpose of the information requested.

(c) *Direct costs* mens those expenditures which an agency actually incurs in searching for and duplication documents to respond to a Freedom of Information Act (FOIA) request. In the case of commercial use requests, the term shall also include expenditures for reviewing documents.

(d) *Duplication* means the process of making a copy of a document necessary to respond to a FOIA request. Such copies may be in the form of paper, microfilm, machine readable documents, or other materials.

(e) *Educational institution* means a preschool, elementary, or secondary school, an institution of graduate or undergraduate higher education, an institution of professional education, or an institution of vocational education, which operates a program or programs of scholarly research.

(f) *Non-commercial scientific institution* means an institution that is not operated on a "commercial use" basis as defined in paragraph (b) of this section and which is operated solely for the purposes of conducting scientific research the results of which are not intended to promote any particular product or industry.

(g) *Representative of the news media* means any person actively gathering news for an entity that is organized and operated to publish or broadcast information that is about current events or that would be of current interest to the public. Freelance journalists may be regarded as working for a news organization if they can demonstrate a sound basis for expecting publication though that organization, even though not actually employed by it.

(h) *Review* means the process of examining a document located in response to a commercial use request to determine whether any portion is permitted to be withheld. Review includes processing documents for disclosure, including all that is necessary to excise them and otherwise prepare them for release. Review does not include time spent resolving general legal or policy issues regarding the application of exemptions.

(i) *Search* means all the time that is spent looking for material that responds to a request, including page-by-page or line-by-line identification of material in documents. Searches may be done manually or by computer using exisiting programs.

[52 FR 48266, Dec. 21, 1987, as amended at 79 FR 9621, Feb. 20, 2014]

§ 1100.2 Organization.

The National Foundation on the Arts and the Humanities was established by the National Foundation on the Arts and the Humanities Act of 1965, 20

U.S.C. 951 *et seq.* The Foundation is composed of the National Endowment for the Arts, the National Endowment for the Humanities, the Institute of Museum and Library Services, and the Federal Council on the Arts and the Humanities. The Institute of Museum and Library Services became a part of the National Foundation on the Arts and the Humanities pursuant to the Museum and Library Services Act, as amended (20 U.S.C. 9102). Each Endowment is headed by a Chairman and has an advisory national council composed of 26 presidential appointees. The Institute of Museum and Library Services is headed by a Director and has a National Museum and Library Services Board composed of 20 presidential appointees, the Director, and IMLS's Deputy Directors for the Offices of Library Services, and Museum Services. The Federal Council on the Arts and the Humanities, comprised of Executive branch officials and appointees of the legislative branch, is authorized to make agreements to indemnify against loss or damage for certain exhibitions and advise on arts and humanities matters. The National Endowment for the Humanities, the Federal Council on the Arts and Humanities, and the Institute of Museum and Library Services no longer follow the regulations under this part. The procedures for disclosing records of the National Endowment for the Humanities and the Federal Council on the Arts and the Humanities are available at 45 CFR part 1171. The procedures for disclosing records of the Institute of Museum and Library Services are available at 45 CFR part 1184.

[79 FR 9621, Feb. 20, 2014]

§ 1100.3 **Availability of information to the public.**

(a) Descriptive brochures of the organization, programs, and function of the National Endowment for the Arts are available upon request. Inquiries involving work of the National Endowment for the Arts should be addressed to the National Endowment for the Arts, 1100 Pennsylvania Avenue NW., Washington, DC 20506. The telephone number of the National Endowment for the Arts is (202) 682–5400.

(b) The head of the National Endowment for the Arts is responsible for the effective administration of the Freedom of Information Act. The head of the National Endowment for the Arts pursuant to this responsibility hereby directs that every effort be expended to facilitate service to the public with respect to the obtaining of information and records.

(c) Requests for access to records of the National Endowment for the Arts may be filed by mail with the General Counsel of the National Endowment for the Arts or by email at *FOIA@arts.gov*. All requests should reasonably describe the record or records sought. Requests submitted should be clearly identified as being made pursuant to the Freedom of Information Act.

[79 FR 9622, Feb. 20, 2014]

§ 1100.4 **Current index.**

The National Endowment for the Arts shall maintain and make available for public inspection and copying a current index providing identifying information for the public as to any matter which is issued, adopted, or promulgated and which is required to be made available pursuant to 5 U.S.C. 552(a)(1) and (2). Publication and distribution of such indices has been determined by the Foundation to be unnecessary and impracticable. The indices will be provided upon request at a cost not to exceed the direct cost of the duplication.

[79 FR 9622, Feb. 20, 2014]

§ 1100.5 **Agency procedures for handling requests for documents.**

(a) Upon receiving a request for documents in accordance with the rules of this part, the General Counsel or respective Assistant General Counsel serving as the Freedom of Information Act Officer of the National Endowment for the Arts shall determine whether or not the request shall be granted in whole or in part.

(1) The determination shall be made within ten (10) days (excepting Saturdays, Sundays, and legal holidays) after receipt of such request.

(2) The requestor shall be notified of the determination and the reasons that support it. When a request is denied in whole or in part, the requestor, will be notified of his or her rights to appeal

National Foundation on the Arts and the Humanities § 1100.6

the determination to the head of the agency.

(b)(1) Any party whose request for documents has been denied in whole or in part may file an appeal no later than ten (10) working days following receipt of the notification of denial. Appeals must be addressed to the Chairman, National Endowment for the Arts, Washington, DC 20506.

(2) The head of the agency or his delegatee shall make a determination with respect to the appeal within twenty (20) days (excepting Saturdays, Sundays, and legal holidays) after the agency has received the appeal, except as provided in paragraph (c) of this section. If, on appeal, the denial is upheld either in whole or in part, the head of the agency shall notify the party submitting the appeal of the judicial review provisions of 5 U.S.C. 552(a)(4)(B).

(c) In unusual circumstances, the time limits prescribed to determine a request for documents with respect to initial actions or actions on appeal may be extended by written notice from the General Counsel or respective Assistant General Counsel serving as the Freedom of Information Act Officer of the National Endowment for the Arts. The notice shall describe the reason for the extension and the date on which the determination is expected to be made. No notice shall specify a date that would result in an extension of more than ten (10) days (excepting Saturdays, Sundays, and legal holidays). As is used in this paragraph, *unusual circumstances* means:

(1) The need to search for and collect the requested records from field facilities or other establishments that are separate from the office processing the request;

(2) The need to search for, collect, and appropriately examine a voluminous amount of separate and distinct records which are demanded in a single request; or

(3) The need for consultation, which shall be conducted with all practicable speed, with another agency having a substantial interest in the determination of the request or among two or more components of the agency having a substantial subject-matter interest in the request.

[52 FR 48266, Dec. 21, 1987, as amended at 79 FR 9622, Feb. 20, 2014]

§ 1100.6 Fees.

(a) *Categories of fees.* Fees will be charged according to the Category of the FOIA request.

(1) *Commercial use requests.* The agency will assess charges to recover the full direct cost of searching for, reviewing, and duplicating the requested document. The agency may recover the cost of searching for and reviewing records even if there is ultimately no disclosure.

(2) *Requests from educational and noncommercial scientific institutions.* The agency will charge for duplication costs. To qualify for this category the requestor must show: (i) That requested records are being sought under the auspices of a qualified institution as defined in § 1100.1 (e) or (f) of this part; (ii) the records are not sought for commercial use; and (iii) the records are being sought in furtherance of scholarly or scientific research of the institution.

(3) *Requests by representatives of the news media.* The agency will charge duplication costs for the requests in this category.

(4) *All other requests.* All other requests shall be charged fees which, recover the full reasonable cost for searching for and duplicating the requested records.

(b) *General fee schedule.* The agency shall use the most efficient and least costly method to comply with requests for documents made under the FOIA. The agency will charge fees to recover all allowable direct costs incurred. The agency may charge fees for searching for and reviewing requested documents even if the documents are determined to be exempt from disclosure or cannot be located. If search charges are likely to exceed $25, the agency shall notify the requestor, unless the requestor has indicated in advance the willingness to pay higher fees. The following fees shall be charged in accordance with paragraph (a) of this section.

(1) *Searches*—(i) *Manual.* The fee charged will be the salary rate(s) (i.e.,

§ 1100.7

basic pay plus 16.1 percent) of the employee(s) conducting the search.

(ii) *Computer.* The fee charged will be the actual direct cost of providing the service including the cost of operating the central processing unit for the operating time that is directly attributed to searching for records responsive to a request and the operator/programmer salary apportionable to the search.

(2) *Review.* The fee charged will equal the salary rate(s) (basic pay plus 16.1 percent) of the employee(s) conducting the review.

(3) *Duplication.* Copies of documents photocopied on one-side of a 8½ × 11 inch sheet of paper will be provided at $.10 per page. Photocopies on two sides of a single 8½ × 11 inch sheet of paper will be provided at $.20 per page. For duplication of other materials, the charge will be the direct cost of duplication.

(c) *Restrictions on charging fees.* (1) Except for documents provided in response to a commercial use request, the first 100 pages of duplication or the first two (2) hours of search time shall be provided at no charge. For the purposes of this section, two (2) hours of search time by computer entitles the requestor to two (2) hours of computer operator salary translated into computer search costs. Computer search costs consist of operator salary plus central proceeding unit operating time costs for the duration of the search.

(2) Fees shall not be charged to any requestor, including commercial use requestors, if the cost of collecting a fee would be equal to or greater than the fee itself.

(d) *Waiver or reduction of fees.* (1) Documents shall be furnished without charge or at reduced charge if disclosure of the information is in the public interest because it is likely to contribute significantly to public understanding of the operations or activities of the government and is not primarily in the commercial interest of the requestor.

(2) The following factors shall be used to determine whether a fee will be waived or reduced:

(i) *The subject of the request.* Whether the subject of the requested records concerns "the operations or activities of the government";

(ii) *The informative value of the information to be disclosed.* Whether the disclosure is "likely to contribute" to an understanding of government operations or activities;

(iii) *The contribution to an understanding of the subject by the general public likely to result from disclosure.* Whether disclosure of the requested information will contribute to "public understanding";

(iv) *The significance of the contribution to public understanding.* Whether disclosure is likely to contribute "significantly" to public understanding of government operations or activities;

(v) *The existence and magnitude of a commercial interest.* Whether the requestor has a commercial interest that would be furthered by the disclosure; and if so

(vi) *The primary interest in disclosure.* Whether the magnitude of the identified commercial interest of the requestor is sufficiently large in comparison with the public interest in disclosure, that disclosure is "primarily in the commercial interest of the requester."

(e) *Assessment and collection of fees.* (1) Interest will accrue from the date the bill is mailed if the fee is not paid within thirty (30) days. Interest will be assessed at the rate prescribed in 31 U.S.C. 3717.

(2) If the agency reasonably believes that a requestor(s) is making multiple requests to avoid the assessment of fees, the agency may aggregate such requests and charge accordingly.

(3) The agency may request an advance payment of the fee if

(i) The allowable charges are likely to exceed $250; or

(ii) The requestor has failed previously to pay a fee in a timely fashion.

(4) When the agency requests an advance payment, the time limits prescribed in section (a)(6) of the Freedom of Information Act will begin only after the agency has received full payment.

§ 1100.7 Foundation report of actions.

On or before March 1 of each calendar year, the National Endowment for the Arts shall submit a report of its activities with regard to public information requests during the preceding calendar year to the Speaker of the House of Representatives and to the President of the Senate. The report shall include:

(a) The number of determinations made by National Endowment for the Arts not to comply with requests for records made to the agency under the provisions of this part and the reasons for each such determination;

(b) The number of appeals made by persons under such provision, the result of such appeals, and the reasons for the action upon each appeal that results in the denial of information;

(c) The names and titles or positions of each person responsible for the denial of records requested under the provisions of this part and the number of instances of participation for each;

(d) The results of each proceeding conducted pursuant to 5 U.S.C. 552(a)(4)(F), as amended, including a report of the disciplinary action taken against the officer of employee who was primarily responsible for improperly withholding records or an explanation of why disciplinary action was not taken;

(e) A copy of every rule made by the Foundation implementing the provisions of the FOIA.

(f) A copy of the fee schedule and the total amount of fees collected by the agency for making records available under this section; and

(g) Such other information as indicates efforts to administer the provisions of the FOIA, as amended.

[52 FR 48266, Dec. 21, 1987, as amended at 79 FR 9622, Feb. 20, 2014]

PART 1105—STANDARDS OF CONDUCT FOR EMPLOYEES

AUTHORITY: 5 U.S.C. 7301.

SOURCE: 68 FR 52702, Sept. 5, 2003, unless otherwise noted.

§ 1105.1 Cross-reference to employee ethical conduct standards and financial disclosure and financial interests regulations.

Employees of the National Endowment for the Arts and the National Endowment for the Humanities are subject to the executive branchwide standards of ethical conduct at 5 CFR part 2635; the executive branch employees responsibilities and conduct regulations at 5 CFR part 735; the executive branch financial disclosure regulations at 5 CFR part 2634, and the executive branch financial interests regulations at 5 CFR part 2640. Employees of the National Endowment for the Arts are also subject to that Agency's regulations at 5 CFR part 6501, which supplement the executive branchwide standards of conduct at 5 CFR part 2635. Employees of the National Endowment for the Humanities are also subject to that Agency's regulations at 5 CFR part 6601, which supplement the executive branchwide standards of conduct at 5 CFR part 2635.

PART 1110—NONDISCRIMINATION IN FEDERALLY ASSISTED PROGRAMS

Sec.
1110.1 Purpose.
1110.2 Application of part.
1110.3 Discrimination prohibited.
1110.4 Assurances required.
1110.5 Illustrative applications.
1110.6 Compliance information.
1110.7 Conduct of investigations.
1110.8 Procedure for effecting compliance.
1110.9 Hearings.
1110.10 Decisions and notices.
1110.11 Judicial review.
1110.12 Effect on other regulations; forms and instructions.
1110.13 Definitions.

APPENDIX A TO PART 1110—FEDERAL FINANCIAL ASSISTANCE TO WHICH THIS PART APPLIES

AUTHORITY: 42 U.S.C. 2000d–2000d–7.

SOURCE: 38 FR 17991, July 5, 1973, unless otherwise noted.

§ 1110.1 Purpose.

The purpose of this part is to effectuate the provisions of title VI of the Civil Rights Act of 1964 (hereafter referred to as the "Act"), 42 U.S.C. 2000d et seq., to the end that no person in the United States shall, on the ground of race, color, or national origin, be excluded from participation in, be denied the benefits of, or be otherwise subjected to discrimination under any program or activity receiving Federal financial assistance from the National Endowment for the Arts, the National Endowment for the Humanities, or the

§ 1110.2

Institute of Museum and Library Services.

[62 FR 66826, Dec. 22, 1997]

§ 1110.2 Application of part.

This part applies to any program for which Federal financial assistance is authorized under a law administered by the National Endowment for the Arts, the National Endowment for Humanities, or the Institute of Museum and Library Services, including the types of Federal financial assistance listed in appendix A of this part. It applies to money paid, property transferred, or other Federal financial assistance extended after the effective date of the part, including assistance pursuant to an application approved prior to such date. It also applies to federal financial assistance extended to any such program prior to the effective date of this part under a contract or grant where the term of the contract or grant continues beyond such date or where the assistance was to provide real or personal property and the recipient or his transferee continues to use or retain ownership or possession of the property (see § 1110.4(a)(1)). This part does not apply to (a) any Federal financial assistance by way of insurance or guaranty contract, (b) any assistance to any individual who is the ultimate beneficiary under any such program, or (c) any employment practice, under any such program, of any employer, employment agency, or labor organization, except to the extent described in § 1110.3. The fact that a type of Federal financial assistance is not listed in appendix A shall not mean, if title VI of the Act is otherwise applicable, that a program is not covered. Other types of Federal financial assistance under statutes now in force or hereinafter enacted may be added to this list by notice published in the FEDERAL REGISTER.

[38 FR 17991, July 5, 1973, as amended at 62 FR 66826, Dec. 22, 1997; 68 FR 51384, Aug. 26, 2003]

§ 1110.3 Discrimination prohibited.

(a) *General.* No person in the United States shall, on grounds of race, color, or national origin be excluded from participation in, be denied the benefits of, or be otherwise subjected, to discrimination under any program to which this part applies.

(b) *Specific discriminatory actions prohibited.* (1) A recipient under any program to which this part applies may not directly or through contractual or other arrangements, on the ground of race, color, or national origin:

(i) Deny an individual any service, financial aid, or other benefit provided under the program;

(ii) Provide any service, financial aid, or other benefit to an individual which is different, or is provided in a different manner, from that provided to others under the program;

(iii) Subject an individual to segregation or separate treatment in any matter related to his receipt of any service, financial aid, or other benefit under the program;

(iv) Restrict an individual in any way in the enjoyment of any advantage or privilege enjoyed by others receiving any service, financial aid, or other benefit under the program;

(v) Treat an individual differently from others in determining whether he satisfies any admission, enrollment, quota, eligibility, membership, or other requirement or condition which individuals must meet in order to be provided any service, financial aid, or other benefit provided under the program;

(vi) Deny an individual an opportunity to participate in the program through the provision of services or otherwise or afford him an opportunity to do so which is different from that afforded others under the program (including the opportunity to participate in the program as an employee but only to the extent set forth in paragraph (c) of this section).

(2) A recipient, in determining the types of services, financial aid, or other benefits, or facilities which will be provided under any such program, or the class of individuals to whom, or the situations in which, such services, financial aid, other benefits, or facilities will be provided under any such program, or the class of individuals to be afforded an opportunity to participate in any such program, may not directly or through contractual or other arrangements, utilize criteria or methods

of administration which have the effect of subjecting individuals to discrimination because of their race, color, or national origin, or have the effect of defeating or substantially impairing accomplishment of the objectives of the program as respects individuals of a particular race, color, or national origin.

(3) In determining the site or location of facilities, a recipient or applicant may not make selections with the purpose or effect of excluding individuals from, denying them the benefits of, or subjecting them to discrimination under any program to which this regulation applies, on the grounds of race, color, or national origin; or with the purpose or effect of defeating or substantially impairing the accomplishment of the objectives of the Act or this regulation.

(4) As used in this section, the services, financial aid, or other benefits provided under a program receiving Federal financial assistance shall be deemed to include any service, financial aid, or other benefit provided in or through a facility provided with the aid of Federal financial assistance.

(5) The enumeration of specific forms of prohibited discrimination in this paragraph and paragraph (c) of this section does not limit the generality of the prohibition in paragraph (a) of this section.

(6) This regulation does not prohibit the consideration of race, color, or national origin if the purpose and effect are to remove or overcome the consequences of practices or impediments which have restricted the availability of, or participation in, the program or activity receiving Federal financial assistance, on the grounds of race, color, or national origin. Where previous discriminatory practice or usage tends, on the grounds of race, color, or national origin, to exclude individuals from participation in, to deny them the benefits of, or to subject them to discrimination under any program or activity to which this regulation applies the applicant or recipient has an obligation to take reasonable action to remove or overcome the consequences of the prior discriminatory practice or usage, and to accomplish the purposes of the Act.

(c) *Employment practices.* (1) Where a primary objective of the Federal financial assistance to a program to which this part applies is to provide employment, a recipient may not directly or through contractual or other arrangements subject an individual to discrimination on the ground of race, color, or national origin in its employment practices under such program (including recruitment or recruitment advertising employment, layoff or termination, upgrading, demotion, or transfer, rates of pay or other forms of compensation and use of facilities), including programs where a primary objective of the Federal financial assistance is (i) to assist such individuals through employment to meet expenses incident to the commencement or continuation of their education or training or (ii) to provide work experience which contributes to the education or training of such individuals or (iii) to reduce the unemployment of such individuals or to help them through employment to meet subsistence needs.

(2) The requirements applicable to construction employment under any such program shall be those specified in or pursuant to Executive Order 11246 or any executive order which supersedes it.

(3) Where a primary objective of the Federal financial assistance is not to provide employment, but discrimination on the grounds of race, color, or national origin in the employment practices of the recipient or other persons subject to the regulation tends, on the grounds of race, color, or national origin, to exclude individuals from participation in, to deny them the benefits of, or to subject them to discrimination under any program to which this regulation applies, the provisions of the foregoing subparagraph of this paragraph (c) shall apply to the employment practices of the recipient or other persons subject to the regulation, to the extent necessary to assure equality of opportunity to and nondiscriminatory treatment of, beneficiaries.

(d) *Medical emergencies.* Notwithstanding the foregoing provisions of this section, a recipient of Federal financial assistance shall not be deemed

§ 1110.4

to have failed to comply with paragraph (a) of this section if immediate provision of a service or other benefit to an individual is necessary to prevent his death or serious impairment of his health and such service or other benefit cannot be provided except by or through a medical institution which refuses or fails to comply with paragraph (a) of this section.

§ 1110.4 Assurances required.

(a) *General.* (1) Every application for Federal financial assistance to which this part applies, and every application for Federal financial assistance to provide a facility shall, as a condition to its approval and the extension of any Federal financial assistance pursuant to the application, contain or be accompanied by an assurance that the program will be conducted or the facility operated in compliance with all requirements imposed by or pursuant to this part. In the case where the Federal financial assistance is to provide or is in the form of personal property, or real property or interest therein or structures thereon, the assurance shall obligate the recipient, or, in the case of a subsequent transfer, the transferee, for the period during which the property is used for a purpose for which the Federal financial assistance is extended or for another purpose involving the provision of similar services and benefits, or for as long as the recipient retains ownership or possession of the property, whichever is longer; and any other type or form of assistance, the assurances shall be in effect for the duration of the period during which Federal financial assistance is extended to the program. The responsible Endowment official shall specify the form of the foregoing assurances and the extent to which like assurances will be required of subgrantees, contractors and subcontractors, successors in interest, and other participants. Any such assurance shall include provisions which give the United States a right to seek its judicial enforcement.

(2) In the case of real property, structures or improvements thereon, or interests therein, which was acquired with Federal financial assistance, or in the case where Federal financial assistance is provided in the form of a transfer of real property or interest therein from the Federal Government, the instrument effecting or recording the transfer, shall contain a covenant running with the land assuring nondiscrimination for the period during which the real property is used for a purpose for which the Federal financial assistance is extended or for another purpose involving the provision of similar services or benefits. Where no transfer of property is involved, but property is improved with Federal financial assistance, the recipients shall agree to include such a covenant in any subsequent transfer of such property. Where the property is obtained from the Federal Government, such covenant may also include a condition coupled with a right to be reserved by the Endowment to revert title to the property in the event of a breach of the covenant where, in the discretion of the responsible Endowment official, such a condition and right of reverter is appropriate to the statute under which the real property is obtained and to the nature of the grant and the grantee. In the event a transferee of real property proposes to mortgage or otherwise encumber the real property as security for financing construction of new, or improvement of existing, facilities on such property for the purposes for which the property was transferred, the Chairman of the Endowment concerned may agree, upon request of the transferee and if necessary to accomplish such financing, and upon such conditions as he deems appropriate, to forebear the exercise of such right to revert title for so long as the lien of such mortgage or other encumbrance remains effective.

(3) Transfers of surplus property are subject to regulations issued by the Administrator of the General Services Administration. (41 CFR 101–6.2)

(b) *Continuing Federal financial assistance.* Every application by a State or a State agency for continuing Federal financial assistance to which this part applies shall as a condition to its approval and the extension of any Federal financial assistance pursuant to the application (1) contain or be accompanied by a statement that the program is (or, in the case of a new program, will be) conducted in compliance with all requirements imposed by or pursuant to this part, and (2) provide or be accompanied by provision for such methods of administration for the program as are found by the responsible Endowment official to give reasonable assurance that the applicant and all recipients of Federal financial assistance under such program will comply with all requirements imposed by or pursuant to this part.

(c) *Elementary and secondary schools.* The requirements of paragraph (a) of this section with respect to any elementary or secondary school or school system shall be deemed to be satisfied if such school or school system (1) is subject to a final order of a court of the United States for the desegregation of such school or school system, and provides an assurance that it will comply with such order, including any future modification of such order, or (2) submits a plan for the desegregation of such school or school system which the responsible official of the Department of Health, Education, and Welfare determines is adequate to accomplish the purposes of the Act and this part within the earliest practicable time and provides reasonable assurance that it will carry out such plan. In any case of continuing Federal financial assistance, the responsible official of the Department of Health, Education, and Welfare may reserve the right to redetermine, after such period as may be specified by him, the adequacy of the plan to accomplish the purposes of the Act and this part. In any case in which a final order of a court of the United States for the desegregation of such school or school system is entered after submission of such a plan, such plan shall be revised to conform to such final order, including any future modification of such order.

(d) *Assurances from institutions.* (1) In the case of any application for Federal financial assistance to an institution of higher education (including assistance for construction, for research, for a special training project, or for any other purpose), the assurance required by this section shall extend to admission practices and to all other practices relating to the treatment of students.

(2) The assurance required with respect to an institution of higher education or any other institution, insofar as the assurance relates to the institution's practices with respect to admission or other treatment of individuals as students, or clients of the institution or to the opportunity to participate in the provision of services or other benefits to such individuals, shall be applicable to the entire institution.

[38 FR 17991, July 5, 1973, as amended at 68 FR 51383, Aug. 26, 2003]

§ 1110.5 Illustrative applications.

The following examples will illustrate the application of the foregoing provisions to some of the activities for which Federal financial assistance is provided by the Endowments. (In all cases the discrimination prohibited is discrimination on the ground of race, color, or national origin prohibited by title VI of the Act and this part, as a condition of the receipt of Federal financial assistance.)

(a) In a research, training, or other grant to a university for activities to be conducted in a graduate school, discrimination in the admission and treatment of students in the graduate school is prohibited, and the prohibition extends to the entire university.

(b) In cases of Federal financial assistance to elementary or secondary schools, discrimination by the recipient school district in any of its elementary or secondary schools, or by the recipient private institution, in the admission of students, or in the treatment of its students in any aspect of the educational process, is prohibited. In this and the following illustration the prohibition of discrimination in the treatment of students or other trainees includes the prohibition of discrimination among the students or trainees in the availability or use of any academic, dormitory, eating, recreational, or other facilities of the grantee or other recipient.

(c) In a training grant to a nonacademic institution, discrimination is prohibited in the selection of individuals to be trained and in their treatment by the grantee during their training. In a research or demonstration grant to such an institution, discrimination is prohibited with respect to

§ 1110.6

any educational activity, any provision of medical or other services and any financial aid to individuals incident to the program.

(d) Where Federal financial assistance is provided to assist in the presentation of artistic and cultural productions to the public, assurances will be required that such productions will not be presented before any audience which has been selected on a discriminatory basis.

(e) A recipient may not take action that is calculated to bring about indirectly what this part forbids it to accomplish directly. Thus, a State, in selecting projects to be supported through a State agency, may not base its selections on criteria which have the effect of defeating or substantially impairing accomplishment of the objectives of the Federal financial assistance as respects individuals of a particular race, color, or national origin.

(f) In some situations even though past discriminatory practices have been abandoned, the consequences of such practices continue to impede the full availability of a benefit. If the efforts required of the applicant or recipient under § 1110.6(d) to provide information as to the availability of the program or activity, and the rights of beneficiaries under this regulation, have failed to overcome these consequences, it will become necessary for such applicant or recipient to take additional steps to make the benefits fully available to racial and nationality groups previously subjected to discrimination. This action might take the form, for example of special arrangements for obtaining referrals or making selections which will insure that groups previously subjected to discrimination are adequately served.

(g) Even though an applicant or recipient has never used discriminatory policies, the services and benefits of the program or activity it administers may not in fact be equally available to some racial or nationality groups. In such circumstances an applicant or recipient may properly give special consideration to race, color, or national origin to make the benefits of its program more widely available to such groups, not then being adequately served. For example, where a university is not adequately serving members of a particular racial or nationality group, it may establish special recruitment policies to make its program better known and more readily available to such group, and take other steps to provide that group with more adequate service.

[38 FR 17991, July 5, 1973, as amended at 68 FR 51383, Aug. 26, 2003]

§ 1110.6 Compliance information.

(a) *Cooperation and assistance.* The responsible Endowment official shall, to the fullest extent practicable, seek the cooperation of recipients in obtaining compliance with this part and shall provide assistance and guidance to recipients to help them comply voluntarily with this part.

(b) *Compliance reports.* Each recipient shall keep such records and submit to the responsible Endowment official timely, complete and accurate compliance reports at such times, and in such form and containing such information, as the responsible Endowment official may determine to be necessary to enable him to ascertain whether the recipient has complied or is complying with this part. In the case in which a primary recipient extends Federal financial assistance to any other recipient, such other recipient shall also submit such compliance reports to the primary recipient as may be necessary to enable the primary recipient to carry out its obligations under this part.

(c) *Access to sources of information.* Each recipient shall permit access by the responsible Endowment official or his designee during normal business hours to such of its books, records, accounts, and other sources of information, and its facilities as may be pertinent to ascertain compliance with this part. Where any information required of a recipient is in the exclusive possession of any other agency, institution or person and this agency, institution or person shall fail or refuse to furnish this information, the recipient shall so certify in its report and shall set forth what efforts it has made to obtain the information.

(d) *Information to beneficiaries and participants.* Each recipient shall make available to participants, beneficiaries, and other interested persons such information regarding the provisions of this part and its applicability to the program for which the recipient receives Federal financial assistance, and make such information available to them in such manner, as the responsible Endowment official finds necessary to apprise such persons of the protections against discrimination assured them by the Act and this part.

[38 FR 17991, July 5, 1973, as amended at 68 FR 51384, Aug. 26, 2003]

§ 1110.7 Conduct of investigations.

(a) *Periodic compliance reviews.* The responsible Endowment official shall from time to time review the practices of recipients to determine whether they are complying with this part.

(b) *Complaints.* Any person who believes himself or any specific class of individuals to be subjected to discrimination prohibited by this part may by himself or by a representative file with the responsible Endowment official a written complaint. A complaint must be filed not later than ninety days from the date of the alleged discrimination, unless the time for filing is extended by the responsible Endowment official.

(c) *Investigations.* The responsible Endowment official will make a prompt investigation whenever a compliance review, report, complaint, or any other information indicates a possible failure to comply with this part. The investigation should include, where appropriate, a review of the pertinent practices and policies of the recipient, the circumstances under which the possible noncompliance with this part occurred, and other factors relevant to a determination as to whether the recipient has failed to comply with this part.

(d) *Resolution of matters.* (1) If an investigation pursuant to paragraph (c) of this section indicates a failure to comply with this part, the responsible Endowment official will so inform the recipient and the matter will be resolved by informal means whenever possible. If it has been determined that the matter cannot be resolved by informal means, action will be taken as provided for in § 1110.8.

(2) If an investigation does not warrant action pursuant to paragraph (d)(1) of this section, the responsible Endowment official will so inform the recipient and the complainant, if any, in writing.

(e) *Intimidatory or retaliatory acts prohibited.* No recipient or other person shall intimidate, threaten, coerce, or discriminate against any individual for the purpose of interfering with any right or privilege secured by section 601 of the Act or this part, or because he has made a complaint, testified, assisted, or participated in any manner in an investigation, proceeding, or hearing under this part. The identity of complainants shall be kept confidential except to the extent necessary to carry out the purposes of this part, including the conduct of any investigation, hearing, or judicial proceeding arising thereunder.

§ 1110.8 Procedure for effecting compliance.

(a) *General.* If there appears to be a failure or threatened failure to comply with this part, and if the noncompliance or threatened noncompliance cannot be corrected by informal means, compliance with this part may be effected by the suspension or termination of or refusal to grant or to continue Federal financial assistance or by any other means authorized by law. Such other means may include, but are not limited to, (1) a reference to the Department of Justice with a recommendation that appropriate proceedings be brought to enforce any rights of the United States under any law of the United States (including other titles of the Act), or any assurance or other contractual undertaking, and (2) any applicable proceeding under State or local law.

(b) *Noncompliance with § 1110.4.* If an applicant fails or refuses to furnish an assurance required under § 1110.4 or otherwise fails to comply with that section, Federal financial assistance may be refused in accordance with the procedures of paragraph (c) of this section. The Endowment concerned shall not be required to provide assistance in such a case during the pendency of the administrative proceedings under such paragraph, except that such Endowment shall continue assistance during the pendency of such proceedings where such assistance is due and payable pursuant to an application therefor approved prior to the effective date of this part.

(c) *Termination of or refusal to grant or to continue Federal financial assistance.* No order suspending, terminating, or refusing to grant or continue Federal financial assistance shall become effective until (1) the responsible Endowment official has advised the applicant or recipient of his failure to comply and has determined that compliance cannot be secured by voluntary means, (2) there has been an express finding on the record, after opportunity for hearings, of a failure by the applicant or recipient to comply with a requirement imposed by or pursuant to this part, (3) the action has been approved by the Chairman of the Endowment concerned, and (4) the expiration of 30 days after the Chairman has filed with the Committee of the House and the Committee of the Senate having legislative jurisdiction over the program involved, a full written report of the circumstances and the grounds for such action. Any action to suspend or terminate or to refuse to grant or to continue Federal financial assistance shall be limited to the particular political entity, or part thereof, or other applicant or recipient as to whom such a finding has been made and shall be limited in its effect to the particular program, or part thereof, in which such noncompliance has been so found.

(d) *Other means authorized by law.* No action to effect compliance by any other means authorized by law shall be taken until (1) the responsible Endowment official has determined that compliance cannot be secured by voluntary means, (2) the recipient or other person has been notified of its failure to comply and of the action to be taken to effect compliance, and (3) the expiration of at least 10 days from the mailing of such notice to the recipient or other person. During this period of at least 10 days, additional efforts shall be made to persuade the recipient or other person to comply with this part and to take such corrective action as may be appropriate.

§ 1110.9 Hearings.

(a) *Opportunity for hearing.* Whenever an opportunity for a hearing is required by § 1110.8(c), reasonable notice shall be given by registered or certified mail, return receipt requested, to the affected applicant or recipient. This notice shall advise the applicant or recipient of the action proposed to be taken, the specific provision under which the proposed action against it is to be taken, and the matters of fact or law asserted as the basis for this action, and either:

(1) Fix a date not less than 20 days after the date of such notice within which the applicant or recipient may request of the responsible Endowment official that the matter be scheduled for hearing or

(2) Advise the applicant or recipient that the matter in question has been set down for hearing at a stated place and time. The time and place so fixed shall be reasonable and shall be subject to change for cause. The complainant, if any, shall be advised of the time and place of the hearing. An applicant or recipient may waive a hearing and submit written information and argument for the record. The failure of an applicant or recipient to request a hearing under this paragraph or to appear at a hearing for which a date has been set shall be deemed to be a waiver of the right of a hearing under section 602 of the Act and § 1110.8(c) of this part and consent to the making of a decision on the basis of such information as is available.

(b) *Time and place of hearing.* Hearings shall be held at the offices of the Endowment concerned in Washington, DC, at a time fixed by the responsible Endowment official unless he determines that the convenience of the applicant or recipient or of the Endowment requires that another place be selected. Hearings shall be held before the responsible Endowment official or, at his discretion, before a hearing examiner designated in accordance with section 11 of the Administrative Procedure Act.

(c) *Right to counsel.* In all proceedings under this section, the applicant or recipient and the Endowment shall have the right to be represented by counsel.

National Foundation on the Arts and the Humanities § 1110.10

(d) *Procedures, evidence, and record.* (1) The hearing, decision, and any administrative review thereof shall be conducted in conformity with 5 U.S.C. 554–557 (sections 5–8 of the Administrative Procedure Act), and in accordance with such rules of procedure as are proper (and not inconsistent with this section) relating to the conduct of the hearing, giving of notices subsequent to those provided for in paragraph (a) of this section, taking of testimony, exhibits, arguments and briefs, requests for findings, and other related matters. Both the Endowment and the applicant or recipient shall be entitled to introduce all relevant evidence on the issues as stated in the notice for hearing or as determined by the officer conducting the hearing at the outset of or during the hearing.

(2) Technical rules of evidence shall not apply to hearings conducted pursuant to this part, but rules or principles designed to assure production of the most credible evidence available and to subject testimony to test by cross-examination shall be applied where reasonably necessary by the officer conducting the hearing. The hearing officer may exclude irrelevant, immaterial, or unduly repetitious evidence. All documents and other evidence entered or taken for the record shall be open to examination by the parties and opportunity shall be given to refute facts and arguments advanced on either side of the issues. A transcript shall be made of the oral evidence except to the extent the substance thereof is stipulated for the record. All decisions shall be based upon the hearing record and written findings shall be made.

(e) *Consolidated or joint hearings.* In cases in which the same or related facts are asserted to constitute noncompliance with this Regulation with respect to two or more Federal statutes, authorities, or other means by which Federal financial assistance is extended and to which this part applies, or noncompliance with this part and the regulations of one or more other Federal departments or agencies issued under title VI of the Act, the Chairman of the Endowment concerned may, by agreement with such other departments or agencies where applicable, provide for the conduct of consolidated or joint hearings and for the application to such hearings of rules or procedures not inconsistent with this part. Final decisions in such cases, insofar as this regulation is concerned, shall be made in accordance with § 1110.10.

[38 FR 17991, July 5, 1973, as amended at 68 FR 51384, Aug. 26, 2003]

§ 1110.10 Decisions and notices.

(a) *Decision by person other than the responsible Endowment official.* If the hearing is held by a hearing examiner such hearing examiner shall either make an initial decision, if so authorized, or certify the entire record including his recommended findings and proposed decision to the responsible Endowment official for a final decision, and a copy of such initial decision or certification shall be mailed to the applicant or recipient. Where the initial decision is made by the hearing examiner the applicant or recipient may within 30 days of the mailing of such notice of initial decision file with the responsible Endowment official his exceptions to the initial decision, with his reasons therefor. In the absence of exceptions, the responsible Endowment official may on his own motion within 45 days after the initial decision serve on the applicant or recipient a notice that he will review the decision. Upon the filing of such exceptions or of such notice of review the responsible Endowment official shall review the initial decision and issue his own decision thereon including the reasons therefor. In the absence of either exceptions or a notice of review the initial decision shall constitute the final decision of the responsible Endowment official.

(b) *Decisions on record or review by the responsible Endowment official.* Whenever a record is certified to the responsible Endowment official for decision or he reviews the decision of a hearing examiner pursuant to paragraph (a) of this section, or whenever the responsible Endowment official conducts the hearing, the applicant or recipient shall be given reasonable opportunity to file with him briefs or other written statements of its contentions, and a copy of the final decision of the responsible Endowment official shall be given in writing to the applicant or recipient and to the complainant if any.

(c) *Decisions on record where a hearing is waived.* Whenever a hearing is waived pursuant to § 1110.9(a) a decision shall be made by the responsible Endowment official on the record and a copy of such decision shall be given in writing to the applicant or recipient, and to the complainant, if any.

(d) *Rulings required.* Each decision of a hearing officer or responsible Endowment official shall set forth his ruling on each finding, conclusion, or exception presented, and shall identify the requirement or requirements imposed by or pursuant to this part with which it is found that the applicant or recipient has failed to comply.

(e) *Approval by Chairman.* Any final decision of a responsible Endowment official (other than the Chairman) which provides for the suspension or termination of, or the refusal to grant or continue Federal financial assistance, or the imposition of any other sanction available under this part or the Act, shall promptly be transmitted to the Chairman, who may approve such decision, may vacate it, or remit or mitigate any sanction imposed.

(f) *Content of orders.* The final decision may provide for suspension or termination of, or refusal to grant or continue Federal financial assistance, in whole or in part, to which this regulation applies, and may contain such terms, conditions, and other provisions as are consistent with and will effectuate the purposes of the Act and this part, including provisions designed to assure that no Federal financial assistance to which this regulation applies will thereafter be extended to the applicant or recipient determined by such decision to be in default in its performance of an assurance given by it pursuant to this part, or to have otherwise failed to comply with this part, unless and until it corrects its noncompliance and satisfies the responsible Endowment official that it will fully comply with this part.

(g) *Post termination proceedings.* (1) An applicant or recipient adversely affected by an order issued under paragraph (f) of this section shall be restored to full eligibility to receive Federal financial assistance if it satisfies the terms and conditions of that order for such eligibility or if it brings itself into compliance with this regulation and provides reasonable assurance that it will fully comply with this regulation. (An elementary or secondary school or school system which is unable to file an assurance of compliance with § 1110.3 shall be restored to full eligibility to receive Federal financial assistance, if it files a court order or a plan for desegregation which meets the requirements of § 1110.4(c), and provides reasonable assurance that it will comply with this court order or plan.)

(2) Any applicant or recipient adversely affected by an order entered pursuant to paragraph (f) of this section may at any time request the responsible Endowment official to restore fully its eligibility to receive Federal financial assistance. Any such request shall be supported by information showing that the applicant or recipient has met the requirements of paragraph (g)(1) of this section. If the responsible Endowment official determines that those requirements have been satisfied, he shall restore such eligibility.

(3) If the responsible Endowment official denies any such request, the applicant or recipient may submit a request for a hearing in writing, specifying why it believes such official to have been in error. It shall thereupon be given an expeditious hearing, with a decision on the record, in accordance with rules of procedure issued by the responsible Endowment official. The applicant or recipient will be restored to such eligibility if it proves at such a hearing that it satisfied the requirements of paragraph (g)(1) of this section. While proceedings under this paragraph are pending, the sanctions imposed by the order issued under paragraph (f) of this section shall remain in effect.

[38 FR 17991, July 5, 1973, as amended at 68 FR 51384, Aug. 26, 2003]

§ 1110.11 Judicial review.

Action taken pursuant to section 602 of the Act is subject to judicial review as provided in section 603 of the Act.

§ 1110.12 Effect on other regulations; forms and instructions.

(a) *Effects on other regulations.* Nothing in this part shall be deemed to supersede any of the following (including future amendments thereof): (1) Executive Orders 10925, 11114, and 11246, and regulations issued thereunder, or (2) Executive Order 11063 and regulations issued thereunder or any other regulations or instructions insofar as such order, regulations, or instructions prohibit discrmination on the grounds of race, color, or national origin in any program or situation to which this part is inapplicable, or prohibit discrimination on any other ground.

(b) *Forms and instructions.* Each responsible Endowment official shall issue and promptly make available to interested persons forms and detailed instructions and procedures for effectuating this part as applied to programs to which this part applies and for which he is responsible.

(c) *Supervision and coordination.* The Chairman of an Endowment may from time to time assign to other officials of the Endowment or to officials of other departments or agencies of the Government, with the consent of such departments or agencies, responsibilities in connection with the effectuation of the purposes of title VI of the Act and this part, including the achievement of effective coordination and maximum uniformity within the Endowment and within the executive branch of the Government in the application of title VI and this part of similar programs and in similar situations. Any action taken, determination made, or requirement imposed by an official of another department or agency acting pursuant to an assignment of responsibility under this subsection shall have the same effect as though such action had been taken by the responsible official of this agency.

§ 1110.13 Definitions.

As used in this part:

(a) The term *Foundation* means the National Foundations for the Arts and the Humanities, and includes the National Endowment for the Arts, the National Endowment for the Humanities, the Institute of Museum and Library Services, and each of their organizational units.

(b) The term *Endowment* means the National Endowment for the Arts, the National Endowment for the Humanities, or the Institute of Museum and Library Services.

(c) The term *Chairman* means the Chairman of the National Endowment for the Arts, the Chairman of the National Endowment for the Humanities, or the Director of the Institute of Museum and Library Services.

(d) The term *responsible Endowment official* with respect to any program receiving Federal financial assistance means the Chairman of any Endowment or other Endowment official designated by the Chairman.

(e) The term *United States* means the States of the United States, the District of Columbia, Puerto Rico, the Virgin Islands, American Samoa, Guam, Wake Island, the Canal Zone, and the territories and possessions of the United States, and the term *State* means any one of the foregoing.

(f) The term *Federal financial assistance* includes (1) grants and loans of Federal funds, (2) the grant or the donation of Federal property and interests in property, (3) the detail of Federal personnel, (4) the sale and lease of, and the permission to use (on other than a casual or transient basis), Federal property or any interest in such property without consideration or at a nominal consideration, or at a consideration which is reduced for the purpose of assisting the recipient, or in recognition of the public interest to be served by such sale or lease to the recipient, and (5) any Federal agreement, arrangement, or other contract which has as one of its purposes the provision of assistance.

(g) *Program or activity* and *program* mean all of the operations of any entity described in paragraphs (g)(1) through (4) of this section, any part of which is extended Federal financial assistance:

(1)(i) A department, agency, special purpose district, or other instrumentality of a State or of a local government; or

(ii) The entity of such State or local government that distributes such assistance and each such department or agency (and each other State or local government entity) to which the assistance is extended, in the case of assistance to a State or local government;

(2)(i) A college, university, or other postsecondary institution, or a public system of higher education; or

(ii) A local educational agency (as defined in 20 U.S.C. 7801), system of vocational education, or other school system;

(3)(i) An entire corporation, partnership, or other private organization, or an entire sole proprietorship—

(A) If assistance is extended to such corporation, partnership, private organization, or sole proprietorship as a whole; or

(B) Which is principally engaged in the business of providing education, health care, housing, social services, or parks and recreation; or

(ii) The entire plant or other comparable, geographically separate facility to which Federal financial assistance is extended, in the case of any other corporation, partnership, private organization, or sole proprietorship; or

(4) Any other entity which is established by two or more of the entities described in paragraph (g)(1), (2), or (3) of this section.

(h) The term *facility* includes all or any portion of structures, equipment, or other real or personal property or interests therein, and the provision of facilities includes the construction, expansion, renovation, remodeling, alteration or acquisition of facilities.

(i) The term *recipient* means any State, political subdivision of any State, or instrumentality of any State or political subdivision, any public or private agency, institution, or organization, or other entity or any individual, in any State, to whom Federal financial assistance is extended, directly or through another recipient, including any successor, assign, or transferee thereof, but such term does not include any ultimate beneficiary.

(j) The term *primary recipients* means any recipient which is authorized or required to extend Federal financial assistance to another recipient.

(k) The term *applicant* means one who submits an application, request, or plan required to be approved by a responsible Endowment official, or by a primary recipient, as a condition to eligibility for Federal financial assistance, and the term *application* means such an application, request, or plan.

[38 FR 17991, July 5, 1973, as amended at 62 FR 66826, Dec. 22, 1997; 68 FR 51383, Aug. 26, 2003]

APPENDIX A TO PART 1110—FEDERAL FINANCIAL ASSISTANCE TO WHICH THIS PART APPLIES

1. Assistance to groups for projects and productions in the arts.
2. Surveys, research and planning in the arts.
3. Assistance to State arts agencies for projects and productions in the arts.
4. Support of research in the humanities.
5. Support of educational programs in the humanities, including the training of students and teachers.
6. Assistance to promote the interchange of information in the humanities.
7. Assistance to foster public understanding and appreciation of the humanities.
8. Support of the publication of scholarly works in the humanities.

PART 1115—PRIVACY ACT REGULATIONS

Sec.
1115.1 Purpose and scope.
1115.2 Definitions.
1115.3 Procedures for notification of existence of records pertaining to individuals.
1115.4 Procedures for requests for access to or disclosure of records pertaining to an individual.
1115.5 Correction of records.
1115.6 Disclosure of records to agencies or persons other than the individual to whom the record pertains.
1115.7 Exemptions.

AUTHORITY: 5 U.S.C. 552a(f).

SOURCE: 40 FR 49286, Oct. 21, 1975, unless otherwise noted.

§ 1115.1 Purpose and scope.

This part sets forth the National Foundation on the Arts and the Humanities' procedures under the Privacy Act of 1974 as required by 5 U.S.C. 552a(f). Internal guidance for Foundation staff and other regulations implementing the Privacy Act are contained or will be contained in Foundation circulars.

National Foundation on the Arts and the Humanities § 1115.4

§ 1115.2 Definitions.

For purposes of this part:

(a) *Foundation* means the National Foundation on the Arts and the Humanities.

(b) *Act* means the Privacy Act of 1974 (Pub. L. 93–579).

(c) *Individual* means a citizen of the United States or an alien lawfully admitted for permanent residence.

(d) *Maintain*, used with reference to a record means to collect, to use, to disseminate, to have control over and responsibility for such record.

(e) *Record* means any item, collection or grouping of information about an individual that is maintained by the Foundation and that is retrievable by his or her name or an identifying particular, such as a number, symbol, fingerprint, or photograph of the individual. Information maintained by the Foundation includes, but is not limited to, education, financial transactions, medical history, employment history and criminal history.

(f) *Routine use* means, with respect to the disclosure of a record, the use of such a record for a purpose which is compatible with the purpose for which it was collected. The routine uses of record systems maintained by the Foundation were established pursuant to notice in the FEDERAL REGISTER.

(g) *System of records* means a group of any records under the control of the Foundation from which information about an individual is retrievable by his or her name or by some identifying particular.

§ 1115.3 Procedures for notification of existence of records pertaining to individuals.

(a) The systems of records, as defined in the Privacy Act of 1974, maintained by the National Foundation on the Arts and the Humanities are listed annually in the FEDERAL REGISTER as required by that Act. Any person who wishes to know whether a system of records contains a record pertaining to him may appear in person at the National Endowment for the Arts, Room 1338, 2401 E Street NW., Washington, DC 20506 or the National Endowment for the Humanities, Room 1000, 806 15th Street NW., Washington, DC 20506, on work days between the hours of 9:00 a.m. and 5:30 p.m. or by writing to the Office of the General Counsel, National Endowment for the Arts or National Endowment for the Humanities, Washington, DC 20506. It is recommended that requests be made in writing, since in many cases it will take several days to ascertain whether a record exists.

(b) Requests for notification of the existence of a record should specifically identify the system of records involved and should state, if the requestor is other than the individual to whom the record pertains, the relationship of the requestor to that individual. (Note that requests will not be honored by the Foundation pursuant to the Privacy Act unless made (1) by the individual to whom the record pertains, (2) by such individual's parent if the individual is a minor, or (3) by such individual's legal guardian if the individual has been declared to be incompetent due to physical or mental incapacity or age by a court of competent jurisdiction).

(c) The Foundation will attempt to respond to a request as to whether a record exists within 10 working days from the time it receives the request or from the time any required identification is established, whichever is later.

§ 1115.4 Procedures for requests for access to or disclosure of records pertaining to an individual.

(a) Any person may request review of records pertaining to him by appearing at the National Endowment for the Arts, Room 1338, 2401 E Street, NW., Washington, DC 20506, or the National Endowment for the Humanities, Room 1000, 806 15th Street, NW., Washington, DC 20506 on work days between the hours of 9:00 a.m. and 5:30 p.m. or by writing to the Office of the General Counsel, National Endowment for the Arts, or National Endowment for the Humanities, Washington, DC 20506. (See paragraphs (b) and (c) of this section for identification requirements.) The request should specifically identify the systems or records involved. The Foundation will strive either to make the record available within 15 working days of the request or to inform the requestor of the need for additional identification or the tendering of fees (as specified in paragraph (d) of this section) within 15 working days.

(b) In the case of persons making requests by appearing at the Foundation, the amount of personal identification required will of necessity vary with the sensitivity of the record involved. Except as indicated below, reasonable identification such as employment identification cards, drivers licenses, and credit cards will normally be accepted as sufficient evidence of identity in the absence of any indications to the contrary. Records in the following systems of records, however, are considered to contain relatively sensitive and/or detailed personal information—

GRANT APPLICATIONS—NEA.
GRANT APPLICATIONS—NEH.
GRANTS TO INDIVIDUALS—NEA.
GRANTS TO INDIVIDUALS AND INSTITUTIONS—NEH.
EQUAL EMPLOYMENT OPPORTUNITY CASE FILE—NFAH NEA/NEH.
EMPLOYEE PAYROLL—NFAH.
PERSONNEL RECORDS—NFAH.

Accordingly, with respect to requests for records in these systems the Foundation reserves the rights to require sufficient identification to identify positively the individual making the request. This might involve independent verification by the Foundation as by phone calls to determine whether an individual has made a request, personal identification by Foundation employees who know the individual, or such other means as are considered appropriate under the circumstances.

(c) A written request will be honored only if it contains the following certification before a duly commissioned notary public of any state or territory (or similar official if the request is made outside the United States):

I,_____(Printed name), do hereby certify that I am the individual about whom the record requested in this letter pertains or that I am within the class of persons authorized to act on his behalf in accordance with 5 U.S.C. 552a(h).

_____
                                   Signature
_____
                                   Date
In the County of_____State of_____. On this ___ day of ____

_____
                         (Name of individual)
who is personally known to me, did appear before me and sign the above certificate.

_____
                                   Signature
_____
                                   Date
(s) My Commission expires _____

However, where the record requested is contained in any of the systems of records listed in paragraph (b) of this section, the Foundation reserves the right to require additional identification and/or to independently verify to its satisfaction, the identity of the requestor.

(d) Charges for copies of records will be at the rate of $0.10 per photography of each page. Where records are not susceptible to photo-copying, e.g., punch cards, magnetic tapes or oversize materials, the amount charged will be actual cost as determined on a case-by-case basis. Only one copy of each record requested will be supplied. No charge will be made unless the charge as computed above would exceed $3.00 for each request or related series of requests. If a fee in excess of $25.00 would be required, the requestor shall be notified and the fee must be tendered before the records will be copied.

§ 1115.5 Correction of records.

(a) Any individual is entitled to request amendments of records pertaining to him pursuant to 5 U.S.C. 552a(d)(2). Such a request shall be made in writing and addressed to the Office of the General Counsel, National Endowment for the Arts or National Endowment for the Humanities, Washington, DC 20506.

(b) The request should specify the record and systems of records involved, and should specify the exact correction desired and state that the request is made pursuant to the Privacy Act. An edited copy of the record showing the desired correction is desirable. Within 10 working days of the receipt of a properly addressed request (or within 10 working days of the time the General Counsel, National Endowment for the Arts or the General Counsel, National Endowment for the Humanities becomes aware that a particular communication not addressed as prescribed above is a request for correction of a record under the Privacy Act), the General Counsel's office shall acknowledge receipt of the request.

(c) The General Counsel's office upon receipt of such a request shall promptly confer with the office within the Foundation responsible for the record. In the event it is felt that correction is not warranted in whole or in part, the matter shall be brought to the attention of the Deputy Chairman of the Endowment involved. If, after review by the Deputy Chairman of the involved Endowment and discussion with the requestor, if deemed helpful, it is determined that correction as requested is not warranted, a letter shall be sent by the Deputy Chairman's office to the requestor denying his request and/or explaining what correction might be made if agreeable to the requestor. This letter shall set forth the reasons for the refusal to honor the request for correction. It shall also inform him of his right to appeal this decision and include a description of the appeals procedure set forth in paragraph (d) of this section.

(d) An appeal may be taken from an adverse determination under paragraph (c) of this section to the Assistant Chairman/Management, National Endowment for the Arts or the Chairman, National Endowment for the Humanities. Such appeal must be made in writing and should clearly indicate that it is an appeal. The basis for the appeal should be included, and it should be mailed to the same address as listed in paragraph (a) of this section. A hearing at the Foundation may be requested. Such hearing will be informal, and shall be before the Assistant Chairman/Management, National Endowment for the Arts, the Chairman, National Endowment for the Humanities, or an appointed designee. If no hearing is requested, the request for appeal should include the basis for the appeal. Where no hearing is requested the Assistant Chairman or Chairman before whom the appeal is taken shall render his decision within thirty working days after receipt of the written appeal at the Foundation, unless the Assistant Chairman or Chairman before whom the appeal is taken, for good cause shown, extends the 30-day period and the appellant is advised in writing of such extension. If a hearing is requested, the Foundation will attempt to contact the appellant within five working days and arrange a suitable time for the hearing. In such cases the decision of the Assistant Chairman or Chairman shall be made within 30 working days after the hearing unless the time is extended and the appellant is advised in writing of such extension.

(e) The final decision of the Assistant Chairman or Chairman in an appeal shall be in writing, and, if adverse to the appellant, set forth the reasons for the refusal to amend the record and advise him of his right to appeal the decision under 5 U.S.C. 552a(g)(1)(A). The individual shall also be notified that he has the right to file with the Foundation a concise statement setting forth the reasons for this disagreement with the refusal of the Foundation to amend his record.

§ 1115.6 Disclosure of records to agencies or persons other than the individual to whom the record pertains.

Records subject to the Privacy Act that are requested by any person other than the individual to whom they pertain will not be made available except under the following circumstances:

(a) Records required to be made available by the Freedom of Information Act will be released in response to a request formulated in accordance with Foundation regulations found at 45 CFR part 1100.

(b) Records not required by the Freedom of Information Act to be released may be released, at the discretion of the Foundation, if the written consent of the individual to whom they pertain has been obtained or if such release would be authorized under 5 U.S.C. 552a(b)(1) or (3) through (11).

§ 1115.7 Exemptions.

(a) *Fellowships and grants.* Pursuant to 5 U.S.C. 552a(k)(5), the Foundation hereby exempts from the application of section 552a(d) any materials which would disclose the identity of references for fellowship or grant applicants contained in any of the Foundation's systems of records.

(b) *Applicants for employment.* Pursuant to 5 U.S.C. 552a(k)(5), the Foundation hereby exempts from the application of 5 U.S.C. 552a(d) any materials which would disclose the identity of references of applicants for employment at the Foundation contained in the system of records entitled "Official Personnel Folders".

SUBCHAPTER B—NATIONAL ENDOWMENT FOR THE ARTS

PARTS 1116–1148 [RESERVED]

PART 1149—PROGRAM FRAUD CIVIL REMEDIES ACT REGULATIONS

Subpart A—Purpose and Definitions

Sec.
1149.1 Purpose.
1149.2 Definitions.

Subpart B—Claims and Statements

1149.3 What is a claim?
1149.4 When is a claim made?
1149.5 What is a false claim?
1149.6 What is a statement?
1149.7 What is a false statement?

Subpart C—Basis for Liability

1149.8 What kind of conduct results in program fraud enforcement?
1149.9 What civil penalties and assessments may I be subjected to?

Subpart D—Procedures Leading to the Issuance of a Complaint

1149.10 How is program fraud investigated?
1149.11 May the investigating official issue a subpoena?
1149.12 What happens if program fraud is suspected?
1149.13 When may the NEA issue a complaint?
1149.14 What is contained in a complaint?
1149.15 How will the complaint be served?
1149.16 What constitutes proof of service?

Subpart E—Procedures Following Service of a Complaint

1149.17 How do you respond to the complaint?
1149.18 May I file a general answer?
1149.19 What happens once an answer is filed?
1149.20 What must the notice of hearing include?
1149.21 When must the ALJ serve the notice of oral hearing?
1149.22 What happens if you fail to file an answer?
1149.23 May I file a motion to reopen my case?
1149.24 What happens if my motion to reopen is denied?
1149.25 When, if ever, will time be tolled?

Subpart F—Hearing Procedures

1149.26 What kind of hearing is contemplated?
1149.27 What is the role of the ALJ?
1149.28 What does the ALJ have the authority to do?
1149.29 What rights do you have at the hearing?
1149.30 How are the functions of the ALJ separated from those of the investigating official and the reviewing official?
1149.31 Can the reviewing official or the ALJ be disqualified?
1149.32 Do you have a right to review documents?
1149.33 What type of discovery is authorized and how is it conducted?
1149.34 How are motions for discovery handled?
1149.35 When may an ALJ grant a motion for discovery?
1149.36 How are depositions handled?
1149.37 Are witness lists and exhibits exchanged before the hearing?
1149.38 Can witnesses be subpoenaed?
1149.39 Who pays the costs for a subpoena?
1149.40 When may I file a motion to quash a subpoena?
1149.41 Are protective orders available?
1149.42 What does a protective order protect?
1149.43 How are documents filed and served with the ALJ?
1149.44 What must documents filed with the ALJ include?
1149.45 How is time computed?
1149.46 Where is the hearing held?
1149.47 How will the hearing be conducted?
1149.48 Who has the burden of proof?
1149.49 How is evidence presented at the hearing?
1149.50 How is witness testimony presented?
1149.51 How can I exclude a witness?
1149.52 Will the hearing proceedings be recorded?
1149.53 Are ex parte communications between a party and the ALJ permitted?
1149.54 Are there sanctions for misconduct?
1149.55 What happens if I fail to comply with an order?
1149.56 Are post-hearing briefs required?

Subpart G—Decisions and Appeals

1149.57 How is the case decided?
1149.58 When will the ALJ serve the initial decision?
1149.59 How are penalty and assessment amounts determined?
1149.60 What factors are considered in determining the amount of penalties and assessments to impose?

§ 1149.1

1149.61 Can a party request reconsideration of the initial decision?
1149.62 When does the initial decision of the ALJ become final?
1149.63 What are the procedures for appealing the ALJ decision?
1149.64 What happens if an initial decision is appealed?
1149.65 Are there any limitations on the right to appeal to the authority head?
1149.66 How does the authority head dispose of an appeal?
1149.67 Who represents the NEA on an appeal?
1149.68 What judicial review is available?
1149.69 Can the administrative complaint be settled voluntarily?
1149.70 How are civil penalties and assessments collected?
1149.71 Is there a right to administrative offset?
1149.72 What happens to collections?
1149.73 What if the investigation indicates criminal misconduct or a violation of the False Claims Act?
1149.74 How does the NEA protect your rights?

AUTHORITY: 5 U.S.C. App. 8G(a)(2); 20 U.S.C. 959; 28 U.S.C. 2461 note; 31 U.S.C. 3801–3812.

SOURCE: 79 FR 67081, Nov. 12, 2014, unless otherwise noted.

Subpart A—Purpose and Definitions

§ 1149.1 Purpose.

This part implements the Program Fraud Civil Remedies Act of 1986, 31 U.S.C. 3801–3812 (PFCRA). The PFCRA provides the NEA, and other Federal agencies, with an administrative remedy to impose civil penalties and assessments against you if you make or cause to be made false, fictitious, or fraudulent claims or written statements to the NEA. The PFCRA also provides due process protections to you if you are subject to administrative proceedings under this part.

§ 1149.2 Definitions.

For the purposes of this part—

Authority means the National Endowment for the Arts.

Authority Head means the Chairperson/head of the National Endowment for the Arts or the Chairperson/authority head/s designee.

Benefit means anything of value, including but not limited to, any advantage, preference, privilege, license, permit, favorable decision, ruling, status, or loan guarantee.

Defendant means any person alleged in a complaint to be liable for a civil penalty or assessment pursuant to the PFCRA.

Government means the United States Government.

Group of related claims submitted at the same time means only those claims arising from the same transaction (such as a grant, loan, application, or contract) which are submitted together as part of a single request, demand, or submission.

Initial decision means the written decision of the Administrative Law Judge (ALJ), and includes a revised initial decision issued following a remand or a motion for reconsideration.

Investigating official means:

(1) The NEA Inspector General; or

(2) A designee of the NEA Inspector General.

Knows or *has reason to know* means that a person:

(1) Has actual knowledge that the claim or statement is false, fictitious, or fraudulent; or

(2) Acts in deliberate ignorance of the truth or falsity of the claim or statement; or

(3) Acts in reckless disregard of the truth or falsity of the claim or statement.

Makes, whenever it appears, must include the terms *presents*, *submits*, and *causes to be made, presented, or submitted*. As the context requires, *making* or *made* must likewise include the corresponding forms of such terms.

Person means any individual, partnership, corporation, association, or private organization, and includes the plural of that term.

Representative means an attorney who is in good standing of the bar of any State, Territory, or possession of the United States, or of the District of Columbia, or the Commonwealth of Puerto Rico, or any other individual designated in writing by you.

Reviewing official means the General Counsel of the NEA or the General Counsel's designee.

National Foundation on the Arts and the Humanities

Subpart B—Claims and Statements

§ 1149.3 What is a claim?

(a) Claim means any request, demand, or submission:

(1) Made to the NEA for property, services, or money (including money representing grants, loans, insurance or benefits);

(2) Made to a recipient of property or services from the NEA, or to a party to a contract with the NEA for property or services if the United States:

(i) Provided such property or services;

(ii) Provided any portion of the funds for the purchase of such property or services; or

(iii) Will reimburse such recipient or party for the purchase of such property or services;

(3) Made to the NEA for the payment of money (including money representing grants, loans, insurance, or benefits) if the United States:

(i) Provided any portion of the money requested or demanded; or

(ii) Will reimburse such recipient or party for any portion of the money paid on such request or demand; or

(4) Made to the NEA which has the effect of decreasing an obligation to pay or account for property, services, or money.

(b) A claim can relate to grants, loans, insurance, or other benefits, and includes the NEA guaranteed loans made by participating lenders.

(c) Each voucher, invoice, claim form, or individual request or demand for property, services, or money constitutes a separate claim.

§ 1149.4 When is a claim made?

A claim is made to the NEA, when such claim is actually made to:

(a) An agent, fiscal intermediary, or other person or entity, including any State or political subdivision of a State, acting for or on behalf of the NEA; or

(b) A recipient of property, services, or money from the Government, or the party to a contract with the NEA.

§ 1149.5 What is a false claim?

(a) A claim submitted to the NEA is "false" if it:

(1) Is false, fictitious or fraudulent;

(2) Includes or is supported by a written statement which asserts or contains a material fact which is false, fictitious, or fraudulent;

(3) Includes or is supported by a written statement which is false, fictitious or fraudulent because it omits a material fact that you have a duty to include in the statement; or

(4) Is for payment for the provision of property or services which you have not provided as claimed.

(b) [Reserved]

§ 1149.6 What is a statement?

(a) A *statement* means any written representation, certification, affirmation, document, record, or accounting or bookkeeping entry made with respect to a claim (including relating to eligibility to make a claim) or to obtain the approval or payment of a claim (including relating to eligibility to make a claim); or with respect to (including relating to eligibility for) a contract, bid or proposal for a contract with the NEA, or a grant, loan or other benefit from the NEA, including applications and proposals for such grants, loans, or other benefits, if the United States Government provides any portion of the money or property under such contract or for such grant, loan or benefit, or if the Government will reimburse any party for any portion of the money or property under such contract or for such grant, loan, or benefit.

(b) A statement is made, presented, or submitted to the NEA when such statement is actually made to an agent, fiscal intermediary, or other person or entity acting for or on behalf of the NEA, including any State or political subdivision of a State, acting for or on behalf of the NEA; or the recipient of property, services, or money from the Government; or the party to a contract with the NEA.

§ 1149.7 What is a false statement?

(a) A statement submitted to the NEA is a *false statement* if you make the statement, or cause the statement to be made, while knowing or having reason to know that the statement:

(1) Asserts a material fact that is false, fictitious, or fraudulent; or

§ 1149.8

(2) Is false, fictitious, or fraudulent because it omits a material fact that you have a duty to include in the statement and contains or is accompanied by an express certification or affirmation of the truthfulness and accuracy of the contents of the statement.

(b) Each written representation, certification, or affirmation constitutes a separate statement.

Subpart C—Basis for Liability

§ 1149.8 What kind of conduct results in program fraud enforcement?

If you make false claims or false statements, you may be subject to civil penalties and assessments under the PFCRA.

§ 1149.9 What civil penalties and assessments may I be subjected to?

(a) In addition to any other penalties that may be prescribed by law, the PFCRA may subject you to the following:

(1) A civil penalty of not more than $10,957 for each false, fictitious or fraudulent statement or claim; and

(2) If the NEA has made any payment, transferred property, or provided services in reliance on a false claim, you are also subject to an assessment of not more than twice the amount of the false claim. This assessment is in lieu of damages sustained by the NEA because of the false claim.

(b) Each false, fictitious, or fraudulent claim for property, services, or money is subject to a civil penalty regardless of whether such property, services, or money is actually delivered or paid.

(c) No proof of specific intent to defraud is required to establish liability under this section for either false claims or false statements.

(d) [Reserved]

(e) In any case in which it is determined that more than one person is liable for making a false, fictitious, or fraudulent claim or statement under this section, each such person may be held liable for a civil penalty and assessment under this section.

(f) In any case in which it is determined that more than one person is liable for making a claim under this section on which the Government has made payment (including transferred property or provided services), an assessment may be imposed against any such person or jointly and severally against any combination of persons.

[79 FR 67081, Nov. 12, 2014, as amended at 82 FR 27434, June 15, 2017]

Subpart D—Procedures Leading to the Issuance of a Complaint

§ 1149.10 How is program fraud investigated?

The Inspector General, or his/her designee, is the investigating official responsible for investigating allegations that you have made a false claim or statement.

§ 1149.11 May the investigating official issue a subpoena?

(a) Yes. The Inspector General has authority to issue administrative subpoenas for the production of records and documents. If an investigating official concludes that a subpoena is warranted, he/she may issue a subpoena.

(1) The issued subpoena must notify you of the authority under which it is issued and must identify the records or documents sought;

(2) The investigating official may designate a person to act on his or her behalf to receive the documents sought; and

(3) You are required to tender to the investigating official, or the person designated to receive the documents, a certification that:

(i) The documents sought have been produced;

(ii) Such documents are not available and the reasons therefore; or

(iii) Such documents, suitably identified, have been withheld based upon the assertion of an identified privilege.

(b) Nothing in this section precludes or limits an investigating official's discretion to refer allegations within the Department of Justice for suit under the False Claims Act or other civil relief, or to defer or postpone a report or referral to the reviewing official to avoid interference with a criminal investigation or prosecution.

(c) Nothing in this section modifies any responsibility of an investigating official to report violations of criminal

§ 1149.12 What happens if program fraud is suspected?

(a) If the investigating official concludes that an action under this part is warranted, the investigating official submits a report containing the findings and conclusions of the investigation to the reviewing official.

(b) If the reviewing official determines that the report provides adequate evidence that you have made a false, fictitious or fraudulent claim or statement, the reviewing official shall transmit to the Attorney General written notice of an intention to refer the matter for adjudication, with a request for approval of such referral. This notice will include the reviewing official's statements concerning:

(1) The reasons for the referral;

(2) The claims or statements upon which liability would be based;

(3) The evidence that supports liability;

(4) An estimate of the amount of money or the value of property, services, or other benefits requested or demanded in the false claim or statement;

(5) Any exculpatory or mitigating circumstances that may relate to the claims or statements known by the reviewing official or the investigating official; and

(6) A statement that there is a reasonable prospect of collecting an appropriate amount of penalties and assessments.

(c) If, at any time, the Attorney General or his or her designee requests in writing that this administrative process be stayed, the authority head must stay the process immediately. The authority head may order the process resumed only upon receipt of the written authorization of the Attorney General.

§ 1149.13 When may the NEA issue a complaint?

The NEA may issue a complaint:

(a) If the Attorney General, or his/her designee, approves the referral of the allegations for adjudication in a written statement; and

(b) In a case of submission of false claims, if the amount of money or the value of property or services demanded or requested in a false claim, or a group of related claims submitted at the same time, does not exceed $150,000.

§ 1149.14 What is contained in a complaint?

(a) A *complaint* is a written statement giving you notice of the specific allegations being referred for adjudication and of your right to request a hearing regarding those allegations.

(b) The reviewing official may join in a single complaint, false claims or statements that are unrelated, or that were not submitted simultaneously, so long as each claim made does not exceed the amount provided in 31 U.S.C. 3803(c).

(c) The complaint must state that the NEA seeks to impose civil penalties, assessments, or both, against you and will include:

(1) The allegations of liability against you, including the statutory basis for liability, identification of the claims or statements involved, and the reasons liability allegedly arises from such claims or statements;

(2) The maximum amount of penalties and assessments for which you may be held liable;

(3) A statement that you may request a hearing by filing an answer and may be represented by a representative;

(4) Instructions for filing such an answer; and

(5) A warning that failure to file an answer within 30 days of service of the complaint will result in imposition of the maximum amount of penalties and assessments.

(d) The reviewing official must serve you with any complaint and, if you request a hearing, provide a copy to the ALJ assigned to the case.

§ 1149.15 How will the complaint be served?

(a) The complaint must be served on you as an individual directly, on a partnership through a general partner, and on corporations or on unincorporated associations through an executive officer or a director. Service may also be made on any person authorized by appointment or by law to receive process for you or a legal entity.

§ 1149.16

(b) The complaint may be served either by:
(1) Registered or certified mail; or
(2) Personal delivery by anyone 18 years of age or older.
(c) The date of service is the date of personal delivery or, in the case of service by registered or certified mail, the date of postmark.

§ 1149.16 What constitutes proof of service?

(a) Proof of service is established by the following:
(1) When service is made by registered or certified mail, the return postal receipt will serve as proof of service.
(2) When service is made by personal delivery, an affidavit of the individual serving the complaint, or written acknowledgment of your receipt or of receipt by a representative, will serve as proof of service.
(b) When served with the complaint, the serving party must also serve you with a copy of this part and 31 U.S.C. 3801–3812.

Subpart E—Procedures Following Service of a Complaint

§ 1149.17 How do you respond to the complaint?

(a) You may respond to the complaint by filing an answer with the reviewing official within 30 days of service of the complaint. A timely answer will be considered a request for an oral hearing.
(b) In the answer, you—
(1) Must admit or deny each of the allegations of liability contained in the complaint (a failure to deny an allegation is considered an admission);
(2) Must state any defense on which you intend to rely;
(3) May state any reasons why you believe the penalties, assessments, or both should be less than the statutory maximum; and
(4) Must state the name, address, and telephone number of the person authorized by you to act as your representative, if any.

§ 1149.18 May I file a general answer?

(a) If you are unable to file a timely answer which meets the requirements set forth in § 1149.17(b), you may file with the reviewing official a general answer denying liability, requesting a hearing, and requesting an extension of time in which to file a complete answer. A general answer must be filed within 30 days of service of the complaint.

(b) If you file a general answer requesting an extension of time, the reviewing official must promptly file with the ALJ the complaint, the general answer, and the request for an extension of time.

(c) For good cause shown, the ALJ may grant you up to 30 additional days within which to file an answer meeting the requirements of paragraph (b) of this section. You must file the answer with the ALJ and serve a copy on the reviewing official.

§ 1149.19 What happens once an answer is filed?

(a) When the reviewing official receives an answer, he/she must simultaneously file the complaint, the answer, and a designation of the NEA's representative with the ALJ.

(b) When the ALJ receives the complaint and the answer, he/she will promptly serve a notice of hearing upon you and the NEA representative, in the same manner as the complaint. At the same time, the ALJ must send a copy of such notice to the reviewing official or his designee.

§ 1149.20 What must the notice of hearing include?

The notice must include:
(a) The tentative time, place, and nature of the hearing;
(b) The legal authority and jurisdiction under which the hearing is being held;
(c) The matters of fact and law to be asserted;
(d) A description of the procedures for the conduct of the hearing;
(e) The name, address, and telephone number of your representative and the NEA's representative; and
(f) Such other matters as the ALJ deems appropriate.

§ 1149.21 When must the ALJ serve the notice of oral hearing?

Unless the parties agree otherwise, the ALJ must serve the notice of oral hearing within six years of the date on which the claim or statement is made.

§ 1149.22 What happens if you fail to file an answer?

(a) If you do not file any answer within 30 days after service of the complaint, the reviewing official may refer the complaint to the ALJ.

(b) Once the complaint is referred, the ALJ will promptly serve on you a notice that he/she will issue an initial decision.

(c) The ALJ will assume the facts alleged in the complaint are true. If such facts establish liability under the statute, the ALJ will issue an initial decision imposing the maximum amount of penalties and assessments allowed under the PFCRA.

(d) Except as otherwise provided in this section, when you fail to file a timely answer, you waive any right to further review of the penalties and assessments imposed in the initial decision. This initial decision will become final and binding 30 days after it is issued.

§ 1149.23 May I file a motion to reopen my case?

(a) You may file a motion with the ALJ asking him/her to reopen the case at any time before an initial decision becomes final. The ALJ may only reopen a case if, in this motion, he/she determines that you set forth extraordinary circumstances that prevented you from filing a timely answer. The initial decision will be stayed until the ALJ makes a decision on your motion to reopen. The reviewing official may respond to the motion.

(b) If the ALJ determines that you have demonstrated extraordinary circumstances excusing your failure to file a timely answer, the ALJ will withdraw the initial decision and grant you an opportunity to answer the complaint.

(c) A decision by the ALJ to deny your motion to reopen a case is not subject to review or reconsideration.

§ 1149.24 What happens if my motion to reopen is denied?

(a) You may appeal the decision denying a motion to reopen to the authority head by filing a notice of appeal with the authority head within 15 days after the ALJ denies the motion. The timely filing of a notice of appeal must stay the initial decision until the authority head decides the issue.

(b) If you file a timely notice of appeal with the authority head, the ALJ must forward the record of the proceeding to the authority head.

(c) The authority head must decide promptly, based solely on the record previously before the ALJ, whether extraordinary circumstances excuse your failure to file a timely answer.

(d) If the authority head decides that extraordinary circumstances excused your failure to file a timely answer, the authority head must remand the case to the ALJ with instructions to grant you an opportunity to answer.

(e) If the authority head decides that your failure to file a timely answer is not excused, the authority head must reinstate the initial decision of the ALJ, which becomes final and binding upon the parties 30 days after the authority head issues such a decision.

§ 1149.25 When, if ever, will time be tolled?

Time will be tolled in the following instances:

(a) If you are granted a 30 day extension to file your answer, the 30 days will be tolled to the six year oral hearing limitation thereby providing the ALJ six years and 30 days to serve the notice of oral hearing as discussed in § 1149.18(c);

(b) If a notice of appeal is filed as discussed in § 1149.24(a);

(c) If a motion is filed to disqualify a reviewing official or an ALJ disqualifies himself/herself as discussed in § 1149.31(c); or

(d) In any other instance in which time is suspended or delayed as a result of an appeal, request for reconsideration, untimely filing, or extensions.

Subpart F—Hearing Procedures

§ 1149.26 What kind of hearing is contemplated?

The hearing is a formal proceeding conducted by the ALJ during which you will have the opportunity to dispute liability, present testimony, and cross-examine witnesses.

§ 1149.27 What is the role of the ALJ?

(a) An ALJ, who will be retained by the NEA, serves as the presiding officer at all hearings. ALJs are selected by the Office of Personnel Management. The ALJ is assigned to cases in rotation so far as practicable, and may not perform duties inconsistent with their duties and responsibilities as administrative law judges.

(b) The ALJ must conduct a fair and impartial hearing, avoid delay, maintain order, and assure that a record of the proceeding is made.

§ 1149.28 What does the ALJ have the authority to do?

(a) The ALJ has the authority to—

(1) Set and change the date, time, and place of the hearing upon reasonable notice to the parties;

(2) Continue or recess the hearing, in whole or in part, for a reasonable period of time;

(3) Hold conferences to identify or simplify the issues or to consider other matters that may aid in the expeditious disposition of the proceeding;

(4) Administer oaths and affirmations;

(5) Issue subpoenas requiring the attendance of witnesses and the production of documents at depositions or at hearings;

(6) Rule on motions and other procedural matters;

(7) Regulate the scope and timing of discovery;

(8) Regulate the course of the hearing and the conduct of representatives and parties;

(9) Examine witnesses;

(10) Receive, rule on, exclude, or limit evidence;

(11) Upon motion of a party, take official notice of facts;

(12) Upon motion of a party, decide cases, in whole or in part, by summary judgment where there is no disputed issue of material fact;

(13) Conduct any conference, argument or hearing on motions in person or by telephone; and

(14) Exercise such other authority as is necessary to carry out the responsibilities of the ALJ under this part.

(b) The ALJ does not have the authority to find Federal statutes or regulations invalid.

§ 1149.29 What rights do you have at the hearing?

Each party to the hearing has the right to:

(a) Be represented by a representative;

(b) Request a pre-hearing conference and participate in any conference held by the ALJ;

(c) Conduct discovery;

(d) Agree to stipulations of fact or law which will be made a part of the record;

(e) Present evidence relevant to the issues at the hearing;

(f) Present and cross-examine witnesses;

(g) Present arguments at the hearing as permitted by the ALJ; and

(h) Submit written briefs and proposed findings of fact and conclusions of law after the hearing, as permitted by the ALJ.

§ 1149.30 How are the functions of the ALJ separated from those of the investigating official and the reviewing official?

(a) The investigating official, the reviewing official, and any employee or agent of the authority who takes part in investigating, preparing, or presenting a particular case may not, in such case or a factually related case:

(1) Participate in the hearing as the ALJ;

(2) Participate or advise in the review of the initial decision by the authority head; or

(3) Make the collection of penalties and assessment.

(b) The ALJ must not be responsible to or subject to the supervision or direction of the investigating official or the reviewing official.

§ 1149.31 Can the reviewing official or the ALJ be disqualified?

(a) A reviewing official or an ALJ may disqualify himself or herself at any time.

(b) Upon motion of any party, the reviewing official or ALJ may be disqualified as follows:

(1) The motion must be supported by an affidavit containing specific facts establishing that personal bias or other reason for disqualification exists, including the time and circumstances of the discovery of such facts;

(2) The motion must be filed promptly after discovery of the grounds for disqualification or the objection will be deemed waived; and

(3) The party, or representative of record, must certify in writing that the motion is made in good faith.

(c) Once a motion has been filed to disqualify the reviewing official or the ALJ, the ALJ will halt the proceedings until resolving the matter of disqualification. If the ALJ determines that the reviewing official is disqualified, the ALJ will dismiss the complaint without prejudice. If the ALJ disqualifies himself/herself, the case will be promptly reassigned to another ALJ. However, if the ALJ denies a motion to disqualify, the matter will be determined by the authority head only during his/her review of the initial decision on appeal.

§ 1149.32 Do you have a right to review documents?

(a) Yes. Once the ALJ issues a hearing notice, and upon written request to the reviewing official, you may:

(1) Review any relevant and material documents, transcripts, records, and other materials that relate to the allegations set out in the complaint and upon which the findings and conclusions of the investigating official are based, unless such documents are subject to a privilege under Federal law. Upon payment of fees for duplication, you may obtain copies of such documents; and

(2) Obtain a copy of all exculpatory information in the possession of the reviewing official or investigating official relating to the allegations in the complaint. You may obtain exculpatory information even if it is contained in a document that would otherwise be privileged. If the document would otherwise be privileged, only that portion containing exculpatory information must be disclosed.

(b) The notice sent to the Attorney General from the reviewing official is not discoverable under any circumstances.

(c) If the reviewing official does not respond to your request within 20 days, you may file a motion to compel disclosure of the documents with the ALJ subject to the provisions of this section. Such a motion may only be filed with the ALJ following the filing of an answer.

§ 1149.33 What type of discovery is authorized and how is it conducted?

(a) The following types of discovery are authorized:

(1) Requests for production of documents for inspection and copying;

(2) Requests for admissions of the authenticity of any relevant document or of the truth of any relevant fact;

(3) Written interrogatories; and

(4) Depositions.

(b) For the purpose of this section, the term *documents* includes information, documents, reports, answers, records, accounts, papers, electronic data and other data and documentary evidence. Nothing contained herein must be interpreted to require the creation of a document.

(c) Unless mutually agreed to by the parties, discovery is available only as ordered by the ALJ. The ALJ must regulate the timing of discovery.

§ 1149.34 How are motions for discovery handled?

Motions for discovery must be handled according to the following:

(a) A party seeking discovery may file a motion with the ALJ. Such a motion must be accompanied by a copy of the requested discovery, or in the case of depositions, a summary of the scope of the proposed deposition.

(b) Within 10 days of service, a party may file an opposition to the motion and/or a motion for protective order.

§ 1149.35 When may an ALJ grant a motion for discovery?

(a) The ALJ may grant a motion for discovery only if he/she finds that the discovery sought—

(1) Is necessary for the expeditious, fair, and reasonable consideration of the issues;

(2) Is not unduly costly or burdensome;

(3) Will not unduly delay the proceeding; and

(4) Does not seek privileged information.

(b) The burden of showing that discovery should be allowed is on the party seeking discovery.

(c) The ALJ may grant discovery subject to a protective order.

§ 1149.36 How are depositions handled?

(a) Depositions are to be handled in the following manner:

(1) If a motion for deposition is granted, the ALJ must issue a subpoena for the deponent, which may require the deponent to produce documents. The subpoena must specify the time and place at which the deposition will be held.

(2) The party seeking to depose must serve the subpoena in the manner prescribed by § 1149.12.

(3) The deponent may file with the ALJ a motion to quash the subpoena or a motion for a protective order within 10 days of service.

(4) The party seeking to depose must provide for the taking of a verbatim transcript of the deposition, which it must make available to all other parties for inspection and copying.

(b) Each party must bear its own costs of discovery.

§ 1149.37 Are witness lists and exhibits exchanged before the hearing?

(a) The parties must exchange witness lists and copies of proposed hearing exhibits at least 15 days before the hearing or at such other time as ordered by the ALJ. This includes copies of any written statements or transcripts of deposition testimony that each party intends to offer in lieu of live testimony.

(b) If a party objects, the ALJ will not admit into evidence the testimony of any witness whose name does not appear on the witness list or any exhibit not provided to an opposing party in advance unless the ALJ finds good cause for the omission or concludes that there is no prejudice to the objecting party.

(c) Documents exchanged in accordance with this section are deemed to be authentic for the purpose of admissibility at the hearing unless a party objects within the time set by the ALJ.

§ 1149.38 Can witnesses be subpoenaed?

(a) A party wishing to procure the appearance and testimony of any individual at the hearing may request that the ALJ issue a subpoena.

(b) A subpoena requiring the attendance and testimony of an individual may also require the individual to produce documents at the hearing.

(c) A party seeking a subpoena must file a written request not less than 15 days before the date of the hearing unless otherwise allowed by the ALJ upon a showing of good cause. Such request must specify any documents to be produced, must designate the witnesses, and describe the address and location of the desired witness with sufficient particularity to permit such witnesses to be found.

(d) The subpoena must specify the time and place at which the witness is to appear and any documents the witness is to produce.

(e) The party seeking the subpoena must serve it in the manner prescribed in § 1149.11. A subpoena on a party or upon an individual under the control of a party may be served by first class mail.

§ 1149.39 Who pays the costs for a subpoena?

The party requesting a subpoena must pay the cost of the fees and mileage of any witness subpoenaed in the amounts that would be payable to a witness in a proceeding in United States District Court. A check for witness fees and mileage must accompany the subpoena when served, except that when a subpoena is issued on behalf of the NEA, a check for witness fees and mileage need not accompany the subpoena.

§ 1149.40 When may I file a motion to quash a subpoena?

A party, entity or the person to whom the subpoena is directed, may file with the ALJ a motion to quash the subpoena:

(a) Within 10 days after service; or

(b) On or before the time specified in the subpoena for compliance if it is less than 10 days after service.

§ 1149.41 Are protective orders available?

A party or prospective witness or deponent may file a motion for a protective order with respect to discovery sought by an opposing party or with respect to the hearing, seeking to limit the availability of an individual or disclosure of evidence.

§ 1149.42 What does a protective order protect?

In issuing a protective order, the ALJ may make any order which justice requires to protect a party or person from annoyance, embarrassment, oppression, or undue burden or expense, including one or more of the following:

(a) That the discovery not be had;

(b) That the discovery may be had only under specified terms and conditions, including a designation of the time or place;

(c) That the discovery may be had only through a different method of discovery than requested;

(d) That certain matters are not inquired into, or that the scope of discovery is limited to certain matters;

(e) That only those persons designated by the ALJ may be present during discovery;

(f) That the contents of the discovery or evidence are sealed;

(g) That a sealed deposition is opened only by order of the ALJ;

(h) That a trade secret or other confidential research, development, commercial information, or facts pertaining to any criminal investigation, proceeding, or other administrative investigation not be disclosed or be disclosed only in a designated way; or

(i) That the parties simultaneously file specified documents or information enclosed in sealed envelopes to be opened as directed by the ALJ.

§ 1149.43 How are documents filed and served with the ALJ?

(a) Documents are considered filed when they are mailed. The date of mailing may be established by a certificate from the party or his/her representative, or by proof that the document was sent by certified or registered mail.

(b) A party filing a document with the ALJ must, at the time of filing, serve a copy of such document on every other party. When a party is represented by a representative, the party's representative must be served in lieu of the party.

(c) A certificate of the individual serving the document by personal delivery or mail and setting forth the manner of service will be proof of service.

(d) Service upon any party of any document other than the complaint must be made by delivering a copy or by placing a copy in the United States mail, postage prepaid and addressed to the party's last known address.

(e) If a party consents in writing, documents may be sent electronically. In this instance, service is complete upon transmission unless the serving party receives electronic notification that transmission of the communication was not completed.

§ 1149.44 What must documents filed with the ALJ include?

(a) Documents filed with the ALJ must include:

(1) An original; and

(2) Two copies.

(b) Every document filed in the proceeding must contain:

(1) A title, for example, "motion to quash subpoena";

(2) A caption setting forth the title of the action; and

(3) The case number assigned by the ALJ.

(c) Every document must be signed by the filer, or his/her representative, and contain the address or telephone number of that person.

§ 1149.45 How is time computed?

(a) In computing any period of time under this part or in an order issued under it, the time begins with the day following the act, event, or default, and

§ 1149.46

includes the last day of the period, unless it is a Saturday, Sunday, or legal holiday observed by the Federal government, in which event it includes the next business day.

(1) *Time calculating example.* If the ALJ denies your motion for an appeal on Wednesday, December 10th you have 15 days to file the notice of appeal. Since the 15th day falls on Christmas, a legal holiday observed by the Federal government, the deadline will be the next business day, Friday, December 26th.

(2) [Reserved]

(b) When the period of time allowed is less than seven days, intermediate Saturdays, Sundays, and legal holidays observed by the Federal government must be excluded from the computation.

(c) Where a document has been served or issued by placing it in the mail, an additional five days will be added to the time permitted for any response.

§ 1149.46 Where is the hearing held?

The ALJ may hold the hearing:

(a) In any judicial district of the United States;

(b) In which you reside or transact business; or

(c) In which the claim or statement on which liability is based was made to the NEA; or

(d) In such other place as agreed upon by you and the ALJ.

§ 1149.47 How will the hearing be conducted?

(a) The ALJ conducts a hearing on the record in order:

(1) To determine whether you are liable for a civil penalty, assessment, or both; and

(2) If so, to determine the appropriate amount of the penalty and/or assessment, considering any aggravating or mitigating factors.

(b) The hearing will be recorded and transcribed, and the transcript of testimony, exhibits admitted at the hearing, and all papers filed in the proceeding constitute the record for a decision by the ALJ.

(c) The hearing will be open to the public unless otherwise ordered by the ALJ for good cause shown.

§ 1149.48 Who has the burden of proof?

(a) The NEA must prove your liability and any aggravating factors by a preponderance of the evidence.

(b) You must prove any affirmative defenses and any mitigating factors by a preponderance of the evidence.

§ 1149.49 How is evidence presented at the hearing?

(a) The ALJ determines the admissibility of evidence.

(b) Except as provided in this part, the ALJ is not bound by the Federal Rules of Evidence. However, the ALJ may choose to apply the Federal Rules of Evidence where he/she deems appropriate, for example, to exclude unreliable evidence.

(c) The ALJ must exclude irrelevant and immaterial evidence.

(d) Although relevant, evidence may be excluded if its probative value is substantially outweighed by the danger of unfair prejudice, confusion of the issues, or by considerations of undue delay or needless presentation of cumulative evidence.

(e) Although relevant, evidence may be excluded if it is privileged under Federal law.

(f) The following evidence concerning offers of compromise or settlement is inadmissible when offered to prove liability for, invalidity of, or amount of a claim that was disputed as to validity or amount, or to impeach through a prior inconsistent statement or contradiction:

(1) Providing, offer, or promising to provide a valuable consideration in compromising or attempting to compromise the claim;

(2) Accepting, offering, or promising to accept a valuable consideration in compromising or attempting to compromise the claim; and

(3) Conduct or statements made in compromise negotiations regarding the claim, except when offered in a criminal case and the negotiations related to a claim by a public office or authority in the exercise of regulatory, investigative, or enforcement authority.

(g) The ALJ must permit the parties to introduce rebuttal witnesses and evidence.

(h) All documents and other evidence taken for the record must be open to examination by all parties unless otherwise ordered by the ALJ.

§ 1149.50 How is witness testimony presented?

(a) Except as provided in paragraph (b) of this section, testimony at the hearing must be given orally by witnesses under oath or affirmation.

(b) At the discretion of the ALJ, testimony may be admitted in the form of a written statement or deposition.

(1) Any such statement must be provided to all other parties along with the last known address of such witness, in a manner which allows sufficient time for other parties to subpoena the witness for cross-examination at the hearing.

(2) Prior written statements of witnesses proposed to testify at the hearing and deposition transcripts must be exchanged.

(c) The ALJ must exercise reasonable control over the mode and order of interrogating witnesses and presenting evidence so as to:

(1) Make the interrogation and presentation effective for ascertaining the truth;

(2) Avoid needless consumption of time; and

(3) Protect witnesses from harassment and undue embarrassment.

(d) The ALJ must permit the parties to conduct such cross examination as may be required for a full and true disclosure of the facts.

(e) At the discretion of the ALJ, a witness may be cross examined on matters relevant to the proceeding without regard to the scope of his or her direct examination. To the extent permitted by the ALJ, cross-examination on matters outside the scope of direct examination must be conducted in the manner of direct examination. Leading questions may be used only if the witness is a hostile witness, an adverse party, or a witness identified with an adverse party.

§ 1149.51 How can I exclude a witness?

Upon motion of any party, the ALJ must order witnesses excluded from the hearing room so that they cannot hear the testimony of other witnesses. This rule does not authorize exclusion of—

(a) A party who is an individual;

(b) In the case of a party that is not an individual, an officer or employee of the party appearing for the entity pro se or designated by the party's representative; or

(c) An individual whose presence is shown by a party to be essential to the presentation of its case, including an individual employed by the Government engaged in assisting the representative for the Government.

§ 1149.52 Will the hearing proceedings be recorded?

(a) The hearing will be recorded and transcribed. Transcripts may be obtained after the conclusion of the hearing and at a cost no greater than the actual cost of duplication.

(b) The transcript of testimony, exhibits and other evidence admitted at the hearing, and all papers and requests filed in the proceeding constitute the record for the decision by the ALJ and the authority head.

(c) The hearings will be recorded either electronically or by a court reporter. If the authority does not intend to arrange for a court reporter, you can arrange for one. If you do, you have to pay the reporter's appearance fees.

(d) Upon payment of a reasonable fee, the record may be inspected and copied by anyone, unless otherwise ordered by the ALJ.

§ 1149.53 Are ex parte communications between a party and the ALJ permitted?

Ex parte communications between a party and the ALJ are not permitted unless the other party consents to such a communication taking place. This does not prohibit a party from inquiring about the status of a case or asking routine questions concerning administrative functions or procedures.

§ 1149.54 Are there sanctions for misconduct?

(a) The ALJ may sanction a person, including any party or representative, as outlined in § 1149.55, for the following:

(1) Failing to comply with an order, rule, or procedure governing the proceeding;

(2) Failing to prosecute or defend an action; or

(3) Engaging in other misconduct that interferes with the speedy, orderly, and fair conduct of a hearing.

(b) Any sanction issued under this section must reasonably relate to the severity and nature of the misconduct.

§ 1149.55 What happens if I fail to comply with an order?

(a) When a party fails to comply with an order, including an order for taking a deposition, the production of evidence within the party's control, or a request for admission, the ALJ may:

(1) Draw an inference in favor of the requesting party with regard to the information sought;

(2) In the case of requests for admission, deem each matter of which an admission is requested to be admitted;

(3) Prohibit the party failing to comply with such order from introducing evidence concerning, or otherwise relying upon testimony relating to the information sought; and

(4) Strike any part of the pleadings or other submissions of the party failing to comply with such a request.

(b) If a party fails to prosecute or defend an action under this part commenced by service of a notice of hearing, the ALJ may dismiss the action or may issue an initial decision imposing penalties and assessments.

(c) The ALJ may refuse to consider any motion, request, response, brief or other document which is not filed in a timely fashion.

§ 1149.56 Are post-hearing briefs required?

Any party may file a post-hearing brief; but, such briefs are not required, unless ordered by the ALJ. The ALJ must fix the time for filing such briefs, not to exceed 60 days from the date the parties receive the transcript of the hearing or, if applicable, the stipulated record. Such briefs may be accompanied by proposed findings of fact and conclusions of law. The ALJ may permit the parties to file reply briefs.

Subpart G—Decisions and Appeals

§ 1149.57 How is the case decided?

(a) The ALJ will issue an initial decision based only on the record. The record must contain findings of fact, conclusions of law, and the amount of any penalties and assessments imposed.

(b) The findings of fact must include a finding on each of the following issues:

(1) Whether any one or more of the claims or statements identified in the complaint, in whole or in part, violate this part; and

(2) If you are liable for penalties or assessments, the appropriate amount of any such penalties or assessments, considering any mitigating or aggravating factors that are proven by a preponderance of the evidence during the hearing.

§ 1149.58 When will the ALJ serve the initial decision?

(a) The ALJ will serve the initial decision on all parties within 90 days after the close of the hearing, or within 90 days after the final post-hearing brief was filed.

(b) At the same time as the initial decision, the ALJ must serve a statement describing your rights if you are found liable for a civil penalty or assessment to file a motion for reconsideration with the ALJ or a notice of appeal with the authority head.

(c) If the ALJ fails to meet the deadline contained in this section, he or she must notify the parties of the reason for the delay and must set a new deadline.

(d) Unless the initial decision of the ALJ is timely appealed to the authority head, or a motion for reconsideration of the initial decision is timely filed, the initial decision must constitute the final decision of the authority head and must be final and binding on the parties 30 days after it is issued by the ALJ.

§ 1149.59 How are penalty and assessment amounts determined?

In determining an appropriate amount of civil penalties and assessments, the ALJ and the authority head, upon appeal, should evaluate any circumstances that mitigate or aggravate the violation and should articulate in their opinions the reasons that support the penalties and assessments they impose.

§ 1149.60 What factors are considered in determining the amount of penalties and assessments to impose?

(a) Although not exhaustive, the following factors are among those that may influence the ALJ and the authority head in determining the amount of penalties and assessments to impose with respect to the misconduct charged in the complaint:

(1) The number of false, fictitious, or fraudulent claims or statements;

(2) The time period over which such claims or statements were made;

(3) The degree of your culpability with respect to the misconduct;

(4) The amount of money or the value of the property, services, or benefit falsely claimed;

(5) The value of the Government's actual loss as a result of the misconduct, including foreseeable consequential damages and the cost of the investigation;

(6) The relationship of the amount imposed as civil penalties to the amount of the Government's loss;

(7) The potential or actual impact of the misconduct upon national defense, public health or safety, or public confidence in the management of Government programs and operations, especially upon the public confidence of those intended to benefit from Government programs;

(8) Whether you have engaged in a pattern of the same or similar misconduct;

(9) Whether you attempted to conceal the misconduct;

(10) The degree to which you have involved others in the misconduct or in concealing it;

(11) Where the misconduct of employees or agents is imputed to you, the extent to which your practices fostered or attempted to preclude such misconduct;

(12) Whether you cooperated in or obstructed an investigation of the misconduct;

(13) Whether you assisted in identifying and prosecuting other wrongdoers;

(14) The complexity of the program or transaction, and the degree of your sophistication with respect to it, including the extent of your prior participation in the program or in similar transactions;

(15) Whether you have been found, in any criminal, civil, or administrative proceeding, to have engaged in similar misconduct or dealt dishonestly with the Government of the United States or a state, directly or indirectly; and

(16) The need to deter you and others from engaging in the same or similar misconduct.

(b) Nothing in this section must be construed to limit the ALJ or the authority head from considering any other factors that in any given case may mitigate or aggravate the offense for which penalties and assessments are imposed.

§ 1149.61 Can a party request reconsideration of the initial decision?

(a) Any party may file a motion for reconsideration of the initial decision with the ALJ within 20 days of receipt of the initial decision. If the initial decision was served by mail, there is a rebuttable presumption that the initial decision was received by the party 5 days from the date of mailing.

(b) A motion for reconsideration shall be accompanied by a supporting brief and must specifically describe the issue and nature of each allegedly erroneous decision.

(c) Responses to a motion for reconsideration will only be allowed if it is requested by the ALJ.

(d) The ALJ will dispose of a motion for reconsideration by denying it or by issuing a revised initial decision.

(e) If the ALJ issues a revised initial decision upon motion of a party, no further motions for reconsideration may be filed by any party.

(f) If the ALJ issues a revised initial decision, that decision shall constitute the final decision of the authority head and shall be final and binding on the parties 30 days after it is issued, unless it is timely appealed to the authority head.

§ 1149.62 When does the initial decision of the ALJ become final?

(a) The initial decision of the ALJ becomes the final decision of the NEA and binds all parties 30 days after it is issued, unless a party timely files a motion for reconsideration or timely

§ 1149.63

appeals to the authority head of NEA, as set forth in § 1149.64.

(b) If the ALJ disposes of a motion for reconsideration by denying it or by issuing a revised initial decision, the ALJ's order on the motion for reconsideration becomes the final decision of NEA 30 days after the order is issued.

§ 1149.63 What are the procedures for appealing the ALJ decision?

(a) Any defendant who submits a timely answer and is found liable for a civil penalty or assessment in an initial decision may appeal the decision to the authority head by filing a notice of appeal with the authority head in accordance with this section.

(b) You may file a notice of appeal with the authority head within 30 days following issuance of the initial decision, serving a copy of the notice of appeal on all parties and the ALJ. The authority head may extend this deadline for up to an additional 30 days if an extension request is filed within the initial 30-day period and shows good cause.

(c) Your appeal will not be considered until all timely motions for reconsideration have been resolved.

(d) If a timely motion for reconsideration is denied, a notice of appeal may be filed within 30 days following such denial or issuance of a revised initial decision, whichever applies.

(e) A notice of appeal must be supported by a written brief specifying why the initial decision should be reversed or modified.

(f) The NEA representative may file a brief in opposition to the notice of appeal within 30 days of receiving your appeal and supporting brief.

(g) If you timely file a notice of appeal, and the time for filing reconsideration motions has expired, the ALJ will forward the record of the proceeding to the authority head.

§ 1149.64 What happens if an initial decision is appealed?

(a) An initial decision is stayed automatically pending disposition of a motion for reconsideration or of an appeal to the authority head.

(b) No administrative stay is available following a final decision of the authority head.

§ 1149.65 Are there any limitations on the right to appeal to the authority head?

(a) You have no right to appear personally, or through a representative, before the authority head.

(b) There is no right to appeal any interlocutory ruling.

(c) The authority head will not consider any objection or evidence that was not raised before the ALJ, unless you demonstrate that the failure to object was caused by extraordinary circumstances. If you demonstrate to the satisfaction of the authority head that extraordinary circumstances prevented the presentation of evidence at the hearing, and that the additional evidence is material, the authority head may remand the matter to the ALJ for consideration of the additional evidence.

§ 1149.66 How does the authority head dispose of an appeal?

(a) The authority head may affirm, reduce, reverse, compromise, remand, or settle any penalty or assessment imposed by the ALJ in the initial decision or reconsideration decision.

(b) The authority head will promptly serve each party to the appeal and the ALJ with a copy of his or her decision. This decision must contain a statement describing the right of any person, against whom a penalty or assessment has been made, to seek judicial review.

§ 1149.67 Who represents the NEA on an appeal?

The authority head will designate the NEA's representative in the event of an appeal.

§ 1149.68 What judicial review is available?

Section 3805 of title 31, United States Code, authorizes Judicial review by the appropriate United States District Court of any final NEA decision by the authority head imposing penalties or assessments under this part. To obtain judicial review, you must file a petition with the appropriate court in a timely manner. (See paragraphs (a) through (e) of 31 U.S.C. 3805 for a description of how judicial review is authorized.)

§ 1149.69 Can the administrative complaint be settled voluntarily?

(a) Parties may make offers of compromise or settlement at any time. Any compromise or settlement must be in writing.

(b) The reviewing official has the exclusive authority to compromise or settle the case anytime after the date on which the reviewing official is permitted to issue a complaint and before the ALJ issues an initial decision.

(c) The authority head has exclusive authority to compromise or settle the case anytime after the date of the ALJ's initial decision until the initiation of any judicial review or any action to collect the penalties and assessments.

(d) The Attorney General has exclusive authority to compromise or settle a case once any judicial review or any action to recover penalties and assessments is initiated.

(e) The investigating official may recommend settlement terms to the reviewing official, the authority head, or the Attorney General, as appropriate.

§ 1149.70 How are civil penalties and assessments collected?

(a) Civil actions to recover penalties or assessments must commence within 3 years after the date of a final decision determining your liability.

(b) The Attorney General is responsible for judicial enforcement of civil penalties or assessments imposed. He/she has exclusive authority to compromise or settle any penalty or assessment during the pendency of any action to collect penalties or assessments under 31 U.S.C. 3806.

(c) Penalties or assessments imposed by a final decision may be recovered in a civil action brought by the Attorney General.

(1) The district courts of the United States have jurisdiction of such civil actions.

(2) The United States Court of Federal Claims has jurisdiction of any civil action to recover any penalty or assessment if the cause of action is asserted by the government as a counterclaim in a matter pending in such court.

(3) Civil actions may be joined and consolidated with or asserted as a counterclaim, cross-claim, or set off by the government in any other civil action which includes you and the government as parties.

(4) Defenses raised at the hearing, or that could have been raised, may not be raised as a defense in the civil action. Determination of liability and of the amounts of penalties and assessments must not be subject to review.

§ 1149.71 Is there a right to administrative offset?

The amount of any penalty or assessment which has become final, or for which a judgment has been entered, or any amount agreed upon in a compromise or settlement, may be collected by administrative offset, except that an administrative offset may not be made under this subsection against a refund of an overpayment of Federal taxes, then or later owing by the United States to you.

§ 1149.72 What happens to collections?

All amounts collected pursuant to this part must be deposited as miscellaneous receipts in the Treasury of the United States.

§ 1149.73 What if the investigation indicates criminal misconduct or a violation of the False Claims Act?

(a) Investigating officials may:

(1) Refer allegations of criminal misconduct or a violation of the False Claims Act directly to the Department of Justice for prosecution and/or civil action, as appropriate;

(2) Defer or postpone a report or referral to the reviewing official to avoid interference with a criminal or civil investigation, prosecution or litigation; or

(3) Issue subpoenas under any other statutory authority.

(b) Nothing in this part limits the requirement that NEA employees report suspected false or fraudulent conduct, claims or statements, and violations of criminal law to the NEA Office of Inspector General or to the Attorney General.

§ 1149.74 How does the NEA protect your rights?

These procedures separate the functions of the investigating official, reviewing official, and the ALJ, each of whom report to a separate organizational authority. Except for purposes of settlement, or as a witness or a representative in public proceedings, no investigating official, reviewing official, or NEA employee or agent who helps investigate, prepare, or present a case may (in such case, or a factually related case) participate in the initial decision or the review of the initial decision by the authority head. This separation of functions and organization is designed to assure the independence and impartiality of each government official during every stage of the proceeding. The representative for the NEA may be employed in the offices of either the investigating official or the reviewing official.

PART 1150—COLLECTION OF CLAIMS

Subpart A—General Provisions

Sec.
1150.1 What definitions apply to the regulations in this part?
1150.2 What is the Endowment's authority to issue these regulations?
1150.3 What other regulations also apply to the Endowment's debt collection efforts?
1150.4 What types of claims are excluded from these regulations?
1150.5 What notice will I be provided if I owe a debt to the Endowment?
1150.6 What opportunity do I have to obtain a review of my debt within the Endowment?
1150.7 What interest, penalty charges, and administrative costs will I have to pay on a debt owed to the Endowment?
1150.8 Will failure to pay my debt affect my eligibility for Endowment programs?
1150.9 How can I resolve the Endowment's claim through a voluntary repayment agreement?
1150.10 What is the extent of the Chairperson's authority to compromise debts owed to the Endowment, or to suspend or terminate collection action on such debts?
1150.11 How does subdividing or joining debts owed to the Endowment affect the Chairperson's compromise, suspension, or termination authority?
1150.12 How will the Endowment use credit reporting agencies to collect its claims?
1150.13 How will the Endowment contract for collection services?
1150.14 When will the Endowment refer claims to the DOJ?
1150.15 Will the Endowment use a cross-servicing agreement with the Treasury to collect its claims?
1150.16 May I use the Endowment's failure to comply with these regulations as a defense?

Subpart B—Salary Offset

1150.20 What debts are included or excluded from coverage of these regulations on salary offset?
1150.21 May I ask the Endowment to waive an overpayment that otherwise would be collected by offsetting my salary as a Federal employee?
1150.22 What are the Endowment's procedures for salary offset?
1150.23 How will the Endowment coordinate salary offsets with other agencies?
1150.24 Under what conditions will the Endowment make a refund of amounts collected by salary offset?
1150.25 Will the collection of a claim by salary offset act as a waiver of my rights to dispute the claimed debt?

Subpart C—Tax Refund Offset

1150.30 Which debts can the Endowment refer to the Treasury for collection by offsetting tax refunds?
1150.31 What are the Endowment's procedures for collecting debts by tax refund offset?

Subpart D—Administrative Offset

1150.40 Under what circumstances will the Endowment collect amounts that I owe to the Endowment (or some other Federal agency) by offsetting the debt against payments that the Endowment (or some other Federal agency) owes me?
1150.41 How will the Endowment request that my debt to the Endowment be collected by offset against some payment that another Federal agency owes me?
1150.42 What procedures will the Endowment use to collect amounts I owe to a Federal agency by offsetting a payment that the Endowment would otherwise make to me?
1150.43 When may the Endowment make an offset in an expedited manner?
1150.44 Can a judgment I have obtained against the United States be used to satisfy a debt that I owe to the Endowment?

AUTHORITY: 31 U.S.C. 3711, 3716–3718, 3720A; 5 U.S.C. 5514.

SOURCE: 65 FR 37486, June 15, 2000, unless otherwise noted.

Subpart A—General Provisions

§ 1150.1 What definitions apply to the regulations in this part?

As used in this part:

(a) *Administrative offset* means the withholding of funds payable by the United States (including funds payable by the United States on behalf of a State government) to any person, or the withholding of funds held by the United States for any person, in order to satisfy a debt owed to the United States.

(b) *Agency* means a department, agency, court, court administrative office, or instrumentality in the executive, judicial, or legislative branch of government, including a government corporation.

(c) *Chairperson* means the Chairperson of the Endowment, or his or her designee.

(d) *Creditor agency* means the agency to which the debt is owed.

(e) *Day* means calendar day. To count days, include the last day of the period unless it is a Saturday, a Sunday, or a Federal legal holiday.

(f) *Debt* and *claim* are deemed synonymous and interchangeable. These terms mean money owed by a person to the United States for any reason, including loans made or guaranteed by the United States, fees, leases, rents, royalties, services, sales of real or personal property, overpayments, damages, interests, penalties, fines, forfeitures, and all other similar sources. For the purpose of administrative offset under 31 U.S.C. 3716 and subpart D of these regulations, the terms debt and claim also include money or property owed by a person to a State, the District of Columbia, American Samoa, Guam, the United States Virgin Islands, the Commonwealth of the Northern Marina Islands, or the Commonwealth of Puerto Rico.

(g) *Debtor* means a person who owes a debt. Uses of the terms "I," "you," "me," and similar references to the reader of the regulations in this part are meant to apply to debtors as defined in this paragraph (g).

(h) *Delinquent debt* means a debt that has not been paid within the time limit prescribed by the Endowment.

(i) *Disposable pay* means the part of an employee's pay that remains after deductions that are required to be withheld by law have been made.

(j) *Employee* means a current employee of an agency, including a current member of the Armed Forces or Reserve of the Armed Forces of the United States.

(k) *Endowment* means the National Endowment for the Arts.

(l) *Federal Claims Collection Standards* means the standards currently published at 4 CFR Chapter II. The DOJ and the Treasury have proposed a revision that would move the Federal Claims Collection Standards to 31 CFR parts 900–904. The Endowment will amend these regulations, as necessary, after the revised Federal Claims Collection Standards have been issued as final regulations.

(m) *Paying agency* means the agency that employs the individual who owes a debt to the United States. In some cases, the Endowment may be both the creditor agency and the paying agency.

(n) *Payroll office* means the office in the paying agency that is primarily responsible for payroll records and the coordination of pay matters with the appropriate personnel office.

(o) *Person* includes a natural person or persons, profit or non-profit corporation, partnership, association, trust, estate, consortium, state or local government, or other entity that is capable of owing a debt to the United States; however, agencies of the United States are excluded.

(p) *Private collection contractor* means a private debt collector under contract with an agency to collect a non-tax debt owed to the United States.

(q) *Salary offset* means a payroll procedure to collect a debt under 5 U.S.C. 5514 by deduction(s) at one or more officially established pay intervals from the current pay account of an employee, without his or her consent.

(r) *Tax refund offset* means the reduction of a tax refund by the amount of a past-due legally enforceable debt owed to the Endowment or any other Federal agency.

§ 1150.2 What is the Endowment's authority to issue these regulations?

The Endowment is issuing the regulations in this part under 31 U.S.C. 3711, 3716–3718, and 3720A. These sections reflect the Federal Claims Collection Act of 1966, as amended by the Debt Collection Act of 1982 and the Debt Collection Improvement Act of 1996. The Endowment is also issuing the regulations in this part in conformity with the Federal Claims Collection Standards, which prescribe standards for the handling of the Federal government's claims for money or property. The Endowment is further issuing the regulations in this part in conformity with 5 U.S.C. 5514 and the salary offset regulations published by the OPM at 5 CFR part 550, subpart K.

§ 1150.3 What other regulations also apply to the Endowment's debt collection efforts?

All provisions of the Federal Claims Collection Standards also apply to the regulations in this part. This part supplements the Federal Claims Collection Standards by prescribing procedures and directives necessary and appropriate for operations of the Endowment.

§ 1150.4 What types of claims are excluded from these regulations?

(a) The regulations in this part do not apply to any claim as to which there is an indication of fraud or misrepresentation, as described in the Federal Claims Collection Standards, unless returned to the Endowment by the DOJ for handling.

(b) The regulations in this subpart, subpart B, and subpart D do not apply to debts arising under the Internal Revenue Code of 1986, as amended (26 U.S.C. 1 et seq.); the Social Security Act (42 U.S.C. 301 et seq.); and the tariff laws of the United States.

(c) Remedies and procedures described in this part may be authorized with respect to claims that are exempt from the Debt Collection Act of 1982 and the Debt Collection Improvement Act of 1996, to the extent that they are authorized under some other statute or the common law.

§ 1150.5 What notice will I be provided if I owe a debt to the Endowment?

(a) When the Chairperson determines that you owe a debt to the Endowment, he or she will send you a written notice (Notice). The Notice will be hand-delivered or sent to you by certified mail, return receipt requested at the most current address known to the Endowment. The Notice will inform you of the following:

(1) The amount, nature, and basis of the debt;

(2) That a designated Endowment official has reviewed the claim and determined that it is valid;

(3) That payment of the debt is due as of the date of the Notice, and that the debt will be considered delinquent if you do not pay it within 30 days of the date of the Notice;

(4) The Endowment's policy concerning interest, penalty charges, and administrative costs (see § 1150.7), including a statement that such assessments must be made against you unless excused in accordance with the Federal Claims Collection Standards and this part;

(5) That you have the right to inspect and copy Endowment records pertaining to your debt, or to receive copies of those records if personal inspection is impractical;

(6) That you have the opportunity to enter into an agreement, in writing and signed by both you and the Chairperson, for voluntary repayment of the debt (see § 1150.9); and

(7) The address, telephone number, and name of the Endowment official available to discuss the debt.

(b) Notice of possible collection actions. The Notice provided by the Chairperson under paragraph (a) of this section will also advise you that, if your debt (including any interest, penalty charges, and administrative costs) is not paid within 60 days of the date of the Notice, or you do not enter into a voluntary repayment agreement within 60 days of the date of the Notice, then the Endowment may enforce collection of the debt by any or all of the following methods:

(1) By referral to a credit reporting agency (see § 1150.12), a collection agency (see § 1150.13), or the DOJ (see § 1150.14);

National Foundation on the Arts and the Humanities § 1150.6

(2) By transferring any debt delinquent for more than 180 days to the Treasury for collection under a cross-servicing agreement with the Treasury (see § 1150.15);

(3) If you are an Endowment employee, by deducting money from your disposable pay account (in the amount and with the frequency, approximate beginning date, and duration specified by the Endowment) until the debt (and all accumulated interest, penalty charges, and administrative costs) is paid in full (see subpart B). Such proceedings are governed by 5 U.S.C. 5514;

(4) If you are an employee of a Federal agency other than the Endowment, by initiating certification procedures to implement a salary offset by that Federal agency (see subpart B). Such proceedings are governed by 5 U.S.C. 5514;

(5) By referring the debt to the Treasury for offset against any refund of overpayment of tax (see subpart C);

(6) By administrative offset (see subpart D); or

(7) By liquidation of security or collateral. When the Endowment holds security or collateral that may be liquidated and the proceeds applied to your debt through the exercise of a power of sale in the security instrument or a nonjudicial foreclosure, such procedures may be followed unless the cost of disposing of the collateral will be disproportionate to its value or special circumstances require judicial foreclosure.

(c) *Notice of opportunity for review.* The Notice provided by the Chairperson under paragraph (a) of this section will also advise you of the opportunity to obtain a review within the Endowment concerning the existence or amount of the debt, the proposed schedule for offset of Federal employee salary payments, or whether the debt is past due or legally enforceable. The Notice shall also advise you of the following:

(1) The name, address, and telephone number of an officer or employee of the Endowment whom you may contact concerning procedures for requesting a review;

(2) The method and time period for requesting a review;

(3) That the filing of a request for a review on or before the 60th day following the date of the Notice will stay the commencement of collection proceedings;

(4) The name and address of the officer or employee of the Endowment to whom you should send the request for a review;

(5) That a final decision on the review (if one is requested) will be issued at the earliest practical date, but not later than 60 days after the receipt of the request for a review, unless you request, and the review official grants, a delay in the proceedings;

(6) That any knowingly false or frivolous statements, representations, or evidence may subject you to:

(i) Disciplinary procedures appropriate under 5 U.S.C. Chapter 75, 5 CFR part 752, or any other applicable statute or regulations;

(ii) Penalties under the False Claims Act (31 U.S.C. 3729–3733) or any other applicable statutory authority; and

(iii) Criminal penalties under 18 U.S.C. 286, 287, 1001, and 1002, or any other applicable statutory authority;

(7) Any other rights available to you to dispute the validity of the debt or to have recovery of the debt waived, or remedies available to you under statutes or regulations governing the program for which the collection is being made; and

(8) That unless there are applicable contractual or statutory provisions to the contrary, amounts paid on or deducted for the debt that are later waived or found not owed will be promptly refunded to you.

(d) The Endowment will respond promptly to communications from you.

§ 1150.6 What opportunity do I have to obtain a review of my debt within the Endowment?

(a) *Request for review.* If you desire a review within the Endowment concerning the existence or amount of your debt, the proposed schedule for offset of Federal employee salary payments, or whether the debt is past due or legally enforceable, you must send such a request to the officer or employee of the Endowment designated in the Notice (see § 1150.5(c)(4)).

(1) Your request for review must carry your signature and fully identify and explain with reasonable specificity all the facts and evidence that support your position. Your request for review should be accompanied by available evidence to support your contentions.

(2) Your request for review must be received by the designated officer or employee of the Endowment on or before the 60th day following the date of the Notice. Timely filing will stay the commencement of collection procedures. If you file a request for a review after the 60-day period provided for in this section, the Endowment will accept the request if you can show that the delay was the result of circumstances beyond your control or because you did not receive notice of the filing deadline (unless you had actual notice of the filing deadline).

(b) *Inspection of Endowment records related to the debt.* (1) In accordance with §1150.5, if you want to inspect or copy Endowment records related to the debt, you must send a letter to the Endowment official designated in the Notice stating your intention. Your letter must be received within 30 days of the date of the Notice.

(2) In response to the timely request described in paragraph (b)(1) of this section, the designated Endowment official will notify you of the location and time when you may inspect and copy records related to the debt.

(3) If personal inspection of Endowment records related to the debt is impractical, reasonable arrangements will be made to send you copies of those records.

(c) *Review official.* The Chairperson shall designate an officer or employee of the Endowment (who was not involved in the determination of the debt) as the review official. When required by law or regulation, the Endowment may request an administrative law judge to conduct the review, or may obtain a review official who is an official, employee, or agent of the United States, but who is not under the supervision or control of the Chairperson. However, unless the review is conducted by an official or employee of the Endowment, any unresolved dispute you have regarding whether all or part of the debt is past due or legally enforceable (for purposes of collection by tax refund offset under §1150.31) must be referred to the Chairperson for ultimate administrative disposition, and the Chairperson must notify you of his or her determination.

(d) *Review procedure.* After you request a review, the review official will notify you of the form of the review to be provided. The review official shall determine whether an oral hearing is required, or if a review of the written record is sufficient, in accordance with the Federal Claims Collection Standards. In either case, the review official shall conduct the review in accordance with the Federal Claims Collection Standards. If the review will include an oral hearing, the notice sent to you by the review official will set forth the date, time, and location of the hearing.

(e) *Date of decision.* The review official will issue a written decision, based upon either the written record or documentary evidence and information developed at an oral hearing, as soon as practical, but not later than 60 days after the date on which the Endowment received your request for a review, unless you request, and the review official grants, a delay in the proceedings.

(f) *Content of review decision.* The review official will prepare a written decision that includes:

(1) A statement of the facts presented to support the origin, nature, and amount of the debt;

(2) The review official's findings, analysis, and conclusions; and

(3) The terms of any repayment schedule, if applicable.

(g) *Interest, penalty charge, and administrative cost accrual during review period.* Interest, penalty charges, and administrative costs authorized by law will continue to accrue during the review period.

§1150.7 **What interest, penalty charges, and administrative costs will I have to pay on a debt owed to the Endowment?**

(a) *Interest.* (1) The Endowment will assess interest on all delinquent debts unless prohibited by statute, regulation, or contract.

(2) Interest begins to accrue on all debts from the date that the debt becomes delinquent. The Endowment will

not recover interest if you pay the debt within 30 days of the date on which interest begins to accrue. The Endowment shall assess interest at the rate established annually by the Secretary of the Treasury under 31 U.S.C. 3717, unless a different rate is either necessary to protect the interests of the Endowment or established by a contract, repayment agreement, or statute. The Endowment will notify you of the basis for its finding when a different rate is necessary to protect the interests of the Endowment.

(3) The Chairperson may extend the 30-day period for payment without interest where he or she determines that such action is in the best interest of the Endowment. A decision to extend or not to extend the payment period is final and is not subject to further review.

(b) *Penalty.* The Endowment will assess a penalty charge, not to exceed 6 percent a year, on any portion of a debt that is delinquent for more than 90 days.

(c) *Administrative costs.* The Endowment will assess charges to cover administrative costs incurred as a result of your failure to pay a debt before it becomes delinquent. Administrative costs include the additional costs incurred in processing and handling the debt because it became delinquent, such as costs incurred in obtaining a credit report or in using a private collection contractor, or service fees charged by a Federal agency for collection activities undertaken on behalf of the Endowment.

(d) *Allocation of payments.* A partial or installment payment by a debtor will be applied first to outstanding penalty assessments, second to administrative costs, third to accrued interest, and fourth to the outstanding debt principal.

(e) *Additional authority.* The Endowment may assess interest, penalty charges, and administrative costs on debts that are not subject to 31 U.S.C. 3717 to the extent authorized under common law or other applicable statutory authority.

(f) *Waiver.* (1) The Chairperson may (without regard to the amount of the debt) waive collection of all or part of accrued interest, penalty charges, or administrative costs, if he or she determines that collection of these charges would be against equity and good conscience or not in the best interest of the Endowment.

(2) A decision to waive interest, penalty charges, or administrative costs may be made at any time before a debt is paid. However, where these charges have been collected before the waiver decision, they will not be refunded. The Chairperson's decision to waive or not waive collection of these charges is final and is not subject to further review.

§ 1150.8 **Will failure to pay my debt affect my eligibility for Endowment programs?**

In the event that you fail to pay your debt to the Endowment within a reasonable period of time after the date of the Notice of debt, the General Counsel of the Endowment shall place your name on the Endowment's list of debarred, suspended, and ineligible contractors, grantees, and other participants in programs sponsored by the Endowment. You will be advised of this action.

§ 1150.9 **How can I resolve the Endowment's claim through a voluntary repayment agreement?**

In response to a Notice of debt, you may propose to the Endowment that you be allowed to repay the debt through a voluntary repayment agreement in lieu of the Endowment taking other collection actions under this part.

(a) Your request to enter into a voluntary repayment agreement must:

(1) Be in writing;

(2) Admit the existence of the debt; and

(3) Either propose payment of the debt (together with interest, penalty charges, and administrative costs) in a lump sum, or set forth a proposed repayment schedule.

(b) The Endowment will collect claims in full or one lump sum whenever feasible. However, if you are unable to pay your debt in one lump sum, the Endowment may accept payment in regular installments that bear a reasonable relationship to the size of the debt and your ability to pay.

(c) The Endowment will consider a request to enter into a voluntary repayment agreement in accordance with the Federal Claims Collection Standards. The Chairperson may request additional information from you, including financial statements if you request to make payments in installments, in order to make a determination of whether to accept a voluntary repayment agreement. It is within the Chairperson's discretion to accept a repayment agreement instead of proceeding with other collection actions under this part, and to set the necessary terms of any voluntary repayment agreement. No repayment agreement will be binding on the Endowment unless it is in writing and signed by both you and the Chairperson. At the Endowment's option, you may be required to enter into a confess-judgment note or bond of indemnity with surety as part of an agreement to make payments in installments. Notwithstanding the provisions of this section, any reduction or compromise of a claim will be governed by 31 U.S.C. 3711.

§ 1150.10 What is the extent of the Chairperson's authority to compromise debts owed to the Endowment, or to suspend or terminate collection action on such debts?

(a) The Chairperson may exercise his or her authority to compromise, or to suspend or terminate collection action on, those debts owed to the Endowment and not exceeding $100,000, excluding interest, in conformity with the Federal Claims Collection Act of 1966, as amended; the Federal Claims Collection Standards issued thereunder; and this part, except where standards are established by other statutes or authorized regulations issued pursuant to them.

(b) The portion of a debt owed to the Endowment that is unrecovered as the result of a compromise shall be reported to the Internal Revenue Service (IRS) as income to the debtor.

§ 1150.11 How does subdividing or joining debts owed to the Endowment affect the Chairperson's compromise, suspension, or termination authority?

A debtor's liability arising from a particular transaction or contract will be considered as a single claim in determining whether the claim is one of not more than $100,000, excluding interest, for the purpose of compromise or suspension or termination of collection action. Such a claim may not be subdivided to avoid the monetary ceiling established by the Federal Claims Collection Act of 1966, as amended. Joining two or more claims in a demand upon a debtor for payment of more than $100,000 does not preclude compromise or suspension or termination of collection action with regard to any one claim not exceeding $100,000, excluding interest.

§ 1150.12 How will the Endowment use credit reporting agencies to collect its claims?

(a) The Endowment may report delinquent debts to appropriate credit reporting agencies by providing the following information:

(1) A statement that the debt is valid and overdue;

(2) The name, address, taxpayer identification number, and any other information necessary to establish the identity of the debtor;

(3) The amount, status, and history of the debt; and

(4) The program or pertinent activity under which the debt arose.

(b) Before disclosing debt information to a credit reporting agency, the Endowment will:

(1) Take reasonable action to locate the debtor if a current address is not available;

(2) Provide the notice required under § 1150.5 if a current address is available; and

(3) Obtain satisfactory assurances from the credit reporting agency that it complies with the Fair Credit Reporting Act (15 U.S.C. 1681 *et seq.*) and other Federal laws governing the provision of credit information.

(c) At the time debt information is submitted to a credit reporting agency, the Endowment will provide a written

National Foundation on the Arts and the Humanities § 1150.16

statement to the reporting agency that all required actions have been taken. In addition, the Endowment will, thereafter, ensure that the credit reporting agency is promptly informed of any substantive change in the conditions or amount of the debt, and promptly verify or correct information relevant to the debt.

(d) If a debtor disputes the validity of the debt, the credit reporting agency will refer the matter to the appropriate Endowment official. The credit reporting agency will exclude the debt from its reports until the Endowment certifies in writing that the debt is valid.

(e) The Endowment may disclose to a commercial credit bureau information concerning a commercial debt, including the following:

(1) Information necessary to establish the name, address, and employer identification number of the commercial debtor;

(2) The amount, status, and history of the debt; and

(3) The program or pertinent activity under which the debt arose.

§ 1150.13 How will the Endowment contract for collection services?

The Endowment will use the services of a private collection contractor where it determines that such use is in the best interest of the Endowment. When the Endowment determines that there is a need to contract for collection services, it will:

(a) Retain sole authority to:

(1) Resolve any dispute with the debtor regarding the validity of the debt;

(2) Compromise the debt;

(3) Suspend or terminate collection action;

(4) Refer the debt to the DOJ for litigation; and

(5) Take any other action under this part which does not result in full collection of the debt;

(b) Require the contractor to comply with the Privacy Act of 1974, as amended, to the extent specified in 5 U.S.C. 552a(m); with the Fair Debt Collection Practices Act (15 U.S.C. 1692–1692o) and other applicable Federal and State laws pertaining to debt collection practices; and with the applicable regulations of the Endowment in this chapter;

(c) Require the contractor to account accurately and fully for all amounts collected; and

(d) Require the contractor to provide to the Endowment, upon request, all data and reports contained in its files related to its collection actions on a debt.

§ 1150.14 When will the Endowment refer claims to the DOJ?

The Chairperson will refer to the DOJ for litigation claims on which aggressive collection actions have been taken but which could not be collected, compromised, suspended, or terminated. Referrals will be made as early as possible, consistent with aggressive Endowment collection action, and within the period for bringing a timely suit against the debtor.

§ 1150.15 Will the Endowment use a cross-servicing agreement with the Treasury to collect its claims?

(a) The Endowment will enter into a cross-servicing agreement that authorizes the Treasury to take the collection actions described in this part on behalf of the Endowment. These debt collection services will be provided to the Endowment in accordance with 31 U.S.C. Chapter 37.

(b) The Endowment shall transfer to the Treasury any past due, legally enforceable, non-tax debt that has been delinquent for a period of 180 days or more so that the Secretary of the Treasury may take appropriate action in accordance with 31 U.S.C. 3716, 5 U.S.C. 5514, the Federal Claims Collection Standards, 5 CFR 550.1108, and 31 CFR part 285. The categories of debts described in 31 U.S.C. 3711(g)(2) are excluded from transfer under this paragraph (b).

§ 1150.16 May I use the Endowment's failure to comply with these regulations as a defense?

No. The failure of the Endowment to comply with any standard prescribed in the Federal Claims Collection Standards or these regulations shall not be available to any debtor as a defense.

Subpart B—Salary Offset

§ 1150.20 What debts are included or excluded from coverage of these regulations on salary offset?

(a) The regulations in this subpart provide Endowment procedures for the collection by salary offset of a Federal employee's pay to satisfy certain debts owed to the Endowment or to other Federal agencies.

(b) The regulations in this subpart do not apply to any case where collection of a debt by salary offset is explicitly provided for or prohibited by another statute.

(c) Nothing in the regulations in this subpart precludes the compromise, suspension, or termination of collection actions under the Federal Claims Collection Act of 1966, as amended, or the Federal Claims Collection Standards.

(d) A levy pursuant to the Internal Revenue Code takes precedence over a salary offset under this subpart, as provided in 5 U.S.C. 5514(d).

(e) This subpart does not apply to any adjustment to pay arising out of your election of coverage or a change in coverage under a Federal benefits program requiring periodic deductions from pay, if the amount to be recovered was accumulated over four or fewer pay periods.

§ 1150.21 May I ask the Endowment to waive an overpayment that otherwise would be collected by offsetting my salary as a Federal employee?

Yes. The regulations in this subpart do not preclude you from requesting waiver of an overpayment under 5 U.S.C. 5584 or 8346(b), 10 U.S.C. 2774, 32 U.S.C. 716, or other statutory provisions pertaining to the particular debts being collected.

§ 1150.22 What are the Endowment's procedures for salary offset?

(a) The Endowment will coordinate salary deductions under this subpart as appropriate.

(b) If you are an Endowment employee, the Endowment's payroll office will determine the amount of your disposable pay and will implement the salary offset.

(c) Deductions will begin within three official pay periods following receipt by the Endowment's payroll office of certification of debt from the creditor agency.

(d) *Types of collection*—(1) *Lump-sum offset.* If the amount of the debt is equal to or less than 15 percent of disposable pay, the debt generally will be collected through one lump-sum offset.

(2) *Installment deductions.* Installment deductions will be made over a period not greater than the anticipated period of employment. The size and frequency of installment deductions will bear a reasonable relation to the size of the debt and your ability to pay. However, the amount deducted from any period will not exceed 15 percent of the disposable pay from which the deduction is made unless you have agreed in writing to the deduction of a greater amount. If possible, installment payments will be sufficient in size and frequency to liquidate the debt in three years or less.

(3) *Deductions from final check.* A deduction exceeding the 15 percent of disposable pay limitation may be made from any final salary payment under 31 U.S.C. 3716 and the Federal Claims Collection Standards, in order to liquidate the debt, whether the employee is being separated voluntarily or involuntarily.

(4) *Deductions from other sources.* If an employee subject to salary offset is separated from the Endowment, and the balance of the debt cannot be liquidated by offset of the final salary check, then the Endowment may offset later payments of any kind against the balance of the debt, as allowed by 31 U.S.C. 3716 and the Federal Claims Collection Standards.

(e) Multiple debts. In instances where two or more creditor agencies are seeking salary offsets, or where two or more debts are owed to a single creditor agency, the Endowment's payroll office may, at its discretion, determine whether one or more debts should be offset simultaneously within the 15 percent limitation.

§ 1150.23 How will the Endowment coordinate salary offsets with other agencies?

(a) *Responsibilities of the Endowment as the creditor agency.* Upon completion of the procedures established in this subpart and pursuant to 5 U.S.C. 5514, the Endowment must submit a claim to a paying agency.

(1) In its claim, the Endowment must certify, in writing, the following:

(i) That the employee owes the debt;

(ii) The amount and basis of the debt;

(iii) The date the Endowment's right to collect the debt first accrued; and

(iv) That the Endowment's regulations in this subpart have been approved by OPM under 5 CFR part 550, subpart K.

(2) If the collection must be made in installments, the Endowment's claim will also advise the paying agency of the amount or percentage of disposable pay to be collected in each installment. The Endowment may also advise the paying agency of the number of installments to be collected and the date of the first installment, if that date is other than the next officially established pay period.

(3) The Endowment shall also include in its claim:

(i) The employee's written consent to the salary offset;

(ii) The employee's signed statement acknowledging receipt of the procedures required by 5 U.S.C. 5514; or

(iii) Information regarding the completion of procedures required by 5 U.S.C. 5514, including the actions taken and the dates of those actions.

(4) If the employee is in the process of separating and has not received a final salary check or other final payment(s) from the paying agency, the Endowment must submit its claim to the paying agency for collection under 31 U.S.C. 3716. The paying agency will (under its regulations adopted under 5 U.S.C. 5514 and 5 CFR part 550, subpart K), certify the total amount of its collection on the debt and notify the employee and the Endowment. If the paying agency's collection does not fully satisfy the debt, and the paying agency is aware that the debtor is entitled to payments from the Civil Service Retirement and Disability Fund or other similar payments that may be due the debtor employee from other Federal government sources, then (under its regulations adopted under 5 U.S.C. 5514 and 5 CFR part 550, subpart K), the paying agency will provide written notice of the outstanding debt to the agency responsible for making the other payments to the debtor employee. The written notice will state that the employee owes a debt, the amount of the debt, and that the provisions of this section have been fully complied with. However, the Endowment must submit a properly certified claim under this paragraph (a)(4) to the agency responsible for making the payments before the collection can be made.

(5) *Separated employee.* If the employee is already separated and all payments due from his or her former paying agency have been paid, the Endowment may request, unless otherwise prohibited, that money due and payable to the employee from the Civil Service Retirement and Disability Fund or other similar funds be administratively offset to collect the debt.

(6) *Employee transfer.* When an employee transfers from one paying agency to another paying agency, the Endowment will not repeat the due process procedures described in 5 U.S.C. 5514 and this subpart to resume the collection. The Endowment will submit a properly certified claim to the new paying agency and will subsequently review the debt to ensure that the collection is resumed by the new paying agency.

(b) *Responsibilities of the Endowment as the paying agency.* (1) Complete claim. When the Endowment receives a certified claim from a creditor agency (under the creditor agency's regulations adopted under 5 U.S.C. 5514 and 5 CFR part 550, subpart K), deductions should be scheduled to begin within three officially established pay intervals. Before deductions can begin, the employee will receive a written notice from the Endowment including:

(i) A statement that the Endowment has received a certified claim from the creditor agency;

(ii) The amount of the claim;

(iii) The date salary offset deductions will begin; and

(iv) The amount of such deductions.

(2) Incomplete claim. When the Endowment receives an incomplete certification of debt from a creditor agency, the Endowment will return the claim with a notice that the creditor agency must comply with the procedures required under 5 U.S.C. 5514 and 5 CFR part 550, subpart K, and must properly certify a claim to the Endowment before the Endowment will take action to collect from the employee's current pay account.

(3) The Endowment is not authorized to review the merits of the creditor agency's determination with respect to the amount or validity of the debt certified by the creditor agency.

(4) Employees who transfer from the Endowment to another paying agency. If, after the creditor agency has submitted the claim to the Endowment, the employee transfers from the Endowment to a different paying agency before the debt is collected in full, the Endowment will certify the total amount collected on the debt and notify the employee and the creditor agency in writing. The notification to the creditor agency will include information on the employee's transfer.

§ 1150.24 Under what conditions will the Endowment make a refund of amounts collected by salary offset?

(a) If the Endowment is the creditor agency, it will promptly refund any amount deducted under the authority of 5 U.S.C. 5514, when:

(1) The debt is waived or all or part of the funds deducted are otherwise found not to be owed (unless expressly prohibited by statute or regulation); or

(2) An administrative or judicial order directs the Endowment to make a refund.

(b) Unless required or permitted by law or contract, refunds under this section will not bear interest.

§ 1150.25 Will the collection of a claim by salary offset act as a waiver of my rights to dispute the claimed debt?

Your involuntary payment of all or any portion of a debt under this subpart will not be construed as a waiver of any rights that you may have under 5 U.S.C. 5514 or other provisions of a law or written contract, unless there are statutory or contractual provisions to the contrary.

Subpart C—Tax Refund Offset

§ 1150.30 Which debts can the Endowment refer to the Treasury for collection by offsetting tax refunds?

(a) The regulations in this subpart implement 31 U.S.C. 3720A, which authorizes the Treasury to reduce a tax refund by the amount of a past-due, legally enforceable debt owed to a Federal agency.

(b) For purposes of this section, a past-due, legally enforceable debt referable to the Treasury for tax refund offset is a debt that is owed to the Endowment and:

(1) Is at least $25.00;

(2) Except in the case of a judgment debt, has been delinquent for at least three months and will not have been delinquent more than 10 years at the time the offset is made;

(3) Cannot currently be collected under the salary offset provisions of 5 U.S.C. 5514;

(4) Is ineligible for administrative offset under 31 U.S.C. 3716(a) by reason of 31 U.S.C. 3716(c)(2) or cannot be collected by administrative offset under 31 U.S.C. 3716(a) by the Endowment against amounts payable to the debtor by the Endowment;

(5) With respect to which the Endowment has

(i) given the debtor at least 60 days to present evidence that all or part of the debt is not past due or legally enforceable,

(ii) considered evidence presented by the debtor, and

(iii) determined that an amount of the debt is past due and legally enforceable;

(6) Has been disclosed by the Endowment to a credit reporting agency as authorized by 31 U.S.C. 3711(e) and § 1150.12 of this part, unless the credit reporting agency would be prohibited from reporting information concerning the debt by reason of 15 U.S.C. 1681c;

(7) With respect to which the Endowment has notified or has made a reasonable attempt to notify the debtor that:

(i) The debt is past due, and

(ii) Unless repaid within 60 days of the date of the Notice, the debt may be referred to the Treasury for offset against any refund of overpayment of tax; and

(8) All other requirements of 31 U.S.C. 3720A and the Treasury regulations relating to the eligibility of a debt for tax return offset (31 CFR 285.2) have been satisfied.

§ 1150.31 What are the Endowment's procedures for collecting debts by tax refund offset?

(a) The Chairperson will be the point of contact with the Treasury for administrative matters regarding the offset program.

(b) The Endowment will ensure that the procedures prescribed by the Treasury are followed in developing information about past-due debts and submitting the debts to the Treasury.

(c) The Endowment will submit to the Treasury a notification of a taxpayer's liability for past-due legally enforceable debt. This notification will contain the following:

(1) The name and taxpayer identification number of the debtor;

(2) The amount of the past-due and legally enforceable debt;

(3) The date on which the original debt became past due; and

(4) A statement certifying that, with respect to each debt reported, all of the requirements of § 1150.30(b) have been satisfied.

(d) For purposes of this section, notice that collection of the debt is affected by a bankruptcy proceeding involving the debtor will bar referral of the debt to the Treasury.

(e) The Endowment shall promptly notify the Treasury to correct data when it:

(1) Determines that an error has been made with respect to a debt that has been referred;

(2) Receives or credits a payment on the debt; or

(3) Receives notice that the person owing the debt has filed for bankruptcy under Title 11 of the United States Code or has been adjudicated bankrupt and the debt has been discharged.

(f) When advising debtors of an intent to refer a debt to the Treasury for offset, the Endowment will also advise debtors of remedial actions available to defer the offset or prevent it from taking place.

Subpart D—Administrative Offset

§ 1150.40 Under what circumstances will the Endowment collect amounts that I owe to the Endowment (or some other Federal agency) by offsetting the debt against payments that the Endowment (or some other Federal agency) owes me?

(a) The regulations in this subpart apply to the collection of any debts you owe to the Endowment, or to any request from another Federal agency that the Endowment collect a debt you owe by offsetting your debt against a payment the Endowment owes you. Administrative offset is authorized under Section 5 of the Federal Claims Collection Act of 1966, as amended (31 U.S.C. 3716). The Endowment shall carry out administrative offset in accordance with the provisions of the Federal Claims Collection Standards; the regulations in this subpart are intended only to supplement the provisions of the Federal Claims Collection Standards.

(b) The Chairperson, after attempting to collect a debt you owe to the Endowment under Section 3(a) of the Federal Claims Collection Act of 1966, as amended (31 U.S.C. 3711(a)), may collect the debt by administrative offset, subject to the following:

(1) The debt you owe is certain in amount; and

(2) It is in the best interest of the Endowment to collect your debt by administrative offset because of the decreased costs of collection and acceleration in the payment of the debt.

(c) No collection by administrative offset will be made on any debt that has been outstanding for more than 10 years unless facts material to the Endowment or a federal agency's right to collect the debt were not known, and reasonably could not have been known, by the official or officials responsible for discovering and collecting the debt.

(d) The regulations in this subpart do not apply to:

(1) A case in which administrative offset of the type of debt involved is explicitly prohibited by statute; or

§ 1150.41

(2) Debts owed to the Endowment by Federal agencies.

§ 1150.41 How will the Endowment request that my debt to the Endowment be collected by offset against some payment that another Federal agency owes me?

The Chairperson may request that funds due and payable to you by another Federal agency instead be paid to the Endowment to satisfy a debt you owe to the Endowment. In requesting administrative offset, the Endowment will certify in writing to the Federal agency that is holding funds for you:

(a) That you owe the debt;

(b) The amount and basis of the debt; and

(c) That the Endowment has complied with the requirements of 31 U.S.C. 3716, its own administrative offset regulations in this subpart, and the applicable provisions of the Federal Claims Collection Standards with respect to providing you with due process.

§ 1150.42 What procedures will the Endowment use to collect amounts I owe to a Federal agency by offsetting a payment that the Endowment would otherwise make to me?

(a) Any Federal agency may request that the Endowment administratively offset funds due and payable to you in order to collect a debt you owe to that agency. The Endowment will initiate the requested offset only upon:

(1) Receipt of written certification from the creditor agency stating:

(i) That you owe the debt;

(ii) The amount and basis of the debt;

(iii) That the agency has prescribed regulations for the exercise of administrative offset; and

(iv) That the agency has complied with its own administrative offset regulations and with the applicable provisions of the Federal Claims Collection Standards, including providing you with any required hearing or review; and

(2) A determination by the Chairperson that offsetting funds payable to you by the Endowment in order to collect a debt owed by you would be in the best interest of the United States as determined by the facts and circumstances of the particular case, and that such an offset would not otherwise be contrary to law.

(b) *Multiple debts.* In instances where two or more creditor agencies are seeking administrative offsets, or where two or more debts are owed to a single creditor agency, the Endowment may, in its discretion, allocate the amount it owes to you to the creditor agencies in accordance with the best interest of the United States as determined by the facts and circumstances of the particular case, paying special attention to applicable statutes of limitations.

§ 1150.43 When may the Endowment make an offset in an expedited manner?

The Endowment may effect an administrative offset against a payment to be made to you before completion of the procedures required by §§ 1150.41 and 1150.42 if failure to take the offset would substantially jeopardize the Endowment's ability to collect the debt and the time before the payment is to be made does not reasonably permit the completion of those procedures. An expedited offset will be followed promptly by the completion of those procedures. Amounts recovered by offset, but later found not to be owed to the Endowment, will be promptly refunded.

§ 1150.44 Can a judgment I have obtained against the United States be used to satisfy a debt that I owe to the Endowment?

Collection by offset against a judgment obtained by a debtor against the United States will be accomplished in accordance with 31 U.S.C. 3728.

PART 1151—NONDISCRIMINATION ON THE BASIS OF HANDICAP

Subpart A—General Provisions

Sec.
1151.1 Purpose.
1151.2 Application.
1151.3 Definitions.
1151.4 Notice.
1151.5 Inconsistent State laws and effect of employment opportunities.
1151.6–1151.10 [Reserved]

National Foundation on the Arts and the Humanities § 1151.3

Subpart B—Standards for Determining Who Are Handicapped Persons

1151.11 Handicapped person.
1151.12 Qualified handicapped person.
1151.13–1151.15 [Reserved]

Subpart C—Discrimination Prohibited

GENERAL

1151.16 General prohibitions against discrimination.
1151.17 Specific discriminatory actions prohibited.
1151.18 Illustrative examples.
1151.19–1151.20 [Reserved]

ACCESSIBILITY

1151.21 Discrimination prohibited.
1151.22 Existing facilities.
1151.23 New construction.
1151.24 Historic properties. [Reserved]
1151.25–1151.30 [Reserved]

EMPLOYMENT

1151.31 Discrimination prohibited.
1151.32 Reasonable accommodation.
1151.33 Employment criteria.
1151.34 Preemployment inquiries.
1151.35–1151.40 [Reserved]

Subpart D—Enforcement

1151.41 Assurances required.
1151.42 Self evaluation.
1151.43 Adoption of grievance procedures.
1151.44 Endowment enforcement and compliance procedures.
1151.45–1151.50 [Reserved]

AUTHORITY: 29 U.S.C. 794.

SOURCE: 44 FR 22734, Apr. 17, 1979, unless otherwise noted.

Subpart A—General Provisions

§ 1151.1 Purpose.

The purpose of this part is to implement section 504 of the Rehabilitation Act of 1973, which is designed to eliminate discrimination on the basis of handicap in any program or activity receiving Federal financial assistance.

§ 1151.2 Application.

This part applies to each recipient of financial assistance from the National Endowment for the Arts and to each program or activity that receives such assistance.

[44 FR 22734, Apr. 17, 1979, as amended at 68 FR 51384, Aug. 26, 2003]

§ 1151.3 Definitions.

As used in this part, the term:

(a) *The Act* means the Rehabilitation Act of 1973, Public Law 93–112, as amended by the Rehabilitation Act Amendments of 1974, (Pub. L. 93–516, 29 U.S.C. 706 *et seq.*) and the Comprehensive Rehabilitation Services Amendments of 1978, (Pub. L. 95–602).

(b) *Section 504* means section 504 of the Act.

(c) *Endowment* means the National Endowment for the Arts.

(d) *Chairman* means the Chairman, National Endowment for the Arts.

(e) *Recipient* means any state or its political subdivision, any instrumentality of a state or its political subdivision, any public or private agency, institution, organization, or other entity, or any person to which federal financial assistance is extended directly or through another recipient, including any successor, assignee, or transferee of a recipient, but excluding the ultimate beneficiary of the assistance.

(f) *Federal financial assistance* means any grant, loan, contract (other than a procurement contract or a contract of insurance or guaranty), or any other arrangement by which the Endowment provides or otherwise makes available assistance in the form of:

(1) Funds;

(2) Services of federal personnel; or

(3) Real and personal property or any interest in or use of such property, including:

(i) Transfers of leases of such property for less than fair market value or for reduced consideration; and,

(ii) proceeds from a subsequent transfer or lease of such property if the federal share of its fair market value is not returned to the Federal Government.

(g) *Facility* means all or any portion of buildings, structures, equipment, roads, walks, parking lots, or other real or personal property or interest in such property.

(h) *Program or activity* means all of the operations of any entity described in paragraphs (h)(1) through (4) of this section, any part of which is extended Federal financial assistance:

(1)(i) A department, agency, special purpose district, or other instrumentality of a State or of a local government; or

(ii) The entity of such State or local government that distributes such assistance and each such department or agency (and each other State or local government entity) to which the assistance is extended, in the case of assistance to a State or local government;

(2)(i) A college, university, or other postsecondary institution, or a public system of higher education; or

(ii) A local educational agency (as defined in 20 U.S.C. 7801), system of vocational education, or other school system;

(3)(i) An entire corporation, partnership, or other private organization, or an entire sole proprietorship—

(A) If assistance is extended to such corporation, partnership, private organization, or sole proprietorship as a whole; or

(B) Which is principally engaged in the business of providing education, health care, housing, social services, or parks and recreation; or

(ii) The entire plant or other comparable, geographically separate facility to which Federal financial assistance is extended, in the case of any other corporation, partnership, private organization, or sole proprietorship; or

(4) Any other entity which is established by two or more of the entities described in paragraph (h)(1), (2), or (3) of this section.

[44 FR 22734, Apr. 17, 1979, as amended at 68 FR 51384, Aug. 26, 2003]

§ 1151.4 Notice.

(a) A recipient shall take appropriate initial and continuing steps to notify participants, beneficiaries, applicants, and employees, including those with impaired vision or hearing, and unions or professional organizations holding collective bargaining or professional agreements with the recipient that it does not discriminate on the basis of handicap in violation of section 504 and this part. The notification shall state, where appropriate, that the recipient does not discriminate in admission or access to, or employment in, its programs or activities. Methods of initial and continuing notification may include the posting of notices, publication in print, audio, and visual media, placement of notices in a recipient's publication, and distribution of other written and verbal communications.

(b) If a recipient publishes or uses recruitment materials or publications containing general information that it makes available to participants, beneficiaries, applicants, or employees, it shall include in those materials or publications a statement of the policy described in paragraph (a) of this section. A recipient may meet the requirement of this paragraph either by including appropriate inserts in existing materials and publications or by revising and reprinting the materials and publications.

[44 FR 22734, Apr. 17, 1979, as amended at 68 FR 51384, Aug. 26, 2003]

§ 1151.5 Inconsistent State laws and effect of employment opportunities.

(a) Recipients are not excused from complying with this part as a result of state or local laws which limit the eligibility of handicapped persons to receive services or to practice a profession or occupation.

(b) The presence of limited employment opportunities in a particular profession does not excuse a recipient from complying with the regulation. For example, a music school receiving Endowment financial assistance could not deny admission to a qualified blind applicant because a blind singer may experience more difficulty than a non-handicapped singer in finding a job.

§§ 1151.6–1151.10 [Reserved]

Subpart B—Standards for Determining Who Are Handicapped Persons

§ 1151.11 Handicapped person.

(a) *Handicapped person* means any person who has a physical or mental impairment that substantially limits one or more major life activities, has a record of such an impairment, or is regarded as having such an impairment. For purposes of section 504, in connection with employment, this term does not include any individual who is an alcoholic or drug abuser whose current use of alcohol or drugs prevents such individual from performing the duties of the job in question or whose employment, by reason of such current alcohol or drug abuse, would constitute a direct threat to the property or safety of others.

(b) As used in paragraph (a) of this section, the phrase:

(1) *Physical or mental impairment* means:

(i) Any physiological disorder or condition, cosmetic disfigurement, or anatomical loss affecting one or more of the following body systems: Neurological; musculoskeletal; special sense organs; respiratory, including speech organs; cardiovascular; reproductive; digestive; genito-urinary; hemic and lymphatic; skin; and endocrine; or

(ii) Any mental or psychological disorder, such as mental retardation, organic brain syndrome, emotional and mental illness, and specific learning disabilities. The term *physical or mental impairment* includes, but is not limited to, such diseases and conditions as orthopedic, visual, speech, and hearing impairments, cerebral palsy, epilepsy, muscular dystrophy, multiple sclerosis, cancer, heart disease, diabetes, mental retardation, emotional illness, and drug addiction and alcoholism.

(2) *Major life activities* means functions such as caring for one's self, performing manual tasks, walking, seeing, hearing, speaking, breathing, learning, and working.

(3) *Has a record of such an impairment* means has a history of, or has been misclassified as having, a mental or physical impairment that substantially limits one or more major life activities.

(4) *Is regarded as having an impairment* means:

(i) Has a physical or mental impairment that does not substantially limit major life activities but that is treated by a recipient as constituting such a limitation;

(ii) Has a physical or mental impairment that substantially limits major life activities only as a result of the attitudes of others toward such impairment;

(iii) Has none of the impairments defined in paragraph (b)(1) of this section but is treated by a recipient as having such an impairment.

§ 1151.12 Qualified handicapped person.

Qualified handicapped person means:

(a) With respect to employment, a handicapped person who, with reasonable accommodation, can perform the essential functions of the job in question; and

(b) With respect to services, a handicapped person who meets the essential eligibility requirements for the receipt of such services.

§§ 1151.13–1151.15 [Reserved]

Subpart C—Discrimination Prohibited

GENERAL

§ 1151.16 General prohibitions against discrimination.

(a) No qualified handicapped person shall, on the basis of handicap, be excluded from participation in, be denied the benefits of, or otherwise be subjected to discrimination under any program or activity which receives federal financial assistance.

(b) These regulations do not prohibit the exclusion of nonhandicapped persons or persons with a specific type of handicap from aid, benefits, or services limited by Federal statute or executive order to handicapped persons or persons with a different type of handicap.

(c) Recipients shall take appropriate steps to insure that no handicapped individual is denied the benefits of, excluded from participation in, or otherwise subjected to discrimination in any program or activity receiving Endowment financial assistance because of the absence of appropriate auxiliary aids for individuals with impaired sensory, manual, or speaking skills.

(d) Recipients shall take appropriate steps to insure that communications with their applicants, employees, and beneficiaries are available to persons with impaired vision and hearing.

§ 1151.17

(e) Recipients shall administer programs or activities in the most integrated setting appropriate to the needs of qualified handicapped persons.

[44 FR 22734, Apr. 17, 1979, as amended at 68 FR 51384, Aug. 26, 2003]

§ 1151.17 Specific discriminatory actions prohibited.

(a) A recipient, in providing any aid, benefit, or service, either directly or through contractual, licensing, or other arrangements, shall not, on the basis of handicap:

(1) Deny a qualified handicapped person the opportunity to participate in or benefit from the aid, benefit, or service;

(2) Afford a qualified handicapped person an opportunity to participate in or benefit from the aid, benefit, or service that is not equal to that afforded others;

(3) Provide a qualified handicapped person with an aid, benefit, or service that is not as effective in affording equal opportunity to obtain the same result, to gain the same benefit, or to reach the same level of achievement as that provided to others;

(4) Provide different or separate aid, benefits, or services to handicapped persons or to any class of handicapped persons unless such action is necessary to provide qualified handicapped persons with aid, benefits, or services that are as effective as those provided to others;

(5) Aid or perpetuate discrimination against a qualified handicapped person by providing significant assistance to an agency, organization, or person that discriminates on the basis of handicap in providing any aid, benefit, or service to beneficiaries of the recipient's program or activity;

(6) Deny a qualified handicapped person the opportunity to participate as a member of planning or advisory boards; or

(7) Otherwise limit a qualified handicapped person in the enjoyment of any right, privilege, advantage, or opportunity enjoyed by others receiving an aid, benefit, or service.

(b) Despite the existence of separate or different aid, benefits, or services provided in accordance with this part, a recipient may not deny a qualified handicapped person the opportunity to participate in such aid, benefits, or services that are not separate or different.

(c) A recipient may not, directly or through contractual or other arrangements, utilize criteria or methods of administration:

(1) That have the effect of subjecting qualified handicapped persons to discrimination on the basis of handicap;

(2) That have the purpose or effect of defeating or substantially impairing accomplishment of the objectives of the recipient's program or activity with respect to handicapped persons; or

(3) That perpetuate the discrimination of another recipient if both recipients are subject to common administrative control or are agencies of the same state.

(d) A recipient may not, in determining the site or location of a facility, make selections:

(1) That have the effect of excluding handicapped persons from, denying them the benefits of, or otherwise subjecting them to discrimination under any program or activity that receives federal financial assistance; or

(2) That have the purpose or effect of defeating or substantially impairing the accomplishment of the objectives of the program or activity with respect to handicapped persons.

(e) As used in this section, the aid, benefit, or service provided under a program or activity receiving federal financial assistance includes any aid, benefit, or service provided in or through a facility that has been constructed, expanded, altered, leased or rented, or otherwise acquired, in whole or in part, with federal financial assistance.

[44 FR 22734, Apr. 17, 1979, as amended at 68 FR 51384, Aug. 26, 2003]

§ 1151.18 Illustrative examples.

(a) The following examples will illustrate the application of the foregoing provisions to some of the activities funded by the National Endowment for the Arts.

(1) A museum exhibition catalogue or small press editions supported by the Endowment may be made usable by the blind and the visually impaired through cassette tapes, records, discs,

braille, readers and simultaneous publications;

(2) A theatre performance supported by Federal funds may be made available to deaf and hearing impaired persons through the use of a sign language interpreter or by providing scripts in advance of the performance.

(3) A performing arts organization receiving Federal funds and offering, for example, a specific event in an inaccessible facility may arrange to provide a reasonable opportunity for that specific event to be offered to the public at large in an alternative accessible space; e.g., a theatre offering four different plays a season may offer at least one performance of each play in an alternative accessible space.

(4) Recipients of federal funds should make every effort to assure that they do not support organizations or individuals that discriminate;

(5) A handicapped person with experience and expertise equal to qualification standards established by a planning or advisory board may not be excluded from participation on the board on the basis of handicap. This does not mean that every planning or advisory board necessarily must include a handicapped person.

(b) Despite the existence of permissible separate or different aid, benefits, or services, e.g., periodic performances in alternative accessible spaces, a physically handicapped person who wishes to be, and can be, escorted to a seat, may not be denied such access to an otherwise inaccessible theatre.

(c) State arts agencies are obligated to develop methods of administering federal funds so as to ensure that handicapped persons are not subjected to discrimination on the basis of handicap either by sub-grantees or by the manner in which the funds are distributed.

(d) In the event Endowment funds are utilized to construct, expand, alter, lease or rent a facility, the aid, benefits, or services provided in or through that facility must be conducted in accordance with these regulations, e.g., a museum receiving a grant to renovate an existing facility must assure that all museum aid, benefits, or services conducted in that facility are accessible to handicapped persons.

(e) In carrying out the mandate of section 504 and these implementing regulations recipients should make every effort to administer Endowment assisted programs or activities in a setting in which able-bodied and disabled persons are integrated, e.g., tours made available to the hearing impaired should be open to the public at large and everyone should be permitted to enjoy the benefits of a tactile experience in a museum.

[44 FR 22734, Apr. 17, 1979, as amended at 68 FR 51384, Aug. 26, 2003]

§§ 1151.19–1151.20 [Reserved]

ACCESSIBILITY

§ 1151.21 Discrimination prohibited.

No qualified handicapped person shall, because a recipient's facilities are inaccessible to or unusable by handicapped persons, be denied the benefits of, be excluded from participation in, or otherwise be subjected to discrimination under any program or activity to which this part applies.

§ 1151.22 Existing facilities.

(a) A recipient shall operate each program or activity to which this part applies so that when each part is viewed in its entirety it is readily accessible to and usable by handicapped persons. This paragraph does not necessarily require a recipient to make each of its existing facilities or every part of a facility accessible to and usable by handicapped persons.

(b) A recipient may comply with the requirement f paragraph (a) of this section through alteration of existing facilities, the construction of new facilities, or any other methods that result in making its program or activity accessible to handicapped persons. A recipient is not required to make structural changes in existing facilities where other methods are effective in achieving compliance with paragraph (a) of this section. In choosing among available methods for meeting the requirement of paragraph (a) of this section, a recipient shall give priority to those methods that serve handicapped persons in the most integrated setting appropriate.

(c) *Time period.* A recipient shall comply with the requirement of paragraph (a) of this section within sixty days of the effective date of this part except that where structural changes are necessary such changes shall be made as soon as possible but in no event later than three years after the effective date of this part.

(d) *Transition plan.* In the event structural changes to facilities are necessary to meet the requirement of paragraph (a) of this section, a recipient shall develop, within one year of the effective date of this part, a transition plan setting forth the steps necessary to complete such changes. The plan shall be developed with the assistance of interested persons, including handicapped persons or organizations representing handicapped persons. Upon request, the recipient shall make available for public inspection a copy of the transition plan. The plan shall, at a minimum:

(1) Identify physical obstacles in the recipient's facilities that limit the accessibility of its program or activity to handicapped persons;

(2) Describe in detail the methods that will be used to make the facilities accessible;

(3) Specify the schedule for taking the steps necessary to achieve full accessibility under paragraph (a) of this section and, if the time period of the transition plan is longer than one year, identify steps that will be taken during each year of the transition period; and

(4) Indicate the person responsible for implementation of the plan.

[44 FR 22734, Apr. 17, 1979, as amended at 68 FR 51384, Aug. 26, 2003]

§ 1151.23 New construction.

(a) *Design, construction, and alteration.* New facilities shall be designed and constructed to be readily accessible to and usable by handicapped persons. Alterations to existing facilities shall, to the maximum extent feasible, be designed and constructed to be readily accessible to and usable by handicapped persons.

(b) *Conformance with Uniform Federal Accessibility Standards.* (1) Effective as of January 18, 1991, design, construction, or alteration of buildings in conformance with sections 3-8 of the Uniform Federal Accessibility Standards (USAF) (appendix A to 41 CFR subpart 101–19.6) shall be deemed to comply with the requirements of this section with respect to those buildings. Departures from particular technical and scoping requirements of UFAS by the use of other methods are permitted where substantially equivalent or greater access to and usability of the building is provided.

(2) For purposes of this section, section 4.1.6(1)(g) of UFAS shall be interpreted to exempt from the requirements of UFAS only mechanical rooms and other spaces that, because of their intended use, will not require accessibility to the public or beneficiaries or result in the employment or residence therein of persons with physical handicaps.

(3) This section does not require recipients to make building alterations that have little likelihood of being accomplished without removing or altering a load-bearing structural member.

[44 FR 22734, Apr. 17, 1979, as amended at 55 FR 52138, 52142, Dec. 19, 1990]

§ 1151.24 Historic properties. [Reserved]

§§ 1151.25–1151.30 [Reserved]

EMPLOYMENT

§ 1151.31 Discrimination prohibited.

(a) No qualified handicapped person shall, on the basis of handicap, be subjected to discrimination in employment under any program or activity that receives federal financial assistance.

(b) A recipient shall make all decisions concerning employment under any program or activity to which this part applies in a manner which ensures that discrimination on the basis of handicap does not occur and may not limit, segregate, or classify applicants or employees in any way that adversely affects their opportunities or status because of handicap.

(c) A recipient may not participate in a contractual or other relationship that has the effect of subjecting qualified handicapped applicants or employees to discrimination prohibited by this subpart. The relationships referred

National Foundation on the Arts and the Humanities § 1151.34

to in this paragraph include relationships with employment and referral agencies, with labor unions, with organizations providing or administering fringe benefits to employees of the recipients, and with organizations providing training and apprenticeships.

(d) The prohibition against discrimination in employment applies to the following activities:

(1) Recruitment, advertising, and the processing of applications for employment;

(2) Hiring, upgrading, promotion, award of tenure, demotion, transfer, layoff, termination, right of return from layoff, and rehiring;

(3) Rates of pay or any other form of compensation and changes in compensation;

(4) Job assignments, job classifications, organizational structures, position descriptions, lines of progression, and seniority lists;

(5) Leaves of absences, sick leave, or any other leave;

(6) Fringe benefits available by virtue of employment, whether or not administered by the recipient;

(7) Selection and financial support for training, including apprenticeship, professional meetings, conferences, and other related activities, and selection for leaves of absence to pursue training;

(8) Employer sponsored activities, including those that are social or recreational; and

(9) Any other term, condition, or privilege of employment.

(e) A recipient's obligation to comply with this subpart is not affected by any inconsistent term of any collective bargaining agreement to which it is a party.

[44 FR 22734, Apr. 17, 1979, as amended at 68 FR 51384, Aug. 26, 2003]

§ 1151.32 Reasonable accommodation.

(a) A recipient shall make reasonable accommodation to the known physical or mental limitations of an otherwise qualified handicapped applicant or employee unless the recipient can demonstrate that the accommodation would impose an undue hardship on the operation of its program or activity.

(b) Reasonable accommodation may include:

(1) Making facilities used by employees readily accessible to and usable by handicapped persons; and

(2) Job restructuring, part-time or modified work schedules, acquisition, or modification of equipment or devices, such as use of telecommunication devices and amplifiers on telephones, the provision of readers or interpreters, and other similar actions.

(c) In determining pursuant to paragraph (a) of this section whether an accommodation would impose an undue hardship on the operation of a recipient's program or activity, factors to be considered include:

(1) The overall size of the recipient's program or activity with respect to number of employees, number and type of facilities, and size of budget;

(2) The type of the recipient's operation, including the composition and structure of the recipient's workforce; and

(3) The nature and cost of the accommodation needed.

[44 FR 22734, Apr. 17, 1979, as amended at 68 FR 51384, Aug. 26, 2003]

§ 1151.33 Employment criteria.

(a) A recipient may not make use of any employment test or other selection criterion that screens out or tends to screen out handicapped persons or any class of handicapped persons unless:

(1) The test score or other selection criterion, as used by the recipient, is shown to be job-related for the position in question; and

(2) Alternative job-related tests or criteria are unavailable.

(b) A recipient shall select and administer tests concerning employment so as best to ensure that, when administered to an applicant or employee who has a handicap that impairs sensory, manual, or speaking skills, the test results accurately reflect the applicant's or employee's job skills, aptitude, or other factors relevant to adequate performance of the job in question.

§ 1151.34 Preemployment inquiries.

A recipient may not, except as provided below, conduct a preemployment medical examination, make preemployment inquiry as to whether the applicant is a handicapped person, or inquire as to the nature or severity of a handicap. A recipient may, however, make preemployment inquiry into an applicant's ability to perform job-related functions.

(a) When a recipient is taking remedial action to correct the effects of past discrimination, when a recipient is taking voluntary action to overcome the effects of conditions that resulted in limited participation in its federally assisted program or activity, or when a recipient is taking affirmative action pursuant to section 504 of the Act, the recipient may invite applicants for employment to indicate whether and to what extent they are handicapped, provided, that:

(1) The recipient states clearly on any written questionnaire used for this purpose or makes clear orally if no written questionnaire is used that the information requested is intended for use solely in connection with its remedial action obligations or its voluntary or affirmative action efforts; and

(2) The recipient states clearly that the information is being requested on a voluntary basis, that it will be kept confidential as provided in paragraph (c) of this section, that refusal to provide it will not subject the applicant or employee to any adverse treatment, and that it will be used only in accordance with this part.

(b) Nothing in this section shall prohibit a recipient from conditioning an offer of employment on the results of a medical examination conducted prior to the employee's entrance on duty, provided, that:

(1) All entering employees are subjected to such an examination regardless of handicap; and

(2) The results of such an examination are used only in accordance with the requirements of this part.

(c) Information obtained in accordance with this section as to the medical condition or history of the applicant shall be collected and maintained on separate forms that shall be accorded confidentiality as medical records, except that:

(1) Supervisors and managers may be informed regarding restrictions on the work or duties of handicapped persons and regarding necessary accommodations;

(2) First aid and safety personnel may be informed, where appropriate, if the condition might require emergency treatment; and

(3) Government officials investigating compliance with the Act shall be provided relevant information upon request.

[44 FR 22734, Apr. 17, 1979; 45 FR 57129, Aug. 27, 1980]

§§ 1151.35–1151.40 [Reserved]

Subpart D—Enforcement

§ 1151.41 Assurances required.

(a) An applicant for federal financial assistance to which this part applies shall submit an assurance, on a form specified by the Chairman, that the program or activity will be operated in compliance with this part. An applicant may incorporate these assurances by reference in subsequent applications to the Endowment.

(b) *Duration of obligation.* (1) In the case of federal financial assistance extended to provide personal property, the assurance will obligate the recipient for the period during which it retains ownership or possession of the property.

(2) In all other cases the assurance will obligate the recipient for the period during which federal financial assistance is extended.

(c) *Covenants.* Where property is purchased or improved with federal financial assistance, the recipient shall agree to include in any instrument effecting or recording any transfer of the property a covenant running with the property assuring nondiscrimination for the period during which the real property is used for a purpose for which the federal financial assistance is extended or for another purpose involving the provision of similar services or benefits.

[44 FR 22734, Apr. 17, 1979, as amended at 68 FR 51384, Aug. 26, 2003]

§ 1151.42 Self evaluation.

(a) A recipient shall within six months of the effective date of this part:

(1) Evaluate, with the assistance of interested persons, including handicapped persons or organizations representing handicapped persons, its current policies and practices and the effects thereof that do not or may not meet the requirements of this part;

(2) Modify, after consultation with interested persons, including handicapped persons or organizations representing handicapped persons, any policies and practices that do not meet the requirements of this part; and

(3) Take, after consultation with interested persons, including handicapped persons or organizations representing handicapped persons, appropriate remedial steps to eliminate the effects of any discrimination that resulted from adherence to these policies and practices.

(4) Maintain on file, make available for public inspection, and provide to the Endowment upon request, for at least three years following completion of the self-evaluation:

(i) A list of the interested persons consulted;

(ii) A description of areas examined and any problems identified; and,

(iii) A description of any modifications made and of any remedial steps taken.

(5) The completed self-evaluation should be signed by a responsible official designated to coordinate the recipient's efforts in connection with this section.

§ 1151.43 Adoption of grievance procedures.

A recipient may adopt an internal grievance procedure in order to provide for the prompt and equitable resolution of complaints alleging any action prohibited by this part. A responsible official should be designated to coordinate the recipient's efforts in connection with this section. Such procedures need not be established with respect to complaints from applicants for employment.

§ 1151.44 Endowment enforcement and compliance procedures.

The procedural provisions applicable to title VI of the Civil Rights Act of 1964 apply to this part. These procedures are found in §§ 1110.8 through 1110.11 of part 1110 of this title.

§§ 1151.45–1151.50 [Reserved]

PART 1152—INTERGOVERNMENTAL REVIEW OF NATIONAL ENDOWMENT FOR THE ARTS PROGRAMS AND ACTIVITIES

Sec.
1152.1 What is the purpose of these regulations?
1152.2 What definitions apply to these regulations?
1152.3 What programs and activities of the Endowment are subject to these regulations?
1152.4 What are the Chairman's general responsibilities under the Order?
1152.5 What is the Chairman's obligation with respect to Federal interagency coordination?
1152.6 What procedures apply to the selection of programs and activities under these regulations?
1152.7 How does the Chairman communicate with state and local officials concerning the Endowment's programs and activities?
1152.8 How does the Chairman provide states with an opportunity to comment on proposed Federal financial assistance?
1152.9 How does the Chairman receive and respond to comments?
1152.10 How does the Chairman make efforts to accommodate intergovernmental concerns?
1152.11 What are the Chairman's obligations in interstate situations?
1152.12 How may a state simplify, consolidate, or substitute federally required state plans?
1152.13 May the Chairman waive any provision of these regulations?

AUTHORITY: E.O. 12372, July 14, 1982 (47 FR 30959), as amended April 8, 1983 (48 FR 15887); sec. 401 of the Intergovernmental Cooperation Act of 1968, as amended (31 U.S.C. 6506).

SOURCE: 48 FR 29352, June 24, 1983, unless otherwise noted.

§ 1152.1 What is the purpose of these regulations?

(a) The regulations in this part implement Executive Order 12372, "Intergovernmental Review of Federal Programs," issued July 14, 1982 and amended on April 8, 1983. These regulations also implement applicable provisions of section 401 of the Intergovernmental Cooperation Act of 1968.

(b) these regulations are intended to foster an intergovernmental partnership and a strengthened Federalism by relying on state processes and on state, areawide, regional and local coordination for review of proposed Federal financial assistance and direct Federal development.

(c) These regulations are intended to improve the internal management of the Endowment, and are not intended to create any right or benefit enforceable at law by a party against the Endowment or its officers.

§ 1152.2 What definitions apply to these regulations?

Chairman means the Chairman of the National Endowment for the Arts or an official or employee of the Endowment acting for the Chairman under a delegation of authority.

Endowment means the National Endowment for the Arts.

Order means Executive Order 12372, issued July 14, 1982, and amended April 8, 1983 and titled "Intergovernmental Review of Federal Programs."

State means any of the 50 states, the District of Columbia, the Commonwealth of Puerto Rico, the Commonwealth of the Northern Mariana Islands, Guam, American Samoa, the U.S. Virgin Islands, or the Trust Territory of the Pacific Islands.

§ 1152.3 What programs and activities of the Endowment are subject to these regulations?

The Chairman publishes in the FEDERAL REGISTER a list of the Endowment's programs and activities that are subject to these regulations.

§ 1152.4 What are the Chairman's general responsibilities under the Order?

(a) The Chairman provides opportunities for consultation by elected officials of those state and local governments that would provide the non-Federal funds for, or that would be directly affected by, proposed Federal financial assistance from the Endowment.

(b) If a state adopts a process under the Order to review and coordinate proposed Federal financial assistance the Chairman, to the extent permitted by law:

(1) Uses the state process to determine official views of state and local elected officials;

(2) Communicates with state and local elected officials as early in a program planning cycle as is reasonably feasible to explain specific plans and actions;

(3) Makes efforts to accommodate state and local elected officials' concerns with proposed Federal financial assistance that is communicated through the state process;

(4) Allows the states to simplify and consolidate existing federally required state plan submissions;

(5) Where state planning and budgeting systems are sufficient and where permitted by law, encourages the substitution of state plans for federally required state plans;

(6) Seeks the coordination of views of affected state and local elected officials in one state with those of another state when proposed Federal financial assistance has an impact on interstate metropolitan urban centers or other interstate areas; and

(7) Supports state and local governments by discouraging the reauthorization or creation of any planning organization which is federally-funded, which has a limited purpose, and which is not adequately representative of, or accountable to, state or local elected officials.

§ 1152.5 What is the Chairman's obligation with respect to Federal interagency coordination?

The Chairman to the extent practicable, consults with and seeks advice from all other substantially affected Federal departments and agencies in an effort to assure full coordination between such agencies and the Endowment regarding programs and activities covered under these regulations.

§ 1152.6 What procedures apply to the selection of programs and activities under these regulations?

(a) A state may select any program or activity published in the FEDERAL REGISTER in accordance with § 1152.3 of this part for intergovernmental review under these regulations. Each state, before selecting programs and activities shall consult with local elected officials.

(b) Each state that adopts a process shall notify the Chairman of the Endowment's programs and activities selected for that process.

(c) A state may notify the Chairman of changes in its selections at any time. For each change, the state shall submit to the Chairman an assurance that the state has consulted with elected local officials regarding the change. The Endowment may establish deadlines by which states are required to inform the Chairman of changes in their program selections.

(d) The Chairman uses a state's process as soon as feasible, depending on individual programs and activities, after the Chairman is notified of its selections.

§ 1152.7 How does the Chairman communicate with state and local officials concerning the Endowment's programs and activities?

(a) [Reserved]

(b) The Chairman provides notice to directly affected state, areawide, regional, and local entities in a state of proposed Federal financial assistance if—

(1) The state has not adopted a process under the Order; or

(2) The assistance or development is under program or activity not selected for the state process.

This notice is made by the publication in the FEDERAL REGISTER or other appropriate means which the Endowment in its discretion deems appropriate.

§ 1152.8 How does the Chairman provide states with an opportunity to comment on proposed Federal financial assistance?

(a) Except in unusual circumstances, the Chairman gives state processes or directly affected state, areawide, regional and local officials and entities—

(1) [Reserved]

(2) At least 60 days from the date established by the Chairman to comment on proposed Federal financial assistance.

(b) This section also applies to comments in cases in which the review, coordination, and communication with the Endowment have been delegated.

§ 1152.9 How does the Chairman receive and respond to comments?

(a) The Chairman follows the procedures in § 1152.10 if:

(1) A state office or official is designated to act as a single point of contact between a state process and all Federal agencies; and

(2) That office or official transmits a state process recommendation for a program selected under § 1152.6.

(b)(1) The single point of contact is not obligated to transmit comments from state, areawide, regional or local officials and entities where there is no state process recommendation.

(2) If a state process recommendation is transmitted by a single point of contact, all comments from state, areawide, regional, and local officials and entities that differ from it must also be transmitted.

(c) If a state has not established a process, or is unable to submit a state process recommendation, state, areawide, regional and local officials and entities may submit comments to the Endowment.

(d) If a program or activity is not selected for a state process, state, areawide, regional and local officials and entities may submit comments to the Endowment. In addition, if a state process recommendation for a nonselected program or activity is transmitted to the Endowment by the single point of contact, the Chairman follows the procedure of § 1152.10 of this part.

(e) The Chairman considers comments which do not constitute a state process recommendation submitted under these regulations and for which the Chairman is not required to apply the procedures of § 1152.10 of this part, when such comments are provided by a single point of contact or directly to the Endowment by a commenting party.

§ 1152.10 How does the Chairman make efforts to accommodate intergovernmental concerns?

(a) If a state process provides a state process recommendation to the Endowment through its single point of contact, the Chairman either:

(1) Accepts the recommendation;

(2) Reaches a mutually agreeable solution with the state process; or

(3) Provides the single point of contact with such written explanation of the decision, as the Chairman in his or her discretion deems appropriate. The Chairman may supplement the written explanation by also providing the explanation to the single point of contact by telephone other telecommunication, or other means.

(b) In any explanation under paragraph (a)(3) of this section the Chairman informs the single point of contact that:

(1) The Endowment will not implement its decision for ten days after the single point of contact receives the explanation; or

(2) The Chairman has reviewed the decision and determined that, because of unusual circumstances, the ten-day waiting period is not feasible.

(c) For purposes of computing the waiting period under paragraph (b)(1) of this section, a single point of contact is presumed to have received written notification 5 days after the date of mailing of such notification.

§ 1152.11 What are the Chairman's obligations in interstate situations?

(a) The Chairman is responsible for:

(1) Identifying proposed Gederal financial assistance that has an impact on interstate areas;

(2) Notifying appropriate officials and entities in states which have adopted a process and which select the Endowment's program or activity;

(3) Making efforts to identify and notify the affected state, areawide, regional, and local officials and entities in those states that have not adopted a process under the Order or do not select the Endowment's program or activity;

(4) Responding pursuant to § 1152.10 of this part if the Chairman receives a recommendation from a designated areawide agency transmitted by a single point of contact, in cases in which the review, coordination, and communication with the Endowment have been delegated.

(b) The Chairman uses the procedures in § 1152.10 if a state process provides a state process recommendation to the Endowment through a single point of contact.

§ 1152.12 How may a state simplify, consolidate, or substitute federally required state plans?

(a) As used in this section:

(1) *Simplify* means that a state may develop its own format, choose its own submission date, and select the planning period for a state plan.

(2) *Consolidate* means that a state may meet statutory and regulatory requirements by combining two or more plans into one document and that the state can select the format, submission date, and planning period for the consolidated plan.

(3) *Substitute* means that a state may use a plan or other document that it has developed for its own purposes to meet Federal requirements.

(b) If not inconsistent with law, a state may decide to try to simplify, consolidate, or substitute Federally required state plans without prior approval by the Chairman.

(c) The Chairman reviews each state plan that a state has simplified, consolidated, or substituted and accepts the plan only if it meets Federal requirements.

§ 1152.13 May the Chairman waive any provision of these regulations?

In an emergency, the Chairman may waive any provision of these regulations.

PART 1153—ENFORCEMENT OF NONDISCRIMINATION ON THE BASIS OF HANDICAP IN PROGRAMS OR ACTIVITIES CONDUCTED BY THE NATIONAL ENDOWMENT FOR THE ARTS

Sec.
1153.101 Purpose.
1153.102 Application.
1153.103 Definitions.
1153.104–1153.109 [Reserved]
1153.110 Self-evaluation.

National Foundation on the Arts and the Humanities § 1153.103

1153.111 Notice.
1153.112–1153.129 [Reserved]
1153.130 General prohibitions against discrimination.
1153.131–1153.139 [Reserved]
1153.140 Employment.
1153.141–1153.148 [Reserved]
1153.149 Program accessibility: Discrimination prohibited.
1153.150 Program accessibility: Existing facilities.
1153.151 Program accessibility: New construction and alterations.
1153.152–1153.159 [Reserved]
1153.160 Communications.
1153.161–1153.169 [Reserved]
1153.170 Compliance procedures.
1153.171–1153.999 [Reserved]

AUTHORITY: 29 U.S.C. 794.

SOURCE: 51 FR 22895, 22896, June 23, 1986, unless otherwise noted.

§ 1153.101 Purpose.

This part effectuates section 119 of the Rehabilitation, Comprehensive Services, and Developmental Disabilities Amendments of 1978, which amended section 504 of the Rehabilitation Act of 1973 to prohibit discrimination on the basis of handicap in programs or activities conducted by Executive agencies or the United States Postal Service.

§ 1153.102 Application.

This part applies to all programs or activities conducted by the agency.

§ 1153.103 Definitions.

For purposes of this part, the term—

Assistant Attorney General means the Assistant Attorney General, Civil Rights Division, United States Department of Justice.

Auxiliary aids means services or devices that enable persons with impaired sensory, manual, or speaking skills to have an equal opportunity to participate in, and enjoy the benefits of, programs or activities conducted by the agency. For example, auxiliary aids useful for persons with impaired vision include readers, brailled materials, audio recordings, telecommunications devices and other similar services and devices. Auxiliary aids useful for persons with impaired hearing include telephone handset amplifiers, telephones compatible with hearing aids, telecommunication devices for deaf persons (TDD's), interpreters, notetakers, written materials, and other similar services and devices.

Complete complaint means a written statement that contains the complainant's name and address and describes the agency's alleged discriminatory action in sufficient detail to inform the agency of the nature and date of the alleged violation of section 504. It shall be signed by the complainant or by someone authorized to do so on his or her behalf. Complaints filed on behalf of classes or third parties shall describe or identify (by name, if possible) the alleged victims of discrimination.

Facility means all or any portion of buildings, structures, equipment, roads, walks, parking lots, rolling stock or other conveyances, or other real or personal property.

Handicapped person means any person who has a physical or mental impairment that substantially limits one or more major life activities, has a record of such an impairment, or is regarded as having such an impairment.

As used in this definition, the phrase:

(1) *Physical or mental impairment* includes—

(i) Any physiological disorder or condition, cosmetic disfigurement, or anatomical loss affecting one or more of the following body systems: Neurological; musculoskeletal; special sense organs; respiratory, including speech organs; cardiovascular; reproductive; digestive; genitourinary; hemic and lymphatic; skin; and endocrine; or

(ii) Any mental or psychological disorder, such as mental retardation, organic brain syndrome, emotional or mental illness, and specific learning disabilities. The term *physical or mental impairment* includes, but is not limited to, such diseases and conditions as orthopedic, visual, speech, and hearing impairments, cerebral palsy, epilepsy, muscular dystrophy, multiple sclerosis, cancer, heart disease, diabetes, mental retardation, emotional illness, and drug addiction and alocoholism.

(2) *Major life activities* includes functions such as caring for one's self, performing manual tasks, walking, seeing, hearing, speaking, breathing, learning, and working.

(3) *Has a record of such an impairment* means has a history of, or has been misclassified as having, a mental or

physical impairment that substantially limits one or more major life activities.

(4) *Is regarded as having an impairment* means—

(i) Has a physical or mental impairment that does not substantially limit major life activities but is treated by the agency as constituting such a limitation;

(ii) Has a physical or mental impairment that substantially limits major life activities only as a result of the attitudes of others toward such impairment; or

(iii) Has none of the impairments defined in paragraph (1) of this definition but is treated by the agency as having such an impairment.

Historic preservation programs means programs conducted by the agency that have preservation of historic properties as a primary purpose.

Historic properties means those properties that are listed or eligible for listing in the National Register of Historic Places or properties designated as historic under a statute of the appropriate State or local government body.

Qualified handicapped person means—

(1) With respect to preschool, elementary, or secondary education services provided by the agency, a handicapped person who is a member of a class of persons otherwise entitled by statute, regulation, or agency policy to receive education services from the agency.

(2) With respect to any other agency program or activity under which a person is required to perform services or to achieve a level of accomplishment, a handicapped person who meets the essential eligibility requirements and who can acheive the purpose of the program or activity without modifications in the program or activity that the agency can demonstrate would result in a fundamental alteration in its nature;

(3) With respect to any other program or activity, a handicapped person who meets the essential eligibility requirements for participation in, or receipt of benefits from, that program or activity; and

(4) *Qualified handicapped person* is defined for purposes of employment in 29 CFR 1613.702(f), which is made applicable to this part by § 1153.140.

Section 504 means section 504 of the Rehabilitation Act of 1973 (Pub. L. 93–112, 87 Stat. 394 (29 U.S.C. 794)), as amended by the Rehabilitation Act Amendments of 1974 (Pub. L. 93–516, 88 Stat. 1617), and the Rehabilitation, Comprehensive Services, and Developmental Disabilities Amendments of 1978 (Pub. L. 95–602, 92 Stat. 2955). As used in this part, section 504 applies only to programs or activities conducted by Executive agencies and not to federally assisted programs.

Substantial impairment means a significant loss of the integrity of finished materials, design quality, or special character resulting from a permanent alteration.

§§ 1153.104–1153.109 [Reserved]

§ 1153.110 Self-evaluation.

(a) The agency shall, by August 24, 1987, evaluate its current policies and practices, and the effects thereof, that do not or may not meet the requirements of this part, and, to the extent modification of any such policies and practices is required, the agency shall proceed to make the necessary modifications.

(b) The agency shall provide an opportunity to interested persons, including handicapped persons or organizations representing handicapped persons, to participate in the self-evaluation process by submitting comments (both oral and written).

(c) The agency shall, until three years following the completion of the self-evaluation, maintain on file and make available for public inspection:

(1) A description of areas examined and any problems identified, and

(2) A description of any modifications made.

§ 1153.111 Notice.

The agency shall make available to employees, applicants, participants, beneficiaries, and other interested persons such information regarding the provisions of this part and its applicability to the programs or activities conducted by the agency, and make such information available to them in such manner as the head of the agency finds necessary to apprise such persons

National Foundation on the Arts and the Humanities § 1153.130

of the protections against discrimination assured them by section 504 and this regulation.

§§ 1153.112–1153.129 [Reserved]

§ 1153.130 General prohibitions against discrimination.

(a) No qualified handicapped person shall, on the basis of handicap, be excluded from participation in, be denied the benefits of, or otherwise be subjected to discrimination under any program or activity conducted by the agency.

(b)(1) The agency, in providing any aid, benefit, or service, may not, directly or through contractual, licensing, or other arrangements, on the basis of handicap—

(i) Deny a qualified handicapped person the opportunity to participate in or benefit from the aid, benefit, or service;

(ii) Afford a qualified handicapped person an opportunity to participate in or benefit from the aid, benefit, or service that is not equal to that afforded others;

(iii) Provide a qualified handicapped person with an aid, benefit, or service that is not as effective in affording equal opportunity to obtain the same result, to gain the same benefit, or to reach the same level of achievement as that provided to others;

(iv) Provide different or separate aid, benefits, or services to handicapped persons or to any class of handicapped persons than is provided to others unless such action is necessary to provide qualified handicapped persons with aid, benefits, or services that are as effective as those provided to others;

(v) Deny a qualified handicapped person the opportunity to participate as a member of planning or advisory boards; or

(vi) Otherwise limit a qualified handicapped person in the enjoyment of any right, privilege, advantage, or opportunity enjoyed by others receiving the aid, benefit, or service.

(2) The agency may not deny a qualified handicapped person the opportunity to participate in programs or activities that are not separate or different, despite the existence of permissibly separate or different programs or activities.

(3) The agency may not, directly or through contractual or other arrangements, utilize criteria or methods of administration the purpose or effect of which would—

(i) Subject qualified handicapped persons to discrimination on the basis of handicap; or

(ii) Defeat or substantially impair accomplishment of the objectives of a program or activity with respect to handicapped persons.

(4) The agency may not, in determining the site or location of a facility, make selections the purpose or effect of which would—

(i) Exclude handicapped persons from, deny them the benefits of, or otherwise subject them to discrimination under any program or activity conducted by the agency; or

(ii) Defeat or substantially impair the accomplishment of the objectives of a program or activity with respect to handicapped persons.

(5) The agency, in the selection of procurement contractors, may not use criteria that subject qualified handicapped persons to discrimination on the basis of handicap.

(6) The agency may not administer a licensing or certification program in a manner that subjects qualified handicapped persons to discrimination on the basis of handicap, nor may the agency establish requirements for the programs or activities of licensees or certified entities that subject qualified handicapped persons to discrimination on the basis of handicap. However, the programs or activities of entities that are licensed or certified by the agency are not, themselves, covered by this part.

(c) The exclusion of nonhandicapped persons from the benefits of a program limited by Federal statute or Executive order to handicapped persons or the exclusion of a specific class of handicapped persons from a program limited by Federal statute or Executive order to a different class of handicapped persons is not prohibited by this part.

(d) The agency shall administer programs and activities in the most integrated setting appropriate to the needs of qualified handicapped persons.

§§ 1153.131–1153.139 [Reserved]

§ 1153.140 Employment.

No qualified handicapped person shall, on the basis of handicap, be subjected to discrimination in employment under any program or activity conducted by the agency. The definitions, requirements, and procedures of section 501 of the Rehabilitation Act of 1973 (29 U.S.C. 791), as established by the Equal Employment Opportunity Commission in 29 CFR part 1613, shall apply to employment in federally conducted programs or activities.

§§ 1153.141–1153.148 [Reserved]

§ 1153.149 Program accessibility: Discrimination prohibited.

Except as otherwise provided in § 1153.150, no qualified handicapped person shall, because the agency's facilities are inaccessible to or unusable by handicapped persons, be denied the benefits of, be excluded from participation in, or otherwise be subjected to discrimination under any program or activity conducted by the agency.

§ 1153.150 Program accessibility: Existing facilities.

(a) *General.* The agency shall operate each program or activity so that the program or activity, when viewed in its entirety, is readily accessible to and usable by handicapped persons. This paragraph does not—

(1) Necessarily require the agency to make each of its existing facilities accessible to and usable by handicapped persons;

(2) In the case of historic preservation programs, require the agency to take any action that would result in a substantial impairment of significant historic features of an historic property; or

(3) Require the agency to take any action that it can demonstrate would result in a fundamental alteration in the nature of a program or activity or in undue financial and administrative burdens. In those circumstances where agency personnel believe that the proposed action would fundamentally alter the program or activity or would result in undue financial and administrative burdens, the agency has the burden of proving that compliance with § 1153.150(a) would result in such alteration or burdens. The decision that compliance would result in such alteration or burdens must be made by the agency head or his or her designee after considering all agency resources available for use in the funding and operation of the conducted program or activity, and must be accompanied by a written statement of the reasons for reaching that conclusion. If an action would result in such an alteration or such burdens, the agency shall take any other action that would not result in such an alteration or such burdens but would nevertheless ensure that handicapped persons receive the benefits and services of the program or activity.

(b) *Methods*—(1) *General.* The agency may comply with the requirements of this section through such means as redesign of equipment, reassignment of services to accessible buildings, assignment of aides to beneficiaries, home visits, delivery of services at alternate accessible sites, alteration of existing facilities and construction of new facilities, use of accessible rolling stock, or any other methods that result in making its programs or activities readily accessible to and usable by handicapped persons. The agency is not required to make structural changes in existing facilities where other methods are effective in achieving compliance with this section. The agency, in making alterations to existing buildings, shall meet accessibility requirements to the extent compelled by the Architectural Barriers Act of 1968, as amended (42 U.S.C. 4151 through 4157), and any regulations implementing it. In choosing among available methods for meeting the requirements of this section, the agency shall give priority to those methods that offer programs and activities to qualified handicapped persons in the most integrated setting appropriate.

(2) *Historic preservation programs.* In meeting the requirements of § 1153.150(a) in historic preservation

programs, the agency shall give priority to methods that provide physical access to handicapped persons. In cases where a physical alteration to an historic property is not required because of § 1153.150(a)(2) or (a)(3), alternative methods of achieving program accessibility include—

(i) Using audio-visual materials and devices to depict those portions of an historic property that cannot otherwise be made accessible;

(ii) Assigning persons to guide handicapped persons into or through portions of historic properties that cannot otherwise be made accessible; or

(iii) Adopting other innovative methods.

(c) *Time period for compliance.* The agency shall comply with the obligations established under this section by October 21, 1986, except that where structural changes in facilities are undertaken, such changes shall be made by August 22, 1989, but in any event as expeditiously as possible.

(d) *Transition plan.* In the event that structural changes to facilities will be undertaken to achieve program accessibility, the agency shall develop, by February 23, 1987, a transition plan setting forth the steps necessary to complete such changes. The agency shall provide an opportunity to interested persons, including handicapped persons or organizations representing handicapped persons, to participate in the development of the transition plan by submitting comments (both oral and written). A copy of the transition plan shall be made available for public inspection. The plan shall, at a minimum—

(1) Identify physical obstacles in the agency's facilities that limit the accessibility of its programs or activities to handicapped persons;

(2) Describe in detail the methods that will be used to make the facilities accessible;

(3) Specify the schedule for taking the steps necessary to achieve compliance with this section and, if the time period of the transition plan is longer than one year, identify steps that will be taken during each year of the transition period; and

(4) Indicate the official responsible for implementation of the plan.

§ 1153.151 **Program accessibility: New construction and alterations.**

Each building or part of a building that is constructed or altered by, on behalf of, or for the use of the agency shall be designed, constructed, or altered so as to be readily accessible to and usable by handicapped persons. The definitions, requirements, and standards of the Architectural Barriers Act (42 U.S.C. 4151 through 4157), as established in 41 CFR 101–19.600 to 101–19.607, apply to buildings covered by this section.

§§ 1153.152–1153.159 **[Reserved]**

§ 1153.160 **Communications.**

(a) The agency shall take appropriate steps to ensure effective communication with applicants, participants, personnel of other Federal entities, and members of the public.

(1) The agency shall furnish appropriate auxiliary aids where necessary to afford a handicapped person an equal opportunity to participate in, and enjoy the benefits of, a program or activity conducted by the agency.

(i) In determining what type of auxiliary aid is necessary, the agency shall give primary consideration to the requests of the handicapped person.

(ii) The agency need not provide individually prescribed devices, readers for personal use or study, or other devices of a personal nature.

(2) Where the agency communicates with applicants and beneficiaries by telephone, telecommunication devices for deaf person (TDD's) or equally effective telecommunication systems shall be used.

(b) The agency shall ensure that interested persons, including persons with impaired vision or hearing, can obtain information as to the existence and location of accessible services, activities, and facilities.

(c) The agency shall provide signage at a primary entrance to each of its inaccessible facilities, directing users to a location at which they can obtain information about accessible facilities. The international symbol for accessibility shall be used at each primary entrance of an accessible facility.

(d) This section does not require the agency to take any action that it can demonstrate would result in a fundamental alteration in the nature of a program or activity or in undue financial and adminstrative burdens. In those circumstances where agency personnel believe that the proposed action would fundamentally alter the program or activity or would result in undue financial and administrative burdens, the agency has the burden of proving that compliance with § 1153.160 would result in such alteration or burdens. The decision that compliance would result in such alteration or burdens must be made by the agency head or his or her designee after considering all agency resources available for use in the funding and operation of the conducted program or activity, and must be accompanied by a written statement of the reasons for reaching that conclusion. If an action required to comply with this section would result in such an alteration or such burdens, the agency shall take any other action that would not result in such an alteration or such burdens but would nevertheless ensure that, to the maximum extent possible, handicapped persons receive the benefits and services of the program or activity.

§§ 1153.161–1153.169 [Reserved]

§ 1153.170 Compliance procedures.

(a) Except as provided in paragraph (b) of this section, this section applies to all allegations of discrimination on the basis of handicap in programs or activities conducted by the agency.

(b) The agency shall process complaints alleging violations of section 504 with respect to employment according to the procedures established by the Equal Employment Opportunity Commission in 29 CFR part 1613 pursuant to section 501 of the Rehabilitation Act of 1973 (29 U.S.C. 791).

(c) The Director, Office for Civil Rights, shall be responsible for coordinating implementation of this section. Complaints may be sent to the Office of General Counsel, National Endowment for the Arts, 1100 Pennsylvania Avenue NW., Washington, DC 20506.

(d) The agency shall accept and investigate all complete complaints for which it has jurisdiction. All complete complaints must be filed within 180 days of the alleged act of discrimination. The agency may extend this time period for good cause.

(e) If the agency receives a complaint over which it does not have jurisdiction, it shall promptly notify the complainant and shall make reasonable efforts to refer the complaint to the appropriate government entity.

(f) The agency shall notify the Architectural and Transportation Barriers Compliance Board upon receipt of any complaint alleging that a building or facility that is subject to the Architectural Barriers Act of 1968, as amended (42 U.S.C. 4151–4157), or section 502 of the Rehabilitation Act of 1973, as amended (29 U.S.C. 792), is not readily accessible to and usable by handicapped persons.

(g) Within 180 days of the receipt of a complete complaint for which it has jurisdiction, the agency shall notify the complainant of the results of the investigation in a letter containing—

(1) Findings of fact and conclusions of law;

(2) A description of a remedy for each violation found; and

(3) A notice of the right to appeal.

(h) Appeals of the findings of fact and conclusions of law or remedies must be filed by the complainant within 90 days of receipt from the agency of the letter required by § 1153.170(g). The agency may extend this time for good cause.

(i) Timely appeals shall be accepted and processed by the head of the agency.

(j) The head of the agency shall notify the complainant of the results of the appeal within 60 days of the receipt of the request. If the head of the agency determines that additional information is needed from the complainant, he or she shall have 60 days from the date of receipt of the additional information to make his or her determination on the appeal.

(k) The time limits cited in paragraphs (g) and (j) of this section may be extended with the permission of the Assistant Attorney General.

(l) The agency may delegate its authority for conducting complaint investigations to other Federal agencies, except that the authority for making

National Foundation on the Arts and the Humanities § 1156.3

the final determination may not be delegated to another agency.

[51 FR 22895, 22896, June 23, 1986, as amended at 51 FR 22895, June 23, 1986]

§§ 1153.171-1153.999 [Reserved]

PART 1156—NONDISCRIMINATION ON THE BASIS OF AGE

Subpart A—General

Sec.
1156.1 Purpose.
1156.2 Application.
1156.3 Definitions.
1156.4 [Reserved]

Subpart B—Standards for Determining Discriminatory Practices

1156.5 Purpose.
1156.6 Rules against age discrimination.
1156.7 Exceptions to the rules against age discrimination.
1156.8 Burden of proof.

Subpart C—Responsibilities of Endowment Recipients

1156.9 [Reserved]
1156.10 General responsibilities.
1156.11 Notice to subrecipients.
1156.12 Self-evaluation.
1156.13 Information requirements.

Subpart D—Investigation, Conciliation, and Enforcement Procedures

1156.14 Compliance reviews.
1156.15 Complaints.
1156.16 Mediation.
1156.17 Investigation.
1156.18 Prohibition against intimidation or retaliation.
1156.19 Compliance procedure.
1156.20 Alternate funds disbursal procedure.
1156.21 Exhaustion of administrative remedies.

AUTHORITY: 42 U.S.C. 6101 et seq.; 45 CFR part 90.

SOURCE: 63 FR 6876, Feb. 11, 1998, unless otherwise noted.

Subpart A—General

§ 1156.1 Purpose.

The purpose of this part is to implement the Age Discrimination Act of 1975 ("Act"), as amended, and as required by the general age discrimination regulations at 45 CFR part 90. The Age Discrimination Act of 1975, as amended, is designed to prohibit discrimination on the basis of age in programs or activities receiving Federal financial assistance. The Act also permits federally assisted programs or activities, and recipients of Federal funds to continue to use certain age distinctions and factors other than age which meet the requirements of the Act and the regulations in this part.

[63 FR 6876, Feb. 11, 1998, as amended at 68 FR 51385, Aug. 26, 2003]

§ 1156.2 Application.

(a) The Age Discrimination Act of 1975 and the regulations in this part apply to any program or activity receiving financial assistance from the National Endowment for the Arts.

(b) The Age Discrimination Act of 1975 does not apply to:

(1) Any age distinction contained in that part of Federal, State, or local statute or ordinance adopted by an elected general purpose legislative body which:

(i) Provides benefits or assistance to persons based on age; or

(ii) Establishes criteria for participation in age-related terms; or

(iii) Describes intended beneficiaries or target groups in age related terms.

(2) Any employment practice of any employer, employment agency, labor organization, or any labor-management joint apprenticeship training program, except for any program or activity receiving Federal financial assistance for public service employment under the Job Training Partnership Act (JTPA).

[63 FR 6876, Feb. 11, 1998, as amended at 68 FR 51385, Aug. 26, 2003]

§ 1156.3 Definitions.

As used in the regulation in this part, the term:

(a) *Act* means the Age Discrimination Act of 1975, as amended (Title III of Pub. L. 94-135).

(b) *Action* means any act, activity, policy, rule, standard, or method of administration; or the use of any policy, rule, standard, or method of administration.

(c) *Age* means how old a person is or the number of elapsed years from the date of a person's birth.

401

(d) *Age distinction* means any action using age or any age-related term.

(e) *Age-related term* means a word or words which necessarily imply a particular age or range of ages (for example, "children," "adult," "older person," but not "student").

(f) *Federal financial assistance* means any grant, entitlement, loan, cooperative agreement, contract (other than a procurement contract or a contract of insurance or guaranty), or any other arrangement by which the agency provides or otherwise makes available assistance in the form of:

(1) Funds;

(2) Services of Federal personnel; or

(3) Real and personal property including:

(i) Transfers or leases of property for less than fair market value or for reduced consideration; and

(ii) Proceeds from a subsequent transfer or lease of property if the Federal share of its fair market value is not returned to the Federal government.

(g) *Normal operation* means the operation of a program or activity without significant changes that would impair its ability to meet its objectives.

(h) *Program or activity* means all of the operations of any entity described in paragraphs (h)(1) through (4) of this section, any part of which is extended Federal financial assistance:

(1)(i) A department, agency, special purpose district, or other instrumentality of a State or of a local government; or

(ii) The entity of such State or local government that distributes such assistance and each such department or agency (and each other State or local government entity) to which the assistance is extended, in the case of assistance to a State or local government;

(2)(i) A college, university, or other postsecondary institution, or a public system of higher education; or

(ii) A local educational agency (as defined in 20 U.S.C. 7801), system of vocational education, or other school system;

(3)(i) An entire corporation, partnership, or other private organization, or an entire sole proprietorship—

(A) If assistance is extended to such corporation, partnership, private organization, or sole proprietorship as a whole; or

(B) Which is principally engaged in the business of providing education, health care, housing, social services, or parks and recreation; or

(ii) The entire plant or other comparable, geographically separate facility to which Federal financial assistance is extended, in the case of any other corporation, partnership, private organization, or sole proprietorship; or

(4) Any other entity which is established by two or more of the entities described in paragraph (h)(1), (2), or (3) of this section.

(i) *Recipient* means any State or its political subdivision, any instrumentality of a State or its political subdivision, any public or private agency, institution, organization, or other entity, or any person to which Federal financial assistance is extended, directly or through another recipient. Recipient includes any successor, assignee, or transferee, but excludes the ultimate beneficiary of the assistance.

(j) *Statutory objective* means any purpose of a program or activity expressly stated in any Federal statute, state statute, or local statute or ordinance adopted by an elected, general purpose legislative body.

(k) *Sub-recipient* means any of the entities in the definition of recipient to which a recipient extends or passes on Federal financial assistance and has all the duties of a recipient in the regulations in this part.

(l) *Endowment* means the National Endowment for the Arts.

(m) *Chairperson* means the Chairperson of the National Endowment for the Arts.

(n) *Secretary* means the Secretary of the Department of Health and Human Services.

(o) *United States* means the fifty States, the District of Columbia, Puerto Rico, the Virgin Islands, American Somoa, Guam, Wake Island, the Canal Zone, the Federated States of Micronesia and the Republic of Palau, the Northern Marianas, and the territories and possessions of the United States.

[63 FR 6876, Feb. 11, 1998, as amended at 68 FR 51385, Aug. 26, 2003]

§ 1156.4 [Reserved]

Subpart B—Standards for Determining Discriminatory Practices

§ 1156.5 Purpose.

The purpose of this subpart is to set forth the prohibitions against age discrimination and the exceptions to those prohibitions.

§ 1156.6 Rules against age discrimination.

The rules stated in this section are limited by the exceptions contained in § 1156.7 (b) and (c).

(a) *General rule.* No person in the United States shall, on the basis of age, be excluded from participation in, be denied the benefits of, or be subjected to discrimination under any program or activity receiving Federal financial assistance.

(b) *Specific rules.* A recipient may not, in any program or activity receiving Federal financial assistance, directly or through contractual, licensing, or other arrangements use age distinctions or take any other actions which have the effect, on the basis of age, of:

(1) Excluding individuals from, denying them the benefits of, or subjecting them to discrimination under a program or activity receiving Federal financial assistance; or

(2) Denying or limiting individuals in their opportunity to participate in any program or activity receiving Federal financial assistance.

(c) The specific forms of age discrimination listed in paragraph (b) of this section do not necessarily constitute a complete list of discriminatory actions.

§ 1156.7 Exceptions to the rules against age discrimination.

(a) *Normal operation or statutory objective of any program or activity.* A recipient is permitted to take an action otherwise prohibited by § 1156.6 if the action reasonably takes into account age as a factor necessary to the normal operation or the achievement of any statutory objective of a program or activity, if:

(1) Age is used as a measure or approximation of one or more other characteristics; and

(2) The other characteristic(s) must be measured or approximated in order for the normal operation of the program or activity to continue, or to achieve any statutory objective of the program or activity; and

(3) The other characteristic(s) can be reasonably measured or approximated by the use of age; and

(4) The other characteristic(s) are impractical to measure directly on an individual basis.

(b) *Reasonable factors other than age.* A recipient is permitted to take an action otherwise prohibited by § 1156.6 which is based on a factor other than age, even though that action may have a disproportionate effect on persons of different ages. An action may be based on a factor other than age only if the factor bears a direct and substantial relationship to the normal operation of the program or activity or to the achievement of a statutory objective.

(c) *Remedial and affirmative action by recipients.* If a recipient operating a program or activity which serves the elderly or children in addition to persons of other ages, provides special benefits to the elderly or to children the provision of those benefits shall be presumed to be voluntary affirmative action provided that it does not have the effect of excluding otherwise eligible persons from participation in the program or activity.

[63 FR 6876, Feb. 11, 1998, as amended at 68 FR 51385, Aug. 26, 2003]

§ 1156.8 Burden of proof.

The recipient of Federal financial assistance bears the burden of proving that an age distinction or other action falls within the exceptions outlined in § 1156.7.

Subpart C—Responsibilities of Endowment Recipients

§ 1156.9 [Reserved]

§ 1156.10 General responsibilities.

A recipient has primary responsibility to ensure that its programs or activities are in compliance with the Age Discrimination Act, to take steps to eliminate violations of the Act, and to provide notice to beneficiaries of its programs and activities concerning protection against discrimination provided by the Act and the regulations in this part. A recipient also has responsibility to maintain records, provide information, and to afford access to its records to the Endowment to the extent required to determine whether it is in compliance with the Act.

[63 FR 6876, Feb. 11, 1998, as amended at 68 FR 51385, Aug. 26, 2003]

§ 1156.11 Notice to subrecipients.

Where a recipient passes on Federal financial assistance from the Endowment to subrecipients, the recipient shall provide the subrecipients with written notice regarding the subrecipient's obligations under the Act and the regulations in this part.

§ 1156.12 Self-evaluation.

(a) Each recipient employing the equivalent of 15 or more full time employees may be required to complete a written self-evaluation, in a manner specified by the responsible Endowment official during the course of an investigation, of any age distinction imposed in its program or activity receiving Federal financial assistance from the Endowment to assess the recipient's compliance with the Act.

(b) Each recipient shall take corrective and remedial action whenever a self-evaluation indicates a violation of the Act.

(c) Each recipient shall make the self-evaluation available on request to the Endowment and to the public for a period of three years following its completion.

§ 1156.13 Information requirements.

Each recipient shall:

(a) Make available to the Endowment, upon request, information necessary to determine whether the recipient is complying with the regulations in this part.

(b) Permit reasonable access by the Endowment to the books, accounts and other recipient facilities and sources of information to the extent necessary to determine whether the recipient is in compliance with the Act.

Subpart D—Investigation, Conciliation, and Enforcement Procedures

§ 1156.14 Compliance reviews.

The Endowment may conduct compliance reviews, pre-award reviews and other similar procedures in order to investigate and correct violations of the Act and regulations. The Endowment may conduct these reviews in the absence of a complaint against the recipient. In the event a compliance review or pre-award review indicates a violation of the regulations in this part, the Endowment will attempt to achieve voluntary compliance with the Act. If voluntary compliance cannot be achieved, enforcement efforts will proceed as described in § 1156.19.

§ 1156.15 Complaints.

(a) Any person, individually or as a member of a class or on behalf of others, may file a complaint with the Endowment, alleging discrimination prohibited by the Act and the regulations in this part based on an action occurring on or after July 1, 1979. A complainant shall file a complaint within 180 days from the date that the complainant first had knowledge of the alleged act of discrimination. However, for good cause, the Endowment may extend this time limit. The Endowment will consider the date a complaint is filed to be the date upon which the complaint is sufficient to be processed.

(b) Complaints must include a written statement identifying the parties involved, describing the alleged violation, and stating the date on which the complainant first had knowledge of the alleged violation. Complaints must be signed by the complainant. The Endowment will return any complaint that does not contain the necessary information, that is not signed by the complainant, or that is not within the Endowment's jurisdiction for any other reason. The Endowment will provide an explanation for all such returned complaints.

(c) The Endowment will attempt to facilitate the filing of complaints wherever possible, including taking the following measures:

(1) Widely disseminating information regarding the obligations of recipients

National Foundation on the Arts and the Humanities § 1156.17

under the Act and the regulations in this part.

(2) Notifying the complainant and the recipient of their rights and obligations under the complaint procedure, including the right to have a representative at all stages of the complaint procedure.

(3) Notifying the complainant and the recipient (or their representatives) of their right to contact the Endowment for information and assistance regarding the complaint resolution process.

§ 1156.16 Mediation.

(a) *Referral of complaints for mediation.* The Endowment will promptly refer all complaints to the agency designated by the Secretary of HHS to manage the mediation process that:

(1) Fall within the jurisdiction of the regulations in this part; and

(2) Contain all information necessary for further processing.

(b) Both the complainant and the recipient shall participate in the mediation process to the extent necessary to reach an agreement or make an informal judgment that an agreement is not possible. There must be at least one meeting with the mediator before the Endowment will accept a judgment that an agreement is not possible. However, the recipient and the complainant need not meet with the mediator at the same time.

(c) If the complainant and recipient reach a mutually satisfactory resolution of the complaint during the mediation period, they shall reduce the agreement to wiring. The mediator shall send a copy of the settlement to the Endowment. No further action shall be taken by the Endowment based on that complaint unless it appears that the complainant or the recipient has failed to comply with the agreement.

(d) The mediator shall protect the confidentiality of all information obtained in the course of the mediation process. No mediator shall testify in any adjudicative proceeding, produce any document, or otherwise disclose any information obtained in the course of the mediation process without prior approval of the head of the mediation agency.

(e) Not more than 60 days after the Endowment receives the complaint, the mediator shall return a still unresolved complaint to the Endowment for initial investigation. The mediator may return a complaint at any time before the end of the 60-day period if it appears that the complaint cannot be resolved through mediation. The mediator may extend this 60-day period, provided the Endowment concurs, for not more than 30 days, if the mediator determines that resolution is likely to occur within such period.

§ 1156.17 Investigation.

(a) *Informal investigation.* (1) The Endowment will investigate complaints that are unresolved after mediation or are reopened because of a violation of a mediation agreement.

(2) As part of the initial investigation, the Endowment will use informal fact-finding methods, including joint or separate discussions with the complainant and the recipient to establish the facts, and, if possible, resolve the complaint to the mutual satisfaction of the parties. The Endowment may seek the assistance of any involved State agency.

(3) The Endowment will put any agreement in writing and have it signed by the parties and an authorized official at the Endowment.

(4) The settlement shall not affect the operation of any other enforcement effort of the Endowment, including compliance reviews and investigation of other complaints which may involve the recipient.

(5) The settlement is not a finding of discrimination against a recipient.

(b) *Formal investigation, conciliation, and hearing.* If the Endowment cannot resolve the complaint during the early stages of the investigation, it shall:

(1) Complete the investigation of the complaint.

(2) Attempt to achieve voluntary compliance satisfactory to the Endowment, if the investigation indicates a violation.

(3) Arrange for enforcement as described in § 1156.19, if necessary.

[63 FR 6876, Feb. 11, 1998, as amended at 68 FR 51385, Aug. 26, 2003]

§ 1156.18 Prohibition against intimidation or retaliation.

A recipient may not engage in acts of intimidation or retaliation against any person who:

(a) Attempts to assert a right protected by the Act; or

(b) Cooperates in any mediation, investigation, hearing, or other part of the Endowment's investigation, conciliation and enforcement process.

§ 1156.19 Compliance procedure.

(a) The Endowment may enforce the Act and the regulations in this part through:

(1) Termination of a recipient's Federal financial assistance from the Endowment under the program or activity involved where the recipient has violated the Act and the regulations in this part. The determination of the recipient's violation may be made only after a recipient has had an opportunity for a hearing on the record before an administrative law judge. Therefore, a case which is settled in mediation, or prior to a hearing, will not involve termination of a recipient's Federal financial assistance from the Endowment unless it is reopened because of a violation of the agreement.

(2) Any other means authorized by law including, but not limited to:

(i) Referral to the Department of Justice for proceedings to enforce any rights of the United States or obligations of the recipient created by the Act or the regulations in this part.

(ii) Use of any requirement of or referral to any Federal, State, or local government agency that will have the effect of correcting a violation of the Act or the regulations in this part.

(b) The Endowment will limit any termination under paragraph (a)(1) of this section to the particular recipient and particular program or activity or portion thereof that the Endowment finds in violation of the regulations in this part. The Endowment will not base any part of a termination on a finding with respect to any program or activity of the recipient which does not receive Federal financial assistance from the Endowment.

(c) The Endowment will not take action under paragraph (a) of this section until:

(1) The Chairperson has advised the recipient of its failure to comply with the Act and the regulations in this part and has determined that voluntary compliance cannot be obtained.

(2) Thirty days have elapsed after the Chairperson has sent a written report of the circumstances and grounds of the action to the committees of the Congress having legislative jurisdiction over the program or activity involved. The Chairperson will file a report whenever any action is taken under paragraph (a) of this section.

(d) The Chairperson also may defer granting new Federal financial assistance from the Endowment to a recipient when a hearing under paragraph (a)(1) of this section is initiated.

(1) New Federal financial assistance from the Endowment includes all assistance for which the Endowment requires an application or approval, including renewal or continuation of existing activities, or authorization of new activities, during the deferral period. New Federal financial assistance from the Endowment does not include assistance approved prior to the beginning of a termination hearing under paragraph (a)(1) of this section or increases in funding as a result of changed computation of formula awards.

(2) The Endowment will not begin a deferral until the recipient has received a notice of an opportunity for a hearing under paragraph (a)(1) of this section. The Endowment will not continue a deferral for more than 60 days unless a hearing has begun within that time or the time for beginning the hearing has been extended by mutual consent of the recipient and the Chairperson. The Endowment will not continue a deferral for more than 30 days after the close of the hearing, unless the hearing results in a finding against the recipient. If the hearing results in a finding against the recipient, the Endowment must terminate funds.

[63 FR 6876, Feb. 11, 1998, as amended at 68 FR 51385, Aug. 26, 2003]

§ 1156.20 Alternate funds disbursal procedure.

(a) When the endowment withholds funds from a recipient under the regulations in this part, the Chairperson may disburse the withheld funds directly to an alternate recipient otherwise eligible for Endowment support: any public or nonprofit private organization or agency, or State or political subdivision of the State.

(b) The Chairperson will require any alternate recipient to demonstrate:

(1) The ability to comply with the regulations in this part; and

(2) The ability to achieve the goals of the Federal statute authorizing the Federal financial assistance.

[63 FR 6876, Feb. 11, 1998, as amended at 68 FR 51385, Aug. 26, 2003]

§ 1156.21 Exhaustion of administrative remedies.

(a) A complainant may file a civil action following the exhaustion of administrative remedies under the Act. Administrative remedies are exhausted if:

(1) 180 days have elapsed since the complainant filed the complaint and the Endowment has made no finding with regard to the complaint; or

(2) The Endowment issues a finding in favor of the recipient.

(b) If the Endowment fails to make a finding within 180 days or issues a finding in favor of the recipient, the Endowment will:

(1) Promptly advise the complainant if either of the conditions of paragraph (a) of this section has been met;

(2) Advise the complainant of his or her right to bring a civil action for injunctive relief that will effect the purpose of the Act;

(3) Inform the complainant:

(i) That the complainant may bring a civil action only in the United States district court for the district in which the recipient is located or transacts business;

(ii) That a complainant prevailing in a civil action has the right to be awarded the costs of the action, including reasonable attorney's fees, but that the complainant must demand these costs in the complaint;

(iii) That before commencing the action the complainant shall give 30 days notice by registered mail to the Chairperson of the Endowment, the Secretary, the Attorney General of the United States, and the recipient;

(iv) That the notice must state: the alleged violation of the Act; the relief requested; the court in which the complainant is bringing the action; and whether or not the attorney's fees are demanded in the event the complainant prevails; and

(v) That the complainant may not bring an action if the same alleged violation of the Act by the same recipient is the subject of a pending action in any court of the United States.

PART 1157 [RESERVED]

PART 1158—NEW RESTRICTIONS ON LOBBYING

Subpart A—General

Sec.
1158.100 Conditions on use of funds.
1158.105 Definitions.
1158.110 Certification and disclosure.

Subpart B—Activities by Own Employees

1158.200 Agency and legislative liaison.
1158.205 Professional and technical services.
1158.210 Reporting.

Subpart C—Activities by Other Than Own Employees

1158.300 Professional and technical services.

Subpart D—Penalties and Enforcement

1158.400 Penalties.
1158.405 Penalty procedures.
1158.410 Enforcement.

Subpart E—Exemptions

1158.500 Secretary of Defense.

Subpart F—Agency Reports

1158.600 Semi-annual compilation.
1158.605 Inspector General report.

APPENDIX A TO PART 1158—CERTIFICATION REGARDING LOBBYING

APPENDIX B TO PART 1158—DISCLOSURE FORM TO REPORT LOBBYING

AUTHORITY: 20 U.S.C. 959; 28 U.S.C. 2461; 31 U.S.C. 1352.

SOURCE: 55 FR 6737, 6755, Feb. 26, 1990, unless otherwise noted.

CROSS REFERENCE: See also Office of Management and Budget notice published at 54 FR 52306, December 20, 1989.

Subpart A—General

§ 1158.100 Conditions on use of funds.

(a) No appropriated funds may be expended by the recipient of a Federal contract, grant, loan, or cooperative ageement to pay any person for influencing or attempting to influence an officer or employee of any agency, a Member of Congress, an officer or employee of Congress, or an employee of a Member of Congress in connection with any of the following covered Federal actions: the awarding of any Federal contract, the making of any Federal grant, the making of any Federal loan, the entering into of any cooperative agreement, and the extension, continuation, renewal, amendment, or modification of any Federal contract, grant, loan, or cooperative agreement.

(b) Each person who requests or receives from an agency a Federal contract, grant, loan, or cooperative agreement shall file with that agency a certification, set forth in appendix A, that the person has not made, and will not make, any payment prohibited by paragraph (a) of this section.

(c) Each person who requests or receives from an agency a Federal contract, grant, loan, or a cooperative agreement shall file with that agency a disclosure form, set forth in appendix B, if such person has made or has agreed to make any payment using nonappropriated funds (to include profits from any covered Federal action), which would be prohibited under paragraph (a) of this section if paid for with appropriated funds.

(d) Each person who requests or receives from an agency a commitment providing for the United States to insure or guarantee a loan shall file with that agency a statement, set forth in appendix A, whether that person has made or has agreed to make any payment to influence or attempt to influence an officer or employee of any agency, a Member of Congress, an officer or employee of Congress, or an employee of a Member of Congress in connection with that loan insurance or guarantee.

(e) Each person who requests or receives from an agency a commitment providing for the United States to insure or guarantee a loan shall file with that agency a disclosure form, set forth in appendix B, if that person has made or has agreed to make any payment to influence or attempt to influence an officer or employee of any agency, a Member of Congress, an officer or employee of Congress, or an employee of a Member of Congress in connection with that loan insurance or guarantee.

§ 1158.105 Definitions.

For purposes of this part:

(a) *Agency*, as defined in 5 U.S.C. 552(f), includes Federal executive departments and agencies as well as independent regulatory commissions and Government corporations, as defined in 31 U.S.C. 9101(1).

(b) *Covered Federal action* means any of the following Federal actions:

(1) The awarding of any Federal contract;

(2) The making of any Federal grant;

(3) The making of any Federal loan;

(4) The entering into of any cooperative agreement; and,

(5) The extension, continuation, renewal, amendment, or modification of any Federal contract, grant, loan, or cooperative agreement.

Covered Federal action does not include receiving from an agency a commitment providing for the United States to insure or guarantee a loan. Loan guarantees and loan insurance are addressed independently within this part.

(c) *Federal contract* means an acquisition contract awarded by an agency, including those subject to the Federal Acquisition Regulation (FAR), and any other acquisition contract for real or personal property or services not subject to the FAR.

(d) *Federal cooperative agreement* means a cooperative agreement entered into by an agency.

(e) *Federal grant* means an award of financial assistance in the form of money, or property in lieu of money, by the Federal Government or a direct appropriation made by law to any person. The term does not include technical assistance which provides services instead of money, or other assistance in the form of revenue sharing, loans, loan guarantees, loan insurance, interest subsidies, insurance, or direct

United States cash assistance to an individual.

(f) *Federal loan* means a loan made by an agency. The term does not include loan guarantee or loan insurance.

(g) *Indian tribe* and *tribal organization* have the meaning provided in section 4 of the Indian Self-Determination and Education Assistance Act (25 U.S.C. 450B). Alaskan Natives are included under the definitions of Indian tribes in that Act.

(h) *Influencing or attempting to influence* means making, with the intent to influence, any communication to or appearance before an officer or employee or any agency, a Member of Congress, an officer or employee of Congress, or an employee of a Member of Congress in connection with any covered Federal action.

(i) *Loan guarantee* and *loan insurance* means an agency's guarantee or insurance of a loan made by a person.

(j) *Local government* means a unit of government in a State and, if chartered, established, or otherwise recognized by a State for the performance of a governmental duty, including a local public authority, a special district, an intrastate district, a council of governments, a sponsor group representative organization, and any other instrumentality of a local government.

(k) *Officer or employee of an agency* includes the following individuals who are employed by an agency:

(1) An individual who is appointed to a position in the Government under title 5, U.S. Code, including a position under a temporary appointment;

(2) A member of the uniformed services as defined in section 101(3), title 37, U.S. Code;

(3) A special Government employee as defined in section 202, title 18, U.S. Code; and,

(4) An individual who is a member of a Federal advisory committee, as defined by the Federal Advisory Committee Act, title 5, U.S. Code appendix 2.

(l) *Person* means an individual, corporation, company, association, authority, firm, partnership, society, State, and local government, regardless of whether such entity is operated for profit or not for profit. This term excludes an Indian tribe, tribal organization, or any other Indian organization with respect to expenditures specifically permitted by other Federal law.

(m) *Reasonable compensation* means, with respect to a regularly employed officer or employee of any person, compensation that is consistent with the normal compensation for such officer or employee for work that is not furnished to, not funded by, or not furnished in cooperation with the Federal Government.

(n) *Reasonable payment* means, with respect to perfessional and other technical services, a payment in an amount that is consistent with the amount normally paid for such services in the private sector.

(o) *Recipient* includes all contractors, subcontractors at any tier, and subgrantees at any tier of the recipient of funds received in connection with a Federal contract, grant, loan, or cooperative agreement. The term excludes an Indian tribe, tribal organization, or any other Indian organization with respect to expenditures specifically permitted by other Federal law.

(p) *Regularly employed* means, with respect to an officer or employee of a person requesting or receiving a Federal contract, grant, loan, or cooperative agreement or a commitment providing for the United States to insure or guarantee a loan, an officer or employee who is employed by such person for at least 130 working days within one year immediately preceding the date of the submission that initiates agency consideration of such person for receipt of such contract, grant, loan, cooperative agreement, loan insurance commitment, or loan guarantee commitment. An officer or employee who is employed by such person for less than 130 working days within one year immediately preceding the date of the submission that initiates agency consideration of such person shall be considered to be regularly employed as soon as he or she is employed by such person for 130 working days.

(q) *State* means a State of the United States, the District of Columbia, the Commonwealth of Puerto Rico, a territory or possession of the United States, an agency or instrumentality of a State, and a multi-State, regional, or

§ 1158.110

interstate entity having governmental duties and powers.

§ 1158.110 Certification and disclosure.

(a) Each person shall file a certification, and a disclosure form, if required, with each submission that initiates agency consideration of such person for:

(1) Award of a Federal contract, grant, or cooperative agreement exceeding $100,000; or

(2) An award of a Federal loan or a commitment providing for the United States to insure or guarantee a loan exceeding $150,000.

(b) Each person shall file a certification, and a disclosure form, if required, upon receipt by such person of:

(1) A Federal contract, grant, or cooperative agreement exceeding $100,000; or

(2) A Federal loan or a commitment providing for the United States to insure or guarantee a loan exceeding $150,000,

unless such person previously filed a certification, and a disclosure form, if required, under paragraph (a) of this section.

(c) Each person shall file a disclosure form at the end of each calendar quarter in which there occurs any event that requires disclosure or that materially affects the accuracy of the information contained in any disclosure form previously filed by such person under paragraph (a) or (b) of this section. An event that materially affects the accuracy of the information reported includes:

(1) A cumulative increase of $25,000 or more in the amount paid or expected to be paid for influencing or attempting to influence a covered Federal action; or

(2) A change in the person(s) or individual(s) influencing or attempting to influence a covered Federal action; or,

(3) A change in the officer(s), employee(s), or Member(s) contacted to influence or attempt to influence a covered Federal action.

(d) Any person who requests or receives from a person referred to in paragraph (a) or (b) of this section:

(1) A subcontract exceeding $100,000 at any tier under a Federal contract;

(2) A subgrant, contract, or subcontract exceeding $100,000 at any tier under a Federal grant;

(3) A contract or subcontract exceeding $100,000 at any tier under a Federal loan exceeding $150,000; or,

(4) A contract or subcontract exceeding $100,000 at any tier under a Federal cooperative agreement,

shall file a certification, and a disclosure form, if required, to the next tier above.

(e) All disclosure forms, but not certifications, shall be forwarded from tier to tier until received by the person referred to in paragraph (a) or (b) of this section. That person shall forward all disclosure forms to the agency.

(f) Any certification or disclosure form filed under paragraph (e) of this section shall be treated as a material representation of fact upon which all receiving tiers shall rely. All liability arising from an erroneous representation shall be borne solely by the tier filing that representation and shall not be shared by any tier to which the erroneous representation is forwarded. Submitting an erroneous certification or disclosure constitutes a failure to file the required certification or disclosure, respectively. If a person fails to file a required certification or disclosure, the United States may pursue all available remedies, including those authorized by section 1352, title 31, U.S. Code.

(g) For awards and commitments in process prior to December 23, 1989, but not made before that date, certifications shall be required at award or commitment, covering activities occurring between December 23, 1989, and the date of award or commitment. However, for awards and commitments in process prior to the December 23, 1989 effective date of these provisions, but not made before December 23, 1989, disclosure forms shall not be required at time of award or commitment but shall be filed within 30 days.

(h) No reporting is required for an activity paid for with appropriated funds if that activity is allowable under either subpart B or C.

Subpart B—Activities by Own Employees

§ 1158.200 Agency and legislative liaison.

(a) The prohibition on the use of appropriated funds, in § 1158.100 (a), does not apply in the case of a payment of reasonable compensation made to an officer or employee of a person requesting or receiving a Federal contract, grant, loan, or cooperative agreement if the payment is for agency and legislative liaison activities not directly related to a covered Federal action.

(b) For purposes of paragraph (a) of this section, providing any information specifically requested by an agency or Congress is allowable at any time.

(c) For purposes of paragraph (a) of this section, the following agency and legislative liaison activities are allowable at any time only where they are not related to a specific solicitation for any covered Federal action:

(1) Discussing with an agency (including individual demonstrations) the qualities and characteristics of the person's products or services, conditions or terms of sale, and service capabilities; and,

(2) Technical discussions and other activities regarding the application or adaptation of the person's products or services for an agency's use.

(d) For purposes of paragraph (a) of this section, the following agencies and legislative liaison activities are allowable only where they are prior to formal solicitation of any covered Federal action:

(1) Providing any information not specifically requested but necessary for an agency to make an informed decision about initiation of a covered Federal action;

(2) Technical discussions regarding the preparation of an unsolicited proposal prior to its official submission; and,

(3) Capability presentations by persons seeking awards from an agency pursuant to the provisions of the Small Business Act, as amended by Pub. L. 95–507 and other subsequent amendments.

(e) Only those activities expressly authorized by this section are allowable under this section.

§ 1158.205 Professional and technical services.

(a) The prohibition on the use of appropriated funds, in § 1158.100 (a), does not apply in the case of a payment of reasonable compensation made to an officer or employee of a person requesting or receiving a Federal contract, grant, loan, or cooperative agreement or an extension, continuation, renewal, amendment, or modification of a Federal contract, grant, loan, or cooperative agreement if payment is for professional or technical services rendered directly in the preparation, submission, or negotiation of any bid, proposal, or application for that Federal contract, grant, loan, or cooperative agreement or for meeting requirements imposed by or pursuant to law as a condition for receiving that Federal contract, grant, loan, or cooperative agreement.

(b) For purposes of paragraph (a) of this section, *professional and technical services* shall be limited to advice and analysis directly applying any professional or technical discipline. For example, drafting of a legal document accompanying a bid or proposal by a lawyer is allowable. Similarly, technical advice provided by an engineer on the performance or operational capability of a piece of equipment rendered directly in the negotiation of a contract is allowable. However, communications with the intent to influence made by a professional (such as a licensed lawyer) or a technical person (such as a licensed accountant) are not allowable under this section unless they provide advice and analysis directly applying their professional or technical expertise and unless the advice or analysis is rendered directly and solely in the preparation, submission or negotiation of a covered Federal action. Thus, for example, communications with the intent to influence made by a lawyer that do not provide legal advice or analysis directly and solely related to the legal aspects of his or her client's proposal, but generally advocate one proposal over another are not allowable under this section because the lawyer is not providing professional legal services. Similarly, communications with the intent to influence made by an engineer providing an engineering analysis prior to the preparation or submission of a bid or proposal are not allowable under this section since the engineer is providing technical services but not directly in the preparation, submission or negotiation of a covered Federal action.

(c) Requirements imposed by or pursuant to law as a condition for receiving a covered Federal award include those required by law r regulation, or reasonably expected to be required by law or regulation, and any other requirements in the actual award documents.

(d) Only those services expressly authorized by this section are allowable under this section.

§ 1158.210 **Reporting.**

No reporting is required with respect to payments of reasonable compensation made to regularly employed officers or employees of a person.

Subpart C—Activities by Other Than Own Employees

§ 1158.300 **Professional and technical services.**

(a) The prohibition on the use of appropriated funds, in § 1158.100 (a), does not apply in the case of any reasonable payment to a person, other than an officer or employee of a person requesting or receiving a covered Federal action, if the payment is for professional or technical services rendered directly in the preparation, submission, or negotiation of any bid, proposal, or application for that Federal contract, grant, loan, or cooperative agreement or for meeting requirements imposed by or pursuant to law as a condition for receiving that Federal contract, grant, loan, or cooperative agreement.

(b) The reporting requirements in § 1158.110 (a) and (b) regarding filing a disclosure form by each person, if required, shall not apply with respect to professional or technical services rendered directly in the preparation, submission, or negotiation of any commitment providing for the United States to insure or guarantee a loan.

(c) For purposes of paragraph (a) of this section, *professional and technical services* shall be limited to advice and analysis directly applying any professional or technical discipline. For example, drafting of a legal document accompanying a bid or proposal by a lawyer is allowable. Similarly, technical advice provided by an engineer on the performance or operational capability of a piece of equipment rendered directly in the negotiation of a contract is allowable. However, communications with the intent to influence made by a professional (such as a licensed lawyer) or a technical person (such as a licensed accountant) are not allowable under this section unless they provide advice and analysis directly applying their professional or technical expertise and unless the advice or analysis is rendered directly and solely in the preparation, submission or negotiation of a covered Federal action. Thus, for example, communications with the intent to influence made by a lawyer that do not provide legal advice or analysis directly and solely related to the legal aspects of his or her client's proposal, but generally advocate one proposal over another are not allowable under this section because the lawyer is not providing professional legal services. Similarly, communications with the intent to influence made by an engineer providing an engineering analysis prior to the preparation or submission of a bid or proposal are not allowable under this section since the engineer is providing technical services but not directly in the preparation, submission or negotiation of a covered Federal action.

(d) Requirements imposed by or pursuant to law as a condition for receiving a covered Federal award include those required by law or regulation, or reasonably expected to be required by law or regulation, and any other requirements in the actual award documents.

(e) Persons other than officers or employees of a person requesting or receiving a covered Federal action include consultants and trade associations.

(f) Only those services expressly authorized by this section are allowable under this section.

Subpart D—Penalties and Enforcement

§ 1158.400 Penalties.

(a) Any person who makes an expenditure prohibited herein shall be subject to a civil penalty of not less than $19,246 and not more than $192,459 for each such expenditure.

(b) Any person who fails to file or amend the disclosure form (see appendix B) to be filed or amended if required herein, shall be subject to a civil penalty of not less than $19,246 and not more than $192,459 for each such failure.

(c) A filing or amended filing on or after the date on which an administrative action for the imposition of a civil penalty is commenced does not prevent the imposition of such civil penalty for a failure occurring before that date. An administrative action is commenced with respect to a failure when an investigating official determines in writing to commence an investigation of an allegation of such failure.

(d) In determining whether to impose a civil penalty, and the amount of any such penalty, by reason of a violation by any person, the agency shall consider the nature, circumstances, extent, and gravity of the violation, the effect on the ability of such person to continue in business, any prior violations by such person, the degree of culpability of such person, the ability of the person to pay the penalty, and such other matters as may be appropriate.

(e) First offenders under paragraph (a) or (b) of this section shall be subject to a civil penalty of $10,000, absent aggravating circumstances. Second and subsequent offenses by persons shall be subject to an appropriate civil penalty between $10,000 and $100,000, as determined by the agency head or his or her designee.

(f) An imposition of a civil penalty under this section does not prevent the United States from seeking any other remedy that may apply to the same conduct that is the basis for the imposition of such civil penalty.

[55 FR 6737, 6755, Feb. 26, 1990, as amended at 82 FR 27434, June 15, 2017]

§ 1158.405 Penalty procedures.

Agencies shall impose and collect civil penalties pursuant to the provisions of the Program Fraud and Civil Remedies Act, 31 U.S.C. sections 3803 (except subsection (c)), 3804, 3805, 3806, 3807, 3808, and 3812, insofar as these provisions are not inconsistent with the requirements herein.

§ 1158.410 Enforcement.

The head of each agency shall take such actions as are necessary to ensure that the provisions herein are vigorously implemented and enforced in that agency.

Subpart E—Exemptions

§ 1158.500 Secretary of Defense.

(a) The Secretary of Defense may exempt, on a case-by-case basis, a covered Federal action from the prohibition whenever the Secretary determines, in writing, that such an exemption is in the national interest. The Secretary shall transmit a copy of each such written exemption to Congress immediately after making such a determination.

(b) The Department of Defense may issue supplemental regulations to implement paragraph (a) of this section.

Subpart F—Agency Reports

§ 1158.600 Semi-annual compilation.

(a) The head of each agency shall collect and compile the disclosure reports (see appendix B) and, on May 31 and November 30 of each year, submit to the Secretary of the Senate and the Clerk of the House of Representatives a report containing a compilation of the information contained in the disclosure reports received during the six-month period ending on March 31 or September 30, respectively, of that year.

(b) The report, including the compilation, shall be available for public inspection 30 days after receipt of the report by the Secretary and the Clerk.

(c) Information that involves intelligence matters shall be reported only to the Select Committee on Intelligence of the Senate, the Permanent Select Committee on Intelligence of the House of Representatives, and the Committees on Appropriations of the Senate and the House of Representatives in accordance with procedures agreed to by such committees. Such information shall not be available for public inspection.

(d) Information that is classified under Executive Order 12356 or any successor order shall be reported only to the Committee on Foreign Relations of the Senate and the Committee on Foreign Affairs of the House of Representatives or the Committees on Armed Services of the Senate and the House of Representatives (whichever such committees have jurisdiction of matters involving such information) and to the Committees on Appropriations of the Senate and the House of Representatives in accordance with procedures agreed to by such committees. Such information shall not be available for public inspection.

(e) The first semi-annual compilation shall be submitted on May 31, 1990, and shall contain a compilation of the disclosure reports received from December 23, 1989 to March 31, 1990.

(f) Major agencies, designated by the Office of Management and Budget (OMB), are required to provide machine-readable compilations to the Secretary of the Senate and the Clerk of the House of Representatives no later than with the compilations due on May 31, 1991. OMB shall provide detailed specifications in a memorandum to these agencies.

(g) Non-major agencies are requested to provide machine-readable compilations to the Secretary of the Senate and the Clerk of the House of Representatives.

(h) Agencies shall keep the originals of all disclosure reports in the official files of the agency.

§ 1158.605 Inspector General report.

(a) The Inspector General, or other official as specified in paragraph (b) of this section, of each agency shall prepare and submit to Congress each year, commencing with submission of the President's Budget in 1991, an evaluation of the compliance of that agency with, and the effectiveness of, the requirements herein. The evaluation may include any recommended changes that may be necessary to strengthen or improve the requirements.

(b) In the case of an agency that does not have an Inspector General, the agency official comparable to an Inspector General shall prepare and submit the annual report, or, if there is no such comparable official, the head of the agency shall prepare and submit the annual report.

(c) The annual report shall be submitted at the same time the agency submits its annual budget justifications to Congress.

(d) The annual report shall include the following: All alleged violations relating to the agency's covered Federal actions during the year covered by the report, the actions taken by the head of the agency in the year covered by the report with respect to those alleged violations and alleged violations in previous years, and the amounts of civil penalties imposed by the agency in the year covered by the report.

APPENDIX A TO PART 1158—
CERTIFICATION REGARDING LOBBYING

Certification for Contracts, Grants, Loans, and Cooperative Agreements

The undersigned certifies, to the best of his or her knowledge and belief, that:

(1) No Federal appropriated funds have been paid or will be paid, by or on behalf of the undersigned, to any person for influencing or attempting to influence an officer or employee of an agency, a Member of Congress, an officer or employee of Congress, or an employee of a Member of Congress in connection with the awarding of any Federal contract, the making of any Federal grant, the making of any Federal loan, the entering into of any cooperative agreement, and the extension, continuation, renewal, amendment, or modification of any Federal contract, grant, loan, or cooperative agreement.

(2) If any funds other than Federal appropriated funds have been paid or will be paid to any person for influencing or attempting to influence an officer or employee of any agency, a Member of Congress, an officer or employee of Congress, or an employee of a Member of Congress in connection with this Federal contract, grant, loan, or cooperative agreement, the undersigned shall complete and submit Standard Form-LLL, "Disclosure Form to Report Lobbying," in accordance with its instructions.

(3) The undersigned shall require that the language of this certification be included in the award documents for all subawards at all tiers (including subcontracts, subgrants, and

contracts under grants, loans, and cooperative agreements) and that all subrecipients shall certify and disclose accordingly.

This certification is a material representation of fact upon which reliance was placed when this transaction was made or entered into. Submission of this certification is a prerequisite for making or entering into this transaction imposed by section 1352, title 31, U.S. Code. Any person who fails to file the required certification shall be subject to a civil penalty of not less than $19,246 and not more than $192,459 for each such failure.

Statement for Loan Guarantees and Loan Insurance

The undersigned states, to the best of his or her knowledge and belief, that:

If any funds have been paid or will be paid to any person for influencing or attempting to influence an officer or employee of any agency, a Member of Congress, an officer or employee of Congress, or an employee of a Member of Congress in connection with this commitment providing for the United States to insure or guarantee a loan, the undersigned shall complete and submit Standard Form-LLL, "Disclosure Form to Report Lobbying," in accordance with its instructions.

Submission of this statement is a prerequisite for making or entering into this transaction imposed by section 1352, title 31, U.S. Code. Any person who fails to file the required statement shall be subject to a civil penalty of not less than $19,246 and not more than $192,459 for each such failure.

[55 FR 6737, 6755, Feb. 26, 1990, as amended at 82 FR 27434, June 15, 2017]

Pt. 1158, App. B 45 CFR Ch. XI (10-1-17 Edition)

APPENDIX B TO PART 1158—DISCLOSURE FORM TO REPORT LOBBYING

DISCLOSURE OF LOBBYING ACTIVITIES

Complete this form to disclose lobbying activities pursuant to 31 U.S.C. 1352
(See reverse for public burden disclosure.)

Approved by OMB
0348-0046

1. **Type of Federal Action:**
   - ☐ a. contract
   - b. grant
   - c. cooperative agreement
   - d. loan
   - e. loan guarantee
   - f. loan insurance

2. **Status of Federal Action:**
   - ☐ a. bid/offer/application
   - b. initial award
   - c. post-award

3. **Report Type:**
   - ☐ a. initial filing
   - b. material change

   For Material Change Only:
   year _____ quarter _____
   date of last report _____

4. **Name and Address of Reporting Entity:**
   ☐ Prime   ☐ Subawardee
   Tier _____ , if known:

   Congressional District, if known:

5. **If Reporting Entity in No. 4 is Subawardee, Enter Name and Address of Prime:**

   Congressional District, if known:

6. **Federal Department/Agency:**

7. **Federal Program Name/Description:**

   CFDA Number, if applicable: _____

8. **Federal Action Number**, if known:

9. **Award Amount**, if known:
   $

10. a. **Name and Address of Lobbying Entity**
    (if individual, last name, first name, MI):

    b. **Individuals Performing Services** (including address if different from No. 10a)
    (last name, first name, MI):

    (attach Continuation Sheet(s) SF-LLL-A, if necessary)

11. **Amount of Payment** (check all that apply):
    $ _____ ☐ actual ☐ planned

12. **Form of Payment** (check all that apply):
    ☐ a. cash
    ☐ b. in-kind; specify: nature _____
    value _____

13. **Type of Payment** (check all that apply):
    ☐ a. retainer
    ☐ b. one-time fee
    ☐ c. commission
    ☐ d. contingent fee
    ☐ e. deferred
    ☐ f. other; specify: _____

14. **Brief Description of Services Performed or to be Performed and Date(s) of Service, including officer(s), employee(s), or Member(s) contacted, for Payment Indicated in Item 11:**

    (attach Continuation Sheet(s) SF-LLL-A, if necessary)

15. **Continuation Sheet(s) SF-LLL-A attached:**   ☐ Yes   ☐ No

16. Information requested through this form is authorized by title 31 U.S.C. section 1352. This disclosure of lobbying activities is a material representation of fact upon which reliance was placed by the tier above when this transaction was made or entered into. This disclosure is required pursuant to 31 U.S.C. 1352. This information will be reported to the Congress semi-annually and will be available for public inspection. Any person who fails to file the required disclosure shall be subject to a civil penalty of not less than $10,000 and not more than $100,000 for each such failure.

Signature: _____
Print Name: _____
Title: _____
Telephone No.: _____ Date: _____

Federal Use Only:

Authorized for Local Reproduction
Standard Form - LLL

National Foundation on the Arts and the Humanities   Pt. 1158, App. B

INSTRUCTIONS FOR COMPLETION OF SF-LLL, DISCLOSURE OF LOBBYING ACTIVITIES

This disclosure form shall be completed by the reporting entity, whether subawardee or prime Federal recipient, at the initiation or receipt of a covered Federal action, or a material change to a previous filing, pursuant to title 31 U.S.C. section 1352. The filing of a form is required for each payment or agreement to make payment to any lobbying entity for influencing or attempting to influence an officer or employee of any agency, a Member of Congress, an officer or employee of Congress, or an employee of a Member of Congress in connection with a covered Federal action. Use the SF-LLL-A Continuation Sheet for additional information if the space on the form is inadequate. Complete all items that apply for both the initial filing and material change report. Refer to the implementing guidance published by the Office of Management and Budget for additional information.

1. Identify the type of covered Federal action for which lobbying activity is and/or has been secured to influence the outcome of a covered Federal action.

2. Identify the status of the covered Federal action.

3. Identify the appropriate classification of this report. If this is a followup report caused by a material change to the information previously reported, enter the year and quarter in which the change occurred. Enter the date of the last previously submitted report by this reporting entity for this covered Federal action.

4. Enter the full name, address, city, state and zip code of the reporting entity. Include Congressional District, if known. Check the appropriate classification of the reporting entity that designates if it is, or expects to be, a prime or subaward recipient. Identify the tier of the subawardee, e.g., the first subawardee of the prime is the 1st tier. Subawards include but are not limited to subcontracts, subgrants and contract awards under grants.

5. If the organization filing the report in item 4 checks "Subawardee", then enter the full name, address, city, state and zip code of the prime Federal recipient. Include Congressional District, if known.

6. Enter the name of the Federal agency making the award or loan commitment. Include at least one organizational level below agency name, if known. For example, Department of Transportation, United States Coast Guard.

7. Enter the Federal program name or description for the covered Federal action (item 1). If known, enter the full Catalog of Federal Domestic Assistance (CFDA) number for grants, cooperative agreements, loans, and loan commitments.

8. Enter the most appropriate Federal identifying number available for the Federal action identified in item 1 (e.g., Request for Proposal (RFP) number; Invitation for Bid (IFB) number; grant announcement number; the contract, grant, or loan award number; the application/proposal control number assigned by the Federal agency). Include prefixes, e.g., "RFP-DE-90-001."

9. For a covered Federal action where there has been an award or loan commitment by the Federal agency, enter the Federal amount of the award/loan commitment for the prime entity identified in item 4 or 5.

10. (a) Enter the full name, address, city, state and zip code of the lobbying entity engaged by the reporting entity identified in item 4 to influence the covered Federal action.

    (b) Enter the full names of the individual(s) performing services, and include full address if different from 10 (a). Enter Last Name, First Name, and Middle Initial (MI).

11. Enter the amount of compensation paid or reasonably expected to be paid by the reporting entity (item 4) to the lobbying entity (item 10). Indicate whether the payment has been made (actual) or will be made (planned). Check all boxes that apply. If this is a material change report, enter the cumulative amount of payment made or planned to be made.

12. Check the appropriate box(es). Check all boxes that apply. If payment is made through an in-kind contribution, specify the nature and value of the in-kind payment.

13. Check the appropriate box(es). Check all boxes that apply. If other, specify nature.

14. Provide a specific and detailed description of the services that the lobbyist has performed, or will be expected to perform, and the date(s) of any services rendered. Include all preparatory and related activity, not just time spent in actual contact with Federal officials. Identify the Federal official(s) or employee(s) contacted or the officer(s), employee(s), or Member(s) of Congress that were contacted.

15. Check whether or not a SF-LLL-A Continuation Sheet(s) is attached.

16. The certifying official shall sign and date the form, print his/her name, title, and telephone number.

Public reporting burden for this collection of information is estimated to average 30 minutes per response, including time for reviewing instructions, searching existing data sources, gathering and maintaining the data needed, and completing and reviewing the collection of information. Send comments regarding the burden estimate or any other aspect of this collection of information, including suggestions for reducing this burden, to the Office of Management and Budget, Paperwork Reduction Project (0348-0046), Washington, D.C. 20503.

Pt. 1158, App. B   **45 CFR Ch. XI (10-1-17 Edition)**

DISCLOSURE OF LOBBYING ACTIVITIES
CONTINUATION SHEET

Approved by OMB
0348-0046

Reporting Entity: _____ Page _____ of _____

Authorized for Local Reproduction
Standard Form - LLL-A

National Foundation on the Arts and the Humanities § 1159.1

PART 1159—IMPLEMENTATION OF THE PRIVACY ACT OF 1974

Sec.
1159.1 What definitions apply to these regulations?
1159.2 What is the purpose of these regulations?
1159.3 Where should individuals send inquiries about the Endowment's systems of records or implementation of the Privacy Act?
1159.4 How will the public receive notification of the Endowment's systems of records?
1159.5 What government entities will the Endowment notify of proposed changes to its systems of records?
1159.6 What limits exist as to the contents of the Endowment's systems of records?
1159.7 Will the Endowment collect information from me for its records?
1159.8 How can I acquire access to Endowment records pertaining to me?
1159.9 What identification will I need to show when I request access to Endowment records pertaining to me?
1159.10 How can I pursue amendments to or corrections of an Endowment record?
1159.11 How can I appeal a refusal to amend or correct an Endowment record?
1159.12 Will the Endowment charge me fees to locate, review, or copy records?
1159.13 In what other situations will the Endowment disclose its records?
1159.14 Will the Endowment maintain a written account of disclosures made from its systems of records?
1159.15 Who has the responsibility for maintaining adequate technical, physical, and security safeguards to prevent unauthorized disclosure or destruction of manual and automatic record systems?
1159.16 Will the Endowment take steps to ensure that its employees involved with its systems of records are familiar with the requirements and implications of the Privacy Act?
1159.17 Which of the Endowment's systems of records are covered by exemptions in the Privacy Act?
1159.18 What are the penalties for obtaining an Endowment record under false pretenses?
1159.19 What restrictions exist regarding the release of mailing lists?

AUTHORITY: 5 U.S.C. 552a(f).

SOURCE: 65 FR 46371, July 28, 2000, unless otherwise noted.

§ 1159.1 What definitions apply to these regulations?

The definitions of the Privacy Act apply to this part. In addition, as used in this part:

(a) *Agency* means any executive department, military department, government corporation, or other establishment in the executive branch of the Federal government, including the Executive Office of the President or any independent regulatory agency.

(b) *Business day* means a calendar day, excluding Saturdays, Sundays, and legal public holidays.

(c) *Chairperson* means the Chairperson of the Endowment, or his or her designee;

(d) *Endowment* means the National Endowment for the Arts;

(e) *Endowment* system means a system of records maintained by the Endowment;

(f) *General Counsel* means the General Counsel of the Endowment, or his or her designee.

(g) *Individual* means any citizen of the United States or an alien lawfully admitted for permanent residence;

(h) *Maintain* means to collect, use, store, or disseminate records, as well as any combination of these recordkeeping functions. The term also includes exercise of control over and, therefore, responsibility and accountability for, systems of records;

(i) *Privacy Act* means the Privacy Act of 1974, as amended (5 U.S.C. 552a);

(j) *Record* means any item, collection, or grouping of information about an individual that is maintained by an agency and contains the individual's name or another identifying particular, such as a number or symbol assigned to the individual, or his or her fingerprint, voice print, or photograph. The term includes, but is not limited to, information regarding an individual's education, financial transactions, medical history, and criminal or employment history;

(k) *Routine* use means, with respect to the disclosure of a record, the use of a record for a purpose that is compatible with the purpose for which it was collected;

(l) *Subject individual* means the individual to whom a record pertains. Uses of the terms "I", "you", "me", and

419

§ 1159.2

other references to the reader of the regulations in this part are meant to apply to subject individuals as defined in this paragraph (l); and

(m) *System of records* means a group of records under the control of any agency from which information is retrieved by use of the name of the individual or by some number, symbol, or other identifying particular assigned to the individual.

§ 1159.2 What is the purpose of these regulations?

The regulations in this part set forth the Endowment's procedures under the Privacy Act, as required by 5 U.S.C. 552a(f), with respect to systems of records maintained by the Endowment. These regulations establish procedures by which an individual may exercise the rights granted by the Privacy Act to determine whether an Endowment system contains a record pertaining to him or her; to gain access to such records; and to request correction or amendment of such records. These regulations also set identification requirements, prescribe fees to be charged for copying records, and establish exemptions from certain requirements of the Act for certain Endowment systems or components thereof.

§ 1159.3 Where should individuals send inquiries about the Endowment's systems of records or implementation of the Privacy Act?

Inquiries about the Endowment's systems of records or implementation of the Privacy Act should be sent to the following address: National Endowment for the Arts; Office of the General Counsel; 1100 Pennsylvania Avenue, NW; Room 518; Washington, DC 20506.

§ 1159.4 How will the public receive notification of the Endowment's systems of records?

(a) From time to time, the Endowment shall review its systems of records in the FEDERAL REGISTER, and publish, if necessary, any amendments to those systems of records. Such publication shall not be made for those systems of records maintained by other agencies while in the temporary custody of the Endowment.

(b) At least 30 days prior to publication of information under paragraph (a) of this section, the Endowment shall publish in the FEDERAL REGISTER a notice of its intention to establish any new routine uses of any of its systems of records, thereby providing the public an opportunity to comment on such uses. This notice published by the Endowment shall contain the following:

(1) The name of the system of records for which the routine use is to be established;

(2) The authority for the system;

(3) The purpose for which the record is to be maintained;

(4) The proposed routine use(s);

(5) The purpose of the routine use(s); and

(6) The categories of recipients of such use.

(c) Any request for additions to the routine uses of Endowment systems should be sent to the Office of the General Counsel (see § 1159.3 of this part).

(d) Any individual who wishes to know whether an Endowment system contains a record pertaining to him or her should write to the Office of the General Counsel (see § 1159.3 of this part). Such individuals may also call the Office of the General Counsel at (202) 682–5418 on business days, between the hours of 9 a.m. and 5:30 p.m., to schedule an appointment to make an inquiry in person. In either case, inquiries should be presented in writing and should specifically identify the Endowment systems involved. The Endowment will attempt to respond to an inquiry as to whether a record exists within 10 business days of receiving the inquiry.

§ 1159.5 What government entities will the Endowment notify of proposed changes to its systems of records?

When the Endowment proposes to establish or significantly changes any of its systems of records, it shall provide adequate advance notice of such proposal to the Committee on Government Reform of the House of Representatives, the Committee on Governmental Affairs of the Senate, and the Office of Management and Budget (OMB), in order to permit an evaluation of the probable or potential effect of such proposal on the privacy or other rights of individuals. This report will be submitted in accordance with guidelines provided by the OMB.

§ 1159.6 What limits exist as to the contents of the Endowment's systems of records?

(a) The Endowment shall maintain only such information about an individual as is relevant and necessary to accomplish a purpose of the agency required by statute or by executive order of the President. In addition, the Endowment shall maintain all records that are used in making determinations about any individual with such accuracy, relevance, timeliness, and completeness as is reasonably necessary to ensure fairness to that individual in the making of any determination about him or her. However, the Endowment shall not be required to update retired records.

(b) The Endowment shall not maintain any record about any individual with respect to or describing how such individual exercises rights guaranteed by the First Amendment of the Constitution of the United States, unless expressly authorized by statute or by the subject individual, or unless pertinent to and within the scope of an authorized law enforcement activity.

§ 1159.7 Will the Endowment collect information from me for its records?

The Endowment shall collect information, to the greatest extent practicable, directly from you when the information may result in adverse determinations about your rights, benefits, or privileges under Federal programs. In addition, the Endowment shall inform you of the following, either on the form it uses to collect the information or on a separate form that you can retain, when it asks you to supply information:

(a) The statutory or executive order authority that authorizes the solicitation of the information;

(b) Whether disclosure of such information is mandatory or voluntary;

(c) The principal purpose(s) for which the information is intended to be used;

(d) The routine uses that may be made of the information, as published pursuant to § 1159.4 of this part; and

(e) Any effects on you of not providing all or any part of the required or requested information.

§ 1159.8 How can I acquire access to Endowment records pertaining to me?

The following procedures apply to records that are contained in an Endowment system:

(a) You may request review of records pertaining to you by writing to the Office of the General Counsel (see § 1159.3 of this part). You may also call the Office of the General Counsel at (202) 682–5418 on business days, between the hours of 9 a.m. and 5:30 p.m., to schedule an appointment to make such a request in person. In either case, your request should be presented in writing and should specifically identify the Endowment systems involved.

(b) Access to the record, or to any other information pertaining to you that is contained in the system, shall be provided if the identification requirements of § 1159.9 of this part are satisfied and the record is otherwise determined to be releasable under the Privacy Act and these regulations. The Endowment shall provide you an opportunity to have a copy made of any such record about you. Only one copy of each requested record will be supplied, based on the fee schedule in § 1159.12 of this part.

(c) The Endowment will comply promptly with requests made in person at scheduled appointments, if the requirements of this section are met and the records sought are immediately available. The Endowment will acknowledge mailed requests, or personal requests for documents that are not immediately available, within 10 business days, and the information requested will be provided promptly thereafter.

(d) If you make your request in person at a scheduled appointment, you may, upon your request, be accompanied by a person of your choice to review your record. The Endowment may require that you furnish a written statement authorizing discussion of your record in the accompanying person's presence. A record may be disclosed to a representative chosen by you upon your proper written consent.

(e) Medical or psychological records pertaining to you shall be disclosed to you unless, in the judgment of the Endowment, access to such records might have an adverse effect upon you. When such determination has been made, the Endowment may refuse to disclose such information directly to you. The Endowment will, however, disclose this information to a licensed physician designated by you in writing.

§ 1159.9 What identification will I need to show when I request access to Endowment records pertaining to me?

The Endowment shall require reasonable identification of all individuals who request access to records in an Endowment system to ensure that they are disclosed to the proper person.

(a) The amount of personal identification required will of necessity vary with the sensitivity of the record involved. In general, if you request disclosure in person, you shall be required to show an identification card, such as a driver's license, containing your photograph and sample signature. However, with regard to records in Endowment systems that contain particularly sensitive and/or detailed personal information, the Endowment reserves the right to require additional means of identification as are appropriate under the circumstances. These means include, but are not limited to, requiring you to sign a statement under oath as to your identity, acknowledging that you are aware of the penalties for improper disclosure under the provisions of the Privacy Act.

(b) If you request disclosure by mail, the Endowment will request such information as may be necessary to ensure that you are properly identified. Authorized means to achieve this goal include, but are not limited to, requiring that a mail request include certification that a duly commissioned notary public of any State or territory (or a similar official, if the request is made outside of the United States) received an acknowledgment of identity from you.

(c) If you are unable to provide suitable documentation or identification, the Endowment may require a signed, notarized statement asserting your identity and stipulating that you understand that knowingly or willfully seeking or obtaining access to records about another person under false pretenses is punishable by a fine of up to $5,000.

§ 1159.10 How can I pursue amendments to or corrections of an Endowment record?

(a) You are entitled to request amendments to or corrections of records pertaining to you pursuant to the provisions of the Privacy Act, including 5 U.S.C. 552a(d)(2). Such a request should be made in writing and addressed to the Office of the General Counsel (see § 1159.3 of this part).

(b) Your request for amendments or corrections should specify the following:

(1) The particular record that you are seeking to amend or correct;

(2) The Endowment system from which the record was retrieved;

(3) The precise correction or amendment you desire, preferably in the form of an edited copy of the record reflecting the desired modification; and

(4) Your reasons for requesting amendment or correction of the record.

(c) The Endowment will acknowledge a request for amendment or correction of a record within 10 business days of its receipt, unless the request can be processed and the individual informed of the General Counsel's decision on the request within that 10-day period.

(d) If after receiving and investigating your request, the General Counsel agrees that the record is not accurate, timely, or complete, based on a preponderance of the evidence, then the record will be corrected or amended promptly. The record will be deleted without regard to its accuracy, if the record is not relevant or necessary to accomplish the Endowment function for which the record was provided or is maintained. In either case, you will be informed in writing of the amendment, correction, or deletion. In addition, if accounting was made of prior disclosures of the record, all previous recipients of the record will be informed of the corrective action taken.

(e) If after receiving and investigating your request, the General Counsel does not agree that the record should be amended or corrected, you will be informed promptly in writing of the refusal to amend or correct the record and the reason for this decision. You will also be informed that you may appeal this refusal in accordance with § 1159.11 of this part.

(f) Requests to amend or correct a record governed by the regulations of another agency will be forwarded to such agency for processing, and you will be informed in writing of this referral.

§ 1159.11 How can I appeal a refusal to amend or correct an Endowment record?

(a) You may appeal a refusal to amend or correct a record to the Chairperson. Such appeal must be made in writing within 10 business days of your receipt of the initial refusal to amend or correct your record. Your appeal should be sent to the Office of the General Counsel (see § 1159.3 of this part), should indicate that it is an appeal, and should include the basis for the appeal.

(b) The Chairperson will review your request to amend or correct the record, the General Counsel's refusal, and any other pertinent material relating to the appeal. No hearing will be held.

(c) The Chairperson shall render his or her decision on your appeal within 30 business days of its receipt by the Endowment, unless the Chairperson, for good cause shown, extends the 30-day period. Should the Chairperson extend the appeal period, you will be informed in writing of the extension and the circumstances of the delay.

(d) If the Chairperson determines that the record that is the subject of the appeal should be amended or corrected, the record will be so modified, and you will be informed in writing of the amendment or correction. Where an accounting was made of prior disclosures of the record, all previous recipients of the record will be informed of the corrective action taken.

(e) If your appeal is denied, you will be informed in writing of the following:

(1) The denial and the reasons for the denial;

(2) That you may submit to the Endowment a concise statement setting forth the reasons for your disagreement as to the disputed record. Under the procedures set forth in paragraph (f) of this section, your statement will be disclosed whenever the disputed record is disclosed; and

(3) That you may seek judicial review of the Chairperson's determination under 5 U.S.C. 552a(g)(1)(a).

(f) Whenever you submit a statement of disagreement to the Endowment in accordance with paragraph (e)(2) of this section, the record will be annotated to indicate that it is disputed. In any subsequent disclosure, a copy of your statement of disagreement will be disclosed with the record. If the Endowment deems it appropriate, a concise statement of the Chairperson's reasons for denying your appeal may also be disclosed with the record. While you will have access to this statement of the Chairperson's reasons for denying your appeal, such statement will not be subject to correction or amendment. Where an accounting was made of prior disclosures of the record, all previous recipients of the record will be provided a copy of your statement of disagreement, as well as any statement of the Chairperson's reasons for denying your appeal.

§ 1159.12 Will the Endowment charge me fees to locate, review, or copy records?

(a) The Endowment shall charge no fees for search time or for any other time expended by the Endowment to review a record. However, the Endowment may charge fees where you request that a copy be made of a record to which you have been granted access. Where a copy of the record must be made in order to provide access to the record (e.g., computer printout where no screen reading is available), the copy will be made available to you without cost.

(b) Copies of records made by photocopy or similar process will be charged to you at the rate of $0.10 per page. Where records are not susceptible to photocopying (e.g., punch cards, magnetic tapes, or oversize materials), you will be charged actual cost as determined on a case-by-case basis. A copying fee totaling $3.00 or less shall be

§ 1159.13

waived, but the copying fees for contemporaneous requests by the same individual shall be aggregated to determine the total fee.

(c) Special and additional services provided at your request, such as certification or authentication, postal insurance, and special mailing arrangement costs, will be charged to you.

(d) A copying fee shall not be charged or, alternatively, it may be reduced, when the General Counsel determines, based on a petition, that the petitioning individual is indigent and that the Endowment's resources permit a waiver of all or part of the fee.

(e) All fees shall be paid before any copying request is undertaken. Payments shall be made by check or money order payable to the "National Endowment for the Arts."

§ 1159.13 In what other situations will the Endowment disclose its records?

(a) The Endowment shall not disclose any record that is contained in a system of records to any person or to another agency, except pursuant to a written request by or with the prior written consent of the subject individual, unless disclosure of the record is:

(1) To those officers or employees of the Endowment who maintain the record and who have a need for the record in the performance of their official duties;

(2) Required under the provisions of the Freedom of Information Act (5 U.S.C. 552). Records required to be made available by the Freedom of Information Act will be released in response to a request to the Endowment formulated in accordance with the National Foundation on the Arts and the Humanities regulations published at 45 CFR part 1100;

(3) For a routine use as published in the annual notice in the FEDERAL REGISTER;

(4) To the Census Bureau for purposes of planning or carrying out a census, survey, or related activity pursuant to the provisions of Title 13 of the United States Code;

(5) To a recipient who has provided the Endowment with adequate advance written assurance that the record will be used solely as a statistical research or reporting record, and the record is to be transferred in a form that is not individually identifiable;

(6) To the National Archives and Records Administration as a record that has sufficient historical or other value to warrant its continued preservation by the United States government, or for evaluation by the Archivist of the United States, or his or her designee, to determine whether the record has such value;

(7) To another agency or to an instrumentality of any governmental jurisdiction within or under the control of the United States for a civil or criminal law enforcement activity, if the activity is authorized by law, and if the head of the agency or instrumentality has made a written request to the Endowment for such records specifying the particular portion desired and the law enforcement activity for which the record is sought. The Endowment may also disclose such a record to a law enforcement agency on its own initiative in situations in which criminal conduct is suspected, provided that such disclosure has been established as a routine use, or in situations in which the misconduct is directly related to the purpose for which the record is maintained;

(8) To a person pursuant to a showing of compelling circumstances affecting the health or safety of an individual if, upon such disclosure, notification is transmitted to the last known address of such individual;

(9) To either House of Congress, or, to the extent of matter within its jurisdiction, any committee or subcommittee thereof, any joint committee of Congress, or subcommittee of any such joint committee;

(10) To the Comptroller General, or any of his or her authorized representatives, in the course of the performance of official duties of the General Accounting Office;

(11) To a consumer reporting agency in accordance with 31 U.S.C. 3711(e); or

(12) Pursuant to an order of a court of competent jurisdiction. In the event that any record is disclosed under such compulsory legal process, the Endowment shall make reasonable efforts to notify the subject individual after the

National Foundation on the Arts and the Humanities § 1159.15

process becomes a matter of public record.

(b) Before disseminating any record about any individual to any person other than an Endowment employee, the Endowment shall make reasonable efforts to ensure that such records are, or at the time they were collected were, accurate, complete, timely, and relevant for Endowment purposes. This paragraph (b) does not apply to disseminations made pursuant to the provisions of the Freedom of Information Act (5 U.S.C. 552) and paragraph (a)(2) of this section.

§ 1159.14 Will the Endowment maintain a written account of disclosures made from its systems of records?

(a) The Office of the General Counsel shall maintain a written log containing the date, nature, and purpose of each disclosure of a record to any person or to another agency. Such accounting shall also contain the name and address of the person or agency to whom each disclosure was made. This log need not include disclosures made to Endowment employees in the course of their official duties, or pursuant to the provisions of the Freedom of Information Act (5 U.S.C. 552).

(b) The Endowment shall retain the accounting of each disclosure for at least five years after the accounting is made or for the life of the record that was disclosed, whichever is longer.

(c) The Endowment shall make the accounting of disclosures of a record pertaining to you available to you at your request. Such a request should be made in accordance with the procedures set forth in § 1159.8 of this part. This paragraph (c) does not apply to disclosures made for law enforcement purposes under 5 U.S.C. 552a(b)(7) and § 1159.13(a)(7) of this part.

§ 1159.15 Who has the responsibility for maintaining adequate technical, physical, and security safeguards to prevent unauthorized disclosure or destruction of manual and automatic record systems?

The Deputy Chairman for Management and Budget has the responsibility of maintaining adequate technical, physical, and security safeguards to prevent unauthorized disclosure or destruction of manual and automatic record systems. These security safeguards shall apply to all systems in which identifiable personal data are processed or maintained, including all reports and outputs from such systems that contain identifiable personal information. Such safeguards must be sufficient to prevent negligent, accidental, or unintentional disclosure, modification or destruction of any personal records or data, and must furthermore minimize, to the extent practicable, the risk that skilled technicians or knowledgeable persons could improperly obtain access to modify or destroy such records or data and shall further insure against such casual entry by unskilled persons without official reasons for access to such records or data.

(a) *Manual systems.* (1) Records contained in a system of records as defined herein may be used, held or stored only where facilities are adequate to prevent unauthorized access by persons within or outside the Endowment.

(2) All records, when not under the personal control of the employees authorized to use the records, must be stored in a locked metal filing cabinet. Some systems of records are not of such confidential nature that their disclosure would constitute a harm to an individual who is the subject of such record. However, records in this category shall also be maintained in locked metal filing cabinets or maintained in a secured room with a locking door.

(3) Access to and use of a system of records shall be permitted only to persons whose duties require such access within the Endowment, for routine uses as defined in § 1159.1 as to any given system, or for such other uses as may be provided herein.

(4) Other than for access within the Endowment to persons needing such records in the performance of their official duties or routine uses as defined in § 1159.1, or such other uses as provided herein, access to records within a system of records shall be permitted only to the individual to whom the record pertains or upon his or her written request to the General Counsel.

(5) Access to areas where a system of records is stored will be limited to

§ 1159.16

those persons whose duties require work in such areas. There shall be an accounting of the removal of any records from such storage areas utilizing a written log, as directed by the Deputy Chairman for Management and Budget. The written log shall be maintained at all times.

(6) The Endowment shall ensure that all persons whose duties require access to and use of records contained in a system of records are adequately trained to protect the security and privacy of such records.

(7) The disposal and destruction of records within a system of records shall be in accordance with rules promulgated by the General Services Administration.

(b) *Automated systems.* (1) Identifiable personal information may be processed, stored or maintained by automated data systems only where facilities or conditions are adequate to prevent unauthorized access to such systems in any form. Whenever such data, whether contained in punch cards, magnetic tapes or discs, are not under the personal control of an authorized person, such information must be stored in a locked or secured room, or in such other facility having greater safeguards than those provided for herein.

(2) Access to and use of identifiable personal data associated with automated data systems shall be limited to those persons whose duties require such access. Proper control of personal data in any form associated with automated data systems shall be maintained at all times, including maintenance of accountability records showing disposition of input and output documents.

(3) All persons whose duties require access to processing and maintenance of identifiable personal data and automated systems shall be adequately trained in the security and privacy of personal data.

(4) The disposal and disposition of identifiable personal data and automated systems shall be done by shredding, burning or in the case of tapes or discs, degaussing, in accordance with any regulations now or hereafter proposed by the General Services Administration or other appropriate authority.

§ 1159.16 Will the Endowment take steps to ensure that its employees involved with its systems of records are familiar with the requirements and implications of the Privacy Act?

(a) The Chairperson shall ensure that all persons involved in the design, development, operation or maintenance of any Endowment system are informed of all requirements necessary to protect the privacy of subject individuals. The Chairperson shall also ensure that all Endowment employees having access to records receive adequate training in their protection, and that records have adequate and proper storage with sufficient security to assure the privacy of such records.

(b) All employees shall be informed of the civil remedies provided under 5 U.S.C. 552a(g)(1) and other implications of the Privacy Act, and the fact that the Endowment may be subject to civil remedies for failure to comply with the provisions of the Privacy Act and these regulations.

§ 1159.17 Which of the Endowment's systems of records are covered by exemptions in the Privacy Act?

(a) Pursuant to and limited by 5 U.S.C. 552a(j)(2), the Endowment system entitled "Office of the Inspector General Investigative Files" shall be exempted from the provisions of 5 U.S.C. 552a, except for subsections (b); (c)(1) and (2); (e)(4)(A) through (F); (e)(6), (7), (9), (10), and (11); and (i), insofar as that Endowment system contains information pertaining to criminal law enforcement investigations.

(b) Pursuant to and limited by 5 U.S.C. 552a(k)(2), the Endowment system entitled "Office of the Inspector General Investigative Files" shall be exempted from 5 U.S.C. 552a(c)(3); (d); (e)(1); (e)(4)(G), (H), and (I); and (f), insofar as that Endowment system consists of investigatory material compiled for law enforcement purposes, other than material within the scope of the exemption at 5 U.S.C. 552a(j)(2).

(c) The Endowment system entitled "Office of the Inspector General Investigative Files" is exempt from the above-noted provisions of the Privacy Act because their application might alert investigation subjects to the existence or scope of investigations; lead to suppression, alteration, fabrication, or destruction of evidence; disclose investigative techniques or procedures; reduce the cooperativeness or safety of witnesses; or otherwise impair investigations.

§ 1159.18 **What are the penalties for obtaining an Endowment record under false pretenses?**

(a) Under 5 U.S.C. 552a(i)(3), any person who knowingly and willfully requests or obtains any record concerning an individual from the Endowment under false pretenses shall be guilty of a misdemeanor and fined not more than $5,000.

(b) A person who falsely or fraudulently attempts to obtain records under the Privacy Act may also be subject to prosecution under other statutes, including 18 U.S.C. 494, 495, and 1001.

§ 1159.19 **What restrictions exist regarding the release of mailing lists?**

The Endowment may not sell or rent an individual's name and address unless such action is specifically authorized by law. This section shall not be construed to require the withholding of names and addresses otherwise permitted to be made public.

SUBCHAPTER C—FEDERAL COUNCIL ON THE ARTS AND THE HUMANITIES

PART 1160—INDEMNITIES UNDER THE ARTS AND ARTIFACTS INDEMNITY ACT

Sec.
1160.1 Purpose and scope.
1160.2 Federal Council on the Arts and the Humanities.
1160.3 Definitions.
1160.4 Eligibility for international exhibitions.
1160.5 Eligibility for domestic exhibitions.
1160.6 Application for indemnification.
1160.7 Certificate of national interest.
1160.8 Indemnity agreement.
1160.9 Letter of intent.
1160.10 Loss adjustment.
1160.11 Certification of claim and amount of loss to the Congress.
1160.12 Appraisal procedures.
1160.13 Indemnification limits.

AUTHORITY: 20 U.S.C. 971–977.

SOURCE: 56 FR 49848, Oct. 2, 1991, unless otherwise noted.

§ 1160.1 Purpose and scope.

(a) This part sets forth the exhibition indemnity procedures of the Federal Council on the Arts and Humanities under the Arts and Artifacts Indemnity Act (Pub. L. 94–158) as required by section 2(a)(2) of the Act.
(1) Eligible items from outside the United States while on exhibition in the United States or
(2) Eligible items from the United States while on exhibition outside this country, preferably when they are part of an exchange of exhibitions.

(b) Program guidelines and further information are available from the Indemnity Administrator, c/o Museum Program, National Endowment for the Arts, 1100 Pennsylvania Avenue, NW., Washington, DC 20506.

[56 FR 49848, Oct. 2, 1991, as amended at 60 FR 42465, Aug. 16, 1995]

§ 1160.2 Federal Council on the Arts and the Humanities

For the purposes of this part (45 CFR part 1160) the Federal Council on the Arts and the Humanities shall be composed of the Chairman of the National Endowment for the Arts, the Chairman of the National Endowment for the Humanities, the Secretary of Education, the Director of the National Science Foundation, the Librarian of Congress, the Chairman of the Commission of Fine Arts, the Archivist of the United States, the Commissioner, Public Buildings Service, General Services Administration, the Administrator of the General Services Administration, the Director of the United States Information Agency, the Secretary of the Interior, the Secretary of Commerce, the Secretary of Transportation, the Chairman of the National Museum Services Board, the Director of the Institute of Museum and Library Services, the Secretary of Housing and Urban Development, the Secretary of Labor, the Secretary of Veterans Affairs, and the Commissioner of the Administration on Aging.

§ 1160.3 Definitions.

For the purposes of this part:

(a) *Council* means the Federal Council on the Arts and the Humanities as defined in § 1160.2.

(b) *Letter of Intent* means an agreement by the Council to provide an indemnity covering a future exhibition subject to compliance with all requirements at the date the indemnity is to be effective.

(c) *Lender* means the owner of an object.

(d) *Eligible item* means an object which qualifies for coverage under the Arts and Artifacts Indemnity Act.

(e) *Exhibition* means a public display of an indemnified items(s) at one or more locations, as approved by the Council, presented by any person, nonprofit agency or institution, or Government, in the United States or elsewhere.

(f) *On Exhibition* means the period of time beginning on the date an indemnified item leaves the place designated by the lender and ending on the termination date.

(g) *Indemnity Agreement* means the contract between the Council and the indemnitee covering loss or damage to indemnified items under the authority of the Arts and Artifacts Indemnity Act.

(h) *Indemnitee* means the party or parties to an indemnity agreement issued by the Council, to whom the promise of indemnification is made.

(i) *Participating institution(s)* means the location(s) where an exhibition indemnified under this part will be displayed.

(j) *Termination date* means the date thirty (30) calendar days after the date specified in the indemnity Certificate by which an indemnified item is to be returned to the place designated by the lender or the date on which the item is actually so returned, whichever date is earlier. (In museum terms this means wall-to-wall coverage.) After 11:59 p.m. on the termination date, the item is no longer covered by the indemnity agreement unless an extension has theretofore been requested by the indemnitee and granted in writing by the Council.

§ 1160.4 Eligibility for international exhibitions.

An indemnity agreement for an international exhibition made under these regulations shall cover:

(a) Eligible items from outside the United States while on exhibition in the United States;

(b) Eligible items from the United States while on exhibition outside this country, preferably when they are part of an exchange of exhibitions; and

(c) Eligible items from the United States while on exhibition in the United States, in connection with other eligible items from outside the United States which are integral to the exhibition as a whole.

(d)(1) *Example.* An American art museum is organizing a retrospective exhibition which will include more than 150 works of art by Impressionist painter Auguste Renoir. Museums in Paris and London have agreed to lend 125 works of art, covering every aspect of his career, many of which have not been seen together since the artist's death in 1919. The organizer is planning to include 25 masterpieces by Renoir from American public and private collections. The show will open in Chicago and travel to San Francisco and Washington.

(2) *Discussion.* This example is a common application for coverage of both foreign- and domestic-owned objects in an international exhibition. The foreign-owned objects are eligible for indemnity coverage under paragraph (a) of this section, and the domestic-owned objects may be eligible for indemnity coverage under paragraph (c) of this section if the foreign-owned objects are integral to the purposes of the exhibition as a whole. In reviewing this application, the Federal Council would evaluate the exhibition as a whole and determine whether the loans of 125 foreign-owned objects are integral to the educational, cultural, historical, or scientific significance of the exhibition on Renoir. It would also be necessary for the U.S. Department of State to determine whether or not the exhibition was in the national interest.

[73 FR 21056, Apr. 18, 2008]

§ 1160.5 Eligibility for domestic exhibitions.

An indemnity agreement for a domestic exhibition made under these regulations shall cover eligible items from the United States while on Exhibition in the United States.

(a)(1) *Example 1.* An American museum is undergoing renovation and will be closed to the public for one year. During that time, masterpieces from the collection will go on tour to three other museums in the United States. Many of these works have never been lent for travel, and this will be a unique and the last opportunity for museum visitors in other parts of the country to see them exhibited together. Once the new building opens, they will be permanently installed and dispersed throughout the museum's galleries.

(2) *Discussion.* (i) This is a straightforward example of a domestic exhibition which would be eligible for consideration for indemnity coverage. Under the previous regulations, eligibility was limited to:

(A) Exhibitions in the United States of entirely foreign-owned objects;

(B) Exhibitions outside of the United States of domestic-owned objects; or

(C) Exhibitions in the United States of both foreign- and domestic-owned objects, with the foreign-owned objects having integral importance to the exhibition.

(ii) In this example, the Federal Council will consider the educational, cultural, historical, or scientific significance of the proposed domestic exhibition of the domestic-owned objects. It would not be necessary for the U.S. Department of State to determine whether or not the exhibition was in the national interest.

(b)(1) *Example 2.* An American museum is organizing an exhibition of works by 20th century American artists, which will travel to one other U.S. museum. There are more than 100 objects in the exhibition. The majority of the paintings, drawings and sculpture, valued at more than $500,000,000, are from galleries, museums and private collections in the United States. The organizing curator has selected ten works of art, mostly drawings and preparatory sketches relating to paintings in the exhibition, valued at less than $5,000,000, which will be borrowed from foreign lenders.

(2) *Discussion.* (i) This example raises the question of whether this applicant should submit an application for indemnity coverage for a domestic exhibition or an international exhibition. If the applicant submitted an application for an international exhibition requesting coverage for only the foreign-owned objects eligible under Section 1160.4(a), the Federal Council would evaluate whether the ten foreign-owned objects further the exhibition's educational, cultural, historical, or scientific purposes. It would also be necessary for the U.S. Department of State to determine whether or not the exhibition was in the national interest. In this case, the applicant would have to insure the loans of the domestic-owned objects by other means.

(ii) In the case of an application for an international exhibition requesting coverage for both domestic-owned and foreign-owned objects eligible under section 1160.4(a) and (c), the Federal Council would evaluate the exhibition as a whole to determine if the ten foreign-owned objects are integral to achieving the exhibition's educational, cultural, historical, or scientific purposes. It would also be necessary for the U.S. Department of State to determine whether or not the exhibition was in the national interest.

(iii) If the applicant submitted an application for a domestic exhibition, however, only the loans of domestic-owned objects, the highest valued part of the exhibition, would be eligible for coverage. The Federal Council would consider if the U.S. loans were of educational, cultural or historic interest. It would not be necessary for the U.S. Department of State to determine whether or not the exhibition was in the national interest. In this case, the applicant would have to insure the loans of the foreign-owned objects by other means.

[73 FR 21056, Apr. 18, 2008]

§ 1160.6 Application for indemnification.

An applicant for an indemnity shall submit an Application for Indemnification, addressed to the Indemnity Administrator, National Endowment for the Arts, Washington, DC 20506, which shall described as fully as possible:

(a) The time, place, nature and Project Director/Curator of the exhibition for which the indemnity is sought;

(b) Evidence that the owner and present possessor are willing to lend the eligible items, and both are prepared to be bound by the terms of the indemnity agreement;

(c) The total value of all items to be indemnified, including a description of each item to be covered by the agreement and each item's value;

(d) The source of valuations of each item, plus an opinion by a disinterested third party of the valuations established by lenders;

(e) The significance, and the educational, cultural, historical, or scientific value of the items to be indemnified, and of the exhibition as a whole;

(f) Statements describing policies, procedures, techniques, and methods to be employed with respect to:

(1) Packing of items at the premises of, or the place designated by the lender;

(2) Shipping arrangements;

(3) Condition reports at lender's location;

(4) Condition reports at borrower's location;

(5) Condition reports upon return of items to lender's location;

(6) Security during the exhibition and security during transportation, including couriers were applicable;

(7) Maximum values to be transported in a single vehicle of transport.

(g) Insurance arrangements, if any, which are proposed to cover the deductible amount provided by law or the excess over the amount indemnified;

(h) Any loss incurred by the indemnitee or participating institutions during the three years prior to the Application for Indemnification which involved a borrowed or loaned item(s) or item(s) in their permanent collections where the amount of loss or damage exceeded $5,000. Details should include the date of loss, nature and cause of damage, and appraised value of the damaged items(s) both before and after loss;

(i) If the application is for an exhibition of loans from the United States, which are being shown outside the United States, the applicant should describe in detail the nature of the exchange of exhibitions of which it is a part if any, including all circumstances surrounding the exhibition being shown in the United States, with particular emphasis on facts concerning insurance or indemnity arrangements.

(j) Upon proper submission of the above required information an application will be selected or rejected for indemnification by the Council. The review criteria include:

(1) Review of educational, cultural, historical, or scientific value as required under the provisions of the Arts and Artifacts Indemnity Act;

(2) Certification by the Secretary of State or his designee that the international exhibition with eligible items under § 1160.4 is in the national interest; and

(3) Review of the availability of indemnity obligational authority under section 5(b) of the Arts and Artifacts Indemnity Act (20 U.S.C. 974).

(Approved under OMB control number 3135–0094)

[56 FR 49848, Oct. 2, 1991; 56 FR 51842, Oct. 16, 1991. Redesignated at 60 FR 42465, Aug. 16, 1995, and further redesignated and amended at 73 FR 21056, Apr. 18, 2008]

§ 1160.7 Certificate of national interest.

After preliminary review applications for international exhibitions with eligible items under § 1160.4 will be submitted to the Secretary of State or his designee for determination of national interest and issuance of a Certificate of National Interest.

[56 FR 49848, Oct. 2, 1991. Redesignated at 60 FR 42465, Aug. 16, 1995, and further redesignated and amended at 73 FR 21056, Apr. 18, 2008]

§ 1160.8 Indemnity agreement.

In cases where the requirements of §§ 1160.4 and 1160.5 have been met to the satisfaction of the Council, an Indemnity Agreement pledging the full faith and credit of the United States for the agreed value of the exhibition in question may be issued to the indemnitee by the Council, subject to the provisions of § 1160.7.

[56 FR 49848, Oct. 2, 1991. Redesignated at 60 FR 42465, Aug. 16, 1995, and further redesignated at 73 FR 21056, Apr. 18, 2008]

§ 1160.9 Letter of intent.

In cases where an exhibition proposed for indemnification is planned to begin on a date more than twelve (12) months after the submission of the application, the Council, upon approval of such a preliminary application, may provide a Letter of Intent stating that it will, subject to the conditions set forth therein, issue an Indemnity Agreement prior to commencement of the exhibition. In such cases, the Council will examine a final application during the twelve (12) month period prior to the date the exhibition is to commence, and shall, upon being satisfied that such conditions have been fulfilled, issue an Indemnity Agreement.

[56 FR 49848, Oct. 2, 1991. Redesignated at 60 FR 42465, Aug. 16, 1995, and further redesignated at 73 FR 21056, Apr. 18, 2008]

§ 1160.10 Loss adjustment.

(a) In the event of loss or damage covered by an Indemnity Agreement, the indemnitee without delay shall file a Notice of Loss or Damage with the Council and shall exercise reasonable care in order to minimize the amount of loss. Within a reasonable time after

§ 1160.11

a loss has been sustained, the claimant shall file a Proof of Loss or Damage on forms provided by the Council. Failure to report such loss or damage and to file such Proof of Loss within sixty (60) days after the termination date as defined in § 1160.3(k) shall invalidate any claim under the Indemnity Agreement.

(b) In the event of total loss or destruction of an indemnified item, indemnification will be made on the basis of the amount specified in the Indemnity Agreement.

(c) In the event of partial loss, or damage, and reduction in the fair market value, as a result thereof, to an indemnified item, indemnification will be made on the basis provided for in the Indemnity Agreement.

(d) No loss or damage claim will be paid in excess of the Indemnification Limits specified in § 1160.11.

[56 FR 49848, Oct. 2, 1991. Redesignated at 60 FR 42465, Aug. 16, 1995, and further redesignated at 73 FR 21056, Apr. 18, 2008]

§ 1160.11 Certification of claim and amount of loss to the Congress.

Upon receipt of a claim of total loss or a claim in which the Council is in agreement with respect to the amount of partial loss, or damage and reduction in fair market value as a result thereof, the Council shall certify the validity of the claim and the amount of such loss or damage and reduction in fair market value as a result thereof, to the Speaker of the House of Representatives and the President pro tempore of the Senate.

[56 FR 49848, Oct. 2, 1991. Redesignated at 60 FR 42465, Aug. 16, 1995, and further redesignated at 73 FR 21056, Apr. 18, 2008]

§ 1160.12 Appraisal procedures.

(a) In the event the Council and the indemnitee fail to agree on the amount of partial loss, or damage to, or any reduction in the fair market value as a result thereof, to the indemnified item(s), each shall select a competent appraiser(s) with evidence to be provided to show that the indemnitee's selection is satisfactory to the owner. The appraiser(s) selected by the Council and the indemnitee shall then select a competent and disinterested arbitrator.

(b) After selection of an arbitrator, the appraisers shall assess the partial loss, or damage to, or where appropriate, any reduction in the fair market value of, the indemnified item(s). The appraisers' agreement with respect to these issues shall determine the dollar value of such loss or damage or repair costs, and where appropriate, such reduction in the fair market value. Disputes between the appraisers with respect to partial loss, damage repair costs, and fair market value reduction of any item shall be submitted to the arbitrator for determination. The appraisers' agreement or the arbitrator's determination shall be final and binding on the parties, and agreement on amount or such determination on amount shall be certified to the Speaker of the House and the President pro tempore of the Senate by the Council.

(c) Each appraiser shall be paid by the party selecting him or her. The arbitrator and all other expenses of the appraisal shall be paid by the parties in equal shares.

[56 FR 49848, Oct. 2, 1991. Redesignated at 60 FR 42465, Aug. 16, 1995, and further redesignated at 73 FR 21056, Apr. 18, 2008]

§ 1160.13 Indemnification limits.

The dollar amounts of the limits described below are found in the guidelines referred to in § 1160.1 and are based upon the statutory limits in the Arts and Artifacts Indemnity Act (20 U.S.C. 974).

(a) There is a maximum amount of loss or damage covered in a single exhibition or an Indemnity Agreement.

(b) A sliding scale deductible amount is applicable to loss or damage arising out of a single exhibition for which an indemnity is issued.

(c) There is an aggregate amount of loss or damage covered by indemnity agreements at any one time.

(d) The maximum value of eligible items carried in or upon any single instrumentality of transportation at any one time, is established by the Council.

[56 FR 49848, Oct. 2, 1991. Redesignated at 60 FR 42465, Aug. 16, 1995, and further redesignated at 73 FR 21056, Apr. 18, 2008]

SUBCHAPTER D—NATIONAL ENDOWMENT FOR THE HUMANITIES

PART 1168—NEW RESTRICTIONS ON LOBBYING

Subpart A—General

Sec.
1168.100 Conditions on use of funds.
1168.105 Definitions.
1168.110 Certification and disclosure.

Subpart B—Activities by Own Employees

1168.200 Agency and legislative liaison.
1168.205 Professional and technical services.
1168.210 Reporting.

Subpart C—Activities by Other Than Own Employees

1168.300 Professional and technical services.

Subpart D—Penalties and Enforcement

1168.400 Penalties.
1168.405 Penalty procedures.
1168.410 Enforcement.

Subpart E—Exemptions

1168.500 Secretary of Defense.

Subpart F—Agency Reports

1168.600 Semi-annual compilation.
1168.605 Inspector General report.
APPENDIX A TO PART 1168—CERTIFICATION REGARDING LOBBYING
APPENDIX B TO PART 1168—DISCLOSURE FORM TO REPORT LOBBYING

AUTHORITY: Sec. 319, Pub. L. 101-121 (31 U.S.C. 1352); 20 U.S.C. 959 (a) (1).

SOURCE: 55 FR 6737, 6755, Feb. 26, 1990, unless otherwise noted.

CROSS REFERENCE: See also Office of Management and Budget notice published at 54 FR 52306, December 20, 1989.

Subpart A—General

§ 1168.100 Conditions on use of funds.

(a) No appropriated funds may be expended by the recipient of a Federal contract, grant, loan, or cooperative ageement to pay any person for influencing or attempting to influence an officer or employee of any agency, a Member of Congress, an officer or employee of Congress, or an employee of a Member of Congress in connection with any of the following covered Federal actions: the awarding of any Federal contract, the making of any Federal grant, the making of any Federal loan, the entering into of any cooperative agreement, and the extension, continuation, renewal, amendment, or modification of any Federal contract, grant, loan, or cooperative agreement.

(b) Each person who requests or receives from an agency a Federal contract, grant, loan, or cooperative agreement shall file with that agency a certification, set forth in appendix A, that the person has not made, and will not make, any payment prohibited by paragraph (a) of this section.

(c) Each person who requests or receives from an agency a Federal contract, grant, loan, or a cooperative agreement shall file with that agency a disclosure form, set forth in appendix B, if such person has made or has agreed to make any payment using nonappropriated funds (to include profits from any covered Federal action), which would be prohibited under paragraph (a) of this section if paid for with appropriated funds.

(d) Each person who requests or receives from an agency a commitment providing for the United States to insure or guarantee a loan shall file with that agency a statement, set forth in appendix A, whether that person has made or has agreed to make any payment to influence or attempt to influence an officer or employee of any agency, a Member of Congress, an officer or employee of Congress, or an employee of a Member of Congress in connection with that loan insurance or guarantee.

(e) Each person who requests or receives from an agency a commitment providing for the United States to insure or guarantee a loan shall file with that agency a disclosure form, set forth in appendix B, if that person has made or has agreed to make any payment to influence or attempt to influence an officer or employee of any agency, a

§ 1168.105

Member of Congress, an officer or employee of Congress, or an employee of a Member of Congress in connection with that loan insurance or guarantee.

§ 1168.105 Definitions.

For purposes of this part:

(a) *Agency,* as defined in 5 U.S.C. 552(f), includes Federal executive departments and agencies as well as independent regulatory commissions and Government corporations, as defined in 31 U.S.C. 9101(1).

(b) *Covered Federal action* means any of the following Federal actions:

(1) The awarding of any Federal contract;

(2) The making of any Federal grant;

(3) The making of any Federal loan;

(4) The entering into of any cooperative agreement; and,

(5) The extension, continuation, renewal, amendment, or modification of any Federal contract, grant, loan, or cooperative agreement.

Covered Federal action does not include receiving from an agency a commitment providing for the United States to insure or guarantee a loan. Loan guarantees and loan insurance are addressed independently within this part.

(c) *Federal contract* means an acquisition contract awarded by an agency, including those subject to the Federal Acquisition Regulation (FAR), and any other acquisition contract for real or personal property or services not subject to the FAR.

(d) *Federal cooperative agreement* means a cooperative agreement entered into by an agency.

(e) *Federal grant* means an award of financial assistance in the form of money, or property in lieu of money, by the Federal Government or a direct appropriation made by law to any person. The term does not include technical assistance which provides services instead of money, or other assistance in the form of revenue sharing, loans, loan guarantees, loan insurance, interest subsidies, insurance, or direct United States cash assistance to an individual.

(f) *Federal loan* means a loan made by an agency. The term does not include loan guarantee or loan insurance.

(g) *Indian tribe* and *tribal organization* have the meaning provided in section 4 of the Indian Self-Determination and Education Assistance Act (25 U.S.C. 450B). Alaskan Natives are included under the definitions of Indian tribes in that Act.

(h) *Influencing or attempting to influence* means making, with the intent to influence, any communication to or appearance before an officer or employee or any agency, a Member of Congress, an officer or employee of Congress, or an employee of a Member of Congress in connection with any covered Federal action.

(i) *Loan guarantee* and *loan insurance* means an agency's guarantee or insurance of a loan made by a person.

(j) *Local government* means a unit of government in a State and, if chartered, established, or otherwise recognized by a State for the performance of a governmental duty, including a local public authority, a special district, an intrastate district, a council of governments, a sponsor group representative organization, and any other instrumentality of a local government.

(k) *Officer or employee of an agency* includes the following individuals who are employed by an agency:

(1) An individual who is appointed to a position in the Government under title 5, U.S. Code, including a position under a temporary appointment;

(2) A member of the uniformed services as defined in section 101(3), title 37, U.S. Code;

(3) A special Government employee as defined in section 202, title 18, U.S. Code; and,

(4) An individual who is a member of a Federal advisory committee, as defined by the Federal Advisory Committee Act, title 5, U.S. Code appendix 2.

(l) *Person* means an individual, corporation, company, association, authority, firm, partnership, society, State, and local government, regardless of whether such entity is operated for profit or not for profit. This term excludes an Indian tribe, tribal organization, or any other Indian organization with respect to expenditures specifically permitted by other Federal law.

National Foundation on the Arts and the Humanities § 1168.110

(m) *Reasonable compensation* means, with respect to a regularly employed officer or employee of any person, compensation that is consistent with the normal compensation for such officer or employee for work that is not furnished to, not funded by, or not furnished in cooperation with the Federal Government.

(n) *Reasonable payment* means, with respect to perfessional and other technical services, a payment in an amount that is consistent with the amount normally paid for such services in the private sector.

(o) *Recipient* includes all contractors, subcontractors at any tier, and subgrantees at any tier of the recipient of funds received in connection with a Federal contract, grant, loan, or cooperative agreement. The term excludes an Indian tribe, tribal organization, or any other Indian organization with respect to expenditures specifically permitted by other Federal law.

(p) *Regularly employed* means, with respect to an officer or employee of a person requesting or receiving a Federal contract, grant, loan, or cooperative agreement or a commitment providing for the United States to insure or guarantee a loan, an officer or employee who is employed by such person for at least 130 working days within one year immediately preceding the date of the submission that initiates agency consideration of such person for receipt of such contract, grant, loan, cooperative agreement, loan insurance commitment, or loan guarantee commitment. An officer or employee who is employed by such person for less than 130 working days within one year immediately preceding the date of the submission that initiates agency consideration of such person shall be considered to be regularly employed as soon as he or she is employed by such person for 130 working days.

(q) *State* means a State of the United States, the District of Columbia, the Commonwealth of Puerto Rico, a territory or possession of the United States, an agency or instrumentality of a State, and a multi-State, regional, or interstate entity having governmental duties and powers.

§ 1168.110 Certification and disclosure.

(a) Each person shall file a certification, and a disclosure form, if required, with each submission that initiates agency consideration of such person for:

(1) Award of a Federal contract, grant, or cooperative agreement exceeding $100,000; or

(2) An award of a Federal loan or a commitment providing for the United States to insure or guarantee a loan exceeding $150,000.

(b) Each person shall file a certification, and a disclosure form, if required, upon receipt by such person of:

(1) A Federal contract, grant, or cooperative agreement exceeding $100,000; or

(2) A Federal loan or a commitment providing for the United States to insure or guarantee a loan exceeding $150,000,

unless such person previously filed a certification, and a disclosure form, if required, under paragraph (a) of this section.

(c) Each person shall file a disclosure form at the end of each calendar quarter in which there occurs any event that requires disclosure or that materially affects the accuracy of the information contained in any disclosure form previously filed by such person under paragraph (a) or (b) of this section. An event that materially affects the accuracy of the information reported includes:

(1) A cumulative increase of $25,000 or more in the amount paid or expected to be paid for influencing or attempting to influence a covered Federal action; or

(2) A change in the person(s) or individual(s) influencing or attempting to influence a covered Federal action; or,

(3) A change in the officer(s), employee(s), or Member(s) contacted to influence or attempt to influence a covered Federal action.

(d) Any person who requests or receives from a person referred to in paragraph (a) or (b) of this section:

(1) A subcontract exceeding $100,000 at any tier under a Federal contract;

(2) A subgrant, contract, or subcontract exceeding $100,000 at any tier under a Federal grant;

§ 1168.200

(3) A contract or subcontract exceeding $100,000 at any tier under a Federal loan exceeding $150,000; or,

(4) A contract or subcontract exceeding $100,000 at any tier under a Federal cooperative agreement,

shall file a certification, and a disclosure form, if required, to the next tier above.

(e) All disclosure forms, but not certifications, shall be forwarded from tier to tier until received by the person referred to in paragraph (a) or (b) of this section. That person shall forward all disclosure forms to the agency.

(f) Any certification or disclosure form filed under paragraph (e) of this section shall be treated as a material representation of fact upon which all receiving tiers shall rely. All liability arising from an erroneous representation shall be borne solely by the tier filing that representation and shall not be shared by any tier to which the erroneous representation is forwarded. Submitting an erroneous certification or disclosure constitutes a failure to file the required certification or disclosure, respectively. If a person fails to file a required certification or disclosure, the United States may pursue all available remedies, including those authorized by section 1352, title 31, U.S. Code.

(g) For awards and commitments in process prior to December 23, 1989, but not made before that date, certifications shall be required at award or commitment, covering activities occurring between December 23, 1989, and the date of award or commitment. However, for awards and commitments in process prior to the December 23, 1989 effective date of these provisions, but not made before December 23, 1989, disclosure forms shall not be required at time of award or commitment but shall be filed within 30 days.

(h) No reporting is required for an activity paid for with appropriated funds if that activity is allowable under either subpart B or C.

Subpart B—Activities by Own Employees

§ 1168.200 Agency and legislative liaison.

(a) The prohibition on the use of appropriated funds, in § 1168.100 (a), does not apply in the case of a payment of reasonable compensation made to an officer or employee of a person requesting or receiving a Federal contract, grant, loan, or cooperative agreement if the payment is for agency and legislative liaison activities not directly related to a covered Federal action.

(b) For purposes of paragraph (a) of this section, providing any information specifically requested by an agency or Congress is allowable at any time.

(c) For purposes of paragraph (a) of this section, the following agency and legislative liaison activities are allowable at any time only where they are not related to a specific solicitation for any covered Federal action:

(1) Discussing with an agency (including individual demonstrations) the qualities and characteristics of the person's products or services, conditions or terms of sale, and service capabilities; and,

(2) Technical discussions and other activities regarding the application or adaptation of the person's products or services for an agency's use.

(d) For purposes of paragraph (a) of this section, the following agencies and legislative liaison activities are allowable only where they are prior to formal solicitation of any covered Federal action:

(1) Providing any information not specifically requested but necessary for an agency to make an informed decision about initiation of a covered Federal action;

(2) Technical discussions regarding the preparation of an unsolicited proposal prior to its official submission; and,

(3) Capability presentations by persons seeking awards from an agency pursuant to the provisions of the Small Business Act, as amended by Pub. L. 95–507 and other subsequent amendments.

(e) Only those activities expressly authorized by this section are allowable under this section.

§ 1168.205 Professional and technical services.

(a) The prohibition on the use of appropriated funds, in § 1168.100 (a), does not apply in the case of a payment of reasonable compensation made to an officer or employee of a person requesting or receiving a Federal contract, grant, loan, or cooperative agreement or an extension, continuation, renewal, amendment, or modification of a Federal contract, grant, loan, or cooperative agreement if payment is for professional or technical services rendered directly in the preparation, submission, or negotiation of any bid, proposal, or application for that Federal contract, grant, loan, or cooperative agreement or for meeting requirements imposed by or pursuant to law as a condition for receiving that Federal contract, grant, loan, or cooperative agreement.

(b) For purposes of paragraph (a) of this section, "professional and technical services" shall be limited to advice and analysis directly applying any professional or technical discipline. For example, drafting of a legal document accompanying a bid or proposal by a lawyer is allowable. Similarly, technical advice provided by an engineer on the performance or operational capability of a piece of equipment rendered directly in the negotiation of a contract is allowable. However, communications with the intent to influence made by a professional (such as a licensed lawyer) or a technical person (such as a licensed accountant) are not allowable under this section unless they provide advice and analysis directly applying their professional or technical expertise and unless the advice or analysis is rendered directly and solely in the preparation, submission or negotiation of a covered Federal action. Thus, for example, communications with the intent to influence made by a lawyer that do not provide legal advice or analysis directly and solely related to the legal aspects of his or her client's proposal, but generally advocate one proposal over another are not allowable under this section because the lawyer is not providing professional legal services. Similarly, communications with the intent to influence made by an engineer providing an engineering analysis prior to the preparation or submission of a bid or proposal are not allowable under this section since the engineer is providing technical services but not directly in the preparation, submission or negotiation of a covered Federal action.

(c) Requirements imposed by or pursuant to law as a condition for receiving a covered Federal award include those required by law or regulation, or reasonably expected to be required by law or regulation, and any other requirements in the actual award documents.

(d) Only those services expressly authorized by this section are allowable under this section.

§ 1168.210 Reporting.

No reporting is required with respect to payments of reasonable compensation made to regularly employed officers or employees of a person.

Subpart C—Activities by Other Than Own Employees

§ 1168.300 Professional and technical services.

(a) The prohibition on the use of appropriated funds, in § 1168.100 (a), does not apply in the case of any reasonable payment to a person, other than an officer or employee of a person requesting or receiving a covered Federal action, if the payment is for professional or technical services rendered directly in the preparation, submission, or negotiation of any bid, proposal, or application for that Federal contract, grant, loan, or cooperative agreement or for meeting requirements imposed by or pursuant to law as a condition for receiving that Federal contract, grant, loan, or cooperative agreement.

(b) The reporting requirements in § 1168.110 (a) and (b) regarding filing a disclosure form by each person, if required, shall not apply with respect to professional or technical services rendered directly in the preparation, submission, or negotiation of any commitment providing for the United States to insure or guarantee a loan.

§ 1168.400

(c) For purposes of paragraph (a) of this section, "professional and technical services" shall be limited to advice and analysis directly applying any professional or technical discipline. For example, drafting or a legal document accompanying a bid or proposal by a lawyer is allowable. Similarly, technical advice provided by an engineer on the performance or operational capability of a piece of equipment rendered directly in the negotiation of a contract is allowable. However, communications with the intent to influence made by a professional (such as a licensed lawyer) or a technical person (such as a licensed accountant) are not allowable under this section unless they provide advice and analysis directly applying their professional or technical expertise and unless the advice or analysis is rendered directly and solely in the preparation, submission or negotiation of a covered Federal action. Thus, for example, communications with the intent to influence made by a lawyer that do not provide legal advice or analysis directly and solely related to the legal aspects of his or her client's proposal, but generally advocate one proposal over another are not allowable under this section because the lawyer is not providing professional legal services. Similarly, communications with the intent to influence made by an engineer providing an engineering analysis prior to the preparation or submission of a bid or proposal are not allowable under this section since the engineer is providing technical services but not directly in the preparation, submission or negotiation of a covered Federal action.

(d) Requirements imposed by or pursuant to law as a condition for receiving a covered Federal award include those required by law or regulation, or reasonably expected to be required by law or regulation, and any other requirements in the actual award documents.

(e) Persons other than officers or employees of a person requesting or receiving a covered Federal action include consultants and trade associations.

(f) Only those services expressly authorized by this section are allowable under this section.

Subpart D—Penalties and Enforcement

§ 1168.400 Penalties.

(a) Any person who makes an expenditure prohibited herein shall be subject to a civil penalty of not less than $10,000 and not more than $100,000 for each such expenditure.

(b) Any person who fails to file or amend the disclosure form (see appendix B) to be filed or amended if required herein, shall be subject to a civil penalty of not less than $10,000 and not more than $100,000 for each such failure.

(c) A filing or amended filing on or after the date on which an administrative action for the imposition of a civil penalty is commenced does not prevent the imposition of such civil penalty for a failure occurring before that date. An administrative action is commenced with respect to a failure when an investigating official determines in writing to commence an investigation of an allegation of such failure.

(d) In determining whether to impose a civil penalty, and the amount of any such penalty, by reason of a violation by any person, the agency shall consider the nature, circumstances, extent, and gravity of the violation, the effect on the ability of such person to continue in business, any prior violations by such person, the degree of culpability of such person, the ability of the person to pay the penalty, and such other matters as may be appropriate.

(e) First offenders under paragraph (a) or (b) of this section shall be subject to a civil penalty of $10,000, absent aggravating circumstances. Second and subsequent offenses by persons shall be subject to an appropriate civil penalty between $10,000 and $100,000, as determined by the agency head or his or her designee.

(f) An imposition of a civil penalty under this section does not prevent the United States from seeking any other remedy that may apply to the same conduct that is the basis for the imposition of such civil penalty.

§ 1168.405 Penalty procedures.

Agencies shall impose and collect civil penalties pursuant to the provisions of the Program Fraud and Civil Remedies Act, 31 U.S.C. sections 3803 (except subsection (c)), 3804, 3805, 3806, 3807, 3808, and 3812, insofar as these provisions are not inconsistent with the requirements herein.

§ 1168.410 Enforcement.

The head of each agency shall take such actions as are necessary to ensure that the provisions herein are vigorously implemented and enforced in that agency.

Subpart E—Exemptions

§ 1168.500 Secretary of Defense.

(a) The Secretary of Defense may exempt, on a case-by-case basis, a covered Federal action from the prohibition whenever the Secretary determines, in writing, that such an exemption is in the national interest. The Secretary shall transmit a copy of each such written exemption to Congress immediately after making such a determination.

(b) The Department of Defense may issue supplemental regulations to implement paragraph (a) of this section.

Subpart F—Agency Reports

§ 1168.600 Semi-annual compilation.

(a) The head of each agency shall collect and compile the disclosure reports (see appendix B) and, on May 31 and November 30 of each year, submit to the Secretary of the Senate and the Clerk of the House of Representatives a report containing a compilation of the information contained in the disclosure reports received during the six-month period ending on March 31 or September 30, respectively, of that year.

(b) The report, including the compilation, shall be available for public inspection 30 days after receipt of the report by the Secretary and the Clerk.

(c) Information that involves intelligence matters shall be reported only to the Select Committee on Intelligence of the Senate, the Permanent Select Committee on Intelligence of the House of Representatives, and the Committees on Appropriations of the Senate and the House of Representatives in accordance with procedures agreed to by such committees. Such information shall not be available for public inspection.

(d) Information that is classified under Executive Order 12356 or any successor order shall be reported only to the Committee on Foreign Relations of the Senate and the Committee on Foreign Affairs of the House of Representatives or the Committees on Armed Services of the Senate and the House of Representatives (whichever such committees have jurisdiction of matters involving such information) and to the Committees on Appropriations of the Senate and the House of Representatives in accordance with procedures agreed to by such committees. Such information shall not be available for public inspection.

(e) The first semi-annual compilation shall be submitted on May 31, 1990, and shall contain a compilation of the disclosure reports received from December 23, 1989 to March 31, 1990.

(f) Major agencies, designated by the Office of Management and Budget (OMB), are required to provide machine-readable compilations to the Secretary of the Senate and the Clerk of the House of Representatives no later than with the compilations due on May 31, 1991. OMB shall provide detailed specifications in a memorandum to these agencies.

(g) Non-major agencies are requested to provide machine-readable compilations to the Secretary of the Senate and the Clerk of the House of Representatives.

(h) Agencies shall keep the originals of all disclosure reports in the official files of the agency.

§ 1168.605 Inspector General report.

(a) The Inspector General, or other official as specified in paragraph (b) of this section, of each agency shall prepare and submit to Congress each year, commencing with submission of the President's Budget in 1991, an evaluation of the compliance of that agency with, and the effectiveness of, the requirements herein. The evaluation may include any recommended changes that may be necessary to strengthen or improve the requirements.

(b) In the case of an agency that does not have an Inspector General, the agency official comparable to an Inspector General shall prepare and submit the annual report, or, if there is no such comparable official, the head of the agency shall prepare and submit the annual report.

(c) The annual report shall be submitted at the same time the agency submits its annual budget justifications to Congress.

(d) The annual report shall include the following: All alleged violations relating to the agency's covered Federal actions during the year covered by the report, the actions taken by the head of the agency in the year covered by the report with respect to those alleged violations and alleged violations in previous years, and the amounts of civil penalties imposed by the agency in the year covered by the report.

APPENDIX A TO PART 1168—
CERTIFICATION REGARDING LOBBYING

Certification for Contracts, Grants, Loans, and Cooperative Agreements

The undersigned certifies, to the best of his or her knowledge and belief, that:

(1) No Federal appropriated funds have been paid or will be paid, by or on behalf of the undersigned, to any person for influencing or attempting to influence an officer or employee of an agency, a Member of Congress, an officer or employee of Congress, or an employee of a Member of Congress in connection with the awarding of any Federal contract, the making of any Federal grant, the making of any Federal loan, the entering into of any cooperative agreement, and the extension, continuation, renewal, amendment, or modification of any Federal contract, grant, loan, or cooperative agreement.

(2) If any funds other than Federal appropriated funds have been paid or will be paid to any person for influencing or attempting to influence an officer or employee of any agency, a Member of Congress, an officer or employee of Congress, or an employee of a Member of Congress in connection with this Federal contract, grant, loan, or cooperative agreement, the undersigned shall complete and submit Standard Form-LLL, "Disclosure Form to Report Lobbying," in accordance with its instructions.

(3) The undersigned shall require that the language of this certification be included in the award documents for all subawards at all tiers (including subcontracts, subgrants, and contracts under grants, loans, and cooperative agreements) and that all subrecipients shall certify and disclose accordingly.

This certification is a material representation of fact upon which reliance was placed when this transaction was made or entered into. Submission of this certification is a prerequisite for making or entering into this transaction imposed by section 1352, title 31, U.S. Code. Any person who fails to file the required certification shall be subject to a civil penalty of not less than $10,000 and not more than $100,000 for each such failure.

Statement for Loan Guarantees and Loan Insurance

The undersigned states, to the best of his or her knowledge and belief, that:

If any funds have been paid or will be paid to any person for influencing or attempting to influence an officer or employee of any agency, a Member of Congress, an officer or employee of Congress, or an employee of a Member of Congress in connection with this commitment providing for the United States to insure or guarantee a loan, the undersigned shall complete and submit Standard Form-LLL, "Disclosure Form to Report Lobbying," in accordance with its instructions.

Submission of this statement is a prerequisite for making or entering into this transaction imposed by section 1352, title 31, U.S. Code. Any person who fails to file the required statement shall be subject to a civil penalty of not less than $10,000 and not more than $100,000 for each such failure.

National Foundation on the Arts and the Humanities Pt. 1168, App. B

APPENDIX B TO PART 1168—DISCLOSURE FORM TO REPORT LOBBYING

DISCLOSURE OF LOBBYING ACTIVITIES

Approved by OMB
0348-0046

Complete this form to disclose lobbying activities pursuant to 31 U.S.C. 1352
(See reverse for public burden disclosure.)

1. Type of Federal Action:
- a. contract
- b. grant
- c. cooperative agreement
- d. loan
- e. loan guarantee
- f. loan insurance

2. Status of Federal Action:
- a. bid/offer/application
- b. initial award
- c. post-award

3. Report Type:
- a. initial filing
- b. material change

For Material Change Only:
year _____ quarter _____
date of last report _____

4. Name and Address of Reporting Entity:
☐ Prime   ☐ Subawardee
Tier _____, if known:

Congressional District, if known:

5. If Reporting Entity in No. 4 is Subawardee, Enter Name and Address of Prime:

Congressional District, if known:

6. Federal Department/Agency:

7. Federal Program Name/Description:

CFDA Number, if applicable:

8. Federal Action Number, if known:

9. Award Amount, if known:
$

10. a. Name and Address of Lobbying Entity (if individual, last name, first name, MI):

b. Individuals Performing Services (including address if different from No. 10a)
(last name, first name, MI):

(attach Continuation Sheet(s) SF-LLL-A, if necessary)

11. Amount of Payment (check all that apply):
$ _____ ☐ actual ☐ planned

12. Form of Payment (check all that apply):
- ☐ a. cash
- ☐ b. in-kind; specify: nature _____
  value _____

13. Type of Payment (check all that apply):
- ☐ a. retainer
- ☐ b. one-time fee
- ☐ c. commission
- ☐ d. contingent fee
- ☐ e. deferred
- ☐ f. other; specify: _____

14. Brief Description of Services Performed or to be Performed and Date(s) of Service, including officer(s), employee(s), or Member(s) contacted, for Payment Indicated in Item 11:

(attach Continuation Sheet(s) SF-LLL-A, if necessary)

15. Continuation Sheet(s) SF-LLL-A attached: ☐ Yes ☐ No

16. Information requested through this form is authorized by title 31 U.S.C. section 1352. This disclosure of lobbying activities is a material representation of fact upon which reliance was placed by the tier above when this transaction was made or entered into. This disclosure is required pursuant to 31 U.S.C. 1352. This information will be reported to the Congress semi-annually and will be available for public inspection. Any person who fails to file the required disclosure shall be subject to a civil penalty of not less than $10,000 and not more than $100,000 for each such failure.

Signature: _____
Print Name: _____
Title: _____
Telephone No.: _____ Date: _____

Federal Use Only:

Authorized for Local Reproduction
Standard Form - LLL

INSTRUCTIONS FOR COMPLETION OF SF-LLL, DISCLOSURE OF LOBBYING ACTIVITIES

This disclosure form shall be completed by the reporting entity, whether subawardee or prime Federal recipient, at the initiation or receipt of a covered Federal action, or a material change to a previous filing, pursuant to title 31 U.S.C. section 1352. The filing of a form is required for each payment or agreement to make payment to any lobbying entity for influencing or attempting to influence an officer or employee of any agency, a Member of Congress, an officer or employee of Congress, or an employee of a Member of Congress in connection with a covered Federal action. Use the SF-LLL-A Continuation Sheet for additional information if the space on the form is inadequate. Complete all items that apply for both the initial filing and material change report. Refer to the implementing guidance published by the Office of Management and Budget for additional information.

1. Identify the type of covered Federal action for which lobbying activity is and/or has been secured to influence the outcome of a covered Federal action.

2. Identify the status of the covered Federal action.

3. Identify the appropriate classification of this report. If this is a followup report caused by a material change to the information previously reported, enter the year and quarter in which the change occurred. Enter the date of the last previously submitted report by this reporting entity for this covered Federal action.

4. Enter the full name, address, city, state and zip code of the reporting entity. Include Congressional District, if known. Check the appropriate classification of the reporting entity that designates if it is, or expects to be, a prime or subaward recipient. Identify the tier of the subawardee, e.g., the first subawardee of the prime is the 1st tier. Subawards include but are not limited to subcontracts, subgrants and contract awards under grants.

5. If the organization filing the report in item 4 checks "Subawardee", then enter the full name, address, city, state and zip code of the prime Federal recipient. Include Congressional District, if known.

6. Enter the name of the Federal agency making the award or loan commitment. Include at least one organizational level below agency name, if known. For example, Department of Transportation, United States Coast Guard.

7. Enter the Federal program name or description for the covered Federal action (item 1). If known, enter the full Catalog of Federal Domestic Assistance (CFDA) number for grants, cooperative agreements, loans, and loan commitments.

8. Enter the most appropriate Federal identifying number available for the Federal action identified in item 1 (e.g., Request for Proposal (RFP) number; Invitation for Bid (IFB) number; grant announcement number; the contract, grant, or loan award number; the application/proposal control number assigned by the Federal agency). Include prefixes, e.g., "RFP-DE-90-001."

9. For a covered Federal action where there has been an award or loan commitment by the Federal agency, enter the Federal amount of the award/loan commitment for the prime entity identified in item 4 or 5.

10. (a) Enter the full name, address, city, state and zip code of the lobbying entity engaged by the reporting entity identified in item 4 to influence the covered Federal action.

    (b) Enter the full names of the individual(s) performing services, and include full address if different from 10 (a). Enter Last Name, First Name, and Middle Initial (MI).

11. Enter the amount of compensation paid or reasonably expected to be paid by the reporting entity (item 4) to the lobbying entity (item 10). Indicate whether the payment has been made (actual) or will be made (planned). Check all boxes that apply. If this is a material change report, enter the cumulative amount of payment made or planned to be made.

12. Check the appropriate box(es). Check all boxes that apply. If payment is made through an in-kind contribution, specify the nature and value of the in-kind payment.

13. Check the appropriate box(es). Check all boxes that apply. If other, specify nature.

14. Provide a specific and detailed description of the services that the lobbyist has performed, or will be expected to perform, and the date(s) of any services rendered. Include all preparatory and related activity, not just time spent in actual contact with Federal officials. Identify the Federal official(s) or employee(s) contacted or the officer(s), employee(s), or Member(s) of Congress that were contacted.

15. Check whether or not a SF-LLL-A Continuation Sheet(s) is attached.

16. The certifying official shall sign and date the form, print his/her name, title, and telephone number.

Public reporting burden for this collection of information is estimated to average 30 minutes per response, including time for reviewing instructions, searching existing data sources, gathering and maintaining the data needed, and completing and reviewing the collection of information. Send comments regarding the burden estimate or any other aspect of this collection of information, including suggestions for reducing this burden, to the Office of Management and Budget, Paperwork Reduction Project (0348-0046), Washington, D.C. 20503.

National Foundation on the Arts and the Humanities Pt. 1168, App. B

DISCLOSURE OF LOBBYING ACTIVITIES
CONTINUATION SHEET

Approved by OMB
0348-0046

Reporting Entity: _____ Page _____ of _____

Authorized for Local Reproduction
Standard Form - LLL-A

PART 1170—NONDISCRIMINATION ON THE BASIS OF HANDICAP IN FEDERALLY ASSISTED PROGRAMS OR ACTIVITIES

Subpart A—General Provisions

Sec.
1170.1 Purpose.
1170.2 Application.
1170.3 Definitions.
1170.4 Effect of State or local law or other requirements and effect of employment opportunities.
1170.5–1170.10 [Reserved]

Subpart B—Discrimination Prohibited

1170.11 General prohibition against discrimination.
1170.12 Discriminatory actions prohibited.
1170.13 Illustrative examples.
1170.14–1170.20 [Reserved]

Subpart C—Employment Practices

1170.21 Discrimination prohibited.
1170.22 Reasonable accommodation.
1170.23 Employment criteria.
1170.24 Preemployment inquiries.
1170.25–1170.30 [Reserved]

Subpart D—Accessibility

1170.31 Discrimination prohibited.
1170.32 Existing facilities.
1170.33 New construction.
1170.34 Historic properties. [Reserved]
1170.35–1170.40 [Reserved]

Subpart E—Postsecondary Education

1170.41 Application of this subpart.
1170.42 Admissions and recruitment.
1170.43 Treatment of students; general.
1170.44 Academic adjustments.
1170.45 Housing.
1170.46 Financial and employment assistance to students.
1170.47 Nonacademic services.
1170.48–1170.50 [Reserved]

Subpart F—Enforcement

1170.51 Assurances required.
1170.52 Remedial action, voluntary action, and self-evaluation.
1170.53 Designation of responsible employee and adoption of grievance procedures.
1170.54 Notice.
1170.55 Endowment enforcement and compliance procedures.
1170.56–1170.99 [Reserved]

AUTHORITY: 29 U.S.C. 794.

SOURCE: 46 FR 55897, Nov. 12, 1981, unless otherwise noted.

Subpart A—General Provisions

§ 1170.1 Purpose.

The purpose of this part is to implement section 504 of the Rehabilitation Act of 1973, which is designed to eliminate discrimination on the basis of handicap in any program or activity receiving Federal financial assistance.

§ 1170.2 Application.

This part applies to each recipient of Federal financial assistance from the National Endowment for the Humanities and to each program or activity that receives such assistance.

[46 FR 55897, Nov. 12, 1981, as amended at 68 FR 51386, Aug. 26, 2003]

§ 1170.3 Definitions.

As used in this part:

(a) *Section 504* means section 504 of the Rehabilitation Act of 1973, Pub. L. 93–112, as amended by the Rehabilitation Act Amendments of 1974, Pub. L. 93–516, 29 U.S.C. 794 *et seq.* by the Rehabilitation, Comprehensive Services Developmental Disabilities Amendments of 1978, Pub. L. 95–602, and by the Civil Rights Restoration Act of 1987, Pub. L. 100–259.

(b) The term *Endowment* or the term *agency* means the National Endowment for the Humanities.

(c) The term *Chairman* means the Chairman of the National Endowment for the Humanities.

(d) The term *responsible Endowment official* with respect to any program or activity receiving Federal financial assistance means the Chairman of the Endowment, the Director of the Office of Equal Employment Opportunity, or other Endowment official designated by the Chairman.

(e) The term *United States* means the States of the United States, the District of Columbia, Puerto Rico, the Virgin Islands, American Samoa, Guam, the Northern Mariana Islands, Wake Island, the Canal Zone, and the territories and possessions of the United States, and the term *State* means any one of the foregoing.

(f) *Federal financial assistance* means any grant, loan, contract (other than a procurement contract or a contract of insurance or guaranty), or any other

National Foundation on the Arts and the Humanities § 1170.3

arrangement by which the agency provides or otherwise makes available assistance in the form of:

(1) Funds;

(2) Services of Federal personnel; or

(3) Real and personal property or any interest in or use of such property, including:

(i) Transfers or leases of such property for less than fair market value or for reduced consideration; and

(ii) Proceeds from a subsequent transfer or lease of such property if the Federal share of its fair market value is not returned to the Federal government.

(g) The term *program or activity* means all of the operations of any entity described in paragraphs (g)(1) through (4) of this section, any part of which is extended Federal financial assistance:

(1)(i) A department, agency, special purpose district, or other instrumentality of a State or of a local government; or

(ii) The entity of such State or local government that distributes such assistance and each such department or agency (and each other State or local government entity) to which the assistance is extended, in the case of assistance to a State or local government;

(2)(i) A college, university, or other postsecondary institution, or a public system of higher education; or

(ii) A local educational agency (as defined in 20 U.S.C. 7801), system of vocational education, or other school system;

(3)(i) An entire corporation, partnership, or other private organization, or an entire sole proprietorship—

(A) If assistance is extended to such corporation, partnership, private organization, or sole proprietorship as a whole; or

(B) Which is principally engaged in the business of providing education, health care, housing, social services, or parks and recreation; or

(ii) The entire plant or other comparable, geographically separate facility to which Federal financial assistance is extended, in the case of any other corporation, partnership, private organization, or sole proprietorship; or

(4) Any other entity which is established by two or more of the entities described in paragraph (g)(1), (2), or (3) of this section.

(h) *Facility* means all or any portion of buildings, structures, equipment, roads, walks, parking lots, or other real or personal property or interest in such property.

(i) *Recipient* means any state or its political subdivision, any instrumentality of a state or its political subdivision, any public or private agency, institution, organization, or other entity, or any person to which Federal financial assistance is extended directly or through another recipient, including any successor, assignee, or transferee of a recipient, but excluding the ultimate beneficiary of the assistance.

(j) *Handicapped person* means any person who has a physical or mental impairment that substantially limits one or more major life activities, has a record of such an impairment, or is regarded as having such an impairment. For purposes of section 504, in connection with employment, this term does not include any individual who is an alcoholic or drug abuser whose current use of alcohol or drugs prevents such individual from performing the duties of the job in question or whose employment, by reason of such current alcohol or drug abuse, would constitute a direct threat to the property or the safety of others. As used in this paragraph, the phrase:

(1) *Physical or mental impairment* means:

(i) Any physiological disorder or condition, cosmetic disfigurement, or anatomical loss affecting one or more of the following body systems: Neurological; musculoskeletal; special sense organs; respiratory, including speech organs; cardiovascular; reproductive; digestive; genitourinary; hemic and lymphatic; skin; and endocrine; or

(ii) Any mental or psychological disorder, such as mental retardation, organic brain syndrome, emotional or mental illness, and specific learning disabilities. The term *physical or mental impairment* includes, but is not limited to, such diseases and conditions as orthopedic, visual, speech, and hearing impairments, cerebral palsy, epilepsy, muscular dystrophy, multiple sclerosis,

§ 1170.4

cancer, heart disease, diabetes, mental retardation, emotional illness, and drug addiction and alcoholism.

(2) *Major life activities* means functions such as caring for one's self, performing manual tasks, walking, seeing, hearing, speaking, breathing, learning, and working.

(3) *Has a record of such impairment* means has a history of, or has been misclassified as having, a mental or physical impairment that substantially limits one or more major life activities.

(4) *Is regarded as having an impairment* means

(i) Has a physical or mental impairment that does not substantially limit major life activities but is treated by a recipient as constituting such a limitation;

(ii) Has a physical or mental impairment that substantially limits major life activities only as a result of the attitudes of others toward such impairment; or

(iii) Has none of the impairments defined in paragraph (j)(1) of this section but is treated by a recipient as having such an impairment.

(k) *Qualified handicapped person* means:

(1) With respect to employment, a handicapped person who, with reasonable accommodation, can perform the essential functions of the job in question and

(2) With respect to postsecondary and vocational education services, a handicapped person who meets the academic and technical standards requisite to admission or participation in the recipient's education program or activity;

(3) With respect to services, a handicapped person who meets the essential eligibility requirements for the receipt of such services.

[46 FR 55897, Nov. 12, 1981, as amended at 68 FR 51386, Aug. 26, 2003]

§ 1170.4 **Effect of State or local law or other requirements and effect of employment opportunities.**

(a) The obligation to comply with this part is not obviated or alleviated by the existence of any state or local law or other requirement that, on the basis of handicap, imposes prohibitions or limits upon the eligibility of qualified handicapped persons to receive services or to practice any occupation or profession.

(b) The obligation to comply with this part is not obviated or alleviated because employment opportunities in any occupation or profession are or may be more limited for handicapped persons than for nonhandicapped persons.

§§ 1170.5–1170.10 [Reserved]

Subpart B—Discrimination Prohibited

§ 1170.11 **General prohibition against discrimination.**

No qualified handicapped person shall, on the basis of handicap, be excluded from participation in, be denied the benefits of, or otherwise be subjected to discrimination under any program or activity that receives Federal financial assistance.

[46 FR 55897, Nov. 12, 1981, as amended at 68 FR 51386, Aug. 26, 2003]

§ 1170.12 **Discriminatory actions prohibited.**

(a) A recipient, in providing any aid, benefit, or service, may not, directly or through contractual, licensing, or other arrangements, on the basis of handicap:

(1) Deny a qualified handicapped person the opportunity to participate in or benefit from the aid, benefit, or service;

(2) Afford a qualified handicapped person an opportunity to participate in or benefit from the aid, benefit, or service that is not equal to that afforded others;

(3) Provide a qualified handicapped person with an aid, benefit, or service that is not as effective in affording equal opportunity to obtain the same result, to gain the same benefit, or to reach the same level of achievement as that provided to others;

(4) Provide different or separate aid, benefits, or services to handicapped persons or to any class of handicapped persons than is provided to others unless such action is necessary to provide qualified handicapped persons with aid,

benefits, or services that are as effective as those provided to others;

(5) Aid or perpetuate discrimination against a qualified handicapped person by providing significant assistance to an agency, organization, or person that discriminates on the basis of handicap in providing any aid, benefit, or service to beneficiaries of the recipient's program or activity;

(6) Deny a qualified handicapped person the opportunity to participate as a member of planning or advisory boards; or

(7) Otherwise limit a qualified handicapped person in the enjoyment of any right, privilege, advantage, or opportunity enjoyed by others receiving the aid, benefit, or service.

(b) A recipient may not deny a qualified handicapped person the opportunity to participate in aid, benefits, or services that are not separate or different, despite the existence of permissibly separate or different aid, benefits, or services.

(c) A recipient may not, directly or through contractual or other arrangements, utilize criteria or methods of administration.

(1) that have the effect of subjecting qualified handicapped persons to discrimination on the basis of handicap,

(2) that have the purpose or effect of defeating or substantially impairing accomplishment of the objectives of the recipient's program or activity with respect to handicapped persons, or

(3) that perpetuate the discrimination of another recipient if both recipients are subject to common administrative control or are agencies of the same state.

(d) A recipient may not, in determining the site or location of a facility, make selections

(1) that have the effect of excluding handicapped persons from, denying them the benefits of, or otherwise subjecting them to discrimination under any program or activity that receives Federal financial assistance or

(2) that have the purpose or effect of defeating or substantially impairing the accomplishment of the objectives of the program or activity with respect to handicapped persons.

(e) The exclusion of nonhandicapped persons from aid, benefits, or services limited by Federal statute or executive order to handicapped persons or the exclusion of a specific class of handicapped persons from aid, benefits, or services limited by Federal statute or executive order to a different class of handicapped persons is not prohibited by this part.

(f) Recipients shall administer programs or activities in the most integrated setting appropriate to the needs of qualified handicapped persons.

(g) Recipients shall take appropriate steps to ensure that communications with their applicants, employees, and beneficiaries are available to persons with impaired vision and hearing.

[46 FR 55897, Nov. 12, 1981, as amended at 68 FR 51386, Aug. 26, 2003]

§ 1170.13 Illustrative examples.

(a) The following examples will illustrate the application of the foregoing provisions to some of the activities funded by the National Endowment for the Humanities.

(1) A publication or a museum catalogue supported by the Endowment may be made usable by the blind and the visually impaired through cassette tapes, records, discs, braille, readers and simultaneous publications.

(2) A lecture, meeting or symposium supported by Federal funds may be made available to deaf and hearing impaired persons through the use of a sign language interpreter or by providing scripts in advance of the performance.

(3) Specific aid, benefits, or services supported by Federal funds may be offered in an inaccessible facility provided that the same aid, benefit, or service is also offered to the public at large in an accessible space.

(4) A qualified handicapped person is one who is able to meet all requirements in spite of his handicap. An educational institution is not required to disregard the disabilities of handicapped individuals or to lower or to make substantial modifications of standards to accommodate a handicapped person.

(b) State humanities committees are obligated to develop methods of administering Federal funds so as to ensure that handicapped persons are not subjected to discrimination on the basis of handicap either by sub-grantees or by the manner in which the funds are distributed.

(c) In the event Endowment funds are utilized to construct, expand, alter, lease or rent a facility, the benefits of the program or activity provided in or through that facility must be conducted in accordance with these regulations, e.g., a museum receiving a grant to renovate an existing facility must assure that all museum aid, benefits, or services conducted in that facility are accessible to handicapped persons.

(d) In carrying out the mandate of section 504 and these implementing regulations recipients should administer Endowment assisted programs or activities in the most integrated setting appropriate, e.g., tours made available to the hearing impaired should be open to the public at large and everyone should be permitted to enjoy the benefits of a tactile experience in a museum.

[46 FR 55897, Nov. 12, 1981, as amended at 68 FR 51386, Aug. 26, 2003]

§§ 1170.14–1170.20 [Reserved]

Subpart C—Employment Practices

§ 1170.21 Discrimination prohibited.

(a) *General.* No qualified handicapped person shall, on the basis of handicap, be subjected to discrimination in employment under any program or activity that receives Federal financial assistance.

(b) A recipient shall make all decisions concerning employment under any program or activity to which this part applies in a manner which ensures that discrimination on the basis of handicap does not occur and may not limit, segregate, or classify applicants or employees in any way that adversely affects their opportunities or status because of handicap.

(c) A recipient may not participate in a contractual or other relationship that has the effect of subjecting qualified handicapped applicants or employees to discrimination prohibited by this subpart. The relationships referred to in this paragraph include relationships with employment and referral agencies, with labor unions, with organizations providing or administering fringe benefits to employees of the recipient, and with organizations providing training and apprenticeships.

(d) *Specific activities.* The provisions of this subpart apply to:

(1) Recruitment, advertising, and the processing of applications for employment;

(2) Hiring, upgrading, promotion, award of tenure, demotion, transfer, layoff, termination, right of return from layoff and rehiring;

(3) Rates of pay or any other form of compensation and changes in compensation;

(4) Job assignments, job classifications, organizational structures, position descriptions, lines of progression, and seniority lists;

(5) Leaves of absence, sick leave, or any other leave;

(6) Fringe benefits available by virtue of employment, whether or not administered by the recipient;

(7) Selection and financial support for training, including apprenticeship, professional meetings, conferences, and other related activities, and selection for leaves of absence to pursue training;

(8) Employer sponsored activities, including those that are social or recreational; and

(9) Any other term, condition, or privilege of employment.

(e) A recipient's obligation to comply with this subpart is not affected by any inconsistent term of any collective bargaining agreement to which it is a party.

[46 FR 55897, Nov. 12, 1981, as amended at 68 FR 51386, Aug. 26, 2003]

§ 1170.22 Reasonable accommodation.

(a) A recipient shall make reasonable accommodation to the known physical or mental limitations of an otherwise qualified handicapped applicant or employee unless the recipient can demonstrate that the accommodation would impose an undue hardship on the operation of its program or activity.

(b) Reasonable accommodation may include:

(1) Making facilities used by employees readily accessible to and usable by handicapped persons, and

(2) Job restructuring, part-time or modified work schedules, acquisition or modification of equipment or devices, the provision of readers or interpreters, and other similar actions.

(c) In determining pursuant to paragraph (a) of this section whether an accommodation would impose an undue hardship on the operation of a recipient's program or activity, factors to be considered include:

(1) The overall size of the recipient's program or activity with respect to number of employees, number and type of facilities, and size of budget;

(2) The type of the recipient's operation, including the composition and structure of the recipient's workforce; and

(3) The nature and cost of the accommodation needed.

[46 FR 55897, Nov. 12, 1981, as amended at 68 FR 51386, Aug. 26, 2003]

§ 1170.23 Employment criteria.

(a) A recipient may not make use of any employment test or other selection criterion that screens out or tends to screen out handicapped persons or any class of handicapped persons unless:

(1) The test score or other selection criterion, as used by the recipient, is shown to be job-related for the position in question; and

(2) Alternative job-related tests or criteria are unavailable.

(b) A recipient shall select and administer tests concerning employment so as best to ensure that, when administered to an applicant or employee who has a handicap that impairs sensory, manual, or speaking skills, the test results accurately reflect the applicant's or employee's job skills, aptitude, or other factors relevant to adequate performance of the job in question.

§ 1170.24 Preemployment inquiries.

(a) A recipient may not, except as provided below, conduct a preemployment medical examination, make preemployment inquiry as to whether the applicant is a handicapped person, or inquire as to the nature or severity of a handicap. A recipient may, however, make preemployment inquiry into an applicant's ability to perform job-related functions.

(b) If a recipient is taking remedial action to correct the effects of past discrimination, if a recipient is taking voluntary action to overcome the effects of conditions that resulted in limited participation in its federally assisted program or activity, or if a recipient is taking affirmative action under section 503 of the Rehabilitation Act, the recipient may invite applicants for employment to indicate whether and to what extent they are handicapped, provided, that:

(1) The recipient states clearly on any written questionnaire used for this purpose or makes clear orally if no written questionnaire is used that the information requested is intended for use solely in connection with its remedial action obligations or its voluntary or affirmative action efforts; and

(2) The recipient states clearly that the information is being requested on a voluntary basis, that it will be kept confidential as provided in paragraph (d) of this section, that refusal to provide it will not subject the applicant or employee to any adverse treatment, and that it will be used only in accordance with this part.

(c) Nothing in this section shall prohibit a recipient from conditioning an offer of employment on the results of a medical examination conducted prior to the employee's entrance on duty, provided, that:

(1) All entering employees are subjected to such an examination regardless of handicap; and

(2) The results of such an examination are used only in accordance with the requirements of this part.

(d) Information obtained in accordance with this section as to the medical condition or history of the applicant shall be collected and maintained on separate forms that shall be accorded confidentiality as medical records, except that:

(1) Supervisors and managers may be informed regarding restrictions on the work or duties of handicapped persons and regarding necessary accommodations;

(2) First aid and safety personnel may be informed, where appropriate, if the condition might require emergency treatment; and

(3) Government officials investigating compliance with the Act shall be provided relevant information upon request.

§§ 1170.25–1170.30 [Reserved]

Subpart D—Accessibility

§ 1170.31 Discrimination prohibited.

No qualified handicapped person shall, because recipient's facilities are inaccessible to or unusable by handicapped persons, be denied the benefits of, be excluded from participation in, or otherwise be subjected to discrimination under any program or activity to which this part applies.

§ 1170.32 Existing facilities.

(a) *Accessibility.* A recipient shall operate each program or activity to which this part applies so that when each part is viewed in its entirety it is readily accessible to handicapped persons. This paragraph does not necessarily require a recipient to make each of its existing facilities or every part of a facility accessible to and usable by handicapped persons.

(b) *Methods.* A recipient may comply with the requirements of paragraph (a) of this section through such means as redesign of equipment, reassignment of classes or other services to accessible buildings, alteration of existing facilities and construction of new facilities in conformance with the requirements of § 1170.33, or any other methods that result in making its program or activity accessible to handicapped persons. A recipient is not required to make structural changes in existing facilities where other methods are effective in achieving compliance with paragraph (a) of this section. In choosing among available methods for meeting the requirement of paragraph (a) of this section, a recipient shall give priority to those methods that serve handicapped persons in the most integrated setting appropriate.

(c) *Time period.* A recipient shall comply with the requirement of paragraph (a) of this section within sixty days of the effective date of this part except that where structural changes in facilities are necessary, such changes shall be made within three years of the effective date of this part, but in any event as expeditiously as possible.

(d) *Transition plan.* In the event that structural changes to facilities are necessary to meet the requirement of paragraph (a) of this section, a recipient shall develop, within one year of the effective date of this part, a transition plan setting forth the steps necessary to complete such changes. The plan shall be developed with the assistance of interested persons, including handicapped persons or organizations representing handicapped persons. A copy of the transition plan shall be made available upon request for public inspection. The plan shall, at a minimum:

(1) Identify physical obstacles in the recipient's facilities that limit the accessibility of its program or activity to handicapped persons;

(2) Describe in detail the methods that will be used to make the facilities accessible;

(3) Specify the schedule for taking the steps necessary to achieve full accessibility under paragraph (a) of this section and, if the time period of the transition plan is longer than one year, identify the steps that will be taken during each year of the transition period; and

(4) Indicate the person responsible for implementation of the plan.

(e) *Notice.* The recipient shall adopt and implement procedures to ensure that interested persons, including persons with impaired vision or hearing can obtain information as to the existence and location of services, activities, and facilities that are accessible to and usable by handicapped persons.

[46 FR 55897, Nov. 12, 1981, as amended at 68 FR 51386, Aug. 26, 2003]

§ 1170.33 New construction.

(a) *Design, construction, and alteration.* New facilities shall be designed and constructed to be readily accessible to and usable by handicapped persons. Alterations to existing facilities shall, to the maximum extent feasible, be designed and constructed to be readily accessible to and usable by handicapped persons.

(b) *Conformance with Uniform Federal Accessibility Standards.* (1) Effective as of January 18, 1991, design, construction, or alteration of buildings in conformance with sections 3–8 of the Uniform Federal Accessibility Standards (USAF) (appendix A to 41 CFR subpart 101–19.6) shall be deemed to comply with the requirements of this section with respect to those buildings. Departures from particular technical and scoping requirements of UFAS by the use of other methods are permitted where substantially equivalent or greater access to and usability of the building is provided.

(2) For purposes of this section, section 4.1.6(1)(g) of UFAS shall be interpreted to exempt from the requirements of UFAS only mechanical rooms and other spaces that, because of their intended use, will not require accessibility to the public or beneficiaries or result in the employment or residence therein of persons with physical handicaps.

(3) This section does not require recipients to make building alterations that have little likelihood of being accomplished without removing or altering a load-bearing structural member.

[46 FR 55897, Nov. 12, 1981, as amended at 55 FR 52138, 52142, Dec. 19, 1990]

§ 1170.34 Historic properties. [Reserved]

§§ 1170.35–1170.40 [Reserved]

Subpart E—Postsecondary Education

§ 1170.41 Application of this subpart.

Subpart E applies to postsecondary education programs or activities, including postsecondary vocational education programs or activities, that receive Federal financial assistance and to recipients that operate, or that receive Federal financial assistance for the operation of, such programs or activities.

[46 FR 55897, Nov. 12, 1981, as amended at 68 FR 51386, Aug. 26, 2003]

§ 1170.42 Admissions and recruitment.

(a) *General.* Qualified handicapped persons may not, on the basis of handicap, be denied admission or be subjected to discrimination in admission or recruitment by a recipient to which this subpart applies.

(b) *Admissions.* In administering its admission policies, a recipient to which this subpart applies:

(1) May not apply limitations upon the number or proportion of handicapped persons who may be admitted;

(2) May not make use of any test or criterion for admission that has a disproportionate, adverse effect on handicapped persons or any class of handicapped persons unless

(i) The test or criterion, as used by the recipient, has been validated as a predictor of success in the education program or activity in question and

(ii) Alternate tests or criteria that have a less disproportionate, adverse effect are not shown by the Chairman to be available.

(3) Shall assure itself that:

(i) Admissions tests are selected and administered so as best to ensure that, when a test is administered to an applicant who has a handicap that impairs sensory, manual, or speaking skills, the test results accurately reflect the applicant's aptitude or achievement level or whatever other factor the test purports to measure, rather than reflecting the applicant's impaired sensory, manual, or speaking skills (except where those skills are the factors that the test purports to measure);

(ii) Admissions tests that are designed for persons with impaired sensory, manual, or speaking skills are offered as often and in as timely a manner as are other admissions tests; and

(iii) Admissions tests are administered in facilities that, on the whole, are accessible to handicapped persons; and

(4) Except as provided in paragraph (c) of this section, may not make preadmission inquiry as to whether an applicant for admission is a handicapped person but, after admission, may make inquiries on a confidential basis as to handicaps that may require accommodation.

(c) *Preadmission inquiry exception.* When a recipient is taking remedial action to correct the effects of past discrimination pursuant to § 1170.52(a) or when a recipient is taking voluntary

§ 1170.43

action to overcome the effects of conditions that resulted in limited participation in its federally assisted program or activity pursuant to § 1170.52(b), the recipient may invite applicants for admission to indicate whether and to what extent they are handicapped, provided, that:

(1) The recipient states clearly on any written questionnaire used for this purpose or makes clear orally if no written questionnaire is used that the information requested is intended for use solely in connection with its remedial action obligations or its voluntary action efforts; and

(2) The recipient states clearly that the information is being requested on a voluntary basis, that it will be kept confidential, that refusal to provide it will not subject the applicant to any adverse treatment, and that it will be used only in accordance with this part.

(d) *Validity studies.* For the purpose of paragraph (b)(2) of this section, a recipient may base prediction equations on first year grades, but shall conduct periodic validity studies against the criterion of overall success in the education program or activity in question in order to monitor the general validity of the test scores.

§ 1170.43 Treatment of students; general.

(a) No qualified handicapped student shall, on the basis of handicap, be excluded from participation in, be denied the benefits of, or otherwise be subjected to discrimination under any academic, research, occupational training, housing, health insurance, counseling, financial aid, physical education, athletics, recreation, transportation, or other postsecondary education aid, benefit, or service to which this subpart applies.

(b) A recipient to which this subpart applies that considers participation by students in education programs or activities not operated wholly by the recipient as part of, or equivalent to, an education program or activity operated by the recipient shall assure itself that the other education program or activity, as a whole, provides an equal opportunity for the participation of qualified handicapped persons.

(c) A recipient to which this subpart applies may not, on the basis of handicap, exclude any qualified handicapped student from any course, course of study, or other part of its education program or activity.

(d) A recipient to which this subpart applies shall operate its program or activity in the most integrated setting appropriate.

[46 FR 55897, Nov. 12, 1981, as amended at 68 FR 51386, Aug. 26, 2003]

§ 1170.44 Academic adjustments.

(a) *Academic requirements.* A recipient to which this subpart applies shall make such modifications to its academic requirements as are necessary to ensure that such requirements do not discriminate or have the effect of discriminating, on the basis of handicap, against a qualified handicapped applicant or student. Academic requirements that the recipient can demonstrate are essential to the instruction being pursued by such student or to any directly related licensing requirement will not be regarded as discriminatory within the meaning of this section. Modifications may include changes in the length of time permitted for the completion of degree requirements, substitution of specific courses required for the completion of degree requirements, and adaptation of the manner in which specific courses are conducted.

(b) *Other rules.* A recipient to which this subpart applies may not impose upon handicapped students other rules, such as the prohibition of tape recorders in classrooms or of dog guides in campus buildings, that have the effect of limiting the participation of handicapped students in the recipient's education program or activity.

(c) *Course examinations.* In its course examinations or other procedures for evaluating students' academic achievement, a recipient to which this subpart applies shall provide such methods for evaluating the achievement of students who have a handicap that impairs sensory, manual, or speaking skills as will best ensure that the results of the evaluation represents the student's achievement in the course, rather than reflecting the student's impaired sensory, manual, or speaking skills (except where such skills are the factors that the test purports to measure).

(d) *Auxiliary aids.* (1) A recipient to which this subpart applies shall take such steps as are necessary to ensure that no handicapped student is denied the benefits of, excluded from participation in, or otherwise subjected to discrimination because of the absence of educational auxiliary aids for students with impaired sensory, manual, or speaking skills.

(2) Auxiliary aids may include taped texts, interpreters or other effective methods of making orally delivered materials available to students with hearing impairments, readers in libraries for students with visual impairments, classroom equipment adapted for use by students with manual impairments, and other similar services and actions. Recipients need not provide attendants, individually prescribed devices, readers for personal use or study, or other devices or services of a personal nature.

[46 FR 55897, Nov. 12, 1981, as amended at 68 FR 51386, Aug. 26, 2003]

§ 1170.45 Housing.

(a) *Housing provided by the recipient.* A recipient that provides housing to its nonhandicapped students shall provide comparable, convenient, and accessible housing to handicapped students at the same cost as to others. At the end of the transition period provided for in Subpart D, such housing shall be available in sufficient quantity and variety so that the scope of handicapped students' choice of living accommodations is, as a whole, comparable to that of nonhandicapped students.

(b) *Other housing.* A recipient that assists any agency, organization, or person in making housing available to any of its students shall take such action as may be necessary to assure itself that such housing is, as a whole, made available in a manner that does not result in discrimination on the basis of handicap.

§ 1170.46 Financial and employment assistance to students.

(a) *Provision of financial assistance.* (1) In providing financial assistance to qualified handicapped persons, a recipient to which this subpart applies may not

(i) On the basis of handicap, provide less assistance than is provided to nonhandicapped persons, limit eligibility for assistance, or otherwise discriminate or

(ii) Assist any entity or person that provides assistance to any of the recipient's students in a manner that discriminates against qualified handicapped persons on the basis of handicap.

(2) A recipient may administer or assist in the administration of scholarships, fellowships, or other forms of financial assistance established under wills, trusts, bequests, or similar legal instruments that require awards to be made on the basis of factors that discriminate or have the effect of discriminating on the basis of handicap only if the overall effect of the award of scholarships, fellowships, and other forms of financial assistance is not discriminatory on the basis of handicap.

(b) *Assistance in making available outside employment.* A recipient that assists any agency, organization, or person in providing employment opportunities to any of its students shall assure itself that such employment opportunities, as a whole, are made available in a manner that would not violate subpart C if they were provided by the recipient.

(c) *Employment of students by recipients.* A recipient that employs any of its students may not do so in a manner that violates subpart C.

§ 1170.47 Nonacademic services.

(a) *Physical education and athletics.* (1) In providing physical education courses and athletics and similar aid, benefits, or services to any of its students, a recipient to which this subpart applies may not discriminate on the basis of handicap. A recipient that offers physical education courses or that operates or sponsors intercollegiate, club, or intramural athletics shall provide to qualified handicapped students an equal opportunity for participation in these activities.

(2) A recipient may offer to handicapped students physical education and athletic activities that are separate or

different only if separation or differentiation is consistent with the requirements of §1170.43(d) and only if no qualified handicapped student is denied the opportunity to compete for teams or to participate in courses that are not separate or different.

(b) *Counseling and placement services.* A recipient to which this subpart applies that provides personal, academic, or vocational counseling, guidance, or placement services to its students shall provide these services without discrimination on the basis of handicap. The recipient shall ensure that qualified handicapped students are not counseled toward more restrictive career objectives than are nonhandicapped students with similar interests and abilities. This requirement does not preclude a recipient from providing factual information about licensing and certification requirements that may present obstacles to handicapped persons in their pursuit of particular careers.

(c) *Social organizations.* A recipient that provides significant assistance to fraternities, sororities, or similar organizations shall assure itself that the membership practices of such organizations do not permit discrimination otherwise prohibited by this subpart.

[46 FR 55897, Nov. 12, 1981, as amended at 68 FR 51386, Aug. 26, 2003]

§§ 1170.48–1170.50 [Reserved]

Subpart F—Enforcement

§ 1170.51 Assurances required.

(a) *Assurances.* An applicant for Federal financial assistance to which this part applies shall submit an assurance, on a form specified by the responsible Endowment official, that the program or activity will be operated in compliance with this part. An applicant may incorporate these assurances by reference in subsequent applications to the Endowment.

(b) *Duration of obligation.* (1) In the case of Federal financial assistance extended in the form of real property or to provide real property or structures on the property, the assurance will obligate the recipient or, in the case of a subsequent transfer, the transferee, for the period during which the real property or structures are used for the purpose for which Federal financial assistance is extended or for another purpose involving the provision of similar services or benefits.

(2) In the case of Federal financial assistance extended to provide personal property, the assurance will obligate the recipient for the period during which it retains ownership or possession of the property.

(3) In all other cases the assurance will obligate the recipient for the period during which Federal financial assistance is extended.

(c) *Covenants.* (1) Where Federal financial assistance is provided in the form of real property or interest in the property from the Endowment, the instrument effecting or recording this transfer shall contain a covenant running with the land to assure nondiscrimination for the period during which the real property is used for a purpose for which the Federal financial assistance is extended or for another purpose involving the provision of similar services or benefits.

(2) Where no transfer of property is involved but property is purchased or improved with Federal financial assistance, the recipient shall agree to include the covenant described in paragraph (b)(2) of this section in the instrument effecting or recording any subsequent transfer of the property.

(3) Where Federal financial assistance is provided in the form of real property or interest in the property from the Endowment, the covenant shall also include a condition coupled with a right to be reserved by the Endowment to revert title to the property in the event of a breach of the covenant. If a transferee of real property proposes to mortgage or to otherwise encumber the real property as security for financing construction of new, or improvement of existing, facilities on the property for the purposes for which the property was transferred, the responsible Endowment official may, upon request of the transferee and if necessary to accomplish such financing and upon such conditions as he or she deems appropriate, agree to forbear the exercise of such right to revert title for

so long as the lien of such mortgage or other encumbrance remains effective.

[46 FR 55897, Nov. 12, 1981, as amended at 68 FR 51386, Aug. 26, 2003]

§ 1170.52 Remedial action, voluntary action, and self-evaluation.

(a) *Remedial action.* (1) If the Chairman finds that a recipient has discriminated against persons on the basis of handicap in violation of section 504 or this part, the recipient shall take such remedial action as the Chairman deems necessary to overcome the effects of the discrimination.

(2) Where a recipient is found to have discriminated against persons on the basis of handicap in violation of section 504 or this part and where another recipient exercises control over the recipient that has discriminated, the Chairman, where appropriate, may require either or both recipients to take remedial action.

(3) The Chairman may, where necessary to overcome the effects of discrimination in violation of section 504 or this part, require a recipient to take remedial action:

(i) With respect to handicapped persons who are no longer participants in the recipient's program or activity but who were participants in the program or activity when such discrimination occurred, or

(ii) With respect to handicapped persons who would have been participants in the program or activity had the discrimination not occurred.

(b) *Voluntary action.* A recipient may take steps, in addition to any action that is required by this part, to overcome the effects of conditions that resulted in limited participation in the recipient's program or activity by qualified handicapped persons.

(c) A recipient shall within one year of the effective date of this part:

(1) Evaluate, with the assistance of interested persons, including handicapped persons or organizations representing handicapped persons, its current policies and practices and the effects thereof that do not or may not meet the requirements of this part;

(2) Modify, after consultation with interested persons, including handicapped persons or organizations representing handicapped persons, any policies and practices that do not meet the requirements of this part;

(3) Take, after consultation with interested persons, including handicapped persons or organizations representing handicapped persons, appropriate remedial steps to eliminate the effects of any discrimination that resulted from adherence to these policies and practices.

(4) A recipient that employs fifteen or more persons shall maintain on file, make available for public inspection, and provide to the Endowment upon request, for at least three years following completion of the self-evaluation:

(i) A list of the interested persons consulted;

(ii) A description of areas examined and any problems identified; and

(iii) A description of any modifications made and of any remedial steps taken.

(5) The completed self-evaluation should be signed by a responsible official designated to coordinate the recipient's efforts in connection with this section.

[46 FR 55897, Nov. 12, 1981, as amended at 68 FR 51386, Aug. 26, 2003]

§ 1170.53 Designation of responsible employee and adoption of grievance procedures.

(a) *Designation of responsible employee.* A recipient that employs fifteen or more persons shall designate at least one person to coordinate its efforts to comply with this part.

(b) *Adoption of grievance procedures.* A recipient that employs fifteen or more persons shall adopt grievance procedures that incorporate appropriate due process standards and that provide for the prompt and equitable resolution of complaints alleging any action prohibited by this part. Such procedures need not be established with respect to complaints from applicants for employment or from applicants for admission to postsecondary educational institutions.

§ 1170.54 Notice.

(a) A recipient that employs fifteen or more persons shall take appropriate initial and continuing steps to notify participants, beneficiaries, applicants, and employees, including those with

§ 1170.55

impaired vision or hearing, and unions or professional organizations holding collective bargaining or professional agreements with the recipient that it does not discriminate on the basis of handicap in violation of section 504 and this part. The notification shall state, where appropriate, that the recipient does not discriminate in admission or access to, or treatment or employment in, its programs or activities. The notification shall also include an identification of the responsible employee designated pursuant to § 1170.53(a). A recipient shall make the initial notification required by this paragraph within 90 days of the effective date of this part. Methods of initial and continuing notification may include the posting of notices, publication in newspapers and magazines, placement of notices in recipients' publication, and distribution of memoranda or other written communications.

(b) If a recipient publishes or uses recruitment materials or publications containing general information that it makes available to participants, beneficiaries, applicants, or employees, it shall include in those materials or publications a statement of the policy described in paragraph (a) of this section. A recipient may meet the requirement of this paragraph either by including appropriate inserts in existing materials and publications or by revising and reprinting the materials and publications.

[46 FR 55897, Nov. 12, 1981, as amended at 68 FR 51386, Aug. 26, 2003]

§ 1170.55 Endowment enforcement and compliance procedures.

The procedural provisions applicable to Title VI of the Civil Rights Act of 1964 apply to this part. These procedures are found in §§ 1110.6 through 1110.11 of part 1100 of this title.

§§ 1170.56–1170.99 [Reserved]

PART 1171—PUBLIC ACCESS TO NEH RECORDS UNDER THE FREEDOM OF INFORMATION ACT

Sec.
1171.1 About the National Endowment for the Humanities.
1171.2 General provisions.
1171.3 Information policy.
1171.4 Public availability of records.
1171.5 Requests for records.
1171.6 Responsibilities for processing and responding to requests.
1171.7 Timing of responses to requests.
1171.8 Responses to requests.
1171.9 Confidential commercial information.
1171.10 Administrative appeals.
1171.11 Fees.
1171.12 Preservation of records.
1171.13 Other rights and services.

AUTHORITY: 5 U.S.C. 552; 20 U.S.C. 959; 31 U.S.C. 3717; E.O. 12600.

SOURCE: 79 FR 9415, Feb. 19, 2014, unless otherwise noted.

§ 1171.1 About the National Endowment for the Humanities.

The National Endowment for the Humanities (NEH) was established by the National Foundation on the Arts and Humanities Act of 1965, 20 U.S.C. 951 *et seq.*, and is an independent grant-making agency of the United States government dedicated to supporting research, education, preservation, and public programs in the humanities. The NEH is directed by a Chairman and has an advisory council composed of twenty-six presidentially-appointed and Senate-confirmed members.

§ 1171.2 General provisions.

This part contains the regulations the NEH follows in processing requests for NEH records under the Freedom of Information Act (FOIA), 5 U.S.C. 552, as amended. The NEH also follows these regulations to process all FOIA requests made to the Federal Council on the Arts and the Humanities (FCAH), an organization established by the National Foundation on the Arts and Humanities Act of 1965 for which the NEH provides legal counsel. These regulations should be read together with the FOIA and OMB's Free Guidelines, which provides additional information about access to NEH and FCAH records. FOIA applies to requests for records concerning the general activities of the government and of the NEH in particular. When individuals seek records about themselves under the Privacy Act of 1974, 5 U.S.C. 552a, NEH processes those requests under both NEH's Privacy regulations at part 1115 of this chapter, and this part. Although

National Foundation on the Arts and the Humanities §1171.5

requests are considered either FOIA requests or Privacy Act requests, agencies process requests in accordance with both laws, which provides the greatest degree of lawful access while safeguarding an individual's personal privacy.

§1171.3 Information policy.

The NEH may provide information the agency routinely makes available to the public through its regular activities (for example, program announcements and solicitations, press releases, and summaries of awarded grant applications) without following this part. As a matter of policy, the NEH makes discretionary disclosures of records or information otherwise exempt under the FOIA whenever disclosure would not foreseeably harm an interest protected by a FOIA exemption. This policy, however, does not create any right enforceable in court.

§1171.4 Public availability of records.

(a) In accordance with 5 U.S.C. 552(a)(2), the NEH will make the following records available for public inspection in an electronic format (unless they are published and copies are offered for sale) without a FOIA request:

(1) Final opinions, including concurring and dissenting opinions, as well as orders made in the adjudication of cases,

(2) Statements of policy and interpretations which have been adopted by the agency and are not published in the FEDERAL REGISTER,

(3) Administrative staff manuals and instructions to staff that affect a member of the public,

(4) Copies of all records, regardless of format, which have been released to any person under 5 U.S.C. 552(a)(3) and which because of their subject matter, the NEH determines have become or are likely to become subject to subsequent requests for substantially the same records, or have been requested three (3) or more times; and

(5) A general index of the records referred to in paragraph (b) of this section.

(b) The NEH will also maintain and make available for public inspection in an electronic format current indexes as required by 5 U.S.C. 552(a)(2) of the FOIA. However, since the NEH has determined that publication and distribution of these indexes is unnecessary and impracticable, the NEH will provide these indexes upon request at a cost not to exceed the direct cost of the duplication.

(c) NEH proactively identifies records of interest to the public, such as past awards, press releases, grant guidelines, and grant terms and conditions, and makes these records available on the NEH's Web site at *www.neh.gov*. In addition, copies of the NEH's policy statements, information about the NEH's FOIA program, sample grant narratives, and other frequently requested records are available in the NEH's Electronic Library.

[79 FR 9415, Feb. 19, 2014, as amended at 82 FR 45, Jan. 3, 2017]

§1171.5 Requests for records.

(a) *How to make a request.* Your FOIA request need not be in any particular format, but it must be in writing, include your full name, mailing address, daytime telephone number. If you choose to submit your request on the NEH Web site, the request must also include your email address. Your request should be clearly identified as a FOIA request in both the text of the request and on the envelope (or on the facsimile or in the subject heading of an email message) and must describe the requested records in enough detail to enable NEH staff to locate them with a reasonable amount of effort. Whenever possible, your request should include specific information about each record sought, such as the date, title or name, author, recipient, and subject matter of the record. The NEH has no obligation to answer questions posed as FOIA requests or to create records to satisfy a FOIA request.

(b) *Agreement to pay fees.* If you make a FOIA request, the NEH will consider it an agreement by you to pay all applicable fees charged under this part, subject to the fee limitations of §1171.11(d). When making a request, you may specify a willingness to pay a greater or lesser amount.

(c) *Where to send a request.* (1) For NEH records (except NEH Office of the Inspector General records) and/or

§ 1171.6

FCAH records, write to: The General Counsel, Office of the General Counsel, National Endowment for the Humanities, 400 7th Street SW., Room 4060, Washington, DC, 20506. You may also send your request to the NEH General Counsel by facsimile at 202–606–8600, by email at *gencounsel@neh.gov*, or through the NEH's electronic FOIA request system, which is available on the NEH Web site at *www.neh.gov*.

(2) For NEH Office of the Inspector General records, write to: The Inspector General, Office of the Inspector General, National Endowment for the Humanities, 400 7th Street SW., Room 2200, Washington, DC 20506. You may also send your request to the Inspector General by facsimile at 202–606–8329 or by email at *oig@neh.gov*.

[79 FR 9415, Feb. 19, 2014, as amended at 80 FR 42066, July 16, 2015]

§ 1171.6 Responsibilities for processing and responding to requests.

(a) *Processing requests.* The NEH Office of the General Counsel (OGC) is the central office for processing requests for records, except when it's necessary for the NEH Office of Inspector General (OIG) to process a request to maintain the OIG's independence or ability to carry out its statutorily mandated duties. If the request is for OIG records, the NEH will inform the requester which office will be processing the request.

(b) *Authority to grant or deny requests.* The NEH General Counsel (or designee) is authorized to grant or deny requests for NEH records (excluding requests for OIG records), and/or FCAH records. The NEH Deputy Inspector General (or designee) is authorized to grant or deny requests for OIG records. The NEH General Counsel (or designee) is authorized to grant or deny requests on any fee matters and requests for expedited treatment, including OIG-related requests.

(c) *Consultations and referrals.* When the NEH receives a request for a record in its possession, the agency will determine whether another Federal government agency is better able to decide whether the record should or should not be disclosed under the FOIA. Ordinarily, the agency that originated a record will be presumed to be best able to determine whether to disclose it.

(1) If the NEH determines that it is the agency best able to process the record in response to the request, then it will do so, after consultation with the other agency that has a substantial interest in the requested records.

(2) If the NEH determines that it is not the agency best able to process the record, then it will refer the record (or portion thereof) to the other Federal agency, but only if that agency is subject to the FOIA.

(d) *Notice of referral.* Whenever the NEH refers all or any part of the responsibility for responding to a request to another agency, the NEH will notify the requester of the referral, provide the name of the agency to which the referral was directed, and include that agency's FOIA contact information. NEH will notify the requester of the part of the request that has been referred, unless such notification would disclose information otherwise exempt. If notification to the requester about the referral would cause a harm meant to be protected against by the FOIA, NEH will coordinate with the agency rather than referring the records to it.

§ 1171.7 Timing of responses to requests.

(a) *In general.* The NEH customarily will respond to requests according to their order of receipt. In determining which records are responsive to a request, the NEH will include only those records in its possession as of the date it begins its search for records. If any other date is used, the NEH will inform the requester of that date.

(b) *Timing for initial response.* Ordinarily, the NEH will determine whether to grant or deny a request for records within twenty (20) days (weekends and Federal holidays excluded) of when the NEH receives a request.

(c) *Tolling of time limits.* The NEH may toll the 20-day time period to:

(1) Make one request for information it reasonably requests from the requester; or

(2) Clarify the applicability or amount of any fees, if necessary, with the requester.

(3) Under paragraphs (c)(1) or (2) of this section, the tolling period ends

upon the NEH's receipt of the information or clarification from the requester.

(d) *Unusual circumstances.* (1) When the NEH cannot meet the statutory time limits for processing a request because of unusual circumstances as defined in the FOIA, the NEH may extend the response time as follows:

(i) If the extension will be for ten (10) or fewer working days (i.e., weekends and Federal holidays excluded), the NEH will notify the requester as soon as practicable in writing of the unusual circumstances and the expected response date; and

(ii) If the extension will be for more than ten (10) working days, the NEH will provide the requester with an opportunity either to modify the request so that it may be processed within the time limit or to arrange an alternative time period to process the request or a modified request. To aid the requester, NEH shall make available its FOIA Public Liaison, who shall assist in the resolution of any disputes between the requester and the agency, and shall notify the requester of his or her right to seek dispute resolution services from the Office of Government Information Services.

(2) If the NEH reasonably believes that multiple requests submitted by a requester, or a group of requesters acting in concert, constitute a single request that would otherwise involve unusual circumstances, and the requests involve clearly related matters, the NEH may aggregate the requests. The NEH will not aggregate multiple requests involving unrelated matters.

(e) *Expedited processing.* (1) The NEH will process requests and appeals on an expedited basis whenever it determines that they involve:

(i) Circumstances in which the lack of expedited treatment could reasonably be expected to pose an imminent threat to the life or physical safety of an individual; or

(ii) An urgency to inform the public about actual or alleged Federal government activity if the expedited processing request is made by a person primarily engaged in disseminating information.

(2) A requester may seek expedited processing at the time of the requester's initial request for records or at any later time.

(3) To request expedited processing, a requester must submit a statement, certified to be true and correct to the requester's best knowledge and belief, explaining in detail the basis for requesting expedited processing.

(4) Within ten (10) calendar days of receipt of a request for expedited processing, the NEH will decide whether to grant it and will notify the requester of the decision. If the NEH grants a request for expedited processing, the NEH will place the request in the expedited processing track and then process the request as soon as practicable. If the NEH denies a request for expedited processing, the NEH will act upon any appeal of that decision expeditiously.

[79 FR 9415, Feb. 19, 2014, as amended at 82 FR 45, Jan. 3, 2017]

§ 1171.8 **Responses to requests.**

(a) *Acknowledgment of requests.* Upon receipt of a request that will take longer than ten (10) days to process, the NEH will send the requester an acknowledgment letter that assigns the request an individualized tracking number.

(b) *Grants of requests.* If the NEH makes a determination to grant a request in whole or in part, it will notify the requester in writing of such determination and the reasons therefore, and the requester's right to seek assistance from NEH's FOIA Public Liaison. The NEH will inform the requester of any applicable fees and will disclose records to the requester promptly on payment of any applicable fees. The NEH will mark or annotate records disclosed in part to show the amount of information deleted pursuant to a FOIA exemption, unless doing so would harm an interest protected by an applicable FOIA exemption. If technically feasible, the NEH will also indicate, on the agency record(s) it provides, the location of the information deleted.

(c) *Denials of requests.* If the NEH makes a determination to deny a request in any respect, the NEH will also notify the requester in writing of:

(1) The name and title or position of the person responsible for the denial;

§ 1171.9

(2) A brief statement of the reason(s) for the denial, including any FOIA exemption applied by the NEH in denying the request;

(3) An estimate of the volume of records or information withheld, if applicable, although such an estimate is not required if the volume is otherwise indicated through deletion on the records disclosed in part, or if providing such an estimate would harm an interest protected by an applicable exemption;

(4) The requester's right to seek dispute resolution services from NEH's FOIA Public Liaison or the Office of Government Information Services; and

(5) A statement that the requester may appeal the denial under § 1171.10 and a description of the requirements to appeal.

[79 FR 9415, Feb. 19, 2014, as amended at 82 FR 45, Jan. 3, 2017]

§ 1171.9 Confidential commercial information.

(a) *In general.* The NEH will not disclose confidential commercial information in response to a FOIA request, except as described in this section.

(b) *Definitions.* For purposes of this section:

(1) *Confidential commercial information* means commercial or financial information obtained by the NEH from a submitter that may be protected from disclosure under Exemption 4 of the FOIA.

(2) *Submitter* means any person or entity from whom the NEH obtains confidential commercial information, directly or indirectly. The term includes corporations; state, local, and tribal governments; and foreign governments.

(c) *Designation of confidential commercial information.* A submitter of confidential commercial information will use good-faith efforts to designate by appropriate markings, either at the time of submission or at a reasonable time thereafter, any portions of its submission that it considers to be protected from disclosure under Exemption 4. These designations will expire ten years after the date of the submission unless the submitter requests, and provides justification for, a longer designation period.

(d) *When notice to submitters is required.* (1) The NEH will give notice to a submitter whenever:

(i) The submitter, in good faith, has designated the requested information as information considered protected from disclosure under Exemption 4; or

(ii) The NEH has reason to believe that the information may be protected from disclosure under Exemption 4.

(2) The notice will either describe the confidential commercial information requested or include copies of the requested records or record portions containing the information. In cases involving a voluminous number of submitters, the NEH may make notice by posting or publishing the notice in a place reasonably likely to accomplish it.

(e) *Exceptions to submitter notice requirements.* The notice requirements of this section will not apply if:

(1) The NEH determines that the requested information is exempt under the FOIA;

(2) The information lawfully has been published or has been officially made available to the public;

(3) Disclosure of the information is required by statute (other than the FOIA) or by a regulation issued in accordance with the requirements of Executive Order 12600 of June 23, 1987; or

(4) The designation made by the submitter under paragraph (c) of this section appears obviously frivolous, except that, in such a case, the NEH will give the submitter written notice of any final decision to disclose the information within a reasonable number of days prior to a specified disclosure date.

(f) *Opportunity to object to disclosure.* (1) The NEH will specify a reasonable time period within which the submitter must respond to the notice described in paragraph (d)(2) of this section. If a submitter has any objection to disclosure, it must submit a detailed written statement to the NEH specifying all grounds for withholding any portion of the information under any exemption of the FOIA. If the submitter relies on Exemption 4 as a basis of nondisclosure, the submitter must explain why the information constitutes a trade secret, or commercial or financial information that is privileged or confidential.

(2) The NEH will consider a submitter who fails to respond with the time period specified on the notice to have no objection to disclosure of the information. The NEH will not consider information it receives from a submitter after the date of any disclosure decision. Any information provided by a submitter under this section may itself be subject to disclosure under the FOIA.

(g) *Notice of intent to disclose.* The NEH will consider a submitter's objections and specific grounds for nondisclosure in deciding whether to disclose confidential commercial information. Whenever the NEH decides to disclose confidential commercial information over the objection of a submitter, the NEH will provide the submitter written notice, which will include:

(1) A statement of the reason(s) why each of the submitter's disclosure objections was not sustained;

(2) A description of the business information to be disclosed; and

(3) A specified disclosure date, which will be a reasonable time after the notice.

(h) *Notice of FOIA lawsuit.* Whenever a requester files a lawsuit seeking to compel the disclosure of confidential commercial information, the NEH will promptly notify the submitter.

(i) *Requester notification.* The NEH will notify the requester whenever the NEH provides the submitter with notice and an opportunity to object to disclosure; whenever the NEH notifies the submitter of its intent to disclose the requested information; and whenever a submitter files a lawsuit to prevent the disclosure of the information.

§ 1171.10 Administrative appeals.

(a) You may appeal a denial of your request for NEH records (except NEH OIG records) and/or FCAH records to The Deputy Chairman, National Endowment for the Humanities, 400 7th Street SW., Room 4053, Washington, DC 20506. You may also send your appeal to the NEH General Counsel by facsimile at 202–606–8600, by email at gencounsel@neh.gov, or through the NEH's electronic FOIA request system, which is available on the NEH Web site at *www.neh.gov.* For a denial of your request for OIG records, you may appeal by facsimile at 202–606–8329, by email at *oig@neh.gov* or by mail to The Inspector General, National Endowment for the Humanities, 400 7th Street SW., Room 2200, Washington, DC 20506. Your appeal must be in writing and received by NEH within ninety (90) days of the date of the letter denying your request in whole or in part. Your appeal letter must clearly identify the NEH decision that you are appealing and contain the tracking number, if assigned. You should clearly mark your appeal letter and envelope "Freedom of Information Act Appeal."

(b) *Responses to appeals.* The Deputy Chairman (or designee) or the Inspector General (or designee) will make a written determination on your appeal within twenty (20) days (weekends and Federal holidays excluded) after the agency receives your appeal, except as provided by 1171.7(d). If the appeal decision affirms the denial of your request, the NEH will notify you in writing of the reason(s) for the decision, including the applicable FOIA exemption(s), and inform you of the FOIA provisions for court review of the decision. If the denial of your request is reversed or modified, in whole or in part, the NEH will reprocess your request in accordance with that appeal decision and notify you of that decision in writing. A response to an appeal will advise the requester that the 2007 amendments to FOIA created the Office of Government Information Services (OGIS) to offer mediation services to resolve disputes between FOIA requesters and Federal agencies as a non-exclusive alternative to litigation. A requester may contact OGIS in any of the following ways: Office of Government Information Services, National Archives and Records Administration, 8601 Adelphi Road—OGIS, College Park, MD 20740; *https:// ogis.archives.gov;* email: *ogis@nara.gov;* telephone: 202–741–5770; facsimile: 202–741–5769; toll-free: 1–877–684–6448.

(c) *When appeal is required.* If you wish to seek review by a court of any denial by the NEH, you must first submit a timely administrative appeal to the NEH.

[79 FR 9415, Feb. 19, 2014, as amended at 80 FR 42066, July 16, 2015; 82 FR 46, Jan. 3, 2017]

§ 1171.11 Fees.

(a) *In general.* The NEH will assess fees for processing FOIA requests in accordance with this section and with the Uniform Freedom of Information Fee Schedule and Guidelines published by the Office of Management and Budget at 52 FR 10012 (Mar. 27, 1987). In order to resolve any fee issues that arise under this section, the NEH may contact a requester for additional information. The NEH ordinarily will collect all applicable fees before sending copies of records to a requester. Requesters must pay fees by check or money order made payable to the Treasury of the United States.

(b) *Definitions.* For purposes of this section:

(1) *Commercial use request* means a request from or on behalf of a person who seeks information for a use or purpose that furthers his or her commercial, trade, or profit interest, which can include furthering those interests through litigation. When it appears that the requester will put the records to a commercial use, either because of the nature of the request itself or because the NEH has reasonable cause to doubt a requester's stated use, the NEH will provide the requester a reasonable opportunity to submit further clarification.

(2) *Direct costs* means those expenses that an agency actually incurs in searching for and duplicating (and, in the case of commercial use requests, reviewing) records to respond to a FOIA request. Direct costs include, for example, the salary of the employee performing the work (the basic rate of pay for the employee, plus 16 percent of that rate to cover benefits) and the cost of operating duplication machinery. Not included in direct costs are overhead expenses such as the costs of space and heating or lighting of the facility in which the records are kept.

(3) *Duplication* means the making of a copy of a record, or of the information contained in it, necessary to respond to a FOIA request. Copies can take the form of paper, microform, audiovisual materials, or electronic records among others.

(4) *Educational institution* means any school that operates a program of scholarly research. A requester in this category must show that the request is authorized by and made under the auspices of a qualifying institution and that the records are not sought for a commercial use, but are sought to further scholarly research.

(5) *Noncommercial scientific institution* means an institution that is not operated on a "commercial" basis, as defined in paragraph (b)(1) above, and that is operated solely for the purpose of conducting scientific research, the results of which are not intended to promote any particular product or industry. A requester in this category must show that the request is authorized by and made under the auspices of a qualifying institution and that the records are not sought for a commercial use or to promote any particular product or industry, but are sought to further scientific research.

(6) *Representative of the news media* means any person or entity that gathers information of potential interest to a segment of the public, uses its editorial skills to turn the raw materials into a distinct work, and distributes that work to an audience. The term "news" means information that is about current events or that would be of current interest to the public. Examples of news-media entities include television or radio stations broadcasting to the public at large, and publishers of periodicals (but only if such entities qualify as disseminators of "news") who make their products available for purchase or by subscription or by free distribution to the general public. The NEH will regard "freelance" journalists as working for a news-media organization if they demonstrate a solid basis for expecting publication though that organization. A publication contract would provide the clearest evidence, but the NEH will also consider a requester's past publication record in making this determination.

(7) *Review* means the process of examining a record located in response to a request in order to determine whether

National Foundation on the Arts and the Humanities §1171.11

any portion of it is exempt from disclosure. Review includes processing any record for disclosure, such as doing all that is necessary to redact it and prepare it for disclosure. It also includes time spent both obtaining and considering any formal objection to disclosure made by a confidential commercial information submitter under §1171.9, but it does not include time spent resolving general legal or policy issues regarding the application of exemptions. Review costs are recoverable even if the NEH ultimately does not disclose a record.

(8) *Search* means the process of looking for and retrieving records or information responsive to a request. It includes page-by-page or line-by-line identification of information within records and the reasonable efforts expended to locate and retrieve information from electronic records. The NEH will ensure that searches are done in the most efficient and least expensive manner reasonably possible.

(c) *Fee schedule.* In responding to FOIA requests, the NEH will charge the following fees for requests, subject to paragraphs (d), (e), and (f) of this section:

(1) *Search.* (i) The NEH will charge $4.00 for each quarter hour spent by clerical personnel in searching for and retrieving a requested record. When clerical personnel cannot perform the search and retrieval (e.g. identification of records within scope of request requires professional personnel), the NEH will charge $7.00 for each quarter hour of search time spent by professional personnel. Where the time of managerial personnel is required, the fee will be $10.00 for each quarter hour of time spent by those personnel. The NEH may charge for time spent searching even if it does not locate any responsive records or if it determines that the records are entirely exempt from disclosure.

(ii) For computer searches of records, the NEH will charge the actual direct cost of conducting the search.

(2) *Duplication.* The fee for a photocopy of a record on one-side of an 8½ × 11 inch sheet of paper is ten cents per page. For copies of records produced on tapes, disks, or other electronic media, the NEH will charge the direct costs of producing the copy, including operator time. For other forms of duplication, the NEH will charge the direct costs of that duplication. The NEH will honor a requester's preference for receiving a record in a particular form or format where it is readily reproducible by the NEH in the form or format requested.

(3) *Review.* The NEH will charge review fees to requesters who make a commercial use request. Review fees will be charged only for the initial record review (i.e., the review the NEH conducted to determine whether an exemption applies to a particular record or record portion at the initial request stage). No charge will be made for review at the administrative appeal stage for exemptions applied at the initial review stage. However, if the NEH re-reviews the records for the applicability of other exemptions that it did not previously consider, then the costs for the subsequent review are assessable. Review fees will be charged at the same rates as those charged for a search under paragraph (c)(1)(i). The NEH may charge for review even if it ultimately decides not to disclose a record.

(d) *Limitations on charging requesters.* (1) Except for requesters seeking records for commercial use, the NEH will provide without charge:

(i) The first 100 pages of duplication (or the cost equivalent); and

(ii) The first two hours of search (or the cost equivalent).

(2) When, after first deducting the 100 pages (or its cost equivalent) and the first two hours of search, the total fee is $25.00 or less for any request, the NEH will not charge a fee.

(3) If NEH fails to comply with the FOIA's time limits in which to respond to a request, it may not charge search fees, or, in the instances of requests from requesters described in paragraphs (b)(4) through (6) of this section, may not charge duplication fees, except as described in paragraphs (d)(3)(i) through (iii) of this section.

(i) If NEH has determined that unusual circumstances, as defined by the FOIA, apply and NEH has provided timely written notice to the requester in accordance with the FOIA, a failure to comply with the time limit shall be excused for an additional ten (10) working days.

(ii) If NEH has determined that unusual circumstances, as defined by the FOIA, apply and more than 5,000 pages are necessary to respond to the request, NEH may charge search fees, or, in the case of requesters described in paragraphs (b)(4) through (6) of this section, may charge duplication fees, provided NEH provided timely written notice of unusual circumstances to the requester in accordance with the FOIA and NEH discussed with the requester via written mail, email, or telephone (or made not less than three good-faith attempts to do so) how the requester could effectively limit the scope of the request in accordance with 5 U.S.C. 552(a)(6)(B)(ii).

(iii) If a court has determined that exceptional circumstances exist, as defined by the FOIA, a failure to comply with the time limits shall be excused for the length of time provided by the court order.

(e) *Categories of requesters.* There are four categories of FOIA requesters: commercial use requesters; educational and non-commercial scientific institutions; representatives of the news media; and all other requesters. The NEH will assess fees for these categories of requesters as follows:

(1) *Commercial use requesters.* The NEH will charge the full direct costs for searching for, reviewing, and duplicating requested records.

(2) *Educational and non-commercial scientific institution requesters.* The NEH will charge for duplication only, excluding costs for the first 100 pages.

(3) *News media requesters.* The NEH will charge for duplication only, excluding costs for the first 100 pages.

(4) *All other requesters.* The NEH will charge requesters who do not fit into any of the categories above the full reasonable direct cost of searching for and reproducing records, excluding costs for the first 100 pages and the first two hours of search time.

(f) *Requirements for fee waivers or reduction of fees.* (1) The NEH will furnish responsive records without charge or at a reduced charge if it determines, based on all available information, that the requester has demonstrated that:

(i) Disclosure of the requested information is in the public interest because it is likely to contribute significantly to public understanding of the operations or activities of the government, and

(ii) Disclosure of the information is not primarily in the commercial interest of the requester.

(2) To determine whether the first fee requirement is met, the NEH will consider the following factors:

(i) The subject of the requested records must concern identifiable operations or activities of the Federal government, with a connection that is direct and clear, not remote or attenuated.

(ii) The disclosable portions of the requested records must be meaningfully informative about government operations or activities in order to be "likely to contribute" to an increased public understanding of those operations or activities. Disclosure of information already in the public domain, in either duplicative or substantially identical form, is unlikely to contribute to such understanding where nothing new would be added to the public's understanding.

(iii) The disclosure must contribute to the understanding of a reasonably broad audience of persons interested in the subject, as opposed to the individual understanding of the requester. A requester's expertise in the subject area as well as his or her ability and intention to effectively convey information to the public will be considered. It will ordinarily be presumed that a representative of the news media satisfies this consideration.

(iv) The public's understanding of the subject in question must be enhanced by the disclosure to a significant extent. The NEH will make no value judgments about whether the information at issue is "important" enough to be made public.

(3) To determine whether the second fee waiver requirement is met, the NEH will consider the following factors:

(i) The NEH will identify any commercial interest of the requester, as defined in paragraph (b)(1) of this section, that would be furthered by the requested disclosure. Requesters will be given an opportunity to provide explanatory information regarding this consideration.

(ii) A fee waiver or reduction is justified where the public interest is greater than any identified commercial interest in disclosure.

(4) Where only some of the requested records satisfy the requirements for a fee waiver, a waiver will be granted for those records.

(5) Requesters should make fee waiver or reduction requests when they first submit a FOIA request to the NEH. Fee waiver or reduction requests should address the factors listed in paragraphs (f)(2) and (3) of this section. Fee waiver or reduction requests may be submitted at a later time so long as the underlying record request is pending or on administrative appeal.

(g) *Notice of anticipated fees in excess of $25.00.* (1) When the NEH determines or estimates that the fees to be charged under this section will exceed $25.00, it will notify the requester of the actual or estimated fees, unless the requester has indicated a willingness to pay fees as high as those anticipated. If the NEH can only readily estimate a portion of the fees, it will advise the requester that the estimated fee may be only a portion of the total fee.

(2) The notice will offer the requester an opportunity to confer with NEH personnel in order to reformulate the request to meet the requester's needs at a lower cost and inform the requester of paragraph (d)(1) of this section, if applicable. A commitment by the requester to pay the anticipated fee must be in writing and must be received by the NEH within thirty (30) calendar days from the date of notification of the fee estimate. Until the requester agrees to pay the anticipated fee, the NEH will not consider the request as received by the agency and no further work will be done on the request. If a requester fails to respond within this timeframe, the NEH will administratively close the request.

(h) *Charges for other services.* When the NEH chooses, in its sole discretion, to provide a requested special service (e.g. certifying that records are true copies or sending them by other than ordinary mail), it will charge the direct costs of providing the service to the requester.

(i) *Charging interest.* The NEH may charge interest on any unpaid bill starting on the 31st day following the date of billing the requester. The NEH will assess interest charges at the rate provided in 31 U.S.C. 3717 and such charges will accrue from the billing date until the NEH receives payment from the requester. The NEH will follow the provisions of the Debt Collection Act of 1982 (Pub. L. 97–365, 96 Stat. 1749), as amended, and its administrative procedures, including the use of consumer reporting agencies, collection agencies, and offset.

(j) *Advance payment.* (1) For requests other than those described in paragraphs (j)(2) and (3) of this section, the NEH will not require the requester to make an advance payment before it commences or continues work on a request. Payment owed for work already completed (i.e., payment before copies are sent to a requester) is not an advance payment.

(2) When the NEH determines or estimates that a total fee to be charged under this section will be more than $250.00, it may require the requester to make an advance payment of an amount up to the amount of the entire anticipated fee before beginning to process the request, except where it receives a satisfactory assurance of full payment from a requester that has a history of prompt payment.

(3) When a requester has previously failed to pay a properly charged fee to the NEH within thirty (30) days of the billing date, the NEH may require the requester to pay the full amount due, plus any applicable interest, and to make an advance payment of the full amount of any anticipated fee, before the NEH begins to process a new request or continues to process a pending request from that requester.

(4) When there is an advance payment request, the NEH will not consider the request as received by the agency and no further work will be done on the request until the required payment is received. If the requester fails to respond within thirty (30) calendar days after the date of the advance payment request, the NEH will administratively close the request.

§ 1171.12

(k) *Aggregating requests.* When the NEH reasonably believes that a requester or a group of requesters acting together is attempting to divide a request into a series of requests for the purpose of avoiding fees, the NEH may aggregate those requests and charge accordingly. The NEH may presume that multiple requests of this type made within a 30-day period have been made in order to avoid fees. For requests separated by a longer period, the NEH will aggregate them only when there is a reasonable basis for determining that aggregation is warranted in view of all the circumstances involved. The NEH will not aggregate multiple requests involving unrelated matters.

[79 FR 9415, Feb. 19, 2014, as amended at 82 FR 46, Jan. 3, 2017]

§ 1171.12 Preservation of records.

NEH will preserve all correspondence pertaining to the requests that it receives as well as copies of all requested records, until disposition or destruction is authorized by the agency's General Records Schedule of the National Archives and Records Administration (NARA) or other NARA-approved records schedule. Records will not be disposed of while they are the subject of a pending request, appeal, or lawsuit under the Act.

§ 1171.13 Other rights and services.

Nothing in this part will be construed to entitle any person, as of right, to any service or to the disclosure of any record to which such person is not entitled under the FOIA.

PART 1172—NONDISCRIMINATION ON THE BASIS OF AGE IN FEDERALLY ASSISTED PROGRAMS OR ACTIVITIES

Subpart A—General

Sec.
1172.1 Purpose.
1172.2 Application.
1172.3 Definitions.

Subpart B—Standards for Determining Age Discrimination

1172.11 Rules against age discrimination.

1172.12 Exceptions to the rules against age discrimination.
1172.13 Burden of proof.

Subpart C—Responsibilities of NEH Recipients

1172.21 General responsibilities.
1172.22 Notice to subrecipients.
1172.23 Self-evaluation.
1172.24 Information requirements.

Subpart D—Investigation, Conciliation, and Enforcement Procedures

1172.31 Compliance reviews.
1172.32 Complaints.
1172.33 Mediation.
1172.34 Investigation.
1172.35 Prohibition against intimidation or retaliation.
1172.36 Enforcement procedure.
1172.37 Hearings, decisions, post-termination proceedings.
1172.38 Remedial action by recipients.
1172.39 Alternate funds disbursal procedure.
1172.40 Exhaustion of administrative remedies.

AUTHORITY: 42 U.S.C. 6101–6107; 45 CFR 90.

SOURCE: 79 FR 26633, May 9, 2014, unless otherwise noted.

Subpart A—General

§ 1172.1 Purpose.

The purpose of this part is to set out the National Endowment for the Humanities' (NEH) policies and procedures for implementing the Age Discrimination Act of 1975, as amended, 42 U.S.C. 6101 *et seq.*, (the Act or the Age Act). The Act is designed to prohibit discrimination on the basis of age in programs or activities receiving Federal financial assistance. The Act also permits federally assisted programs or activities, and recipients of Federal funds, to continue to use certain age distinctions and factors other than age which meet the requirements of the Act and the regulations in this part. The regulations in this part are based upon the general, government-wide age discrimination regulations issued by the United States Department of Health and Human Services (HHS) at 45 CFR part 90. Complaints of employment discrimination based on age may be subject to the Age Discrimination in Employment Act of 1967, as amended, 29 U.S.C. 621 *et seq.*, (ADEA) and should be filed administratively with the

National Foundation on the Arts and the Humanities § 1172.3

Equal Employment Opportunity Commission (EEOC) (29 CFR part 1626).

§ 1172.2 Application.

(a) The Act and the regulations in this part apply to each recipient and to any program or activity receiving financial assistance from the NEH.

(b) The Act does not apply to:

(1) Any age distinction contained in that part of a Federal, State or local statute or ordinance adopted by an elected, general purpose legislative body which:

(i) Provides any benefits or assistance to persons based on age;

(ii) Establishes criteria for participation in age-related terms; or

(iii) Describes intended beneficiaries or target groups in age-related terms.

(2) Any employment practice of any employer, employment agency, labor organization, or with respect to any labor-management joint apprenticeship training program.

(3) The rights or responsibilities of any person or party pursuant to the ADEA, the EEOC regulations under the ADEA, or any statements of policy promulgated by the EEOC under the ADEA.

§ 1172.3 Definitions.

As used in this part, the term:

Act means the Age Discrimination Act of 1975, as amended, 42 U.S.C. 6101 *et seq.* (Pub. L. 94-135).

Action means any act, activity, policy, rule, standard, or method of administration; or the use of any policy, rule, standard, or method of administration.

ADEA means the Age Discrimination in Employment Act of 1967, as amended, 29 U.S.C. 621 *et seq.* (Pub. L. 90-202).

Age means how old a person is, or the number of elapsed years from the date of a person's birth.

Age distinction means any action using age or an age-related term.

Age-related term means a word or words which necessarily imply a particular age or range of ages (for example, *children, adult, older persons*, but not *student*).

Agency means a Federal department or agency that is empowered to extend financial assistance.

Chairman means the Chairman of the National Endowment for the Humanities.

Federal financial assistance means any grant, entitlement, loan, cooperative agreement, contract (other than a procurement contract or a contract of insurance or guaranty), or any other arrangement by which NEH provides or otherwise makes available assistance in the form of:

(1) Funds;

(2) Services of Federal personnel; or

(3) Real and personal property or any interest in or use of property, including:

(i) Transfers or leases of property for less than fair market value or for reduced consideration; and

(ii) Proceeds from a subsequent transfer or lease of property if the Federal share of its fair market value is not returned to the Federal Government.

Normal operation means the operation of a program or activity without significant changes that would impair its ability to meet its objectives.

Program or activity means all of the operations of:

(1)(i) A department, agency, special purpose district, or other instrumentality of a State or local government, or

(ii) The entity of such State or local government that distributes Federal financial assistance and each such department or agency (and each other State or local government entity) to which the assistance is extended, in the case of assistance to a State or local government;

(2)(i) A college, university, or other postsecondary institution, or a public system of higher education, or

(ii) A local educational agency (as defined in 20 U.S.C. 7801), system of vocational education, or other school system;

(3)(i) An entire corporation, partnership, or other private organization, or an entire sole proprietorship—

(A) If assistance is extended to such corporation, partnership, private organization, or sole proprietorship as a whole, or

(B) Which is principally engaged in the business of providing education, health care, housing, social services, or parks and recreation; or

(ii) The entire plant or other comparable, geographically separate facility to which Federal financial assistance is extended, in the case of any other corporation, partnership, private organization, or sole proprietorship; or

(4) Any other entity which is established by two or more of the entities described in paragraph (1), (2), or (3) of this definition, any part of which is extended Federal financial assistance.

Recipient means any State or its political subdivision, any instrumentality of a State or its political sub-division, any public or private agency, institution, organization, or other entity, or any person to which Federal financial assistance is extended, directly or through another recipient. Recipient includes any successor, assignee, or transferee, but excludes the ultimate beneficiary of the assistance.

Secretary means the Secretary of the Department of Health and Human Services.

Statutory objective means any purpose of a program or activity expressly stated in any Federal statute, State statute, or local statute or ordinance adopted by an elected, general purpose legislative body.

Subrecipient means any of the entities in the definition of recipient to which a recipient extends or passes on Federal financial assistance. A subrecipient is generally regarded as a recipient of Federal financial assistance and has all the duties of a recipient in the regulations in this part.

United States means the fifty states, the District of Columbia, Puerto Rico, the Virgin Islands, American Samoa, Guam, Wake Island, the Trust Territory of the Pacific Islands, the Northern Marianas, and the territories and possessions of the United States.

Subpart B—Standards for Determining Age Discrimination

§ 1172.11 Rules against age discrimination.

The rules stated in this section are limited by the exceptions contained in § 1172.12.

(a) *General rule.* No person in the United States shall, on the basis of age, be excluded from participation in, be denied the benefits of, or be subjected to discrimination under, any program or activity receiving Federal financial assistance.

(b) *Specific rules.* A recipient may not, in any program or activity receiving Federal financial assistance, directly or through contractual, licensing, or other arrangements use age distinctions or take any other actions which have the effect, on the basis of age, of:

(1) Excluding individuals from, denying them the benefits of, or subjecting them to discrimination under, a program or activity receiving Federal financial assistance, or

(2) Denying or limiting individuals in their opportunity to participate in any program or activity receiving Federal financial assistance.

(c) The specific forms of age discrimination listed in paragraph (b) of this section do not necessarily constitute a complete list of discriminatory actions.

§ 1172.12 Exceptions to the rules against age discrimination.

(a) *Normal operation or statutory objective of any program or activity.* A recipient may take an action otherwise prohibited by § 1172.11 if the action reasonably takes into account age as a factor necessary to the normal operation or the achievement of any statutory objective of a program or activity, if:

(1) Age is used as a measure or approximation of one or more other characteristics;

(2) The other characteristic(s) must be measured or approximated in order for the normal operation of the program or activity to continue, or to achieve any statutory objective of the program or activity;

(3) The other characteristic(s) can be reasonably measured or approximated by the use of age; and

(4) The other characteristic(s) are impractical to measure directly on an individual basis.

(b) *Reasonable factors other than age.* A recipient may take an action otherwise prohibited by § 1172.11 which is based on a reasonable factor other than age, even though that action may have a disproportionate effect on persons of different ages. An action may be based on a reasonable factor other than age only if the factor bears a direct and substantial relationship to the normal operation of the program or activity or to the achievement of a statutory objective.

(c) *Affirmative action by recipient.* Even in the absence of a finding of discrimination, a recipient may take affirmative action to overcome the effects or conditions that resulted in limited participation in the recipient's program or activity on the basis of age.

(d) *Special benefits for children and the elderly.* If a recipient operating a program or activity provides special benefits to the elderly or to children, such use of age distinctions shall be presumed to be necessary to the normal operation of the program or activity, notwithstanding the provisions of § 1172.12(a).

(e) *Age distinctions in NEH regulations.* Any age distinction in a regulation issued by NEH is presumed to be necessary to the achievement of a statutory objective of the program or activity to which the regulation applies, notwithstanding the provisions of § 1172.12(a).

§ 1172.13 Burden of proof.

The recipient of Federal financial assistance bears the burden of proving that an age distinction or other action falls within the exceptions outlined in § 1172.12.

Subpart C—Responsibilities of NEH Recipients

§ 1172.21 General responsibilities.

A recipient has responsibility to ensure that its programs or activities are in compliance with the Act and the regulations in this part and to take steps to eliminate violations of the Act and the regulations in this part. A recipient also has responsibility to maintain records, provide information, and afford NEH access to its records to the extent NEH finds necessary to determine whether the recipient is in compliance with the Act and the regulations in this part.

§ 1172.22 Notice to subrecipients.

Where a recipient passes on Federal financial assistance from NEH to subrecipients, the recipient must provide the subrecipients with written notice of their obligations under the Act and the regulations in this part. Each recipient must also make necessary information available to its beneficiaries in order to inform them about the protections against discrimination provided by the Act and the regulations in this part.

§ 1172.23 Self-evaluation.

As part of a compliance review under § 1172.31 or a complaint investigation under § 1172.34, NEH may require a recipient employing the equivalent of fifteen (15) or more full time employees to complete a written self-evaluation, in a manner specified by NEH, of any age distinction imposed in its program or activity receiving Federal financial assistance. A recipient must take corrective and remedial action whenever a self-evaluation indicates a violation of the Act, and the recipient must make the self-evaluation available upon request to NEH and to the public for a period of three (3) years following its completion.

§ 1172.24 Information requirements.

Each recipient shall keep records containing information necessary for NEH to determine whether the recipient is in compliance with the Act and the regulations in this part, and shall provide any such records to NEH upon request and in the preferred format specified by NEH. Each recipient shall also permit reasonable access by NEH to its books, records, accounts, and other facilities and sources of information, to the extent necessary for NEH to determine whether the recipient is in compliance with the Act and this part.

Subpart D—Investigation, Conciliation, and Enforcement Procedures

§ 1172.31 Compliance reviews.

(a) NEH may conduct compliance reviews, pre-award reviews, and other similar procedures in order to investigate and correct violations of the Act and the regulations in this part. NEH may conduct these reviews even in the absence of a complaint against the recipient. Reviews may be as comprehensive as necessary to determine whether a recipient is in compliance with the Act and this part.

(b) If a compliance review or pre-award review indicates a violation of the Act and the regulations in this part, NEH will attempt to contact the recipient and achieve the recipient's voluntary compliance. If the recipient does not comply voluntarily, NEH may pursue enforcement efforts as described in § 1172.36.

§ 1172.32 Complaints.

(a) Any person, individually or as a member of a class or on behalf of others, may file a complaint with NEH, alleging discrimination prohibited by the Act and the regulations in this part based on an action occurring on or after July 1, 1979. A complainant must file a complaint in writing within one hundred eighty (180) days from the date that the complainant first had knowledge of the alleged act of discrimination. However, for good cause, NEH may extend this time limit. NEH will consider the date a complaint is filed as the date when the complaint is sufficient to be processed.

(b) Complaints must include a written and signed statement identifying the parties involved, describing the alleged violation, and stating the date on which the complainant first had knowledge of the alleged violation.

(c) NEH will attempt to facilitate the filing of complaints wherever possible, including taking the following measures, as appropriate:

(1) Widely disseminating information regarding the obligations of recipients under the Act and this part,

(2) Permitting a complainant to add information to the complaint to meet the requirements of a sufficient complaint,

(3) Notifying the complainant and the recipient (or their representatives) of their rights and obligations under the complaint procedure, including the right to have a representative at all stages of the complaint procedure, and/or

(4) Notifying the complainant and the recipient (or their representatives) of their right to contact NEH for information and assistance regarding the complaint resolution process.

(d) NEH will return any complaint that is unsigned or that is not within NEH's jurisdiction for any other reason, and NEH will provide an explanation for the return.

§ 1172.33 Mediation.

(a) *Referral of complaints for mediation.* Unless the age distinction complained of is clearly within an exception, NEH will promptly refer all complaints that fall within the jurisdiction of the regulations in this part, and that contain all information necessary for further processing, to the Mediation Agency designated by the Secretary of the Department of Health and Human Services.

(b) Both the complainant and the recipient shall participate in the mediation process to the extent necessary to reach an agreement, or for the mediator to make an informed judgment that an agreement is impossible.

(c) If the complainant and recipient reach a mutually satisfactory resolution of the complaint during the mediation period, the mediator shall prepare a mediation agreement in writing, to be signed by the complainant and recipient, and send a copy of the signed agreement to NEH. NEH will take no further action based on that complaint unless the complainant or the recipient has failed to comply with the agreement.

(d) The mediator shall protect the confidentiality of all information obtained in the course of the mediation process, and no mediator shall testify in any adjudicative proceeding, produce any document, or otherwise disclose any information obtained in the course of the mediation process without prior approval of the head of the mediation agency.

(e) If the complainant and recipient do not reach a mutually satisfactory resolution during mediation within sixty (60) days after NEH receives the complaint, the mediator shall return the complaint to NEH for investigation. The mediator may return a complaint at any time before the end of the sixty-day period if it appears that the complaint cannot be resolved through mediation or if an agreement is reached. The mediator may extend this sixty-day period, provided NEH concurs, for not more than thirty (30) days, if the mediator determines that resolution is likely to occur within such period.

§ 1172.34 Investigation.

(a) *Initial investigation.* (1) NEH will investigate complaints that are unresolved after mediation or are reopened because of a violation of a mediation agreement.

(i) As part of this initial investigation, NEH will use informal fact-finding methods, including joint or separate discussions with the complainant and the recipient to establish the facts, and, if possible, resolve the complaint to the mutual satisfaction of the parties. NEH may seek the assistance of any involved State agency.

(ii) NEH will put any settlement agreement in writing and have it signed by the parties and NEH. The settlement is not a finding of discrimination against a recipient.

(2) The settlement shall not affect the operation of any other enforcement effort of NEH, including compliance reviews and investigation of other complaints which may involve the recipient.

(b) *Formal investigation and finding.* If NEH cannot resolve the complaint during the initial investigation, it will complete the investigation of the complaint and make a formal finding. If the formal investigation indicates a violation of the Act or the regulations in this part, NEH will attempt to achieve voluntary compliance. If NEH cannot obtain voluntary compliance, it will begin appropriate enforcement action as provided in § 1172.36.

§ 1172.35 Prohibition against intimidation or retaliation.

A recipient may not engage in acts of intimidation or retaliation against any person who attempts to assert a right protected by the Act or this part, or cooperates in any mediation, investigation, hearing, or other part of NEH's investigation, conciliation, and enforcement process.

§ 1172.36 Enforcement procedure.

(a) NEH may enforce the Act and the regulations in this part through:

(1) Termination of a recipient's Federal financial assistance under the program or activity involved where the recipient has violated the Act or the regulations in this part. Prior to such termination, a recipient must have the opportunity for a hearing on record before an administrative law judge who must determine that a violation has occurred. Therefore, NEH will not terminate a recipient's Federal financial assistance in a case that has been settled in mediation, or prior to a hearing, unless the case is reopened because of a violation of the settlement agreement.

(2) Any other means authorized by law, including but not limited to:

(i) Referral to the Department of Justice for proceedings to enforce any rights of the United States or obligations of the recipient created by the Act or the regulations in this part.

(ii) Use of any requirement of, or referral to, any Federal, State, or local government agency that will have the effect of correcting a violation of the Act or this part.

(b) NEH will limit any termination under § 1172.36(a)(1) to the particular recipient and particular program or activity, or portion thereof, that NEH finds in violation of the Act or the regulations in this part. NEH will not base its decision to terminate on any findings with respect to any other program or activity of the recipient that does not receive Federal financial assistance from NEH.

(c) NEH will not take action under § 1172.36(a) until:

(1) The Chairman has advised the recipient of its failure to comply with the Act or the regulations in this part, and that NEH has determined that voluntary compliance cannot be obtained, and

(2) Thirty (30) days have elapsed after the Chairman has sent a written report of the circumstances and grounds of the action to the Congressional Committee(s) having legislative jurisdiction over the program or activity involved. The Chairman will file such report whenever it takes action under § 1172.36(a).

(d) NEH also may defer granting new Federal financial assistance to a recipient when a hearing under § 1172.36(a)(1) is initiated.

(1) New Federal financial assistance includes all assistance for which NEH requires an application or approval, including renewal or continuation of existing activities, or authorization of new activities, during the deferral period. New Federal financial assistance does not include assistance approved prior to the beginning of a termination hearing under § 1172.36(a)(1), or increases in funding as a result of changed computation of formula awards.

(2) NEH will not begin a deferral until the recipient has received a notice of an opportunity for a hearing under § 1172.36(a)(1). NEH will not continue a deferral for more than sixty (60) days unless a hearing has begun within that time, or the time for beginning the hearing has been extended by mutual written consent of the recipient and NEH. NEH will not continue a deferral for more than thirty (30) days after the close of the hearing, unless the hearing results in a finding against the recipient.

(3) NEH will limit any deferral to the particular recipient and particular program or activity, or portion thereof, that NEH finds in violation of the Act or the regulations in this part. NEH will not base the deferral decision any finding with respect to any other program or activity of the recipient that does not receive Federal financial assistance from NEH.

§ 1172.37 Hearings, decisions, post-termination proceedings.

Certain NEH procedural provisions applicable to Title VI of the Civil Rights Act of 1964 apply to NEH enforcement of the regulations in this part. They are found at 45 CFR chapter XI, subchapter A, 1110.9 through 1110.11.

§ 1172.38 Remedial action by recipients.

Where NEH finds a recipient has discriminated on the basis of age, the recipient shall take any remedial action that NEH may require to overcome the effects of discrimination. If another recipient exercises control over the recipient that has discriminated, NEH may require both recipients to take remedial action.

§ 1172.39 Alternate funds disbursal procedure.

When NEH withholds funds from a recipient under the regulations in this part, the Chairman may disburse the withheld funds directly to an alternate recipient otherwise eligible for NEH support. NEH will require any alternate recipient to demonstrate the ability to comply with the regulations in this part and to achieve the goals of the National Foundation on the Arts and the Humanities Act of 1965, Pub. L. 89–209 (20 U.S.C. 951)—the Federal statute authorizing the Federal financial assistance.

§ 1172.40 Exhaustion of administrative remedies.

(a) A complainant may file a civil action under the Act and the regulations in this part following the exhaustion of administrative remedies. Administrative remedies are exhausted if one hundred eighty (180) days have elapsed since the complainant filed the complaint and NEH has made no finding with regard to the complaint, or NEH issues any finding in favor of the recipient.

(b) If either of the conditions set forth in § 1172.40(a) is satisfied, NEH will:

(1) Promptly advise the complainant of this fact,

(2) Advise the complainant of his or her right, to bring a civil action for injunctive relief, and

(3) Inform the complainant:

(i) That a civil action can only be brought in a United States district court for the district in which the recipient is found or transacts business,

(ii) That a complainant prevailing in a civil action has the right to be awarded the costs of the action, including reasonable attorney's fees, but that these costs must be demanded in the complaint,

(iii) That before commencing the action, the complainant must give thirty (30) days' notice by registered mail to the Secretary, the Attorney General of the United States, the Chairman, and the recipient,

(iv) That the notice must state the alleged violation of the Act, the relief requested, the court in which the complainant is bringing the action, and, whether or not attorney's fees are demanded in the event the complainant prevails, and

(v) That no action may be brought if the same alleged violation of the Act by the same recipient is the subject of a pending action in any court of the United States.

PART 1174 [RESERVED]

PART 1175—ENFORCEMENT OF NONDISCRIMINATION ON THE BASIS OF HANDICAP IN PROGRAMS OR ACTIVITIES CONDUCTED BY THE NATIONAL ENDOWMENT FOR THE HUMANITIES

Sec.
1175.101 Purpose.
1175.102 Application.
1175.103 Definitions.
1175.104–1175.109 [Reserved]
1175.110 Self-evaluation.
1175.111 Notice.
1175.112–1175.129 [Reserved]
1175.130 General prohibitions against discrimination.
1175.131–1175.139 [Reserved]
1175.140 Employment.
1175.141–1175.148 [Reserved]
1175.149 Program accessibility: Discrimination prohibited.
1175.150 Program accessibility: Existing facilities.
1175.151 Program accessibility: New construction and alterations.
1175.152–1175.159 [Reserved]
1175.160 Communications.
1175.161–1175.169 [Reserved]
1175.170 Compliance procedures.
1175.171–1175.999 [Reserved]

AUTHORITY: 29 U.S.C. 794.

SOURCE: 51 FR 4578, 4579, Feb. 5, 1986, unless otherwise noted.

§ 1175.101 Purpose.

This part effectuates section 119 of the Rehabilitation, Comprehensive Services, and Developmental Disabilities Amendments of 1978, which amended section 504 of the Rehabilitation Act of 1973 to prohibit discrimination on the basis of handicap in programs or activities conducted by Executive agencies or the United States Postal Service.

§ 1175.102 Application.

This part applies to all programs or activities conducted by the agency.

§ 1175.103 Definitions.

For purposes of this part, the term—

Assistant Attorney General means the Assistant Attorney General, Civil Rights Division, United States Department of Justice.

Auxiliary aids means services or devices that enable persons with impaired sensory, manual, or speaking skills to have an equal opportunity to participate in, and enjoy the benefits of, programs or activities conducted by the agency. For example, auxiliary aids useful for persons with impaired vision include readers, Brailled materials, audio recordings, telecommunications devices and other similar services and devices. Auxiliary aids useful for persons with impaired hearing include telephone handset amplifiers, telephones compatible with hearing aids, telecommunication devices for deaf persons (TDD's), interpreters, notetakers, written materials, and other similar services and devices.

Complete complaint means a written statement that contains the complainant's name and address and describes the agency's alleged discriminatory action in sufficient detail to inform the agency of the nature and date of the alleged violation of section 504. It shall be signed by the complainant or by someone authorized to do so on his or her behalf. Complaints filed on behalf of classes or third parties shall describe or identify (by name, if possible) the alleged victims of discrimination.

Facility means all or any portion of buildings, structures, equipment, roads, walks, parking lots, rolling stock or other conveyances, or other real or personal property.

Handicapped person means any person who has a physical or mental impairment that substantially limits one or more major life activities, has a record of such an impairment, or is regarded as having such an impairment.

As used in this definition, the phrase:

(1) *Physical or mental impairment* includes—

(i) Any physiological disorder or condition, cosmetic disfigurement, or anatomical loss affecting one of more of the following body systems: Neurological; musculoskeletal; special sense organs; respiratory, including speech organs; cardiovascular; reproductive; digestive; genitourinary; hemic and lymphatic; skin; and endocrine; or

(ii) Any mental or psychological disorder, such as mental retardation, organic brain syndrome, emotional or mental illness, and specific learning disabilities. The term *physical or mental impairment* includes, but is not limited to, such diseases and conditions as orthopedic, visual, speech, and hearing impairments, cerebral palsy, epilepsy, muscular dystrophy, multiple sclerosis, cancer, heart disease, diabetes, mental retardation, emotional illness, and drug addition and alcholism.

(2) *Major life activities* includes functions such as caring for one's self, performing manual tasks, walking, seeing, hearing, speaking, breathing, learning, and working.

(3) *Has a record of such an impairment* means has a history of, or has been misclassified as having, a mental or physical impairment that substantially limits one or more major life activities.

(4) *Is regarded as having an impairment* means—

(i) Has a physical or mental impairment that does not substantially limit major life activities but is treated by the agency as constituting such a limitation;

(ii) Has a physical or mental impairment that substantially limits major life activities only as a result of the attitudes of others toward such impairment; or

(iii) Has none of the impairments defined in paragraph (1) of this definition but is treated by the agency as having such an impairment.

Qualified handicapped person means—

(1) With respect to any agency program or activity under which a person is required to perform services or to achieve a level of accomplishment, a handicapped person who meets the essential eligibility requirements and who can achieve the purpose of the program or activity without modifications in the program or activity that the agency can demonstrate would result in a fundamental alteration in its nature; or

(2) With respect to any other program or activity, a handicapped person who meets the essential eligibility requirements for participation in, or receipt of benefits from, that program or activity.

(3) *Qualified handicapped person* is defined for purposes of employment in 29 CFR 1613.702(f), which is made applicable to this part by § 1175.140.

Section 504 means section 504 of the Rehabilitation Act of 1973 (Pub. L. 93–112, 87 Stat. 394 (29 U.S.C. 794)), as amended by the Rehabilitation Act Amendments of 1974 (Pub. L. 93–516, 88 Stat. 1617), and the Rehabilitation, Comprehensive Services, and Developmental Disabilities Amendments of 1978 (Pub. L. 95–602, 92 Stat. 2955). As used in this part, section 504 applies only to programs or activities conducted by Executive agencies and not to federally assisted programs.

[51 FR 4578, 4579, Feb. 5, 1986; 51 FR 7543, Mar. 5, 1986]

§§ 1175.104–1175.109 [Reserved]

§ 1175.110 Self-evaluation.

(a) The agency shall, by April 9, 1987, evaluate its current policies and practices, and the effects thereof, that do not or may not meet the requirements of this part, and, to the extent modification of any such policies and practices is required, the agency shall proceed to make the necessary modifications.

(b) The agency shall provide an opportunity to interested persons, including handicapped persons or organizations representing handicapped persons, to participate in the self-evaluation process by submitting comments (both oral and written).

(c) The agency shall, until three years following the completion of the self-evaluation, maintain on file and make available for public inspections:

(1) A description of areas examined and any problems identified, and

(2) A description of any modifications made.

§ 1175.111 Notice.

The agency shall make available to employees, applicants, participants, beneficiaries, and other interested persons such information regarding the provisions of this part and its applicability to the programs or activities conducted by the agency, and make such information available to them in such manner as the head of the agency finds necessary to apprise such persons of the protections against discrimination assured them by section 504 and this regulation.

§§ 1175.112–1175.129 [Reserved]

§ 1175.130 General prohibitions against discrimination.

(a) No qualified handicapped person shall, on the basis of handicap, be excluded from participation in, be denied the benefits of, or otherwise be subjected to discrimination under any program or activity conducted by the agency.

(b)(1) The agency, in providing any aid, benefit, or service, may not, directly or through contractual, licensing, or other arrangements, on the basis of handicap—

(i) Deny a qualified handicapped person the opportunity to participate in or benefit from the aid, benefit, or service;

(ii) Afford a qualfied handicapped person an opportunity to participate in or benefit from the aid, benefit, or service that is not equal to that afforded others;

(iii) Provide a qualified handicapped person with an aid, benefit, or service that is not as effective in affording equal opportunity to obtain the same result, to gain the same benefit, or to reach the same level of achievement as that provided to others;

(iv) Provide different or separate aid, benefits, or services to handicapped persons or to any class of handicapped persons than is provided to others unless such action is necessary to provide qualified handicapped persons with aid, benefits, or services that are as effective as those provided to others;

(v) Deny a qualified handicapped person the opportunity to participate as a member of planning or advisory boards; or

(vi) Otherwise limit a qualified handicapped person in the enjoyment of any right, privilege, advantage, or opportunity enjoyed by others receiving the aid, benefit, or service.

(2) The agency may not deny a qualified handicapped person the opportunity to participate in programs or activities that are not separate or different, despite the existence of permissibly separate or different programs or activities.

(3) The agency may not, directly or through contractual or other arrangements, utilize criteria or methods of administration the purpose or effect of which would—

(i) Subject qualified handicapped persons to discrimination on the basis of handicap; or

(ii) Defeat or substantially impair accomplishment of the objectives of a program or activity with respect to handicapped persons.

(4) The agency may not, in determining the site or location of a facility, make selections the purpose or effect of which would—

(i) Exclude handicapped persons from, deny them the benefits of, or otherwise subject them to discrimination under any program or activity conducted by the agency; or

(ii) Defeat or substantially impair the accomplishment of the objectives of a program or activity with respect to handicapped persons.

(5) The agency, in the selection of procurement contractors, may not use criteria that subject qualified handicapped persons to discrimination on the basis of handicap.

(c) The exclusion of nonhandicapped persons from the benefits of a program limited by Federal statute or Executive order to handicapped persons or the exclusion of a specific class of handicapped persons from a program limited by Federal statute or Executive order to a different class of handicapped persons is not prohibited by this part.

(d) The agency shall administer programs and activities in the most integrated setting appropriate to the needs of qualified handicapped persons.

§§ 1175.131–1175.139 [Reserved]

§ 1175.140 Employment.

No qualified handicapped person shall, on the basis of handicap, be subjected to discrimination in employment under any program or activity conducted by the agency. The definitions, requirements, and procedures of section 501 of the Rehabilitation Act of 1973 (29 U.S.C. 791), as established by the Equal Employment Opportunity Commission in 29 CFR part 1613, shall apply to employment in federally conducted programs or activities.

§§ 1175.141–1175.148 [Reserved]

§ 1175.149 Program accessibility: Discrimination prohibited.

Except as otherwise provided in § 1175.150, no qualified handicapped person shall, because the agency's facilities are inaccessible to or unusable by handicapped persons, be denied the benefits of, be excluded from participation in, or otherwise be subjected to discrimination under any program or activity conducted by the agency.

§ 1175.150 Program accessibility: Existing facilities.

(a) *General.* The agency shall operate each program or activity so that the program or activity, when viewed in its entirety, is readily accessible to and usable by handicapped persons. This paragraph does not—

(1) Necessarily require the agency to make each of its existing facilities accessible to and usable by handicapped persons; or

(2) Require the agency to take any action that it can demonstrate would result in a fundamental alteration in the nature of a program or activity or in undue financial and administrative burdens. In those circumstances where agency personnel believe that the proposed action would fundamentally alter the program or activity or would result in undue financial and administrative burdens, the agency has the burden of proving that compliance with § 1175.150(a) would result in such alteration or burdens. The decision that compliance would result in such alteration or burdens must be made by the agency head or his or her designee after considering all agency resources available for use in the funding and operation of the conducted program or activity, and must be accompanied by a written statement of the reasons for reaching that conclusion. If an action would result in such an alteration or such burdens, the agency shall take any other action that would not result in such an alteration or such burdens but would nevertheless ensure that handicapped persons receive the benefits and services of the program or activity.

(b) *Methods.* The agency may comply with the requirements of this section through such means as redesign of equipment, reassignment of services to accessible buildings, assignment of aides to beneficiaries, home visits, delivery of services at alternate accessible sites, alteration of existing facilities and construction of new facilities, use of accessible rolling stock, or any other methods that result in making its programs or activities readily accessible to and usable by handicapped persons. The agency is nor required to make structural changes in existing facilities where other methods are effective in achieving compliance with this section. The agency, in making alterations to existing buildings, shall meet accessibility requirements to the extent compelled by the Architectural Barriers Act of 1968, as amended (42 U.S.C. 4151 through 4157), and any regulations implementing it. In choosing among available methods for meeting the requirements of this section, the agency shall give priority to those methods that offer programs and activities to qualified handicapped persons in the most integrated setting appropriate.

(c) *Time period for compliance.* The agency shall comply with the obligations established under this section by June 6, 1986, except that where structural changes in facilities are undertaken, such changes shall be made by April 7, 1989, but in any event as expeditiously as possible.

(d) *Transition plan.* In the event that structural changes to facilities will be undertaken to achieve program accessibility, the agency shall develop, by

October 7, 1986, a transition plan setting forth the steps necessary to complete such changes. The agency shall provide an opportunity to interested persons, including handicapped persons or organizations representing handicapped persons, to participate in the development of the transition plan by submitting comments (both oral and written). A copy of the transition plan shall be made available for public inspection. The plan shall, at a minimum—

(1) Identify physical obstacles in the agency's facilities that limit the accessibility of its programs or activities to handicapped persons;

(2) Describe in detail the methods that will be used to make the facilities accessible;

(3) Specify the schedule for taking the steps necessary to achieve compliance with this section and, if the time period of the transition plan is longer than one year, identify steps that will be taken during each year of the transition period; and

(4) Indicate the official responsible for implementation of the plan.

[51 FR 4578, 4579, Feb. 5, 1986; 51 FR 7543, Mar. 5, 1986]

§ 1175.151 Program accessibility: New construction and alterations.

Each building or part of a building that is constructed or altered by, on behalf of, or for the use of the agency shall be designed, constructed, or altered so as to be readily accessible to and usable by handicapped persons. The definitions, requirements, and standards of the Architectural Barriers Act (42 U.S.C. 4151 through 4157), as established in 41 CFR 101–19.600 to 101–19.607, apply to buildings covered by this section.

§§ 1175.152–1175.159 [Reserved]

§ 1175.160 Communications.

(a) The agency shall take appropriate steps to ensure effective communication with applicants, participants, personnel of other Federal entities, and members of the public.

(1) The agency shall furnish appropriate auxiliary aids where necessary to afford a handicapped person an equal opportunity to participate in, and enjoy the benefits of, a program or activity conducted by the agency.

(i) In determining what type of auxiliary aid is necessary, the agency shall give primary consideration to the requests of the handicapped person.

(ii) The agency need not provide individually prescribed devices, readers for personal use or study, or other devices of a personal nature.

(2) Where the agency communicates with applicants and beneficiaries by telephone, telecommunication devices for deaf persons (TDD's) or equally effective telecommunication systems shall be used.

(b) The agency shall ensure that interested persons, including persons with impaired vision or hearing, can obtain information as to the existence and location of accessible services, activities, and facilities.

(c) The agency shall provide signage at a primary entrance to each of its inaccessible facilities, directing users to a location at which they can obtain information about accessible facilities. The international symbol for accessibility shall be used at each primary entrance of an accessible facility.

(d) This section does not require the agency to take any action that it can demonstrate would result in a fundamental alteration in the nature of a program or activity or in undue financial and administrative burdens. In those circumstances where agency personnel believe that the proposed action would fundamentally alter the program or activity or would result in undue financial and administrative burdens, the agency has the burden of proving that compliance with § 1175.160 would result in such alteration or burdens. The decision that compliance would result in such alteration or burdens must be made by the agency head or his or her designee after considering all agency resources available for use in the funding and operation of the conducted program or activity, and must be accompanied by a written statement of the reasons for reaching that conclusion. If an action required to comply with this section would result in such an alteration or such burdens, the agency shall take any other action that would not result in such an alteration or such burdens but would nevertheless ensure that, to the maximum extent possible, handicapped persons receive the benefits and services of the program or activity.

§§ 1175.161–1175.169 [Reserved]

§ 1175.170 Compliance procedures.

(a) Except as provided in paragraph (b) of this section, this section applies to all allegations of discrimination on the basis of handicap in programs or activities conducted by the agency.

(b) The agency shall process complaints alleging violations of section 504 with respect to employment according to the procedures established by the Equal Employment Opportunity Commission in 29 CFR part 1613 pursuant to section 501 of the Rehabilitation Act of 1973 (29 U.S.C. 791).

(c) The Director, Office of Equal Opportunity shall be responsible for coordinating implementation of this section. Complaints may be sent to Director, Office of Equal Opportunity, National Endowment for the Humanities, 1100 Pennsylvania Avenue, NW., Room 419, Washington, DC 20506.

(d) The agency shall accept and investigate all complete complaints for which it has jurisdiction. All complete complaints must be filed within 180 days of the alleged act of discrimination. The agency may extend this time period for good cause.

(e) If the agency receives a complaint over which it does not have jurisdiction, it shall promptly notify the complainant and shall make reasonable efforts to refer the complaint to the appropriate government entity.

(f) The agency shall notify the Architectural and Transportation Barriers Compliance Board upon receipt of any complaint alleging that a building or facility that is subject to the Architectural Barriers Act of 1968, as amended (42 U.S.C. 4151 through 4157), or section 502 of the Rehabilitation Act of 1973, as amended (29 U.S.C. 792), is not readily accessible to and usable by handicapped persons.

(g) Within 180 days of the receipt of a complete complaint for which it has jurisdiction, the agency shall notify the complainant of the results of the investigation in a letter containing—

(1) Findings of fact and conclusions of law;

(2) A description of a remedy for each violation found;

(3) A notice of the right to appeal.

(h) Appeals of the findings of fact and conclusions of law or remedies must be filed by the complainant within 90 days of receipt from the agency of the letter required by § 1175.170(g). The agency may extend this time for good cause.

(i) Timely appeals shall be accepted and processed by the head of the agency.

(j) The head of the agency shall notify the complainant of the results of the appeal within 60 days of the receipt of the request. If the head of the agency determines that additional information is needed from the complainant, he or she shall have 60 days from the date of receipt of the additional information to make his or her determination on the appeal.

(k) The time limits cited in paragraphs (g) and (j) of this section may be extended with the permission of the Assistant Attorney General.

(l) The agency may delegate its authority for conducting complaint investigations to other Federal agencies, except that the authority for making the final determination may not be delegated to another agency.

[51 FR 4578, 4579, Feb. 5, 1986, as amended at 51 FR 4578, Feb. 5, 1986]

§§ 1175.171–1175.999 [Reserved]

PART 1176—PART-TIME CAREER EMPLOYMENT

Sec.
1176.1 General.
1176.2 Definitions.
1176.3 Criteria.
1176.4 Establishing and converting part-time positions.
1176.5 Annual plan.
1176.6 Review and evaluation.
1176.7 Publicizing vacancies.
1176.8 Exceptions.
1176.9–1176.99 [Reserved]

AUTHORITY: Federal Employees Part-Time Career Employment Act of 1978, Pub. L. 95–437, 92 Stat. 1055, 5 U.S.C. 3401–3408.

SOURCE: 46 FR 35647, July 10, 1981, unless otherwise noted.

National Foundation on the Arts and the Humanities § 1176.8

§ 1176.1 General.

(a) *Purpose.* Many individuals in society possess great productive potential which goes unrealized because they cannot meet the requirements of a standard workweek. Permanent part-time employment also provides benefits to other individuals in a variety of ways, such as providing older individuals with a gradual transition into retirement, providing employment opportunities to handicapped individuals or others who require a reduced workweek, providing parents with opportunities to balance family responsibilities with the need for added income, and assisting students who must finance their own education or vocational training. In view of this, the National Endowment for the Humanities will operate a part-time career employment program, consistent with its responsibilities and in accordance with Public Law 95-437, the Federal Employees' Part-Time Career Employment Act of 1978.

(b) *Program Coordinator.* The Personnel Officer is responsible for program operation and coordination.

§ 1176.2 Definitions.

(a) *Part-time employment* means employment of 16 to 32 hours a week under a schedule consisting of an equal or varied number of hours per day, whether in a position which would be part-time without regard to the Act or one established to allow job-sharing or comparable arrangements, but does not include employment on a temporary or intermittent basis.

(b) *Career employment* includes competitive and excepted service employees in tenure groups I and II.

§ 1176.3 Criteria.

Positions becoming vacant, unless excepted as provided by § 1176.8, will be reviewed to determine the feasibility of converting them to part-time. Among the criteria which may be used when conducting this review are:

(a) Mission requirements.
(b) Workload.
(c) Employment ceilings and budgetary considerations.
(d) Availability of qualified applicants willing to work part-time.

§ 1176.4 Establishing and converting part-time positions.

Position management and other internal reviews may indicate that positions may be either converted from full-time or initially established as part-time positions. Criteria listed in § 1176.3 may be used during these reviews. If a decision is made to convert to or to establish a part-time position, regular position management and classification procedures will be followed.

§ 1176.5 Annual plan.

(a) An agencywide plan for promoting part-time employment opportunities will be developed annually. This plan will establish annual goals and set interim and final deadlines for achieving these goals. This plan will be applicable throughout the agency, and will be transmitted to the Office of Personnel Management with the required report to OPM on the status of the program as of September 30 of each year.

(b) Beginning in FY 1981 in administering personnel ceilings, part-time career employees shall be counted against ceiling authorizations as a fraction. This will be determined by dividing 40 hours into the average number of hours of such employee's regularly scheduled workweek.

§ 1176.6 Review and evaluation.

Regular employment reports will be used to determine levels of part-time employment. This program will also be designated an item of special interest to be reviewed during personnel management reviews.

§ 1176.7 Publicizing vacancies.

When applicants from outside the Federal service are desired, part-time vacancies may be publicized through various recruiting means, such as:

(a) Federal Job Information Centers.
(b) State Employment Offices.
(c) Veterans' Administration Recruiting Bulletins.

§ 1176.8 Exceptions.

(a) The Personnel Officer may except positions from inclusion in this program to provide fewer than 16 hours per week. This will normally be done in furtherance of special hiring programs such as the Stay-in-School or Handicapped Employment Program.

(b) On occasions when it becomes necessary to allow supervisors and managers to temporarily increase the hours of duty of employees above 32 hours per week for limited and specific periods of time to meet heavy workloads, perform special assignments, permit employee training, etc., the Endowment policy is as follows:

(1) Requests to work NEH employees on a 32 hour/week appointment more than 32 hours must be submitted in advance to the Personnel Office;

(2) Justification should be concise but specific and must state the exact time frame for the increase in hours above 32 hours per week; and

(3) The Program Coordinator will decide if the request meets the intent of the law and this agency's policy.

§§ 1176.9–1176.99 [Reserved]

PART 1177—CLAIMS COLLECTION

Sec.
1177.1 Purpose and scope.
1177.2 Definitions.
1177.3 Other remedies.
1177.4 Claims involving criminal activity or misconduct.
1177.5 Collection.
1177.6 Notice to debtor.
1177.7 Interest, penalties, and administrative costs.
1177.8 Administrative offset.
1177.9 Use of credit reporting agencies.
1177.10 Collection services.
1177.11 Referral to the Department of Justice or the General Accounting Office.
1177.12 Compromise, suspension and termination.
1177.13 Omissions not a defense.
1177.14–1177.99 [Reserved]

AUTHORITY: 31 U.S.C. 3711, 3716–3719.

SOURCE: 51 FR 20484, June 5, 1986, unless otherwise noted.

§ 1177.1 Purpose and scope.

This part prescribes standards and procedures for officers and employees of the National Endowment for the Humanities who are responsible for the collection and disposition of debts owed to the United States. The authority for this part is the Federal Claims Collection Act of 1966, as amended, 31 U.S.C. 3711 and 3716 through 3719; the Federal Claims Collection Standards at 4 CFR parts 101 through 105, as amended by 49 FR 8889, 5 U.S.C. 552a, and Office of Management and Budget Circular A–129. The activities covered include: collecting claims in any amount; compromising claims, or suspending or terminating the collection of claims that do not exceed $20,000 exclusive of interest and charges, and referring debts that cannot be disposed of by the Endowment to the Department of Justice or to the General Accounting Office for further administrative action or litigation.

§ 1177.2 Definitions.

For the purpose of this part the following definitions will apply:

(a) *Claim* or *debt* means an amount of property owed to the United States. These include but are not limited to: Overpayments to program beneficiaries; overpayments to contractors and grantees, including overpayments arising from audit disallowances; excessive cash advances to grantees and contractors; and civil penalties and assessments. A debt is overdue or delinquent if it is not paid by the due date specified in the initial notice of the debt (see § 1177.6 of this part) or if the debtor fails to satisfy his or her obligation under a repayment agreement.

(b) *Debtor* means an individual, organization, group, association, partnership, or corporation indebted to the United States, or the person or entity with legal responsibility for assuming the debtor's obligation.

(c) *Endowment* means the National Endowment for the Humanities.

(d) *Administrative offset* means satisfying a debt by withholding money payable by the United States to or held by the United States for a debtor.

§ 1177.3 Other remedies.

The remedies and sanctions available to the National Endowment for the Humanities under this part are not intended to be exclusive. The Chairperson of the National Endowment for the Humanities or his designee may impose other appropriate sanctions upon a debtor for prolonged or repeated failure to pay a debt. For example, the Chairperson or his designee may place the debtor's name on a list of debarred, suspended, or ineligible grantees and contractors, convert the method of payment under a grant from an advance to a reimbursement method, or revoke a grantee's letter of credit. In such cases the debtor will be advised of the Endowment's action.

§ 1177.4 Claims involving criminal activity or misconduct.

(a) A debtor whose indebtedness involves criminal activity such as fraud, embezzlement, theft, or misuse of government funds or property is subject to punishment by fine or imprisonment as well as to a civil claim by the United States for compensation for the misappropriated funds. The Endowment will refer these cases to the appropriate law enforcement agency for prosecution.

(b) Debts involving fraud, false, claims, or misrepresentation shall not be compromised, terminated, suspended, or otherwise disposed of under this rule. Only the Department of Justice is authorized to compromise, terminate, suspend, or otherwise dispose of such debts.

§ 1177.5 Collection.

(a) The Endowment will take aggressive action to collect debts and reduce delinquencies. Collection efforts shall include sending to the debtor's last known address a total of three progressively stronger written demands for payment at not more than 30 day intervals. When necessary to protect the Government's interest, written demand may be preceded by other appropriate action, including immediate referral for litigation. Other contact with the debtor or his or her representative or guarantor by telephone, in person and/or in writing may be appropriate to demand prompt payment, to discuss the debtor's position regarding the existence, amount and repayment of the debt, and to inform the debtor of his or her rights and the effect of nonpayment or delayed payment. A debtor who disputes a debt must promptly provide available supporting evidence.

(b) If a debtor is involved in insolvency proceedings, the debt will be referred to the appropriate United States Attorney to file a claim. The United States may have a priority over other creditors under 31 U.S.C. 3713.

§ 1177.6 Notice to debtor.

The first written demand for payment must inform the debtor of the following:

(a) The amount and nature of the debt:

(b) The date payment is due, which will generally be 30 days from the date the notice was mailed;

(c) The assessment of interest under § 1177.7 from the date the notice was mailed if payment is not received within the 30 days;

(d) The right to dispute the debt;

(e) The office, address and telephone number that the debtor should contact to discuss repayment and reconsideration of the debt and;

(f) The sanctions available to the National Endowment for the Humanities to collect a delinquent debt including, but not limited to, referral of the debt to a credit reporting agency, a private collection bureau, or the Department of Justice for litigation.

§ 1177.7 Interest, penalties, and administrative costs.

(a) Interest will accrue on all debts from the date when the first notice of the debt and the interest requirement is mailed to the last known address or hand-delivered to the debtor if the debt is not paid within 30 days from the date the first notice was mailed. The Endowment will charge an annual rate of interest that is equal to the average investment rate for the Treasury tax and loan accounts on September 30 of each year, rounded to the nearest whole per centum. This rate, which represents the current value of funds to the United States Treasury, may be revised quarterly by the Secretary of the Treasury and is published by the Secretary of the Treasury annually or quarterly in the FEDERAL REGISTER and the Treasury Financial Manual Bulletins.

(b) The rate of interest initially assessed will remain fixed for the duration of the indebtedness, except that if a debtor defaults on a repayment agreement interest may be set at the Treasury rate in effect on the date a new agreement is executed.

(c) The Endowment shall charge debtors for administrative costs incurred in handling overdue debts.

§ 1177.8

(d) Interest will not be charged on administrative costs.

(e) The Endowment shall assess a penalty charge, not to exceed 6 per cent per year on debts which have been delinquent for more than 90 days. This charge shall accrue from the date that the debt became delinquent.

(f) The Chairperson or his designee may waive in whole or in part the collection of interest and administrative and penalty charges if determined that collection would be against equity or not in the best interests of the United States. The Endowment shall waive the collection of interest on the debt or any part of the debt which is paid within 30 days after the date on which interest began to accrue.

§ 1177.8 Administrative offset.

(a) The Endowment may collect debts owed by administrative offset if:

(1) The debt is certain in amount;

(2) Efforts to obtain direct payment have been, or would most likely be unsuccessful, or the Endowment and the debtor agree to the offset;

(3) Offset is cost effective or has significant deterrent value; and

(4) Offset is best suited to further and protect the Government's interest.

(b) The Endowment may offset a debt owed to another Federal agency from amounts due or payable by the Endowment to the debtor or request another Federal agency to offset a debt owed to the Endowment;

(c) Prior to initiating administrative offset, the National Endowment for the Humanities will send the debtor written notice of the following:

(1) The nature and amount of the debt and the agency's intention to collect the debt by offset 30 days from the date the notice was mailed if neither payment nor a satisfactory response is received by that date;

(2) The debtor's right to an opportunity to submit a good faith alternative repayment schedule to inspect and copy agency records pertaining to the debt, to request a review of the determination of indebtedness; and to enter into a written agreement to repay the debt and;

(3) The applicable interest.

(d) The National Endowment for the Humanities may effect an administrative offset against a payment to be made to a debtor prior to the completion of the procedures required by paragraph (c) of this section if:

(1) Failure to offset would substantially prejudice the Government's ability to collect the debt and

(2) The time before the payment is to be made does not reasonably permit completion of those procedures.

§ 1177.9 Use of credit reporting agencies.

(a) The Endowment may report delinquent accounts to credit reporting agencies consistent with the notice requirements contained in the § 1177.6 of this part. Individual debtors must be given at least 60 days written notice that the debt is overdue and will be reported to a credit reporting agency.

(b) Debts may be reported to consumer or commercial reporting agencies. Consumer reporting agencies are defined in 31 U.S.C. 3701(a)(3) pursuant to 5 U.S.C. 552a(b)(12) and 31 U.S.C. 3711(f). The Endowment may disclose only an individual's name, address, social security number, and the nature, amount, status and history of the debt and the program under which the claim arose.

§ 1177.10 Collection services.

(a) The Endowment may contract for collection services to recover outstanding debts. The Endowment may refer delinquent debts to private collection agencies listed on the schedule compiled by the General Services Administration. In such contracts, the National Endowment for the Humanities will retain the authority to resolve disputes, compromise claims, terminate or suspend collection, and refer the matter to the Department of Justice or the General Accounting Office.

(b) The contractor shall be subject to the disclosure provisions of the Privacy Act of 1974, as amended (5 U.S.C. 552a(m)), and to applicable federal and state laws and regulations pertaining to debt collection practices, including the Fair Debt Collection Practices Act, 15 U.S.C. 1692. The contractor shall be strictly accountable for all amounts collected.

(c) The contractor shall be required to provide to the Endowment any data contained in its files relating to the debt account upon agency request or upon returning an account to the Endowment for referral to the Department of Justice for litigation.

§ 1177.11 Referral to the Department of Justice or the General Accounting Office.

Debts over $600 but less than $100,000 which the Endowment determines can neither be collected nor otherwise disposed of will be referred for litigation to the United States Attorney in whose judicial district the debtor is located. Claims for amounts exceeding $100,000 shall be referred for litigation to the Commercial Litigation Branch, Civil Division of the Department of Justice.

§ 1177.12 Compromise, suspension and termination.

(a) The Chairperson of the National Endowment for the Humanities or his designee may compromise, suspend or terminate the collection of debts where the outstanding principal is not greater than $20,000. Endowment procedures for writing off outstanding accounts are available to the public.

(b) The Chairperson of the National Endowment for the Humanities may compromise, suspend or terminate collection of debts where the outstanding principal is greater than $20,000 only with the approval of, or by referral to the United States Attorney or the Department of Justice.

(c) The Chairman of the National Endowment for the Humanities will refer to the General Accounting Office (GAO) debts arising from GAO audit exceptions.

§ 1177.13 Omissions not a defense.

Failure to comply with any provisions of this rule may not serve as a defense to any debtor.

§§ 1177.14–1177.99 [Reserved]

PART 1178—USE OF PENALTY MAIL IN THE LOCATION AND RECOVERY OF MISSING CHILDREN

Sec.
1178.1 Purpose and scope.
1178.2 Withdrawal of information.

AUTHORITY: 39 U.S.C. 3220.

§ 1178.1 Purpose and scope.

(a) The Chairperson of the National Endowment for the Humanities (NEH) may direct the agency to use penalty mail to assist in the location and recovery of missing children. When determined to be appropriate and cost-effective, the National Endowment for the Humanities may print, insert or use any other effective method to affix pictures and biographical data relating to missing children on NEH mail. The contact person for matters related to the implementation of this part is Tracy J. Joselson, Esq. Office of the General Counsel, National Endowment for the Humanities, 1100 Pennsylvania Avenue, NW., Washington, DC 20506, (202) 786–0322.

(b) The National Center for Missing and Exploited Children will be the exclusive source from which the National Endowment for the Humanities will obtain photographic and biographical information for dissemination to the public.

(c) It is estimated that the National Endowment for the Humanities will incur no additional costs to implement this program during its initial year. This estimate is based on a review of Endowment mailings that would maximize dissemination of this information.

[51 FR 20974, June 10, 1986]

§ 1178.2 Withdrawal of information.

The National Endowment for the Humanities will withdraw or exhaust the supply of all materials bearing the photograph and biographical information of a missing child within a three month period from the date the National Center for Missing and Exploited Children receives notice that the child has been recovered or that the parents or guardian of the child have revoked permission to use the information. The National Center for Missing and Exploited Children will be responsible for immediately notifying the agency contact, in writing, of the need to withdraw or remove this material.

[51 FR 20974, June 10, 1986]

PART 1179—SALARY OFFSET

Sec.
1179.1 Purpose and scope.
1179.2 Definitions.
1179.3 Applicability.
1179.4 Notice requirements.
1179.5 Hearing.
1179.6 Written decision.
1179.7 Coordinating offset with another Federal agency.
1179.8 Procedures for salary offset.
1179.9 Refunds.
1179.10 Statute of limitations.
1179.11 Non-waiver of rights.
1179.12 Interest, penalties, and administrative costs.

AUTHORITY: 5 U.S.C. 5514, E.O. 11809 (redesignated E.O. 12107), and 5 CFR part 550, subpart K.

SOURCE: 52 FR 28472, July 30, 1987, unless otherwise noted.

§ 1179.1 Purpose and scope.

(a) This regulation provides procedures for the collection by administrative offset of a Federal employee's salary without his/her consent to satisfy certain debts owed to the Federal government. These regulations apply to all Federal employees who owe debts to the National Endowment for the Humanities (NEH) and to current employees of the National Endowment for the Humanities who owe debts to other Federal agencies. This regulation does not apply when the employee consents to recovery from his/her current pay account.

(b) This regulation does not apply to debts or claims arising under:

(1) The Internal Revenue Code of 1954, as amended, 26 U.S.C. 1 *et seq*;

(2) The Social Security Act, 42 U.S.C. 301 *et seq*;

(3) The tariff laws of the United States; or

(4) Any case where a collection of a debt by salary offset is explicitly provided for or prohibited by another statute.

(c) This regulation does not apply to any adjustment to pay arising out of an employee's selection of coverage or a change in coverage under a Federal benefits program requiring periodic deductions from pay if the amount to be recovered was accumulated over four pay periods or less.

(d) This regulation does not preclude the compromise, suspension, or termination of collection action where appropriate under the standards implementing the Federal Claims Collection Act 31 U.S.C. 3711 *et seq*. 4 CFR parts 101 through 105 45 CFR part 1177.

(e) This regulation does not preclude an employee from requesting waiver of an overpayment under 5 U.S.C. 5584, 10 U.S.C. 2774 or 32 U.S.C. 716 or in any way questioning the amount or validity of the debt by submitting a subsequent claim to the General Accounting Office. This regulation does not preclude an employee from requesting a waiver pursuant to other statutory provisions applicable to the particular debt being collected.

(f) Matters not addressed in these regulations should be reviewed in accordance with the Federal Claims Collection Standards at 4 CFR 101.1 *et seq*.

§ 1179.2 Definitions.

For the purposes of the part the following definitions will apply:

Agency means an executive agency as is defined at 5 U.S.C. 105 including the U.S. Postal Service, the U.S. Postal Commission, a military department as defined at 5 U.S.C. 102, an agency or court in the judicial branch, an agency of the legislative branch including the U.S. Senate and House of Representatives and other independent establishments that are entities of the Federal government.

Chairperson means the Chairperson of the National Endowment for the Humanities or the Chairperson's designee.

Creditor agency means the agency to which the debt is owed.

Debt means an amount owed to the United States from sources which include loans insured or guaranteed by the United States and all other amounts due the United States from fees, leases, rents, royalties, services, sales or real or personal property, overpayments, penalties, damages, interests, fines, forfeitures, (except those arising under the Uniform Code of Military Justice) and all other similar sources.

Disposable pay means the amount that remains from an employee's Federal pay after required deductions for social security, Federal, state or local income tax, health insurance premiums, retirement contributions, life insurance premiums, Federal employment taxes, and any other deductions that are required to be withheld by law.

Hearing official means an individual responsible for conducting any hearing with respect to the existence or amount of a debt claimed, and who renders a decision on the basis of such hearing. A hearing official may not be under the supervision or control of the Chairperson of the National Endowment for the Humanities.

Paying Agency means the agency that employs the individual who owes the debt and authorizes the payment of his/her current pay.

Salary offset means an administrative offset to collect a debt pursuant to 5 U.S.C. 5514 by deduction(s) at one or more officially established pay intervals from the current pay account of an employee without his/her consent.

§ 1179.3 Applicability.

(a) These regulations are to be followed when:

(1) The National Endowment for the Humanities is owed a debt by an individual currently employed by another Federal agency;

(2) The National Endowment for the Humanities is owed a debt by an individual who is a current employee of the National Endowment for the Humanities; or

(3) The National Endowment for the Humanities employs an individual who owes a debt to another Federal agency.

§ 1179.4 Notice requirements.

(a) Deductions shall not be made unless the employee is provided with written notice signed by the Chairperson of the debt at least 30 days before salary offset commences.

(b) The written notice shall contain:

(1) A statement that the debt is owed and an explanation of its nature, and amount;

(2) The agency's intention to collect the debt by deducting from the employee's current disposable pay account;

(3) The amount, frequency proposed beginning date, and duration of the intended deduction(s);

(4) An explanation of interest, penalties, and administrative charges, including a statement that such charges will be assessed unless excused in accordance with the Federal Claims Collections Standards at 4 CFR 101.1 *et seq.;*

(5) The employee's right to inspect, request, or receive a copy of government records relating to the debt;

(6) The opportunity to establish a written schedule for the voluntary repayment of the debt;

(7) The right to a hearing conducted by an impartial hearing official;

(8) The methods and time period for petitioning for hearings;

(9) A statement that the timely filing of a petition for a hearing will stay the commencement of collection proceedings;

(10) A statement that a final decision on the hearing will be issued not later than 60 days after the filing of the petition requesting the hearing unless the employee requests and the hearing official grants a delay in the proceedings;

(11) A statement that knowingly false or frivolous statements, representations, or evidence may subject the employee to appropriate disciplinary procedures;

(12) A statement of other rights and remedies available to the employee under statutes or regulations governing the program for which the collection is being made; and

(13) Unless there are contractual or statutory provisions to the contrary, a statement that amounts paid on or deducted for the debt which are later waived or found not owed to the United States will be promptly refunded to the employee.

§ 1179.5 Hearing.

(a) *Request for hearing.* (1) An employee must file a petition for a hearing in accordance with the instructions outlined in the agency's notice to offset. (2) A hearing may be requested by filing a written petition addressed to the Chairperson of the National Endowment for the Humanities stating why the employee disputes the existence or amount of the debt. The petition for a hearing must be received by the Chairperson no later than fifteen (15) calendar days after the date of the notice to offset unless the employee can show good cause for failing to meet the deadline date.

(b) Hearing procedures. (1) The hearing will be presided over by an impartial hearing official. (2) The hearing shall conform to procedures contained in the Federal Claims Collection Standards 4 CFR 102.3(c). The burden shall be on the employee to demonstrate that the existence or the amount of the debt is in error.

§ 1179.6 Written decision.

(a) The hearing official shall issue a written opinion no later than 60 days after the hearing.

(b) The written opinion will include: a statement of the facts presented to demonstrate the nature and origin of the alleged debt; the hearing official's analysis, findings and conclusions; the amount and validity of the debt, and the repayment schedule.

§ 1179.7 Coordinating offset with another Federal agency.

(a) *The Endowment as the creditor agency.* (1) When the Chairperson determines that an employee of a Federal agency owes a delinquent debt to the National Endowment for the Humanities, the Chairperson shall as appropriate:

(i) Arrange for a hearing upon the proper petitioning by the employee;

(ii) Certify in writing that the employee owes the debt, the amount and basis of the debt, the date on which payment is due, the date the Government's right to collect the debt accrued, and that Endowment regulations for salary offset have been approved by the Office of Personnel Management;

(iii) If collection must be made in installments, the Chairperson must advise the paying agency of the amount or percentage of disposable pay to be collected in each installment;

(iv) Advise the paying agency of the actions taken under 5 U.S.C. 5514(b) and provide the dates on which action was taken unless the employee has consented to salary offset in writing or signed a statement acknowledging receipt of procedures required by law. The written consent or acknowledgment must be sent to the paying agency;

(v) If the employee is in the process of separating, the Endowment must submit its debt claim to the paying agency as provided in this part. The paying agency must certify any amounts already collected, notify the employee, and send a copy of the certification and notice of the employee's separation to the creditor agency. If the paying agency is aware that the employee is entitled to Civil Service Retirement and Disability Fund or similar payments, it must certify to the agency responsible for making such payments the amount of the debt and that the provisions of this part have been followed; and

(vi) If the employee has already separated and all payments due from the paying agency have been paid, the Chairperson may request unless otherwise prohibited, that money payable to the employee from the Civil Service Retirement and Disability Fund or other similar funds be collected by administrative offset.

(b) *The Endowment as the paying agency.* (1) Upon receipt of a properly certified debt claim from another agency, deductions will be scheduled to begin at the next established pay interval. The employee must receive written notice that the National Endowment for the Humanities has received a certified debt claim from the creditor agency, the amount of the debt, the date salary offset will begin, and the amount of the deduction(s). The National Endowment for the Humanities shall not review the merits of the creditor agency's determination of the validity or the amount of the certified claim.

(2) If the employee transfers to another agency after the creditor agency has submitted its debt claim to the National Endowment for the Humanities and before the debt is collected completely, the National Endowment for the Humanities must certify the total amount collected. One copy of the certification must be furnished to the employee. A copy must be furnished the creditor agency with notice of the employee's transfer.

§ 1179.8 Procedures for salary offset.

(a) Deductions to liquidate an employee's debt will be by the method and in the amount stated in the Chairperson's notice of intention to offset as provided in § 1179.4. Debts will be collected in one lump sum where possible. If the employee is financially unable to pay in one lump sum, collection must be made in installments.

(b) Debts will be collected by deduction at officially established pay intervals from an employee's current pay account unless alternative arrangements for repayment are made.

(c) Installment deductions will be made over a period not greater than the anticipated period of employment. The size of installment deductions must bear a reasonable relationship to the size of the debt and the employee's ability to pay. The deduction for the pay intervals for any period must not exceed 15% of disposable pay unless the employee has agreed in writing to a deduction of a greater amount.

(d) Unliquidated debts may be offset against any financial payment due to a separated employee including but not limited to final salary payment or leave in accordance with 31 U.S.C. 3716.

§ 1179.9 Refunds.

(a) The National Endowment for the Humanities will refund promptly any amounts deducted to satisfy debts owed to the NEH when the debt is waived, found not owed to the NEH, or when directed by an administrative or judicial order.

(b) The creditor agency will promptly return any amounts deducted by NEH to satisfy debts owed to the creditor agency when the debt is waived, found not owed, or when directed by an administrative or judicial order.

(c) Unless required by law, refunds under this section shall not bear interest.

§ 1179.10 Statute of limitations.

If a debt has been outstanding for more than 10 years after the agency's right to collect the debt first accrued, the agency may not collect by salary offset unless facts material to the Government's right to collect were not known and could not reasonably have been known by the official or officials who were charged with the responsibility for discovery and collection of such debts.

§ 1179.11 Non-waiver of rights.

An employee's involuntary payment of all or any part of a debt collected under these regulations will not be construed as a waiver of any rights that employee may have under 5 U.S.C. 5514 or any other provision of contract law unless there are statutes or contract(s) to the contrary.

§ 1179.12 Interest, penalties, and administrative costs.

Charges may be assessed for interest, penalties, and administrative costs in accordance with the Federal Claims Collection Standards, 4 CFR 102.13.

SUBCHAPTER E—INSTITUTE OF MUSEUM AND LIBRARY SERVICES

PART 1180 [RESERVED]

PART 1181—ENFORCEMENT OF NONDISCRIMINATION ON THE BASIS OF HANDICAP IN PROGRAMS OR ACTIVITIES CONDUCTED BY THE INSTITUTE OF MUSEUM AND LIBRARY SERVICES

Sec.
1181.101 Purpose.
1181.102 Application.
1181.103 Definitions.
1181.104–1181.109 [Reserved]
1181.110 Self-evaluation.
1181.111 Notice.
1181.112–1181.129 [Reserved]
1181.130 General prohibitions against discrimination.
1181.131–1181.139 [Reserved]
1181.140 Employment.
1181.141–1181.148 [Reserved]
1181.149 Program accessibility: Discrimination prohibited.
1181.150 Program accessibility: Existing facilities.
1181.151 Program accessibility: New construction and alterations.
1181.152–1175.159 [Reserved]
1181.160 Communications.
1181.161–1181.169 [Reserved]
1181.170 Compliance procedures.
1181.171–1181.999 [Reserved]

AUTHORITY: 29 U.S.C. 794.

SOURCE: 51 FR 4578, 4579, Feb. 5, 1986, unless otherwise noted.

§ 1181.101 Purpose.

This part effectuates section 119 of the Rehabilitation, Comprehensive Services, and Developmental Disabilities Amendments of 1978, which amended section 504 of the Rehabilitation Act of 1973 to prohibit discrimination on the basis of handicap in programs or activities conducted by Executive agencies or the United States Postal Service.

§ 1181.102 Application.

This part applies to all programs or activities conducted by the agency.

§ 1181.103 Definitions.

For purposes of this part, the term—

Assistant Attorney General means the Assistant Attorney General, Civil Rights Division, United States Department of Justice.

Auxiliary aids means services or devices that enable persons with impaired sensory, manual, or speaking skills to have an equal opportunity to participate in, and enjoy the benefits of, programs or activities conducted by the agency. For example, auxiliary aids useful for persons with impaired vision include readers, Brailled materials, audio recordings, telecommunications devices and other similar services and devices. Auxiliary aids useful for persons with impaired hearing include telephone handset amplifiers, telephones compatible with hearing aids, telecommunication devices for deaf persons (TDD's), interpreters, notetakers, written materials, and other similar services and devices.

Complete complaint means a written statement that contains the complainant's name and address and describes the agency's alleged discriminatory action in sufficient detail to inform the agency of the nature and date of the alleged violation of section 504. It shall be signed by the complainant or by someone authorized to do so on his or her behalf. Complaints filed on behalf of classes or third parties shall describe or identify (by name, if possible) the alleged victims of discrimination.

Facility means all or any portion of buildings, structures, equipment, roads, walks, parking lots, rolling stock or other conveyances, or other real or personal property.

Handicapped person means any person who has a physical or mental impairment that substantially limits one or more major life activities, has a record of such an impairment, or is regarded as having such an impairment.

As used in this definition, the phrase:

(1) *Physical or mental impairment* includes—

(i) Any physiological disorder or condition, cosmetic disfigurement, or anatomical loss affecting one or more of the following body systems: Neurological; musculoskeletal; special sense organs; respiratory, including speech organs; cardiovascular; reproductive; digestive; genitourinary; hemic and lymphatic; skin; and endocrine; or

(ii) Any mental or psychological disorder, such as mental retardation, organic brain syndrome, emotional or mental illness, and specific learning disabilities. The term *physical or mental impairment* includes, but is not limited to, such diseases and conditions as orthopedic, visual, speech, and hearing impairments, cerebral palsy, epilepsy, muscular dystrophy, multiple sclerosis, cancer, heart disease, diabetes, mental retardation, emotional illness, and drug addition and alcholism.

(2) *Major life activities* includes functions such as caring for one's self, performing manual tasks, walking, seeing, hearing, speaking, breathing, learning, and working.

(3) *Has a record of such an impairment* means has a history of, or has been misclassified as having, a mental or physical impairment that substantially limits one or more major life activities.

(4) *Is regarded as having an impairment* means—

(i) Has a physical or mental impairment that does not substantially limit major life activities but is treated by the agency as constituting such a limitation;

(ii) Has a physical or mental impairment that substantially limits major life activities only as a result of the attitudes of others toward such impairment; or

(iii) Has none of the impairments defined in paragraph (1) of this definition but is treated by the agency as having such an impairment.

Qualified handicapped person means—

(1) With respect to any agency program or activity under which a person is required to perform services or to achieve a level of accomplishment, a handicapped person who meets the essential eligibility requirements and who can achieve the purpose of the program or activity without modifications in the program or activity that the agency can demonstrate would result in a fundamental alteration in its nature; or

(2) With respect to any other program or activity, a handicapped person who meets the essential eligibility requirements for participation in, or receipt of benefits from, that program or activity.

(3) *Qualified handicapped person* is defined for purposes of employment in 29 CFR 1613.702(f), which is made applicable to this part by § 1181.140.

Section 504 means section 504 of the Rehabilitation Act of 1973 (Pub. L. 93–112, 87 Stat. 394 (29 U.S.C. 794)), as amended by the Rehabilitation Act Amendments of 1974 (Pub. L. 93–516, 88 Stat. 1617), and the Rehabilitation, Comprehensive Services, and Developmental Disabilities Amendments of 1978 (Pub. L. 95–602, 92 Stat. 2955). As used in this part, section 504 applies only to programs or activities conducted by Executive agencies and not to federally assisted programs.

[51 FR 4578, 4579, Feb. 5, 1986; 51 FR 7543, Mar. 5, 1986]

§§ 1181.104–1181.109 [Reserved]

§ 1181.110 Self-evaluation.

(a) The agency shall, by April 9, 1987, evaluate its current policies and practices, and the effects thereof, that do not or may not meet the requirements of this part, and, to the extent modification of any such policies and practices is required, the agency shall proceed to make the necessary modifications.

(b) The agency shall provide an opportunity to interested persons, including handicapped persons or organizations representing handicapped persons, to participate in the self-evaluation process by submitting comments (both oral and written).

(c) The agency shall, until three years following the completion of the self-evaluation, maintain on file and make available for public inspections:

(1) A description of areas examined and any problems identified, and

(2) A description of any modifications made.

§ 1181.111 Notice.

The agency shall make available to employees, applicants, participants, beneficiaries, and other interested persons such information regarding the provisions of this part and its applicability to the programs or activities conducted by the agency, and make such information available to them in such manner as the head of the agency finds necessary to apprise such persons of the protections against discrimination assured them by section 504 and this regulation.

§§ 1181.112–1181.129 [Reserved]

§ 1181.130 General prohibitions against discrimination.

(a) No qualified handicapped person shall, on the basis of handicap, be excluded from participation in, be denied the benefits of, or otherwise be subjected to discrimination under any program or activity conducted by the agency.

(b)(1) The agency, in providing any aid, benefit, or service, may not, directly or through contractual, licensing, or other arrangements, on the basis of handicap—

(i) Deny a qualified handicapped person the opportunity to participate in or benefit from the aid, benefit, or service;

(ii) Afford a qualfied handicapped person an opportunity to participate in or benefit from the aid, benefit, or service that is not equal to that afforded others;

(iii) Provide a qualified handicapped person with an aid, benefit, or service that is not as effective in affording equal opportunity to obtain the same result, to gain the same benefit, or to reach the same level of achievement as that provided to others;

(iv) Provide different or separate aid, benefits, or services to handicapped persons or to any class of handicapped persons than is provided to others unless such action is necessary to provide qualified handicapped persons with aid, benefits, or services that are as effective as those provided to others;

(v) Deny a qualified handicapped person the opportunity to participate as a member of planning or advisory boards; or

(vi) Otherwise limit a qualified handicapped person in the enjoyment of any right, privilege, advantage, or opportunity enjoyed by others receiving the aid, benefit, or service.

(2) The agency may not deny a qualified handicapped person the opportunity to participate in programs or activities that are not separate or different, despite the existence of permissibly separate or different programs or activities.

(3) The agency may not, directly or through contractual or other arrangements, utilize criteria or methods of administration the purpose or effect of which would—

(i) Subject qualified handicapped persons to discrimination on the basis of handicap; or

(ii) Defeat or substantially impair accomplishment of the objectives of a program or activity with respect to handicapped persons.

(4) The agency may not, in determining the site or location of a facility, make selections the purpose or effect of which would—

(i) Exclude handicapped persons from, deny them the benefits of, or otherwise subject them to discrimination under any program or activity conducted by the agency; or

(ii) Defeat or substantially impair the accomplishment of the objectives of a program or activity with respect to handicapped persons.

(5) The agency, in the selection of procurement contractors, may not use criteria that subject qualified handicapped persons to discrimination on the basis of handicap.

(c) The exclusion of nonhandicapped persons from the benefits of a program limited by Federal statute or Executive order to handicapped persons or the exclusion of a specific class of handicapped persons from a program limited by Federal statute or Executive order to a different class of handicapped persons is not prohibited by this part.

(d) The agency shall administer programs and activities in the most integrated setting appropriate to the needs of qualified handicapped persons.

§§ 1181.131–1181.139 [Reserved]

§ 1181.140 Employment.

No qualified handicapped person shall, on the basis of handicap, be subjected to discrimination in employment under any program or activity conducted by the agency. The definitions, requirements, and procedures of section 501 of the Rehabilitation Act of 1973 (29 U.S.C. 791), as established by the Equal Employment Opportunity Commission in 29 CFR part 1613, shall apply to employment in federally conducted programs or activities.

§§ 1181.141-1181.148 [Reserved]

§ 1181.149 Program accessibility: Discrimination prohibited.

Except as otherwise provided in § 1181.150, no qualified handicapped person shall, because the agency's facilities are inaccessible to or unusable by handicapped persons, be denied the benefits of, be excluded from participation in, or otherwise be subjected to discrimination under any program or activity conducted by the agency.

§ 1181.150 Program accessibility: Existing facilities.

(a) *General.* The agency shall operate each program or activity so that the program or activity, when viewed in its entirety, is readily accessible to and usable by handicapped persons. This paragraph does not—

(1) Necessarily require the agency to make each of its existing facilities accessible to and usable by handicapped persons; or

(2) Require the agency to take any action that it can demonstrate would result in a fundamental alteration in the nature of a program or activity or in undue financial and administrative burdens. In those circumstances where agency personnel believe that the proposed action would fundamentally alter the program or activity or would result in undue financial and administrative burdens, the agency has the burden of proving that compliance with § 1181.150(a) would result in such alteration or burdens. The decision that compliance would result in such alteration or burdens must be made by the agency head or his or her designee after considering all agency resources available for use in the funding and operation of the conducted program or activity, and must be accompanied by a written statement of the reasons for reaching that conclusion. If an action would result in such an alteration or such burdens, the agency shall take any other action that would not result in such an alteration or such burdens but would nevertheless ensure that handicapped persons receive the benefits and services of the program or activity.

(b) *Methods.* The agency may comply with the requirements of this section through such means as redesign of equipment, reassignment of services to accessible buildings, assignment of aides to beneficiaries, home visits, delivery of services at alternate accessible sites, alteration of existing facilities and construction of new facilities, use of accessible rolling stock, or any other methods that result in making its programs or activities readily accessible to and usable by handicapped persons. The agency is nor required to make structural changes in existing facilities where other methods are effective in achieving compliance with this section. The agency, in making alterations to existing buildings, shall meet accessibility requirements to the extent compelled by the Architectural Barriers Act of 1968, as amended (42 U.S.C. 4151–4157), and any regulations implementing it. In choosing among available methods for meeting the requirements of this section, the agency shall give priority to those methods that offer programs and activities to qualified handicapped persons in the most integrated setting appropriate.

(c) *Time period for compliance.* The agency shall comply with the obligations established under this section by June 6, 1986, except that where structural changes in facilities are undertaken, such changes shall be made by April 7, 1989, but in any event as expeditiously as possible.

(d) *Transition plan.* In the event that structural changes to facilities will be undertaken to achieve program accessibility, the agency shall develop, by October 7, 1986, a transition plan setting forth the steps necessary to complete such changes. The agency shall provide an opportunity to interested persons, including handicapped persons or organizations representing handicapped persons, to participate in the development of the transition plan by submitting comments (both oral and written). A copy of the transition plan shall be made available for public inspection. The plan shall, at a minimum—

(1) Identify physical obstacles in the agency's facilities that limit the accessibility of its programs or activities to handicapped persons;

(2) Describe in detail the methods that will be used to make the facilities accessible;

(3) Specify the schedule for taking the steps necessary to achieve compliance with this section and, if the time period of the transition plan is longer than one year, identify steps that will be taken during each year of the transition period; and

(4) Indicate the official responsible for implementation of the plan.

[51 FR 4578, 4579, Feb. 5, 1986; 51 FR 7543, Mar. 5, 1986]

§ 1181.151 Program accessibility: New construction and alterations.

Each building or part of a building that is constructed or altered by, on behalf of, or for the use of the agency shall be designed, constructed, or altered so as to be readily accessible to and usable by handicapped persons. The definitions, requirements, and standards of the Architectural Barriers Act (42 U.S.C. 4151–4157), as established in 41 CFR 101–19.600 to 101–19.607, apply to buildings covered by this section.

§§ 1181.152–1181.159 [Reserved]

§ 1181.160 Communications.

(a) The agency shall take appropriate steps to ensure effective communication with applicants, participants, personnel of other Federal entities, and members of the public.

(1) The agency shall furnish appropriate auxiliary aids where necessary to afford a handicapped person an equal opportunity to participate in, and enjoy the benefits of, a program or activity conducted by the agency.

(i) In determining what type of auxiliary aid is necessary, the agency shall give primary consideration to the requests of the handicapped person.

(ii) The agency need not provide individually prescribed devices, readers for personal use or study, or other devices of a personal nature.

(2) Where the agency communicates with applicants and beneficiaries by telephone, telecommunication devices for deaf persons (TDD's) or equally effective telecommunication systems shall be used.

(b) The agency shall ensure that interested persons, including persons with impaired vision or hearing, can obtain information as to the existence and location of accessible services, activities, and facilities.

(c) The agency shall provide signage at a primary entrance to each of its inaccessible facilities, directing users to a location at which they can obtain information about accessible facilities. The international symbol for accessibility shall be used at each primary entrance of an accessible facility.

(d) This section does not require the agency to take any action that it can demonstrate would result in a fundamental alteration in the nature of a program or activity or in undue financial and administrative burdens. In those circumstances where agency personnel believe that the proposed action would fundamentally alter the program or activity or would result in undue financial and administrative burdens, the agency has the burden of proving that compliance with § 1181.160 would result in such alteration or burdens. The decision that compliance would result in such alteration or burdens must be made by the agency head or his or her designee after considering all agency resources available for use in the funding and operation of the conducted program or activity, and must be accompanied by a written statement of the reasons for reaching that conclusion. If an action required to comply with this section would result in such an alteration or such burdens, the agency shall take any other action that would not result in such an alteration or such burdens but would nevertheless ensure that, to the maximum extent possible, handicapped persons receive the benefits and services of the program or activity.

§§ 1181.161–1181.169 [Reserved]

§ 1181.170 Compliance procedures.

(a) Except as provided in paragraph (b) of this section, this section applies to all allegations of discrimination on the basis of handicap in programs or activities conducted by the agency.

(b) The agency shall process complaints alleging violations of section 504 with respect to employment according to the procedures established by the Equal Employment Opportunity Commission in 29 CFR part 1613 pursuant to section 501 of the Rehabilitation Act of 1973 (29 U.S.C. 791).

(c) The Director shall be responsible for coordinating implementation of this section. Complaints may be sent to Director, Institute of Museum and Library Services, 1100 Pennsylvania Ave., NW., room 510, Washington, DC 20506.

(d) The agency shall accept and investigate all complete complaints for which it has jurisdiction. All complete complaints must be filed within 180 days of the alleged act of discrimination. The agency may extend this time period for good cause.

(e) If the agency receives a complaint over which it does not have jurisdiction, it shall promptly notify the complainant and shall make reasonable efforts to refer the complaint to the appropriate government entity.

(f) The agency shall notify the Architectural and Transportation Barriers Compliance Board upon receipt of any complaint alleging that a building or facility that is subject to the Architectural Barriers Act of 1968, as amended (42 U.S.C. 4151–4157), or section 502 of the Rehabilitation Act of 1973, as amended (29 U.S.C. 792), is not readily accessible to and usable by handicapped persons.

(g) Within 180 days of the receipt of a complete complaint for which it has jurisdiction, the agency shall notify the complainant of the results of the investigation in a letter containing—

(1) Findings of fact and conclusions of law;

(2) A description of a remedy for each violation found;

(3) A notice of the right to appeal.

(h) Appeals of the findings of fact and conclusions of law or remedies must be filed by the complainant within 90 days of receipt from the agency of the letter required by § 1181.170(g). The agency may extend this time for good cause.

(i) Timely appeals shall be accepted and processed by the head of the agency.

(j) The head of the agency shall notify the complainant of the results of the appeal within 60 days of the receipt of the request. If the head of the agency determines that additional information is needed from the complainant, he or she shall have 60 days from the date of receipt of the additional information to make his or her determination on the appeal.

(k) The time limits cited in paragraphs (g) and (j) of this section may be extended with the permission of the Assistant Attorney General.

(l) The agency may delegate its authority for conducting complaint investigations to other Federal agencies, except that the authority for making the final determination may not be delegated to another agency.

[51 FR 4578, 4579, Feb. 5, 1986, as amended at 51 FR 4578, Feb. 5, 1986]

§§ 1181.171–1181.999 [Reserved]

PART 1182—IMPLEMENTATION OF THE PRIVACY ACT OF 1974

Sec.
1182.1 Purpose and scope of these regulations.
1182.2 Definitions.
1182.3 Inquiries about the Institute's systems of records or implementation of the Privacy Act.
1182.4 Procedures for notifying the public of the Institute's systems of records.
1182.5 Procedures for notifying government entities of the Institute's proposed changes to its systems of records.
1182.6 Limits that exist as to the contents of the Institute's systems of records.
1182.7 Institute procedures for collecting information from individuals for its records.
1182.8 Procedures for acquiring access to Institute records pertaining to an individual.
1182.9 Identification required when requesting access to Institute records pertaining to an individual.
1182.10 Procedures for amending or correcting an individual's Institute record.
1182.11 Procedures for appealing a refusal to amend or correct an Institute record.
1182.12 Fees charged to locate, review, or copy records.
1182.13 Policies and procedures for Institute disclosure of its records.

1182.14 Procedures for maintaining accounts of disclosures made by the Institute from its systems of records.
1182.15 Institute responsibility for maintaining adequate technical, physical, and security safeguards to prevent unauthorized disclosure or destruction of manual and automatic record systems.
1182.16 Procedures to ensure that Institute employees involved with its systems of records are familiar with the requirements and of the Privacy Act.
1182.17 Institute systems of records that are covered by exemptions in the Privacy Act.
1182.18 Penalties for obtaining an Institute record under false pretenses.
1182.19 Restrictions that exist regarding the release of mailing lists.

AUTHORITY: 5 U.S.C. 552a(f).

SOURCE: 71 FR 6375, Feb. 8, 2006, unless otherwise noted.

§ 1182.1 Purpose and scope of these regulations.

The regulations in this part set forth the Institute's procedures under the Privacy Act, as required by 5 U.S.C. 552a(f), with respect to systems of records maintained by the Institute. These regulations establish procedures by which an individual may exercise the rights granted by the Privacy Act to determine whether an Institute system contains a record pertaining to him or her; to gain access to such records; and to request correction or amendment of such records. These regulations also set identification requirements, prescribe fees to be charged for copying records, and establish exemptions from certain requirements of the Act for certain Institute systems or components thereof:

§ 1182.2 Definitions.

The definitions of the Privacy Act apply to this part. In addition, as used in this part:

(a) *Agency* means any executive department, military department, government corporation, or other establishment in the executive branch of the Federal government, including the Executive Office of the President or any independent regulatory agency.

(b) *Business day* means a calendar day, excluding Saturdays, Sundays, and legal public holidays.

(c) *Director* means the Director of the Institute, or his or her designee;

(d) *General Counsel* means the General Counsel of the Institute, or his or her designee.

(e) *Individual* means any citizen of the United States or an alien lawfully admitted for permanent residence;

(f) *Institute* means the Institute of Museum and Library Services;

(g) *Institute system* means a system of records maintained by the Institute;

(h) *Maintain* means to collect, use, store, or disseminate records, as well as any combination of these record-keeping functions. The term also includes exercise of control over and, therefore, responsibility and accountability for, systems of records;

(i) *Privacy Act* or *Act* means the Privacy Act of 1974, as amended (5 U.S.C. 552a);

(j) *Record* means any item, collection, or grouping of information about an individual that is maintained by an agency and contains the individual's name or another identifying particular, such as a number or symbol assigned to the individual, or his or her fingerprint, voice print, or photograph. The term includes, but is not limited to, information regarding an individual's education, financial transactions, medical history, and criminal or employment history;

(k) *Routine use* means, with respect to the disclosure of a record, the use of a record for a purpose that is compatible with the purpose for which it was collected;

(l) *Subject individual* means the individual to whom a record pertains. Uses of the terms "I", "you", "me", and other references to the reader of the regulations in this part are meant to apply to subject individuals as defined in this paragraph (l); and

(m) *System of records* means a group of records under the control of any agency from which information is retrieved by use of the name of the individual or by some number, symbol, or other identifying particular assigned to the individual.

§ 1182.3 Inquiries about the Institute's systems of records or implementation of the Privacy Act.

Inquiries about the Institute's systems of records or implementation of the Privacy Act should be sent to the following address: Institute of Museum and Library Services; Office of the General Counsel; 1800 M Street, NW., 9th Floor, Washington, DC 20036.

§ 1182.4 Procedures for notifying the public of the Institute's systems of records.

(a) From time to time, the Institute shall review its systems of records in the FEDERAL REGISTER, and publish, if necessary, any amendments to those systems of records. Such publication shall not be made for those systems of records maintained by other agencies while in the temporary custody of the Institute.

(b) At least 30 days prior to publication of information under paragraph (a) of this section, the Institute shall publish in the FEDERAL REGISTER a notice of its intention to establish any new routine uses of any of its systems of records, thereby providing the public an opportunity to comment on such uses. This notice published by the Institute shall contain the following:

(1) The name of the system of records for which the routine use is to be established;

(2) The authority for the system;

(3) The purpose for which the record is to be maintained;

(4) The proposed routine use(s);

(5) The purpose of the routine use(s); and

(6) The categories of recipients of such use.

(c) Any request for additions to the routine uses of Institute systems should be sent to the Office of the General Counsel (see § 1182.3).

(d) Any individual who wishes to know whether an Institute system contains a record pertaining to him or her should write to the Office of the General Counsel (see § 1182.3). Such individuals may also call the Office of the General Counsel at (202) 653–4787 on business days, between the hours of 9 a.m. and 5 p.m., to schedule an appointment to make an inquiry in person. Inquiries should be presented in writing and should specifically identify the Institute systems involved. The Institute will attempt to respond to an inquiry regarding whether a record exists within 10 business days of receiving the inquiry.

§ 1182.5 Procedures for notifying government entities of the Institute's proposed changes to its systems of records.

When the Institute proposes to establish or significantly change any of its systems of records, it shall provide adequate advance notice of such proposal to the Committee on Government Reform of the House of Representatives, the Committee on Governmental Affairs of the Senate, and the Office of Management and Budget (OMB), in order to permit an evaluation of the probable or potential effect of such proposal on the privacy or other rights of individuals. This report will be submitted in accordance with guidelines provided by the OMB.

§ 1182.6 Limits that exist as to the contents of the Institute's systems of records.

(a) The Institute shall maintain only such information about an individual as is relevant and necessary to accomplish a purpose of the agency required by statute or by executive order of the President. In addition, the Institute shall maintain all records that are used in making determinations about any individual with such accuracy, relevance, timeliness, and completeness as is reasonably necessary to ensure fairness to that individual in the making of any determination about him or her. However, the Institute shall not be required to update retired records.

(b) The Institute shall not maintain any record about any individual with respect to or describing how such individual exercises rights guaranteed by the First Amendment of the Constitution of the United States, unless expressly authorized by statute or by the subject individual, or unless pertinent to and within the scope of an authorized law enforcement activity.

§ 1182.7 Institute procedures for collecting information from individuals for its records.

The Institute shall collect information, to the greatest extent practicable, directly from you when the information may result in adverse determinations about your rights, benefits, or privileges under Federal programs. In addition, the Institute shall inform

§ 1182.8

you of the following, either on the form it uses to collect the information or on a separate form that you can retain, when it asks you to supply information:

(a) The statutory or executive order authority that authorizes the solicitation of the information;

(b) Whether disclosure of such information is mandatory or voluntary;

(c) The principal purpose(s) for which the information is intended to be used;

(d) The routine uses that may be made of the information, as published pursuant to § 1182.4; and

(e) Any effects on you of not providing all or any part of the required or requested information.

§ 1182.8 Procedures for acquiring access to Institute records pertaining to an individual.

The following procedures apply to records that are contained in an Institute system:

(a) You may request review of records pertaining to you by writing to the Office of the General Counsel (see § 1182.3). You also may call the Office of the General Counsel at (202) 653–4787 on business days, between the hours of 9 a.m. and 5 p.m., to schedule an appointment to make such a request in person. A request for records should be presented in writing and should identify specifically the Institute systems involved.

(b) Access to the record, or to any other information pertaining to you that is contained in the system shall be provided if the identification requirements of § 1182.9 are satisfied and the record is determined otherwise to be releasable under the Privacy Act and these regulations. The Institute shall provide you an opportunity to have a copy made of any such record about you. Only one copy of each requested record will be supplied, based on the fee schedule in § 1182.12.

(c) The Institute will comply promptly with requests made in person at scheduled appointments, if the requirements of this section are met and the records sought are immediately available. The institute will acknowledge, within 10 business days, mailed requests or personal requests for documents that are not immediately available, and the information requested will be provided promptly thereafter.

(d) If you make your request in person at a scheduled appointment, you may, upon your request, be accompanied by a person of your choice to review your record. The Institute may require that you furnish a written statement authorizing discussion of your record in the accompanying person's presence. A record may be disclosed to a representative chosen by you upon your proper written consent.

(e) Medical or psychological records pertaining to you shall be disclosed to you unless, in the judgment of the Institute, access to such records might have an adverse effect upon you. When such a determination has been made, the Institute may refuse to disclose such information directly to you. The Institute will, however, disclose this information to a licensed physician designated by you in writing.

§ 1182.9 Identification required when requesting access to Institute records pertaining to an individual.

The Institute shall require reasonable identification of all individuals who request access to records in an Institute system to ensure that they are disclosed to the proper person.

(a) The amount of personal identification required will of necessity vary with the sensitivity of the record involved. In general, if you request disclosure in person, you shall be required to show an identification card, such as a driver's license, containing your photograph and sample signature. However, with regard to records in Institute systems that contain particularly sensitive and/or detailed personal information, the Institute reserves the right to require additional means of identification as are appropriate under the circumstances. These means include, but are not limited to, requiring you to sign a statement under oath as to your identity, acknowledging that you are aware of the penalties for improper disclosure under the provisions of the Privacy Act.

(b) If you request disclosure by mail, the Institute will request such information as may be necessary to ensure

National Foundation on the Arts and the Humanities § 1182.11

that you are properly identified. Authorized means to achieve this goal include, but are not limited to, requiring that a mail request include certification that a duly commissioned notary public of any State or territory (or a similar official, if the request is made outside of the United States) received an acknowledgment of identity from you.

(c) If you are unable to provide suitable documentation or identification, the Institute may require a signed, notarized statement asserting your identity and stipulating that you understand that knowingly or willfully seeking or obtaining access to records about another person under false pretenses is punishable by a fine of up to $5,000.

§ 1182.10 Procedures for amending or correcting an individual's Institute record.

(a) You are entitled to request amendments to or corrections of records pertaining to you pursuant to the provisions of the Privacy Act, including 5 U.S.C. 552a(d)(2). Such a request should be made in writing and addressed to the Office of the General Counsel (see § 1182.3).

(b) Your request for amendments or corrections should specify the following:

(1) The particular record that you are seeking to amend or correct;

(2) The Institute system from which the record was retrieved;

(3) The precise correction or amendment you desire, preferably in the form of an edited copy of the record reflecting the desired modification; and

(4) Your reasons for requesting amendment or correction of the record.

(c) The Institute will acknowledge a request for amendment or correction of a record within 10 business days of its receipt, unless the request can be processed and the individual informed of the General Counsel's decision on the request within that 10-day period.

(d) If after receiving and investigating your request, the General Counsel agrees that the record is not accurate, timely, or complete, based on a preponderance of the evidence, then the record will be corrected or amended promptly. The record will be deleted without regard to its accuracy, if the record is not relevant or necessary to accomplish the Institute function for which the record was provided or is maintained. In either case, you will be informed in writing of the amendment, correction, or deletion. In addition, if accounting was made of prior disclosures of the record, all previous recipients of the record will be informed of the corrective action taken.

(e) If after receiving and investigating your request, the General Counsel does not agree that the record should be amended or corrected, you will be informed promptly in writing of the refusal to amend or correct the record and the reason for this decision. You also will be informed that you may appeal this refusal in accordance with § 1182.11.

(f) Requests to amend or correct a record governed by the regulations of another agency will be forwarded to such agency for processing, and you will be informed in writing of this referral.

§ 1182.11 Procedures for appealing a refusal to amend or correct an Institute record.

(a) You may appeal a refusal to amend or correct a record to the Director. Such appeal must be made in writing within 10 business days of your receipt of the initial refusal to amend or correct your record. Your appeal should be sent to the Office of the General Counsel (see § 1182.3), should indicate that it is an appeal, and should include the basis for the appeal.

(b) The Director will review your request to amend or correct the record, the General Counsel's refusal, and any other pertinent material relating to the appeal. No hearing will be held.

(c) The Director shall render his or her decision on your appeal within 30 business days of its receipt by the Institute, unless the Director, for good cause shown, extends the 30-day period. Should the Director extend the appeal period, you will be informed in writing of the extension and the circumstances of the delay.

(d) If the Director determines that the record that is the subject of the appeal should be amended or corrected, the record will be so modified, and you will be informed in writing of the amendment or correction. Where an accounting was made of prior disclosures of the record, all previous recipients of the record will be informed of the corrective action taken.

(e) If your appeal is denied, you will be informed in writing of the following:

(1) The denial and the reasons for the denial;

(2) That you may submit to the Institute a concise statement setting forth the reasons for your disagreement as to the disputed record. Under the procedures set forth in paragraph (f) of this section, your statement will be disclosed whenever the disputed record is disclosed; and

(3) That you may seek judicial review of the Director's determination under 5 U.S.C. 552a(g)(1)(a).

(f) Whenever you submit a statement of disagreement to the Institute in accordance with paragraph (e)(2) of this section, the record will be annotated to indicate that it is disputed. In any subsequent disclosure, a copy of your statement of disagreement will be disclosed with the record. If the Institute deems it appropriate, a concise statement of the Director's reasons for denying our appeal also may be disclosed with the record. While you will have access to this statement of the Director's reasons for denying your appeal, such statement will not be subject to correction or amendment. Where an accounting was made of prior disclosures of the record, all previous recipients of the record will be provided a copy of your statement of disagreement, as well as any statement of the Director's reasons for denying your appeal.

§ 1182.12 Fees charged to locate, review, or copy records.

(a) The Institute shall charge no fees for search time or for any other time expended by the Institute to review a record. However, the Institute may charge fees where you request that a copy be made of a record to which you have been granted access. Where a copy of the record must be made in order to provide access to the record (e.g., computer printout where no screen reading is available), the copy will be made available to you without cost.

(b) Copies of records made by photocopy or similar process will be charged to you at the rate of $0.10 per page. Where records are not susceptible to photocopying (e.g., punch cards, magnetic tapes, or oversize materials), you will be charged actual cost as determined on a case-by-case basis. A copying fee totaling $3.00 or less shall be waived, but the copying fees for contemporaneous requests by the same individual shall be aggregated to determine the total fee.

(c) Special and additional services provided at your request, such as certification or authentication, postal insurance, and special mailing arrangement costs, will be charged to you.

(d) A copying fee shall not be charged or, alternatively, it may be reduced, when the General Counsel determines, based on a petition, that the petitioning individual is indigent and that the Institute's resources permit a waiver of all or part of the fee.

(e) All fees shall be paid before any copying request is undertaken. Payments shall be made by check or money order payable to the "Institute of Museum and Library Services."

§ 1182.13 Policies and procedures for Institute disclosure of its records.

(a) The Institute not disclose any record that is contained in a system of records to any person or to another agency, except pursuant to a written request by or with the prior written consent of the subject individual, unless disclosure of the record is:

(1) To those officers or employees of the Institute who maintain the record and who have a need for the record in the performance of their official duties;

(2) Required under the provisions of the Freedom of Information Act (5 U.S.C. 552). Records required to be made available by the Freedom of Information Act will be released in response to a request to the Institute formulated in accordance with the National Foundation on the Arts and the Humanities regulations published at 45 CFR part 1100;

(3) For a routine use as published in the annual notice in the FEDERAL REGISTER;

(4) To the Census Bureau for purpose of planning or carrying out a census;

National Foundation on the Arts and the Humanities § 1182.14

survey, or related activity pursuant to the provisions of Title 13 of the United States Code;

(5) To a recipient who has provided the Institute with adequate advance written assurance that the record will be used solely as a statistical research or reporting record, and the record is to be transferred in a form that is not individually identifiable;

(6) To the National Archives and Records Administration as a record that has sufficient historical or other value to warrant its continued preservation by the United States government, or for evaluation by the Archivist of the United States, or his or her designee, to determine whether the record has such value;

(7) To another agency or to an instrumentality of any governmental jurisdiction within or under the control of the United States for a civil or criminal law enforcement activity, if the activity is authorized by law, and if the head of the agency or instrumentality has made a written request to the Institute for such records specifying the particular portion desired and the law enforcement activity for which the record is sought. The Institute also may disclose such a record to a law enforcement agency on its own initiative in situations in which criminal conduct is suspected, provided that such disclosure has been established as a routine use, or in situations in which the misconduct is directly related to the purpose for which the record is maintained;

(8) To a person pursuant to a showing of compelling circumstances affecting the health or safety of an individual if, upon such disclosure, notification is transmitted to the last known address of such individual;

(9) To either House of Congress, or, to the extent of matter within its jurisdictions, any committee or subcommittee thereof, any joint committee of Congress, or subcommittee of any such joint committee;

(10) To the Comptroller General, or any of his or her authorized representatives, in the course of the performance of official duties of the General Accounting Office;

(11) To a consumer reporting agency in accordance with 31 U.S.C. 3711(e); or

(12) Pursuant to an order of a court of competent jurisdiction. In the event that any record is disclosed under such compulsory legal process, the Institute shall make reasonable efforts to notify the subject individual after the process becomes a matter of public record.

(b) Before disseminating any record about any individual to any person other than an Institute employee, the Institute shall make reasonable efforts to ensure that such records are, or at the time they were collected were, accurate, complete, timely, and relevant for Institute purposes. This paragraph (b) does not apply to dissemination made pursuant to the provisions of the Freedom of Information Act (5 U.S.C. 552) and paragraph (a)(2) of this section.

§ 1182.14 Procedures for maintaining accounts of disclosures made by the Institute from its systems of records.

(a) The Office of the General Counsel shall maintain a log containing the date, nature, and purpose of each disclosure of a record to any person or to another agency. Such accounting also shall contain the name and address of the person or agency to whom each disclosure was made. This log need not include disclosures made to Institute employees in the course of their official duties, or pursuant to the provisions of the Freedom of Information Act (5 U.S.C. 552).

(b) The Institute shall retain the accounting of each disclosure for at least five years after the accounting is made or for the life of the record that was disclosed, whichever is longer.

(c) The Institute shall make the accounting of disclosures of a record pertaining to you available to you at your request. Such a request should be made in accordance with the procedures set forth in § 1182.8. This paragraph (c) does not apply to disclosures made for law enforcement purposes under 5 U.S.C. 552a(b)(7) and § 1182.13(a)(7).

§ 1182.15 Institute responsibility for maintaining adequate technical, physical, and security safeguards to prevent unauthorized disclosure or destruction of manual and automatic record systems.

The Chief Information Officer has the responsibility of maintaining adequate technical, physical, and security safeguards to prevent unauthorized disclosure or destruction of manual and automatic record systems. These security safeguards shall apply to all systems in which identifiable personal data are processed or maintained, including all reports and outputs from such systems that contain identifiable personal information. Such safeguards must be sufficient to prevent negligent, accidental, or unintentional disclosure, modification or destruction of any personal records or data, and must furthermore minimize, to the extent practicable, the risk that skilled technicians or knowledgeable persons could improperly obtain access to modify or destroy such records or data and shall further insure against such casual entry by unskilled persons without official reasons for access to such records or data.

(a) *Manual systems.* (1) Records contained in a system of records as defined in this part may be used, held, or stored only where facilities are adequate to prevent unauthorized access by persons within or outside the Institute.

(2) All records, when not under the personal control of the employees authorized to use the records, must be stored in a locked filing cabinet. Some systems of records are not of such confidential nature that their disclosure would constitute a harm to an individual who is the subject of such record. However, records in this category also shall be maintained in locked filing cabinets or maintained in a secured room with a locking door.

(3) Access to and use of a system of records shall be permitted only to persons whose duties require such access within the Institute, for routine uses as defined in § 1182.1 as to any given system, or for such other uses as may be provided in this part.

(4) Other than for access within the Institute to persons needing such records in the performance of their official duties or routine uses as defined in § 1182.1, or such other uses as provided in this part, access to records within a system of records shall be permitted only to the individual to whom the record pertains or upon his or her written request to the General Counsel.

(5) Access to areas where a system of records is stored will be limited to those persons whose duties require work in such areas. There shall be an accounting of the removal of any records from such storage areas utilizing a log, as directed by the Chief Information Officer. The log shall be maintained at all times.

(6) The Institute shall ensure that all persons whose duties require access to and use of records contained in a system of records are adequately trained to protect the security and privacy of such records.

(7) The disposal and destruction of records within a system of records shall be in accordance with rules promulgated by the General Services Administration.

(b) *Automated systems.* (1) Identifiable personal information may be processed, stored, or maintained by automated data systems only where facilities or conditions are adequate to prevent unauthorized access to such systems in any form. Whenever such data, whether contained in punch cards, magnetic tapes, or discs, are not under the personal control of an authorized person, such information must be stored in a locked or secured room, or in such other facility having greater safeguards than those provided for in this part.

(2) Access to and use of identifiable personal data associated with automated data systems shall be limited to those persons whose duties require such access. Proper control of personal data in any form associated with automated data systems shall be maintained at all times, including maintenance of accountability records showing disposition of input and output documents.

(3) All persons whose duties require access to processing and maintenance of identifiable personal data and automated systems shall be adequately

trained in the security and privacy of personal data.

(4) The disposal and disposition of identifiable personal data and automated systems shall be done by shredding, burning, or, in the case of tapes or discs, degaussing, in accordance with regulations of the General Services Administration or other appropriate authority.

§ 1182.16 Procedures to ensure that Institute employees involved with its systems of records are familiar with the requirements and of the Privacy Act.

(a) The Director shall ensure that all persons involved in the design, development, operation, or maintenance of any Institute system are informed of all requirements necessary to protect the privacy of subject individuals. The Director also shall ensure that all Institute employees having access to records receive adequate training in their protection, and that records have adequate and proper storage with sufficient security to assure the privacy of such records.

(b) All employees shall be informed of the civil remedies provided under 5 U.S.C. 552a(g)(1) and other implications of the Privacy Act, and the fact that the Institute may be subject to civil remedies for failure to comply with the provisions of the Privacy Act and the regulations in this part.

§ 1182.17 Institute systems of records that are covered by exemptions in the Privacy Act.

(a) Pursuant to and limited by 5 U.S.C. 552a(j)(2), the Institute system entitled "Office of the Inspector General Investigative Files" shall be exempted from the provisions of 5 U.S.C. 552a, except for subsections (b); (c)(1) and (2); (e)(4)(A) through (F); (e)(6), (7), (9), (10), and (11); and (i), insofar as that Institute system contains information pertaining to criminal law enforcement investigations.

(b) Pursuant to and limited by 5 U.S.C. 552a(k)(2), the Institute system entitled "Office of the Inspector General Investigative Files" shall be exempted from 5 U.S.C. 552a(c)(3); (d); (e)(1); (e)(4)(G), (H), and (I); and (f), insofar as that Institute system consists of investigatory material compiled for law enforcement purposes, other than material within the scope of the exemption at 5 U.S.C. 552a(j)(2).

(c) The Institute system entitled "Office of the Inspector General Investigative Files" is exempt from the provisions of the Privacy Act noted in this section because their application might alert investigation subjects to the existence or scope of investigations; lead to suppression, alteration, fabrication, or destruction of evidence; disclose investigative techniques or procedures; reduce the cooperativeness or safety of witnesses; or otherwise impair investigations.

§ 1182.18 Penalties for obtaining an Institute record under false pretenses.

(a) Under 5 U.S.C. 552a(i)(3), any person who knowingly and willfully requests or obtains any record from the Institute concerning an individual under false pretenses shall be guilty of a misdemeanor and fined not more than $5,000.

(b) A person who falsely or fraudulently attempts to obtain records under the Privacy Act also may be subject to prosecution under other statutes, including 18 U.S.C. 494, 495, and 1001.

§ 1182.19 Restrictions that exist regarding the release of mailing lists.

The Institute may not sell or rent an individual's name and address unless such action specifically is authorized by law. This section shall not be construed to require the withholding of names and addresses otherwise permitted to be made public.

PART 1183 [RESERVED]

PART 1184—IMPLEMENTATION OF THE FREEDOM OF INFORMATION ACT

Sec.
1184.1 What is the purpose and scope of these regulations?
1184.2 What are IMLS's general policies with respect to FOIA?
1184.3 How do I request records?
1184.4 When will I receive a response to my request?
1184.5 How will my request be processed?

§ 1184.1

1184.6 How can I appeal a denial of my request?
1184.7 How will fees be charged?
1184.8 How can I address concerns regarding my request?
1184.9 What are IMLS' policies regarding disclosure of confidential business information?
1184.10 Disclaimer.

AUTHORITY: 5 U.S.C. 552.

SOURCE: 79 FR 9423, Feb. 19, 2014, unless otherwise noted.

§ 1184.1 What is the purpose and scope of these regulations?

(a) The regulations in this part describe how the Institute of Museum and Library Services (IMLS) processes requests for records under the Freedom of Information Act (FOIA), 5 U.S.C. 552 as amended. The regulations in this part apply only to records that are both:

(1) Created or obtained by IMLS; and
(2) Under the agency's control at the time of the FOIA request.

(b) The rules in this part should be read in conjunction with the text of the FOIA and the Uniform Freedom of Information Fee Act Schedule and Guidelines published by the Office of Management and Budget at 52 FR 10012 (Mar. 27, 1987) (the "OMB Guidelines"). Requests made by individuals for records about themselves under the Privacy Act of 1974, 5 U.S.C. 552a, are processed under 45 CFR part 1182 as well as under this part.

§ 1184.2 What are IMLS's general policies with respect to FOIA?

(a) *Non-exempt records available to the public.* Except for records exempt or excluded from disclosure by 5 U.S.C. 552 or published in the FEDERAL REGISTER under 5 U.S.C. 552(a)(1), IMLS records subject to the FOIA are available to any person who requests them in accordance with these regulations.

(b) *Records available at the IMLS FOIA Electronic Reading Room.* IMLS makes records available on its Web site in accordance with 5 U.S.C. 552(a)(2), as amended, and other documents that, because of the nature of their subject matter, are likely to be the subject of FOIA requests. IMLS establishes categories of records that can be disclosed regularly and proactively identifies and discloses additional records of interest to the public. To save time and money, IMLS strongly urges you to review documents available at the IMLS FOIA Electronic Reading Room before submitting a FOIA request.

(c) *Definitions.* For purposes of this part, all of the terms defined in the Freedom of Information Act, and the OMB Guidelines apply, unless otherwise defined in this part.

(1) *Commercial use request.* A request by or on behalf of anyone who seeks information for a use or purpose that furthers his or her commercial, trade, or profit interests, which can include furthering those interests through litigation.

(2) *Direct costs.* Those expenses that IMLS actually incurs in searching for and duplicating (and, in the case of commercial use requests, reviewing) records in order to respond to a FOIA request. Direct costs include, for example, the salary of the employee performing the work (the basic rate of pay for the employee, plus 16.1 percent of that rate to cover benefits) and the cost of operating duplication machinery. Not included in direct costs are overhead expenses such as the costs of space and heating or lighting of the facility in which the records are kept.

(3) *Duplication.* The making of a copy of a record, or of the information contained in it, necessary to respond to a FOIA request. Copies can take the form of paper, audiovisual materials, or electronic records (for example, magnetic tape or disk), among others.

(4) *Educational institution.* Any school that operates a program of scholarly research. A requester in this category must show that the request is authorized by, and is made under the auspices of, a qualifying institution and that the records are not sought for a commercial use, but rather are sought to further scholarly research.

(5) *Fee waiver.* The waiver or reduction of processing fees if a requester can demonstrate that certain statutory standards are satisfied including that the information is in the public interest and is not requested for a commercial interest.

(6) *FOIA Public Liaison.* An IMLS official who is responsible for assisting in

National Foundation on the Arts and the Humanities § 1184.3

reducing delays, increasing transparency and understanding of the status of FOIA requests, and assisting in the resolution of disputes.

(7) *Non-commercial scientific institution.* An institution that is not operated on a "commercial" basis, as defined in paragraph (c)(1) of this section, and that is operated solely for the purpose of conducting scientific research the results of which are not intended to promote any particular product or industry. A requester in this category must show that the request is authorized by and is made under the auspices of a qualifying institution and that the records are sought to further scientific research and not for a commercial use.

(8) *Representative of news media.* Any person or entity organized and operated to publish or broadcast news to the public that actively gathers information of potential interest to a segment of the public, uses its editorial skills to turn raw materials into a distinct work, and distributes that work to an audience. The term "news" means information that is about current events or that would be of current interest to the public. Examples of news media entities include television or radio stations that broadcast news to the public at large and publishers of periodicals that disseminate news and make their products available through a variety of means to the general public. A request for records that supports the news-dissemination function of the requester will not be considered to be for a commercial use. "Freelance" journalists who demonstrate a solid basis for expecting publication through a news media entity will be considered as working for that entity. A publishing contract would provide the clearest evidence that publication is expected; however, IMLS will also consider a requester's past publication record in making this determination.

(9) *Requester Category.* One of the three categories that IMLS places requesters in for the purpose of determining whether a requester will be charged fees for search, review and duplication, and include commercial requesters; non-commercial scientific or educational institutions or news media requesters, and all other requesters.

(10) *Review.* The examination of a record located in response to a request in order to determine whether any portion of it is exempt from disclosure. Review time includes processing any record for disclosure, such as doing all that is necessary to prepare the record for disclosure, including the process of redacting the record and marking the appropriate exemptions. Review costs are properly charged even if a record ultimately is not disclosed. Review time also includes time spent both obtaining and considering any formal objection to disclosure made by a confidential business information submitter under § 1184.8 but it does not include time spent resolving general legal or policy issues regarding the application of exemptions.

(11) *Search.* The process of looking for and retrieving records or information responsive to a FOIA request. Search time includes page-by-page or line-by-line identification of information within records; and the reasonable efforts expended to locate and retrieve information from electronic records.

(12) *Working day.* A regular Federal working day. It does not include Saturdays, Sundays, or legal Federal holidays.

§ 1184.3 How do I request records?

(a) *Where to send a request.* You may make a FOIA request for IMLS records by writing directly to the FOIA Officer, Institute of Museum and Library Services, 1800 M Street NW., 9th Floor, Washington, DC 20036–5802. Requests may also be sent by facsimile to the FOIA Officer at (202) 653–4625 or by email to *foia@imls.gov.* You may also submit your FOIA request online through the IMLS FOIA Request Form located at: *http://www.imls.gov/about/ foia_request_form.aspx.*

(b) *Form of request.* Your FOIA request need not be in any particular format, but it must be in writing, include your name and mailing address, and should be clearly identified as a Freedom of Information Act or "FOIA" request. You must describe the records sought with sufficient specificity to enable the agency to identify and locate the records, including, if possible, dates, subjects, titles, or authors of the records requested. If IMLS determines

§ 1184.4

that your request does not reasonably describe the requested records, the agency will advise you what additional information is required to perfect your request, or why your request is otherwise insufficient. You should also indicate if you have a preferred form or format in which you would like to receive the requested records.

(c) *Electronic format records.* IMLS will provide the responsive records in the form or format you request if the records are readily reproducible by IMLS in that form or format. IMLS will make reasonable efforts to maintain its records in forms or formats that are reproducible for the purpose of disclosure. IMLS may disclose records in electronic format if the records can be downloaded or transferred intact through electronic media currently in use by the agency. In responding to a request for records, IMLS will make reasonable efforts to search for the records in electronic form or format, except where such efforts would significantly interfere with the operation of the agency's automated information system(s).

(d) *Date of receipt.* IMLS considers a request that complies with paragraphs (a) and (b) of this section to be a perfected request. The agency considers a request to be received on the date that the request is perfected.

§ 1184.4 When will I receive a response to my request?

(a) *Responses within 20 working days.* IMLS will ordinarily grant, partially grant, or deny your request for records within 20 working days after receiving a perfected request.

(b) *Extensions of response time in "unusual circumstances".* (1) Where the time limits for processing a request cannot be met because of "unusual circumstances," as defined in the FOIA, the FOIA Officer will notify you as soon as practicable in writing of the unusual circumstances and may extend the response period for up to ten (10) working days.

(2) Where the extension is for more than ten (10) working days, the FOIA Officer will provide you with an opportunity either to modify the request so that it may be processed within the time limits or to arrange an agreed upon alternative time period for processing the request or a modified request.

§ 1184.5 How will my request be processed?

(a) *Acknowledgment of requests.* IMLS will assign a tracking number to your request and will, as soon as practicable, advise you in writing of this tracking number, and, as appropriate, a brief description of the request, and relevant IMLS contact information, including the name and contact information of the FOIA Public Liaison.

(b) *Clarifications.* If there is any uncertainty, IMLS will attempt to communicate with you to clarify the scope of your request.

(c) *Referrals of requests.* Whenever IMLS refers all or any part of the responsibility for responding to a request to another agency, IMLS will notify you of the name of the agency to which the request has been referred.

(d) *Grants of requests.* When responsive records are located, IMLS will apply a presumption of disclosure and openness. If IMLS decides to grant your request in whole or in part, the agency will notify you in writing. The notice will include any applicable fee and the agency will disclose records to you promptly upon payment of applicable fees. IMLS will mark or annotate any records disclosed in part to show the amount, the location, and the FOIA exemptions under which the redaction is made, unless doing so would harm an interest protected by an applicable exemption.

(e) *Denials of requests.* Denials of your FOIA request, either whole or in part, will be made in writing by the FOIA Officer. IMLS will inform you of the reasons for the denial, including any FOIA exemption(s) applied by the agency in denying the request, and notify you of your right to appeal the determination as described in § 1184.6. IMLS will, as appropriate, provide a brief description of the information being withheld.

§ 1184.6 How can I appeal a denial of my request?

(a) *Submission of an appeal.* If your FOIA request has been denied in whole or in part, or if the agency has not

National Foundation on the Arts and the Humanities § 1184.7

found any records in response to your request, you may file an appeal no later than thirty (30) calendar days following the date of the notification of denial. Your appeal must include a description of the initial request, the reason for the appeal, and why you believe the agency's response was incorrect. Your appeal must be in writing, signed, and filed with the IMLS Director, c/o Office of the General Counsel, 1800 M Street NW., 9th Floor, Washington, DC 20036–5802. Appeals may also be sent by email to *foia@imls.gov*, or by facsimile to (202) 653–4625.

(b) *Decisions on appeal.* The Director of IMLS will make a determination with respect to your appeal within twenty (20) working days after the agency has received the appeal, except as provided in § 1184.4(b). If the decision on appeal is favorable to you, the Director of IMLS will take action to assure prompt dispatch of the records to you. If the decision on appeal is adverse to you, in whole or in part, you will be informed by the Director of IMLS of the reasons for the decision and of the provisions for judicial review set forth in the FOIA. As appropriate, IMLS will advise you in a response to an appeal that the 2007 FOIA amendments created the Office of Government Services (OGIS) to offer mediation services to resolve disputes between FOIA requesters and Federal agencies as a non-exclusive alternative to litigation.

§ 1184.7 How will fees be charged?

(a) *In general.* IMLS will use the most efficient and least costly methods to comply with FOIA requests. IMLS will charge fees to recover all allowable direct costs incurred, and may charge fees for searching for and reviewing requested records even if the records are determined to be exempt from disclosure or cannot be located. IMLS will charge fees in accordance with the category of the FOIA requester.

(1) *Commercial use requests.* IMLS will assess charges to recover the full direct cost of searching for, reviewing and duplicating the requested records. IMLS may recover the cost of searching for and reviewing records even if there is ultimately no disclosure.

(2) *Requests from educational and noncommercial scientific institutions.* IMLS will charge for duplication costs.

(3) *Requests by representatives of the news media.* IMLS will charge for duplication costs.

(4) *All other requests.* IMLS will assess charges to recover the full direct cost for searching for and duplicating the requested records.

(5) *Status of Requester.* IMLS' decision regarding the categorization of a requester will be made on a case-by-case basis based upon the requester's intended use of the requested records.

(b) *General fee schedule.* The following fees will be charged in accordance with paragraph (a) of this section.

(1) *Manual search fee.* The fee charged will be the salary rate(s) (i.e., basic pay plus 16.1 percent) of the employee(s) conducting the search.

(2) *Computer search fee.* The fee charged will be the actual direct cost of providing the service including the cost of operating the central processing unit for the operating time that is directly attributed to searching for records responsive to a request and the operator/programmer salary apportionable to the search.

(3) *Review fee.* The fee charged will equal the salary rate(s) (i.e., basic pay plus 16.1 percent) of the employee(s) conducting the review.

(4) *Duplication fee.* Copies of records photocopied on an 8½ × 11 inch sheet of paper will be provided at $.10 per page. For duplication of other materials, the charge will be the direct cost of duplication.

(c) *Restrictions on charging fees.* (1) Except for records provided in response to a commercial use request, the first 100 pages of duplication and the first two (2) hours of search time will be provided at no charge.

(2) Fees will not be charged to any requester, including commercial use requesters, if the total amount calculated under this section is less than $25.

(d) *Fees likely to exceed $25.* If the total fee charges are likely to exceed $25, IMLS will notify you of the estimated amount of the charges, including a breakdown of the fees for search, review and/or duplication, unless you have indicated in advance that you are

§ 1184.8

willing to pay higher fees and will offer you an opportunity to confer with the FOIA Public Liaison to revise the request to meet your needs at a lower cost.

(e) *Waiver or reduction of fees.* (1) IMLS will disclose records without charge or at a reduced charge if the agency determines that disclosure of the information is in the public interest because it is likely to contribute significantly to public understanding of the operations or activities of the government and is not primarily in the commercial interest of the requester.

(2) IMLS will use the following factors to determine whether a fee will be waived or reduced:

(i) *The subject of the request.* Whether the subject of the requested records concerns the "operations or activities of the government";

(ii) *The informative value of the information to be disclosed.* Whether the disclosure is "likely to contribute" to an understanding of government operations or activities;

(iii) *The contribution to an understanding of the subject by the general public likely to result from disclosure.* Whether disclosure of the requested information will contribute to "public understanding";

(iv) *The significance of the contribution to public understanding.* Whether disclosure is likely to contribute "significantly" to public understanding of government operations or activities;

(v) *The existence and magnitude of a commercial interest.* Whether you have a commercial interest that would be furthered by the disclosure; and if so

(vi) *The primary interest in disclosure.* Whether the magnitude of your commercial interest is sufficiently large in comparison with the public interest in disclosure, that disclosure is primarily in the your commercial interest.

(f) *Assessment and collection of fees.* (1) If you fail to pay your bill within thirty (30) days, interest will accrue from the date the bill was mailed, and will be assessed at the rate prescribed in 31 U.S.C. 3717.

(2) If IMLS reasonably believes that you are attempting to divide a request into a series of requests to avoid the assessment of fees, the agency may aggregate such requests and charge accordingly.

(3) *Advance payment.* (i) Advance payment of fees will generally not be required. IMLS may request an advance payment of the fee, however, if:

(A) The charges are likely to exceed $250; or

(B) You have failed previously to pay a fee in a timely fashion.

(ii) When IMLS requests an advance payment, the time limits described in section (a)(6) of the FOIA will begin only after IMLS has received full payment.

(g) *Failure to comply.* In the absence of unusual or exceptional circumstances, IMLS will not assess fees if the agency fails to comply with any time limit set forth in these regulations.

(h) *Waivers.* IMLS may waive fees in other circumstances solely at its discretion, consistent with 5 U.S.C. 552.

§ 1184.8 How can I address concerns regarding my request?

(a) *FOIA Public Liaison.* If you have questions or concerns regarding your request, your first point of contact should be the FOIA Public Liaison, who is responsible for reducing delays, increasing transparency and understanding of the status of requests, and assisting in the resolution of disputes.

(b) *Additional resource.* The National Archives and Records Administration (NARA), Office of Government Information Services (OGIS) offers non-compulsory, non-binding mediation services to help resolve FOIA disputes. If you seek information regarding OGIS and/or the services it offers, please contact OGIS directly at Office of Government Information Services, National Archives and Records Administration, Room 2510, 8601 Adelphi Road, College Park, MD 20740–6001, Email: *ogis@nara.gov*, Phone: (301) 837–1996, Fax: (301) 837–0348. This information is provided as a public service only. By providing this information, IMLS does not commit to refer disputes to OGIS, or to defer to OGIS' mediation decision in particular cases.

§ 1184.9 What are IMLS' policies regarding disclosure of confidential business information?

(a) *In general.* Confidential business information obtained by IMLS from a submitter will be disclosed under FOIA only under this section.

(b) *Definitions.* For purposes of this section, the following definitions apply:

(1) *Confidential business information.* Commercial or financial information obtained by IMLS from a submitter that may be protected from disclosure under Exemption 4 of FOIA.

(2) *Submitter.* Any person or entity from whom IMLS obtains confidential business information, directly or indirectly. The term includes corporations; state, local and tribal governments; and foreign governments.

(c) *Designation of confidential business information.* A submitter of confidential business information will use good-faith efforts to designate, either at the time of submission or at a reasonable time thereafter, any portions of its submission that it considers to be protected from disclosure under Exemption 4. These designations will expire ten years after the date of the submission unless the submitter requests, and provides justification for, a longer designation period.

(d) *Notice to submitters.* When required under paragraph (e) of this section, subject to the exceptions in paragraph (h) of this section, IMLS will provide a submitter with prompt written notice of a FOIA request or administrative appeal that seeks its confidential business information, in order to give the submitter an opportunity to object to disclosure of any specified portion of that information. The notice will either describe the confidential business information requested or include copies of the requested records or record portions containing the information. When notification of a voluminous number of submitters is required, notification may be made by posting or publishing the notice in a place reasonably likely to accomplish it.

(e) *Where notice is required.* IMLS will give notice to a submitter wherever:

(1) The information has been designated in good faith by the submitter as information considered protected from disclosure under Exemption 4; or

(2) IMLS has reason to believe that the information may be protected from disclosure under Exemption 4.

(f) *Opportunity to object to disclosure.* IMLS will allow a submitter a reasonable time to respond to the notice described in paragraph (d) of this section and will specify that time period within the notice. If a submitter has any objection to disclosure, it must submit a detailed written statement to IMLS. The statement must specify all grounds for withholding any portion of the information under any exemption of FOIA and, in the case of Exemption 4, it must show why the information is a trade secret or commercial or financial information that is privileged or confidential. If a submitter fails to respond to the notice within the time specified, the submitter will be considered to have no objection to disclosure of the information. Information provided by the submitter that is not received by IMLS until after the agency's disclosure decision has been made will not be considered by IMLS. Information provided by a submitter under this paragraph may itself be subject to disclosure under FOIA.

(g) *Notice of intent to disclose.* IMLS will consider a submitter's objections and specific grounds for nondisclosure in deciding whether to disclose confidential business information. If IMLS decides to disclose confidential business information over the objection of a submitter, IMLS will give the submitter written notice, which will include:

(1) A statement of the reason(s) why each of the submitter's disclosure objections was not sustained;

(2) A description of the confidential business information to be disclosed; and

(3) A specified disclosure date, which will be a reasonable time subsequent to the notice.

(h) *Exceptions to notice requirements.* The notice requirements of paragraphs (d) and (g) of this section will not apply if:

(1) IMLS determines that the information should not be disclosed;

(2) The information lawfully has been published or has been officially made available to the public;

(3) Disclosure of the information is required by statute (other than FOIA) or by a regulation issued in accordance with the requirements of Executive Order 12600; or

(4) The designation made by the submitter under paragraph (c) of this section appears obviously frivolous—except that, in such a case, IMLS will, within a reasonable time prior to a specified disclosure date, give the submitter written notice of any final decision to disclose the information.

(i) *Notice of FOIA lawsuit.* If a requester files a lawsuit seeking to compel the disclosure of confidential business information, IMLS will promptly notify the submitter of the filing of the lawsuit.

(j) *Corresponding notice to requesters.* If IMLS provides a submitter with notice and an opportunity to object to disclosure under paragraph (d) of this section, IMLS will also notify the requester(s). If IMLS notifies a submitter of its intent to disclose requested information under paragraph (g) of this section, IMLS will also notify the requester(s). If a submitter files a lawsuit seeking to prevent the disclosure of confidential business information, IMLS will notify the requester(s) of the filing of the lawsuit.

§ 1184.10 **Disclaimer.**

Nothing in the regulations in this part will be construed to entitle any person, as a right, to any service or to the disclosure of any record to which such person is not entitled under FOIA.

PARTS 1185–1199 [RESERVED]

FINDING AIDS

A list of CFR titles, subtitles, chapters, subchapters and parts and an alphabetical list of agencies publishing in the CFR are included in the CFR Index and Finding Aids volume to the Code of Federal Regulations which is published separately and revised annually.

Table of CFR Titles and Chapters
Alphabetical List of Agencies Appearing in the CFR
List of CFR Sections Affected

Table of CFR Titles and Chapters
(Revised as of October 1, 2017)

Title 1—General Provisions

I	Administrative Committee of the Federal Register (Parts 1—49)
II	Office of the Federal Register (Parts 50—299)
III	Administrative Conference of the United States (Parts 300—399)
IV	Miscellaneous Agencies (Parts 400—599)
VI	National Capital Planning Commission (Parts 600—699)

Title 2—Grants and Agreements

SUBTITLE A—OFFICE OF MANAGEMENT AND BUDGET GUIDANCE FOR GRANTS AND AGREEMENTS

I	Office of Management and Budget Governmentwide Guidance for Grants and Agreements (Parts 2—199)
II	Office of Management and Budget Guidance (Parts 200—299)

SUBTITLE B—FEDERAL AGENCY REGULATIONS FOR GRANTS AND AGREEMENTS

III	Department of Health and Human Services (Parts 300—399)
IV	Department of Agriculture (Parts 400—499)
VI	Department of State (Parts 600—699)
VII	Agency for International Development (Parts 700—799)
VIII	Department of Veterans Affairs (Parts 800—899)
IX	Department of Energy (Parts 900—999)
X	Department of the Treasury (Parts 1000—1099)
XI	Department of Defense (Parts 1100—1199)
XII	Department of Transportation (Parts 1200—1299)
XIII	Department of Commerce (Parts 1300—1399)
XIV	Department of the Interior (Parts 1400—1499)
XV	Environmental Protection Agency (Parts 1500—1599)
XVIII	National Aeronautics and Space Administration (Parts 1800—1899)
XX	United States Nuclear Regulatory Commission (Parts 2000—2099)
XXII	Corporation for National and Community Service (Parts 2200—2299)
XXIII	Social Security Administration (Parts 2300—2399)
XXIV	Housing and Urban Development (Parts 2400—2499)
XXV	National Science Foundation (Parts 2500—2599)
XXVI	National Archives and Records Administration (Parts 2600—2699)

Title 2—Grants and Agreements—Continued

Chap.	
XXVII	Small Business Administration (Parts 2700—2799)
XXVIII	Department of Justice (Parts 2800—2899)
XXIX	Department of Labor (Parts 2900—2999)
XXX	Department of Homeland Security (Parts 3000—3099)
XXXI	Institute of Museum and Library Services (Parts 3100—3199)
XXXII	National Endowment for the Arts (Parts 3200—3299)
XXXIII	National Endowment for the Humanities (Parts 3300—3399)
XXXIV	Department of Education (Parts 3400—3499)
XXXV	Export-Import Bank of the United States (Parts 3500—3599)
XXXVI	Office of National Drug Control Policy, Executive Office of the President (Parts 3600—3699)
XXXVII	Peace Corps (Parts 3700—3799)
LVIII	Election Assistance Commission (Parts 5800—5899)
LIX	Gulf Coast Ecosystem Restoration Council (Parts 5900—5999)

Title 3—The President

I	Executive Office of the President (Parts 100—199)

Title 4—Accounts

I	Government Accountability Office (Parts 1—199)

Title 5—Administrative Personnel

I	Office of Personnel Management (Parts 1—1199)
II	Merit Systems Protection Board (Parts 1200—1299)
III	Office of Management and Budget (Parts 1300—1399)
IV	Office of Personnel Management and Office of the Director of National Intelligence (Parts 1400—1499)
V	The International Organizations Employees Loyalty Board (Parts 1500—1599)
VI	Federal Retirement Thrift Investment Board (Parts 1600—1699)
VIII	Office of Special Counsel (Parts 1800—1899)
IX	Appalachian Regional Commission (Parts 1900—1999)
XI	Armed Forces Retirement Home (Parts 2100—2199)
XIV	Federal Labor Relations Authority, General Counsel of the Federal Labor Relations Authority and Federal Service Impasses Panel (Parts 2400—2499)
XVI	Office of Government Ethics (Parts 2600—2699)
XXI	Department of the Treasury (Parts 3100—3199)
XXII	Federal Deposit Insurance Corporation (Parts 3200—3299)
XXIII	Department of Energy (Parts 3300—3399)
XXIV	Federal Energy Regulatory Commission (Parts 3400—3499)
XXV	Department of the Interior (Parts 3500—3599)
XXVI	Department of Defense (Parts 3600—3699)

Title 5—Administrative Personnel—Continued

Chap.	
XXVIII	Department of Justice (Parts 3800—3899)
XXIX	Federal Communications Commission (Parts 3900—3999)
XXX	Farm Credit System Insurance Corporation (Parts 4000—4099)
XXXI	Farm Credit Administration (Parts 4100—4199)
XXXIII	Overseas Private Investment Corporation (Parts 4300—4399)
XXXIV	Securities and Exchange Commission (Parts 4400—4499)
XXXV	Office of Personnel Management (Parts 4500—4599)
XXXVI	Department of Homeland Security (Parts 4600—4699)
XXXVII	Federal Election Commission (Parts 4700—4799)
XL	Interstate Commerce Commission (Parts 5000—5099)
XLI	Commodity Futures Trading Commission (Parts 5100—5199)
XLII	Department of Labor (Parts 5200—5299)
XLIII	National Science Foundation (Parts 5300—5399)
XLV	Department of Health and Human Services (Parts 5500—5599)
XLVI	Postal Rate Commission (Parts 5600—5699)
XLVII	Federal Trade Commission (Parts 5700—5799)
XLVIII	Nuclear Regulatory Commission (Parts 5800—5899)
XLIX	Federal Labor Relations Authority (Parts 5900—5999)
L	Department of Transportation (Parts 6000—6099)
LII	Export-Import Bank of the United States (Parts 6200—6299)
LIII	Department of Education (Parts 6300—6399)
LIV	Environmental Protection Agency (Parts 6400—6499)
LV	National Endowment for the Arts (Parts 6500—6599)
LVI	National Endowment for the Humanities (Parts 6600—6699)
LVII	General Services Administration (Parts 6700—6799)
LVIII	Board of Governors of the Federal Reserve System (Parts 6800—6899)
LIX	National Aeronautics and Space Administration (Parts 6900—6999)
LX	United States Postal Service (Parts 7000—7099)
LXI	National Labor Relations Board (Parts 7100—7199)
LXII	Equal Employment Opportunity Commission (Parts 7200—7299)
LXIII	Inter-American Foundation (Parts 7300—7399)
LXIV	Merit Systems Protection Board (Parts 7400—7499)
LXV	Department of Housing and Urban Development (Parts 7500—7599)
LXVI	National Archives and Records Administration (Parts 7600—7699)
LXVII	Institute of Museum and Library Services (Parts 7700—7799)
LXVIII	Commission on Civil Rights (Parts 7800—7899)
LXIX	Tennessee Valley Authority (Parts 7900—7999)
LXX	Court Services and Offender Supervision Agency for the District of Columbia (Parts 8000—8099)
LXXI	Consumer Product Safety Commission (Parts 8100—8199)
LXXIII	Department of Agriculture (Parts 8300—8399)

Title 5—Administrative Personnel—Continued

Chap.

LXXIV	Federal Mine Safety and Health Review Commission (Parts 8400—8499)
LXXVI	Federal Retirement Thrift Investment Board (Parts 8600—8699)
LXXVII	Office of Management and Budget (Parts 8700—8799)
LXXX	Federal Housing Finance Agency (Parts 9000—9099)
LXXXIII	Special Inspector General for Afghanistan Reconstruction (Parts 9300—9399)
LXXXIV	Bureau of Consumer Financial Protection (Parts 9400—9499)
LXXXVI	National Credit Union Administration (Parts 9600—9699)
XCVII	Department of Homeland Security Human Resources Management System (Department of Homeland Security—Office of Personnel Management) (Parts 9700—9799)
XCVIII	Council of the Inspectors General on Integrity and Efficiency (Parts 9800—9899)
XCIX	Military Compensation and Retirement Modernization Commission (Parts 9900—9999)
C	National Council on Disability (Parts 10000—10049)

Title 6—Domestic Security

I	Department of Homeland Security, Office of the Secretary (Parts 1—199)
X	Privacy and Civil Liberties Oversight Board (Parts 1000—1099)

Title 7—Agriculture

SUBTITLE A—OFFICE OF THE SECRETARY OF AGRICULTURE (PARTS 0—26)

SUBTITLE B—REGULATIONS OF THE DEPARTMENT OF AGRICULTURE

I	Agricultural Marketing Service (Standards, Inspections, Marketing Practices), Department of Agriculture (Parts 27—209)
II	Food and Nutrition Service, Department of Agriculture (Parts 210—299)
III	Animal and Plant Health Inspection Service, Department of Agriculture (Parts 300—399)
IV	Federal Crop Insurance Corporation, Department of Agriculture (Parts 400—499)
V	Agricultural Research Service, Department of Agriculture (Parts 500—599)
VI	Natural Resources Conservation Service, Department of Agriculture (Parts 600—699)
VII	Farm Service Agency, Department of Agriculture (Parts 700—799)
VIII	Grain Inspection, Packers and Stockyards Administration (Federal Grain Inspection Service), Department of Agriculture (Parts 800—899)
IX	Agricultural Marketing Service (Marketing Agreements and Orders; Fruits, Vegetables, Nuts), Department of Agriculture (Parts 900—999)

Title 7—Agriculture—Continued

Chap.	
X	Agricultural Marketing Service (Marketing Agreements and Orders; Milk), Department of Agriculture (Parts 1000—1199)
XI	Agricultural Marketing Service (Marketing Agreements and Orders; Miscellaneous Commodities), Department of Agriculture (Parts 1200—1299)
XIV	Commodity Credit Corporation, Department of Agriculture (Parts 1400—1499)
XV	Foreign Agricultural Service, Department of Agriculture (Parts 1500—1599)
XVI	Rural Telephone Bank, Department of Agriculture (Parts 1600—1699)
XVII	Rural Utilities Service, Department of Agriculture (Parts 1700—1799)
XVIII	Rural Housing Service, Rural Business-Cooperative Service, Rural Utilities Service, and Farm Service Agency, Department of Agriculture (Parts 1800—2099)
XX	Local Television Loan Guarantee Board (Parts 2200—2299)
XXV	Office of Advocacy and Outreach, Department of Agriculture (Parts 2500—2599)
XXVI	Office of Inspector General, Department of Agriculture (Parts 2600—2699)
XXVII	Office of Information Resources Management, Department of Agriculture (Parts 2700—2799)
XXVIII	Office of Operations, Department of Agriculture (Parts 2800—2899)
XXIX	Office of Energy Policy and New Uses, Department of Agriculture (Parts 2900—2999)
XXX	Office of the Chief Financial Officer, Department of Agriculture (Parts 3000—3099)
XXXI	Office of Environmental Quality, Department of Agriculture (Parts 3100—3199)
XXXII	Office of Procurement and Property Management, Department of Agriculture (Parts 3200—3299)
XXXIII	Office of Transportation, Department of Agriculture (Parts 3300—3399)
XXXIV	National Institute of Food and Agriculture (Parts 3400—3499)
XXXV	Rural Housing Service, Department of Agriculture (Parts 3500—3599)
XXXVI	National Agricultural Statistics Service, Department of Agriculture (Parts 3600—3699)
XXXVII	Economic Research Service, Department of Agriculture (Parts 3700—3799)
XXXVIII	World Agricultural Outlook Board, Department of Agriculture (Parts 3800—3899)
XLI	[Reserved]
XLII	Rural Business-Cooperative Service and Rural Utilities Service, Department of Agriculture (Parts 4200—4299)

Chap.

Title 8—Aliens and Nationality

I   Department of Homeland Security (Immigration and Naturalization) (Parts 1—499)

V   Executive Office for Immigration Review, Department of Justice (Parts 1000—1399)

Title 9—Animals and Animal Products

I   Animal and Plant Health Inspection Service, Department of Agriculture (Parts 1—199)

II   Grain Inspection, Packers and Stockyards Administration (Packers and Stockyards Programs), Department of Agriculture (Parts 200—299)

III   Food Safety and Inspection Service, Department of Agriculture (Parts 300—599)

Title 10—Energy

I   Nuclear Regulatory Commission (Parts 0—199)

II   Department of Energy (Parts 200—699)

III   Department of Energy (Parts 700—999)

X   Department of Energy (General Provisions) (Parts 1000—1099)

XIII   Nuclear Waste Technical Review Board (Parts 1300—1399)

XVII   Defense Nuclear Facilities Safety Board (Parts 1700—1799)

XVIII   Northeast Interstate Low-Level Radioactive Waste Commission (Parts 1800—1899)

Title 11—Federal Elections

I   Federal Election Commission (Parts 1—9099)

II   Election Assistance Commission (Parts 9400—9499)

Title 12—Banks and Banking

I   Comptroller of the Currency, Department of the Treasury (Parts 1—199)

II   Federal Reserve System (Parts 200—299)

III   Federal Deposit Insurance Corporation (Parts 300—399)

IV   Export-Import Bank of the United States (Parts 400—499)

V   Office of Thrift Supervision, Department of the Treasury (Parts 500—599)

VI   Farm Credit Administration (Parts 600—699)

VII   National Credit Union Administration (Parts 700—799)

VIII   Federal Financing Bank (Parts 800—899)

IX   Federal Housing Finance Board (Parts 900—999)

X   Bureau of Consumer Financial Protection (Parts 1000—1099)

XI   Federal Financial Institutions Examination Council (Parts 1100—1199)

XII   Federal Housing Finance Agency (Parts 1200—1299)

Title 12—Banks and Banking—Continued

Chap.
XIII Financial Stability Oversight Council (Parts 1300—1399)
XIV Farm Credit System Insurance Corporation (Parts 1400—1499)
XV Department of the Treasury (Parts 1500—1599)
XVI Office of Financial Research (Parts 1600—1699)
XVII Office of Federal Housing Enterprise Oversight, Department of Housing and Urban Development (Parts 1700—1799)
XVIII Community Development Financial Institutions Fund, Department of the Treasury (Parts 1800—1899)

Title 13—Business Credit and Assistance

I Small Business Administration (Parts 1—199)
III Economic Development Administration, Department of Commerce (Parts 300—399)
IV Emergency Steel Guarantee Loan Board (Parts 400—499)
V Emergency Oil and Gas Guaranteed Loan Board (Parts 500—599)

Title 14—Aeronautics and Space

I Federal Aviation Administration, Department of Transportation (Parts 1—199)
II Office of the Secretary, Department of Transportation (Aviation Proceedings) (Parts 200—399)
III Commercial Space Transportation, Federal Aviation Administration, Department of Transportation (Parts 400—1199)
V National Aeronautics and Space Administration (Parts 1200—1299)
VI Air Transportation System Stabilization (Parts 1300—1399)

Title 15—Commerce and Foreign Trade

SUBTITLE A—OFFICE OF THE SECRETARY OF COMMERCE (PARTS 0—29)

SUBTITLE B—REGULATIONS RELATING TO COMMERCE AND FOREIGN TRADE

I Bureau of the Census, Department of Commerce (Parts 30—199)
II National Institute of Standards and Technology, Department of Commerce (Parts 200—299)
III International Trade Administration, Department of Commerce (Parts 300—399)
IV Foreign-Trade Zones Board, Department of Commerce (Parts 400—499)
VII Bureau of Industry and Security, Department of Commerce (Parts 700—799)
VIII Bureau of Economic Analysis, Department of Commerce (Parts 800—899)
IX National Oceanic and Atmospheric Administration, Department of Commerce (Parts 900—999)

Title 15—Commerce and Foreign Trade—Continued

Chap.

XI   National Technical Information Service, Department of Commerce (Parts 1100—1199)
XIII East-West Foreign Trade Board (Parts 1300—1399)
XIV Minority Business Development Agency (Parts 1400—1499)

SUBTITLE C—REGULATIONS RELATING TO FOREIGN TRADE AGREEMENTS

XX   Office of the United States Trade Representative (Parts 2000—2099)

SUBTITLE D—REGULATIONS RELATING TO TELECOMMUNICATIONS AND INFORMATION

XXIII National Telecommunications and Information Administration, Department of Commerce (Parts 2300—2399) [Reserved]

Title 16—Commercial Practices

I   Federal Trade Commission (Parts 0—999)
II Consumer Product Safety Commission (Parts 1000—1799)

Title 17—Commodity and Securities Exchanges

I   Commodity Futures Trading Commission (Parts 1—199)
II Securities and Exchange Commission (Parts 200—399)
IV Department of the Treasury (Parts 400—499)

Title 18—Conservation of Power and Water Resources

I   Federal Energy Regulatory Commission, Department of Energy (Parts 1—399)
III   Delaware River Basin Commission (Parts 400—499)
VI   Water Resources Council (Parts 700—799)
VIII Susquehanna River Basin Commission (Parts 800—899)
XIII Tennessee Valley Authority (Parts 1300—1399)

Title 19—Customs Duties

I   U.S. Customs and Border Protection, Department of Homeland Security; Department of the Treasury (Parts 0—199)
II   United States International Trade Commission (Parts 200—299)
III International Trade Administration, Department of Commerce (Parts 300—399)
IV   U.S. Immigration and Customs Enforcement, Department of Homeland Security (Parts 400—599) [Reserved]

Title 20—Employees' Benefits

I   Office of Workers' Compensation Programs, Department of Labor (Parts 1—199)
II Railroad Retirement Board (Parts 200—399)

Title 20—Employees' Benefits—Continued

Chap.
- III Social Security Administration (Parts 400—499)
- IV Employees' Compensation Appeals Board, Department of Labor (Parts 500—599)
- V Employment and Training Administration, Department of Labor (Parts 600—699)
- VI Office of Workers' Compensation Programs, Department of Labor (Parts 700—799)
- VII Benefits Review Board, Department of Labor (Parts 800—899)
- VIII Joint Board for the Enrollment of Actuaries (Parts 900—999)
- IX Office of the Assistant Secretary for Veterans' Employment and Training Service, Department of Labor (Parts 1000—1099)

Title 21—Food and Drugs

- I Food and Drug Administration, Department of Health and Human Services (Parts 1—1299)
- II Drug Enforcement Administration, Department of Justice (Parts 1300—1399)
- III Office of National Drug Control Policy (Parts 1400—1499)

Title 22—Foreign Relations

- I Department of State (Parts 1—199)
- II Agency for International Development (Parts 200—299)
- III Peace Corps (Parts 300—399)
- IV International Joint Commission, United States and Canada (Parts 400—499)
- V Broadcasting Board of Governors (Parts 500—599)
- VII Overseas Private Investment Corporation (Parts 700—799)
- IX Foreign Service Grievance Board (Parts 900—999)
- X Inter-American Foundation (Parts 1000—1099)
- XI International Boundary and Water Commission, United States and Mexico, United States Section (Parts 1100—1199)
- XII United States International Development Cooperation Agency (Parts 1200—1299)
- XIII Millennium Challenge Corporation (Parts 1300—1399)
- XIV Foreign Service Labor Relations Board; Federal Labor Relations Authority; General Counsel of the Federal Labor Relations Authority; and the Foreign Service Impasse Disputes Panel (Parts 1400—1499)
- XV African Development Foundation (Parts 1500—1599)
- XVI Japan-United States Friendship Commission (Parts 1600—1699)
- XVII United States Institute of Peace (Parts 1700—1799)

Title 23—Highways

- I Federal Highway Administration, Department of Transportation (Parts 1—999)

Title 23—Highways—Continued

Chap.

II National Highway Traffic Safety Administration and Federal Highway Administration, Department of Transportation (Parts 1200—1299)

III National Highway Traffic Safety Administration, Department of Transportation (Parts 1300—1399)

Title 24—Housing and Urban Development

SUBTITLE A—OFFICE OF THE SECRETARY, DEPARTMENT OF HOUSING AND URBAN DEVELOPMENT (PARTS 0—99)

SUBTITLE B—REGULATIONS RELATING TO HOUSING AND URBAN DEVELOPMENT

I Office of Assistant Secretary for Equal Opportunity, Department of Housing and Urban Development (Parts 100—199)

II Office of Assistant Secretary for Housing-Federal Housing Commissioner, Department of Housing and Urban Development (Parts 200—299)

III Government National Mortgage Association, Department of Housing and Urban Development (Parts 300—399)

IV Office of Housing and Office of Multifamily Housing Assistance Restructuring, Department of Housing and Urban Development (Parts 400—499)

V Office of Assistant Secretary for Community Planning and Development, Department of Housing and Urban Development (Parts 500—599)

VI Office of Assistant Secretary for Community Planning and Development, Department of Housing and Urban Development (Parts 600—699) [Reserved]

VII Office of the Secretary, Department of Housing and Urban Development (Housing Assistance Programs and Public and Indian Housing Programs) (Parts 700—799)

VIII Office of the Assistant Secretary for Housing—Federal Housing Commissioner, Department of Housing and Urban Development (Section 8 Housing Assistance Programs, Section 202 Direct Loan Program, Section 202 Supportive Housing for the Elderly Program and Section 811 Supportive Housing for Persons With Disabilities Program) (Parts 800—899)

IX Office of Assistant Secretary for Public and Indian Housing, Department of Housing and Urban Development (Parts 900—1699)

X Office of Assistant Secretary for Housing—Federal Housing Commissioner, Department of Housing and Urban Development (Interstate Land Sales Registration Program) (Parts 1700—1799)

XII Office of Inspector General, Department of Housing and Urban Development (Parts 2000—2099)

XV Emergency Mortgage Insurance and Loan Programs, Department of Housing and Urban Development (Parts 2700—2799) [Reserved]

XX Office of Assistant Secretary for Housing—Federal Housing Commissioner, Department of Housing and Urban Development (Parts 3200—3899)

Title 24—Housing and Urban Development—Continued

Chap.

XXIV	Board of Directors of the HOPE for Homeowners Program (Parts 4000—4099) [Reserved]
XXV	Neighborhood Reinvestment Corporation (Parts 4100—4199)

Title 25—Indians

I	Bureau of Indian Affairs, Department of the Interior (Parts 1—299)
II	Indian Arts and Crafts Board, Department of the Interior (Parts 300—399)
III	National Indian Gaming Commission, Department of the Interior (Parts 500—599)
IV	Office of Navajo and Hopi Indian Relocation (Parts 700—899)
V	Bureau of Indian Affairs, Department of the Interior, and Indian Health Service, Department of Health and Human Services (Part 900)
VI	Office of the Assistant Secretary, Indian Affairs, Department of the Interior (Parts 1000—1199)
VII	Office of the Special Trustee for American Indians, Department of the Interior (Parts 1200—1299)

Title 26—Internal Revenue

I	Internal Revenue Service, Department of the Treasury (Parts 1—End)

Title 27—Alcohol, Tobacco Products and Firearms

I	Alcohol and Tobacco Tax and Trade Bureau, Department of the Treasury (Parts 1—399)
II	Bureau of Alcohol, Tobacco, Firearms, and Explosives, Department of Justice (Parts 400—699)

Title 28—Judicial Administration

I	Department of Justice (Parts 0—299)
III	Federal Prison Industries, Inc., Department of Justice (Parts 300—399)
V	Bureau of Prisons, Department of Justice (Parts 500—599)
VI	Offices of Independent Counsel, Department of Justice (Parts 600—699)
VII	Office of Independent Counsel (Parts 700—799)
VIII	Court Services and Offender Supervision Agency for the District of Columbia (Parts 800—899)
IX	National Crime Prevention and Privacy Compact Council (Parts 900—999)
XI	Department of Justice and Department of State (Parts 1100—1199)

Chap.	

Title 29—Labor

SUBTITLE A—OFFICE OF THE SECRETARY OF LABOR (PARTS 0—99)
SUBTITLE B—REGULATIONS RELATING TO LABOR

I	National Labor Relations Board (Parts 100—199)
II	Office of Labor-Management Standards, Department of Labor (Parts 200—299)
III	National Railroad Adjustment Board (Parts 300—399)
IV	Office of Labor-Management Standards, Department of Labor (Parts 400—499)
V	Wage and Hour Division, Department of Labor (Parts 500—899)
IX	Construction Industry Collective Bargaining Commission (Parts 900—999)
X	National Mediation Board (Parts 1200—1299)
XII	Federal Mediation and Conciliation Service (Parts 1400—1499)
XIV	Equal Employment Opportunity Commission (Parts 1600—1699)
XVII	Occupational Safety and Health Administration, Department of Labor (Parts 1900—1999)
XX	Occupational Safety and Health Review Commission (Parts 2200—2499)
XXV	Employee Benefits Security Administration, Department of Labor (Parts 2500—2599)
XXVII	Federal Mine Safety and Health Review Commission (Parts 2700—2799)
XL	Pension Benefit Guaranty Corporation (Parts 4000—4999)

Title 30—Mineral Resources

I	Mine Safety and Health Administration, Department of Labor (Parts 1—199)
II	Bureau of Safety and Environmental Enforcement, Department of the Interior (Parts 200—299)
IV	Geological Survey, Department of the Interior (Parts 400—499)
V	Bureau of Ocean Energy Management, Department of the Interior (Parts 500—599)
VII	Office of Surface Mining Reclamation and Enforcement, Department of the Interior (Parts 700—999)
XII	Office of Natural Resources Revenue, Department of the Interior (Parts 1200—1299)

Title 31—Money and Finance: Treasury

SUBTITLE A—OFFICE OF THE SECRETARY OF THE TREASURY (PARTS 0—50)
SUBTITLE B—REGULATIONS RELATING TO MONEY AND FINANCE

I	Monetary Offices, Department of the Treasury (Parts 51—199)
II	Fiscal Service, Department of the Treasury (Parts 200—399)
IV	Secret Service, Department of the Treasury (Parts 400—499)
V	Office of Foreign Assets Control, Department of the Treasury (Parts 500—599)

Title 31—Money and Finance: Treasury—Continued

Chap.

VI	Bureau of Engraving and Printing, Department of the Treasury (Parts 600—699)
VII	Federal Law Enforcement Training Center, Department of the Treasury (Parts 700—799)
VIII	Office of Investment Security, Department of the Treasury (Parts 800—899)
IX	Federal Claims Collection Standards (Department of the Treasury—Department of Justice) (Parts 900—999)
X	Financial Crimes Enforcement Network, Department of the Treasury (Parts 1000—1099)

Title 32—National Defense

SUBTITLE A—DEPARTMENT OF DEFENSE

I	Office of the Secretary of Defense (Parts 1—399)
V	Department of the Army (Parts 400—699)
VI	Department of the Navy (Parts 700—799)
VII	Department of the Air Force (Parts 800—1099)

SUBTITLE B—OTHER REGULATIONS RELATING TO NATIONAL DEFENSE

XII	Defense Logistics Agency (Parts 1200—1299)
XVI	Selective Service System (Parts 1600—1699)
XVII	Office of the Director of National Intelligence (Parts 1700—1799)
XVIII	National Counterintelligence Center (Parts 1800—1899)
XIX	Central Intelligence Agency (Parts 1900—1999)
XX	Information Security Oversight Office, National Archives and Records Administration (Parts 2000—2099)
XXI	National Security Council (Parts 2100—2199)
XXIV	Office of Science and Technology Policy (Parts 2400—2499)
XXVII	Office for Micronesian Status Negotiations (Parts 2700—2799)
XXVIII	Office of the Vice President of the United States (Parts 2800—2899)

Title 33—Navigation and Navigable Waters

I	Coast Guard, Department of Homeland Security (Parts 1—199)
II	Corps of Engineers, Department of the Army, Department of Defense (Parts 200—399)
IV	Saint Lawrence Seaway Development Corporation, Department of Transportation (Parts 400—499)

Title 34—Education

SUBTITLE A—OFFICE OF THE SECRETARY, DEPARTMENT OF EDUCATION (PARTS 1—99)

SUBTITLE B—REGULATIONS OF THE OFFICES OF THE DEPARTMENT OF EDUCATION

I	Office for Civil Rights, Department of Education (Parts 100—199)

Title 34—Education—Continued

Chap.
- II Office of Elementary and Secondary Education, Department of Education (Parts 200—299)
- III Office of Special Education and Rehabilitative Services, Department of Education (Parts 300—399)
- IV Office of Career, Technical and Adult Education, Department of Education (Parts 400—499)
- V Office of Bilingual Education and Minority Languages Affairs, Department of Education (Parts 500—599) [Reserved]
- VI Office of Postsecondary Education, Department of Education (Parts 600—699)
- VII Office of Educational Research and Improvement, Department of Education (Parts 700—799) [Reserved]

SUBTITLE C—REGULATIONS RELATING TO EDUCATION

- XI [Reserved]
- XII National Council on Disability (Parts 1200—1299)

Title 35 [Reserved]

Title 36—Parks, Forests, and Public Property

- I National Park Service, Department of the Interior (Parts 1—199)
- II Forest Service, Department of Agriculture (Parts 200—299)
- III Corps of Engineers, Department of the Army (Parts 300—399)
- IV American Battle Monuments Commission (Parts 400—499)
- V Smithsonian Institution (Parts 500—599)
- VI [Reserved]
- VII Library of Congress (Parts 700—799)
- VIII Advisory Council on Historic Preservation (Parts 800—899)
- IX Pennsylvania Avenue Development Corporation (Parts 900—999)
- X Presidio Trust (Parts 1000—1099)
- XI Architectural and Transportation Barriers Compliance Board (Parts 1100—1199)
- XII National Archives and Records Administration (Parts 1200—1299)
- XV Oklahoma City National Memorial Trust (Parts 1500—1599)
- XVI Morris K. Udall Scholarship and Excellence in National Environmental Policy Foundation (Parts 1600—1699)

Title 37—Patents, Trademarks, and Copyrights

- I United States Patent and Trademark Office, Department of Commerce (Parts 1—199)
- II U.S. Copyright Office, Library of Congress (Parts 200—299)
- III Copyright Royalty Board, Library of Congress (Parts 300—399)
- IV National Institute of Standards and Technology, Department of Commerce (Parts 400—599)

Title 38—Pensions, Bonuses, and Veterans' Relief

Chap.
- I Department of Veterans Affairs (Parts 0—199)
- II Armed Forces Retirement Home (Parts 200—299)

Title 39—Postal Service

- I United States Postal Service (Parts 1—999)
- III Postal Regulatory Commission (Parts 3000—3099)

Title 40—Protection of Environment

- I Environmental Protection Agency (Parts 1—1099)
- IV Environmental Protection Agency and Department of Justice (Parts 1400—1499)
- V Council on Environmental Quality (Parts 1500—1599)
- VI Chemical Safety and Hazard Investigation Board (Parts 1600—1699)
- VII Environmental Protection Agency and Department of Defense; Uniform National Discharge Standards for Vessels of the Armed Forces (Parts 1700—1799)
- VIII Gulf Coast Ecosystem Restoration Council (Parts 1800—1899)

Title 41—Public Contracts and Property Management

SUBTITLE A—FEDERAL PROCUREMENT REGULATIONS SYSTEM [NOTE]

SUBTITLE B—OTHER PROVISIONS RELATING TO PUBLIC CONTRACTS

- 50 Public Contracts, Department of Labor (Parts 50–1—50–999)
- 51 Committee for Purchase From People Who Are Blind or Severely Disabled (Parts 51–1—51–99)
- 60 Office of Federal Contract Compliance Programs, Equal Employment Opportunity, Department of Labor (Parts 60–1—60–999)
- 61 Office of the Assistant Secretary for Veterans' Employment and Training Service, Department of Labor (Parts 61–1—61–999)
- 62—100 [Reserved]

SUBTITLE C—FEDERAL PROPERTY MANAGEMENT REGULATIONS SYSTEM

- 101 Federal Property Management Regulations (Parts 101–1—101–99)
- 102 Federal Management Regulation (Parts 102–1—102–299)
- 103—104 [Reserved]
- 105 General Services Administration (Parts 105–1—105–999)
- 109 Department of Energy Property Management Regulations (Parts 109–1—109–99)
- 114 Department of the Interior (Parts 114–1—114–99)
- 115 Environmental Protection Agency (Parts 115–1—115–99)
- 128 Department of Justice (Parts 128–1—128–99)
- 129—200 [Reserved]

SUBTITLE D—OTHER PROVISIONS RELATING TO PROPERTY MANAGEMENT [RESERVED]

Title 41—Public Contracts and Property Management—Continued

Chap.

SUBTITLE E—FEDERAL INFORMATION RESOURCES MANAGEMENT REGULATIONS SYSTEM [RESERVED]

SUBTITLE F—FEDERAL TRAVEL REGULATION SYSTEM

- 300 General (Parts 300-1—300-99)
- 301 Temporary Duty (TDY) Travel Allowances (Parts 301-1—301-99)
- 302 Relocation Allowances (Parts 302-1—302-99)
- 303 Payment of Expenses Connected with the Death of Certain Employees (Part 303-1—303-99)
- 304 Payment of Travel Expenses from a Non-Federal Source (Parts 304-1—304-99)

Title 42—Public Health

- I Public Health Service, Department of Health and Human Services (Parts 1—199)
- ii—III [Reserved]
- IV Centers for Medicare & Medicaid Services, Department of Health and Human Services (Parts 400—699)
- V Office of Inspector General-Health Care, Department of Health and Human Services (Parts 1000—1099)

Title 43—Public Lands: Interior

SUBTITLE A—OFFICE OF THE SECRETARY OF THE INTERIOR (PARTS 1—199)

SUBTITLE B—REGULATIONS RELATING TO PUBLIC LANDS

- I Bureau of Reclamation, Department of the Interior (Parts 400—999)
- II Bureau of Land Management, Department of the Interior (Parts 1000—9999)
- III Utah Reclamation Mitigation and Conservation Commission (Parts 10000—10099)

Title 44—Emergency Management and Assistance

- I Federal Emergency Management Agency, Department of Homeland Security (Parts 0—399)
- IV Department of Commerce and Department of Transportation (Parts 400—499)

Title 45—Public Welfare

SUBTITLE A—DEPARTMENT OF HEALTH AND HUMAN SERVICES (PARTS 1—199)

SUBTITLE B—REGULATIONS RELATING TO PUBLIC WELFARE

- II Office of Family Assistance (Assistance Programs), Administration for Children and Families, Department of Health and Human Services (Parts 200—299)

Title 45—Public Welfare—Continued

Chap.

III	Office of Child Support Enforcement (Child Support Enforcement Program), Administration for Children and Families, Department of Health and Human Services (Parts 300—399)
IV	Office of Refugee Resettlement, Administration for Children and Families, Department of Health and Human Services (Parts 400—499)
V	Foreign Claims Settlement Commission of the United States, Department of Justice (Parts 500—599)
VI	National Science Foundation (Parts 600—699)
VII	Commission on Civil Rights (Parts 700—799)
VIII	Office of Personnel Management (Parts 800—899)
IX	Denali Commission (Parts 900—999)
X	Office of Community Services, Administration for Children and Families, Department of Health and Human Services (Parts 1000—1099)
XI	National Foundation on the Arts and the Humanities (Parts 1100—1199)
XII	Corporation for National and Community Service (Parts 1200—1299)
XIII	Administration for Children and Families, Department of Health and Human Services (Parts 1300—1399)
XVI	Legal Services Corporation (Parts 1600—1699)
XVII	National Commission on Libraries and Information Science (Parts 1700—1799)
XVIII	Harry S. Truman Scholarship Foundation (Parts 1800—1899)
XXI	Commission of Fine Arts (Parts 2100—2199)
XXIII	Arctic Research Commission (Part 2301)
XXIV	James Madison Memorial Fellowship Foundation (Parts 2400—2499)
XXV	Corporation for National and Community Service (Parts 2500—2599)

Title 46—Shipping

I	Coast Guard, Department of Homeland Security (Parts 1—199)
II	Maritime Administration, Department of Transportation (Parts 200—399)
III	Coast Guard (Great Lakes Pilotage), Department of Homeland Security (Parts 400—499)
IV	Federal Maritime Commission (Parts 500—599)

Title 47—Telecommunication

I	Federal Communications Commission (Parts 0—199)
II	Office of Science and Technology Policy and National Security Council (Parts 200—299)
III	National Telecommunications and Information Administration, Department of Commerce (Parts 300—399)

Chap. ## Title 47—Telecommunication—Continued

IV National Telecommunications and Information Administration, Department of Commerce, and National Highway Traffic Safety Administration, Department of Transportation (Parts 400—499)
V The First Responder Network Authority (Parts 500—599)

Title 48—Federal Acquisition Regulations System

1 Federal Acquisition Regulation (Parts 1—99)
2 Defense Acquisition Regulations System, Department of Defense (Parts 200—299)
3 Health and Human Services (Parts 300—399)
4 Department of Agriculture (Parts 400—499)
5 General Services Administration (Parts 500—599)
6 Department of State (Parts 600—699)
7 Agency for International Development (Parts 700—799)
8 Department of Veterans Affairs (Parts 800—899)
9 Department of Energy (Parts 900—999)
10 Department of the Treasury (Parts 1000—1099)
12 Department of Transportation (Parts 1200—1299)
13 Department of Commerce (Parts 1300—1399)
14 Department of the Interior (Parts 1400—1499)
15 Environmental Protection Agency (Parts 1500—1599)
16 Office of Personnel Management, Federal Employees Health Benefits Acquisition Regulation (Parts 1600—1699)
17 Office of Personnel Management (Parts 1700—1799)
18 National Aeronautics and Space Administration (Parts 1800—1899)
19 Broadcasting Board of Governors (Parts 1900—1999)
20 Nuclear Regulatory Commission (Parts 2000—2099)
21 Office of Personnel Management, Federal Employees Group Life Insurance Federal Acquisition Regulation (Parts 2100—2199)
23 Social Security Administration (Parts 2300—2399)
24 Department of Housing and Urban Development (Parts 2400—2499)
25 National Science Foundation (Parts 2500—2599)
28 Department of Justice (Parts 2800—2899)
29 Department of Labor (Parts 2900—2999)
30 Department of Homeland Security, Homeland Security Acquisition Regulation (HSAR) (Parts 3000—3099)
34 Department of Education Acquisition Regulation (Parts 3400—3499)
51 Department of the Army Acquisition Regulations (Parts 5100—5199)
52 Department of the Navy Acquisition Regulations (Parts 5200—5299)
53 Department of the Air Force Federal Acquisition Regulation Supplement (Parts 5300—5399) [Reserved]

Title 48—Federal Acquisition Regulations System—Continued

Chap.	
54	Defense Logistics Agency, Department of Defense (Parts 5400—5499)
57	African Development Foundation (Parts 5700—5799)
61	Civilian Board of Contract Appeals, General Services Administration (Parts 6100—6199)
99	Cost Accounting Standards Board, Office of Federal Procurement Policy, Office of Management and Budget (Parts 9900—9999)

Title 49—Transportation

SUBTITLE A—OFFICE OF THE SECRETARY OF TRANSPORTATION (PARTS 1—99)

SUBTITLE B—OTHER REGULATIONS RELATING TO TRANSPORTATION

I	Pipeline and Hazardous Materials Safety Administration, Department of Transportation (Parts 100—199)
II	Federal Railroad Administration, Department of Transportation (Parts 200—299)
III	Federal Motor Carrier Safety Administration, Department of Transportation (Parts 300—399)
IV	Coast Guard, Department of Homeland Security (Parts 400—499)
V	National Highway Traffic Safety Administration, Department of Transportation (Parts 500—599)
VI	Federal Transit Administration, Department of Transportation (Parts 600—699)
VII	National Railroad Passenger Corporation (AMTRAK) (Parts 700—799)
VIII	National Transportation Safety Board (Parts 800—999)
X	Surface Transportation Board (Parts 1000—1399)
XI	Research and Innovative Technology Administration, Department of Transportation (Parts 1400—1499) [Reserved]
XII	Transportation Security Administration, Department of Homeland Security (Parts 1500—1699)

Title 50—Wildlife and Fisheries

I	United States Fish and Wildlife Service, Department of the Interior (Parts 1—199)
II	National Marine Fisheries Service, National Oceanic and Atmospheric Administration, Department of Commerce (Parts 200—299)
III	International Fishing and Related Activities (Parts 300—399)
IV	Joint Regulations (United States Fish and Wildlife Service, Department of the Interior and National Marine Fisheries Service, National Oceanic and Atmospheric Administration, Department of Commerce); Endangered Species Committee Regulations (Parts 400—499)
V	Marine Mammal Commission (Parts 500—599)

Title 50—Wildlife and Fisheries—Continued

Chap.

VI Fishery Conservation and Management, National Oceanic and Atmospheric Administration, Department of Commerce (Parts 600—699)

Alphabetical List of Agencies Appearing in the CFR
(Revised as of October 1, 2017)

Agency	CFR Title, Subtitle or Chapter
Administrative Committee of the Federal Register	1, I
Administrative Conference of the United States	1, III
Advisory Council on Historic Preservation	36, VIII
Advocacy and Outreach, Office of	7, XXV
Afghanistan Reconstruction, Special Inspector General for	5, LXXXIII
African Development Foundation	22, XV
Federal Acquisition Regulation	48, 57
Agency for International Development	2, VII; 22, II
Federal Acquisition Regulation	48, 7
Agricultural Marketing Service	7, I, IX, X, XI
Agricultural Research Service	7, V
Agriculture Department	2, IV; 5, LXXIII
Advocacy and Outreach, Office of	7, XXV
Agricultural Marketing Service	7, I, IX, X, XI
Agricultural Research Service	7, V
Animal and Plant Health Inspection Service	7, III; 9, I
Chief Financial Officer, Office of	7, XXX
Commodity Credit Corporation	7, XIV
Economic Research Service	7, XXXVII
Energy Policy and New Uses, Office of	2, IX; 7, XXIX
Environmental Quality, Office of	7, XXXI
Farm Service Agency	7, VII, XVIII
Federal Acquisition Regulation	48, 4
Federal Crop Insurance Corporation	7, IV
Food and Nutrition Service	7, II
Food Safety and Inspection Service	9, III
Foreign Agricultural Service	7, XV
Forest Service	36, II
Grain Inspection, Packers and Stockyards Administration	7, VIII; 9, II
Information Resources Management, Office of	7, XXVII
Inspector General, Office of	7, XXVI
National Agricultural Library	7, XLI
National Agricultural Statistics Service	7, XXXVI
National Institute of Food and Agriculture	7, XXXIV
Natural Resources Conservation Service	7, VI
Operations, Office of	7, XXVIII
Procurement and Property Management, Office of	7, XXXII
Rural Business-Cooperative Service	7, XVIII, XLII
Rural Development Administration	7, XLII
Rural Housing Service	7, XVIII, XXXV
Rural Telephone Bank	7, XVI
Rural Utilities Service	7, XVII, XVIII, XLII
Secretary of Agriculture, Office of	7, Subtitle A
Transportation, Office of	7, XXXIII
World Agricultural Outlook Board	7, XXXVIII
Air Force Department	32, VII
Federal Acquisition Regulation Supplement	48, 53
Air Transportation Stabilization Board	14, VI
Alcohol and Tobacco Tax and Trade Bureau	27, I
Alcohol, Tobacco, Firearms, and Explosives, Bureau of	27, II
AMTRAK	49, VII
American Battle Monuments Commission	36, IV
American Indians, Office of the Special Trustee	25, VII

Agency	CFR Title, Subtitle or Chapter
Animal and Plant Health Inspection Service	7, III; 9, I
Appalachian Regional Commission	5, IX
Architectural and Transportation Barriers Compliance Board	36, XI
Arctic Research Commission	45, XXIII
Armed Forces Retirement Home	5, XI
Army Department	32, V
Engineers, Corps of	33, II; 36, III
Federal Acquisition Regulation	48, 51
Bilingual Education and Minority Languages Affairs, Office of	34, V
Blind or Severely Disabled, Committee for Purchase from People Who Are	41, 51
Broadcasting Board of Governors	22, V
Federal Acquisition Regulation	48, 19
Career, Technical and Adult Education, Office of	34, IV
Census Bureau	15, I
Centers for Medicare & Medicaid Services	42, IV
Central Intelligence Agency	32, XIX
Chemical Safety and Hazardous Investigation Board	40, VI
Chief Financial Officer, Office of	7, XXX
Child Support Enforcement, Office of	45, III
Children and Families, Administration for	45, II, III, IV, X, XIII
Civil Rights, Commission on	5, LXVIII; 45, VII
Civil Rights, Office for	34, I
Council of the Inspectors General on Integrity and Efficiency	5, XCVIII
Court Services and Offender Supervision Agency for the District of Columbia	5, LXX
Coast Guard	33, I; 46, I; 49, IV
Coast Guard (Great Lakes Pilotage)	46, III
Commerce Department	2, XIII; 44, IV; 50, VI
Census Bureau	15, I
Economic Analysis, Bureau of	15, VIII
Economic Development Administration	13, III
Emergency Management and Assistance	44, IV
Federal Acquisition Regulation	48, 13
Foreign-Trade Zones Board	15, IV
Industry and Security, Bureau of	15, VII
International Trade Administration	15, III; 19, III
National Institute of Standards and Technology	15, II; 37, IV
National Marine Fisheries Service	50, II, IV
National Oceanic and Atmospheric Administration	15, IX; 50, II, III, IV, VI
National Technical Information Service	15, XI
National Telecommunications and Information Administration	15, XXIII; 47, III, IV
National Weather Service	15, IX
Patent and Trademark Office, United States	37, I
Secretary of Commerce, Office of	15, Subtitle A
Commercial Space Transportation	14, III
Commodity Credit Corporation	7, XIV
Commodity Futures Trading Commission	5, XLI; 17, I
Community Planning and Development, Office of Assistant Secretary for	24, V, VI
Community Services, Office of	45, X
Comptroller of the Currency	12, I
Construction Industry Collective Bargaining Commission	29, IX
Consumer Financial Protection Bureau	5, LXXXIV; 12, X
Consumer Product Safety Commission	5, LXXI; 16, II
Copyright Royalty Board	37, III
Corporation for National and Community Service	2, XXII; 45, XII, XXV
Cost Accounting Standards Board	48, 99
Council on Environmental Quality	40, V
Court Services and Offender Supervision Agency for the District of Columbia	5, LXX; 28, VIII
Customs and Border Protection	19, I
Defense Contract Audit Agency	32, I
Defense Department	2, XI; 5, XXVI; 32, Subtitle A; 40, VII
Advanced Research Projects Agency	32, I

Agency	CFR Title, Subtitle or Chapter
Air Force Department	32, VII
Army Department	32, V; 33, II; 36, III; 48, 51
Defense Acquisition Regulations System	48, 2
Defense Intelligence Agency	32, I
Defense Logistics Agency	32, I, XII; 48, 54
Engineers, Corps of	33, II; 36, III
National Imagery and Mapping Agency	32, I
Navy Department	32, VI; 48, 52
Secretary of Defense, Office of	2, XI; 32, I
Defense Contract Audit Agency	32, I
Defense Intelligence Agency	32, I
Defense Logistics Agency	32, XII; 48, 54
Defense Nuclear Facilities Safety Board	10, XVII
Delaware River Basin Commission	18, III
Denali Commission	45, IX
District of Columbia, Court Services and Offender Supervision Agency for the	5, LXX; 28, VIII
Drug Enforcement Administration	21, II
East-West Foreign Trade Board	15, XIII
Economic Analysis, Bureau of	15, VIII
Economic Development Administration	13, III
Economic Research Service	7, XXXVII
Education, Department of	2, XXXIV; 5, LIII
Bilingual Education and Minority Languages Affairs, Office of	34, V
Career, Technical and Adult Education, Office of	34, IV
Civil Rights, Office for	34, I
Educational Research and Improvement, Office of	34, VII
Elementary and Secondary Education, Office of	34, II
Federal Acquisition Regulation	48, 34
Postsecondary Education, Office of	34, VI
Secretary of Education, Office of	34, Subtitle A
Special Education and Rehabilitative Services, Office of	34, III
Career, Technical, and Adult Education, Office of	34, IV
Educational Research and Improvement, Office of	34, VII
Election Assistance Commission	2, LVIII; 11, II
Elementary and Secondary Education, Office of	34, II
Emergency Oil and Gas Guaranteed Loan Board	13, V
Emergency Steel Guarantee Loan Board	13, IV
Employee Benefits Security Administration	29, XXV
Employees' Compensation Appeals Board	20, IV
Employees Loyalty Board	5, V
Employment and Training Administration	20, V
Employment Standards Administration	20, VI
Endangered Species Committee	50, IV
Energy, Department of	2, IX; 5, XXIII; 10, II, III, X
Federal Acquisition Regulation	48, 9
Federal Energy Regulatory Commission	5, XXIV; 18, I
Property Management Regulations	41, 109
Energy, Office of	7, XXIX
Engineers, Corps of	33, II; 36, III
Engraving and Printing, Bureau of	31, VI
Environmental Protection Agency	2, XV; 5, LIV; 40, I, IV, VII
Federal Acquisition Regulation	48, 15
Property Management Regulations	41, 115
Environmental Quality, Office of	7, XXXI
Equal Employment Opportunity Commission	5, LXII; 29, XIV
Equal Opportunity, Office of Assistant Secretary for	24, I
Executive Office of the President	3, I
Environmental Quality, Council on	40, V
Management and Budget, Office of	2, Subtitle A; 5, III, LXXVII; 14, VI; 48, 99
National Drug Control Policy, Office of	2, XXXVI; 21, III
National Security Council	32, XXI; 47, 2

Agency	CFR Title, Subtitle or Chapter
Presidential Documents	3
Science and Technology Policy, Office of	32, XXIV; 47, II
Trade Representative, Office of the United States	15, XX
Export-Import Bank of the United States	2, XXXV; 5, LII; 12, IV
Family Assistance, Office of	45, II
Farm Credit Administration	5, XXXI; 12, VI
Farm Credit System Insurance Corporation	5, XXX; 12, XIV
Farm Service Agency	7, VII, XVIII
Federal Acquisition Regulation	48, 1
Federal Aviation Administration	14, I
Commercial Space Transportation	14, III
Federal Claims Collection Standards	31, IX
Federal Communications Commission	5, XXIX; 47, I
Federal Contract Compliance Programs, Office of	41, 60
Federal Crop Insurance Corporation	7, IV
Federal Deposit Insurance Corporation	5, XXII; 12, III
Federal Election Commission	5, XXXVII; 11, I
Federal Emergency Management Agency	44, I
Federal Employees Group Life Insurance Federal Acquisition Regulation	48, 21
Federal Employees Health Benefits Acquisition Regulation	48, 16
Federal Energy Regulatory Commission	5, XXIV; 18, I
Federal Financial Institutions Examination Council	12, XI
Federal Financing Bank	12, VIII
Federal Highway Administration	23, I, II
Federal Home Loan Mortgage Corporation	1, IV
Federal Housing Enterprise Oversight Office	12, XVII
Federal Housing Finance Agency	5, LXXX; 12, XII
Federal Housing Finance Board	12, IX
Federal Labor Relations Authority	5, XIV, XLIX; 22, XIV
Federal Law Enforcement Training Center	31, VII
Federal Management Regulation	41, 102
Federal Maritime Commission	46, IV
Federal Mediation and Conciliation Service	29, XII
Federal Mine Safety and Health Review Commission	5, LXXIV; 29, XXVII
Federal Motor Carrier Safety Administration	49, III
Federal Prison Industries, Inc.	28, III
Federal Procurement Policy Office	48, 99
Federal Property Management Regulations	41, 101
Federal Railroad Administration	49, II
Federal Register, Administrative Committee of	1, I
Federal Register, Office of	1, II
Federal Reserve System	12, II
Board of Governors	5, LVIII
Federal Retirement Thrift Investment Board	5, VI, LXXVI
Federal Service Impasses Panel	5, XIV
Federal Trade Commission	5, XLVII; 16, I
Federal Transit Administration	49, VI
Federal Travel Regulation System	41, Subtitle F
Financial Crimes Enforcement Network	31, X
Financial Research Office	12, XVI
Financial Stability Oversight Council	12, XIII
Fine Arts, Commission of	45, XXI
Fiscal Service	31, II
Fish and Wildlife Service, United States	50, I, IV
Food and Drug Administration	21, I
Food and Nutrition Service	7, II
Food Safety and Inspection Service	9, III
Foreign Agricultural Service	7, XV
Foreign Assets Control, Office of	31, V
Foreign Claims Settlement Commission of the United States	45, V
Foreign Service Grievance Board	22, IX
Foreign Service Impasse Disputes Panel	22, XIV
Foreign Service Labor Relations Board	22, XIV
Foreign-Trade Zones Board	15, IV
Forest Service	36, II
General Services Administration	5, LVII; 41, 105

Agency	CFR Title, Subtitle or Chapter
Contract Appeals, Board of	48, 61
Federal Acquisition Regulation	48, 5
Federal Management Regulation	41, 102
Federal Property Management Regulations	41, 101
Federal Travel Regulation System	41, Subtitle F
General	41, 300
Payment From a Non-Federal Source for Travel Expenses	41, 304
Payment of Expenses Connected With the Death of Certain Employees	41, 303
Relocation Allowances	41, 302
Temporary Duty (TDY) Travel Allowances	41, 301
Geological Survey	30, IV
Government Accountability Office	4, I
Government Ethics, Office of	5, XVI
Government National Mortgage Association	24, III
Grain Inspection, Packers and Stockyards Administration	7, VIII; 9, II
Gulf Coast Ecosystem Restoration Council	2, LIX; 40, VIII
Harry S. Truman Scholarship Foundation	45, XVIII
Health and Human Services, Department of	2, III; 5, XLV; 45, Subtitle A
Centers for Medicare & Medicaid Services	42, IV
Child Support Enforcement, Office of	45, III
Children and Families, Administration for	45, II, III, IV, X, XIII
Community Services, Office of	45, X
Family Assistance, Office of	45, II
Federal Acquisition Regulation	48, 3
Food and Drug Administration	21, I
Indian Health Service	25, V
Inspector General (Health Care), Office of	42, V
Public Health Service	42, I
Refugee Resettlement, Office of	45, IV
Homeland Security, Department of	2, XXX; 5, XXXVI; 6, I; 8, I
Coast Guard	33, I; 46, I; 49, IV
Coast Guard (Great Lakes Pilotage)	46, III
Customs and Border Protection	19, I
Federal Emergency Management Agency	44, I
Human Resources Management and Labor Relations Systems	5, XCVII
Immigration and Customs Enforcement Bureau	19, IV
Transportation Security Administration	49, XII
HOPE for Homeowners Program, Board of Directors of	24, XXIV
Housing and Urban Development, Department of	2, XXIV; 5, LXV; 24, Subtitle B
Community Planning and Development, Office of Assistant Secretary for	24, V, VI
Equal Opportunity, Office of Assistant Secretary for	24, I
Federal Acquisition Regulation	48, 24
Federal Housing Enterprise Oversight, Office of	12, XVII
Government National Mortgage Association	24, III
Housing—Federal Housing Commissioner, Office of Assistant Secretary for	24, II, VIII, X, XX
Housing, Office of, and Multifamily Housing Assistance Restructuring, Office of	24, IV
Inspector General, Office of	24, XII
Public and Indian Housing, Office of Assistant Secretary for	24, IX
Secretary, Office of	24, Subtitle A, VII
Housing—Federal Housing Commissioner, Office of Assistant Secretary for	24, II, VIII, X, XX
Housing, Office of, and Multifamily Housing Assistance Restructuring, Office of	24, IV
Immigration and Customs Enforcement Bureau	19, IV
Immigration Review, Executive Office for	8, V
Independent Counsel, Office of	28, VII
Independent Counsel, Offices of	28, VI
Indian Affairs, Bureau of	25, I, V
Indian Affairs, Office of the Assistant Secretary	25, VI

Agency	CFR Title, Subtitle or Chapter
Indian Arts and Crafts Board	25, II
Indian Health Service	25, V
Industry and Security, Bureau of	15, VII
Information Resources Management, Office of	7, XXVII
Information Security Oversight Office, National Archives and Records Administration	32, XX
Inspector General	
Agriculture Department	7, XXVI
Health and Human Services Department	42, V
Housing and Urban Development Department	24, XII, XV
Institute of Peace, United States	22, XVII
Inter-American Foundation	5, LXIII; 22, X
Interior Department	2, XIV
American Indians, Office of the Special Trustee	25, VII
Endangered Species Committee	50, IV
Federal Acquisition Regulation	48, 14
Federal Property Management Regulations System	41, 114
Fish and Wildlife Service, United States	50, I, IV
Geological Survey	30, IV
Indian Affairs, Bureau of	25, I, V
Indian Affairs, Office of the Assistant Secretary	25, VI
Indian Arts and Crafts Board	25, II
Land Management, Bureau of	43, II
National Indian Gaming Commission	25, III
National Park Service	36, I
Natural Resource Revenue, Office of	30, XII
Ocean Energy Management, Bureau of	30, V
Reclamation, Bureau of	43, I
Safety and Enforcement Bureau, Bureau of	30, II
Secretary of the Interior, Office of	2, XIV; 43, Subtitle A
Surface Mining Reclamation and Enforcement, Office of	30, VII
Internal Revenue Service	26, I
International Boundary and Water Commission, United States and Mexico, United States Section	22, XI
International Development, United States Agency for	22, II
Federal Acquisition Regulation	48, 7
International Development Cooperation Agency, United States	22, XII
International Joint Commission, United States and Canada	22, IV
International Organizations Employees Loyalty Board	5, V
International Trade Administration	15, III; 19, III
International Trade Commission, United States	19, II
Interstate Commerce Commission	5, XL
Investment Security, Office of	31, VIII
James Madison Memorial Fellowship Foundation	45, XXIV
Japan–United States Friendship Commission	22, XVI
Joint Board for the Enrollment of Actuaries	20, VIII
Justice Department	2, XXVIII; 5, XXVIII; 28, I, XI; 40, IV
Alcohol, Tobacco, Firearms, and Explosives, Bureau of	27, II
Drug Enforcement Administration	21, II
Federal Acquisition Regulation	48, 28
Federal Claims Collection Standards	31, IX
Federal Prison Industries, Inc.	28, III
Foreign Claims Settlement Commission of the United States	45, V
Immigration Review, Executive Office for	8, V
Independent Counsel, Offices of	28, VI
Prisons, Bureau of	28, V
Property Management Regulations	41, 128
Labor Department	2, XXIX; 5, XLII
Employee Benefits Security Administration	29, XXV
Employees' Compensation Appeals Board	20, IV
Employment and Training Administration	20, V
Employment Standards Administration	20, VI
Federal Acquisition Regulation	48, 29
Federal Contract Compliance Programs, Office of	41, 60

Agency	CFR Title, Subtitle or Chapter
Federal Procurement Regulations System	41, 50
Labor-Management Standards, Office of	29, II, IV
Mine Safety and Health Administration	30, I
Occupational Safety and Health Administration	29, XVII
Public Contracts	41, 50
Secretary of Labor, Office of	29, Subtitle A
Veterans' Employment and Training Service, Office of the Assistant Secretary for	41, 61; 20, IX
Wage and Hour Division	29, V
Workers' Compensation Programs, Office of	20, I, VII
Labor-Management Standards, Office of	29, II, IV
Land Management, Bureau of	43, II
Legal Services Corporation	45, XVI
Library of Congress	36, VII
Copyright Royalty Board	37, III
U.S. Copyright Office	37, III
Local Television Loan Guarantee Board	7, XX
Management and Budget, Office of	5, III, LXXVII; 14, VI; 48, 99
Marine Mammal Commission	50, V
Maritime Administration	46, II
Merit Systems Protection Board	5, II, LXIV
Micronesian Status Negotiations, Office for	32, XXVII
Military Compensation and Retirement Modernization Commission	5, XCIX
Millennium Challenge Corporation	22, XIII
Mine Safety and Health Administration	30, I
Minority Business Development Agency	15, XIV
Miscellaneous Agencies	1, IV
Monetary Offices	31, I
Morris K. Udall Scholarship and Excellence in National Environmental Policy Foundation	36, XVI
Museum and Library Services, Institute of	2, XXXI
National Aeronautics and Space Administration	2, XVIII; 5, LIX; 14, V
Federal Acquisition Regulation	48, 18
National Agricultural Library	7, XLI
National Agricultural Statistics Service	7, XXXVI
National and Community Service, Corporation for	2, XXII; 45, XII, XXV
National Archives and Records Administration	2, XXVI; 5, LXVI; 36, XII
Information Security Oversight Office	32, XX
National Capital Planning Commission	1, IV, VI
National Commission for Employment Policy	1, IV
National Commission on Libraries and Information Science	45, XVII
National Council on Disability	5, C; 34, XII
National Counterintelligence Center	32, XVIII
National Credit Union Administration	5, LXXXVI; 12, VII
National Crime Prevention and Privacy Compact Council	28, IX
National Drug Control Policy, Office of	2, XXXVI; 21, III
National Endowment for the Arts	2, XXXII
National Endowment for the Humanities	2, XXXIII
National Foundation on the Arts and the Humanities	45, XI
National Geospatial-Intelligence Agency	32, I
National Highway Traffic Safety Administration	23, II, III; 47, VI; 49, V
National Imagery and Mapping Agency	32, I
National Indian Gaming Commission	25, III
National Institute of Food and Agriculture	7, XXXIV
National Institute of Standards and Technology	15, II; 37, IV
National Intelligence, Office of Director of	5, IV; 32, XVII
National Labor Relations Board	5, LXI; 29, I
National Marine Fisheries Service	50, II, IV
National Mediation Board	29, X
National Oceanic and Atmospheric Administration	15, IX; 50, II, III, IV, VI
National Park Service	36, I
National Railroad Adjustment Board	29, III
National Railroad Passenger Corporation (AMTRAK)	49, VII
National Science Foundation	2, XXV; 5, XLIII; 45, VI

Agency	CFR Title, Subtitle or Chapter
Federal Acquisition Regulation	48, 25
National Security Council	32, XXI
National Security Council and Office of Science and Technology Policy	47, II
National Telecommunications and Information Administration	15, XXIII; 47, III, IV, V
National Transportation Safety Board	49, VIII
Natural Resources Conservation Service	7, VI
Natural Resource Revenue, Office of	30, XII
Navajo and Hopi Indian Relocation, Office of	25, IV
Navy Department	32, VI
Federal Acquisition Regulation	48, 52
Neighborhood Reinvestment Corporation	24, XXV
Northeast Interstate Low-Level Radioactive Waste Commission	10, XVIII
Nuclear Regulatory Commission	2, XX; 5, XLVIII; 10, I
Federal Acquisition Regulation	48, 20
Occupational Safety and Health Administration	29, XVII
Occupational Safety and Health Review Commission	29, XX
Ocean Energy Management, Bureau of	30, V
Oklahoma City National Memorial Trust	36, XV
Operations Office	7, XXVIII
Overseas Private Investment Corporation	5, XXXIII; 22, VII
Patent and Trademark Office, United States	37, I
Payment From a Non-Federal Source for Travel Expenses	41, 304
Payment of Expenses Connected With the Death of Certain Employees	41, 303
Peace Corps	2, XXXVII; 22, III
Pennsylvania Avenue Development Corporation	36, IX
Pension Benefit Guaranty Corporation	29, XL
Personnel Management, Office of	5, I, XXXV; 5, IV; 45, VIII
Human Resources Management and Labor Relations Systems, Department of Homeland Security	5, XCVII
Federal Acquisition Regulation	48, 17
Federal Employees Group Life Insurance Federal Acquisition Regulation	48, 21
Federal Employees Health Benefits Acquisition Regulation	48, 16
Pipeline and Hazardous Materials Safety Administration	49, I
Postal Regulatory Commission	5, XLVI; 39, III
Postal Service, United States	5, LX; 39, I
Postsecondary Education, Office of	34, VI
President's Commission on White House Fellowships	1, IV
Presidential Documents	3
Presidio Trust	36, X
Prisons, Bureau of	28, V
Privacy and Civil Liberties Oversight Board	6, X
Procurement and Property Management, Office of	7, XXXII
Public Contracts, Department of Labor	41, 50
Public and Indian Housing, Office of Assistant Secretary for	24, IX
Public Health Service	42, I
Railroad Retirement Board	20, II
Reclamation, Bureau of	43, I
Refugee Resettlement, Office of	45, IV
Relocation Allowances	41, 302
Research and Innovative Technology Administration	49, XI
Rural Business-Cooperative Service	7, XVIII, XLII
Rural Development Administration	7, XLII
Rural Housing Service	7, XVIII, XXXV
Rural Telephone Bank	7, XVI
Rural Utilities Service	7, XVII, XVIII, XLII
Safety and Environmental Enforcement, Bureau of	30, II
Saint Lawrence Seaway Development Corporation	33, IV
Science and Technology Policy, Office of	32, XXIV
Science and Technology Policy, Office of, and National Security Council	47, II
Secret Service	31, IV

Agency	CFR Title, Subtitle or Chapter
Securities and Exchange Commission	5, XXXIV; 17, II
Selective Service System	32, XVI
Small Business Administration	2, XXVII; 13, I
Smithsonian Institution	36, V
Social Security Administration	2, XXIII; 20, III; 48, 23
Soldiers' and Airmen's Home, United States	5, XI
Special Counsel, Office of	5, VIII
Special Education and Rehabilitative Services, Office of	34, III
State Department	2, VI; 22, I; 28, XI
Federal Acquisition Regulation	48, 6
Surface Mining Reclamation and Enforcement, Office of	30, VII
Surface Transportation Board	49, X
Susquehanna River Basin Commission	18, VIII
Technology Administration	15, XI
Technology Policy, Assistant Secretary for	37, IV
Tennessee Valley Authority	5, LXIX; 18, XIII
Thrift Supervision Office, Department of the Treasury	12, V
Trade Representative, United States, Office of	15, XX
Transportation, Department of	2, XII; 5, L
Commercial Space Transportation	14, III
Emergency Management and Assistance	44, IV
Federal Acquisition Regulation	48, 12
Federal Aviation Administration	14, I
Federal Highway Administration	23, I, II
Federal Motor Carrier Safety Administration	49, III
Federal Railroad Administration	49, II
Federal Transit Administration	49, VI
Maritime Administration	46, II
National Highway Traffic Safety Administration	23, II, III; 47, IV; 49, V
Pipeline and Hazardous Materials Safety Administration	49, I
Saint Lawrence Seaway Development Corporation	33, IV
Secretary of Transportation, Office of	14, II; 49, Subtitle A
Transportation Statistics Bureau	49, XI
Transportation, Office of	7, XXXIII
Transportation Security Administration	49, XII
Transportation Statistics Bureau	49, XI
Travel Allowances, Temporary Duty (TDY)	41, 301
Treasury Department	2, X; 5, XXI; 12, XV; 17, IV; 31, IX
Alcohol and Tobacco Tax and Trade Bureau	27, I
Community Development Financial Institutions Fund	12, XVIII
Comptroller of the Currency	12, I
Customs and Border Protection	19, I
Engraving and Printing, Bureau of	31, VI
Federal Acquisition Regulation	48, 10
Federal Claims Collection Standards	31, IX
Federal Law Enforcement Training Center	31, VII
Financial Crimes Enforcement Network	31, X
Fiscal Service	31, II
Foreign Assets Control, Office of	31, V
Internal Revenue Service	26, I
Investment Security, Office of	31, VIII
Monetary Offices	31, I
Secret Service	31, IV
Secretary of the Treasury, Office of	31, Subtitle A
Thrift Supervision, Office of	12, V
Truman, Harry S. Scholarship Foundation	45, XVIII
United States and Canada, International Joint Commission	22, IV
United States and Mexico, International Boundary and Water Commission, United States Section	22, XI
U.S. Copyright Office	37, II
Utah Reclamation Mitigation and Conservation Commission	43, III
Veterans Affairs Department	2, VIII; 38, I
Federal Acquisition Regulation	48, 8
Veterans' Employment and Training Service, Office of the Assistant Secretary for	41, 61; 20, IX
Vice President of the United States, Office of	32, XXVIII

Agency	CFR Title, Subtitle or Chapter
Wage and Hour Division	29, V
Water Resources Council	18, VI
Workers' Compensation Programs, Office of	20, I, VII
World Agricultural Outlook Board	7, XXXVIII

List of CFR Sections Affected

All changes in this volume of the Code of Federal Regulations (CFR) that were made by documents published in the FEDERAL REGISTER since January 1, 2012 are enumerated in the following list. Entries indicate the nature of the changes effected. Page numbers refer to FEDERAL REGISTER pages. The user should consult the entries for chapters, parts and subparts as well as sections for revisions.

For changes to this volume of the CFR prior to this listing, consult the annual edition of the monthly List of CFR Sections Affected (LSA). The LSA is available at *www.fdsys.gov*. For changes to this volume of the CFR prior to 2001, see the "List of CFR Sections Affected, 1949–1963, 1964–1972, 1973–1985, and 1986–2000" published in 11 separate volumes. The "List of CFR Sections Affected 1986–2000" is available at *www.fdsys.gov*.

2012

45 CFR — 77 FR Page

Chapter VI
670.29 Revised 5404

2013

45 CFR — 78 FR Page

Chapter VI
612 Revised 53278

Chapter VIII
800 Added 15587
   Correctly amended 25591
800.20 Correctly amended 18246
800.110 Correctly amended 18246
800.202 (f) correctly amended 18246

Chapter XI
1180.2 (b) introductory text amended 34921
1180.3 Amended 34921
1180.37 (a) revised 34921
1180.55 Revised 34921
1180.70 (Subpart D) removed 34922

2014

45 CFR — 79 FR Page

Chapter VI
602 Removed; interim 76079

Chapter XI
1100.1 (a) revised 9621
1100.2 Revised 9621

45 CFR—Continued — 79 FR Page

Chapter XI—Continued
1100.3 Revised 9622
1100.4 Revised 9622
1100.5 (a) and (b)(1) revised; (c) introductory text amended 9622
1100.7 (a) and introductory text revised 9622
1149 Added 67081
1157 Removed; interim 76091
1171 Added 9415
1172 Added 26633
1174 Removed; interim 76091
1180 Removed; interim 76090
1183 Removed; interim 76090
1184 Added 9423

2015

45 CFR — 80 FR Page

Chapter VIII
800 Republished 9655
   Correctly revised 16577

Chapter XI
1155 Removed 33157
1157 Regulation at 79 FR 76091 confirmed (*Editor's Note:* This is actually supposed to be 2 CFR Part 3255) 36930
1171.5 (c)(1) and (2) amended 42066
1171.10 (a) amended 42066
1174 Regulation at 79 FR 76091 confirmed 55505

45 CFR—Continued

80 FR Page

Chapter XI—Continued
1180 Regulation at 79 FR 76090 confirmed 56893
1183 Regulation at 79 FR 76090 confirmed 56893

2016

45 CFR

81 FR Page

Chapter VI
672.24 Revised; interim 41452
681.3 (f) and (g) added; interim 41452

Chapter IX
Chapter IX Established 53033
900 Added 53033

Chapter X
1000.3 (a) and (b) amended; interim 3021
1050.3 (h) revised 19428

2017

(Regulations published from January 1, 2017, through October 1, 2017)

45 CFR

82 FR Page

Chapter V
500 Authority citation revised; interim 16126

45 CFR—Continued

82 FR Page

Chapter V—Continued
500.3 (c) added; interim 16126
500.4 (a)(3) revised; interim 16126
510 (Subchapter D) Added; interim 16126

Chapter VI
690 Revised; eff. 1-19-18 7273

Chapter XI
1149 Authority citation revised; interim 27434
1149.9 (a)(1) amended; interim 27434
1158 Authority citation revised; interim 27434
1158.400 (a) and (b) amended; interim 27434
1158 Appendix A amended; interim 27434
1171 Authority citation revised 45
1171.4 (a) and (b) revised 45
1171.7 (d)(1)(ii) revised 45
1171.8 (b) and (c) revised 45
1171.10 (a) revised 46
1171.11 (d)(3) revised 46